The Beta Sigma Phi Party Cookbook

D1539691

The Beta Sigma Phi

Party Cookbook

Prize-Winning
Menus and Recipes

EDITORIAL STAFF

Managing Editor	Mary Jane Blount
Project Manager	Debbie Seigenthaler
Cookbook Editors	Georgia Brazil
	Mary Cummings
	Jane Hinshaw
	Linda Jones
	Mary Wilson
Typography	William Maul
	Sharon Whitehurst

Cover Photographer: John Guider; Page 1, Florida Citrus Commission; Page 2, CocoRibe

© Favorite Recipes Press, A Division of Heritage House, Inc. MCMLXXXVIII
P. O. Box 305141, Nashville, Tennessee 37230

Library of Congress Cataloging-in-Publication Data
Main entry under title:
The Beta Sigma Phi Party Cookbook
      Includes index.
         1. Cookery.   I. Beta Sigma Phi.
1988   88-21741
ISBN 0-87197-237-9

Manufactured in the United States of America
First Printing 1988
Second Printing 1988

Recipes for Page 1 on pages 59 and 216
Recipes for Page 2 on pages 2, 82 and 108

Contents

Introduction

When we invited Beta Sigma Phi members to send us their favorite party recipes and tips, we expected to receive an outstanding array of festive menus and wonderful food ideas. After all, this is a sorority known for its entertaining expertise.

What surprised even us, though, was the sheer number of sorority sisters we heard from—some 3,200, representing 1,675 chapters—plus their remarkable abilities to launch a great party at what seemed to be the drop of a hat! Needless to say, our task here at Favorite Recipes Press was a delightful one, sorting through the more than 6,500 favorite recipes to come up with the *crème de la crème* for this **Beta Sigma Phi Party Cookbook.**

In the pages that follow, you will find ideas and recipes for nearly every conceivable type of party fare. We have selected easy but elegant buffets, all-out seated dinners, parties for the small set, trend-setting theme parties and seasonal celebrations.

Our panel of food experts from both the Beta Sigma Phi and Favorite Recipes Press staffs have chosen from among these recipes a number of award-winners we feel will become your favorites too. You will find them throughout the book with ribbon artwork, signifying the winners in several categories. There is a list of winning recipes as well as an index of menu recipes in the back of the book.

Our Grand Prize-winning menu is a special treat for those who love great parties, an up-to-the-minute version of a classic holiday meal. The Xi Beta chapter of Peoria, Arizona has won a $500 party of its choice for a "Thanksgiving Day Celebration." We found it to be a celebration indeed, with such tempting delicacies as Red Pepper Pasta with Salmon Champagne Sauce, Barbecued Turkey, and Frozen Waldorf Salad.

What we found especially appealing about this award-winner is what we think is the hallmark of all great festive food: a creative, new approach to familiar favorites, uncomplicated preparation that leaves the hostess as fresh as her guests, careful attention to color, texture, taste and presentation, and a style that is elegant without being fussy.

We hope you will use the recipes and menus that follow as an inspiration for your memorable social events, whether they are chapter get-togethers, family parties, or formal entertaining. Even more creative ideas for lots more different occasions can be found on pages 25 and 26. Adapt them to your own needs and style, embellish or simplify them, and make them your very own. We are confident this Beta Sigma Phi cookbook will occupy a favored spot on your cookbook shelf and will offer you a wealth of enjoyment, ease and excitement in your entertaining.

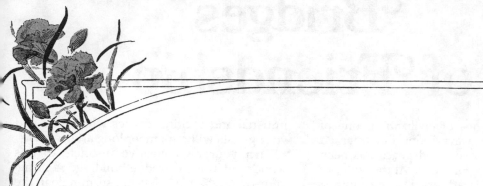

Party Menus

Bridges of Friendship

Since the beginnings of civilization, one of the most important ways people have marked friendship, cooperation and peace has been through the sharing of meals. At the table we are at our best—relaxed, open to one another, ready to enjoy.

Beta Sigma Phi members work hard to build bridges of friendship between people everywhere, and parties are one of the very best ways to accomplish this.

In this chapter we have brought together a veritable world tour that covers nearly every continent and includes menus close-to-home in their flavor as well as the truly exotic. These tried and true suggestions make for unusual and exciting parties which you and your guests will remember long afterwards.

Turn your own creative instincts to this wonderful way of bridge-building. A bring-your-own-wok party lets guests mingle in the kitchen while they prepare their personal stir-fry choices. Or try the Iditarod Trail Party, where Alaskan dog-sled racing provides the theme with such one-of-a-kind items as Musher's Whips, Tundra Greens and Mountain Peaks make up the menu.

Use the menus below to take you and your guests to Indonesia, Finland, Mexico, the Casbah and Cajun country. These might be the most enjoyable trips you have ever taken.

AROUND THE WORLD

Eta Xi, Sterling Heights, Michigan

Sweet and Sour Chicken Wings

Spice Nuts   Pierogi

Sweet and Sour Kielbasa

Cauliflower-Broccoli Casserole

Potatoes O'Brien   Glorified Rice

German Nut Loaf

Scotch Shortbread   Pavlova

Angel Wings   Dublin Tea Cakes

Sweet German Chocolate Cake

Kentucky Bourbon Balls

Cider Punch

SOUTH OF THE BORDER FIESTA

Xi Delta Pi, Del Norte, Colorado

Stuffed Chili Verde

Cheese Olé

Tostados de Harina

Chilies Rellenos

Ensalada "La Bamba"

Manicotti con Queso

Pollo de Kiev con Salsa

Chicarrones de Arroz

Mexicana Spoon Bread

Fiesta Fruta Dip   Flan

Margaritas   Acapulco Sunrise Ponche

INTERNATIONAL BRUNCH

Iota Sigma, Hiawatha, Kansas

Swedish Fruit Soup
Parisian Pancake
German Apple Coffee Cake
Fraises Romanoff   Koulouria
(Strawberries)   (Butter Cookies)
Champagne à l'Orange
African Tea and Coffee

INTERNATIONAL POT LUCK

Epsilon Beta, Alta Loma, California

Stuffed Snow Peas
Fusilli con Pomodori
Jagerschnitzel
(Veal Chops)
Green Spinach Casserole
American Apple Pie
Scotch Shortbread

GREEK PICNIC

Laureate Alpha Alpha, Pueblo, Colorado

Feta Cheese and Greek Olives
Carrot Curls   Celery Sticks   Radishes
Keftethyakia   Souvlakia
(Spiced Meatballs)   (Kabobs)
Pita Bread
Tzatziki
(Yogurt & Cucumber)
Tomato with Herbs
Walnut Cake

MIDEASTERN SUMMER

Delta Theta, Blue Earth, Minnesota

Fruit and Cheese Plate
Pickles   Vegetubles
Cacik
(Cucumber & Yogurt Salad)
Baba Ghannoush
(Eggplant & Tahini Purée)
Tabbouli   Pita Bread
Baklava
Coffee   Morrocan Tea

FRENCH CRÊPE FANTASIA

Preceptor Beta Psi, Akron, Colorado

Royal Chicken Crêpes
French Enchiladas
Springtime Salad
Strawberries and Crêpes
Waikiki Crêpes
Beverage

INDIAN TANDOORI FEAST

Alpha Pi, Missoula, Montana

Tandoori Cornish Hens
Vegetables with Saffron Rice
Cucumber and Yogurt Salad
Indian Flat Bread
Sweetly Spiced Oranges
Beverage

A BRIDGE TO THE OLD CASBAH

Lambda Sigma, Houston, Texas

Shake
(Strong, sweet tea)

Hummus
(Chick Pea Hors d'Oeuvres)

Persian Beef Stew   Couscous

Cucumbers   Orange Slices   Olives

Dates   Butter Cookies

FINNISH-DANISH DINNER

Xi Gamma Xi, Ames, Iowa

Stegt Rodspaette
(Sautéed Flounder with Shrimp)

Savory Lemon Vegetables

Macaroni Salad

Suomalaisleipa
(Finnish Bread)

Danish Pastry

CHRISTMAS IN GERMANY

Alpha Chi, Findley, Ohio

Relish Tray

Baked Ham Basted in German Beer

German Potato Salad

Barbecued Sauerkraut

Green Bean Casserole

Black Bread

Bavarian Torte

Springerle Cookies

ENGLISH TEA PARTY

Xi Alpha Gamma, Mountain Home, Idaho

Cheese Straws

Sausage Rolls

Plain Scones   Flaky Bars

Maids of Honor Tarts

Victoria Sponge Cake

Shortbread Fingers

Almond Slices

Tea

ORIENTAL BACKYARD BUFFET

Zi Alpha Tau, Sun City, Arizona

Chow Mein Munchie

Shrimp Salad Tomatoes

Classic Fried Rice

Chinese Barbecued Chicken

Spicy Potato Salad

Steamed Spice Cake

Iced Spiced Sun Tea

ORIENTAL COOK-OUT

Zeta Kappa, Virginia Beach, Virginia

Sesame-Soy Cheese

Rice Salad

Oriental Grilled Pork Chops

Grilled Tomatoes

Orangy Rum Sherbet

Fortune Cookies

Iced Tea   Chilled White Wine

SOUTHWESTERN BRUNCH

Alpha Zeta, Los Alamos, California

Frosty Fruit
New Mexico Jalapeño Pinwheels
Green Chili Quiche
Mexican Strata
Sour Cream Enchiladas
Egg Soufflé   Salsa
New Mexico Flan
Biscochitos

HAWAIIAN PARTY

Xi Beta Omicron, Medford, Oklahoma

Bacon-Pineapple Appetizers
Pineapple Bird Fruit Tray
Coconut Bananas
Fruit-Glazed Pork Chops
Orange Sweet Potatoes
Flamed Caramel Pineapple
Kona Krunch Pie
Waikiki Beach Centerpiece

JAVANESE RIJSTTAFEL BUFFET

Pre Laureate Beta Tau, Twenty-nine Palms, California

Nasi Goreng   Sates
(Rice with Special Sauce)   (Kabobs)

Green Vegetable with Nippy Sauce

Side Dishes
(Condiments)

Fruit Compote

Fortune Cookies   Hot Chinese Tea

IDITAROD TRAIL PARTY

Xi Nu, Kenai, Alaska

Tundra Tidbits   Musher's Whips
(Vegetable Tray)   (Breadsticks)

Mountain Peaks   Tundra Greens
(Stuffed Mushrooms)   (Spinach Salad)

Eskimo White Fish
(Halibut)

Snow Drifts   Dog Food Bundles
(Meat Rolls)   (Cabbage Rolls)

Snowball Cake

BRIDGING THE ROCKIES

Xi Alpha Phi, Boulder, Colorado

Buffalo Wings
Rocky Mountain Oysters
Aspen Salad
Buffalo Burgers on Baby Doe Buns
Molly Brown Beans
Rocky Mountain High Dessert
Gold Rush Punch   Boulder Brew

A CAJUN FEAST

Epsilon Beta, Palm Bay, Florida

Tossed Garden Salad
Shrimp Creole
Seafood Gumbo
Yeast Biscuits
Pecan Pie
Buttermilk Poundcake with
Fresh Strawberries

Affairs to Remember

Of all the many parties we attend, undoubtedly those that tend to stand out most in our memories are theme parties. Whether they are wild and woolly or subdued and elegant, theme parties give the hostess a wonderful opportunity to really stretch creatively, tying food, decoration, costume, invitations, music and table settings all together in one great big, beautiful package.

These may be the most "fun" parties of all, where we let our hair down, laugh a little at ourselves and amuse each other with wit and good humor. A party theme can come from almost anywhere—the sky's the limit. In this section, accomplished party-givers have shared ideas for some delightful get-togethers. Tax-time blues got you and your friends down? Why not cheer up with a Tax Payer's Bawl on April 15? Or take advantage of the current exercise craze with a Carbo-Loading Pasta Party.

Current events are often a source of themes, like an Inaugural Gala, where guests come dressed as presidents and first ladies, items from White House menus are served and prizes are given for winners of presidential trivia games. On the zanier side of things, take a (lowbrow) cue from our Couch Potato Party, where all menu items are based on potatoes, or a wonderfully Tacky Party, where you can surrender to that urge to serve up heaps of Moon Pies, Spam, and peanut butter crackers. Just let your imagination lead you where it will. The idea is to have fun!

ACADEMY AWARDS LUNCHEON

Laureate Lambda, Tulsa, Oklahoma

Splendor in the Grass
(Stuffed Zucchini Cups)

Some Like It Hot
(Spicy Bloody Marys)

The Godfather   *Godfather II*
(Pasta Salad)   (Romaine Salad)

The French Connection
(Garlic Bread)

Grapes of Wrath
(Wine Cooler)

An American in Paris
(Chocolate Éclair Dessert)

Selected Short Subjects
(Popcorn—Peanuts—Candy)

SWAMP PARTY

Xi Zeta Phi, Orlando, Florida

Buzzard Eggs
(Deviled Eggs)

Swamp Sandwiches
(Open-faced Sandwiches Topped with Sprouts)

Rocks with Dirty Dip
(Rye Bread Chunks with Green Vegetable Dip)

Bark with Dirty Dip
(Chips & Onion Dip)

Trollhouse Cookies
(Green-Tinted Chocolate Chip Cookies)

Bog Munchies
(Vegetable Tray)

Murky Punch
(Tea Punch)

PREHISTORIC PARTY
Preceptor Theta, Eagle Grove, Iowa

Tyrannosaurus Teeth
Stuffed Ankylosaurus Shell
Prehistoric Paw Prints
Brontosaurus Buns   Pteranodon Wings
Marsh Mush   Gorp

A WILD GAME DESSERT PARTY
Xi Alpha Delta, St. Simons Island, Georgia

Assorted Pastries "Lion" on a Tray
Chocolate Moose
Chocolate Chipmunk Cookies
Koala Karrot Kake   Bear-y Pie
Animal Crackers Everywhere

CARBO LOADING PASTA PARTY
Sigma, Nashville, Tennessee

Antipasto Salad
Fettucini with Scampi
Spaghetti al' Amatriciana
Biscuit Tortoni   Beverage

TACKY PARTY
Xi Mu Kappa, Ocala, Florida

Peanut Butter and Jelly on Ritz
Cheese in a Can
Spam   Beans in a Skillet
Moon Pies   RC Cola

MINER'S GRUBSTAKE
Xi Lambda, Deadwood, South Dakota

Stuffed Mushrooms
Spinach Dip in Bread Bowl
Cornish Pasty
Apple Dickey
Syllabub
Tea

ROMAN BANQUET
Preceptor Kappa, Ludington, Michigan

Roast Cornish Hens
Mushroom and Wild Rice Dressing
Broccoli with Almonds
Natural Grain Bread with Honey
Dates Stuffed with Almonds
Fresh Fruits   Soft Cheeses

PO' FOLKS PARTY
Preceptor Alpha Epsilon, Edmond, Oklahoma

Hamburger Stew
Buttermilk Corn Bread
Sugar-Free Banana Pudding

COUCH POTATO PARTY

Beta Theta, Columbia, Maryland

Potato Chips and Dip
Baked Potatoes with Assorted Toppings
Potato and Cheese Casserole
German-Style Potato Salad
Potato Pancakes
Sweet Potato Pie
Pennsylvania Dutch Potato Candy

FIRST-BORN BABY BASH

Rho Lambda, Levelland, Texas

2:00 a.m. Keep Your Cool Dip
Papa's Cheese Spread
Grandma's Party Sandwiches
Disposable Cheese Pastries
Baby Phyllo Baskets
Teddy Bear Cakes   Ga Ga Gooies
Formula Fruit Punch

TAXPAYER'S BAWL

Epsilon Tau, El Dorado, Kansas

Cocktails   Party Snacks
Ham and Bean Soup
Steak Soup
Corn Bread Sticks
Tossed Salad
Poor Boy Sandwiches
Brownies and Ice Cream

POLITICAL BARBECUE

Eta Delta, Osceola, Iowa

Relish Tray
Fresh Vegetables   Dip
Pickles and Olives
Jackson's Barbecue Sandwiches
Dole Slaw   Gore's Dream Salad
Bush's Baked Beans
Dukakis' Twinkie Cake

BLACK AND WHITE 40TH BIRTHDAY

Xi Lambda Xi, Highland, Illinois

Crab Sticks   Stromboli
Stuffed Mushrooms
Chicken Marengo
Linguine with Asparagus
Marinated Brussels Sprouts
Carrots Rosemary
Amaretto Cheesecake

ROARING 20'S FIVE-STAR DINNER

Xi Iota Epsilon, DuQuoin, Illinois

Swiss Broccoli Soup
Spinach Salad Flambé
Cornish Game Hens with
Crab Meat Stuffing
Apricot-Glazed Carrots
Fabulous Cheesecake
Champagne

Occasional Occasions

Most of the time, we think of social events as Big Occasions, parties that mark particularly important happenings in our lives. These are wonderful gatherings, often characterized by elaborate menus and extensive preparation. But why wait for a "capital O" occasion to roll around for a party? Even the most common-place event can inspire a grand celebration.

The approach of *any* weekend is cause for festivities, and here you will find an "Attitude Adjustment Hour" menu to suit the occasion. You might host a tantalizing dessert buffet in honor of the end of winter doldrums or a foot-ball widow's brunch when the season comes.

Beta Sigma Phi members have come up with many ideas for occasions great and small

on the following pages. Included are menus and recipes for a Bridesmaids' Luncheon and a big-deal luncheon for eight, as well as a delightful first birthday party for a child, geared for both grownup and kiddie tastes. If you think of salad as only an accompaniment to an entrée, you will be impressed with our Salad Luncheon menu, in which all courses — including dessert — are based on salads. And for those with a taste for the latest trends in cookery, a Club Med party menu offers great food with a cosmopolitan flair.

Whatever your preferences and style of en-tertaining, use these suggestions to brighten up your next event. Remember, there is a party out there just waiting to happen!

EASY ELEGANCE

Laureate Beta, Claremont, New Hampshire

Blinkers Dilly Crackers
Sweet and Sour Chicken
Buffet Ham Slices
Company Potato Casserole
Green Beans Italienne
Molded Lime Salad Tossed Salad
Wedges of Warm Corn Bread
Chocolate Outrageous Pie
Strawberries à l'Orange
Coffee Tea

CLUB MED

Tau, Wilmington, Delaware

Margaritas
Homemade Salsa
Tortilla Chips
Teriyaki Ribs Chicken Hoisin
Steamed Artichokes
Fresh Corn on the Cob
Melon Wedges
Grape Clusters
Rum-Raisin Ice Cream
Macadamia Bar Cookies

CHAMPAGNE BRUNCH

Preceptor Alpha Epsilon, Tucson, Arizona

Shrimp with Cocktail Sauce
Sour Cream and Caviar on Toast
Fresh Fruit Compote   Ginger Cream
Mixed Green Salad
Ham and Rice Quiche
Croissants
Chocolate-Raspberry Cheesecake

BRUNCH FOR EIGHT TO TWELVE

Laureate Alpha Eta, Pompano Beach, Florida

Overnight Bloody Marys
Sausage Breakfast Casserole
Hot Fruit Bake
Cheesy Grits Casserole
Banana Nut Bread
Orange Rolls
Beverage

LUNCHEON FOR EIGHT

Epsilon Rho, Magnolia, Arkansas

Spinach Soufflé Roll
Avocado with Tomato Freeze
Fresh Fruit with Dip
Cheese Bread
Oreo Delight

SOUP AND SALAD LUNCHEON

Laureate Iota, Colorado Springs, Colorado

Zucchini Soup
Curried Chicken Salad
Apricot and Apple Salad
Orange Cinnamon Muffins
Sherbet or Ice Cream

SALAD LUNCHEON

Alpha Gamma, Story, Wyoming

Sweet and Sour Meatballs
Lazaran Bread
Raspberry-Applesauce Salad
Green Magic Salad   Pasta Salad
Cauliflower Salad   Blueberry Layer Salad
Almond Pound Cake   Seven Layer Bars

BRIDESMAIDS' LUNCHEON

Xi Alpha Phi, Murray, Kentucky

Molded Turkey Salad
Twice-Baked Potatoes
Frozen Strawberry Salad
Bran Biscuits
Chocolate Éclairs
Party Tea

DINNER PARTY FOR EIGHT

Laureate Epsilon, Alamosa, Colorado

Avocado Soup

Broiled Chicken   Corn Fritters

Asparagus with Hollandaise Sauce

Green Salad with Fresh Pineapple

Raspberry Parfait

DINNER PARTY FOR SIX

Preceptor Kappa, Lutherville, Maryland

Shrimp Cocktail   Caesar Salad

Lobster Alfredo

Mixed Italian Vegetables

Herbed Bread

Kahlua Parfait

DINNER PARTY FOR FOUR

Preceptor Zeta Gamma, Tampa, Florida

Champagne   Cocktail Nuts

Creamed Spinach Soup

Tomato and Mozzarella Salad

Seafood Tortellini

Coffee Ice Cream Brittle   Fudge Sauce

Cookies   Coffee

A FONDUE COOK-IN DINNER

Laureate Eta, Clarksville, Tennessee

Frosted Raspberry Shrub

Beef Fondue

Buttered Green Beans   Curried Onions

Fresh Mushroom and Romaine Salad

Poppy Seed Loaf Bread

Chess Pie

INTIMATE ANNIVERSARY PARTY

Xi Beta Psi, Raleigh, North Carolina

Avocado and Tomato Salad

Chicken à l'Orange

Orange Rice Pilaf   Gingered Carrots

Buttered Green Beans

Extra Special Biscuits

Strawberries Chantilly in Melba Sauce

Viennese Coffee

DINNER PARTY FOR SIX

Preceptor Zeta Chi, Pittsburg, California

Shrimp Appetizer with Crackers

Fresh Mushroom Soup

Pork Au Vin

Fresh Steamed Broccoli

Red Potatoes with Butter and Cheese

Petite Dinner Salad

Lemon Delight Dessert

CHILD'S FIRST BIRTHDAY PARTY

Alpha Upsilon, Danville, Kentucky

Layered Taco Surprise
Smoked Beef Brisket with
Sesame Buns
Freezer Slaw
Seafood Pasta Salad
Relish Tray
"Ice Cream Cone" Ice Cream Sandwiches
Lemonade   Wine
(Children)   (Adults)

ATTITUDE ADJUSTMENT PARTY

Mu Theta, Converse, Texas

Olive Balls   Sausage Balls
Spinach Dip
Seasoned Oyster Crackers
Picadillo   Shrimp Dip
Layered Taco Dip
Artichoke Dip
Party Meat Balls
Red and White Wine

OPEN HOUSE

Kappa Pi, Atchison, Kansas

Shrimp Vinaigrette
Gourmet Pâté
Curried Vegetable Dip
with Assorted Vegetables
Hors d'Oeuvre Pie
Miniature Cheesecakes
Mock Champagne Punch
Gin Fizz

ELEGANT SUPPER PARTY

Beta Omega, Stansbury Park, Utah

Chicken Elegante
Wild Rice Mix with Mushrooms
Tossed Salad with Croutons
and Dijon Vinaigrette
Frozen Fruit Salad Fantasia
White and Wheat Rolls   Butter
Sour Cream Pound Cake
Coffee   Tea

AFTER PRODUCTION PARTY

Delta Kappa, Ellisville, Missouri

Corned Beef Mold
Cheese Ring
Spinach Sandwiches
Cheese Puffs
Three Bean Salad
Hawaiian Aloha Dip
Almond Bark Pretzels
Rocky Road Fudge
Mock Champagne

ARTIST'S RECEPTION

Xi Alpha Rho, Sumter, South Carolina

Chicken Puffs
Cocktail Meatballs
Cheese and Spinach Puffs
Cucumber Tea Sandwiches
Cheese and Fruit Tray
Vegetable Tray
Lemon Squares   Pecan Dainties
Cream Cheese Tarts
Cranberry Punch

Seasonal Sampler

Whether you celebrate Christmas under the palms, or define summer as two months of warmth sandwiched between snowstorms, you undoubtedly associate certain special kinds of entertaining with each season. Seasonal changes present us with wonderful opportunities for party giving, and wise hosts know that one of the secrets of successful entertaining is taking advantage of these.

Fall parties can take on a harvest theme, celebrate the glorious golds, reds and russets of the changing season. With events from football games to Halloween and Thanksgiving, autumn is a great season for entertaining.

In Winter, major holidays take the spotlight. Our suggestions for Christmas include classic dinners as well as lighthearted ideas such as a Christmas Tree Caper. For New Year's, why not try a daytime open house in lieu of the standby New Year's Eve party? Or warm up informally with a Snowy Chili Supper.

In Spring, graduations, weddings and other special days fill our social calendars, along with Easter and Mother's Day. It is also the time when gardens provide the stuff great menus are made of. You can enjoy the season in your Woman of the Year dinner or a charming Merry Month of May luncheon.

Last, but in no way least, on our entertaining calendar, is Summer, the time of the year when easy, breezy parties come into their own. Parties like our River Bank Fish Fry and Screen Porch Supper make the most of the good times and good food of Summer.

Fall

WESTERN ROUND-UP BRUNCH

Zeta Epsilon, Carbondale, Colorado

Western Sunrise   Campfire Coffee

Orange Wagonwheels

Cowboy Casserole

Colorado Crunch   Cowpatties
(French Toast)   (Sausage)

Cast-Iron Skillet Biscuits

Prickly Pear Cake

TAILGATE PARTY

Xi Alpha Sigma, Vienna, West Virginia

Ham and Cheese Rolls

Veggie Bars   Italian Salad

Vegetable Soup

Yummy Oyster Crackers

Beer Bread

Caramel Corn   Beer Nut Clusters

Assorted Soft Drinks and Beer

FALL PARTY

Alpha Omicron Phi, Kingwood, Texas

Pumpkin Soup   Cheese Bites

Rock Cornish Game Hens

Wilted Green Salad   Succotash

Blueberry Crisp

OKTOBERFEST

Preceptor Beta Eta, Bradenton, Florida

Sauerbraten over Noodles

Sauerkraut and Pork Loin with Dumplings

Baked Tomato Casserole   Corn Bread

Apple Dumplings

TRICK OR DRINK

Kappa Omega, Fredonia, Kansas

Porcupine Pumpkin
(Veggies on a Pumpkin)

Costume Cabbage   **Ghost Nuggets**
(Hard-Cooked Eggs)

Bat Wings   **Dracula Dip**
(Chilies Rellenos)   (Chili con Queso)

Black Cat Cheese Ball
(Black Olive Cheese Ball)

Goblin Stew   **Halloween Burgers**
(Chili)   (Cheeseburgers)

Jack-O'-Lantern Cake   **Witches' Brew**

HALLOWEEN PARTY

Xi Zeta Lambda, Fort Stockton, Texas

Eye of Newt Spread
(Shrimp Spread)

Skeleton Wellington
(Beans and Wieners)

Wrapped Lizards
(Pigs in a Blanket)

Yummie Mummie Cake
(Chocolate Chip Fudge Cake)

Peachy Keen Witches' Brew
(Peach Shake)

Bat Bars   **Spider Cider**
(Easy Butter Cake)   (Spiced Cider)

OLD-FASHIONED THANKSGIVING

Laureate Epsilon, Alamosa, Colorado

Roast Turkey
Sausage and Sage Dressing
Yams and Chestnuts   Skillet Cranberries
Mrs. Boylston's Asparagus
Strawberry Flummery

HOLIDAY DINNER

Epsilon Psi, San Angelo, Texas

Roast Cornish Game Hens
Pecan and Rice Dressing
Marinated Green Beans   Glazed Carrots
Fruit Salad
Chocolate Cream Roll

THANKSGIVING CELEBRATION

Xi Beta, Peoria, Arizona

Red Pepper Pasta with
Salmon Champagne Cream Sauce
Frozen Waldorf Salad
Barbecued Turkey
Carrots in Champagne   Whipped Potatoes
Swedish Braid Loaf
Pecan Black Bottom Pie

YOU WERE EXPECTING TURKEY?

Theta Upsilon, Springfield, Missouri

Broc-Olé Soup   Cheese Crisps
!Ay Chihuahua Dip!
Piñata Salad
Grits Garcia
Chicken Very Hot
Caramel Rum Fondue   Carmelitas
White Wine Sangria

Winter

APRÈS SKI PARTY

Zeta Kappa, Virginia Beach, Virginia

Fireside Fondue
Toasted French Bread Cubes
Chalet Salad with Tangy Salad Dressing
Grand Marnier Macaroon Pie
Double-Diamond's Cocoa

CHRISTMAS TREE PARTY

Gamma Nu, Romney, West Virginia

Chicken Liver Bacon Roll-Ups
Treed Vegetables   Sno-Ball Dip
Microwave Chocolate Fondue
Assorted Crackers and Dips
Mulled Cider

CHRISTMAS TREE CAPER

Xi Eta Omega, Visalia, California

Fruits of the Forest
Fluffy Fruit Dip
Paul Bunyon Pie
Monterey Lumberjack Sandwiches
Spruced Up Spuds   Barnstormin' Beans
Snow Tunnel Cake

DECEMBER BRUNCH

Xi Delta Zeta, Richmond, Virginia

Wassail Bowl
Roasted Pecans
Salmon Party Ball with Assorted Crackers
Fabulous Ham and Cheese Soufflé
Cran-Raspberry Ring   Tossed Salad
Cheese Cupcakes

CHRISTMAS DAY DINNER PARTY

Preceptor Beta Zeta, Mt. Clemens, Michigan

Tomato Bouillon
Almond Pilaf
Roast Leg of Lamb
Golden Squash Casserole
Mixed Vegetable Medley
Mandarin Orange Toss with
Sweet-Sour Dressing
Cloverleaf Rolls
Hot Fudge Coconut Snowballs

SOUTHWESTERN CHRISTMAS

Xi Beta Lambda, Chama, New Mexico

Apple-Tequila Cocktail
Green Chili Hors d'Oeuvres
Chilies Rellenos   Atule
Smothered Burritos   Pasalé
Enchilada Casserole   Chicken Chama
Sour Cream Enchiladas   Green Chili Stew
Tortillas de Harina   Sopa
Pumpkin Cake Roll   Biscochitos
Canjilon Pudding   Natilles

HOLIDAY COCKTAIL BUFFET

Laureate Alpha Kappa, Escondido, California

Manhattan Meatballs   Stuffed Mushrooms
Roquefort Log with Melba Rounds
Dill Dip and Fresh Vegetables
Pimento Cheese Ball   Hot Cheese Squares
Tomato and Squash Quiche
Parsley Flat Bread
Penuche Nuts   Glazed Bar Chews
Marvelous Brownies

CHRISTMAS OPEN HOUSE

Laureate Beta, Salt Lake City, Utah

Cheese Ball   Mixed Crackers
Corn Chowder
Curried Turkey on Hot Rice
Tomato Aspic Ring filled with
Green Pea Salad
Cinnamon Apples
Potato Rolls
Fruit Cake   Mixed Nuts

NEW YEAR'S BRUNCH

Gamma Epsilon, Henderson, Kentucky

Baked Eggs and Sausage
Apple Pancakes
Fresh Fruit   Party Mix
Bloody Marys   Champagne

NEW YEAR'S EVE DINNER

Xi Beta Epsilon, Marshall, Minnesota

Beef Tenderloin
Cheese Potatoes   Asparagus Spears
Mock Caesar Salad   Croissants
Coffee with Kahlua or Crème de Menthe

SUPER BOWL SUNDAY

Laureate Alpha Beta, Oak Harbor, Washington

Hot Artichoke Dip   Baked Cheese Dip
Salmon Ball   Taco Salad
Delicious Fruit Salad   Vegetable Tray
Oyster Stew with Crackers
Butch's Chili   Spinach Casserole
Football Field Cake

SNOWY CHILI SUPPER

Beta Kappa, Bartlesville, Oklahoma

Potato Skins
Chili con Queso Dip
Vegetable Relish Tray
Spicy Hot Chili   Jalapeño Bread
Kahlua Chocolate Cake
Sangria

ST. PATRICK'S DAY PARTY

Laureate Iota, Rome, Georgia

Brie with Crackers and Fruit
Spinach-Stuffed Mushrooms
Chocolate Sheathcake Squares
Coconut Almond Logs .   Shamrock Mints

MARDI GRAS PARTY

Alpha Pi, Caldwell, Idaho

Chicken-Sausage Gumbo
Shrimp Amandine   Spicy Green Beans
Calenda Cabbage with Cheese Sauce
French Doughnuts

Spring

LENTEN RUSH BRUNCH

Xi Zetz Mu, Eldridge, Iowa

Stuffed Shells Neopolitan
Under the Sea Salad   Crusty Rolls
Custard with Raspberry Sauce
Iced Tea with Mint Leaves

WOMAN OF THE YEAR DINNER

Preceptor Alpha Beta, Senatobia, Mississippi

Chicken Breasts Wellington
Cheesy Squash Bake   Steamed Asparagus
Layered Salad   Crescent Rolls
Fresh Fruit Napoleons

EASTER BRUNCH BUFFET

Lambda Phi, West Palm Beach, Florida

Mimosas   Ginger Ale Salad
Scallops in Seafood Sauce
Baked Ham   Wild Rice
Steamed Broccoli and Carrots
Sweet Potato Soufflé   Cheese Pudding
Sugar Cookies   Chocolate-Peanut Eggs

FAMILY EASTER DINNER

Alpha Alpha, Glascow, Montana

Stuffed Easter Ham
Golden Potato Squares
Buttered Green Beans
Tangy Slaw
Homemade Dinner Rolls
Chocolate Fudgey Torte

MOTHER'S DAY BRUNCH

Preceptor Theta Rho, Thousand Oaks, California

Fresh Fruit Compote
Egg Fondue   Blueberry Muffins
Fruit with Lemon Yogurt Dressing

MERRY MONTH OF MAY

Laureate Epsilon, Pensacola, Florida

Lobster Mousse   Cheese Wafers
Grapefruit and Avocado Salad
Ice Cream Dessert   May Wine

Summer

SCREEN PORCH SUPPER

Gamma Iota, Berlin, Maryland

Barbecued Franks   Fluffy Rice
Steamed Fresh Broccoli
Peach Yogurt Salad   Cloverleaf Rolls
Jell-O Tapioca Dessert

GARDEN PARTY

Xi Epsilon Nu, Cedar Rapids, Iowa

Stuffed Snow Peas   Cucumber on Rye
Basil Fettuccine in Tomatoes
Chicken and Pineapple Salad
Vanilla Ice Cream   Iced Sun Tea

TEX-MEX PATIO PARTY

Laureate Epsilon, New Braunfels, Texas

Sangria or Tequila Slush
Laredo Dip and Taco Chips
Tamale Bits   Ceviche
King Ranch Casserole
Hot Corn and Flour Tortillas
Mango Salad   Flan

RIVER BANK FISH FRY

Xi Delta Psi, Viburnum, Missouri

Fried Fish
Potato Crisp   Bean Casserole
Marinated Tomatoes and Onions
Skillet Biscuits
Chewy Chocolate Cookies
Tea   Soda

POOL SIDE PARTY

Xi Beta Zeta, Decatur, Alabama

Grilled Beef Tenderloin
Baked Stuffed Tomatoes
Fruit-Filled Watermelon Basket
Layered Salad   Assorted Breads
Strawberry Bucket Cake

ROAD RALLY TAILGATE PARTY

Xi Beta Phi, Clinton, New York

Oysters in Mufflers
"Herbied" Pull-Apart Cheese Puffs
Tail Lights Crudités
"It's A Lemon" Chicken
Rocky Road Fudge Brownies

FOURTH OF JULY BASH

Xi Eta Nu, Bryan, Texas

Little Smokies
Corn on the Cob   Nippy Potato Salad
Marinated Mushrooms   Dilled Pickles
Fritter-Fried Okra
Brownies   Iced Tea Cooler

INDEPENDENCE DAY BLAST

Kappa, Flint Michigan

Philadelphia Dip with Crackers
Firecracker Chicken   Star-Spangled Salad
Yankee Doodle Dandy Salad
Kappa Cake   American Ambrosia
Lady Liberty Fingers   Sparkling Slush

SUMMER PICNIC

Iota Epsilon, Fayetteville, Georgia

Vegetables and Dip   Fruit Kabobs
Cold Broiled Chicken   Barbecued Shrimp
Broccoli Medley   Deviled Eggs
Marbled Brownies   Amaretto Cheesecake
Cranberry Cooler

BEGINNING DAY DINNER

Alpha Phi, Roswell, New Mexico

Apricot-Glazed Cornish Hens
Mushroom Wild Rice   Green Bean Bundles
Spinach Salad with Poppy Seed Dressing
Golden Honey Rolls with Flavored Butters
Chocolate Mousse

Creative Party Ideas

ACADEMY AWARDS LUNCHEON

Oklahoma Laureate Lambda makes invitations as replicas of movie tickets. Serving tables are decorated with black clap-boards, studio lamps, marquee menu recipes and popcorn buckets covered with movie star photos. Games include a written "screen test." *See menu on page 12.*

BACKYARD SUMMER PARTY

Arizona Xi Gamma Gamma serves Garbage Can Dinner (page 114) at this cook-out. Build a small fire pit in backyard with chairs gathered round. Purchase an extra carbage can to ice down beer and wine. Serve snacks and relishes in small decorator plastic garbage cans.

BLACK AND WHITE 40TH BIRTHDAY

Illinois Xi Lambda Xi suggests party invitations, decorations and dress all in black and white for this milestone event. *See menu on page 14.*

A BRIDGE TO THE OLD CASBAH

Texas Lambda Sigma removes all furniture, places red tablecloth in center of room, and arranges pillows around cloth. Centerpieces are red votive candles and flowers floating in flat bowls. Guests eat with their right hands only. Arabic music and a belly dancer demonstration complete the evening. *See menu on page 10.*

BRIDGING THE ROCKIES

Colorado Xi Alpha Phi sends invitations to this interchapter party shaped like Aspen leaves. Tables are decorated with arrangements of the state flower and replicas of the state bird. Table settings include pie tin plates and mason jar glasses on flour sack tablecloths. *See menu of page 11.*

CARBO LOADING PASTA PARTY

Tennessee Sigma knows that complex carbohydrates are a great source of energy, an attribute every good Beta Sigma Phi needs. Bright decorations add extra energy. Shoe laces are napkin rings. Afterwards, guests "race" around to clean up. *See menu on page 13.*

CHINESE SURPISE SUPPER

Montana Xi Alpha Beta asks each member to bring miscellaneous ingredients to the party without revealing the menu or theme ahead of time. After the ingredients arrive, a committee surprises the members by preparing a Chinese dinner.

CHRISTMAS DINNER FOR 100

Pennsylvania Preceptor Phi hosts an annual Christmas dinner for 100 YMCA residents. Favors include cookies and candy tied in bags decorated with candy canes, Christmas jars of candy, poinsettias for each resident and a grand prize of a giant filled stocking.

CHRISTMAS TREE CAPER

California Zi Eta Omega hand prints invitations to this Christmas barn dance on strips of bark. The barn is decorated with evergreen boughs, hay bales and a lighted Christmas tree. Guests eat a hearty feast, gather around a fire to sing Christmas carols, and string cranberries and popcorn for their own Christmas trees. *See menu on page 21.*

COUCH POTATO PARTY

Maryland Beta Thetas know that a Couch Potato is unenergetic, so guests relax and let the host take care of every need. Using leftover fabric swatches, the guests decorate potatoes and awards of potato peelers are given for the "best dressed" potatoes. *See menu on page 14.*

DECEMBER BRUNCH

Virginia Xi Delta Zeta uses traditional Christmas Dinner centerpieces or a pretty glass bowl filled with polished apples or clove-studded oranges interspersed with holly sprigs. Simmer 1½ quarts water, the peel of 1 lemon and 1 orange, 2 bay leaves, 2 or 3 cinnamon sticks and 3 tablespoons whole cloves for a holiday fragrance. *See menu on page 21.*

FIRST BORN BABY BASH

Texas Rho Lambda makes invitations to this shower for couples by using rub-on letters for the printing and the bear from a box of Pampers. Make a master copy, and photo copy invitations on pastel pink or blue paper. *See menu on page 14.*

FRENCH CRÊPE FANTASIA

Colorado Preceptor Beta Psi gives each guest an apron and chef's hat on arrival. Guests cook and fill their own crêpes. Booklets of crêpe recipes are favors. *See menu on page 12.*

HALLOWEEN BACKWARDS FIESTA

Washington Preceptor Gamma Zeta writes invitations backwards so guests must hold them up to the mirror to read. Set the table with kitchen utensils instead of silverware and cups placed on the wrong side of the plates. Guests wear backwards costumes, use the back door, and walk backwards. Dinner begins with desserts and ends with hors d'oeuvres.

HALLOWEEN PARTY

Texas Zi Zeta Lambda serves punch in hollowed out pumpkin. Add gummy worms, if desired. To preserve decorative carved jack-o'-lanterns, spray inside and out with antiseptic spray. *See menu on page 20.*

HAWAIIAN PARTY

Oklahoma Xi Beta Omicron makes a Waikiki Beach centerpiece with palm trees and hut from decorative foods. Score cucumbers to resemble palm tree bark and soak in ice water. Slice bottoms from green peppers, remove seed, and trim to resemble palm leaves. Slice bottom from pineapple, remove fruit, leaving shell. Cut door in shell. Attach cucumbers to florist frogs. Attach leaves with toothpicks. Arrange trees and hut on tray lined with leaves. Decorate hut with flowers or leaves. Decorate tray with flowers and fruit. *See menu on page 11.*

MIDEASTERN SUMMER

Minnesota Delta Theta suggests checking out music and books from the library. Decorate with brass, silver and gold and Indian print bedspreads for tablecloths. Use posters from travel agencies. For entertainment rent *"Lawrence of Arabia"* or *"The Shiek"* from the video store. Serve trays of figs, dates, apricots, quince, apples, oranges and melons. *See menu on page 9.*

MOCK CHINESE NEW YEAR'S PARTY

Wisconsin Xi Beta Eta sends invitations on fans, requesting members to dress as one of the animals used on the Chinese calendar. The symbol for the year is used as a large wall decoration. Bamboo plants and stuffed pandas add to the atmosphere.

PREHISTORIC PARTY

Iowa Preceptor Thets invites guests with dinosaur egg invitations. Decorations include dinosaur name tags, inflatable dinosaurs, palm plants and rocks and bones. Foods include cheese bugle "teeth", hot chicken salad buns, bread shell stuffed with dip, fruit pizza "paw prints" and chicken wings. Table settings use rock place cards, burlap placemats and tissue palm leaf napkins. Dinner music is a recording from the science museum of dinosaur and jungle noises. *See menu on page 13.*

ROARING 20'S FIVE STAR DINNER

Illinois Xi Iota Epsilon has invitations, written on parchment and tied to a long-stemmed red rose delivered by a florist. A tablecloth of deep floral chintz is caught at the corners by long strands of pearls. Lace and ecru napkins, wisteria and azalea blossoms are tucked into pink depression goblets. An elegant floral arrangement, antique dishes and gold flatwear complete the table. Each lady receives a headband and each gentleman receives an armband as favors. *See menu on page 14.*

ROMAN BANQUET

Michigan Preceptor Kappa sends a proclamation inviting all to strengthen their spirits at this Ides of March banquet. Diners, dressed in togas and head wreaths, lie on cushions at low tables decorated with candles and grape clusters. *See menu on page 13.*

SOUTH OF THE BORDER FIESTA

Colorado Xi Delta Pi sends invitations on red chili designs reading "Some like it hot." Decorate with hanging red chilies or ristras intermingled with Christmas lights shaped like red chilies. *See menu on page 8.*

SUPER BOWL SUNDAY

Washington Laureate Alpha Beta couples gather two hours beforehand to socialize and wager in football pools with prizes for quarter, halftime and final scores. Place several television sets in the seating area for easy viewing. Serve fresh popcorn during the game and a buffet at halftime. *See menu on page 22.*

SWAMP PARTY

Florida Xi Zeta Phi sets tables with newspaper tablecloths, grape vines, brown paper towel napkins, tin pie plates and mason jar glasses. A tin bucket and metal cup serve as punch bowl and dipper. All games have a swamp or troll theme. *See menu on page 12.*

TAXPAYER'S BAWL

Kansas Epsilon Tau sends invitations to this April 15th party on brown paper sandwich bags printed with red ink and decorated with a frownie face. Attire should be obsolete or depreciated. *See menu on page 14.*

TRICK OR DRINK PARTY

Kansas Kappa Omega hosts assemble guests by Trick or "Drinking" at each house until the entire group is gathered and returns for a buffet dinner. Make the Jack-O'-Lantern Cake from 2 bundt cakes frosted together to resemble a pumpkin. *See menu on page 20.*

Party
Appetizers
and Beverages

BACON-CHEESE QUICHE SQUARES

1 8-ounce package refrigerator crescent rolls	1 egg, beaten
¾ cup shredded Swiss cheese	¾ cup milk
	½ cup sliced stuffed green olives
¾ cup shredded mozzarella cheese	½ cup mushroom stems and pieces
1 tablespoon minced onion	6 tablespoons bacon bits
	1 tablespoon parsley flakes

Preheat oven to 375 degrees. Separate crescent roll dough into 2 rectangles. Place in ungreased 9x13-inch baking pan; press over bottom and ½ inch up sides of baking pan to form crust. Seal perforations. Sprinkle cheeses over dough. Combine onion, egg, milk, olives and mushrooms in bowl; mix well. Pour over cheeses. Sprinkle with bacon bits and parsley. Bake for 22 to 28 minutes. Cool for 5 minutes; cut into squares.
Yield: 5 dozen.

Joyce Chriss, Laureate Sigma
Richardson, Texas

BARBECUE IN A CUP

1 10-count package refrigerator biscuits	Salt and pepper to taste
1 pound ground beef	⅓ cup catsup
½ medium onion, chopped	⅓ cup barbecue sauce
	2 tablespoons mustard
1 teaspoon sugar	2 cups shredded mozzarella cheese
1 teaspoon vinegar	

Preheat oven to 350 degrees. Separate biscuits. Press into muffin cups. Brown ground beef with onion in skillet, stirring frequently; drain. Combine remaining ingredients except cheese in bowl; mix well. Stir into ground beef. Spoon into prepared muffin cups. Top with cheese. Bake for 10 minutes or until crusts are brown. Serve hot or cooled. Yield: 10 servings.

Helene Eddy, Alpha Delta
Spearfish, South Dakota

BLACK OLIVE CANAPÉS

8 ounces Cheddar cheese, shredded	8 tablespoons mayonnaise
8 ounces mozzarella cheese, shredded	2 tablespoons minced onion flakes
½ cup chopped black olives	12 English muffins, split

Preheat broiler. Mix cheeses, olives, mayonnaise and onion flakes in bowl. Spread on muffins; place on baking sheet. Broil until brown and bubbly. Cut each muffin half into quarters using scissors. May be frozen before or after broiling. Reheat in microwave. Yield: 8 dozen.

Eileen Partise, Xi Delta Rho
LeRoy, New York

BLUE CHEESE PUFFS

4 ounces blue cheese	1 to 2 tablespoons cream
3 ounces cream cheese, softened	½ cup chopped pecans
2 tablespoons butter, softened	1½ to 2 dozen Midget Cream Puffs

Blend cheeses, butter and cream in bowl. Stir in pecans. Spoon into cream puff shells; replace tops. Chill, wrapped in foil, until serving time. May be frozen.
Yield: 1½ to 2 dozen.

Sally Oakes, Laureate Eta
Columbus, Nebraska

MIDGET CREAM PUFFS

1 cup water	1 cup all-purpose flour
½ cup butter or margarine	4 eggs

Preheat oven to 400 degrees. Heat water and butter to a rolling boil in saucepan. Stir in flour. Cook over low heat about 1 minute or until mixture forms a ball, stirring constantly. Remove from heat. Add eggs, beating until smooth. Drop by slightly rounded teaspoonfuls onto ungreased baking sheet. Bake for 25 minutes or until puffed and golden. Cool. Cut off tops. Remove soft dough. Fill as desired; replace tops. Yield: 5 dozen.

Evelina Wright, Xi Delta Psi
Erie, Kansas

CHEESE AND OLIVE ROUNDS

½ cup mayonnaise	1½ cups grated sharp Cheddar cheese
1 cup chopped black olives	1 loaf party rye bread
1 teaspoon curry powder	

Preheat oven to 350 degrees. Mix mayonnaise, olives, curry powder and cheese in bowl. Spread on bread slices; place on baking sheet. Bake for 10 minutes. Serve hot. Yield: 4 dozen.

Esther Hallock, Laureate Lambda
Salmon, Idaho

CHILI CHIPS

1 pound hot pork sausage	1 teaspoon oregano
1 pound ground beef	1 teaspoon chili powder
1 pound Velveeta cheese, cubed	1 teaspoon garlic salt
	1½ loaves party rye bread

Brown sausage and ground beef in skillet, stirring until crumbly; drain. Add cheese and seasonings; mix well. Spread on party rye slices. Place on baking sheet. Freeze until firm. Preheat broiler. Broil canapés for 4 minutes. Yield: 5 dozen.

Alberta Gamble, Laureate Delta
Quincy, Illinois

Jean Singman, Preceptor Kappa, Lutheville, Maryland, suggests using salad bar veggies for your crudités. Available in most grocery stores, there is no waste, and they are already bite-sized—a big time-saver.

CLAM CANAPÉS

2 cloves of garlic, minced	2 tablespoons corn oil
1 tablespoon minced onion	1 8-ounce can minced clams
½ teaspoon parsley	⅛ teaspoon salt
½ teaspoon oregano	Parmesan cheese
¼ cup bread crumbs	Saltine crackers

Preheat oven to 350 degrees. Sauté garlic, onion, parsley, oregano and crumbs in oil in skillet for 2 minutes. Remove from heat when garlic and onion start to brown. Mix in undrained clams and salt. Pour into 3-cup ovenproof dish; sprinkle lightly with additional crumbs and Parmesan cheese. Bake for 25 to 30 minutes or until crusty. Serve on saltines. Yield: 2 to 3 dozen.

Lodema Erbacher, Preceptor Zeta
Williamsville, New York

BROILED CRAB MELTAWAYS

8 ounces crab meat	2 tablespoons mayonnaise
½ cup margarine, softened	½ teaspoon salt
	½ teaspoon garlic salt
1 5-ounce jar Old English cheese spread	6 English muffins, split

Combine first 6 ingredients in mixer bowl; mix well. Cut muffin halves into quarters. Spread with crab meat mixture. Place on baking sheet. Freeze for 30 minutes. Preheat broiler. Broil until just golden brown and bubbly. Yield: 4 dozen.

Marvil J. Hoehn, Xi Lambda Beta
Lynn Haven, Florida

CRAB MEAT CANAPÉS

1 5-ounce jar Old English cheese spread	½ cup melted butter
	1 tablespoon mayonnaise
½ teaspoon seasoned salt	1 7-ounce can crab meat
¼ teaspoon garlic powder	6 English muffins, split

Combine cheese spread, seasonings, butter, mayonnaise and crab meat in bowl; mix well. Spread on muffin halves. Freeze just until firm. Cut into quarters. Store wrapped, in freezer. Preheat oven to 350 degrees. Place on baking sheet. Bake for 15 minutes. Yield: 4 dozen.

Kathleen A. Rocha, Omicron Zeta
Independence, Missouri

CRAB PUFFS

½ cup butter, softened	2 tablespoons mayonnaise
1 5-ounce jar Old English cheese spread	1 7-ounce can crab meat, drained
1½ teaspoons garlic salt	12 bagels, split

Combine butter, cheese spread, garlic salt, mayonnaise and crab meat in bowl; mix well. Spread on bagels. Cut into quarters. Place on baking sheet. Freeze until firm. Preheat broiler. Broil crab puffs for 5 minutes. Yield: 8 dozen.

Rhea Light, Xi Gamma Mu
Grinnell, Iowa

CRACKER BREAD PINWHEELS

1 box Armenian cracker bread	½ pound roast beef, thinly sliced
8 ounces cream cheese, softened	1 package alfalfa sprouts

Rinse crackers under running water; place under damp towels. Let stand for 1 hour or longer to soften. Spread with cream cheese; add roast beef and alfalfa sprouts. Roll as for jelly roll; slice into pinwheels. Yield: 10 servings.

Anne Welsh, Xi Nu
Owensboro, Kentucky

HAM AND CHEESE TARTS

1 10-count package refrigerator biscuits	4 ounces cream cheese with chives, softened
½ cup sour cream	½ cup finely chopped cooked ham
⅛ teaspoon finely grated orange rind	Paprika
¼ teaspoon dry mustard	

Preheat oven to 375 degrees. Separate each biscuit into 2 layers. Fit each layer into miniature muffin cup. Combine next 5 ingredients in bowl; mix well. Spoon 1 tablespoon filling into each muffin cup. Sprinkle with paprika. Bake for 15 minutes or until set. Serve warm. Yield: 20 tarts.

Janet Jarrett, Iota Eta
Havelock, North Carolina

HAM CRUNCH APPETIZER

2 8-count packages refrigerator crescent rolls	1 cup mayonnaise
	3½ cups ground cooked ham
6 ounces cream cheese, softened	1 cup chopped fresh vegetables
1 3½-ounce package Hidden Valley salad dressing mix	1 cup grated Cheddar cheese

Preheat oven to 375 degrees. Unroll roll dough. Press over bottom of 9x13-inch baking pan; seal edges. Bake for 8 minutes or until brown; cool. Combine cream cheese, salad dressing mix and mayonnaise in bowl; mix well. Stir in ham. Spread over crust. Layer vegetables and cheese over top. Cut into squares. Yield: 2 dozen.

Pam Van Ryswyk, Alpha Theta
Chariton, Iowa

HAM PUFFS

1 pound ham, shaved	⅓ cup sour cream
1 tablespoon horseradish	6 dozen Midget Cream Puffs (page 28)
¾ teaspoon pepper	
¾ teaspoon onion salt	

Combine first 5 ingredients in food processor container. Process until smooth. Chill in refrigerator. Fill cream puff shells with ham mixture; replace tops. Yield: 6 dozen.

Cheryl A. Hurt, Omicron Pi
Winter Haven, Florida

MINI HAM SANDWICHES

½ cup butter	1½ teaspoons poppy seed
2 tablespoons onion flakes	2 24-count packages dinner rolls
1½ teaspoons dried mustard	1½ pounds cooked ham, thinly sliced
1 teaspoon Worcestershire sauce	1 18-ounce package sliced Swiss cheese

Preheat oven to 350 degrees. Combine first 5 ingredients in small saucepan. Heat until butter is melted; mix well. Slice dinner rolls in half. Place ham and cheese on bottom portion of rolls. Place top of rolls on ham and cheese to form large sandwich. Replace in foil roll pans. Pour butter mixture over rolls. Bake for 20 minutes. Cut rolls into individual sandwiches. Yield: 4 dozen.

Timmie Brannon, Zeta Omega
Lenoir City, Tennessee

HERB MIRACLE BARS

1 pound pork sausage	2 tablespoons chopped parsley
½ cup chopped onion	1 teaspoon chopped oregano
¼ cup Parmesan cheese	1 cup biscuit mix
½ cup shredded Swiss cheese	¾ cup milk
1 egg, beaten	¼ cup salad dressing
¼ teaspoon cayenne pepper	1 egg yolk
1 teaspoon chopped basil	1 tablespoon water

Preheat oven to 400 degrees. Brown sausage with onion in skillet, stirring frequently; drain well. Add cheeses, egg and seasonings; mix well. Combine biscuit mix, milk and salad dressing in bowl; mix well. Spread half the dough in greased 9x9-inch baking pan. Spoon sausage mixture over dough. Spread remaining dough over sausage. Brush with mixture of egg yolk and water. Bake for 20 minutes or until mixture pulls from sides of pan. Cool for 5 minutes. Cut into squares. Yield: 6 dozen.

Mae A. Ballard, Laureate Beta Epsilon
Houston, Texas

HOT PARTY CANAPÉS

1 cup shredded Swiss cheese	1 envelope Italian salad dressing mix
½ cup mayonnaise	1 tablespoon lemon juice
3 ounces cream cheese, softened	4 to 6 slices crisp-fried bacon, crumbled
¼ cup Dijon-style mustard	Assorted party breads

Preheat broiler. Combine Swiss cheese, mayonnaise, cream cheese, mustard, salad dressing mix and lemon juice in bowl; mix well. Fold in bacon. Spread generously on bread. Place on ungreased baking sheet. Broil until lightly browned. Serve immediately. Yield: 3 dozen.

Vickie Loach, Gamma Theta
Jacksonville, North Carolina

JOSEPHINES

½ cup margarine, softened	1½ cups shredded Monterey Jack cheese
1 large clove of garlic, crushed	1½ cups shredded Cheddar cheese
1 4-ounce can chopped green chilies, drained	½ cup mayonnaise
	18 small French rolls

Preheat broiler. Combine first 3 ingredients in bowl; mix well. Mix cheeses and mayonnaise in bowl. Slice rolls ¼ inch thick. Spread with butter mixture, then cheese mixture. Arrange in broiler pan. Broil for 2 to 4 minutes or until puffed and brown. Serve hot. Yield: 3 dozen.

Nancy Hunter, Xi Omega
Yuma, Arizona

MEXICAN FUDGE HORS D'OEUVRES

8 ounces Monterey Jack cheese, shredded	3 eggs
8 ounces sharp Cheddar cheese, shredded	⅓ cup green taco sauce
	1 package tortilla chips

Preheat oven to 350 degrees. Mix cheeses together. Let stand for 30 to 45 minutes or until slightly dried. Sprinkle half the cheese into 9-inch square baking pan. Beat eggs with taco sauce. Pour into pan. Top with remaining cheese. Bake for 25 minutes or until set. Let stand for 5 to 10 minutes. Cut into 1½-inch squares. Place on tortilla chips. Yield: 3 dozen.

Hazel D. Culbertson, Rho Pi
McHenry, Illinois

MEXICAN PIZZAS

12 flour tortillas	1 8-ounce package sliced pepperoni
3 cups shredded Monterey Jack cheese	1 16-ounce can artichoke hearts, chopped
Jalapeño peppers, chopped	1 8-ounce jar picante sauce
1 green pepper, chopped	
½ cup sliced black olives	

Place tortillas 1 at a time in nonstick skillet. Layer cheese and remaining ingredients over tortillas as desired. Cook, covered, over medium heat for 2 to 3 minutes. Cut into wedges. Serve hot. Yield: 12 pizzas.

Cheri Brown, Preceptor Sigma
Oxon Hill, Maryland

ONION APPETIZERS

2 2½-inch diameter white onions	Mayonnaise
1 loaf party rye bread	Parmesan cheese
	Paprika

Preheat broiler. Slice onions thinly. Spread party rye bread with mayonnaise. Place onion slice on each round. Spread onions with mayonnaise; sprinkle with cheese and paprika. Broil until bubbly. Serve immediately. Yield: 2 dozen.

Sharon G. Crouse, Gamma Nu
Lexington, North Carolina

OWL EYES

1 16-ounce loaf white bread	1 13-ounce jar olives, drained
2 5-ounce jars olive and pimento cheese spread	

Trim crusts from bread. Roll bread thin with rolling pin. Spread each slice with cheese spread. Arrange olives in row touching each other at end of bread slice. Roll as for jelly roll. Chill in covered container overnight. Cut into slices. Place olive side up on serving dish. Yield: 5 dozen.

Mary James, Pi Gamma
Batavia, Illinois

PEPPERS AND CHEESE CRACKERS

1 7¼-ounce jar Progresso fried peppers with onions	2 eggs, beaten
	2 tablespoons milk
	Butter crackers
8 ounces red label Cracker Barrel cheese	

Preheat oven to 350 degrees. Drain peppers. Spread in 9-inch pie plate. Shred cheese; spread over peppers. Beat eggs with milk. Pour over cheese. Bake for 35 minutes or until puffy and golden brown. Place spoonfuls on butter crackers. Serve hot. Yield: 10 servings.

Rita Skedzielewski, Laureate Eta
Pennsauken, New Jersey

PIZZA BAGEL HORS D'OEUVRES

⅔ cup grated Parmesan cheese	1 16-ounce package miniature bagels, split
1½ cups mayonnaise	Paprika
1 cup chopped green onion	

Preheat broiler. Combine first 3 ingredients in bowl; mix well. Spread on bagels. Sprinkle with paprika. Place on baking sheets. Broil for 3 to 5 minutes or until bubbly. Yield: 2½ dozen.

Christina L. Richardson, Mu Phi
Modesto, California

PIZZA HORS D'OEUVRES

1 pound sweet Italian sausage	½ teaspoon Worcestershire sauce
1 pound ground beef	1 pound Velveeta cheese, cubed
1 teaspoon oregano	1 loaf cocktail rye bread
1 teaspoon fennel seed	

Preheat oven to 425 degrees. Remove casings from sausage. Brown with next 3 ingredients in skillet over medium heat, stirring frequently; drain. Add Worcestershire sauce and cheese. Cook until cheese melts, stirring constantly. Spread on cocktail rye bread. Place on baking sheet. Bake for 10 minutes or until bubbly. Yield: 2 dozen.

Jeanne Moore, Preceptor Iota Gamma
La Mesa, California

PIZZA PARTY ROUNDS

1 pound ground beef	2 teaspoons oregano
1 pound hot sausage	1 teaspoon minced garlic
1 pound Velveeta cheese, cubed	2 teaspoons Worcestershire sauce
2 teaspoons seasoned salt	1 loaf party rye bread

Preheat broiler. Brown ground beef and sausage in skillet, stirring frequently; drain. Add cheese and seasonings. Cook over low heat until cheese melts, stirring constantly. Spread on party rye. Place on baking sheet. Broil until brown. Yield: 2 dozen.

Bill Ross, Beta Sigma Phi International
Kansas City, Missouri

QUESADILLAS

5 10-inch flour tortillas	½ cup minced pimento
½ cup unsalted butter, softened	1 4-ounce can green chilies, drained and chopped
1 pound Monterey Jack cheese, shredded	1 teaspoon cumin
8 green onions, minced	

Preheat oven to 400 degrees. Spread tortillas with butter; place on rack in broiler pan. Bake for 5 minutes. Cool. Spread tortillas with mixture of cheese, green onions, pimento, green chilies and cumin. Bake for 5 to 8 minutes or until cheese bubbles. Cut into wedges with pizza cutter. Serve warm. Yield: 40 appetizers.

Susan H. Davis, Xi Delta Zeta
Richmond, Virginia

SHRIMP PUFFS

3 ounces cream cheese, softened	1 cup chopped cooked shrimp
2 tablespoons mayonnaise	¼ cup chopped onion
1 tablespoon catsup	24 Midget Cream Puffs (page 28)
1 teaspoon mustard	
Dash of garlic powder	

Combine first 7 ingredients in bowl; mix well. Spoon into cooled cream puff shells. Yield: 2 dozen.

Mary Louise Wheeler, Laureate Alpha Eta
Bethlehem, Pennsylvania

CHEESE SANDWICHES

2½ loaves bread	2 teaspoons dillweed
2 cups butter, softened	1 teaspoon onion or garlic salt
4 5-ounce jars Old English cheese spread	½ teaspoon cayenne pepper
2 teaspoons Tabasco sauce	

Trim crusts from bread. Combine remaining ingredients in bowl; mix well. Spread between slices of bread; cut into quarters. Ice top and sides of each square with cheese mixture. Freeze until firm. Preheat oven to 350 degrees. Place sandwiches on baking sheet. Bake for 20 minutes. Serve warm. Yield: 30 to 40 servings.

Judie Highmiller, Xi Mu
Las Vegas, Nevada

GREEN BEAN SANDWICHES

1 16-ounce can whole
   green beans, drained
⅔ cup white vinegar
⅔ cup corn oil
⅔ cup sugar
1 onion, sliced

1 8-ounce bottle of
   Italian salad dressing
Sandwich bread
½ cup Durkee Famous
   Sauce
½ cup mayonnaise

Mix first 5 ingredients in bowl. Marinate in refrigerator overnight; drain. Add salad dressing. Marinate overnight; drain. Trim crusts from bread. Spread slices with Durkees and mayonnaise. Place 1 to 3 beans on each slice. Roll up; secure with toothpicks. Chill, covered, overnight. Slice. Arrange on serving tray. Yield: 4 dozen.

Eva Marie Pearson, Member at Large
Pine Bluff, Arkansas

PARTY SANDWICHES

16 slices sandwich bread
Butter, softened
8 pineapple rings
2 cups chicken salad

16 ounces cream cheese,
   softened
Pineapple juice

Cut a circle out of each bread slice with pineapple can. Butter eight slices of bread. Place pineapple slice on each. Spoon ¼ cup chicken salad and unbuttered bread slice on each. Combine cream cheese with enough pineapple juice to make of frosting consistency. Frost top and sides of sandwiches. Yield: 8 sandwiches.

Loretta Kelly, Laureate Tau
Afton, Iowa

RAISIN-CREAM CHEESE SANDWICHES

1 16-ounce loaf iced
   raisin bread

8 ounces cream cheese,
   softened

Trim crusts from bread, leaving iced side. Spread softened cream cheese between 2 slices. Cut into desired shapes. Yield: 2½ dozen.

Emma Purdy, Preceptor Rho
Bossier City, Louisiana

SMOKY SAUSAGE CRESCENTS

1 8-count package
   refrigerator crescent
   rolls
3 ounces cream cheese
   with chives, softened
2 teaspoons Dijon-style
   mustard

1 teaspoon prepared
   horseradish
1 5-ounce package small
   smoked sausage links

Preheat oven to 400 degrees. Unroll crescent rolls; separate into triangles. Cut each triangle in half. Beat cream cheese in mixer bowl for 2 minutes. Add mustard and horseradish; beat until fluffy. Spread on bottom 2 inches of triangles. Add sausage link; roll up. Place seam side down on greased baking sheet. Bake for 10 minutes. Yield: 16 servings.

K. D. Potts, Alpha Nu Xi
Mount Pleasant, Texas

CREAMY TUNA GARDEN WEDGES

2 cups buttermilk baking
   mix
½ cup cold water
8 ounces cream cheese,
   softened
½ cup mayonnaise
½ cup sliced green onions
⅛ teaspoon red pepper
   sauce

2 teaspoons prepared
   horseradish
1 6½-ounce can tuna,
   drained
2 medium stalks celery
Sliced mushrooms
Cherry tomato halves
Chopped broccoli
Shredded cheese

Preheat oven to 450 degrees. Combine baking mix and water in bowl. Beat for 20 strokes. Pat into ungreased pizza pan, forming ½-inch rim. Bake for 10 minutes. Cool. Combine cream cheese, mayonnaise, onions, seasonings and tuna in bowl; mix well. Spread over crust. Slice celery diagonally. Outline 6 wedges with celery slices. Top with vegetables and cheese. Chill, covered, for 1 hour. Cut into wedges. Yield: 16 servings.

Kathleen J. Hash, Xi Alpha Eta
Fruitland, Idaho

VEGGIE BARS

2 8-count packages
   refrigerator crescent
   rolls
¾ cup salad dressing
16 ounces cream cheese,
   softened
1 envelope dry ranch
   dressing mix
¾ cup broccoli flowerets

¾ cup cauliflowerets
¾ cup chopped green
   pepper
¾ cup chopped onion
¾ cup sliced fresh
   mushrooms
¾ cup sliced carrots
2 cups shredded Cheddar
   cheese

Preheat oven to 350 degrees. Unroll crescent roll dough. Press dough over baking sheet; seal edges. Bake for 7 minutes. Cool. Combine salad dressing, cream cheese and ranch dressing mix in bowl; mix well. Spread over crust. Layer vegetables and cheese over top. Chill for 1 to 2 hours. Cut into squares. Yield: 2 dozen.

Mary J. Jacobs, Xi Epsilon Beta
Fort Wayne, Indiana

SWEET AND SOUR WON TONS

1 64-ounce can
   pineapple juice
3 cups sugar
¾ cup catsup
1 teaspoon garlic salt
2 tablespoons red pepper
   sauce
8 ounces ground pork

1 egg
¼ cup chopped onion
3 cloves of garlic, minced
2 packages won ton
   wrappers
1 egg yolk, beaten
Oil for deep-frying

Combine first 5 ingredients in saucepan. Simmer for 1 hour. Cool to room temperature. Combine pork, egg, onion and garlic in bowl; mix well. Chill for 1 hour. Place 1 teaspoon filling in each won ton wrapper. Seal with egg yolk using package instructions. Deep-fry in hot oil until golden brown. Drain on paper towel. Serve with sauce. Yield: 100 servings.

Valerie Lynn Mata, Psi Kappa
Houston, Texas

AMARETTO CHEESE BALL

8 ounces cream cheese, softened	1 3-ounce package slivered almonds, toasted
¼ cup Amaretto	
2 tablespoons sugar	

Beat cream cheese with Amaretto and sugar in mixer bowl. Shape into ball; stud porcupine-fashion with almonds. Chill. Place on serving plate. Serve with grapes and Granny Smith apple wedges. Yield: 1 cheese ball.

Nancy Tanksley, Alpha Zeta
Mitchell, Indiana

BEEFY CHEESE BALL

8 ounces cream cheese, softened	1 tablespoon lemon juice
1 teaspoon prepared horseradish	1 tablespoon dry onion soup mix
1 teaspoon Worcestershire sauce	1 4-ounce package chipped beef

Combine cream cheese, horseradish, Worcestershire sauce, lemon juice and onion soup mix in mixer bowl. Beat at medium speed until well blended. Chop beef into small pieces; fold into cream cheese mixture. Shape into ball. Chill. Serve with crackers. Yield: 12 servings.

Tina Scott, Rho Psi
Frostproof, Florida

BIG CHEESE BALL

8 ounces sharp Cheddar cheese, shredded	1 8-ounce can crushed pineapple, drained
8 ounces cream cheese, softened	1 4-ounce jar stuffed green olives, finely chopped
1 medium green bell pepper, chopped	½ to ¾ cup crushed soda crackers
1 medium onion, finely chopped	2 cups chopped pecans

Combine cheeses, green pepper, onion, pineapple, olives, cracker crumbs and 1 cup pecans in bowl; mix well. Chill for 1 hour. Shape into ball; roll in remaining 1 cup pecans. Chill until serving time. Serve with crackers. Yield: 1 cheese ball.

Cathi Lensch, Nu Alpha
Rock Valley, Iowa

THREE-CHEESE BALL

8 ounces cream cheese, softened	1 teaspoon Worcestershire sauce
2 4-ounce jars pimento cheese	1 teaspoon garlic salt
2 cups Cheddar cheese, shredded	1 cup chopped nuts

Combine first 5 ingredients, except nuts, in bowl; mix well. Chill until firm enough to shape into ball. Roll in nuts; wrap in plastic wrap. Chill until firm. Serve with crackers. Yield: 1 cheese ball.

Carol Gordon, Lambda Pi
Sarasota, Florida

JALAPEÑO CHEESE ROLL

1 pound Velveeta cheese, softened	1 4-ounce can chopped chilies, drained
4 ounces cream cheese, softened	½ cup chopped mild jalapeño peppers
1 4-ounce package chopped pecans	1 bunch green onions, chopped
1 4-ounce jar chopped pimento, drained	

Roll out Velveeta between sheets of waxed paper into large rectangle sheet. Remove top layer of paper. Spread with thin layers of cream cheese. Sprinkle with remaining ingredients. Chill for 30 minutes. Roll as for jelly roll; wrap in plastic wrap. Chill. Serve with crackers. Yield: 1 cheese roll.

Elaine Hanson, Xi Gamma Epsilon
Omaha, Nebraska

CHEESE À LA PRIDDEAUX

24 ounces cold-pack cheese food, softened	½ teaspoon Tabasco sauce
12 ounces cream cheese, softened	1 teaspoon lemon juice
1 tablespoon grated onion	⅛ teaspoon garlic powder
	1 teaspoon Worcestershire sauce

Combine all ingredients in bowl; mix well. Chill in refrigerator overnight. Serve with crackers. May store in refrigerator for 3 to 4 weeks. Yield: 6 cups.

Alma Priddy, Xi Gamma Rho
Alice, Texas

PINEAPPLE-NUT CHEESE BALL

16 ounces cream cheese, softened	1 8-ounce can crushed pineapple, drained
¾ cup chopped green bell pepper	1 tablespoon salt
2 tablespoons chopped onion	2 cups chopped pecans

Combine first 5 ingredients and 1 cup pecans in bowl; mix well. Shape into ball. Chill until firm. Roll in remaining 1 cup pecans. Chill until serving time. Yield: 24 servings.

Bette Deniston, Xi Eta Mu
Carbondale, Illinois

CHILI-COATED CHEESE BALL

1 pound Velveeta cheese	½ to 1 cup chopped pecans
2 ounces cream cheese	Chili powder to taste
1 tablespoon garlic powder	

Soften cheeses. Combine cheeses, garlic powder and pecans in bowl; mix well. Shape into ball. Chill until firm. Roll in chili powder until completely coated. Serve with favorite crackers. Yield: 8 to 12 servings.

Gail Duchamp, Alpha Epsilon
Lafayette, Louisiana

CORNED BEEF CHEESE LOG

2 packages corned beef
16 ounces cream cheese,
softened
2 tablespoons chopped
chives

1½ teaspoons onion salt
1 teaspoon MSG
2 tablespoons
Worcestershire sauce

Reserve 5 slices corned beef. Chop remaining corned beef fine. Combine with cream cheese and remaining ingredients in bowl; mix throughly with hands. Shape into log. Wrap in reserved corned beef, placing 2 slices on top, two on bottom and fifth slice diagonally across top and securing with toothpicks. Chill overnight. Serve with toasted wheat crackers. Yield: 10 to 12 servings.

Sue Fulcher, Xi Alpha Mu
Fayetteville, North Carolina

FAVORITE CHEESE BALL

16 ounces cream cheese
½ cup shredded Cheddar
cheese
2½ ounces dried beef,
finely chopped
½ cup chopped pecans
¼ cup dried parsley

¼ teaspoon minced garlic
⅛ teaspoon red pepper
1 tablespoon
Worcestershire sauce
1 teaspoon dried chives
1 teaspoon dried onion

Soften cheeses in bowl. Reserve small amounts of beef, pecans and parsley. Add remaining beef, pecans and parsley and remaining ingredients to cheeses; mix well. Chill until firm. Shape into ball with buttered hands. Roll in mixture of reserved beef, pecans and parsley. Serve on lettuce-lined plate. Yield: 1 cheese ball.

Bonnie Beck, Xi Beta Rho
Boggstown, Indiana

BLUE CHEESE BALL

8 ounces cream cheese,
softened
1 cup shredded sharp
Cheddar cheese
4 ounces blue cheese,
crumbled

⅓ cup chopped walnuts
1½ teaspoons
Worcestershire sauce
1½ teaspoons minced
onion
Walnuts or parsley flakes

Combine all ingredients in food processor; process until well mixed. Shape into ball. Roll in additional walnuts or parsley flakes. Yield: 1 cheese ball.

Tammy Robbins, Xi Xi
Eielson AFB, Alaska

WALNUT AND BLUE CHEESE BALLS

8 ounces cream cheese
4 ounces blue cheese
1 tablespoon chopped
onion

10 tablespoons margarine
1 4-ounce can chopped
olives
1 cup chopped walnuts

Combine first 5 ingredients in bowl; mix well. Shape into 2 balls. Coat each with walnuts. Yield: 2 cheese balls.

Lola Glee Shanley, Preceptor Beta Upsilon
Hutchinson, Kansas

CHICKEN AND CHILIES CHEESE BALL

8 ounces cream cheese,
softened
½ cup chopped cooked
chicken
3 tablespoons chopped
green chilies
¼ teaspoon garlic powder

1 tablespoon minced
onion
1 tablespoon instant
chicken bouillon
½ cup coarsely chopped
nuts

Combine first 6 ingredients in bowl; mix well. Shape into ball; roll in nuts. Chill until serving time. Serve with assorted crackers. Yield: 2 cups.

Elaine Cumpton, Preceptor Omega
Monroe, Louisiana

SAVORY EDAM SPREAD

1 1¾-pound whole
Edam cheese, softened
1 cup beer
¼ cup butter, softened

1 teaspoon caraway seed
1 teaspoon dry mustard
½ teaspoon celery salt

Remove one-inch thick slice from top of cheese, leaving red wax covering intact. Scoop out cheese; reserve shell. Refrigerate shell. Grate cheese into medium bowl. Let stand at room temperature until very soft. Add beer, butter, caraway seed, mustard and celery salt; mix well. Spoon into reserved shell. Wrap in plastic wrap. Refrigerate or freeze for 2 to 3 days for improved flavor. Serve on crackers, Melba toast or celery. Yield: 4 cups.

JoBeth Vinson, Xi Gamma Sigma
Lubbock, Texas

HERB CHEESE ROUND

8 ounces cream cheese,
softened
1 teaspoon dried basil
leaves
1 teaspoon caraway seed

1 teaspoon dillweed
1 teaspoon chopped fresh
chives
1 clove of garlic, crushed
Lemon-pepper seasoning

Combine first 6 ingredients in bowl; mix well. Shape into 1x5-inch patty. Coat top and sides with lemon-pepper seasoning. Chill, covered, for 10 to 12 hours.
Yield: 25 servings.

Linda Merrihew, Xi Pi Omicron
Alpine, Texas

MACADAMIA NUT CHEESE BALL

16 ounces cream cheese,
softened
1½ cups shredded
Cheddar cheese
2 teaspoons minced onion

½ cup chopped sweet
pickles
1 teaspoon salt
½ cup chopped
macadamia nuts

Combine cream cheese, Cheddar cheese, onion, pickles and salt in bowl; mix well. Shape into ball; roll in macadamia nuts. Chill, covered, for several hours. Serve with crackers. Yield: 1 cheese ball.

Linda Heyland, Theta Mu
Susanville, California

PINE CONE CHEESE BALLS

16 ounces cream cheese, softened
½ cup real mayonnaise
½ tablespoon grated onion
¼ teaspoon dillweed
Dash of pepper
1 5-ounce jar Old English cheese spread, softened
1¼ cups natural brown almonds

Combine cream cheese and mayonnaise in bowl; mix well. Add onion, dillweed and pepper; mix well. Add Old English cheese; mix well. Shape as for 2 pine cones on cheese board. Chill, covered, overnight. Press almonds at slight angle into cheese mixture in overlapping rows, beginning at narrow end, until cheese is covered. Garnish with artificial holly leaves or pine sprigs and ribbon bow. Serve with crackers. Yield: 2 cups.

Helen Bennett, Preceptor Pi
Vernal, Utah

SANDY'S SOUTHWESTERN CHEESE BALL

16 ounces cream cheese, softened
1 cup chopped black olives
1 cup chopped ham
1 cup shredded Cheddar cheese
3 jalapeño peppers
2 tablespoons grated onion
Garlic salt and pepper to taste
Chopped pecans

Combine first 6 ingredients and seasonings in bowl; mix well. Shape into ball. Roll in chopped pecans. Refrigerate until firm. Serve with Ritz or Nutty Wheat Thin crackers. Yield: 1 cheese ball.

Liz Byrom, Pi Psi
Keystone Heights, Florida

PINEAPPLE CHEESE BALL

16 ounces cream cheese, softened
1 8½-ounce can crushed pineapple, drained
1 tablespoon seasoned salt
¼ cup chopped green bell pepper
2 tablespoons chopped onion
2 cups chopped pecans

Combine first 5 ingredients and 1 cup pecans in bowl; mix well. Chill until firm. Shape into ball; coat with remaining 1 cup pecans. Chill until serving time. Serve with crackers. Yield: 1 cheese ball.

Nina McMahon, Xi Alpha Nu
Annandale, Virginia

RANCH-STYLE CHEESE BALL

1 package Hidden Valley Ranch salad dressing mix
½ cup mayonnaise
½ cup milk
8 ounces cream cheese, softened
¼ cup chopped onion
1 teaspoon dillweed
1 teaspoon Beau Monde seasoning
2 cups shredded Cheddar cheese

Combine all ingredients in food processor. Process for 30 to 45 seconds or until well mixed. Shape into ball; place on serving plate. Sprinkle with additional dillweed. Serve with assorted crackers. Yield: 1 cheese ball.

Pam Allen, Theta Iota
Aurelia, Iowa

SALMON BALL

1 15-ounce can salmon, drained, flaked
8 ounces cream cheese, softened
¼ teaspoon salt
¼ teaspoon liquid smoke
1 teaspoon lemon juice
¾ to 1 cup finely chopped pecans
Fresh parsley, chopped

Combine salmon, cream cheese and seasonings in bowl; mix well. Shape into ball. Roll in pecans and parsley. Chill in refrigerator. Serve with crackers. Yield: One 5-inch cheese ball.

Betty McCanless, Laureate Chi
Eureka, Illinois

BRIE WITH BRANDY AND PECANS

¼ cup packed light brown sugar
2 tablespoons Brandy
¼ cup chopped pecans
1 8 to 12-ounce wheel Brie

Preheat oven to 400 degrees. Combine first 3 ingredients in saucepan. Cook over low heat until blended, stirring frequently. Place Brie in baking dish. Pour Brandy mixture over Brie. Bake for 10 minutes or until softened. Serve with apple slices or crackers. Yield: 12 servings.

Elisabeth Hinman-Smith, Iota Theta
Carrboro, North Carolina

SPICY CHEESE MOLD

1 pound Velveeta cheese, chopped
1 pound sharp Cheddar cheese, shredded
1 pound mild Cheddar cheese, shredded
1 pound hot sausage

Melt cheeses in top of double boiler. Cook sausage in skillet until brown and crumbly; drain. Mix cheeses and sausage together. Pour into well-greased bundt or ring mold. Chill until firm. Unmold onto serving platter. Serve with crackers. Yield: 1 cheese mold.

Rebecca Rishe, Preceptor Theta Tau
Houston, Texas

STRAWBERRY AND CHEESE RING

12 ounces sharp Cheddar cheese, shredded
12 ounces medium Cheddar cheese, shredded
1 small onion, chopped
1 cup chopped pecans
1 cup mayonnaise
1 teaspoon red pepper
1 16-ounce jar strawberry jam
1 15-ounce package Triscuits

Combine first 6 ingredients in food processor container. Process until smooth. Press into 6-cup mold. Chill for 4 hours. Unmold onto serving plate. Spoon jam into center. Serve with Triscuits. Yield: 50 servings.

Marie Brackett, Delta Beta
Jonesboro, Arkansas

TUNA BALL

1 6½-ounce can tuna, drained	½ cup chopped onion
8 ounces cream cheese, softened	1 cup chopped nuts
⅓ cup mayonnaise	Pinch of salt
	Parsley flakes

Mix tuna, cream cheese and mayonnaise in bowl with fork. Add onion, nuts and salt; mix well. Shape into ball. Sprinkle generously with parsley flakes. Chill until serving time. Serve with favorite crackers.
Yield: 1 cheese ball.

Margaret Skidmore, Xi Beta Mu
Montrose, West Virginia

HAM AND SAUERKRAUT BALL

1 7-ounce can ham	½ cup mayonnaise
1 16-ounce can sauerkraut, drained	1 tablespoon chopped onion
1 cup shredded Cheddar cheese	½ cup cracker crumbs
1 tablespoon chopped green bell pepper	Pimento strips
	Sliced green olives

Mix first 7 ingredients in bowl. Shape into ball. Chill for 1 hour or longer. Place on serving plate. Garnish with pimento strips and sliced green olives. Serve with assorted crackers. Yield: 1 cheese ball.

Sharon L. Cullen, Xi Kappa
Austin, Minnesota

ZESTY CHEESE BALL

16 ounces cream cheese, softened	1 tablespoon minced onion
2 cups shredded Cheddar cheese	2 teaspoons Worcestershire sauce
1 tablespoon chopped pimento	1 teaspoon lemon juice
1 tablespoon chopped green bell pepper	Dash of salt
	Dash of red pepper
	Chopped pecans

Combine all ingredients, except pecans, in bowl; mix well. Chill for 1 hour. Shape into ball. Coat with pecans. Serve with crackers. Yield: 24 servings.

Bernice Evans, Xi Delta Iota
Jay, Florida

ARTICHOKE DIP

1 6-ounce can marinated artichoke hearts	6 tablespoons mayonnaise
1 8½-ounce can artichoke hearts, drained	2½ cups shredded Cheddar cheese
1 4-ounce can chopped green chilies	1 large package dip-sized corn chips

Drain marinated artichoke hearts, reserving 2 tablespoons marinade. Chop artichoke hearts. Combine with reserved marinade, green chilies and mayonnaise in bowl; mix well. Spoon into 9-inch pie plate. Top with cheese. Bake at 350 degrees for 20 to 25 minutes. Serve with chips. Yield: 6 servings.

Rita Countryman, Upsilon Sigma
Punta Gorda, Florida

EASY ARTICHOKE DIP

1 16-ounce can artichoke hearts	1 cup Parmesan cheese
	1 cup mayonnaise

Preheat oven to 350 degrees. Combine all ingredients in bowl; mix well. Pour into baking dish. Bake until bubbly. Serve with crackers. Yield: 3 cups.

Paula Vanover, Delta Omega
Danville, Kentucky

HOT ARTICHOKE DIP

2 16-ounce cans artichoke hearts	1 2-ounce jar sliced pimentos
½ small onion, chopped	4 ounces Parmesan cheese
1 4-ounce can chopped green chilies	1 2¾-ounce can French-fried onion rings
¾ cup mayonnaise	

Drain and chop artichoke hearts. Mix with onion, green chilies, mayonnaise, pimentos, Parmesan cheese and ½ cup onion rings in large bowl. Spoon into 8x8-inch baking dish. Bake at 350 degrees for 35 to 40 minutes. Crumble remaining onion rings on top. Serve with assorted crackers. Yield: 12 servings.

Martha Ann McAlister, Xi Alpha Mu
Flagstaff, Arizona

CHEESY ARTICHOKE SPREAD

2 cups shredded mozzarella cheese	⅛ teaspoon garlic salt
1 cup mayonnaise	1 16-ounce jar artichoke hearts, drained, chopped
1 cup Parmesan cheese	

Preheat oven to 350 degrees. Mix all ingredients in bowl. Spread in 10-inch pie plate. Bake for 30 minutes. Serve with crackers. Yield: enough for 50 to 60 crackers.

Eileen Wagner, Beta Omicron
Livonia, Michigan

AVOCADO-CHEESE DIP

8 ounces cream cheese, softened	3 tablespoons lemon juice
1 cup mashed avocado	1 teaspoon salt
⅓ cup finely chopped green onions	Dash of Worcestershire sauce

Beat cream cheese in mixer bowl until smooth. Add avocado gradually; beat until smooth. Add onions, lemon juice, salt and Worcestershire sauce; mix well. Spoon into serving dish. Serve with assorted crackers and bite-sized fresh vegetables. Yield: 2 cups.

Edna Painter, Laureate Theta
Oak Hill, West Virginia

AVOCADO DIP FOR VEGETABLES

1 large avocado, mashed	**3 tablespoons sour cream**
4 slices crisp-fried bacon,	**½ teaspoon onion juice**
crumbled	**2 teaspoons lemon juice**
8 ounces cream cheese,	**1 teaspoon grated lemon**
softened	**rind**
½ teaspoon salt	

Combine all ingredients in bowl; mix well. Chill, covered, for 1 hour. Spoon into serving dish. Serve with carrot, celery and cucumber sticks. Yield: 24 servings.

Averil Riffle, Laureate Delta
Marathon, Florida

ZESTY BACON DIP

1 cup low-fat cottage	**1 tablespoon chopped**
cheese	**scallions**
8 ounces cream cheese,	**1 tablespoon chopped**
softened	**parsley**
4 slices bacon, crisp-fried,	**1 tablespoon diced**
crumbled	**pimento**
1 tablespoon horseradish	

Mix cottage cheese and cream cheese in bowl. Stir in bacon, horseradish, scallions, parsley and pimento. Chill for 1 hour. Serve with vegetable crackers. Yield: 2 cups.

Kay McCarrick, Xi Beta Zeta
Decatur, Alabama

BACON AND CHEESE SPREAD

½ cup sliced almonds	**2 cups shredded Cheddar**
4 slices crisp-fried bacon,	**cheese**
crumbled	**¼ cup chopped green**
1 cup mayonnaise	**onions**

Combine all ingredients in bowl; mix well. Chill, covered, overnight. Serve with assorted crackers.

Beverley Moschak, Beta Lambda
Fremont, Nebraska

BEAN DIP

1 pound sausage	**2 16-ounce cans refried**
2 10-ounce cans Ro-Tel	**beans**
tomatoes	**1 bag dip-sized corn chips**

Cook sausage in skillet until brown and crumbly; drain well. Combine with Ro-Tel tomatoes and refried beans in Crock•Pot. Cook on Low until heated through. Serve with corn chips. Yield: 6 to 7 cups.

Vicki Miller, Alpha Phi
Bentonville, Arkansas

HOT BEAN DIP

8 ounces cream cheese,	**2 tablespoons parsley**
softened	**¼ cup chopped green**
1 cup sour cream	**onions**
1 large can bean dip	**8 ounces Cheddar cheese,**
½ envelope taco	**shredded**
seasoning mix	**8 ounces Monterey Jack**
5 drops of Tabasco sauce	**cheese, shredded**

Preheat oven to 350 degrees. Mix cream cheese with sour cream in bowl. Add bean dip, seasonings, parsley, green onions and half the Cheddar and Monterey Jack cheeses. Spoon into baking dish. Top with remaining cheeses. Bake for 20 to 30 minutes or until heated through. Serve with taco chips. Yield: 7 cups.

Judi Schmitt, Alpha Delta
Baker, Oregon

LAYERED BEAN DIP

1 16-ounce can refried	**6 green onions, chopped**
beans	**1½ cups shredded cheese**
1 8-ounce jar taco sauce	**1 2¼-ounce can sliced**
1 tomato, chopped	**olives**

Layer all ingredients in order listed in 10x10-inch serving dish. Serve with tortilla chips. Yield: 6 cups.

Vivian M. Watt, Xi Beta Eta
Mobile, Alabama

HOT CHIPPED BEEF DIP

8 ounces cream cheese,	**2 tablespoons milk**
softened	**2 tablespoons chopped**
½ cup sour cream	**green bell pepper**
¾ teaspoon	**1 bunch green onions,**
Worcestershire sauce	**chopped**
1 4-ounce package dried	**½ cup chopped pecans**
chipped beef	

Combine all ingredients in Crock•Pot. Cook on Low until heated through. Serve hot with Triscuits. Yield: 2 cups.

Marsha Cooper, Gamma Mu
Newton, Kansas

CORNED BEEF DIP

1 12-ounce can corned	**1½ cups mayonnaise**
beef	**2 teaspoons Beau Monde**
2 tablespoons chopped	**seasoning**
onion	**1 teaspoon chives**
2 tablespoons chopped	**1 teaspoon dillweed**
parsley	**1 teaspoon garlic powder**
1½ cups sour cream	**1 round loaf rye bread**

Break corned beef apart with fork in bowl. Add onion, parsley, sour cream, mayonnaise and seasonings; mix well. Scoop out center of loaf to form shell; cut center into pieces. Spoon corned beef mixture into bread shell. Serve with bread pieces. Yield: 4½ cups.

Mary Elizabeth Arnold, Preceptor Alpha Phi
Lebanon, Pennsylvania

BEEFY DIP

1 pound ground beef	½ teaspoon powdered
½ cup chopped onion	oregano
1 clove of garlic, minced	8 ounces cream cheese,
1 8-ounce can tomato	softened
sauce	⅓ cup Parmesan cheese
¼ cup catsup	½ cup shredded Cheddar
1 teaspoon sugar	cheese

Combine ground beef, onion and garlic in 2-quart glass casserole dish. Microwave, covered, on High for 5 to 6 minutes or until ground beef is no longer pink, stirring once; drain. Crumble ground beef. Add tomato sauce, catsup, sugar and oregano; cover. Microwave on High for 8 minutes; drain. Place cream cheese in small glass bowl. Microwave on Low until softened. Add cream cheese, Parmesan cheese and Cheddar cheese to hamburger mixture. Microwave on High for 3 minutes or until cream cheese is melted, stirring once. Keep warm in chafing dish. Serve with Triscuits or tortilla chips.
Yield: 8 servings.

Sharil Carlson, Xi Gamma Eta
Clay Center, Kansas

GROUND BEEF NACHO DIP

2 pounds ground beef	8 to 16 ounces refried
1 onion, chopped	beans, mashed
1 envelope taco seasoning	Salt and pepper to taste
mix	1 cup Velveeta cheese
1 can Mrs. Grimes hot	cubes
chili beans, mashed	1 cup shredded Cheddar
½ cup catsup	cheese

Brown ground beef and onion in skillet; drain. Mix with remaining ingredients except cheeses in bowl. Layer half the mixture, Velveeta cheese, remaining mixture and Cheddar cheese in Crock•Pot. Cook until cheeses melt and mixture can be stirred together. Serve with tortilla chips. Yield: 8 cups.

Pam Ebel, Xi Zeta Pi
Paullina, Iowa

BROCCOLI DIP

1 10-ounce package	2 tablespoons butter
frozen chopped broccoli	1 6-ounce roll garlic
1 4-ounce can water	cheese
chestnuts, chopped	1 10-ounce can cream of
1 4-ounce can chopped	mushroom soup
mushrooms	

Cook broccoli using package directions; drain. Sauté water chestnuts and mushrooms in butter in skillet. Melt cheese with mushroom soup in saucepan. Add broccoli and sautéed vegetables. Serve hot with tortilla chips.
Yield: 3 cups.

Teresa Britt, Eta Pi
Pocahontas, Arkansas

HOT BROCCOLI AND CHEESE DIP

3 stalks celery, thinly	1 10-ounce package
sliced	frozen chopped
1 medium onion, chopped	broccoli, thawed
1 4-ounce can sliced	1 20¾-ounce can
mushrooms, drained	condensed cream of
¼ cup butter	celery soup
3 tablespoons flour	
1 5-ounce roll garlic	
cheese, sliced	

Sauté celery, onion and mushrooms in butter in skillet. Stir in flour. Pour into lightly greased Crock•Pot. Add remaining ingredients. Cook on High until cheese melts, stirring occasionally. Cook on Low for about 2 hours or until serving time. Serve hot with chips, crackers or raw vegetables. Yield: 4 cups.

Margaret Doherty, Xi Alpha Alpha Omicron
Ennis, Texas

BUTTERMILK DIP

1 tablespoon onion	1 (heaping) tablespoon
powder	parsley flakes
1 teaspoon garlic salt	1 quart buttermilk
1 tablespoon MSG	4 cups mayonnaise

Combine all ingredients in bowl; mix well. Serve with fresh vegetables. Yield: 8 cups.

Ervinette Arthur, Beta Delta
Wallace, Idaho

CHAMPAGNE MUSTARD

4 eggs	⅔ cup dry mustard
¾ cup sugar	½ cup Chablis
½ cup cider vinegar	

Beat eggs in saucepan. Add remaining ingredients; blend well. Bring to a simmer, stirring constantly. Simmer for 8 minutes, stirring constantly. Pour into hot sterilized jars; seal. Store in refrigerator. Serve as dip with summer sausage, fresh vegetables or cheese or as spread on sandwiches. Yield: 2 cups.

Jean Pessano, Preceptor Alpha Beta
Ocean City, New Jersey

CHEESE DIP

8 ounces extra sharp	¼ small green bell
Cheddar cheese,	pepper, chopped
shredded	1 tablespoon lemon juice
8 ounces cream cheese,	1 2-ounce jar pimento
softened	1 teaspoon Worcestershire
¼ small onion, chopped	sauce

Combine all ingredients in bowl; mix well. Chill for 1 hour. Serve with vegetables or crackers. Yield: 1½ cups.

Karlene K. Humpal, Alpha Sigma
Decorah, Iowa

HOLIDAY CHEESE DIP

1 24-ounce carton
  cottage cheese
8 ounces cream cheese,
  softened

1 6-ounce jar jalapeño
  cheese spread
1 small package ranch-
  style salad dressing mix

Combine all ingredients in blender container. Process on High until creamy. Serve with crackers, chips and fresh vegetables. Yield: 4 cups.

Betty Jo Hebbert, Xi Psi
Potter, Nebraska

CHILI CHEESE DIP

3 tablespoons onion
  flakes
3 tablespoons water
8 ounces cream cheese,
  softened
3 tablespoons chili sauce

3 tablespoons French
  dressing
1 teaspoon Worcestershire
  sauce
⅛ teaspoon garlic salt
1 tablespoon catsup

Soften onion flakes in water in bowl. Add cream cheese; mix well. Add remaining ingredients; mix well. Chill until serving time. Serve with chips or vegetables. Yield: 1½ cups.

Dottie V. Duda, Laureate Theta
Oak Hill, West Virginia

ABC CHEESE SPREAD

⅓ cup chopped toasted
  almonds
3 slices crisp-fried bacon,
  crumbled
¾ cup mayonnaise

1½ cups shredded sharp
  Cheddar cheese
1 tablespoon minced
  green onion
¼ teaspoon salt

Combine all ingredients in bowl; mix well. Serve on wheat crackers. Yield: 2 cups.

Carol Drake, Preceptor Xi
Winnemucca, Nevada

PIMENTO CHEESE SPREAD

2 pounds Velveeta cheese
1 dozen hard-cooked eggs
½ cup chopped onion
1 jar pimentos

1 cup mayonnaise-type
  salad dressing
½ teaspoon salt

Grind cheese, eggs and onion together. Stir in pimento, salad dressing and salt. Chill, covered, for several hours. Serve with party bread or crackers. Yield: 10 cups.

Reva J. Falk, Preceptor Alpha Epsilon
Tucson, Arizona

THE BEST QUESO IN ANTHONY

2 10-ounce packages
  frozen chopped broccoli
2 10-ounce cans cream of
  mushroom soup
2 pounds Velveeta cheese,
  cubed

1 2-ounce jar chopped
  pimentos
Chopped jalapeño
  peppers to taste

Preheat Crock•Pot to High. Cook broccoli using package directions; drain. Combine with soup, cheese, pimentos and jalapeño peppers in Crock•Pot. Cook until cheese is melted, stirring occasionally. Keep warm on Low. Serve with chips. Yield: 6 cups.

Janice Lunsford, Xi Alpha Zeta
Anthony, New Mexico

CHEESY RO-TEL FONDUE

4 ounces Velveeta cheese
1 cup shredded Cheddar
  cheese

1 6-ounce roll garlic
  cheese
1 can Ro-Tel tomatoes

Combine cheeses in double boiler. Heat until cheeses melt. Add Ro-Tel; mix well. Heat to serving temperature. Spoon into chafing dish. Serve with tortilla chips or dried bread. Yield: 3 to 4 cups.

Marian Zoller, Preceptor Epsilon
Maryland Heights, Missouri

FIRESIDE FONDUE

2 pounds Swiss cheese,
  shredded
5 tablespoons flour
3¼ cups Chablis

¼ teaspoons white pepper
Dash of nutmeg
3 tablespoons Brandy

Coat cheese with flour. Warm Chablis in heavy saucepan; do not boil. Add cheese gradually, stirring constantly. Add seasonings and brandy gradually, blending well. Pour into warm fondue pot. Keep warm over lowest heat; do not boil. Stir occasionally. Serve with plain or toasted French bread cubes for dipping. Yield: 10 to 12 servings.

Peggy W. Ellis, Zeta Kappa
Virginia Beach, Virginia

CHEESY CHILI DIP

8 ounces cream cheese,
  softened
1 4-ounce can diced
  green chilies

1 16-ounce can chili
  without beans
1½ cups shredded cheese

Spread cream cheese in 8x8-inch glass baking dish. Layer green chilies, chili and cheese over top. Microwave on High for 10 minutes or until bubbly. Serve with tortilla chips. Yield: 15 to 20 servings.

Anita Chambers, Epsilon Chi
Pratt, Kansas

CHILI DIP

1 onion, finely chopped
1 green bell pepper, finely
  chopped
2 tablespoons butter
1 16-ounce can chili
  without beans

1 10-ounce can cream of
  mushroom soup
12 ounces sharp Cheddar
  cheese, cubed

Sauté onion and green pepper in butter in skillet until onion is transparent. Stir in chili and soup. Add cheese; heat until cheese is partially melted. Pour into chafing dish. Serve with corn chips. Yield: 12 servings.

Nancy Zsoldos, Laureate Gamma
Williamson, West Virginia

AUDREY'S CHIP DIP

8 ounces cream cheese, softened
2 tablespoons French dressing
1 tablespoon minced onion
2 tablespoons cream
½ cup catsup
½ teaspoon salt
1 teaspoon garlic salt

Combine all ingredients in bowl; mix well. Chill for several hours. Serve with chips. Yield: 1 cup.

Audrey Sasse, Xi Gamma
Miles City, Montana

CHUTNEY DIP

8 ounces cream cheese, softened
¼ cup chutney
¼ teaspoon dry mustard
1 teaspoon curry powder
¼ cup chutney
3 green onions, sliced
Slivered almonds

Combine cream cheese, ¼ cup chutney, mustard and curry powder in blender or container. Chill for 2 hours. Spread on serving plate. Top with ¼ cup chutney, green onion and almonds. Serve with snack crackers. Yield: 6 servings.

Lucille Humbert, Laureate Rho
Greensburg, Indiana

CHUTNEY SUPREME

¾ cup chopped salted peanuts
1 medium bunch green onions, chopped
¾ cup coconut
1 bottle of chutney
8 ounces cream cheese, softened

Line 8-ounce plastic container with plastic wrap. Layer chopped peanuts, chopped green onions, coconut, chutney and softened cream cheese in prepared bowl. Chill in refrigerator until firm. Invert on serving plate; remove plastic wrap. Serve with Triscuits. Yield: 8 servings.

Wanda Gish, Preceptor Alpha Omicron
Marshall, Michigan

CLAM BALL DIP

1 large round loaf French bread
16 ounces cream cheese, softened
3 6½-ounce cans chopped clams
2 tablespoons grated onion
2 tablespoons beer
2 teaspoons Worcestershire sauce
2 teaspoons lemon juice
1 teaspoon hot pepper sauce
½ teaspoon salt
¼ cup clam juice

Preheat oven to 250 degrees. Cut top from bread; set aside. Hollow out loaf, leaving 1½ to 2-inch shell. Cut bread into cubes. Beat cream cheese in bowl until smooth. Stir in remaining ingredients; mix well. Spoon into bread shell, replace top. Wrap in foil. Bake for 3 hours. Toast reserved bread cubes during last 5 minutes. Serve dip hot with toasted bread and fresh vegetables. Yield: 12 servings.

Diane Gustafson, Xi Gamma Psi
Fort Collins, Colorado

CLAM DIP

1 6½-ounce can minced clams, drained
½ cup salad dressing
2 teaspoons minced onions
½ cup sour cream
¼ teaspoon salt
¼ teaspoon pepper
4 slices bacon, crisp-fried, crumbled

Combine all ingredients in bowl; mix well. Chill until serving time. Yield: 2 cups.

Rene Ann Kennedy, Xi Beta Sigma
Sulphur, Oklahoma

MINCED CLAM DIP

1 package dry vegetable soup mix
2 cups sour cream
1 7-ounce can minced clams, drained

Combine all ingredients in bowl; mix well. Chill until serving time. Yield: 3 cups.

Elsie K. Brown, Alpha
Lindale, Georgia

SHOE PEG CORN DIP

1 8-ounce can whole kernel corn, drained
4 ounces Cheddar cheese, shredded
¼ cup Parmesan cheese
1 cup sour cream
½ cup mayonnaise
1 tablespoon grated onion

Combine all ingredients in bowl; mix well. Chill until serving time. Serve with crackers. Yield: 2 cups.

Donna Luse, Preceptor Alpha Sigma
Marion, Ohio

CRAB AND CHILI SAUCE DIP

16 ounces cream cheese, softened
1 medium onion, chopped
1 tablespoon mayonnaise
1 tablespoon Worcestershire sauce
1 teaspoon lemon juice
Garlic salt to taste
1 6-ounce bottle of chili sauce
1 7-ounce can white crab meat
Parsley

Combine first 6 ingredients in bowl; mix well. Spread on serving plate. Chill for 1 hour. Layer chili sauce and crab meat over top. Sprinkle with parsley. Serve with favorite crackers or chips. Yield: 3½ cups.

Sarah K. Roberts, Gamma Nu
Missouri City, Texas

CRAB AND HORSERADISH DIP

1 7-ounce can crab meat
8 ounces cream cheese, softened
2 ounces Cheddar cheese, shredded
½ cup horseradish sauce
⅛ teaspoon garlic powder
1 teaspoon Worcestershire sauce
Dash of salt and pepper

All ingredients should be at room temperature. Rinse crab meat several times. Shred and squeeze out excess water. Combine all ingredients in bowl. Chill. Serve at room temperature with crackers or chips. Yield: 3 cups.

Phyllis Johnson, Xi Eta Lambda
Tampa, Florida

CRAB MEAT IN A BOWL

16 ounces cream cheese, softened
¼ to ½ pound crab meat
2 tablespoons chopped onion
2 tablespoons beer
2 teaspoons Worcestershire sauce
2 teaspoons lemon juice
½ teaspoon salt
1 large round loaf bread

Preheat oven to 250 degrees. Beat cream cheese in bowl until smooth. Add crab meat, onion, beer, Worcestershire sauce, lemon juice and salt. Cut top from bread; hollow out loaf to make shell. Cut bread into bite-sized pieces. Place bread shell on foil-lined baking sheet. Spoon crab meat mixture into shell; wrap with foil. Bake for 3 hours. Serve with reserved bread and fresh vegetables. Yield: 4 cups.

Prudence De Lucca, Beta Phi
Mesa, Arizona

LAYERED CRAB DIP

11 ounces cream cheese, softened
2 tablespoons mayonnaise
2 tablespoons lemon juice
1 tablespoon Worcestershire sauce
2 tablespoons minced onion flakes
½ teaspoon garlic powder
1 12-ounce bottle of chili sauce
1 6-ounce can crab meat
2 cups shredded mozzarella cheese
Parsley flakes
Oregano to taste

Combine cream cheese, mayonnaise, lemon juice, Worcestershire sauce, onion flakes and garlic powder in bowl; mix until smooth. Spread on 10-inch serving platter. Cover with chili sauce. Sprinkle crab meat on top. Top with cheese, parsley and oregano. Chill until serving time. Serve with onion crackers. Yield: 12 servings.

Sharon Steinberger, Xi Gamma
Lexington, Nebraska

CRAB PÂTÉ

1 envelope unflavored gelatin
3 tablespoons cold water
1 10-ounce can cream of mushroom soup
8 ounces cream cheese, softened
¾ cup mayonnaise
1 7-ounce can crab meat, drained, flaked
1 small onion, grated
1 cup finely chopped celery

Soften gelatin in cold water. Heat soup in saucepan over low heat. Add gelatin; stir until dissolved. Mix in remaining ingredients. Pour into oiled 4-cup mold. Chill until firm. Unmold onto serving plate. Serve with crackers, Melba toast or 2-inch bread rounds. Yield: 16 servings.

Sharon A. Crumpton, Xi Gamma Tau
Norman Park, Georgia

Donna Hendricks, Preceptor Alpha Omicron, Cherokee, Oklahoma, uses part of the refreshments, such as a fruit basket or dip tray, as a centerpiece for a serving table.

CRAB DELIGHT

1 envelope unflavored gelatin
3 tablespoons cold water
1 10-ounce can cream of mushroom soup
1 cup mayonnaise
8 ounces cream cheese, softened
1 small onion, grated
1 7-ounce can crab meat

Soften gelatin in cold water. Heat soup in saucepan over low heat. Add gelatin; stir until dissolved. Remove from heat. Blend mayonnaise and cream cheese in bowl. Add soup, onion and crab meat; mix well. Rinse 3-cup mold with cold water. Pour in crab mixture. Chill overnight. Unmold onto serving plate. Yield: 3 cups.

Arlene Facchin Villa, Laureate Gamma Delta
San Marcos, California

CRAB PIZZA

16 ounces cream cheese, softened
¼ cup mayonnaise
1 to 2 tablespoons Worcestershire sauce
1 to 2 teaspoons lemon juice
½ cup chopped onion
½ teaspoon garlic salt
1 12-ounce bottle of seafood cocktail sauce
1 7-ounce can crab meat, drained, flaked

Combine first 6 ingredients in bowl; mix well. Spread mixture on large plate with rim. Spread cocktail sauce over cream cheese layer. Top with crab meat. Serve with crackers. Yield: 10 to 12 servings.

Patsy Ruth Frye, Xi Gamma Beta
Fairfax, Virginia

CUCUMBER-CHEESE DIP

8 ounces cream cheese, softened
2 tablespoons lemon juice
1 large cucumber, coarsely grated
2 tablespoons finely chopped green onions
Dash of salt
Dash of pepper

Combine cream cheese and lemon juice in bowl; mix well. Add ½ cup drained cucumber and green onions. Season with salt and pepper. Thin with cucumber juice if desired. Garnish with cucumber slices. Serve with chips or bacon-flavored crackers. Yield: 1½ cups.

Mary E. Young, Iota Chi
Wagoner, Oklahoma

CURRY DIP

2 cups mayonnaise
1 tablespoon curry powder
1 teaspoon lemon juice
1 teaspoon steak sauce
1 teaspoon pepper
1 teaspoon Worcestershire sauce
Dash of Tabasco sauce
Dash of celery salt
Dash of garlic salt

Combine all ingredients in bowl; mix well. Chill for 1 hour. Serve with fresh vegetables. Yield: 2 cups.

Janet Edmonds, Omicron Lambda
Sarasota, Florida

ZESTY CURRY DIP

1 cup mayonnaise	1 teaspoon dry mustard
1 teaspoon curry powder	1 teaspoon horseradish
1 teaspoon wine vinegar	1 teaspoon garlic salt
1 teaspoon prepared mustard	1 teaspoon chopped onion

Combine all ingredients in bowl; mix well. Chill until serving time. Serve with bite-sized fresh vegetables. Yield: 1 cup.

Patsy Berry, Laureate Pi
Mansfield, Ohio

FRITO DIP

1 pound ground beef	1 8-ounce jar Cheez Whiz
1 10-ounce can tomato soup	1 8-ounce jar salsa
1 10-ounce can cream of mushroom soup	Chopped onion to taste

Brown ground beef in skillet, stirring frequently. Add remaining ingredients. Simmer for 10 to 15 minutes. Serve warm with corn chips. Yield: 6 cups.

Beverly Goates, Xi Theta
Pocatello, Idaho

ALOHA DIP FOR FRUIT

1 large pineapple	2 cups sour cream
1/4 cup packed light brown sugar	12 macaroons, crushed

Cut top off pineapple. Scoop out pulp, reserving shell. Cut pineapple pulp into chunks. Drain pineapple shell and chunks on paper towel. Combine brown sugar, sour cream and macaroons in bowl; mix well. Chill for 3 to 4 hours. Spoon dip into pineapple shell on serving plate. Serve with reserved pineapple chunks, grapes and apple and banana slices. Yield: 3 cups.
Note: May substitute crushed vanilla wafers and 2 tablespoons coconut for macaroons.

Cheryl Miller, Xi Zeta Rho
Muncy, Pennsylvania

AMBROSIA FRUIT DIP

1 cup fruit-flavored yogurt	1/4 cup chopped toasted pecans
1/2 cup cream of coconut	

Combine yogurt and cream of coconut in small bowl; mix well. Stir in pecans. Chill in refrigerator. Serve with fresh fruit. Yield: 2 cups.

Virginia Fawley
Kansas City, Missouri

CARAMEL DIP

8 ounces cream cheese, softened	3/4 cup packed light brown sugar
1/4 cup sugar	1 teaspoon vanilla extract

Combine all ingredients in mixer bowl. Beat until blended. Serve with apple slices and other fresh fruit. Yield: 2 cups.

Jean Rucker, Alpha Rho
Maryville, Missouri

CREAMY CARAMEL DIP

1 pound caramels	1 cup sour cream

Melt caramels in microwave or in double boiler. Stir in sour cream until smooth. Serve with sliced apples, cake or other fruits. Yield: 8 to 10 servings.

Jo Ellen Nelson, Xi Delta Beta
Upland, Indiana

CREAM CHEESE SPREAD FOR FRUIT

16 ounces cream cheese, softened	1 teaspoon grated lemon rind
1/4 cup butter, softened	1 teaspoon vanilla extract
1 cup confectioners' sugar, sifted	2 pounds apples, sliced
2 tablespoons orange juice	

Combine first 6 ingredients in bowl; blend well. Chill for 30 minutes or longer. Place dip in small bowl on serving plate. Arrange apple slices around bowl. Yield: 3 cups.

Linda Necrason, Eta Iota
Winter Park, Florida

EASY FRUIT DIP

8 ounces cream cheese, softened	1 7-ounce jar marshmallow creme

Combine cream cheese and marshmallow creme in mixer bowl. Beat until smooth. Serve with fresh fruit. Yield: 2 cups.

Debbie Garcia, Delta Eta
Clarksburg, West Virginia

MARSHMALLOW DIP

1 11-ounce jar marshmallow creme	1 to 2 tablespoons lemon juice
1/2 cup mayonnaise	

Combine all ingredients in bowl; mix well. Chill in refrigerator. Serve with bite-sized fruit. Yield: 2 cups.

Laura M. Ritzman, Preceptor Alpha Mu
Sunnyvale, California

ORANGE FRUIT DIP

1 6-ounce can frozen orange juice concentrate	1/4 cup milk
1 3-ounce package vanilla instant pudding mix	1/2 cup sour cream

Combine orange juice concentrate, pudding mix and milk in mixer bowl. Beat for 2 minutes. Stir in sour cream. Chill for 2 hours. Serve with fruit. Yield: 2 cups.

Paula Vanover, Delta Omega
Danville, Kentucky

PINEAPPLE FRUIT DIP

8 ounces cream cheese, softened	1 8-ounce jar pineapple preserves
1 8-ounce container whipped topping	

Beat cream cheese until light and fluffy. Add whipped topping; mix well. Fold in preserves. Serve with fresh fruit. Yield: 4 cups.

Nancy J. Hanway, Preceptor Beta Theta
Unionville, Pennsylvania

RASPBERRY FRUIT DIP

1 12-ounce container whipped topping	Fresh or frozen raspberries to taste
1 cup vanilla yogurt	

Mix whipped topping, yogurt and raspberries in bowl with spoon. Spoon into serving dish. Place on large serving plate. Arrange fresh fruit such as strawberries, bananas, pineapple, grapes and apples around dip. Yield: 4 cups.

Carol Stanion, Beta Omega
Stansbury, Utah

ROMANOFF SAUCE

4 cups sour cream	¼ cup cinnamon
2 cups packed light brown sugar	¼ cup Brandy
	Nutmeg to taste

Combine all ingredients in bowl; mix well. Serve with banana slices, pineapple chunks and fresh strawberries. Yield: 4½ cups.

Donna Schnitman, Alpha Omicron Sigma
Plano, Texas

STRAWBERRY-CREAM CHEESE FRUIT DIP

3 ounces cream cheese, softened	¼ cup strawberry jam
	1 cup whipped topping

Mix cream cheese and jam in bowl until well blended. Blend in whipped topping. Serve with assorted fresh fruits such as pineapple, bananas, kiwifruit, orange slices and pear chunks. Yield: 1½ cups.

Carolyn M. Cline, Xi Sigma
Jamestown, New York

SWEET SURPRISE

8 ounces cream cheese, softened	1 16-ounce can fruit cocktail
½ 3-ounce package French vanilla instant pudding mix	Sour cream to taste

Combine all ingredients in blender container. Process until smooth. Serve with vanilla wafers. Yield: 3 cups.

Melanie Winyall, Beta Theta
Columbia, Maryland

PIÑA COLADA FRUIT DIP

1 3-ounce package coconut instant pudding mix	1 8-ounce can crushed pineapple
¾ cup milk	½ cup yogurt

Combine all ingredients in blender container. Process for 30 seconds, stirring once. Refrigerate for several hours. Serve with fresh cherries, melon, apple or pear slices. Yield: 2½ cups.

Chris Johnson, Delta Psi
Farwell, Michigan

HUMMUSBIT-TAHINI

2 16-ounce cans garbanzo beans	½ teaspoon salt
1 clove of garlic, pressed	3 tablespoons tahini (sesame butter)
½ cup lemon juice	1 tablespoon olive oil
⅛ teaspoon cumin	Parsley

Drain 1 can beans. Place in food processor container. Add remaining can undrained beans. Combine garlic, lemon juice, cumin and salt in bowl. Add to food processor. Process until smooth. Add tahini; blend well. Pour into serving dish. Dribble olive oil over top. Garnish with parsley. Serve with pita bread. Yield: 4 cups.

Barbara Sledjeski, Xi Epsilon Eta
Centreville, Virginia

DELICIOUS GUACAMOLE

3 large avocados	1 teaspoon garlic powder
1 tablespoon minced onion	3 tablespoons picante sauce
1 teaspoon celery salt	Tomatoes or black olives

Mash the avocados with fork in bowl. Add remaining ingredients; mix well. Chill for 1 hour. Serve on bed of shredded lettuce. Garnish with diced tomatoes or sliced black olives. Yield: 4 cups.

Linda Bowen, Omega Nu
Lancaster, California

GUACAMOLE DIP

2 8-ounce cartons guacamole dip, softened	Shredded Cheddar cheese to taste
16 ounces cream cheese, softened	½ can black olives, sliced
¼ head lettuce, shredded	½ medium tomato, chopped

Layer mixture of guacamole and cream cheese on glass serving dish. Layer with remaining ingredients in order listed. Serve with tortilla chips. Yield: 4 cups.

Janet Pownell, Xi Beta Zeta
Spokane, Washington

To make guacamole ahead of time, **Patricia McInerney, Xi Beta Zeta, Decatur, Alabama,** leaves an avocado seed in the guacamole until serving time to keep it from turning dark.

HAM SPREAD

8 ounces cream cheese, softened
1/4 cup mayonnaise
2 cups ground cooked ham

1 tablespoon parsley
1 tablespoon finely chopped onion
1/4 teaspoon dry mustard

Combine all ingredients in bowl; mix well. Serve with crackers or vegetables. Yield: 2 cups.

Lynnette S. Groepper, Mu Nu
Eldora, Iowa

LADIES' DELIGHT

12 ounces cream cheese, softened
1/2 cup butter, softened
1/2 cup sour cream
1/2 cup sugar
1 envelope unflavored gelatin

1/4 cup water
1/4 teaspoon grated lemon rind
1/2 cup white raisins
1 cup slivered almonds, toasted

Blend cream cheese, butter and sour cream in large mixer bowl. Mix in sugar. Soften gelatin in water in saucepan. Heat until gelatin is dissolved. Stir into cream cheese mixture. Add remaining ingredients. Pour into greased 1-quart mold. Chill until set. Unmold onto serving plate. Serve with cinnamon graham crackers. Yield: 20 servings.

Susan Edwardson-Johnson, Preceptor Upsilon
Red Oak, Iowa

COMPUESTA

1 16-ounce can refried beans
1 16-ounce can jalapeño refried beans
1 onion, minced
White wine
3 or 4 avocados
Lemon juice to taste
Seasonings to taste
2 tablespoons mayonnaise

1 cup sour cream
1 envelope dry taco seasoning mix
2 cups shredded Monterey Jack cheese
2 cups shredded Cheddar cheese
Sliced black olives
1 tomato, seeded, chopped

Mix beans and onion in bowl. Add a small amount of white wine to make of spreading consistency. Spread in 9x13-inch dish. Mash avocados in bowl. Add lemon juice and seasonings to taste. Spread over bean layer. Blend mayonnaise, sour cream and taco seasoning mix in small bowl. Spread over avocado layer. Sprinkle with mixture of cheeses and add layers of olives and tomato. Serve with large tostado chips. Yield: 20 to 25 servings.

Nadine Coyle, Preceptor Laureate Beta
Corpus Christi, Texas

FESTIVE MEXICAN DIP

1 16-ounce can refried beans
1/4 cup picante sauce
1 cup sour cream
1 4-ounce can chopped green chilies
2 avocados, mashed

1/4 c. chopped olives
1/4 cup minced onions
1 cup shredded longhorn cheese
Shredded lettuce
1/4 cup chopped tomatoes

Mix beans and picante sauce in bowl. Spread on large platter. Layer remaining ingredients over bean mixture in order listed. Serve with nacho chips.
Yield: 12 to 15 servings.

Betty Trembly, Xi Beta Iota
Cortez, Colorado

BAKED MEXICAN DIP

1 pound ground beef
1 medium onion, chopped
1 16-ounce can refried beans
1 4-ounce can chopped green chilies
1 to 2 cups taco sauce

1 pound Cojack cheese, shredded
Chopped green onions
Chopped tomatoes
1 4-ounce can chopped black olives
2 cups sour cream

Preheat oven to 350 degrees. Cook ground beef with onion in skillet, stirring until brown and crumbly; drain. Spread layer of beans in 8x8-inch baking dish. Add layers of ground beef mixture, green chilies, taco sauce and cheese. Bake for 20 minutes. Top with green onions and remaining ingredients. Serve with corn or tortilla chips. Yield: 16 servings.

Glenda Long, Iota Eta
Louisburg, Kansas

LAYERED MEXICAN DIP

3 avocados, mashed
1 clove of garlic, minced
1 tomato, chopped
Chopped green chilies to taste
Tabasco sauce to taste
Salt and pepper to taste
1 16-ounce can refried beans
1 envelope dry taco seasoning mix

1 cup sour cream
2 4-ounce cans sliced black olives
2 medium tomatoes, chopped
1 purple onion, chopped
1 4-ounce can chopped mild green chilies
Shredded Monterey Jack and Cheddar cheeses

Combine first 5 ingredients and salt and pepper in bowl; mix well. Spread refried beans in 9x13-inch dish. Sprinkle with taco seasoning mix. Add layer of avocado mixture and layers of sour cream and remaining ingredients in order listed. Yield: 8 servings.

Dinah Langley, Alpha Mu Epsilon
Hallsville, Texas

THREE-LAYER MEXICAN DIP

1 pound mild sausage
2 15-ounce cans refried beans with sausage
1 envelope dry taco seasoning mix

2 cups sour cream
1 pound sharp Cheddar cheese, shredded

Preheat oven to 350 degrees. Brown sausage in skillet, stirring frequently. Add refried beans and taco seasoning mix; mix well. Spread mixture in bottom of 9x13-inch baking pan. Spread with sour cream. Top with cheese. Bake for 30 minutes. Yield: 16 servings.

Julie Graham, Eta Kappa
St. Marys, Georgia

TRAVELING TACO DIP

1 16-ounce can refried beans	1 4-ounce can diced green chilies
1 8-ounce carton avocado dip	2 green onions, chopped
1 4¼-ounce can chopped ripe olives	1 cup shredded Cheddar cheese
1 tomato, chopped	Sour cream to taste

Spread refried beans in 2-quart rectangular serving dish. Spread avocado dip over beans. Mix olives, tomato, chilies and green onions in bowl; spread over avocado dip. Sprinkle with Cheddar cheese; dot with sour cream. Chill for 1 hour or longer. Yield: 25 servings.

Sara H. Pitcher, Laureate Gamma Alpha
San Jose, California

MEXICAN HOMINY DIP

1 6-ounce jar jalapeño Cheez Whiz	1 16-ounce can hominy, drained
1 10-ounce can cream of mushroom soup	

Melt Cheez Whiz in glass dish in microwave. Add soup and hominy. Microwave until heated through. Serve with tostados. Yield: 12 servings.

Reba T. Cross, Xi Pi Omicron
Alpine, Texas

MEXICAN PARTY DIP

1 16-ounce can tamales	1 16-ounce can chili with beans
1 10-ounce can cheese soup	

Mash tamales with fork in 1½-quart microwave dish. Add soup and chili; mix well. Microwave on High until heated through. Serve with tortilla chips. Yield: 8 servings.

Debbie Goss, Sigma Delta
Kearney, Missouri

MOUNT DIABLO DIP

½ cup chopped green onions	1 cup sour cream
2 ounces black olives, sliced	½ envelope dry taco seasoning mix
1 cup chopped tomatoes	2 avocados, mashed
1 cup shredded Monterey Jack cheese	Lemon juice to taste
1 cup shredded Cheddar cheese	Pinch of salt

Layer first 5 ingredients in order given in round bowl. Mix sour cream with taco seasoning mix in bowl. Spread over layers. Mix avocados with lemon juice and salt in bowl. Spread over top. Chill for 2 hours. Invert bowl onto plate; shake carefully to unmold. Serve with nacho chips. Yield: 12 servings.

Connie Anne Erikson, Xi Beta Delta
Bay City, Michigan

NACHOS PARA SOPEAR

12 corn tortillas	1 4-ounce can chopped green chilies
Oil for deep frying	3 cups shredded Monterey Jack cheese
Salt to taste	
½ pound chorizo sausage	¾ cup taco sauce
½ pound lean ground beef	¼ cup chopped green onions
1 large onion, chopped	1 avocado, mashed
2 16-ounce cans refried beans	1 cup sour cream

Cut tortillas into sixths. Fry in deep hot oil until crisp. Drain on paper towels; salt to taste. Remove casing from sausage; crumble into skillet. Sauté sausage, ground beef and onion in skillet until slightly brown; drain and add salt to taste. Spread refried beans in 10x15-inch baking dish. Layer sausage mixture, green chilies, cheese and taco sauce over beans. Bake, uncovered, for 20 minutes or until heated through. Top with green onions, mound avocado in center and add dollops of sour cream. Insert tortilla chips around edges. Yield: 4 to 6 servings.

Terry A. O'Neil, Sigma Zeta
Lombard, Illinois

SUPER NACHOS

1 pound lean ground beef	1 cup shredded Cheddar cheese
1 large onion, chopped	
1 teaspoon seasoned salt	¾ cup chunky taco sauce
½ teaspoon ground cumin	Fried tortilla chips
2 16-ounce cans refried beans	1 cup guacamole
	½ cup sour cream
1 1¼-ounce package dry taco seasoning mix	¼ cup chopped green onions
2 cups shredded Monterey Jack cheese	1 cup sliced ripe olives
1 4-ounce can chopped green chilies	

Preheat oven to 400 degrees. Brown ground beef with onion in skillet, stirring frequently; drain well. Add seasoned salt and cumin. Combine beans and taco seasoning mix in bowl; blend well. Add Monterey Jack cheese; mix well. Spread in shallow oval 10x15-inch baking dish. Top with ground beef mixture. Layer chilies and Cheddar cheese over top. Pour chunky taco sauce over cheese. Bake for 20 minutes or until heated through. Tuck tortilla chips around edge of platter; top with remaining ingredients. Yield: 10 to 12 servings.

Tammy Dighero, Lambda Eta
Lamar, Missouri

---

*Do a "dry run" before the party as **Alicia Miller, Xi Gamma Beta, Springfield, Virginia**, does. In order to see how many dishes are necessary and how much space is needed, make a list of each dish to be served, and note which serving plate will be used. Set the serving dishes out on the tables with a note card in each showing what will be served in that dish.*

EASY SUPER NACHOS

1 pound ground beef	1½ cups shredded
1 16-ounce can refried	Cheddar cheese
beans	1½ to 2 cups mild taco
1 4-ounce can chopped	sauce
green chilies	

Place ground beef in colander in casserole. Microwave on High for 2½ minutes; stir. Microwave for 2½ minutes longer. Layer beans, ground beef, green chilies, cheese and taco sauce in 3-quart casserole. Microwave on High for 5 to 8 minutes or until heated through. Serve with taco chips. Yield: 6 to 8 servings.

Loretta Kerschen, Alpha Alpha
Anthony, Kansas

PICO DE GALLO

1 bunch scallions, finely chopped	1 4-ounce can chopped jalapeño peppers
4 medium tomatoes, finely chopped	1 pound Monterey Jack cheese, cubed
1 green bell pepper, finely chopped	1 16-ounce bottle of Italian salad dressing
2 5½-ounce cans chopped green chilies	

Combine chopped vegetables, canned peppers and cheese in bowl. Pour salad dressing over all. Chill overnight. Drain excess salad dressing before serving; reserve drained dressing for use on salads. Yield: 6 to 8 servings.

Mariann Smith, Xi Sigma Alpha
El Paso, Texas

PLATTER DIP

1 pound ground beef	½ 4-ounce can chopped green chilies
1 envelope dry taco seasoning mix	2 cans bean dip
1 8-ounce bottle of taco sauce	1 cup sour cream
1 cup sour cream	Shredded lettuce
6 green onions, chopped	Chopped tomatoes
	Shredded cheese

Brown ground beef in skillet, stirring until crumbly; drain. Add taco seasoning mix and taco sauce. Cool. Mix 1 cup sour cream, green onions and green chilies in bowl. Layer bean dip, 1 cup plain sour cream, ground beef mixture, green chili mixture, lettuce, tomatoes and cheese in 16-inch round plate. Serve with taco-flavored chips. Yield: 8 servings.

Deena Gowdy, Mu Iota
Williams, Iowa

QUICK DIP

1 18-ounce jar apple jelly	1 1-ounce can dry mustard
1 10-ounce jar pineapple preserves	1 5-ounce jar horseradish
1 10-ounce jar apricot preserves	8 ounces cream cheese

Combine first 5 ingredients in bowl; mix well. Place cream cheese on serving plate. Pour sauce over top. Serve with crackers. Yield: 20 servings.

Suzy Wilson, Alpha Mu Epsilon
Hallsville, Texas

SALSA SAUCE

1 16-ounce can tomato sauce	½ teaspoon salt
½ teaspoon cumin	Tabasco sauce to taste
⅓ cup chopped green onions	½ teaspoon pepper

Combine all ingredients in saucepan. Heat to serving temperature. Serve with chicken nuggets. Yield: 2½ cups.

Bonnie Wakefield, Xi Delta Pi
Del Norte, Colorado

TEXAS CAVIAR SALSA

2 large tomatoes, finely chopped	6 green onions, chopped
2 4-ounce cans chopped black olives	3 tablespoons olive oil
2 4-ounce cans chopped green chilies	1½ tablespoons wine vinegar
	1 teaspoon garlic salt
	Salt and pepper to taste

Combine all ingredients in bowl; mix well. Chill for several hours. Serve with tortilla chips. Yield: 8 to 10 servings.

Paula D. Whinery, Xi Beta Nu
Dover, Arkansas

TEXAS CAVIAR

2 14-ounce cans jalapeño black-eyed peas, drained	2 cloves of garlic, minced
1 15½-ounce can white hominy, drained	1 medium green bell pepper, chopped
2 medium tomatoes, chopped	½ cup chopped onion
4 green onions, chopped	½ cup chopped fresh parsley
	1 8-ounce bottle of Italian salad dressing

Combine first 8 ingredients in bowl; mix well. Pour salad dressing over black-eyed pea mixture; cover. Marinate in refrigerator for 2 hours. Drain. Serve with tortilla chips. Yield: 3 cups.

Jill A. Spears, Alpha Upsilon Psi
The Colony, Texas

RED BELL PEPPER DIP

6 very large red bell peppers, finely chopped	¾ cup apple cider vinegar
1½ cups sugar	1 teaspoon salt
	1 tablespoon cornstarch

Combine all ingredients in saucepan. Bring to a boil; reduce heat. Simmer for 5 to 6 minutes. Store in refrigerator. Serve over cream cheese with wheat crackers. Yield: 3 cups.

Joyce Lockwood, Preceptor Kappa Kappa
Fairfield, California

RYE BREAD DIP

1⅓ cups mayonnaise	2 tablespoons onion
1⅓ cups sour cream	flakes
2 teaspoons Beau Monde	2 tablespoons parsley
seasoning	flakes
2 teaspoons dillweed	1 loaf unsliced rye bread

Combine first 6 ingredients in bowl; mix well. Chill overnight. Cut top from bread. Hollow out loaf, reserving chunks of bread. Place dip in bread shell just before serving. Use chunks of bread and then shell for dipping. Yield: 3 cups.

Carol Thomas, Xi Gamma Omicron
Evans, Georgia

SALMON SPREAD

1 7-ounce can pink	Garlic powder and onion
salmon, drained	flakes to taste
8 ounces cream cheese,	Chopped celery and
softened	parsley to taste

Mix salmon and cream cheese in bowl. Add remaining ingredients; mix well. Serve with crackers. Yield: 2 cups.

Deloris L. Carriker, Xi Beta Kappa
Hardtner, Kansas

SALMON HORS D'OEUVRE FILLING

1 envelope unflavored	½ cup chili sauce
gelatin	½ cup whipping cream,
3 tablespoons cold water	whipped
½ cup flaked drained	½ cup cream cheese,
salmon	softened
½ cup mayonnaise	1 bunch celery, separated

Soften gelatin in cold water in double boiler. Heat over hot water until gelatin dissolves, stirring constantly. Mix salmon and next 4 ingredients in bowl. Add gelatin. Chill. Stuff celery with salmon mixture. Garnish with chopped parsley or paprika. Yield: 2 cups.

Helen V. Miller, Xi Epsilon Tau
Waterloo, Iowa

VICKIE'S SALSA

1 18-ounce can tomatoes	1 teaspoon cumin
3 or 4 jalapeño peppers	½ teaspoon garlic powder
1½ tablespoons catsup	1 tablespoon onion flakes

Combine first 5 ingredients in food processor container. Process until chopped. Add onion flakes. Refrigerate until serving time. Serve with tortilla chips. Yield: 2 cups.

Barbara Brown, Omega
Jonesboro, Arkansas

CREAMY SHRIMP DIP

½ cup chili sauce	¼ cup chopped onion
8 ounces cream cheese,	2 teaspoons horseradish
softened	1 4-ounce can shrimp,
½ cup mayonnaise	rinsed, drained

Blend chili sauce and cream cheese in bowl. Mix in mayonnaise, onion and horseradish. Fold in shrimp. Chill, covered, for 1 hour. Serve with chips. Yield: 2½ cups.

Regina Smith, Xi Eta Chi
Morton, Illinois

DELICIOUS SHRIMP DIP

3 pounds small cooked	1 4-ounce jar dried
shrimp	chives
1 quart mayonnaise	1 2½-ounce jar
Juice of 1 lemon	horseradish
1 tablespoon onion salt	1 small jar parsley flakes

Combine all ingredients in bowl; mix well. Chill overnight. Serve with chips or crackers. Yield: 5 pounds.

Betty Faggard, Preceptor Zeta Omega
High Island, Texas

MEXICAN SHRIMP DIP

8 ounces cream cheese,	1 6-ounce carton frozen
softened	avocado dip, thawed
2 tablespoons mayonnaise	½ cup picante sauce
Worcestershire sauce to	1 8-ounce can baby
taste	shrimp, drained
1 clove of garlic, minced	2 green onions, chopped

Combine first 4 ingredients in bowl; mix well. Spread on rimmed plate; cover. Chill in refrigerator. Layer avocado dip and picante sauce over top. Sprinkle shrimp and green onions on top. Serve with chips. Yield: 12 servings.

Peggy Warren, Xi Psi Tau
Victoria, Texas

SHRIMP AND EGG DIP

1 cup chopped cooked	¼ cup chopped black
shrimp	olives
2 hard-cooked eggs,	¼ teaspoon garlic juice
chopped	1 teaspoon sugar
8 ounces cream cheese,	¼ teaspoon paprika
softened	⅛ teaspoon salt
¼ cup mayonnaise	

Combine all ingredients in bowl; mix well. Chill, covered, for 1 hour. Serve with melba toast. Yield: 2½ cups.

Virginia Warner, Iota Omega
Cape Coral, Florida

SHRIMP DIP

8 ounces cream cheese,	1 green onion, chopped
softened	1 teaspoon (heaping)
2 tablespoons mayonnaise	horseradish
1 teaspoon lemon juice	Salt and pepper to taste
¼ teaspoon curry powder	½ pound shrimp,
¼ teaspoon dill	chopped

Combine first 8 ingredients in bowl; mix until smooth. Fold in shrimp. Chill until serving time. Serve with butterfly butter crackers or sesame rounds. Yield: 2½ cups.

Janice Wheeles, Eta Iota
Orlando, Florida

SHRIMP CAROUSEL DIP

8 ounces cream cheese, softened	2 cups small curd cottage cheese
¼ teaspoon garlic salt	2 cups mayonnaise
¼ teaspoon salt	1 4-ounce can shrimp
½ teaspoon pepper	½ cup finely chopped onion
½ teaspoon lemon juice	½ cup finely chopped celery
½ teaspoon Worcestershire sauce	

Combine first 6 ingredients in blender container. Process until smooth. Add cottage cheese, mayonnaise, drained shrimp, onion and celery. Chill for 3 hours. Serve with fresh vegetables. Yield: 8 cups.

Terry Hebensperger, Xi Epsilon Tau
Hobart, Oklahoma

SHRIMP MOLD

1 envelope unflavored gelatin	2 cups chopped cooked shrimp
¼ cup cold water	¼ cup chopped green bell pepper
1 10-ounce can tomato soup	¾ cup chopped stuffed green olives
3 ounces cream cheese, softened	¼ cup chopped green onions
1 cup mayonnaise	Tabasco sauce to taste
½ cup chopped celery	

Soften gelatin in cold water. Heat soup and cream cheese in saucepan over low heat until cream cheese melts. Add gelatin; stir until dissolved. Remove from heat. Add mayonnaise and remaining ingredients; mix well. Pour into mold lightly greased with mayonnaise. Chill overnight. Unmold onto lettuce-lined serving plate. Serve with favorite crackers. Yield: 5 cups.

Peggy Camus, Xi Upsilon
Pensacola, Florida

CALIFORNIA SPINACH DIP

1 10-ounce package frozen chopped spinach, thawed	1 cup mayonnaise
½ cup chopped green onions	1 6-ounce carton cottage cheese
½ cup finely chopped parsley	Salt and pepper to taste
	1 round loaf sourdough bread

Squeeze spinach to remove excess moisture. Combine with next 6 ingredients in bowl; mix well. Chill, covered, for 2 to 6 hours. Cut top off bread. Remove inside of bread loaf to make serving bowl. Pour spinach mixture into bread bowl. Serve with remaining bread for dipping. Yield: 6 to 8 servings.

Cindy J. Pollard, Gamma Beta
Las Cruces, New Mexico

SPINACH COCKTAIL DIP

1 10-ounce package frozen chopped spinach, thawed	1 4-ounce can water chestnuts, drained, chopped
1 cup sour cream	1 medium onion, chopped
½ cup mayonnaise	1 envelope dry vegetable soup mix
1 medium tomato, peeled, seeded, chopped	

Dry spinach with paper towel. Combine with remaining ingredients in bowl; mix well. Serve with crackers, chips or fresh vegetables.

Elizabeth D. Bower, Preceptor Delta Xi
Pompano Beach, Florida

CHEESY SPINACH PARTY LOAF

1 1½-pound round loaf sourdough bread	1 pound Velveeta cheese
⅓ cup melted margarine	1 10-ounce package frozen chopped spinach, thawed
⅔ cup chopped red or green bell pepper	¼ teaspoon dried rosemary leaves, crushed
⅓ cup chopped celery	
⅓ cup chopped onion	

Preheat oven to 350 degrees. Cut top from loaf; scoop out and reserve center, leaving 1-inch shell. Cut reserved bread into bite-sized pieces. Brush inside of shell with margarine; place loaf on baking sheet. Bake for 20 minutes. Sauté pepper, celery and onion in any remaining margarine in skillet until tender. Add cheese. Cook over low heat until cheese melts, stirring constantly. Squeeze spinach dry; stir into cheese mixture with rosemary. Pour into bread shell. Serve with bread pieces and assorted fresh vegetable dippers. Yield: 2⅔ cups.

Linda Van Metre, Alpha Lambda
Lewisburg, West Virginia

EXTRA SPECIAL SPINACH DIP

1 envelope dry vegetable soup mix	1 cup chopped apple
1 cup sour cream	2 tablespoons chopped green onion (optional)
½ cup mayonnaise	2 tablespoons chopped radishes (optional)
½ teaspoon lemon juice	2 tablespoons crumbled blue cheese (optional)
1 10-ounce package frozen chopped spinach, thawed	

Combine first 4 ingredients in bowl. Squeeze spinach to remove excess moisture. Add to sour cream mixture; mix well. Fold in apple and optional ingredients as desired. Chill until serving time. Yield: 3 cups.

Carol Cox, Preceptor Gamma Rho
Stinnett, Texas

EASY TACO DIP

1 pound ground beef	1 8-ounce jar mild salsa
1 pound Velveeta cheese	

Brown ground beef in skillet, stirring until crumbly; drain. Melt cheese in double boiler over hot water. Add ground beef and salsa. Heat to serving temperature. Serve warm with taco chips. Yield: 15 to 20 servings.

Dorothy Twyford, Preceptor Beta Alpha
Springfield, Illinois

TACO CHIP DIP OLÉ

½ pound ground turkey	1 8-ounce can pork and
¼ cup finely chopped	beans
onion	½ cup coarsely shredded
1 8-ounce can tomato	cheese
sauce	¼ cup chopped black
1½ teaspoon chili powder	olives
½ teaspoon salt	¼ cup chopped onions

Brown turkey with ¼ cup onion in skillet, stirring frequently. Stir in tomato sauce, chili powder and salt. Bring to a simmer. Mash pork and beans; add to fried mixture. Simmer for 5 minutes. Pour into chafing dish; sprinkle with cheese, olives and remaining ¼ cup chopped onions. Serve hot with chips.
Yield: 4 to 6 servings.

Bonnie J. Carroll, Xi Nu
Evansville, Indiana

TACO DIP

8 ounces cream cheese,	1 small tomato, chopped
softened	1 cup shredded Colby
1 cup sour cream	cheese
2 tablespoons dry taco	1 4-ounce can chopped
seasoning mix	black olives
2 tablespoons taco sauce	Taco chips
2 cups shredded lettuce	

Combine first 4 ingredients in bowl; mix well. Spread on large serving plate. Top with lettuce, tomato, cheese and olives. Arrange taco chips around edge of plate.
Yield: 20 servings.

Nancy Sivinski, Mu Theta
Cherokee, Iowa

TACOS GRANDE

1½ to 2 pounds ground	1 16-ounce can chili
beef	1 can Ro-Tel tomatoes
1 pound Velveeta cheese	2 cups whipping cream

Brown ground beef in skillet, stirring until crumbly; drain. Add cheese. Cook over medium heat until cheese melts. Add chili and Ro-Tel. Cook over medium heat for 30 minutes, stirring frequently. Add whipping cream. Cook until heated through. Keep warm in Crock•Pot. Serve with corn chips. Yield: 25 servings.

Judy Rockett, Xi Beta Kappa
Hardtner, Kansas

TACO WHEELS

16 ounces cream cheese,	1 2-ounce jar pimento
softened	1 4-ounce jar chopped
6 green onions, chopped	black olives
1 7-ounce can mild green	6 flour tortillas
chilies	

Mix first 5 ingredients in bowl. Spread on tortillas; roll as for jelly roll. Slice as desired. Arrange on serving plate. Yield: 3 to 4 dozen.

Jolene Koos, Xi Beta Theta
Roseland, Nebraska

TUNA SPREAD

1 12½-ounce can tuna	¼ teaspoon celery salt
6 ounces cream cheese,	¼ teaspoon onion salt
softened	¼ teaspoon MSG
½ teaspoon soy sauce	1 tablespoon mayonnaise
¼ teaspoon garlic salt	

Combine all ingredients in bowl; mix well. Chill for several hours to overnight. Serve with crackers or thinly sliced bread. Yield: 3 cups.

Marilyn Cullen, Laureate Alpha Phi
Steilacoom, Washington

STARBURST VEGETABLE DIP

¼ cup chopped, peeled	1 cup sour cream
cucumber	3 tablespoons finely
Salt to taste	chopped green bell
1 ¾-ounce package dry	pepper
Italian salad dressing	3 tablespoons finely
mix	chopped pimento

Sprinkle cucumbers with salt. Let stand for 20 minutes. Place cucumbers in colander; rinse well and drain. Press cucumbers between paper towels until barely moist; set aside. Combine Italian salad dressing mix and sour cream in bowl; mix well. Stir in cucumber, green pepper and pimento. Chill for 1 hour. Serve with fresh vegetables. Yield: 1½ cups.

Pat Andazola, Xi Beta Zeta
Decatur, Alabama

ARTICHOKE PARMESAN

4 6-ounce jars artichoke	¼ cup chopped green bell
bottoms	pepper
8 ounces cream cheese,	½ cup melted margarine
softened	1 cup Parmesan cheese
¼ cup minced chives	

Drain and rinse artichokes; pat dry. Mix cream cheese with chives and green pepper in bowl. Fill artichoke bottoms; smooth level with rim. Dip into margarine; coat with cheese. Chill, covered, overnight. Preheat oven to 350 degrees. Place on baking sheet. Bake for 20 minutes. Yield: 8 servings.

Patricia A. Rindo, Xi Iota Chi
Stockton, California

HEAVENLY ARTICHOKE NIBLETS

2 6-ounce jars artichoke hearts	⅛ teaspoon pepper
1 small onion, chopped	⅛ teaspoon oregano
1 clove of garlic, mashed	⅛ teaspoon Tabasco sauce
4 eggs, beaten	2 cups shredded sharp Cheddar cheese
¼ cup fine dry bread crumbs	2 teaspoons minced parsley
¼ teaspoon salt	

Preheat oven to 325 degrees. Drain liquid from 1 jar artichokes into skillet; discard liquid of second jar. Sauté onion and garlic in artichoke liquid in skillet for 5 minutes. Add eggs, bread crumbs, seasonings, cheese and parsley; mix well. Pour into greased 7x11-inch baking dish. Bake for 30 minutes or until set. Cool. Cut into 1-inch squares. Serve cold or reheat in 325-degree oven for 10 minutes. Yield: 4 dozen.

Gloria Church, Preceptor Theta Xi
Dublin, California

BACON POLES

10 slices bacon	20 long, thin bread sticks

Cut bacon into halves lengthwise. Wrap bacon barber pole fashion around bread sticks. Arrange bacon poles not touching on 2 paper towels in bottom of 9x13-inch glass baking dish. Cover with paper towel. Microwave on High for 10 to 13 minutes, rotating dish after 5 minutes. Yield: 20 servings.

Sandi Davison, Preceptor Gamma Upsilon
Kansas City, Missouri

EASY BACON ROLL-UP HORS D'OEUVRES

1 pound bacon	1 10-ounce can cream of mushroom soup
1 loaf sandwich bread, crusts trimmed	

Preheat oven to 400 degrees. Cut bacon slices crosswise and into thirds lengthwise. Flatten bread slices with rolling pin. Spread with soup. Cut bread slices into halves. Roll each half as for jelly roll; wrap sliver of bacon around outside and secure with toothpick. Place on baking sheet. Bake for 15 minutes. Serve warm. Yield: 40 appetizers.

Carey Anne Gray-Tingler, Alpha Alpha
Glasgow, Montana

STUFFED BACON BITES

2 cups soft bread crumbs	⅛ teaspoon pepper
1 cup finely chopped apple	¼ cup milk
1 tablespoon minced parsley	1 egg, beaten
⅛ teaspoon salt	10 to 12 bacon slices, cut into halves

Preheat oven to 375 degrees. Mix first 5 ingredients in bowl. Mix in milk and egg. Shape by tablespoonfuls into balls; wrap in bacon and secure with toothpick. Place on wire rack in baking pan. Bake for 30 minutes or until bacon is brown and crisp. Serve hot. Yield: 20 servings.

Judy Doud, Zeta Lambda
Elgin, Oregon

BACON ROLL-UPS

¼ cup margarine	1 egg, beaten
½ cup water	8 ounces hot sausage
1½ cups herb-seasoned stuffing mix	8 ounces bacon slices, cut into thirds

Melt margarine in water in saucepan; remove from heat. Add stuffing mix, egg and sausage; mix well. Chill for 1 hour. Preheat oven to 375 degrees. Shape into pecan-sized balls; wrap with bacon and secure with toothpicks. Place on rack in baking pan. Bake for 15 minutes; turn over. Bake for 20 minutes. Drain on paper towels. Serve hot. Yield: 2 dozen.

Waunetta Magennis, Laureate Sigma
Whiteland, Indiana

BACON SNACKS

1 pound bacon	1 box Waverly crackers

Preheat oven to 250 degrees. Cut bacon slices into halves. Wrap bacon slices lengthwise around crackers. Place on rack in baking pan. Bake for 2 hours. Yield: 3 dozen.

Retha Weed, Preceptor Tau
Ozark, Alabama

BACON HORS D'OEUVRES

1 pound bacon	1 jar sweet pickled watermelon rind
1 pound brown sugar	

Preheat oven to 425 degrees. Cut bacon slices into halves; place on waxed paper. Coat heavily with brown sugar. Roll watermelon rind with bacon; secure with toothpicks. Place on rack in broiler pan. Bake for 15 minutes or until brown and crisp. Serve warm. Yield: 32 servings.

Sue L. Rhodes, Preceptor Alpha Chi
Glendale, Arizona

MEXICAN-STYLE CARROT APPETIZERS

2 pounds carrots, peeled	Pickled jalapeño peppers to taste
1½ cups water	
1 large white onion, sliced, separated into rings	1 tablespoon lemon pepper
	1½ cups white vinegar

Microwave carrots in water in glass baking dish for 8 minutes or until tender-crisp. Drain, reserving liquid. Cool. Slice carrots diagonally. Combine with onion and jalapeño peppers in glass container. Add reserved liquid, lemon pepper and vinegar. Chill for 2 days. Yield: 7½ cups.

Evelyn Ciolfe, Xi Beta Xi
Lemon Grove, California

CREAM CHEESE-STUFFED CELERY

8 ounces cream cheese, softened	Dash of soy sauce
Cream	Salt and cayenne pepper to taste
12 to 16 stuffed green olives, chopped	1 bunch celery

Blend cream cheese with enough cream in bowl to make spreadable. Add olives and seasonings; mix well. Rinse celery; pat dry. Cut into desired lengths. Fill with cream cheese mixture. Chill until serving time.
Yield: 12 servings.

Carolyn Ferry, Omicron
Greenwood, South Carolina

CHEESY TORTILLA ROLL-UPS

1½ cups shredded sharp cheese	½ cup sour cream
3 tablespoons dry onion soup mix	¼ cup Parmesan cheese
	12 flour tortillas

Mix first 4 ingredients in bowl. Spread about 3 tablespoons on each tortilla; roll as for jelly roll. Cut into 3 portions; secure each with toothpick. Arrange on plate. Microwave for 1 minute or until heated through.
Yield: 3 dozen.

Jeanne Winterfeld, Preceptor Gamma Mu
Toppenish, Washington

CHEESE SURPRISES

½ cup butter, softened	⅛ teaspoon paprika
2 cups shredded sharp Cheddar cheese	1 cup all-purpose flour, sifted
⅛ teaspoon salt	

Beat butter and cheese in bowl until well mixed. Add salt, paprika and flour; mix well. Shape into 1-inch balls; place on baking sheet. Freeze until firm. Store in plastic bag in freezer. Preheat oven to 350 degrees. Place on baking sheet. Bake for 15 minutes. Serve hot. Yield: 3 dozen.

Bonnie K. Simpson, Preceptor Delta Nu
Oak Park, Illinois

CHEESE PUFF

10 eggs	½ cup melted margarine
½ cup all-purpose flour	4 cups shredded Cheddar cheese
1 teaspoon baking powder	
½ teaspoon salt	8 ounces thinly sliced ham
1 cup cottage cheese	

Preheat oven to 350 degrees. Combine eggs and remaining ingredients in bowl; mix well. Pour into 9x11-inch baking dish sprayed with nonstick cooking spray. Bake for 35 minutes. Cool for several minutes. Cut into 1-inch squares. Serve warm. Yield: 8 dozen.

Dianne Moll, Beta Nu
Kingsport, Tennessee

CHEESE AND CHILI TORTILLA STACKS

10 8-inch flour tortillas	⅔ cup thinly sliced green onions
8 ounces Cheddar cheese	
2 cups shredded Monterey Jack cheese	1 or 2 4-ounce cans sliced olives
1 7-ounce can chopped green chilies	

Preheat oven to 400 degrees. Place 1 tortilla on lightly greased rimmed baking pan. Sprinkle evenly with cheeses, chilies, onions and olives. Repeat with remaining tortillas, using five tortillas per stack. Bake for 25 minutes. Cut into wedges. Yield: 16 servings.

Denise Enright, Mu Lambda
Burlingame, California

BLUE CHEESE CRISPS

8 ounces blue cheese	1 teaspoon freshly ground pepper
4 ounces unsalted butter, softened	¾ cup chopped pecans
1 egg	1¾ cups all-purpose flour

Cream blue cheese and butter in bowl. Add egg, pepper, pecans and flour; mix well. Shape into two 1½-inch diameter rolls; wrap in waxed paper. Chill for 4 hours to overnight. Preheat oven to 425 degrees. Slice ¼ inch thick; place on ungreased baking sheet. Bake for 10 minutes or until light brown. Yield: 4 dozen.

Velma J. Barnes, Laureate Gamma Chi
Colorado Springs, Colorado

CHEESE PECAN CRISPIES

2 cups all-purpose flour	10 ounces Cheddar cheese, shredded
¼ teaspoon salt	
½ teaspoon cayenne pepper	¼ cup toasted sesame seed
1 cup margarine	Pecan halves
2 cups crisp rice cereal	

Preheat oven to 350 degrees. Mix first 3 ingredients in bowl. Cut in margarine until crumbly. Mix in cereal, cheese and sesame seed. Shape by tablespoonfuls into balls; place on ungreased baking sheet. Flatten with fork. Top each with pecan. Bake for 15 minutes. Cool on wire rack. Store in refrigerator. Yield: 4 dozen.

June Ellis, Preceptor Rho
Bossier City, Louisiana

FRIED CHEESE CUBES

Oil for deep frying	2 eggs, beaten
10 ounces sharp or extra sharp Cheddar cheese	¾ cup dry bread crumbs
	1 tablespoon sesame seed

Preheat oil to 350 degrees. Cut cheese into ¾-inch cubes. Dip into egg; coat with mixture of crumbs and sesame seed. Deep-fry in hot oil for 1 to 2 minutes or until golden. Drain on paper towel. Serve immediately.
Yield: 20 servings.

Candi Borah, Alpha Eta
Salida, Colorado

CANDIED CHICKEN WINGS

10 pounds chicken wings	*1⅓ cups sugar*
1⅓ cups dark soy sauce	*1⅓ cups water*

Preheat oven to 300 degrees. Disjoint wings; discard tips. Place in large baking pan. Mix soy sauce, sugar and water in saucepan. Bring to a boil, stirring constantly. Boil until reduced by ⅓, stirring constantly. Pour over wings. Bake for 2 hours or until very dark brown, turning every 15 minutes. Yield: 6 servings.

Sharon Kay Wright, Xi Nu Eta
Merkel, Texas

CHICKEN AND ALMOND BITES

1 cup chicken broth	*½ teaspoon paprika*
½ cup butter or margarine	*⅛ teaspoon cayenne*
1 cup all-purpose flour	*pepper*
1 tablespoon snipped	*4 eggs*
parsley	*1 5-ounce can boned*
2 teaspoons seasoned salt	*chicken, drained,*
2 teaspoons	*chopped*
Worcestershire sauce	*¼ cup chopped toasted*
¾ teaspoon celery seed	*almonds*

Preheat oven to 400 degrees. Bring chicken broth and butter to a boil in saucepan. Stir in flour, parsley and seasonings. Cook until mixture forms smooth ball, stirring constantly. Remove from heat. Add eggs 1 at a time, beating well after each addition. Stir in chicken and almonds. Drop by rounded teaspoonfuls onto ungreased baking sheets. Bake for 15 minutes or until brown. Serve hot. Yield: 6 dozen.

Anne Beirth, Laureate Rho
Norristown, Pennsylvania

FOUR-LAYER CHICKEN APPETIZERS

1 12-ounce package	*4 cherry tomatoes, sliced*
chicken nuggets	*1 tablespoon sour cream*
2½ ounces Monterey Jack	
cheese	

Heat chicken nuggets using package directions. Cut cheese into 1 x 1-inch slices. Place on nuggets. Heat for 1 minute longer or until cheese melts. Top each with tomato slice and dab of sour cream. Yield: 16 appetizers.

Laurie Erickson, Alpha Kappa
Hastings, Nebraska

CHICKEN LIVER PÂTÉ

½ cup chopped onion	*3 tablespoons butter*
2 small tart apples,	*1½ tablespoons lemon*
peeled, chopped	*juice*
3 tablespoons butter	*2 tablespoons whipping*
1 pound chicken livers	*cream*
¼ cup butter	*¼ teaspoon nutmeg*
3 tablespoons Brandy	*Salt and pepper to taste*

Sauté onion and apples in 3 tablespoons butter in skillet until apples are soft. Spoon into blender container. Sauté chicken livers in ¼ cup butter in skillet for 5 minutes. Add Brandy; ignite. Let flame subside. Spoon into blender container. Add remaining ingredients. Process until smooth. Pour into 3 or 4-cup soufflé dish. Chill, tightly covered, until firm. Garnish with parsley. Serve with crackers or toast. Yield: 20 servings.

Yvonne Clapp, Laureate Delta Eta
Sunnyvale, California

CHILIES RELLENOS PIES

8 ounces ground round	*8 ounces Cheddar cheese,*
5 eggs	*shredded*
2 cups whipping cream	*16 ounces Monterey Jack*
½ teaspoon cumin	*cheese, shredded*
1 teaspoon salt	*2 unbaked 9-inch pie*
1 4-ounce can chopped	*shells*
green chilies	

Preheat oven to 375 degrees. Brown ground round in skillet, stirring until crumbly; drain. Beat eggs with cream, cumin and salt in bowl. Stir in chilies, ground round and cheeses. Pour into pie shells. Bake for 50 minutes or until set. Cut into wedges. Serve warm. Yield: 12 servings.

Ione Nichols, Preceptor Alpha Beta
Ocean City, New Jersey

CLAMS CASINO

½ cup butter, softened	*¾ teaspoon oregano*
2 medium cloves of garlic,	*⅓ cup Italian bread*
finely chopped	*crumbs*
10 sprigs of parsley,	*35 cherrystone clams*
finely chopped	*Salt and pepper to taste*

Preheat oven to 475 degrees. Combine first 5 ingredients in bowl; mix well. Sprinkle over clams in baking dish. Season with salt and pepper. Bake for 10 to 12 minutes or until brown. Yield: 35 servings.

Kathy Phares, Delta Psi
Lincroft, New Jersey

DEVILED CLAMS

1 28-ounce can minced	*½ teaspoon prepared*
clams	*mustard*
2 tablespoons minced	*¼ teaspoon basil*
onion	*¼ teaspoon dillweed*
2 tablespoons minced	*¼ cup butter*
green bell pepper	*¾ cup cracker crumbs*
¼ cup chopped celery	*Small clam shells for*
⅛ teaspoon pepper	*baking*
3 drops of Tabasco sauce	*Paprika*

Preheat oven to 350 degrees. Drain clams, reserving liquid. Sauté clams, onion, green pepper, celery and seasonings in butter in skillet until onion is transparent. Add cracker crumbs and reserved liquid. Mixture will be of meat loaf consistency. Fill clam shells with mixture; sprinkle with paprika. Bake for 20 minutes.

Jane C. Little, Xi Omicron Delta
Universal City, Texas

CRAB DELIGHT

2 tablespoons butter,
   softened
1/3 cup all-purpose flour
2 cups hot milk
3 tablespoons Dijon-style
   mustard
1 tablespoon dry mustard
2 tablespoons
   Worcestershire sauce

1 teaspoon Tabasco sauce
3 tablespoons Sherry
1 teaspoon MSG
1 or 2   7-ounce cans crab
   meat
2 hard-cooked eggs,
   chopped
2 tablespoons Parmesan
   cheese

Blend butter and flour in casserole. Stir in hot milk gradually. Add next 6 ingredients; mix well. Stir in crab meat and hard-cooked eggs. Sprinkle with cheese. Chill for several hours to overnight if desired. Preheat oven to 450 degrees. Bake for 20 minutes or until heated through. Serve hot in tiny pastry shells or cold in fresh mushroom caps. Yield: 2½ cups.

Rosanna Fahl, Preceptor Alpha Epsilon
Oroville, California

CRAB RANGOON

Oil for deep frying
1   7-ounce can crab meat,
   rinsed, drained
8 ounces cream cheese,
   softened
2 green onions, chopped

½ teaspoon soy sauce
1 teaspoon Worcestershire
   sauce
¼ teaspoon garlic powder
1 package won ton skins

Preheat oil to 370 degrees. Combine next 6 ingredients in bowl; mix well. Spoon onto won ton skins. Fold diagonally into triangle; moisten edges with water and press to seal. Seal other 2 corners together. Deep-fry until golden brown; drain. Serve warm with sweet and sour sauce and Chinese mustard. May freeze and reheat in 375-degree oven for 10 minutes. Yield: 3 dozen.

Evelyn Tallyn, Iota Chi
St. Louis, Missouri

DILL CRACKERS

1 envelope dry ranch
   salad dressing mix
1 teaspoon (heaping)
   dillweed

¾ cup corn oil
1   16-ounce package
   oyster crackers

Combine first 3 ingredients in glass bowl; mix well. Add crackers; mix well. Microwave on High for 4 minutes, stirring once. Yield: 15 to 18 servings.

Marjorie Mattoon, Laureate Gamma
Mobile, Alabama

SNACK CRACKERS

1 cup corn oil
1 envelope dry original
   recipe ranch salad
   dressing mix

½ teaspoon garlic powder
1 teaspoon dillweed
2   12-ounce packages
   oyster crackers

Mix first 4 ingredients in small bowl. Pour over crackers in large bowl; mix well. Let stand for 1 hour or longer. Store in airtight container. Yield: 24 servings.

Estelline Mikeworth, Beta Omega
Bellevue, Texas

STUFFED DATES

8 ounces Cheddar cheese,
   shredded
½ cup margarine,
   softened
1¼ cups sifted
   all-purpose flour

½ teaspoon cayenne
   pepper
1   6-ounce package
   whole dates, pitted
½ cup pecan halves

Preheat oven to 400 degrees. Let cheese and margarine stand in bowl at room temperature. Cut in flour and pepper as for pie dough. Slit dates; stuff with pecan halves. Flatten a small amount of dough in palm of hand. Wrap date in dough, sealing completely. Place on baking sheet. Bake for 15 minutes or until light brown. Store between waxed paper in airtight container. Yield: 15 stuffed dates.

Kathy Wicklund, Xi Alpha Alpha
Jacksonville, Florida

ALMOND DEVILED EGGS

6 hard-cooked eggs
1 tablespoon crumbled
   blue cheese
1 tablespoon thinly sliced
   scallions
1 tablespoon chopped
   pimento
2 tablespoons mayonnaise

1 tablespoon sour cream
4 teaspoons toasted
   slivered almonds
1½ tablespoons cider
   vinegar
Salt and freshly ground
   pepper to taste

Peel eggs; cut into halves lengthwise. Mash yolks in bowl. Add remaining ingredients; mix well. Spoon into egg whites. Garnish with additional pimento. Chill until serving time. Yield: 1 dozen.

Anita K. Short, Nu Phi Mu
Goodland, Kansas

DEVILED EGGS WITH HAM

8 eggs
½ cup finely chopped
   ham
½ cup mayonnaise
2 teaspoons Dijon-style
   mustard

1½ tablespoons rinsed
   capers
2 tablespoons chopped
   chives
Dash of pepper

Bring eggs and water to cover to a boil in 2-quart saucepan; reduce heat. Simmer for 12 minutes. Rinse with cold water. Let stand in cold water for 30 minutes. Peel eggs; cut into halves lengthwise. Mash yolks in bowl; reserve 3 teaspoonfuls for garnish. Reserve 3 teaspoonfuls ham for garnish. Add remaining ham and remaining ingredients to remaining yolks; mix well. Spoon into egg whites. Place on plate lined with shredded lettuce. Garnish with reserved yolk and ham. Yield: 8 servings.

Debbie Heaton, Theta Beta
Peachtree City, Georgia

HEARTY EGG ROLLS

Oil for deep frying
1 pound Italian sausage,
   finely ground
2 5-ounce cans chicken,
   drained
½ to ¾ cup finely
   chopped fresh bean
   sprouts
2 cups shredded carrots
½ cup finely chopped
   onion
3 eggs, beaten
½ cup soy sauce
1 teaspoon garlic powder
1 teaspoon pepper
Salt to taste
2 packages egg roll skins

Preheat oil to 350 degrees. Process sausage and chicken in food processor until well mixed. Combine with vegetables, eggs and seasonings in bowl; mix well. Spray egg roll skins with water. Place 1 to 2 tablespoons sausage mixture in center of each skin. Fold in sides and roll up; press with moistened fingers to seal. Deep-fry until golden brown; drain. Serve with hot mustard or sweet and sour sauce. May reheat at 300 degrees for 10 minutes with oven door ajar. Yield: 12 servings.

Holly Nystrom, Alpha Mu
Spencer, Iowa

MON-DOO (KOREAN EGG ROLLS)

Oil for deep frying
1 pound zucchini, finely
   shredded
½ pound carrots, finely
   shredded
4 large onions, finely
   chopped
½ teaspoon salt
2 pounds ground beef
1 teaspoon salt
1 teaspoon pepper
1 package Mon-Doo
   wrappers
2 egg whites, beaten

Preheat oil to 350 degrees. Mix shredded vegetables with salt; drain and pat dry with paper towels. Mix with ground beef, 1 teaspoon salt and pepper in bowl. Place 1 tablespoon mixture on each wrapper. Moisten edges with egg white; fold over and press to seal. Deep-fry until golden brown; drain on paper towels. May rewarm in 325-degree oven for 8 to 10 minutes.
Yield: 75 to 100 appetizers.

Cindy Shilling, Xi Alpha Theta
Lakewood, New York

HAM CHEESECAKE

½ cup bread crumbs
½ cup half and half
1¼ teaspoons dry mustard
1¼ teaspoons salt
¼ teaspoon ground red
   pepper
24 ounces cream cheese,
   softened
4 eggs
8 ounces cooked smoked
   ham, finely chopped
2 cups shredded Swiss
   cheese
Pimento
Parsley
Sliced olives

Preheat oven to 325 degrees. Sprinkle bread crumbs over bottom and side of greased 9-inch springform pan; spread any remaining crumbs over bottom. Combine half and half, seasonings, cream cheese and eggs in mixer bowl. Beat at medium speed for 5 minutes or until smooth. Stir in ham and cheese. Spread in prepared pan. Bake for 1 hour or until set. Cool. Refrigerate, covered,

for up to 48 hours. Let stand at room temperature for 2 hours. Remove side of pan; place on serving plate. Garnish with pimento, parsley and olives. Yield: 50 servings.

LouAnn Rochford, Xi Alpha Theta
North Platte, Nebraska

HORS D'OEUVRE PIE

1 frozen 9-inch pie shell,
   thawed
8 ounces cream cheese,
   softened
1 ounce blue cheese
½ cup mayonnaise
½ teaspoon onion powder
Cherry tomato halves
Sliced mushrooms
Parsley sprigs
Hard-cooked eggs, sliced
Ripe olives, sliced

Preheat oven to 425 degrees. Pat pie shell into 11-inch circle on large baking sheet; prick with fork. Bake for 5 minutes or until golden. Cool. Place carefully on serving platter. Blend cream cheese and next 3 ingredients in bowl until fluffy. Spread on pastry. Cover. Chill for 4 hours. Arrange garnishes in circles on pie, starting with cherry tomatoes in center. Cut into small pie-shaped wedges to serve. Yield: 12 wedges.

Dayna Dyer, Kappa Pi
Atchison, Kansas

KIELBASA IN CRUST

1⅓ cups plus 1 tablespoon
   all-purpose flour
½ teaspoon salt
½ cup unsalted butter
1 egg
1 tablespoon sour cream
1 tablespoon brown
   mustard
1 pound kielbasa, cut into
   halves
1 egg
1 teaspoon water

Preheat oven to 375 degrees. Process flour, salt and butter in food processor until crumbly. Add mixture of 1 egg, sour cream and mustard gradually, processing constantly until mixture forms ball. Dust with flour; wrap in plastic wrap. Chill for 2 hours. Roll into 2 triangles; spread with additional mustard. Place sausage in center; wrap with dough, sealing edges. Place on baking sheet. Brush with 1 egg beaten with water. Bake for 20 minutes or until golden. Serve with spicy mustard. Yield: 8 servings.

Nancy Lucente, Xi Kappa Xi
Norco, California

BEER NUTS

1 pound raw peanuts
1 cup sugar
½ cup water
1 tablespoon maple
   flavoring

Preheat oven to 300 degrees. Cook all ingredients in heavy skillet over high heat until water evaporates and peanuts begin to separate, stirring constantly. Spread on baking sheet. Bake for 30 minutes. Yield: 1 pound.

Ginny Porter, Iota Delta
Oskaloosa, Iowa

BEER NUT CLUSTERS

8 ounces almond bark
1 cup beer nut peanuts
1 cup Cheerios
1 cup broken pretzels

Melt almond bark in glass bowl in microwave on High for 60 seconds or in double boiler until smooth. Add remaining ingredients. Drop by teaspoonfuls onto waxed paper; cool. Yield: 3 to 4 servings.

Becky Tichy, Xi Alpha Sigma
Vienna, West Virginia

SPICY TOASTED NUTS

2 tablespoons butter	½ teaspoon curry powder
1 tablespoon sugar	½ teaspoon cinnamon
1 teaspoon garlic salt	4 cups mixed nuts

Preheat oven to 350 degrees. Melt butter in small saucepan. Add sugar, garlic salt, curry powder and cinnamon; mix well. Place nuts in 9x9-inch baking pan. Pour butter mixture over nuts; mix until coated. Bake, uncovered, until butter sizzles. Stir. Let stand until cool, stirring frequently. Store in airtight container. Yield: 4 cups.

Deneen Phelps, Eta
Auburn, Washington

PARTY MIX

1 10-ounce box	1 cup pecans
Doo-Dads snack mix	1 cup peanuts
1 cup pretzels	1 cup Cheese Nips
1 cup croutons	1 tablespoon garlic salt
1 cup Twigs, broken	¼ cup margarine
1 cup sesame sticks	

Combine first 9 ingredients in 5-quart baking pan. Dot with margarine. Microwave, covered, on High for 15 minutes, stirring once. Cool. Store in airtight container. Yield: 20 to 25 servings.

Dorothy W. Deslattes, Sigma
Duncanville, Alabama

MEXICAN PARTY MIX

1 large box Crispix cereal	½ cup Parmesan cheese
1 package small pretzels	5 tablespoons
1 package corn spirals	Worcestershire sauce
2 cups mixed nuts	Garlic salt to taste
2 envelopes dry taco	1 tablespoon chili powder
seasoning mix	1 cup melted butter

Preheat oven to 225 degrees. Combine all ingredients in baking pan in order listed; mix well. Bake for 45 minutes, stirring every 15 minutes. Yield: 24 servings.

Linda Harper, Pi Iota
Carrollton, Missouri

VEGETABLE PIZZA

2 8-count packages	1 teaspoon dillweed
refrigerator crescent	1 teaspoon garlic powder
rolls	2 tablespoons chopped
16 ounces cream cheese,	onion
softened	Assorted chopped fresh
⅔ cup mayonnaise-type	vegetables
salad dressing	Shredded cheese
⅓ cup sour cream	

Preheat oven to 375 degrees. Press crescent roll dough into 4 small circles on baking sheet. Bake for 13 minutes. Cool. Combine next 6 ingredients in bowl; mix well. Spread over cooled crusts. Top with vegetables and cheese. Chill until serving time. Yield: 24 servings.

Lisa Gibson, Epsilon Delta
Eagleville, Missouri

PUPPY CHOW (ALPO)

½ cup margarine	1 12 or 15-ounce box
1 cup peanut butter	Crispix cereal
2 cups milk chocolate	4 cups confectioners'
chips	sugar

Melt first 3 ingredients in saucepan, stirring constantly. Pour over cereal in large bowl; mix well. Add confectioners' sugar; stir until coated. Yield: 10 cups.

Diane Burton, Xi Beta
Phoenix, Arizona

WHITE TRASH

½ cup margarine	1 15-ounce package
1 cup crunchy peanut	raisins
butter	1 package Chex cereal
2 cups chocolate chips	1 1-pound package
1 cup peanuts	confectioners' sugar

Melt first 3 ingredients in double boiler. Mix peanuts, raisins and cereal in bowl. Pour chocolate mixture over cereal mixture. Pour half the confectioners' sugar into large paper bag. Add half the cereal mixture. Shake to coat. Repeat with remaining cereal. Yield: 14 cups.

Debbie McMurry, Xi Rho
Spartanburg, South Carolina

BACON-WRAPPED HOT DOGS

1 pound hot dogs, cut into	½ pound light brown
thirds	sugar
½ pound bacon	

Preheat oven to 225 degrees. Wrap hot dogs with ½ slice bacon; secure with toothpicks. Arrange in 9x13-inch baking dish. Cover with brown sugar. Bake for 2½ hours. Drain well. Yield: 2½ dozen.

Mary Margaret Draper, Xi Beta Beta
Boise, Idaho

SAUSAGE ROLLS

1 recipe rich flaky pastry	½ cup bread crumbs
8 ounces ground pork	1 egg, beaten
Sage and pepper to taste	

Preheat oven to 425 degrees. Roll pastry into 3½x15-inch rectangle on floured surface. Mix pork with seasonings and crumbs in bowl. Shape into 15-inch log; place on pastry. Fold pastry to enclose filling; seal edge. Slice diagonally 1½ inches thick. Place on baking sheet, separating slices. Cut vents in pastry. Brush with egg. Bake for 15 minutes or until golden. Yield: 1 dozen.

Janet Weise, Xi Alpha Gamma
Mountain Home, Idaho

GOURMET MUSHROOMS

36 medium mushrooms	Garlic powder to taste
16 ounces lite cream cheese, softened	½ teaspoon lemon juice
1 to 2 7-ounce cans crab meat	¾ to 1 cup shredded Cheddar cheese

Preheat oven to 350 degrees. Wash mushrooms; discard stems. Place caps on baking sheet. Mix cream cheese, crab meat, garlic powder and lemon juice in bowl. Fill mushroom caps; sprinkle with Cheddar cheese. Bake until cheese melts. Serve immediately. Yield: 3 dozen.

Delores Miller, Preceptor Theta
Cody, Wyoming

STUFFED MUSHROOMS

12 large mushrooms	12 Ritz crackers, finely crushed
1 medium onion, finely chopped	3 tablespoons Parmesan cheese
2 ounces pepperoni, finely chopped	1 tablespoon minced parsley
¼ cup finely chopped green bell pepper	½ teaspoon salt
1 small clove of garlic, minced	Dash of pepper
2 tablespoons margarine	¼ teaspoon oregano
	⅓ cup chicken broth

Preheat oven to 325 degrees. Wash mushrooms. Remove stems; chop finely. Drain caps on paper towel. Sauté onion, pepperoni, green pepper, garlic and chopped mushroom stems in margarine in skillet until tender, but not brown. Mix in remaining ingredients. Spoon into mushroom caps, rounding tops. Place in shallow baking dish with ¼ inch water. Bake, uncovered, for 25 minutes. Yield: 12 mushrooms.

Margo Butler, Xi Omicron
Cumberland, Maryland

OLIVE BALLS

½ cup margarine, softened	Dash of cayenne pepper
1 cup all-purpose flour	1 10-ounce jar stuffed green olives, rinsed, drained
¾ pound sharp Cheddar cheese, shredded	

Preheat oven to 400 degrees. Blend margarine and flour in bowl. Add cheese and cayenne pepper. Cover each olive with about 1 teaspoon flour mixture. Place on baking sheet. Bake for 10 minutes. Yield: 15 to 20 servings.

Beverly Caldwell, Preceptor Beta Rho
Rocky Ford, Colorado

STUFFED SNOW PEAS

3 ounces cream cheese, softened	1½ tablespoons chopped pimento
1½ tablespoons catsup	⅓ cup finely chopped pecans
3 tablespoons chopped green bell pepper	¼ teaspoon salt
2 tablespoons finely chopped onion	¼ teaspoon pepper
	30 tender snow peas

Combine first 8 ingredients in bowl; mix well. Chill for 1 hour or longer. String snow peas. Blanch in boiling water in saucepan for 30 seconds. Plunge into cold water; drain. Slit the straight side of each snow pea to open. Spread with 1½ teaspoons filling. Yield: 2½ dozen.

Connie Bender, Xi Epsilon Nu
Cedar Rapids, Iowa

COCKTAIL TURKEY MEATBALLS

1½ pounds ground turkey	½ cup chopped celery
1½ tablespoons instant chicken bouillon	¼ cup margarine
1 teaspoon poultry seasoning	1 cup milk
½ teaspoon pepper	1½ cups stuffing mix
½ cup chopped parsley	1 10-ounce can chicken-mushroom soup
1 cup chopped onion	¼ cup water
	½ cup sour cream

Combine first 5 ingredients in large bowl; mix well. Sauté onion and celery in margarine in skillet. Stir in milk. Heat just until warm. Stir in stuffing mix. Add to turkey mixture; mix well. Shape into 1½-inch meatballs. Place in glass baking dish. Microwave, loosely covered, on High for 7 minutes, turning meatballs once. Blend soup, water and sour cream in large serving dish. Heat in microwave until blended. Add meatballs. Microwave on High for 4 to 6 minutes or until heated through. Yield: 2 dozen.

Ruth Hinsch, Preceptor Alpha Nu
El Paso, Texas

FIESTA ROLL

2 10-ounce packages frozen chopped spinach, thawed	6 green onions, chopped
	¼ to ½ cup bacon bits, crushed
1 small envelope dry Hidden Valley Ranch salad dressing mix	1 cup mayonnaise
	1 cup sour cream
	10 large flour tortillas

Squeeze spinach dry. Combine with next 5 ingredients in bowl; mix well. Spread over tortillas; roll as for jelly roll. Wrap in plastic wrap. Chill for several hours. Cut into thin slices. Arrange on serving plate. Yield: 60 servings.

Jessie R. Ballmer, Laureate Alpha Epsilon
Riverside, California

TORTILLA ROLL-UPS

1 4½-ounce can deviled ham	2 to 3 tablespoons minced fresh parsley
3 ounces cream cheese, softened	4 10-inch flour tortillas
1 cup shredded pepper cheese	

Mix first 4 ingredients in bowl. Spread ⅓ cup on each tortilla; roll up as for jelly roll. Wrap in plastic wrap. Chill for 1 hour. Slice each into 6 to 8 slices; insert toothpick in each. Yield: 24 to 28 appetizers.

Karen Morse, Beta Chi
Arvada, Colorado

PIZZA ROLLS

1½ pounds ground chuck
½ cup chopped onion
½ cup chopped celery
1 2-ounce can mushroom pieces, drained, chopped
½ teaspoon sugar
½ teaspoon salt
⅛ teaspoon pepper
¼ teaspoon oregano
¼ teaspoon basil

¼ teaspoon dried parsley
½ cup tomato sauce
1 package pepperoni, chopped
1 package shredded mozzarella cheese
1 tablespoon all-purpose flour
1 16-ounce package won ton skins
Oil for deep frying

Sauté ground chuck, onion and celery in skillet; drain. Stir in mushrooms, sugar, seasonings, tomato sauce and pepperoni. Simmer, uncovered, for 10 minutes or until thickened. Stir in cheese. Blend flour with a small amount of water to make paste. Brush all 4 corners of 1 won ton skin with paste. Place 1 tablespoon ground beef mixture in center of skin. Fold corners to center alternately; press to seal. Repeat with remaining won ton skins and ground beef mixture. Deep-fry for 1 to 2 minutes or until light brown; drain on paper towels. Yield: 3 dozen.

Kim Thompson, Iota Phi
Independence, Missouri

POCO PEPPER SNACKS

6 ounces cream cheese, softened
½ cup shredded Cheddar cheese
2 tablespoons chopped green chilies
1 teaspoon minced onion

2 tablespoons chopped black olives
6 drops of hot chili sauce
1 8-count package refrigerator crescent rolls

Preheat oven to 450 degrees. Combine first 6 ingredients in small bowl; mix well. Separate rolls into 4 rectangles. Press perforations to seal. Spread ¼ of the mixture over each rectangle. Roll as for jelly roll from long side. Cut each roll into ¾-inch slices. Place cut side down on greased baking sheet. Bake for 12 to 15 minutes or until golden brown. Serve hot. Yield: 4 dozen.

Pam Newman, Alpha Nu
Farmington, New Mexico

COCKTAIL REUBENS

8 ounces cream cheese, softened
1½ cups margarine, softened
4 cups all-purpose flour
1 teaspoon salt
5 eggs, beaten
1 30-ounce can sauerkraut, drained

2 3-ounce packages smoked corned beef, chopped
12 ounces Swiss cheese, shredded
Salt and pepper to taste
4 ounces Cheddar cheese, shredded

Preheat oven to 350 degrees. Beat cream cheese and margarine with wooden spoon in bowl. Add flour and 1 teaspoon salt; mix well. Chill. Shape into 1 inch balls; press into miniature muffin cups. Beat eggs with sauerkraut, corned beef, Swiss cheese, salt and pepper. Fill pastry-lined muffin cups. Top with Cheddar cheese. Bake for 20 minutes. Serve hot. Yield: 4 dozen.

Christella D. Snyder, Xi Delta Omicron
Savannah, Georgia

HOT SAUSAGE AND CHEESE SQUARES

1 pound hot sausage
2 cups buttermilk baking mix
½ cup milk
1 egg
¼ cup mayonnaise
1 medium onion, chopped

½ cup Parmesan cheese
½ cup shredded Swiss cheese
½ cup shredded Cheddar cheese
½ cup chopped green bell pepper

Preheat oven to 350 degrees. Cook sausage in skillet until brown and crumbly; drain. Combine with baking mix and remaining ingredients in bowl; mix well. Pour into greased 7x11-inch baking pan. Bake for 25 to 30 minutes. Cut into squares. Serve warm. Yield: 5 dozen.

Judy A. Shipman, Xi Delta Upsilon
Dumas, Texas

GREEN CHILI HOR D'OEUVRES

1 pound sausage, crumbled
3 cups buttermilk baking mix
1½ cups mixed shredded Cheddar and Monterey Jack cheeses

½ cup chopped mixed black olives, green olives, pimentos and green chilies
Milk
Sour cream

Preheat oven to 375 degrees. Mix uncooked sausage, baking mix, cheese mixture and olive mixture in bowl. Add enough milk to make of consistency of biscuit dough. Shape into walnut-sized balls; place on baking sheet. Bake for 20 minutes. Serve warm with sour cream for dipping. Yield: 2 to 3 dozen.

Pat Intermont, Xi Beta Lambda
Chama, New Mexico

SPINACH BALLS

2 10-ounce packages frozen chopped spinach
1 cup chopped onion
5 eggs, beaten
¾ cup melted butter
⅔ teaspoon thyme

2 cups herb-seasoned stuffing mix
¾ cup Parmesan cheese
1 teaspoon garlic salt
½ teaspoon pepper

Preheat oven to 350 degrees. Cook spinach using package directions; drain until dry. Mix with remaining ingredients in bowl. Shape into balls; place on baking sheet. Bake for 20 minutes. Yield: 4 dozen.

Susan Brock, Zeta Delta
Crestview, Florida

SPINACH AND CHEESE PUFF BALLS

1 10-ounce package frozen chopped spinach	½ cup Parmesan cheese
½ cup chopped onion	2 tablespoons butter, melted
2 eggs, slightly beaten	⅛ teaspoon garlic powder
⅓ cup blue cheese salad dressing	Dijon-style mustard to taste
½ cup shredded Cheddar cheese	1 8½-ounce package corn muffin mix

Cook spinach using package directions, adding onion; drain well and press dry. Combine eggs, salad dressing, cheeses, butter, garlic powder and mustard in bowl; mix well. Stir in spinach and muffin mix. Chill, covered, for 1 hour or until easy to handle. Shape into 1-inch balls; arrange on baking sheet. Chill, covered, until 20 minutes before serving. Preheat oven to 350 degrees. Bake for 10 to 15 minutes or until light brown. Serve warm with mustard. Yield: 50 puff balls.

Deborah J. Hood, Xi Psi Beta
Beeville, Texas

PHYLLO SPINACH TRIANGLES

¾ cup chopped onion	8 ounces mozzarella cheese, shredded
½ cup butter	8 ounces Parmesan cheese
2 10-ounce packages frozen chopped spinach, thawed	3 ounces blue cheese, crumbled
8 ounces Monterey Jack cheese, shredded	¼ teaspoon Tabasco sauce
	1 package phyllo dough

Preheat oven to 400 degrees. Sauté onion in butter in skillet until clear. Add spinach. Cook for 5 minutes. Remove from heat. Add cheeses and Tabasco sauce; mix well. Set aside. Follow direction on phyllo package for handling dough. Cut sheets into strips. Place 1 rounded teaspoonful spinach mixture on each strip and fold like a flag. Bake for 15 to 20 minutes or until golden brown. Yield: 6 to 8 dozen.

Judi Hollomon, Xi Beta
Jackson, Mississippi

STUFFED BABY TOMATOES

4 quarts cherry tomatoes, chilled	½ cup minced onion
1 quart mayonnaise	2 cups chopped fresh spinach
½ cup Parmesan cheese	
¼ cup horseradish	

Cut tomatoes into halves; scoop out and discard pulp. Mix mayonnaise, cheese, horseradish and onion in bowl. Process spinach in food processor. Add to mayonnaise mixture. Spoon into tomatoes. Chill until serving time. Arrange around large tomato or artichoke on serving tray. Yield: 2 dozen.

Carla Lassiter, Theta Theta
Franklin, Kentucky

TERIYAKI WRAP-UPS

1 tablespoon sugar	4 ounces sirloin steak, cut into strips
1 tablespoon chopped onion	1 8-ounce can whole water chestnuts, drained
1 clove of garlic, minced	
¼ teaspoon ginger	
¼ cup soy sauce	

Combine first 5 ingredients in bowl; mix well. Add steak strips; toss to coat. Marinate for 30 minutes, stirring occasionally. Preheat broiler. Drain steak strips. Wrap around water chestnuts; fasten with toothpicks. Arrange on broiler pan. Broil for 5 to 8 minutes or to desired degree of doneness, turning once. Yield: 20 servings.

Shirley Lab, Xi Omicron
Harlingen, Texas

BACON-WRAPPED WATER CHESTNUTS

1 pound bacon	½ cup sugar
1 8-ounce can whole water chestnuts, drained	3 tablespoons pickle relish
1 cup mayonnaise	2 tablespoons catsup

Preheat oven to 425 degrees. Cut bacon slices into thirds. Wrap bacon around water chestnuts; secure with toothpick. Place in baking pan. Bake until bacon is crisp; drain. Combine remaining ingredients in bowl. Pour over water chestnuts. Bake for 10 minutes longer. Yield: 20 servings.

Nancy N. Swingley, Xi Delta Delta
Portland, Indiana

BRANDY SLUSH

2 cups sugar	1 12-ounce can frozen lemonade concentrate
7 cups boiling water	1 12-ounce can frozen orange juice concentrate
4 tea bags	
2 cups boiling water	Ginger ale
1 fifth Brandy	

Dissolve sugar in 7 cups boiling water in saucepan. Combine tea bags and 2 cups boiling water in pitcher; steep until strong. Mix sugar-water, tea, Brandy and concentrates in large freezer container. Freeze, covered, stirring frequently until slushy. Mix ¾ cup slush with ¼ cup ginger ale in glass. Yield: 15 to 20 servings.
Note: Bourbon or Rum may be substituted for Brandy.

Mary Bango, Xi Alpha Sigma
Parkersburg, West Virginia

BURGUNDY PUNCH

¾ cup water	4 to 6 whole cloves
¾ cup sugar	1 quart cranapple juice
1 stick cinnamon	2 cups Burgundy

Boil first 4 ingredients in saucepan for 10 minutes. Let stand for 24 to 48 hours. Strain. Combine syrup with cranapple juice and wine in punch bowl. Garnish with ice ring. Yield: 7 cups.

Avie Roscoe, Preceptor Delta
West Salem, Ohio

HOT BUTTERED RUM BATTER

1 pound butter, softened
1 16-ounce package dark
  brown sugar
1 quart vanilla ice cream,
  softened
1 teaspoon vanilla extract
1 teaspoon nutmeg
1 teaspoon cinnamon
Dark rum to taste
Nutmeg to taste

Blend first 6 ingredients in bowl. Spoon into freezer container. Freeze until firm. Combine 1 heaping tablespoon batter, 1 shot dark rum, dash of nutmeg and boiling water in preheated mug. Yield: 6 cups batter.
Note: May store batter in freezer for 2 months.

Sandy Goedde, Xi Beta Eta
Coeur d' Alene, Idaho

RASPBERRY AND CHAMPAGNE PUNCH

1 6-ounce can frozen
  lemonade concentrate
½ cup water
1 10-ounce package
  frozen raspberries
1 1-liter bottle of 7-Up,
  chilled
1 fifth Champagne,
  chilled

Combine lemonade concentrate and water in punch bowl, stirring until lemonade dissolves. Blend in remaining ingredients. Ladle into serving cups.
Yield: 24 servings.

Phyllis Warden, Xi Mu Epsilon
Venice, Florida

PARTY CHAMPAGNE PUNCH

½ cup sugar
2 cups water
1 18-ounce can
  pineapple juice
4 cups cranberry juice
  cocktail
1 6-ounce can frozen
  lemonade concentrate
4 fifths Champagne
Lemon twists
Grape clusters

Combine sugar and water in saucepan. Cook until sugar is dissolved, stirring constantly. Combine sugar-water with pineapple juice, cranberry juice and lemonade concentrate in glass container. Chill in refrigerator. Pour over ice ring in punch bowl. Add Champagne. Garnish with lemon twists and grape clusters. Yield: 35 servings.

Cindy Christensen, Xi Alpha Theta
Scottsdale, Arizona

SPICED CHERRY TEA

2 quarts apple cider
1 cup sugar
1 6-ounce can frozen
  orange juice concentrate
1 cup water
2 cups pineapple juice
¾ cup lemon juice
1 16-ounce can red
  cherries with juice
5 whole cloves
4 sticks cinnamon
4 drops of peppermint
  extract
8 cups strong tea

Mix all ingredients in large saucepan. Simmer for 1 hour. Strain to remove whole spices. Ladle into serving mugs. Yield: 1 gallon.

Peggy Davis, Laureate Gamma Alpha
Dallas, Texas

COCONUT RUM PUNCH

1 bottle of Chablis,
  chilled
1 cup CocoRibe coconut
  rum
3 tablespoons grenadine
1 32-ounce bottle of club
  soda, chilled
Fresh strawberries, sliced

Combine all ingredients over ice in punch bowl. Garnish with strawberries. Yield: 8 cups.

Photograph for this recipe on Page 2.

CHRISTMAS WASSAIL

2 cups sugar
1 cup packed light brown
  sugar
8 cups apple cider
2 3-inch sticks cinnamon
12 whole cloves
1 cup pineapple juice
4 cups grapefruit juice
4 cups orange juice
Whole cloves
7 orange slices
7 maraschino cherry
  halves

Combine sugars and cider in large saucepan. Cook over low heat until sugar dissolves, stirring constantly. Add cinnamon sticks and 12 cloves. Simmer for 5 minutes. Add juices. Heat just to serving temperature; do not boil. Strain wassail into heatproof punch bowl; discard spices. Insert cloves around edges of orange slices. Place cherry half on each. Float in wassail. Yield: 10 cups.

Photograph for this recipe on page 1.

COFFEE PUNCH

2 ounces instant coffee
  powder
2 cups boiling water
1 cup sugar
4 quarts milk
2 quarts chocolate ice
  cream
2 quarts vanilla ice cream
1 16-ounce container
  whipped topping

Combine coffee powder, water and sugar in bowl; mix well. Chill. Mix with next 3 ingredients in punch bowl. Top with whipped topping. Yield: 50 servings.

Brenda J. Atkins, Preceptor Beta
Hopewell, Virginia

COFFEE MOCHA PUNCH

2 squares unsweetened
  chocolate, melted
1 gallon strong hot coffee
1 cup sugar
Dash of salt
1 teaspoon vanilla extract
½ gallon vanilla ice cream
1 1-liter bottle of club
  soda, chilled
4 cups half and half
2 cups whipped topping
Chocolate syrup

Combine melted chocolate, coffee, sugar, salt and vanilla in large container. Chill for several hours. Slice ice cream into cubes. Pour coffee mixture into punch bowl. Add club soda, half and half and ice cream; mix gently. Ladle into serving cups. Top with dollops of whipped topping. Drizzle chocolate syrup over whipped topping.
Yield: One-hundred twenty eight ½-cup servings.

Jan Hendrickson, Preceptor Zeta Psi
Duncanville, Texas

CRANAPPLE PUNCH

2 quarts cranapple juice
1 quart water
1 cup packed light brown
  sugar
3 sticks cinnamon
1 teaspoon whole allspice
1 teaspoon whole cloves

Combine all ingredients in saucepan. Bring to a boil. Strain into mugs. Yield: 16 servings.

Ellen Traylor, Xi Beta Delta
Midlothian, Virginia

QUICK DAIQUIRI PUNCH

2 pounds fresh
  strawberries, hulled
1 12-ounce can frozen
  lemonade concentrate
½ cup sugar
2 2-liter bottles of
  lemon-lime soda
½ cup rum

Purée strawberries in blender container. Add lemonade concentrate and sugar. Process until blended. Pour into freezer container. Freeze until firm but slushy. Set punch bowl in ice. Scoop slush into punch bowl. Add soda and rum if desired; mix gently. Yield: 20 servings.

Terry A. Walker, Xi Pi
Pittsburg, Kansas

OVERNIGHT BLOODY MARYS

1 46-ounce can cocktail
  vegetable juice
1 46-ounce can tomato
  juice
1 cup lemon juice
2 tablespoons
  Worcestershire sauce
1 teaspoon salt
½ teaspoon seasoned salt
3 cups Vodka

Combine first 6 ingredients in bowl; mix well. Chill, covered, overnight. Stir in Vodka just before serving. Serve over crushed ice. Yield: 15½ cups.

Evelyn Pomper, Laureate Alpha Eta
Pompano Beach, Florida

MARGARITAS

1 12-ounce can frozen
  lemonade concentrate,
  thawed
6 ounces Triple Sec
3 to 6 ounces lime juice
1 12-ounce can frozen
  limeade concentrate,
  thawed
1 12-ounce bottle of
  Tequila

Combine all ingredients in blender container; process until well mixed. Process ⅓ at a time with crushed ice in blender until slushy. Pour into glasses rimmed with coarse salt. Yield: 10 servings.

Robin M. Cheatham, Alpha Phi
Hamilton, Montana

SPRING MAY WINE

1 cup lemon juice
2 cups sugar
2 12-ounce packages
  frozen strawberries
4 cups pineapple juice
2 fifths May wine
2 fifths Champagne

Combine lemon juice and sugar in small container, stirring until sugar is dissolved. Place ice in punch bowl. Add lemon-sugar mixture, strawberries and pineapple juice; mix well. Stir in wines. Ladle into serving cups. Yield: 10 servings.

Wanda Combs, Beta Rho
Independence, Missouri

PEACHY KEEN WITCHES BREW

¼ cup sugar
2 cups water
1 12-ounce can frozen
  orange juice
  concentrate, thawed
3 cups water
2½ cups peach-flavored
  schnapps
⅓ cup lemon juice
2 bottles of ginger ale

Boil sugar and 2 cups water in medium saucepan for 3 minutes; cool. Combine with next 4 ingredients in large glass container; cover. Freeze until firm. Thaw for 15 minutes, stirring occasionally. Spoon ½ cup slush mixture into each serving glass; stir in ¼ cup ginger ale. Yield: 22 servings.

Jody Reddell, Xi Zeta Lambda
Fort Stockton, Texas

PIÑA COLADA FLIP

1 46-ounce can
  pineapple juice, chilled
1 16-ounce can cream
  of coconut
1 quart vanilla ice cream
1 28-ounce bottle of
  club soda, chilled

Combine first 2 ingredients in punch bowl; mix well. Add ice cream. Pour in club soda slowly. Yield: 12 servings.

Rosemary Zambo, Preceptor Epsilon
Allentown, Pennsylvania

SANGRIA SLUSH

1 8-ounce can crushed
  pineapple
2½ cups dry red wine
1½ cups orange juice
½ cup lemon juice
½ cup sugar
2 tablespoons grated
  lemon rind

Combine all ingredients in blender. Process on High for 5 seconds. Pour into 9-inch square dish; freeze until firm. Let stand at room temperature for several minutes. Stir until slushy. Spoon into 8 wine or sherbet glasses. Garnish with orange slices or mint sprigs. Yield: 8 servings.

Lillian Putnam, Delta Kappa
Ellisville, Mississippi

WHITE WINE SANGRIA

3 cups white wine
½ cup Triple Sec
¼ cup sugar
1 orange, sliced
1 lime, sliced
1 10-ounce bottle of
  club soda, chilled

Combine wine, Triple Sec and sugar in glass container; stir to dissolve sugar. Add fruit. Chill, covered, in refrigerator for 1 hour. Add soda and ice. Stir gently to mix. Pour into pitcher. Yield: 6 servings.

June Wheeler, Theta Upsilon
Springfield, Missouri

Party
Salads

ROYAL AMBROSIA SALAD

1 cup sour cream
1 cup miniature
  marshmallows
1 15-ounce can Royal
  Anne cherries, drained

1 8-ounce can mandarin
  oranges, drained
1 8-ounce can pineapple
  tidbits, drained
1 cup seedless grapes

Mix sour cream and marshmallows in bowl. Stir in fruit. Chill, covered, for 24 hours. Garnish with fresh fruit at serving time. Yield: 10 to 12 servings.

Elsie Hansen, Laureate Iota
Grand Island, Nebraska

CARAMEL APPLE SALAD

1 3½-ounce package
  butterscotch instant
  pudding mix
1 cup dry-roasted nuts
1 8-ounce can crushed
  pineapple

1 cup miniature
  marshmallows
3 cups chopped unpeeled
  apples
1 8-ounce container
  whipped topping

Combine all ingredients in bowl; mix well. Chill until serving time. Yield: 6 servings.

JoAnn den Broeder, Preceptor Beta Epsilon
Grand Rapids, Michigan

CONGEALED APPLE SALAD

4 to 6 apples, peeled,
  sliced
½ cup sugar
1 cup water
½ cup cinnamon candies
1 3-ounce package
  strawberry gelatin
2 tablespoons mayonnaise

3 ounces cream cheese,
  softened
1 cup whipped cream
½ cup crushed pineapple,
  drained
⅓ cup finely chopped
  celery
½ cup chopped nuts

Bring apples, sugar, water and candies to a boil in saucepan. Cook until apples are tender. Let stand for 24 hours. Drain. Prepare gelatin using package directions. Stir in apple mixture. Pour into 9x13-inch pan. Chill until firm. Combine mayonnaise, cream cheese, whipped cream, pineapple, celery and nuts in bowl; mix well. Spread over gelatin mixture, sealing to edge. Chill until serving time. Serve on lettuce-lined plate. Yield: 15 servings.

Helen Kirby, Xi Gamma Upsilon
Thorp, Washington

TOFFEE APPLE SALAD

1 8-ounce can crushed
  pineapple
1 tablespoon all-purpose
  flour
½ cup sugar
2 tablespoons apple
  cider vinegar

1 egg, beaten
4 cups chopped
  unpeeled apples
1 8-ounce container
  whipped topping
2 cups salted Spanish
  peanuts, chopped

Drain pineapple, reserving juice. Combine pineapple juice, flour, sugar, vinegar and egg in small saucepan. Cook until thickened, stirring constantly. Cool. Combine apples, pineapple, whipped topping and cooked mixture in 2½-quart bowl; mix well. Chill until serving time. Stir in peanuts just before serving. Yield: 8 servings.

Linda Bahl, Beta Pi
Dubuque, Iowa

APRICOT SALAD

2 3-ounce packages
  apricot gelatin
⅔ cup water
⅔ cup sugar
2 4-ounce jars apricot
  baby food
1 cup nuts

1 14-ounce can
  sweetened condensed
  milk
8 ounces cream cheese,
  softened
1 20-ounce can crushed
  pineapple

Bring gelatin, water and sugar to a boil in saucepan. Remove from heat. Stir in baby food. Add nuts, condensed milk, cream cheese and pineapple; mix well. Spoon into large serving dish. Chill, covered, until set.
Yield: 25 servings.

Juanita Hardin, Laureate Iota
Jonesboro, Arkansas

APRICOT AND PINEAPPLE SALAD

2 3-ounce packages
  orange gelatin
2 cups boiling water
½ cup pineapple juice
½ cup apricot juice
1 17-ounce can crushed
  pineapple, drained
1 17-ounce can apricots,
  diced
2 tablespoons butter,
  melted

3 tablespoons all-purpose
  flour
½ cup sugar
1 egg, slightly beaten
1 cup apricot juice
1 cup pineapple juice
3 ounces cream cheese,
  softened
1 cup whipped topping
8 ounces Cheddar
  cheese, shredded

Dissolve gelatin in boiling water in bowl. Add next 4 ingredients. Pour into 9x13-inch pan. Chill until firm. Blend butter and flour in saucepan. Add sugar, egg, 1 cup apricot juice and 1 cup pineapple juice. Cook until thickened, stirring constantly. Stir in cream cheese. Cool. Add whipped topping. Spread over gelatin. Sprinkle cheese on top. Yield: 15 servings.

Dawn D. Haley, Alpha Chi
Findlay, Ohio

FROZEN BANANA SPLIT SALAD

8 ounces cream cheese,
  softened
¾ cup sugar
3 bananas, sliced
1 15-ounce can crushed
  pineapple, drained

1 16-ounce package
  frozen strawberries,
  thawed
1 envelope whipped
  topping mix, prepared

Blend cream cheese and sugar in bowl. Mix in fruit. Fold in whipped topping. Freeze, covered, for 12 hours or longer. Let stand at room temperature for 15 minutes before serving. Yield: 20 servings.

Helen Ables, Beta Alpha
Mt. Vernon, Ohio

CHERRY SALAD

1 8-ounce can crushed pineapple	1 21-ounce can cherry pie filling
1 3-ounce package cherry gelatin	½ cup chopped celery ½ cup chopped nuts

Drain pineapple, reserving juice. Add enough water to reserved juice to measure 1 cup. Bring to a boil in saucepan. Dissolve gelatin in hot juice mixture. Add remaining ingredients; mix well. Pour into 9x13-inch pan. Chill until firm. Yield: 15 servings.

Susan Turner, Preceptor Zeta
Marysville, Kansas

CHERRY COLA SALAD

8 ounces cream cheese, softened	1 cup boiling water
¼ cup mayonnaise	1 17-ounce can pitted dark sweet cherries
1 3-ounce package cherry gelatin	1 13-ounce can pineapple tidbits
1 3-ounce package strawberry gelatin	14 tablespoons cola 1 cup chopped nuts

Blend cream cheese and mayonnaise in bowl. Dissolve gelatins in boiling water in large bowl. Stir in cheese mixture. Drain cherries and pineapple, reserving 1½ cups syrup. Stir juices and cola into gelatin. Chill until partially set. Add fruit and nuts. Pour into 9x13-inch dish. Chill until firm. Yield: 12 servings.

Sue Troyer, Xi Beta Sigma
Dumfries, Virginia

DONNA'S DELUXE CHRISTMAS SALAD

1½ cups red hot cinnamon candies	8 ounces cream cheese, softened
2 cups boiling water	½ cup mayonnaise
2 3-ounce packages lemon gelatin	½ cup chopped celery ½ cup chopped nuts
3 cups applesauce	

Dissolve candies in boiling water in saucepan over low heat. Add gelatin; stir until dissolved. Add applesauce. Pour half the mixture into mold. Chill until set. Spread with mixture of cream cheese, mayonnaise, celery and nuts. Top with remaining gelatin mixture. Chill until firm. Unmold onto serving plate. Yield: 8 to 10 servings.

Mary Park, Xi Delta Tau
Stillwater, Oklahoma

FROZEN CHRISTMAS SALAD

1 cup sour cream	1 15-ounce can crushed pineapple, drained
½ 8-ounce carton whipped topping	½ cup red candied cherries, sliced
½ cup sugar	½ cup green candied cherries, sliced
1 teaspoon vanilla extract	
2 medium bananas	½ cup chopped walnuts
2 tablespoons lemon juice	

Blend sour cream, whipped topping, sugar and vanilla in bowl. Chop bananas; coat with lemon juice. Let stand for several minutes. Add to sour cream mixture with remaining fruit and walnuts. Pour into 4½-cup ring mold. Freeze until firm. Unmold onto serving plate. Let stand for 10 minutes before serving. Yield: 10 to 12 servings.

June Phillips, Preceptor Alpha
Pocatello, Idaho

COOKIE SALAD

1 cup buttermilk	1 20-ounce can pineapple chunks, drained
1 3-ounce package vanilla instant pudding mix	
8 ounces whipped topping	1 or 2 11-ounce cans mandarin oranges, drained
½ to 1 package chocolate-striped shortbread cookies	1 cup miniature marshmallows

Mix buttermilk and pudding mix in bowl. Add whipped topping. Crumble cookies into very small pieces; fold into mixture. Stir in fruit and marshmallows. Chill until serving time. Yield: 10 to 12 servings.

Kelly Anderson, Beta Rho
Evanston, Wyoming

APPLE AND CRANBERRY SALAD

2 3-ounce packages strawberry gelatin	3 apples, ground
2 cups boiling water	1 cup crushed pineapple
1 12-ounce package cranberries, ground	2 cups sugar
	1 cup cold water
	Miniature marshmallows

Dissolve gelatin in boiling water in bowl. Add next 5 ingredients. Stir in marshmallows. Chill, covered, in refrigerator. Yield: 20 servings.

Denise Barber, Kappa
Sioux City, Nebraska

CRANBERRIES IN THE SNOW

1 12-ounce package fresh cranberries	1 cup chopped celery
¾ cup water	1 cup chopped pecans
1 6-ounce package cherry gelatin	1 11-ounce jar marshmallow creme
2 cups sugar	1 8-ounce container whipped topping
1 cup drained pineapple tidbits	8 ounces cream cheese, softened

Cook cranberries in water in saucepan over medium heat until cranberries pop; remove from heat. Add gelatin and sugar; stir until dissolved. Cool. Add pineapple, celery and pecans. Pour into two 9x13-inch dishes. Chill overnight. Blend marshmallow creme, whipped topping and cream cheese in bowl. Spread over congealed layer. Chill until serving time. Yield: 16 to 24 servings.

Bonnie J. Carroll, Xi Nu
Evansville, Indiana

CRANBERRY SALAD

2 cups cranberries
1½ cups sugar
2 cups water
1 3-ounce package red
   gelatin
¼ cup chopped celery
¼ cup chopped apple
¼ cup chopped walnuts
8 ounces cream cheese,
   softened
1 6-ounce can
   evaporated milk

Combine cranberries, sugar and water in saucepan. Cook for 10 minutes. Dissolve gelatin in 2 cups hot mixture. Combine celery, apple and walnuts in ring mold. Add gelatin mixture. Chill until firm. Unmold onto serving plate. Blend cream cheese with enough evaporated milk to make of sauce consistency. Serve over salad. Yield: 6 servings.

Elaine Benton, Preceptor Omega
Sheffield Lake, Ohio

EGGNOG AND CRANBERRY SALAD

1 3-ounce package
   vanilla pudding and
   pie filling mix
1 3-ounce package
   lemon gelatin
2 cups water
2 tablespoons lemon juice
1 3-ounce package
   raspberry gelatin
1 cup boiling water
1 16-ounce can whole
   cranberry sauce
½ cup finely chopped
   celery
¼ cup chopped pecans
1 envelope whipped
   topping mix
½ teaspoon nutmeg

Mix pudding mix, lemon gelatin and 2 cups water in saucepan. Bring to a boil, stirring constantly. Stir in lemon juice. Chill until partially set. Dissolve raspberry gelatin in 1 cup boiling water. Blend in cranberry sauce. Add celery and pecans. Chill until partially set. Prepare whipped topping mix according to package directions, adding nutmeg. Fold into pudding mixture. Pour half the mixture into 8x8-inch pan. Add layer of cranberry mixture and remaining pudding mixture. Chill for 6 hours to overnight. Yield: 9 servings.

Ruth Orlob, Preceptor Delta
Sandy, Utah

CHERRY AND CRANBERRY FREEZE

1 8-ounce jar red
   maraschino cherries
1 3-ounce package
   cherry gelatin
1 16-ounce can jellied
   cranberry sauce
3 tablespoons lemon juice
1 cup whipping cream
3 tablespoons sugar
¼ teaspoon grated
   lemon rind
1 tablespoon lemon juice
⅓ cup mayonnaise-type
   salad dressing
⅓ cup chopped pecans
Fresh mint leaves

Drain cherries, reserving syrup. Chop cherries; set aside. Add enough water to reserved syrup to measure 1½ cups. Bring to a boil in saucepan; remove from heat. Add gelatin; stir until dissolved. Add cranberry sauce and 3 tablespoons lemon juice. Beat with rotary beater until blended. Chill until slightly thickened; fold in cherries.

Pour into lightly oiled 6-cup mold. Freeze until firm. Whip cream with sugar and lemon rind in bowl until stiff; fold in 1 tablespoon lemon juice, salad dressing and pecans. Spread over frozen cherry layer. Freeze until firm. Unmold onto lettuce-lined salad plate. Garnish with fresh mint and additional cherries.
Yield: 16 to 20 servings.

Beverly L. Sheen, Preceptor Epsilon
Laramie, Wyoming

PECAN AND CRANBERRY SALAD

1 3-ounce package
   orange gelatin
1 3-ounce package
   cherry gelatin
1 cup boiling water
1 16-ounce can whole
   cranberry sauce
1 cup chopped pecans
1 6-ounce can frozen
   orange juice
   concentrate, thawed
1 15-ounce can crushed
   pineapple
½ cup coarsely chopped
   celery

Dissolve gelatins in boiling water in bowl. Add remaining ingredients; mix well. Pour into 6-cup ring mold sprayed with nonstick cooking spray. Chill until firm. Unmold onto serving plate. Yield: 12 servings.

Faye Christiansen, Laureate Mu
Albany, Georgia

LEMONY PECAN SALAD

1 4-ounce package
   lemon pudding and
   pie filling mix
2 cups whipped topping
½ cup mayonnaise
2 tablespoons lemon juice
1 cup miniature
   marshmallows
½ cup chopped pecans
1 16-ounce can fruit
   cocktail, drained

Prepare and cook pudding mix according to package directions. Cool. Fold in remaining ingredients. Pour into 5x9-inch loaf pan. Freeze until firm. Let stand at room temperature for 40 minutes. Cut into thick slices and serve on lettuce-lined salad plates. Yield: 8 servings.

Mary Ann Novak, Laureate Alpha Pi
Elyria, Ohio

PINK LEMONADE SALAD

60 Ritz crackers, crushed
¼ cup confectioners'
   sugar
½ cup melted margarine
1 14-ounce can
   sweetened condensed
   milk
1 8-ounce container
   whipped topping
1 6-ounce can frozen
   pink lemonade, thawed
Several drops of
   red food coloring

Combine first 3 ingredients in 9x13-inch dish. Press down with tablespoon, reserving 2 or 3 tablespoons for topping. Combine condensed milk and remaining ingredients in bowl; mix well. Spread over crumbs. Sprinkle reserved crumbs over top. Chill until serving time.
Yield: 15 servings.

Minnie M. Hopkins, Preceptor Beta Lambda
Garden City, Kansas

LUSCIOUS LEMONY PINEAPPLE SALAD

1 16-ounce can crushed
pineapple
1 3-ounce package
lemon gelatin
6 ounces cream cheese,
softened
⅔ cup chopped pecans
½ cup finely chopped
celery
1 4-ounce can chopped
pimento, drained
1 cup whipping cream,
whipped

Drain pineapple, reserving juice. Bring pineapple juice to a boil. Pour juice over gelatin in bowl; stir until dissolved. Chill until partially congealed. Combine cream cheese, pineapple, pecans, celery and pimento in bowl; mix well. Stir into gelatin. Fold in whipped cream. Pour into greased 2-quart salad mold. Chill overnight. Unmold on lettuce-lined serving plate. Yield: 12 servings.

Freeda Stewart, Preceptor Gamma Sigma
Houston, Missouri

LIME AND CUCUMBER SALAD

1 6-ounce package
lime gelatin
2 cups boiling water
1 20-ounce can
crushed pineapple
1 tablespoon vinegar
1½ teaspoons celery salt
½ teaspoon dillweed
1 cup grated cucumber
1 cup sour cream

Dissolve gelatin in boiling water in bowl. Drain pineapple, reserving juice. Add enough water to reserved juice to measure 1 cup. Add to gelatin with vinegar and seasonings. Chill until partially set. Fold in cucumber, sour cream and pineapple. Pour into 2-quart mold. Chill until firm. Unmold onto lettuce-lined serving plate. Yield: 6 servings.

Elfreda Schlenz, Preceptor Pi
Fresno, California

LIME FRUIT SALAD

2 3-ounce packages
lime gelatin
2 cups boiling water
1 cup cold water
6 ounces cream cheese,
softened
1 cup chopped nuts
1 cup whipping cream,
whipped
1 15-ounce can crushed
pineapple, drained
1 4-ounce bottle of
maraschino cherries,
drained

Dissolve gelatin in boiling water in bowl; stir in cold water. Chill until syrupy. Beat cream cheese until fluffy. Fold in nuts, whipped cream and fruit. Fold into gelatin. Pour into mold. Chill until firm. Unmold onto serving plate. Yield: 8 servings.

Sharon Wiers, Alpha Eta Beta
Spring, Texas

ORANGE AND COTTAGE CHEESE SALAD

1 12-ounce container
cottage cheese
1 3-ounce package
orange gelatin
1 8-ounce container
whipped topping
1 8-ounce can crushed
pineapple
1 11-ounce can
mandarin oranges,
drained

Combine cottage cheese and gelatin in bowl; mix well. Fold in whipped topping. Add pineapple and oranges; mix well. Chill until serving time. Yield: 6 to 8 servings.

Dori Shackelford, Gamma Beta
Hampton, Virginia

FROTHY CONGEALED ORANGE SALAD

1 3-ounce package
orange gelatin
1 4-ounce package
vanilla pudding
and pie filling mix
2 cups mixed fruit juice
1 20-ounce can
pineapple, drained
2 8-ounce cans mandarin
oranges, drained
2 bananas
Maraschino cherries
to taste
1 8-ounce container
whipped topping

Mix gelatin, pudding mix and juice in saucepan. Bring to a boil, stirring constantly. Chill for 4 hours to overnight. Fold in fruit and whipped topping. Chill until serving time. Yield: 6 servings.

Kay Beasley, Xi Delta Lambda
Canon City, Colorado

LOUISIANA POPPY SEED FRUIT SALAD

2 11-ounce cans
mandarin orange
segments
1 16-ounce can freestone
peaches
1 15-ounce can
pineapple tidbits
4 bananas, peeled, sliced
1 10-ounce package
frozen sliced
strawberries with sugar
1 3-ounce package
vanilla instant
pudding mix
1 cup orange juice
1 teaspoon poppy seed

Drain oranges, peaches and pineapple. Combine all fruit in large bowl; toss gently. Combine pudding mix, orange juice and poppy seed in bowl; mix well. Pour over fruit; toss gently. Chill overnight. Yield: 12 servings.

Paige Franklin, Beta Beta Theta
Lampasas, Texas

MINTED FRESH FRUIT COMPOTE

3 or 4 fresh mint leaves
1 cup sugar
2 cups water
¼ cup lemon juice
1 honeydew melon
2 small cantaloupes
2 boxes fresh strawberries
Watermelon chunks
1 or 2 seedless oranges,
sectioned
Red or green seedless
grapes

Combine first 3 ingredients in saucepan. Bring to a boil. Boil rapidly for 5 minutes. Remove from heat; cool. Add lemon juice; remove mint leaves. Cut melons into balls; slice strawberries. Combine fruit in bowl. Pour mint syrup over fruit. Let stand for 1 hour or longer, stirring occasionally. Garnish with fresh mint leaves. Yield: 10 servings.

Janice Crockett, Laureate Alpha Psi
Albany, Missouri

FROSTED PINEAPPLE SALAD

2 3-ounce packages lemon gelatin	1 egg, beaten
2 cups boiling water	2 tablespoons all-purpose flour
2 cups 7-Up	1 cup pineapple juice
1 20-ounce can crushed pineapple, drained	2 tablespoons butter
2 cups miniature marshmallows	3 ounces cream cheese, softened
2 bananas, sliced	½ cup whipping cream
½ cup sugar	½ cup chopped pecans
	½ cup coconut

Dissolve gelatin in boiling water in bowl. Add 7-Up. Pour into 9x13-inch dish. Chill until partially set. Add pineapple, marshmallows and bananas. Chill until firm. Combine sugar, egg, flour and pineapple juice in saucepan. Cook over low heat until thickened, stirring constantly; remove from heat. Add butter. Cool. Blend in cream cheese. Chill. Whip cream until stiff; fold into cheese mixture. Spread over gelatin; sprinkle with pecans and coconut. Yield: 16 to 20 servings.

Carolyn J. McClung, Alpha Chi
Fort Bragg, North Carolina

YUM YUM PINEAPPLE SALAD

1 20-ounce can crushed pineapple	1 teaspoon finely chopped onion
1 cup sugar	1 green bell pepper, finely chopped
2 envelopes unflavored gelatin	3 stalks celery, finely chopped
½ cup cold water	Mayonnaise-type salad dressing to taste
1 cup shredded Velveeta cheese	
1 cup whipping cream, whipped	

Heat pineapple and sugar to a boil in saucepan. Soften gelatin in cold water in bowl. Add to pineapple mixture; cool until slightly thickened, stirring occasionally. Add cheese; fold in whipped cream. Pour into 6-cup mold. Chill overnight. Unmold onto serving plate. Spread mixture of onion, green pepper, celery and salad dressing on top. Yield: 9 to 12 servings.

Maxine Burns, Laureate Lambda
Beloit, Wisconsin

PEACHY TAPIOCA SALAD

2 15-ounce cans peaches	2 3-ounce packages vanilla tapioca pudding mix
1 3-ounce package peach gelatin	

Drain peaches, reserving juice. Add enough water to reserved juice to measure 3 cups. Combine with gelatin and pudding mix in saucepan. Bring to a boil; cool. Add peaches; mix well. Chill in refrigerator. Yield: 4 to 6 servings.

Patsy Wirtz, Iota Phi
West Bend, Iowa

PRETZEL SALAD

1½ cups pretzels	¾ cup sugar
4½ tablespoons sugar	1 6-ounce package strawberry gelatin
¾ cup melted margarine	2 cups boiling water
8 ounces cream cheese, softened	1 16-ounce package strawberries, sliced
1 8-ounce container whipped topping	

Preheat oven to 350 degrees. Crush pretzels coarsely. Combine with sugar and margarine in 9x13-inch baking pan. Bake for 10 minutes. Cool. Combine next 3 ingredients in bowl; mix well. Spread over crust. Dissolve gelatin in boiling water in bowl. Add strawberries. Chill until partially set. Spoon over cream cheese layer. Chill until set. Yield: 12 servings.

Lovea Vaughan, Preceptor Delta Epsilon
Titusville, Florida

RASPBERRY-CHEESE SALAD

1 8-ounce container cottage cheese	3 cups fresh raspberries
1 3-ounce package raspberry gelatin	2 cups whipped topping

Combine cottage cheese and dry gelatin in bowl; mix until gelatin dissolves. Fold in raspberries and whipped topping. Yield: 6 to 8 servings.

Jeannette Needels, Alpha Lambda
Basin, Wyoming

RIBBON SALAD

5 packages various flavors gelatin	1 teaspoon vanilla extract
5 cups boiling water	3 envelopes unflavored gelatin
2 cups milk	½ cup cold water
1 cup sugar	2 cups sour cream

Prepare 5 different gelatin flavors by dissolving each in 1 cup boiling water in small bowl. Pour 1 flavor into 9x13-inch dish. Chill in freezer for 5 minutes. Combine milk and sugar in saucepan. Bring to a boil. Add vanilla; remove from heat. Soften 3 packages unflavored gelatin in ½ cup cold water in bowl. Stir into milk mixture. Cool. Add sour cream; beat well. Alternate white layer with remaining gelatins. Chill in freezer for 5 minutes after each layer is added. Chill until firm. Yield: 24 to 33 servings.
Note: Use colors to accent the occasion or party. Christmas might be red, white and green. Use pastels for Easter and orange, white and blackberry for Halloween.

Dawn Irish, Mu Tau
Ennis, Texas

*To vary the Ribbon Salad, **Angie Cyr, Xi Delta Tau, Stillwater, Oklahoma,** uses cherry and blueberry gelatin for the Fourth of July or strawberry, orange and lime gelatin for a birthday.*

SUGAR-FREE CONGEALED SALAD

1 20-ounce can tart
  cherries
1 20-ounce can crushed
  pineapple
1 6-ounce package sugar-
  free cherry gelatin
2 cups diet cola
4 ounces cream cheese,
  softened
½ cup chopped pecans

Drain fruit, reserving juice. Combine juices with enough water to measure 2 cups. Bring to a boil in saucepan. Add gelatin; stir until dissolved. Add cola. Chill until partially set. Add cream cheese; mix well. Fold in cherries, pineapple and pecans. Pour into 2-quart mold. Chill until firm. Unmold onto serving plate. Yield: 6 to 8 servings.

Fran Maloy, Alpha Delta
Tifton, Georgia

DELUXE FRUIT SALAD

1 8-ounce can
  mandarin oranges
1 8-ounce can pineapple
  chunks
1 4-ounce jar
  maraschino cherries
2 apples, chopped
2 bananas, sliced
1 21-ounce can peach
  pie filling
½ cup chopped pecans

Drain oranges, pineapple and cherries. Combine with remaining ingredients in bowl. Chill until serving time. Yield: 6 servings.

Linda Sides, Alpha Mu Epsilon
Hallsville, Texas

HEALTH FRUIT SALAD

2 pints fresh
  strawberries
1 fresh pineapple
4 to 6 bananas
1 pound seedless grapes
1 6-pack low-fat
  strawberry yogurt
2 cups pecan pieces

Slice strawberries, pineapple and bananas into bite-sized pieces; cut grapes into halves. Layer in large bowl. Cover with yogurt; sprinkle pecans on top. Mix well. Chill, covered, until serving time. Mix well before serving. Yield: 10 to 12 servings.

Margie Akelewicz, Preceptor Tau
Merritt Island, Florida

PRETTY FRUIT SALAD

1 21-ounce can apricot
  pie filling
1 16-ounce can sliced
  peaches, drained
4 bananas, sliced
1 cup maraschino cherries
1 15-ounce can
  pineapple chunks,
  drained
1 11-ounce can mandarin
  oranges, drained

Combine all ingredients in bowl. Toss gently to mix. Chill in refrigerator. Yield: 6 to 8 servings.

Beth Mitchell, Alpha Lambda Sigma
El Campo, Texas

FRUITED PUDDING SALAD

1 4-ounce package
  vanilla instant
  pudding mix
1 15-ounce can crushed
  pineapple
1 8-ounce can mandarin
  oranges, drained
1 12-ounce container
  whipped topping
3 medium bananas, sliced
2 cups miniature
  marshmallows

Mix dry pudding mix and undrained pineapple in large bowl. Add oranges and remaining ingredients; mix well. Chill until serving time. Yield: 10 servings.

Pam Van Buskirk, Omicron Epsilon
Lucerne, Missouri

MIXED FRUIT SALAD

3 egg yolks
6 tablespoons sugar
3 tablespoons
  pineapple juice
2 tablespoons
  lemon juice
2 cups whipped topping
1 16-ounce can fruit
  cocktail
1 16-ounce can
  pineapple chunks
1 8-ounce can mandarin
  oranges
2 or 3 apples, chopped
Coconut to taste

Beat egg yolks in saucepan until fluffy. Add sugar, pineapple juice and lemon juice. Cook until thickened, stirring constantly. Cool. Add whipped topping. Drain canned fruit. Combine all fruit and coconut in bowl. Add cooked mixture; mix well. Chill until serving time. Yield: 10 to 12 servings.

Sally Wassmuth, Gamma Beta
Grangeville, Idaho

FROSTY STRAWBERRY SALAD

1 14-ounce can
  sweetened condensed
  milk
1 16-ounce can crushed
  pineapple, drained
1 21-ounce can
  strawberry pie filling
1 16-ounce container
  whipped topping

Combine all ingredients in bowl; mix well. Pour into 9x12-inch dish. Freeze until firm. Let stand at room temperature for 15 minutes before serving. Yield: 12 servings.

Denise Barber, Kappa
Sioux City, Nebraska

FROZEN STRAWBERRY SALAD

8 ounces cream cheese,
  softened
¾ cup sugar
2 20-ounce cans crushed
  pineapple, drained
3 bananas, sliced
3 pints frozen
  strawberries, thawed
2 9-ounce containers
  whipped topping

Combine cream cheese and sugar in mixer bowl; mix well. Fold in remaining ingredients. Pour into 9x13-inch glass dish. Freeze until firm. Thaw for 20 minutes before serving. Yield: 6 servings.

Peggy Carraway, Xi Alpha Phi
Murray, Kentucky

FROZEN FRUIT SALAD

¾ cup chopped canned
   peaches
¼ cup chopped canned
   apricots
½ cup crushed pineapple
½ cup chopped
   maraschino cherries
1 cup chopped pecans

⅓ cup confectioners'
   sugar
¼ teaspoon salt
4 or 5 marshmallows,
   cut into quarters
¾ cup mayonnaise
1 cup whipping cream,
   whipped

Drain fruit well. Combine in bowl. Add pecans, confectioners' sugar, salt and marshmallows; mix well. Blend in mayonnaise and whipped cream gently. Spoon into molds. Freeze until serving time. Unmold onto lettuce-lined plates. Yield: 8 to 10 servings.

Lois Roth, Preceptor Delta
Salt Lake City, Utah

TWENTY-FOUR HOUR SALAD

4 egg yolks
½ cup sugar
¼ cup canned cream
Juice of 1 lemon
1 cup whipping cream
1 can pineapple
   chunks, drained
1 16-ounce can fruit
   cocktail, drained

2 11-ounce cans
   mandarin oranges,
   drained
½ cup chopped nuts
1 16-ounce package
   miniature
   marshmallows
2 bananas, sliced

Combine first 4 ingredients in saucepan. Cook over low heat until thickened, stirring constantly. Chill. Beat whipping cream until stiff. Fold in cooked mixture. Combine canned fruit in bowl. Add whipped cream mixture; mix well. Add nuts and marshmallows. Pour into 11x13-inch dish. Chill, covered, for 24 hours. Stir in bananas just before serving. Yield: 16 to 20 servings.

Radine Murphy, Xi Iota Tau
Decatur, Illinois

FROZEN WALDORF SALAD

1 9-ounce can crushed
   pineapple
2 eggs, slightly beaten
½ cup sugar
¼ cup lemon juice
⅛ teaspoon salt
¼ cup mayonnaise
2½ cups chopped
   unpeeled Red
   Delicious apples

⅔ cup diced celery
½ cup coarsely chopped
   walnuts
⅓ cup miniature
   marshmallows
½ cup whipping cream,
   whipped

Drain pineapple, reserving syrup. Combine syrup, eggs, sugar, lemon juice and salt in saucepan. Cook over low heat for 20 minutes or until slightly thickened, stirring constantly. Cool. Fold in mayonnaise. Combine pineapple, apples, celery, walnuts and marshmallows in bowl; mix well. Fold whipped cream into cooled egg mixture. Pour over fruit mixture; toss lightly. Spoon into paper-lined muffin cups. Freeze until firm. Place in refrigerator

for 1 hour before serving. Remove paper liners from each salad; invert on lettuce-lined serving plate.
Yield: 12 servings.

 Diane Runo, Xi Beta
Peoria, Arizona

WINE SALAD

2 3-ounce packages
   raspberry gelatin
1¼ cups boiling water
1 16-ounce can whole
   cranberry sauce
1 20-ounce can crushed
   pineapple

½ cup wine
3 ounces cream cheese,
   softened
1 cup sour cream
Chopped nuts

Dissolve gelatin boiling water in bowl; cool. Add cranberry sauce, pineapple and wine. Pour into serving dish. Chill until firm. Spread mixture of cream cheese and sour cream over top. Sprinkle with nuts. Yield: 12 servings.

Marcia Flood, Xi Alpha Delta
Excelsior Springs, Missouri

BEEF SALAD

1 pound boneless
   beef steak
Garlic and onion powder
   to taste
1 cucumber, peeled,
   sliced
1 white onion,
   thinly sliced

1 tomato, chopped
1 green bell pepper,
   chopped
1 red bell pepper,
   chopped
2 chili peppers, chopped
Juice of 1 lemon
Juice of 1 lime

Preheat oven to 350 degrees. Cut beef into 1-inch cubes; place in baking pan. Season with garlic powder and onion powder. Bake for 20 to 30 minutes or until cooked through, stirring occasionally. Mix vegetables and juices in large bowl. Add beef cubes; toss to mix. Chill overnight for improved flavor. Serve on lettuce-lined plate. Yield: 4 to 6 servings.

Jeri Vineyard, Phi
Henderson, Nevada

CONFETTI SALAD

1⅓ cups long grain rice
¼ cup French dressing
¾ cup mayonnaise
1 tablespoon minced
   green onions
½ teaspoon salt
Dash of pepper
½ to 1 teaspoon curry
   powder
½ teaspoon dry mustard

¾ cup chopped ham
¾ cup chopped cooked
   chicken
1 cup thinly sliced fresh
   cauliflower
1 cup frozen peas, cooked,
   chilled
½ cup chopped celery
½ cup sliced radishes
Romaine lettuce

Cook rice using package directions. Add French dressing; toss lightly. Chill for several hours. Mix mayonnaise with next 5 ingredients. Toss with chilled rice in salad bowl. Add ham, chicken and vegetables; toss lightly. Serve on romaine lettuce-lined plate. Yield: 18 servings.

Eloise Hood, Preceptor Epsilon Alpha
Winter Haven, Florida

CHICKEN ALOHA

1 pound chopped cooked chicken	2 teaspoons toasted sesame seed
1 stalk celery, chopped	6 tablespoons mayonnaise
1 medium apple, chopped	1 teaspoon curry powder
1 cup pineapple chunks	
2 tablespoons raisins, plumped	

Combine first 5 ingredients and ⅔ of the sesame seed in bowl. Add mixture of mayonnaise and curry powder; toss to mix. Sprinkle with remaining sesame seed. Yield: 4 servings.

Deborah Scalf, Xi Rho Psi
Port Neches, Texas

FRESH BROCCOLI AND CHICKEN SALAD

2 cups chopped fresh broccoli	12 ounces chopped cooked chicken
⅔ cup sliced pimento-stuffed olives	¼ cup mayonnaise
½ cup chopped onion	2 teaspoons lemon juice
⅔ cup chopped celery	1 teaspoon sugar
⅔ cup chopped bell pepper	1 teaspoon salt
6 hard-cooked eggs	1 teaspoon pepper
	1 teaspoon garlic powder
	6 slices Swiss cheese

Combine first 7 ingredients in bowl. Blend mayonnaise with lemon juice, sugar and seasonings in small bowl. Add to chicken mixture; toss until mixed. Chill overnight if desired. Serve on lettuce-lined plate. Garnish with cheese slice. Yield: 6 servings.

Alta Mary Arnold, Mu
Jackson, Tennessee

CHICKEN AND BROCCOLI SALAD

2 heads broccoli	2 tablespoons wine vinegar
2 tablespoons peanut oil	1 clove of garlic, minced
2 to 3 chicken breasts	1 teaspoon dried dillweed
½ cup cottage cheese	Salt and pepper to taste
½ cup mayonnaise	1 cup chopped parsley
½ cup milk	4 green onions, chopped
1 tablespoon olive oil	

Cut flowerets and upper stems of broccoli into small pieces; discard tough stems. Bring generous amount of water and peanut oil to a boil in saucepan. Add broccoli. Simmer for 5 minutes; drain. Plunge into cold water; drain and chill. Roast or poach chicken until tender; bone, chop and chill. Combine broccoli, chicken and mixture of cottage cheese, mayonnaise and next 6 ingredients in salad bowl; toss to mix. Add parsley and green onions; toss lightly. Serve with crusty French or sourdough bread. Yield: 4 servings.

Rosella Pelling, Xi Rho
Spartanburg, South Carolina

CURRIED CHICKEN SALAD

2 cups mayonnaise	1 6-ounce can sliced water chestnuts, drained
2 tablespoons lemon juice	
2½ tablespoons soy sauce	2 cups seedless white grapes
1 tablespoon (rounded) curry powder	
1 tablespoon onion juice	1 16-ounce can pineapple chunks, well drained
1 tablespoon chutney, chopped	
3 cups chopped cooked chicken breasts	½ cup slivered almonds, toasted
1½ cups chopped celery	

Combine first 6 ingredients in large bowl; mix well. Add chicken, vegetables and fruits; toss lightly. Refrigerate overnight. Sprinkle with almonds. Yield: 8 servings.

Christine L. Morrow, Preceptor Gamma
Smyrna, Delaware

CURRIED CHICKEN AND RICE SALAD

4 chicken breasts, cooked, chopped	1 cup chopped unpeeled apples
1 package wild rice, cooked	½ cup mayonnaise
	1 tablespoon mango chutney
1 cup seedless green grapes	2 tablespoons soy sauce
1 cup diced celery	2 to 3 teaspoons curry powder
1 cup slivered almonds	

Mix chicken, rice, grapes, celery, almonds and apples in bowl. Add mayonnaise; mix well. Add chutney, soy sauce and curry powder; mix well. Adjust seasonings if necessary. Chill for 2 hours. Yield: 4 to 6 servings.

Kathy Berning, Chi
Waterloo, Iowa

DELIGHTFUL CHICKEN SALAD

1 package slivered almonds	2 cups green grape halves
½ tablespoon butter	2 small cans mandarin oranges, drained
2 cups cooked long grain rice	2 cups mayonnaise
2 cups diced celery	2 cups ranch salad dressing
2 tablespoons chopped onion	10 chicken breasts, cooked, chopped

Sauté almonds in butter in skillet until golden brown; drain on paper towels. Combine rice and remaining ingredients in bowl; mix gently. Top with almonds. Chill for 2 hours. Serve in glass bowl. Yield: 15 to 20 servings.

Marlene R. Bartz, Iota Delta
Midland, Michigan

Priscilla Dodd, Xi Delta Lambda, Flint, Michigan, *reserves some of the salad ingredients such as mandarin orange sections, whole nuts, grapes or pineapple chunks to garnish the salad. This not only looks pretty but suggests the taste treats within.*

FLYING FARMER'S CHICKEN SALAD

5 cups chopped cooked chicken	1 11-ounce can mandarin oranges
2 tablespoons orange juice	1½ cups chopped celery
2 tablespoons corn oil	½ cup small green grapes
2 tablespoons vinegar	1 13-ounce can
1 teaspoon salt	pineapple chunks
3 cups cooled cooked rice	1 cup toasted sliced
1½ cups mayonnaise	almonds

Marinate chicken in mixture of orange juice, oil, vinegar and salt in bowl for several minutes. Combine rice and remaining ingredients in salad bowl. Add chicken; toss gently. Chill until serving time. Yield: 6 to 8 servings.

Sherie L. Keck, Beta Kappa
Boise, Idaho

LAYERED CHICKEN SALAD

1 small head lettuce, torn	¼ teaspoon garlic powder
1 10-ounce package frozen peas, thawed	1½ cups shredded carrots
	4 hard-cooked eggs, sliced
3 5-ounce cans chunky chicken	1½ cups thinly sliced celery
1 cup sour cream	1 small red onion, thinly sliced
1½ cups mayonnaise	
⅓ cup minced fresh parsley	¼ cup Parmesan cheese
	8 slices crisp-fried bacon, crumbled
2½ teaspoons dried dillweed	
1½ teaspoons Beau Monde seasoning	

Layer lettuce and peas in large salad bowl. Drain chicken, reserving broth. Mix reserved broth, sour cream and next 5 ingredients in small bowl. Spread half the mixture evenly over peas. Add layers of carrots, chicken, eggs, celery and onion. Spread remaining sour cream mixture over top, sealing to edge of bowl. Sprinkle with Parmesan cheese. Chill, covered, overnight. Sprinkle bacon on top just before serving. Yield: 10 to 12 servings.

Maria Miller, Xi Alpha Alpha
Jacksonville, Florida

MANDARIN CHICKEN SALAD

2 cups chopped cooked chicken	1 cup chopped mandarin oranges
1 tablespoon minced onion	1 cup cooked macaroni rings
½ teaspoon salt	1 cup mayonnaise-type salad dressing
1 cup seedless green grape halves	1 cup whipping cream, whipped
1 cup chopped celery	
⅓ cup slivered almonds	

Combine chicken, onion and salt in bowl. Chill for 1 hour. Add grapes, celery, almonds, oranges and macaroni. Add salad dressing; mix well. Chill until serving time. Fold in whipped cream just before serving. Serve on lettuce-lined plates. Yield: 8 servings.

Andra Stone, Beta Rho
Lewistown, Montana

CHICKEN MOUSSE SUPREME

3 envelopes unflavored gelatin	1½ cups finely diced celery
½ cup cold water	1 teaspoon Worcestershire sauce
1 10-ounce can cream of chicken soup	1½ tablespoons grated onion
2½ cups chicken broth	2 tablespoons lemon juice
2 teaspoons salt	2 tablespoons chopped parsley
¼ teaspoon pepper	
1 cup mayonnaise	1 cup whipping cream, whipped
5 cups chopped cooked chicken	

Soften gelatin in cold water. Combine soup, broth, salt and pepper in saucepan. Cook until hot and blended, stirring frequently. Add gelatin; stir until dissolved. Cool. Blend in mayonnaise. Add chicken and next 5 ingredients. Fold in whipped cream. Spoon into 3-quart ring mold rinsed with cold water. Chill for 4 hours or until set. Unmold onto lettuce-lined serving plate. Serve with French dressing. Yield: 16 servings.

Barbara Restvedt, Preceptor Laureate Alpha
Williston, North Dakota

CHICKEN SALAD SUPREME

2½ cups chopped cooked chicken	1 cup sliced white grapes
2 tablespoons lemon juice	2 tablespoons minced parsley
1 cup finely chopped celery	1 teaspoon salt
½ cup slivered toasted almonds	1 cup mayonnaise
	½ cup whipping cream, whipped
4 hard-cooked eggs, chopped	1 or 2 cantaloupe or honeydew melons

Mix first 9 ingredients in bowl. Fold in whipped cream. Serve in cantaloupe or honeydew rings on lettuce-lined plates. Yield: 8 servings.

Jean Hamner, Xi Rho
Spartanburg, South Carolina

HAM AND MANDARIN SALAD

1 7-ounce package macaroni rings, cooked	1 11-ounce can mandarin oranges, drained
1 clove of garlic, split	⅔ cup mayonnaise
2 cups chopped ham	¼ cup light cream
⅓ cup chopped green onions	2 tablespoons vinegar
1 cup chopped celery	½ teaspoon pepper

Rinse macaroni with cold water; drain. Rub salad bowl with cut side of garlic; discard garlic. Combine macaroni, ham, green onions, celery and orange segments in prepared bowl. Chill, covered, for 2 hours to overnight. Blend mayonnaise, cream, vinegar and pepper in small bowl. Pour over macaroni mixture; toss until well coated. Serve on lettuce-lined plate. Yield: 10 to 12 servings.

Louise Baumgartner, Gamma Upsilon
Bagley, Minnesota

HAM SALAD

1 package wild rice
1 envelope dry vinaigrette
   seasoning mix
½ cup sliced green olives
1 cup (or more) chopped
   celery
1 6-ounce jar artichoke
   hearts, sliced
½ cup chopped tomatoes,
   drained
1 cup chopped ham
½ to ¾ cup lite
   mayonnaise
Salt and pepper to taste
Onion powder to taste
½ cup chopped cucumber

Cook wild rice using package directions. Prepare vinaigrette mix using package directions. Stir vinaigrette into rice. Add remaining ingredients; mix well. Chill, covered, overnight. Yield: 12 to 14 servings.

Gigi Riggs, Xi Alpha Lambda
Sedan, Kansas

CRAB MEAT SALAD

1 medium onion,
   finely chopped
1 pound lump crab meat,
   flaked
Salt and pepper to taste
½ cup corn oil
6 tablespoons cider
   vinegar
½ cup ice water

Layer half the onion in bottom of large bowl. Layer crab meat, remaining onion, salt and pepper on top. Pour mixture of oil, vinegar and ice water over crab meat. Marinate, covered, for 2 to 12 hours. Toss lightly. Serve on lettuce-lined serving plate. Garnish with tomato wedges, radishes or cucumbers. Yield: 4 servings.

Daisy Sport, Preceptor Upsilon
Brantley, Alabama

GOURMET SHRIMP AND PASTA SALAD

16 ounces pasta
1 tablespoon olive oil
¼ cup margarine
Parsley to taste
1 pound shrimp, cooked
2 or 3 slices white cheese
2 or 3 slices ham
½ red onion, chopped
1 cucumber, peeled,
   chopped
1 tomato, peeled, chopped
2 tablespoons Dijon-
   style mustard
¾ cup mayonnaise

Cook pasta using package directions, adding oil to water. Rinse and drain. Add margarine and parsley to pasta. Toss with remaining ingredients. Yield: 12 to 16 servings

Bette Deniston, Xi Eta Mu
Carbondale, Illinois

SHRIMP CABBAGE SALAD

½ cup corn oil
1 package ramen
   noodle soup mix
1 medium head cabbage,
   shredded
½ cup chopped onion
½ cup chopped celery
1 green bell pepper,
   chopped
1 7-ounce can shrimp
Salt and pepper to taste

Combine oil and soup base in bowl; mix well. Add vegetables, crumbled noodles, shrimp and salt and pepper; mix well. Chill, covered, for several hours. Yield: 12 servings.

Lois Bennett, Preceptor Iota
Helena, Montana

SHRIMP AND RICE SALAD

1 cup cooked shrimp
3 cups cooked rice
¼ cup sliced celery
¼ cup sliced pimento-
   stuffed olives
¼ cup chopped green
   bell pepper
¼ cup chopped pimento
¼ cup minced onion
½ teaspoon salt
½ teaspoon pepper
3 tablespoons mayonnaise
Crisp greens
2 tomatoes, cut into
   wedges
French dressing
1 lemon, cut into wedges

Split each shrimp lengthwise. Combine shrimp, rice, celery, olives, green pepper, pimento and onion in bowl. Chill, covered, until serving time. Blend salt, pepper and mayonnaise in bowl. Add to shrimp mixture, tossing to mix. Spoon onto crisp greens. Garnish with tomato wedges and additional whole shrimp. Serve with French dressing and lemon wedges. Yield: 6 servings.

Jeannine Partsch, Xi Alpha Iota
Nebraska City, Nebraska

SHRIMP AND VERMICELLI SALAD

1 16-ounce package
   vermicelli
5 tablespoons olive oil
Salt and pepper to taste
2 cloves of garlic, minced
3 cups finely chopped
   celery
1 small bunch green
   onions, chopped
1 green bell pepper,
   chopped
1 4-ounce jar chopped
   pimento
8 ounces cooked shrimp
1 cup mayonnaise
Juice of 1 lemon
½ cup Champagne
   salad dressing

Break vermicelli into 1-inch pieces. Cook using package directions, adding 1 tablespoon oil to water; drain. Do not rinse. Add remaining ¼ cup oil, salt, pepper and minced garlic; mix well. Cool. Combine with remaining ingredients in serving bowl; toss well. Yield: 24 servings.

Carol Stevens, Xi Delta Omicron
San Jose, California

SHRIMP LOUIS

1 cup mayonnaise
¼ cup chili sauce
2 tablespoons grated
   onion
2 teaspoons lemon juice
1 cup whipping cream,
   whipped
1 head lettuce, shredded
2 pounds shrimp, cooked,
   peeled
12 ripe olives
3 hard-cooked eggs,
   quartered
3 large tomatoes,
   cut into quarters
2 avocados, peeled, sliced

Mix first 4 ingredients in bowl. Fold in whipped cream. Chill in refrigerator. Place shredded lettuce on 6 chilled plates. Arrange shrimp in center of plate. Surround shrimp with olives, eggs, tomatoes and avocados. Spoon sauce over shrimp and vegetables. Serve immediately. Yield: 6 servings.

Phyllis Briggman, Laureate Iota
Colorado Springs, Colorado

SHRIMP AND SHOESTRING SALAD

2 6-ounce cans
   shrimp, drained
1 cup shredded carrots
1 cup diced celery
⅓ cup chopped onion
1 cup mayonnaise
1 10-ounce can
   shoestring potatoes

Combine first 5 ingredients in bowl; mix well. Chill until serving time. Add potatoes just before serving. Yield: 4 to 6 servings.

Rosemary Gallagher, Xi Kappa Phi
Stow, Ohio

SEAFOOD SALAD

10 to 12 ounces crab meat
2 6-ounce cans shrimp
4 hard-cooked eggs,
   chopped
1 head lettuce, torn
½ cup shredded
   Cheddar cheese
¾ to 1 cup Thousand
   Island salad dressing
Croutons

Combine all ingredients in large bowl; mix well. Spoon onto salad plates. Garnish with croutons. Yield: 4 to 6 servings.

Jan Hendrickson, Preceptor Zeta Psi
Duncanville, Texas

SPECIAL TUNA SALAD

1 6½-ounce can oil-pack
   tuna, drained
2 hard-cooked eggs,
   chopped
2 tablespoons sweet
   pickle relish
1 medium apple, chopped
½ cup mayonnaise
1 teaspoon vinegar
1 teaspoon lemon juice
1 teaspoon mustard
½ teaspoon garlic powder
1 teaspoon chopped
   parsley
½ cup finely chopped
   onion
½ cup finely chopped
   green bell pepper
½ cup finely chopped
   celery

Combine all ingredients in bowl; mix well. Serve on lettuce-lined plates or in tomato shells. Yield: 6 servings.

Olivia C. Reid, Laureate Beta
Lafayette, Louisiana

ORIENTAL TUNA SALAD

1 10-ounce package
   frozen peas
¾ cup mayonnaise
1 tablespoon lemon juice
¼ teaspoon curry powder
¼ teaspoon garlic powder
1 teaspoon soy sauce
1 6½-ounce can water-
   pack tuna, drained
1 cup sliced celery
¼ cup thinly sliced
   green onions
1 4-ounce can sliced
   water chestnuts
1 5-ounce can
   Chinese noodles
1 3-ounce package
   slivered almonds

Cook peas using package directions; drain, set aside. Mix next 5 ingredients in bowl. Add tuna, celery, onions, peas and water chestnuts. Chill for 5 hours. Add Chinese noodles just before serving. Top with almonds. Yield: 6 servings.

Susan Rieder, Xi Beta Xi
Jefferson, Iowa

TUNA AND CHOW MEIN SALAD

1 6½-ounce can tuna,
   drained
1 carrot, grated
½ cup chopped celery
¼ cup mayonnaise
¼ cup French onion dip
1 3-ounce can chow
   mein noodles

Combine tuna, carrot and celery in bowl. Add mixture of mayonnaise and dip. Chill until serving time. Add chow mein noodles just before serving. Yield: 4 to 6 servings.

Lyeliene Hoehne, Preceptor Alpha Omicron
Marshall, Michigan

TUNA AND TOMATOES PROVENÇALE

1½ cups cooked rice
½ cup white beans,
   drained
1 6½-ounce can water-
   pack tuna
¼ cup chopped red onion
¼ cup sliced celery
¼ cup oil and vinegar
   salad dressing
1½ tablespoons lemon
   juice
¼ teaspoon salt
⅛ teaspoon pepper
4 large ripe tomatoes
4 lettuce leaves
4 hard-cooked eggs,
   halved
4 lemon slices

Combine first 5 ingredients in large bowl. Add dressing, lemon juice, salt and pepper; toss to mix. Chill, covered, for 2 hours. Cut slice from top of each tomato; scoop out pulp and seeds. Invert on paper towel to drain. Spoon tuna mixture into tomatoes. Arrange on lettuce-lined serving plates; garnish with eggs and lemon slices. Yield: 4 servings.

Vera Roberts, Xi Epsilon
Edmond, Oklahoma

TUNA MOLD SALAD

1 6½-ounce can
   Albacore tuna, drained
3 hard-cooked eggs,
   chopped
⅓ cup sliced stuffed
   green olives
½ cup chopped celery
½ envelope unflavored
   gelatin
½ cup tomato juice
1 3-ounce package
   lemon gelatin
1 cup mayonnaise
1 cup sour cream
1 tablespoon minced
   onion
2 tablespoons dry
   parsley flakes
¼ teaspoon salt

Combine tuna, eggs, olives and celery in bowl. Soften unflavored gelatin in tomato juice in saucepan. Heat until gelatin dissolves, stirring constantly. Add lemon gelatin, stir until dissolved. Add mayonnaise, sour cream, onion, parsley and salt. Stir into tuna mixture. Pour into mold or dish. Chill until firm. Serve on lettuce-lined plates. Yield: 4 to 6 servings.

Anne Carson, Laureate
Mobile, Alabama

Marjorie Norcutt, Xi Alpha Upsilon, Gretna, Virginia,
makes Thousand Island dressing by combining half a small
bottle of catsup, 3 cups mayonnaise, 2 tablespoons mustard, 1
cup chopped sweet pickle and enough pickle juice to make of
desired consistency. Serve on Seafood Salad or tossed salad.

MOCK CHICKEN SALAD WITH TUNA

1 3-ounce package lemon gelatin	1 10-ounce can chicken and rice soup
1 cup boiling water	1 cup diced celery
1 6½-ounce can water-pack tuna	½ cup mayonnaise
1 cup chopped walnuts	½ cup whipped cream

Dissolve gelatin in boiling water in bowl. Add tuna and remaining ingredients. Pour into 9x13-inch dish. Chill until firm. Cut into squares. Serve on lettuce leaf. Yield: 8 servings.

Dora Bailey, Preceptor Delta
Salt Lake City, Utah

FRESH SALMON SALAD

2 pounds fresh salmon	1 8-ounce can water chestnuts, chopped
2 cups water	½ cup minced green bell pepper
2 bay leaves	
2 tablespoons peppercorns	½ cup minced onion
½ cup lemon juice	¾ cup chopped seeded cucumber
½ cup mustard	
2 tablespoons dried onion flakes	20 pimento-stuffed green olives, chopped
½ cup mayonnaise	Pita pockets

Poach salmon in water in saucepan for 20 minutes, adding bay leaves, peppercorns and lemon juice. Turn salmon over. Poach for 15 minutes longer. Cool and flake. Mix mustard with dried onion flakes in small bowl. Let stand at room temperature for 30 minutes. Chill. Mix with mayonnaise. Combine salmon, vegetables, olives and enough mayonnaise mixture to bind in bowl; mix lightly. Serve in pita pockets spread with remaining mayonnaise mixture. May serve on lettuce-lined salad plates garnished with fruit. Yield: 8 servings.

 Muriel Faltz Lembright, Preceptor Beta Alpha
El Dorado, Kansas

ITALIAN MACARONI SALAD

1 pound small shell macaroni	½ cup chopped green bell pepper
4 ounces provolone cheese, chopped	½ cup chopped red bell pepper
4 ounces salami, chopped	¾ cup olive oil
4 ounces pepperoni, chopped	½ cup white vinegar
	3 tablespoons sugar
2 small onions, chopped	1 tablespoon oregano
1 small can pitted black olives, chopped	1 tablespoon salt
	1 teaspoon pepper
1 7-ounce jar green olives, chopped	3 to 5 ripe tomatoes, chopped
½ cup chopped celery	Fresh parsley to taste

Cook macaroni using package directions. Combine with next 9 ingredients in bowl. Add mixture of oil, vinegar, sugar and seasonings; mix well. Chill for 24 hours. Add tomatoes and parsley just before serving. Yield:15 servings.

Susie Myers, Xi Alpha Sigma
Vienna, West Virginia

MACARONI SALAD FOR 100

1 bunch celery, chopped	1 cup sugar
1 12-ounce jar pimento-stuffed olives	⅓ cup mustard
	Salt and pepper to taste
½ cup diced onion	7 5-ounce packages macaroni, cooked
1 pound carrots, grated	
36 hard-cooked eggs, chopped	4 to 6 cups cheese cubes
	6 to 8 cups turkey or ham cubes
4 quarts mayonnaise-type salad dressing	

Combine first 5 ingredients in bowl. Add salad dressing, sugar, mustard, salt and pepper; mix well. Cook macaroni using package directions; rinse. Add to salad with cheese and meat cubes; mix well. Chill for 4 to 5 hours. May chop vegetables up to 2 days before serving and prepare eggs and macaroni 1 day before. Store, tightly covered, in refrigerator. Yield: 8 quarts.

Lois Sanner, Preceptor Tau
Silver Bay, Minnesota

MOSTACELLI SALAD

1 16-ounce package mostacelli noodles	1½ cups sugar
	1½ cups vinegar
¼ cup corn oil	1 cucumber, sliced
1 teaspoon garlic powder	1 onion, sliced
1 teaspoon salt	2 tablespoon mustard
1 teaspoon pepper	

Cook mostacelli noodles using package directions. Add oil; mix lightly. Combine next 5 ingredients in saucepan. Bring to a boil. Simmer for 15 minutes. Combine with noodles, cucumber, onion and mustard in bowl; mix well. Chill for 24 hours. Yield: 12 servings.

Carolyn Tysdal, Mu Omega
West Des Moines, Iowa

MEATY PASTA SALAD

1 16-ounce package small shells, cooked	3 green peppers, chopped
	2 small onions, chopped
4 ounces provolone cheese, cubed	3 stalks celery, chopped
	1 tablespoon oregano
8 ounces salami, cubed	1½ teaspoon salt
4 ounces pepperoni, cubed	1 teaspoon pepper
	¾ cup olive oil
3 tomatoes, chopped	½ cup wine vinegar

Combine all ingredients in bowl; toss to mix well. Chill in refrigerator. Yield: 12 servings.

Maribeth V. Dottore, Pi
Hockessin, Delaware

QUICK PASTA SALAD

1 12-ounce package pasta, cooked	Bermuda onion, sliced
	½ bottle of cheese and garlic salad dressing
Carrots, chopped	
Broccoli flowerets	

Combine all ingredients in bowl; toss to mix. Yield: 8 to 12 servings.

Anne Denk, Alpha
Sandy, Utah

PASTA SALAD

2 tomatoes, chopped
1 cucumber, sliced
1 green bell pepper, sliced
1   16-ounce can artichoke
    hearts
1 pound pasta, cooked
1½ cups vinegar
1½ cups sugar
¾ cup olive oil
2 or 3 tablespoons
    mustard
1 tablespoon garlic salt
1 teaspoon pepper
MSG to taste
1 tablespoon dried parsley

Combine first 5 ingredients in bowl; toss lightly. Blend vinegar, sugar, oil, mustard, seasonings and parsley in bowl; mix well. Add to pasta; mix well. Chill for several hours. Yield: 12 servings.

Twila Morrow, Laureate Alpha Psi
Albany, Missouri

MARINATED SPAGHETTI SALAD

10 ounces thin spaghetti
1 bunch green onions,
    sliced
2 tablespoons chopped
    parsley
2 stalks celery, chopped
½ cup sweet pickle
    juice
2 cloves of garlic, mashed
1½ teaspoon salt
1 teaspoon celery seed
1 tablespoon poppy seed
½ teaspoon caraway seed
1 cup Italian salad
    dressing
Tomato and avocado
    wedges

Cook spaghetti using package directions; drain. Mix with remaining ingredients in bowl. Chill overnight. Garnish with tomato and avocado wedges. Yield: 4 to 6 servings.

Connie Byrd, Xi Alpha Alpha Lambda
Sugar Land, Texas

SPAGHETTI SALAD

1 pound vermicelli
1 cup zesty Italian
    salad dressing
1 cup chopped celery
1 cup sliced radishes
1 green bell pepper,
    chopped
1 onion, chopped
1 tomato, chopped
½ jar salad seasoning

Cook vermicelli using package directions; rinse with cold water and drain. Mix with salad dressing in bowl. Add remaining ingredients. Chill overnight. Yield: 8 cups.

Julia Cooning, Xi Beta Gamma
Warsaw, Indiana

PIZZA PASTA SALAD

8 ounces macaroni,
    cooked
6 ounces Gruyère cheese
⅓ cup Parmesan cheese
2 teaspoons salt
1 teaspoon oregano
¼ teaspoon pepper
3 tomatoes, chopped
1 small red onion,
    chopped
1 head lettuce, chopped
½ cup olive oil
¼ cup vinegar
Onion and garlic croutons

Combine first 3 ingredients and seasonings in salad bowl; mix well. Add vegetables just before serving. Drizzle mixture of oil and vinegar over top; toss lightly. Sprinkle with croutons. Yield: 10 to 12 servings.

Ruth Chapman, Xi Beta
Cumberland, Maryland

SQUASH AND PASTA SALAD

3 cups coarsely chopped
    yellow summer squash
3 cups rigatoni
2 cups cherry tomato
    halves
½ cup fresh basil leaves
¼ cup olive oil
2 large cloves of garlic,
    mashed
3 tablespoons wine
    vinegar
Salt and pepper to taste
¼ cup Parmesan cheese

Steam squash in steamer just until tender-crisp. Cool. Cook rigatoni using package directions just until tender; rinse with cold water and drain. Mix squash, rigatoni, tomatoes and basil in salad bowl. Drizzle mixture of olive oil, garlic, vinegar and salt and pepper over salad. Add cheese; toss lightly. Serve at room temperature. Yield: 6 servings.

Dorothy Rice, Preceptor Beta Nu
St. Louis, Missouri

PASTA AND VEGETABLE SALAD

1   7-ounce package
    macaroni rings
1 small green bell pepper,
    chopped
1 small onion, chopped
1 cup chopped celery
1   2-ounce jar chopped
    pimento, drained
1   16-ounce can red
    kidney beans
Vinegar
1   16-ounce can peas
1   16-ounce can carrots
1   16-ounce can French-
    style green beans
1 cup (scant) sugar
1 cup cream
2 cups salad dressing

Cook macaroni using package directions; cool. Add next 4 ingredients. Drain kidney beans. Marinate in vinegar to cover in bowl for 1 hour; drain. Drain peas, carrots and green beans. Add all vegetables to macaroni mixture. Blend sugar, cream and salad dressing in bowl. Add to pasta and vegetables; mix well. Yield: 12 servings.

Gracia Leone Lee, Preceptor Beta Upsilon
Hutchinson, Kansas

RICE AND ARTICHOKE SALAD

1   6-ounce package
    chicken-flavored rice
3 green onions, chopped
½ green bell pepper,
    chopped
2 small jars marinated
    artichoke hearts
½ teaspoon curry powder
½ cup mayonnaise

Prepare rice using package directions omitting butter or margarine. Cool to room temperature. Add green onions and green pepper. Drain artichokes reserving juice. Add artichokes to rice. Combine artichoke heart juice, curry powder and mayonnaise in bowl; mix well. Add to rice mixture. Serve at room temperature. Yield: 12 servings.

Sandy Easthope, Xi Theta
Scottsdale, Arizona

Serve a delicious rice salad in a pretty glass bowl instead of a hot rice dish to convert a menu for the summer suggests **Angela Galen, Xi Epsilon Upsilon, Herndon, Virginia.**

RICE-A-RONI ARTICHOKE SALAD

2 6-ounce jars marinated
   artichokes
1 package chicken-
   flavored Rice-A-Roni
Chopped parsley to taste
½ green bell pepper,
   chopped

4 green onions, chopped
1 can pitted black
   olives, sliced
¼ cup mayonnaise
¼ teaspoon thyme
Salt and pepper to taste

Drain artichokes, reserving liquid. Cook Rice-A-Roni according to package directions, reducing water to 2 cups. Combine with parsley and vegetables in bowl. Blend reserved artichoke liquid with mayonnaise and thyme in small bowl. Add to vegetable mixture with salt and pepper; mix well. Chill overnight. Yield: 8 to 10 servings.

Vicky Marinelli, Preceptor Epsilon
Galveston, Texas

RICE SALAD

1¼ cups rice
3 cups chicken broth
½ cup corn oil
2 tablespoons vinegar
1 teaspoon salt
⅛ teaspoon pepper
1 cup chopped black
   olives
1½ cups chopped celery

2 hard-cooked eggs,
   chopped
1 small onion, minced
1 2-ounce jar chopped
   pimento
1 medium green bell
   pepper, chopped
½ cup mayonnaise
1 tablespoon mustard

Cook rice in chicken broth using package directions. Stir into mixture of oil, vinegar, salt and pepper in bowl. Let stand until cool. Add olives and remaining ingredients; mix well. Chill overnight. Yield: 10 to 12 servings.

Beverley J. Neff, Laureate Tau
Charleston, West Virginia

RICE AND CHUTNEY SALAD

3 cups cooked rice, chilled
1 cup cooked peas, chilled
½ cup chutney
½ cup finely chopped
   celery
1 tablespoon finely
   chopped onion

⅓ cup chopped parsley
1 tablespoon corn oil
1 tablespoon wine vinegar
⅓ cup mayonnaise
⅓ cup sour cream
Salt and pepper to taste

Combine first 6 ingredients in bowl. Blend oil, wine vinegar, mayonnaise and sour cream in bowl. Add to rice mixture. Season with salt and pepper. Refrigerate for a few hours for better flavor. Serve on crisp salad greens. Yield: 6 to 8 servings.

Maye Zenthoefer, Laureate Alpha Gamma
Denison, Texas

ARTICHOKE AND BLUE CHEESE SALAD

⅓ cup olive oil
2 tablespoons red wine
   vinegar
4 teaspoons lemon juice
1½ teaspoons salt
1 teaspoon sugar

¼ teaspoon pepper
1 large head lettuce, torn
1 16-ounce can artichoke
   hearts
¼ cup crumbled blue
   cheese

Combine first 6 ingredients in bowl; mix well. Add lettuce. Drain artichoke hearts; cut into halves. Add with blue cheese to lettuce. Yield: 8 servings.

Diane Kirkpatrick, Preceptor Beta Zeta
Chambersburg, Pennsylvania

ARTICHOKE HEART SALAD

2 10-ounce packages
   frozen chopped broccoli
1 9-ounce package
   French-style
   green beans
2 6-ounce jars marinated
   artichoke hearts

1 medium cucumber,
   peeled, chopped
1 small onion, chopped
1 envelope buttermilk
   ranch salad dressing
   mix, prepared

Cook broccoli and green beans using package directions for half the time; drain. Cut artichoke hearts into bite-sized pieces. Combine all vegetables and dressing in bowl; mix well. Chill overnight. Yield: 10 to 12 servings.

Carla Hefley, Alpha Epsilon
Tulsa, Oklahoma

PETITE DINNER SALAD

½ cup corn oil
¼ cup white vinegar
½ teaspoon sugar
⅛ teaspoon dried
   dillweed
Salt and pepper to taste
Pinch of onion powder
Pinch of garlic powder

1 avocado, sliced
Juice of 1 lemon
1 head soft butter
   lettuce
1 11-ounce can mandarin
   oranges, drained
1 10-ounce can white
   asparagus spears

Combine first 7 ingredients in blender container. Process until smooth. Dip avocado slices in lemon juice. Place 1 leaf lettuce, 5 orange sections, 2 slices avocado and 2 asparagus spears on individual salad plates. Drizzle dressing over salads just before serving. Yield: 6 servings.

Molly Fatale, Preceptor Zeta Chi
Moraga, California

ASPEN SALAD

4 cups dandelion greens
1 small bunch arugula,
   torn
¼ cup all-purpose flour
1 teaspoon salt
3 tablespoons sugar
3 tablespoons vinegar

1½ cups water or milk
2 tablespoons bacon
   drippings
2 hard-cooked eggs,
   chopped
2 slices crisp-fried bacon,
   crumbled

Gather dandelions in very early spring before buds develop. Wash carefully; drain. Tear into bowl. Add arugula. Combine flour, salt, sugar, vinegar and water or milk and drippings in skillet. Cook until sauce is smooth and thick, stirring constantly. Pour sauce over greens. Stir lightly to coat. Garnish with eggs and bacon bits. Yield: 6 servings.

Dixie Norris, Xi Alpha Phi
Boulder, Colorado

AVOCADO WITH TOMATO FREEZE

1 envelope unflavored
  gelatin
2 tablespoons water
2 6-ounce cans tomato
  paste
2 ounces Roquefort
  cheese
3 ounces cream cheese,
  softened

2 tablespoons (heaping)
  mayonnaise
1 tablespoon grated
  onion
Juice of ½ lemon
¼ teaspoon salt
2 teaspoons
  Worcestershire sauce
4 avocados

Soften gelatin in water. Heat tomato paste in saucepan; stir in gelatin until dissolved. Cool. Cream cheeses and mayonnaise in bowl. Blend in tomato mixture and remaining ingredients except avocados. Pour into freezer trays. Freeze until firm. Peel avocados; cut into halves. Brush with lemon juice to prevent darkening. Scoop frozen mixture into avocados. Serve on lettuce-lined plates. Yield: 8 servings.

Eva Glasgow, Epsilon Rho
Magnolia, Arkansas

AVOCADO AND TOMATO SALAD

½ cup safflower oil
2 tablespoons tarragon
  wine vinegar
1 teaspoon basil
1 teaspoon Chinese
  5 spice
⅛ teaspoon dry mustard

⅛ teaspoon pepper
1 medium tomato, peeled,
  thinly sliced
1 avocado, peeled, sliced
Romaine lettuce leaves
Cucumber slices

Combine first 6 ingredients in bowl; mix well. Let stand for 2 hours. Arrange tomato and avocado slices on Romaine lettuce-lined serving plate. Drizzle dressing over top. Garnish with cucumber slices. Yield: 2 servings.

Nancy K. Henry, Xi Beta Psi
Raleigh, North Carolina

BROCCOLI AND CAULIFLOWER MOLD

1 head cauliflower
2 bunches broccoli

2 16-ounce bottles of
  Italian salad dressing

Cut and break cauliflower into flowerets about the size of a quarter. Place in saucepan of boiling water. Cook for 3 minutes or until tender-crisp; do not overcook. Rinse with cold water. Cut broccoli into quarter-sized flowerets. Blanch in boiling water until tender-crisp. Rinse in cold water. Arrange cauliflower and broccoli alternately in glass bowl, placing flowerettes next to bottom and sides of bowl. Continue pattern over top; press lightly to secure and intertwine stems. Pour salad dressing over top. Marinate, covered, for 24 hours. Drain dressing. Invert onto serving plate. Yield: 40 servings.
Note: Use salad dressing made with olive oil.

Florene Thal, Beta Psi
Fredericktown, Missouri

BROCCOLI CRUNCH DELIGHT

Flowerets of large
  bunch broccoli
1 cup chopped red onion
1 cup dark raisins

1 cup unsalted sunflower
  seed
½ to 1 cup mayonnaise
1 cup bacon bits

Mix broccoli, onion, raisins and sunflower seed in salad bowl. Add enough mayonnaise to coat; mix well. Reserve a small amount of bacon bits. Mix remaining bacon bits into salad. Chill for several hours to overnight. Sprinkle with remaining bacon bits. Yield: 6 to 8 servings.

Jean Robertson, Preceptor Gamma Phi
Fort Walton Beach, Florida

BROCCOLI AND BEAN SALAD

1 bunch broccoli
1 16-ounce can kidney
  beans, drained
1 purple onion, chopped

1 cup shredded sharp
  Cheddar cheese
1 8-ounce bottle of zesty
  Italian salad dressing

Cut broccoli into bite-sized pieces. Combine with kidney beans, onion and cheese in bowl. Add salad dressing. Chill for 6 hours or longer, stirring occasionally. Yield: 6 to 8 servings.

Peggy Warren, Xi Psi Tau
Victoria, Texas

BROCCOLI AND ONION SALAD

Flowerets of 2 bunches
  broccoli
1 medium red onion,
  thinly sliced
8 ounces mozarella
  cheese, shredded

1 cup mayonnaise
½ cup sugar
2 tablespoons vinegar
8 ounces bacon, crisp-
  fried, crumbled

Combine broccoli, onion and cheese in salad bowl. Blend mayonnaise, sugar and vinegar in small bowl. Add to broccoli mixture; mix well. Add bacon just before serving. Yield: 8 servings.

Thelma Higdon, Preceptor Alpha Upsilon
Tustin, California

BROCCOLI AND RAISIN SALAD

5 cups bite-sized pieces
  fresh broccoli
½ medium red onion,
  chopped
8 ounces bacon, crisp-
  fried, crumbled

½ cup golden raisins
½ cup mayonnaise-
  type salad dressing
⅓ cup sugar
2 tablespoons vinegar

Combine broccoli, onion, bacon and raisins in bowl. Blend salad dressing, sugar and vinegar in small bowl. Pour over broccoli mixture. Chill for 4 hours. Yield: 6 to 8 servings.

Pat Schramm, Preceptor Zeta
Marysville, Kansas

BROCCOLI RING

1 10-ounce package frozen chopped broccoli	⅔ cup mayonnaise
	⅓ cup sour cream
	1 tablespoon lemon juice
1 envelope unflavored gelatin	1 tablespoon minced onion
½ cup water	3 hard-cooked eggs, chopped
1 10-ounce can condensed chicken broth	Lettuce

Cook broccoli according to package directions; drain well. Soften gelatin in cold water in medium saucepan. Add chicken broth. Heat until gelatin is dissolved, stirring constantly. Add mayonnaise, sour cream, lemon juice and onion. Beat until smooth. Chill until partially set; mixture will resemble unbeaten egg whites. Fold eggs and broccoli into gelatin. Spoon into 4-cup mold. Chill until firm. Unmold onto serving plate. Garnish with leaf lettuce. Yield: 8 servings.

Linda S. Allen, Iota Chi
Beaver Falls, New York

WINTER VEGETABLE SALAD

1 bunch broccoli	1 tablespoon dillweed
1 head cauliflower	1 tablespoon dillseed
4 medium carrots	1 tablesppoon MSG
1 carton cherry tomatoes	1 tablespoon sugar
1 cup cider vinegar	1 teaspoon pepper
1½ cups corn oil	1 teaspoon garlic salt

Cut broccoli and cauliflower into bite-sized pieces. Slice carrots; cut cherry tomatoes into halves. Combine vegetables in bowl. Blend remaining ingredients in bowl. Pour over vegetables. Refrigerate for 24 hours, stirring frequently. Drain vegetables before serving. Yield: 8 servings.

Kathleen Hess, Alpha Gamma
Lawrence, Kansas

MICHIGAN CAESAR SALAD

½ cup corn oil	½ cup Parmesan cheese
¼ cup red wine vinegar	½ cup crumbled blue cheese
1 tablespoon lemon juice	
1 large clove of garlic, finely minced	1 bunch endive, torn
	1 head romaine, torn
2 teaspoons Worcestershire sauce	1 head leaf lettuce, torn
¼ teaspoon salt	1 cup croutons
¼ teaspoon pepper	1 egg

Blend first 9 ingredients in bowl; chill overnight. Combine greens in bowl. Sprinkle with croutons. Add egg to chilled mixture; mix well. Pour on lettuce; toss to mix well. Yield: 8 servings.

Cathy Helleny, Xi Rho
Energy, Illinois

CAESAR SALAD

3 eggs	1 tablespoon Worcestershire sauce
6 inches anchovy paste	
2 dashes Tabasco sauce	½ cup corn oil
1 tablespoon finely chopped capers	¼ cup white wine vinegar
2½ tablespoons Dijon-style mustard	1 head romaine lettuce
	¼ cup Parmesan cheese
2 cloves of garlic, finely chopped	Croutons

Boil eggs for 2½ minutes. Remove yolks; discard whites. Mix yolks with anchovy paste, Tabasco sauce, capers, mustard, garlic and Worcestershire sauce in bowl. Blend in oil until creamy. Add vinegar gradually, blending well. Tear romaine. Combine with Parmesan cheese and croutons in bowl. Stir in dressing. Yield: 6 servings.

Jean Singman, Preceptor Kappa
Lutherville, Maryland

MOCK CAESAR SALAD

3 eggs	¼ cup red wine vinegar
2 cups corn oil	Salt and freshly ground pepper to taste
¼ cup brown mustard	
2 stalks celery, chopped	1 head romaine lettuce
1 medium onion, chopped	Crisp-fried crumbled bacon to taste
2 cloves of garlic, minced	
1 tablespoon MSG	Seasoned croutons to taste
3 or 4 drops of Tabasco sauce	Parmesan cheese to taste

Combine first 11 ingredients in blender container; process until foamy. Store in refrigerator. Combine romaine and remaining ingredients in salad bowl. Add dressing; toss to mix. Serve immediately. Yield: 8 servings.

Judy Running, Xi Beta Epsilon
Marshall, Minnesota

MARINATED CARROT SALAD

2 pounds carrots, sliced	¼ cup corn oil
1 green bell pepper, chopped	1 cup sugar
	½ cup vinegar
1 onion, chopped	½ teaspoon pepper
1 cup chopped celery	1 teaspoon salt
1 small cauliflower, chopped	1 teaspoon dry mustard
1 10-ounce can tomato soup	1 teaspoon Worcestershire sauce

Cook carrots in salted water in saucepan until tender; drain. Combine all vegetables in bowl; mix well. Bring tomato soup to a boil in saucepan and add remaining ingredients. Cool. Pour over vegetables. Refrigerate for 24 hours. Yield: 10 cups.

Beverly Attebery, Upsilon
Weiser, Idaho

SPECIAL CARROT SALAD

3½ cups grated carrots
1½ cups miniature
 marshmallows
1 20-ounce can
 pineapple, drained
2 cups chopped pecans
1 cup golden raisins
1 cup coconut
1 6-ounce jar maraschino
 cherries, chopped
1 cup mayonnaise
1 16-ounce container
 frozen whipped
 topping

Combine all ingredients in large bowl; mix well. Chill in refrigerator. Yield: 16 servings.

Bonnie Farber, Xi Delta Kappa
Longwood, Florida

MOCK POTATO SALAD

1 head cauliflower
3 stalks celery, chopped
½ green bell pepper,
 chopped
Salt and pepper to taste
2 tablespoons pickle
 relish
½ cup mayonnaise

Cook whole cauliflower as desired until tender. Chill. Break cauliflower into pieces; place in large bowl. Add chopped celery, green pepper and remaining ingredients; mix well. Chill until serving time. Yield: 6 servings.

Judy Williams, Epsilon Beta
Palm Bay, Florida

CHINESE COLESLAW

¼ cup sesame seed
1 5-ounce package
 slivered almonds
1 medium head cabbage
4 green onions, chopped
¼ cup sugar
1 cup corn oil
2 teaspoons salt
2 teaspoons MSG
1 teaspoon pepper
½ cup rice vinegar
1 package ramen noodles

Toast sesame seed and almonds on baking sheet under broiler until golden brown. Chop cabbage finely. Combine with green onions and toasted mixture in bowl. Blend sugar, oil, salt, MSG, pepper and rice vinegar in small bowl with wire whisk. Add to cabbage mixture; toss until coated. Chill overnight if desired. Crush uncooked noodles and add to salad 30 minutes before serving. Reserve seasoning packet from noodles for another purpose. Yield: 10 to 12 servings.

Linda Emry, Xi Beta Beta
Boise, Idaho

SOUR CREAM AND APPLE COLESLAW

1½ cups sour cream
2 egg yolks
2 tablespoons lemon
 juice
3 tablespoons horseradish
¼ teaspoon paprika
1 teaspoon sugar
1 teaspoon salt
8 cups shredded cabbage
1 cup chopped red apple

Mix sour cream and egg yolks in medium bowl. Add seasonings; mix well. Combine cabbage and apple in bowl. Add dressing. Chill in refrigerator. Yield: 6 to 8 servings.

Holly Crowell, Zeta Kappa
Red Oak, Iowa

SOUR CREAM COLESLAW DRESSING

1 cup sour cream
1 tablespoon red wine
 vinegar
1 teaspoon sugar
½ teaspoon caraway seed
1 teaspoon celery seed
1 teaspoon salt
½ cup heavy cream

Mix first 6 ingredients in bowl. Add enough cream to make of desired consistency. Use on favorite coleslaw mixture, adding a small amount of lemon zest.
Yield: 1¼ cups.

Beverly Brown, Laureate Beta Epsilon
Port Angeles, Washington

VEGETABLE COLESLAW

1 head cabbage
¾ small head cauliflower
½ small bunch broccoli
1 cucumber
1 cup chopped tomato
¼ green bell pepper
4 small green onions,
 chopped
1 cup mayonnaise
⅓ cup sugar
1 teaspoon seasoned salt
Salt and pepper to taste

Cut all vegetables into bite-sized pieces; toss well. Mix mayonnaise, sugar and seasoned salt in bowl. Season with salt and pepper; mix well. Pour over vegetables; mix well. Chill until serving time. Yield: 8 servings.

Carma Aikens, Beta
Clinton, Utah

WALDORF COLESLAW

1 red apple, chopped
Lemon juice
6 cups shredded cabbage
1 20-ounce can juice-
 pack pineapple chunks
1 cup red grapes
1 cup sour cream
1 tablespoon sugar
1 teaspoon lemon juice
1 teaspoon salt
⅓ cup chopped walnuts

Sprinkle chopped apples with lemon juice. Combine apples, cabbage, pineapple and grapes in bowl; toss lightly. Combine sour cream, sugar, lemon juice and salt in bowl; mix well. Pour over cabbage mixture; toss until well coated. Chill, covered, in refrigerator. Sprinkle with walnuts just before serving. Yield: 16 servings.

Josephine Monty; Beta Epsilon
Greenville, Mississippi

CORN BREAD SALAD

2 packages jalapeño
 corn bread mix
1 green onion, chopped
1 green bell pepper,
 chopped
2 tomatoes, chopped
1 16-ounce can corn
1 cup shredded Cheddar
 cheese
8 slices bacon, crisp-
 fried, crumbled
1½ cups mayonnaise
½ cup sour cream
½ teaspoon chili powder
Pepper to taste
Avocado slices

Prepare corn bread using package directions. Cool and crumble into bowl. Add vegetables, cheese, bacon, mayonnaise, sour cream and seasonings; mix well. Chill overnight. Garnish with avocado. Yield: 10 to 12 servings.

Nora May Bremser, Preceptor Beta Sigma
Wharton, Texas

CUCUMBER AND GRAPE MOLD

1 3-ounce package lime gelatin	1 cup chopped, seeded, peeled cucumber
1 cup boiling water	½ cup seedless green grape halves
1 tablespoon lemon juice	Lettuce
1 cup lemon-lime soda	

Dissolve gelatin in boiling water in bowl. Cool. Stir in lemon juice and soda gradually. Chill until partially set. Fold in cucumber and grapes. Pour into 5½-cup mold. Chill until firm. Unmold onto lettuce-lined plate. Garnish with mayonnaise and additional grapes.
Yield: 6 servings.

Betty Hadlock, Preceptor Gamma Eta
South Bend, Washington

CUCUMBER SALAD WITH YOGURT

2 large cucumbers, thinly sliced	¼ cup chopped fresh cilantro
1 tablespoon coarse salt	½ teaspoon salt
2 cups low-fat yogurt	2 medium tomatoes, seeded, chopped
½ cup low-fat sour cream	Curly leaf lettuce
1 teaspoon ground cumin	

Sprinkle cucumbers with coarse salt; cover. Let stand, covered, for 30 minutes. Rinse several times in cold water; drain well. Squeeze dry with paper towels. Set aside. Mix yogurt, sour cream, cumin, cilantro and ½ teaspoon salt in small bowl. Chill, covered, until serving time. Combine cucumber, yogurt mixture and tomatoes in large bowl; toss gently to mix well. Spoon into lettuce-lined salad bowl. Yield: 8 servings.

Kathy Kaufman, Alpha Pi
Jeanie Waugh, Alpha Pi
Missoula, Montana

DILLED VEGETABLE COMBO

¼ cup creamy French salad dressing	½ small head cauliflower, sliced, cooked
¼ cup mayonnaise	1 9-ounce package frozen peas, cooked
2 tablespoons chili sauce	1 9-ounce package frozen Italian green beans, cooked
2 teaspoons lemon juice	½ cup chopped celery
1 teaspoon salt	¼ cup chopped onion
½ teaspoon pepper	
Dillweed to taste	
1½ cups chopped carrots, cooked	

Blend French dressing, mayonnaise, chili sauce, lemon juice, salt, pepper and dillweed in bowl. Chill for several hours. Drain cooked vegetables well. Combine all vegetables in salad bowl. Add dressing; toss to coat.
Yield: 8 to 10 servings.

Elaine Smith, Delta Omicron
Lexington, South Carolina

HEALTH SALAD

1 head Boston lettuce, torn	3 tablespoons corn oil
1 small cucumber	1 small onion, minced
2 small tomatoes	2 teaspoons prepared mustard
1 green bell pepper	6 tablespoons lemon juice
5 radishes	¼ teaspoon salt
½ avocado	⅛ teaspoon pepper
1 peach	1 sprig parsley, chopped
1 slice canned pineapple, drained	½ teaspoon dried dillweed
½ cup mandarin oranges, drained	¼ teaspoon dried tarragon
8 ounces fresh strawberries	¼ teaspoon dried basil

Tear lettuce into bite-sized pieces. Cut vegetables and fruits into bite-sized pieces. Combine in large bowl. Mix oil and remaining ingredients in small bowl. Pour over salad; mix gently. Marinate, covered, for 10 minutes. Serve in glass bowl. Yield: 4 to 6 servings.

Janet Blakely, Xi Theta
Phoenix, Arizona

KOREAN SALAD

½ cup corn oil	1 pound spinach, torn
¼ cup vinegar	1 5-ounce can water chestnuts, thinly sliced
¼ cup catsup	2 hard-cooked eggs, chopped
⅓ cup sugar	6 slices crisp-fried bacon, crumbled
½ medium onion, grated	
Salt to taste	
1 16-ounce can bean sprouts, drained	

Combine first 6 ingredients in jar; shake well. Mix bean sprouts, spinach and water chestnuts in salad bowl. Add dressing; toss to mix. Top with eggs and bacon.
Yield: 4 to 6 servings.

Georgine Wasley, Xi Alpha Eta
Nevada City, California

STUFFED HEAD LETTUCE

8 ounces cream cheese, softened	1 tablespoon chopped green bell pepper
1 teaspoon onion juice	2 tablespoons chopped tomato
Salt and pepper to taste	1 head lettuce
2 tablespoons Roquefort cheese	
2 tablespoons chopped carrot	

Blend cream cheese, onion juice, salt and pepper in bowl. Mix in Roquefort cheese and chopped vegetables. Cut lettuce in half through core; remove core. Hollow out halves, leaving 1-inch shell. Stuff lettuce with cheese mixture. Place lettuce halves together. Wrap in waxed paper; chill in refrigerator. Cut into wedges.
Yield: 8 to 10 servings.

Arlene Pankow, Preceptor Epsilon Theta
Westchester, California

MEDITERRANEAN SALAD

1 16-ounce can artichoke
hearts, drained
⅓ cup olive oil
⅓ cup freshly squeezed
lemon juice
1 head romaine, torn
4 green onions, chopped

2 tablespoons crushed
dried mint
1 cup pitted Greek
black olives
1 ripe tomato, peeled,
cut into wedges
Salt to taste

Marinate artichoke hearts in olive oil and lemon juice for
2 to 3 hours. Combine lettuce and remaining ingredients
in large salad bowl. Add artichoke hearts with marinade;
toss lightly. Yield: 6 servings.

Nancy E. Carpenter, Xi Gamma Eta
Paris, Tennessee

MEXICAN SALAD

1 16-ounce can whole
kernel corn, drained
1 16-ounce can kidney
beans, drained
1 16-ounce can garbanzo
beans, drained
1 2-ounce jar chopped
pimento, drained

1 medium green bell
pepper, chopped
1 medium onion, chopped
1 medium tomato,
chopped
1 9-ounce can sliced
black olives
French salad dressing

Combine first 8 ingredients in bowl. Add enough salad
dressing to coat. Marinate for 2 hours. Serve on lettuce-
lined platter. Yield: 8 to 10 servings.

Julia Kay Cervantes, Xi Rho Omicron
Humble, Texas

PIÑATA SALAD

1 16-ounce can French-
cut green beans,
drained
1 16-ounce can tiny
sweet peas, drained
1 cup finely chopped
celery
1 16-ounce can Shoe Peg
corn, drained
1 green bell pepper,
chopped

1 small onion, chopped
1 2-ounce jar chopped
pimento, drained
½ cup sugar
½ cup wine vinegar
½ cup corn oil
2 tablespoons parsley
1 teaspoon salt
½ teaspoon dry mustard
½ teaspoon tarragon
½ teaspoon basil

Combine all vegetables in bowl. Mix sugar, vinegar, oil
and seasonings in bowl; mix well. Pour over vegetables.
Chill, covered, overnight. Yield: 10 to 12 servings.

June Wheeler, Theta Upsilon
Springfield, Missouri

MANDARIN ORANGE TOSS

⅓ cup corn oil
3 tablespoons sugar
3 tablespoons cider
vinegar
1 tablespoon snipped
parsley or mint
½ teaspoon salt
Dash of pepper
Dash of red pepper sauce
⅓ cup sliced almonds

2 tablespoons sugar
½ head lettuce, torn
1 small bunch romaine,
torn
1 cup thinly sliced celery
2 green onions, thinly
sliced
1 11-ounce can mandarin
oranges, drained

Combine oil and next 6 ingredients in tightly covered jar.
Chill in refrigerator. Cook almonds and sugar in skillet
over low heat until sugar is melted and almonds are
coated, stirring constantly. Cool and break apart. Store at
room temperature. Place vegetables in plastic bag. Add
dressing and orange segments. Close bag tightly; shake
until well coated. Add almonds; shake. Pour into salad
bowl. Yield: 12 servings.

Jeanette Azar, Preceptor Beta Zeta
Mt. Clemens, Michigan

MANDARIN SALAD WITH ALMONDS

½ teaspoon salt
Dash of pepper
2 tablespoons sugar
2 tablespoons vinegar
¼ cup corn oil
Dash of Tabasco sauce
½ cup slivered almonds

2 tablespoons sugar
1 head romaine
1 cup chopped celery
4 green onions, sliced
2 8-ounce cans mandarin
oranges, drained

Combine first 6 ingredients in bowl; mix well and set
aside. Cook almonds and sugar in skillet over medium
heat until sugar melts and turns light brown. Cool. Combine lettuce, celery, onions and oranges in salad bowl.
Add dressing and almonds; toss to mix. Serve immediately. Yield: 6 to 8 servings.

Katrina VanderWaal, Xi Gamma Upsilon
Ellensburg, Washington

MANDARIN ORANGES AND RED ONION

½ cup corn oil
¼ cup white wine vinegar
¼ teaspon dry mustard
¼ teaspoon sweet basil
¼ teaspoon sugar
Salt and pepper to taste

2 heads Bibb lettuce
2 medium red onions,
thinly sliced
1 11-ounce can mandarin
oranges, drained

Combine first 7 ingredients in small covered jar. Shake
until well blended. Refrigerate for up to 2 weeks. Wash
lettuce; drain well. Wrap in paper towels; place in plastic
bag. Refrigerate for up to 2 days. Tear lettuce into bite-
sized pieces into salad bowl. Add onion rings and oranges. Pour dressing over salad; toss to coat well.
Yield: 8 servings.

Judy Graves, Laureate Upsilon
Prescott Valley, Arizona

VERY BEST SALAD

½ cup orange juice
1 teaspoon lemon juice
½ cup corn oil
2 tablespoons red vinegar
¼ teaspoon salt
2 tablespoons sugar

½ teaspoon grated orange
rind
1 head butter lettuce
1 cucumber, sliced
1 avocado, sliced
1 cup mandarin oranges

Combine first 7 ingredients in bowl; mix well. Chill in refrigerator. Break lettuce into bite-sized pieces. Combine
with cucumber, avocado and oranges in salad bowl. Drizzle with dressing. Yield: 4 servings.

June Solberg, Preceptor Delta
Midvale, Utah

MINT AND GARLIC SALAD

2 large cloves of garlic	1 tablespoon (heaping)
1½ teaspoons salt	dry mint
¼ cup lemon juice	4 tomatoes, chopped
¼ cup safflower oil	1 large head lettuce, torn

Mash garlic in wooden bowl, spreading garlic around side of bowl while mashing. Add salt to garlic; mix well. Add lemon juice and oil; mix well. Add dry mint; mix well. Add tomatoes. Chill until serving time. Add lettuce just before serving; toss to mix. Yield: 4 to 6 servings.

Barbara Cox, Preceptor Alpha Omega
Oklahoma City, Oklahoma

PARMESAN SALAD

1 small red onion	1 cup Italian salad
1 6-ounce jar marinated	dressing
artichoke hearts	Croutons
2 heads green leaf lettuce,	Parmesan cheese
torn	
2 tomatoes, chopped	

Cut onion into thin strips. Separate leaves of artichoke hearts. Combine with lettuce and tomatoes in salad bowl. Add salad dressing, croutons and generous amount of parmesan cheese; toss lightly. Serve immediately. Yield: 12 servings.

Rita Bouillon, Phi
Moscow, Idaho

BACON-PEA SALAD

1 24-ounce package	2 scallions, thinly sliced
frozen tiny peas,	½ cup mayonnaise
thawed	½ teaspoon salt
¾ cup freshly grated	¼ teaspoon pepper
Parmesan cheese	1 teaspoon sugar
6 slices crisp-fried	⅛ teaspoon nutmeg
bacon, crumbled	1½ tablespoons Dijon-
3 stalks celery, thinly	style mustard
sliced	

Combine peas, cheese, bacon, celery and scallions in bowl. Blend mayonnaise, salt, pepper, sugar, nutmeg and mustard in small bowl. Stir into pea mixture. Chill in refrigerator. Yield: 13 servings.

Carol Drake, Preceptor Xi
Winnemucca, Nevada

PEANUTTY PEA AND POPPY SEED SALAD

2 20-ounce packages	1 12-ounce bottle of
frozen green peas	ranch salad dressing
1½ pounds dry roasted	½ 2-ounce bottle of
salted peanuts	poppy seed
2 or 3 green onions,	
sliced	

Place frozen peas in bowl; break apart. Add peanuts, green onions, dressing and poppy seed; mix well. Let stand for 3½ to 4 hours before serving. Yield: 25 servings.

Barbara Ann Winquist, Preceptor Alpha Zeta
Seattle, Washington

POLYNESIAN GARDEN SALAD

1 6-ounce package	⅓ cup thinly sliced
lemon gelatin	water chestnuts
½ teaspoon salt	1 tablespoon sliced
2 cups boiling water	pimento
1 8-ounce can	1 tablespoon chopped
crushed pineapple	green bell pepper
¾ cup cold water	½ cup mayonnaise
¼ cup white wine	1 teaspoon lemon juice
vinegar	1 tablespoon toasted
½ cup packed bean	sesame seed
sprouts	

Dissolve gelatin and salt in boiling water in bowl. Stir in undrained pineapple, cold water and wine vinegar. Chill until partially set. Fold in bean sprouts, water chestnuts, pimento and green pepper. Pour into oiled 5½-cup ring mold. Chill until firm. Unmold onto serving plate lined with shredded lettuce. Serve with mixture of remaining ingredients. Yield: 6 servings.

Betty Morgan, Laureate Omicron
Dubuque, Iowa

NIPPY POTATO SALAD

36 medium potatoes,	24 hard-cooked eggs,
boiled in skins	peeled, chopped
6 tablespoons white wine	3 4-ounce jars chopped
vinegar	pimento
2 tablespoons melted	1½ cups chopped
butter	green onions
6 tablespoons sugar	3 quarts mayonnaise
2 tablespoons salt	3 5-ounce jars
1 tablespoon pepper	horseradish
1 cup chopped parsley	

Peel and chop cooked potatoes. Combine vinegar, butter, sugar, salt and pepper in bowl. Add to warm potatoes. Chill in refrigerator. Stir in parsley, eggs, pimento and green onions. Chill overnight. Add mayonnaise and horseradish. Chill until serving time. Yield: 36 servings.

Cecile Loudat, Xi Eta Nu
Bryan, Texas

POTATO SALAD

5 or 6 medium potatoes,	1 teaspoon dark mustard
peeled, cooked	½ teaspoon celery seed
½ cup chopped onions	¼ teaspon cumin
½ teaspoon crushed	1 to 2 tablespoons
minced garlic	chopped fresh dill
2 large dill pickles,	Salt and pepper to taste
chopped	2 hard-cooked eggs,
2 tablespoons wine	chopped
vinegar	1½ cups mayonnaise

Chop potatoes into small cubes. Combine with onions, garlic, pickles, wine vinegar and mustard in bowl; mix well. Add seasonings and eggs; mix well. Add mayonnaise; mix well. Chill for 1 to 2 hours. Garnish with olives. Yield: 8 to 10 servings.

Rebecca Albanese, Xi Omicron
Powell, Wyoming

GARDEN DELIGHT POTATO SALAD

1 16-ounce can mixed vegetables	1 package salami
¼ cup chopped green pepper	3 hard-cooked eggs, sliced
2 cups chopped cooked potatoes	¾ cup mayonnaise
1 bunch green onions, cut into ¾-inch pieces	2 teaspoons horseradish
	Dash of hot pepper sauce
	1¼ teaspoons salt

Combine first 4 ingredients, 4 slices salami and eggs; mix well. Chill thoroughly. Combine mayonnaise, horseradish, hot pepper sauce and salt in bowl; mix well. Add to chilled vegetables; toss lightly. Spoon into lettuce-lined salad bowl. Garnish with salami.
Yield: 4 to 6 servings.

Jean Baker, Alpha Beta
Bedford, Indiana

CONFETTI POTATO SALAD

2½ pounds potatoes, peeled, cooked, sliced	2 tablespoons chopped red onion
1 cup chopped red bell pepper	2 tablespoons Dijon-style mustard
1 cup sliced black olives	¾ teaspoon celery seed
1 cup frozen peas, thawed	½ teaspoon salt
1 cup mayonnaise	⅛ teaspoon pepper
⅓ cup cider vinegar	

Combine potatoes, red pepper, olives and peas in large bowl. Combine remaining ingredients in small bowl. Pour over potato mixture; stir gently. Chill, covered, for several hours to blend flavors. Yield: 8 servings.

Photograph for this recipe on page 2.

GRANDMA'S GERMAN POTATO SALAD

6 slices bacon	½ teaspoon celery seed
¾ cup thinly sliced onion	¾ cup water
2 tablespoons all-purpose flour	½ cup vinegar
2 tablespoons sugar	6 potatoes, cooked, thinly sliced

Brown bacon in skillet until crisp. Drain on paper towel, reserving drippings. Add onion, flour, sugar and celery seed to drippings; mix well. Stir in water and vinegar. Boil for 1 minute, stirring constantly. Pour over potatoes in casserole dish. Add crumbled bacon; mix well. Serve immediately or reheat in 300-degree oven.
Yield: 8 servings.

Michelle Schuch, Mu Gamma
Brooklyn, Michigan

ROMAINE SALAD

½ cup slivered almonds	1 large bunch romaine
½ cup corn oil	1 8-ounce can mandarin oranges, drained
¼ cup rice vinegar	4 green onions, chopped
1½ tablespoons orange juice	Salt and pepper to taste
1½ tablespoons honey	

Preheat oven to 350 degrees. Bake slivered almonds in baking pan for 5 minutes or until toasted and golden brown. Cool. Combine oil and next 3 ingredients in jar; shake well. Toss romaine, mandarin oranges and green onions in salad bowl. Add dressing, toasted almonds and salt and pepper; toss lightly. Yield: 6 servings.

Joan Falk, Iota Delta
Midland, Michigan

ROMAN SALAD

9 stalks celery	1 pound large mushrooms, quartered
7 carrots	⅔ cup corn oil
1 6-ounce jar marinated artichoke hearts	½ cup vinegar
1 5-ounce can pitted black olives, drained	2 tablespoons parsley flakes
1 4-ounce jar green olives, drained	2 teaspoons garlic powder
1 tablespoon oregano	2 bunches scallions, sliced

Cut celery, carrots and artichoke hearts into bite-sized pieces. Combine with remaining ingredients in bowl. Marinate overnight or longer in refrigerator. May add other vegetables such as cauliflower and broccoli.
Yield: 6 to 8 servings.

Mary Ann Anthony, Xi Psi
Ocean Springs, Mississippi

MARINATED SAUERKRAUT SALAD

1 cup chopped onion	1 31-ounce can sauerkraut
1 cup chopped celery	1 cup sugar
1 cup chopped green bell pepper	½ cup vinegar
1 cup shredded carrots	½ cup corn oil

Mix vegetables in bowl. Bring sugar, vinegar and oil to a boil in saucepan. Pour over vegetables; mix well. Marinate for up to 3 days. Yield: 16 to 20 servings.

Marty Holz, Preceptor Theta Sigma
Los Angeles, California

SAUERKRAUT SALAD

1 cup diced celery	1 cup sugar
1 large onion, finely chopped	½ tablespoon celery seed
1 large green bell pepper, finely chopped	½ cup vinegar
1 large can sauerkraut, drained	½ cup corn oil
	¼ teaspoon salt
	¼ teaspon pepper

Combine first 4 ingredients in bowl; mix well. Add mixture of sugar, celery seed, vinegar, oil, salt and pepper; toss until well mixed. Chill overnight. Yield: 12 servings.

Pam Closson, Upsilon
Claremore, Oklahoma

---

*A super French salad dressing comes from **Sandra Miller, Preceptor Beta Lambda, Lakewood, Colorado**, who combines 1 can tomato soup, 1 cup salad oil, ½ cup tarragon vinegar and 1 cup sugar. She seasons with ½ teaspoon each dry mustard, salt, pepper and paprika, 1 tablespoon Worcestershire sauce and 1 whole clove.*

CHINATOWN SPINACH SALAD

2 tablespoons red wine
  vinegar
1 tablespoon minced
  onion
2 teaspoons prepared
  mustard
¾ teaspoon salt
¼ teaspoon pepper
½ cup olive oil
1 8½-ounce can sliced
  water chestnuts,
  drained

Fresh bean sprouts to taste
8 ounces fresh spinach,
  torn
8 ounces fresh
  mushrooms, sliced
1 tablespoon lemon juice
4 slices crisp-fried bacon,
  crumbled

Combine vinegar, onion, mustard, salt and pepper in pint jar; cover and shake vigorously until well blended. Add oil ⅓ at a time, shaking well after each addition. Add water chestnuts; cover and shake to coat evenly. Chill for several hours, shaking occasionally. Combine bean sprouts, spinach and mushrooms in salad bowl. Remove water chestnuts from dressing; add to salad. Add desired amount of dressing and lemon juice; toss well. Add bacon; toss. Refrigerate leftover dressing. Yield: 6 servings.

Sharron McDonald, Xi Delta Lambda
Grand Blanc, Michigan

CITRUS SPINACH SALAD

1 10-ounce package
  fresh spinach
1 grapefruit, peeled,
  sectioned
1 orange, peeled,
  sectioned
2 tablespoons chopped
  onion
2 tablespoons corn oil
½ teaspoon sugar

1 tablespoon cider
  vinegar
1 tablespoon grapefruit
  juice
¼ teaspoon grated
  orange rind
⅛ teaspoon salt
Dash of cinnamon
¼ cup toasted slivered
  almonds

Combine spinach, fruit and onion in salad bowl. Add mixture of oil and next 6 ingredients; toss to mix. Sprinkle with almonds. Yield: 6 to 8 servings.

Donna Martin, Pi Gamma
Yorkville, Illinois

EASY SPINACH SALAD

1 cup corn oil
¾ cup white wine
  vinegar
½ cup sugar
¾ cup chili sauce
2 pounds fresh spinach

1 red onion, sliced
  into rings
3 hard-cooked eggs,
  sliced
4 slices crisp-fried
  bacon, crumbled

Mix first 4 ingredients in bowl. Rinse spinach; pat dry. Tear into bite-sized pieces; place in salad bowl. Pour dressing over spinach. Top with onion, eggs and bacon. Yield: 8 to 10 servings.

Diane Domaschki, Xi Alpha Omicron
South Charleston, West Virginia

JEANETTE'S SPINACH SALAD

½ cup mayonnaise type-
  salad dressing
½ cup sugar
¼ cup white vinegar
1 bunch spinach,
  chopped
1 head lettuce

1 small purple onion,
  sliced
8 ounces bacon, crisp-
  fried, crumbled
2 hard-cooked eggs,
  chopped
Garlic croutons

Combine first 3 ingredients in bowl; mix well. Chill for 2 hours. Combine vegetables, bacon and eggs in bowl. Add dressing and croutons. Yield: 8 servings.

Lisa A. Thomsen
Reno, Nevada

PIMA WILTED SALAD

4 slices bacon
3 tablespoons fresh
  lemon juice
1 tablespoon sugar
¼ cup chopped onion

2 bunches spinach
3 medium oranges,
  peeled, chopped
½ cup Swiss cheese strips

Fry bacon in skillet until crisp. Remove from pan; drain and crumble. Add lemon juice, sugar and onion to hot bacon drippings. Heat until onion is transparent but not brown. Tear spinach into bite-sized pieces into large bowl. Pour hot mixture over spinach. Add fried bacon, oranges and cheese; toss lightly. Serve immediately. Yield: 6 servings.

Susanne Patch, Xi Gamma Upsilon
Cle Elum, Washington

SPINACH SALAD FLAMBÉ

1 bunch fresh spinach,
  torn
1 small head Bibb or
  Boston lettuce, torn
8 ounces fresh
  mushrooms, sliced
6 slices bacon cut
  into 1-inch pieces

¼ cup freshly squeezed
  lemon juice
3 tablespoons sugar
2 tablespoons
  Worcestershire sauce
3 tablespoons Brandy

Combine spinach, lettuce and mushrooms in large bowl. Cook bacon in skillet until crisp; do not drain. Add lemon juice, sugar and Worcestershire sauce; bring to a boil. Pour over salad mixture, leaving bacon in skillet. Toss salad well. Divide salad mixture among 8 salad plates. Add Brandy to bacon in skillet; heat and ignite. Spoon over salads. Serve immediately. Yield: 8 servings.

Marlene Kellerman, Xi Iota Epsilon
DuQuoin, Illinois

Renee Diemer, Delta Upsilon, Britt, Iowa, makes a list of all items to be served with the amount of time each takes. This way she knows which items require the longest cooking, refrigeration or preparation time.

SPINACH SALAD WITH POPPY SEED

¾ to 1 cup honey
½ cup olive oil
3 tablespoons poppy seed
½ to ¾ cup pineapple
  juice
1 bunch fresh spinach
1 cup whole pecans
  or halves
1   16-ounce can
    pineapple chunks,
    drained
1   11-ounce can
    mandarin oranges,
    drained

Combine first 4 ingredients in blender container. Process until blended. Chill overnight. Wash spinach leaves; pat dry. Place 2 or 3 leaves on individual salad plates. Arrange 6 to 7 pecans, pineapple chunks and 3 to 4 mandarin orange segments on spinach. Pour dressing over salad just before serving. Yield: 6 to 8 servings.

Gloria F. Mendiola, Alpha Phi
Roswell, New Mexico

SPINACH AND PRUNE SALAD

3 tablespoons creamy
  deluxe French salad
  dressing
1 tablespoon lemon juice
10 pitted prunes, chopped
1   8-ounce can mandarin
    oranges, well drained
1 bunch fresh spinach,
  torn
1 medium red onion,
  thinly sliced
½ cup chopped mixed
  salted nuts

Mix 3 tablespoons French dressing with lemon juice in salad bowl. Add chopped prunes. Let stand for 1 hour. Add oranges, spinach and onion. Add additional French dressing if desired; toss lightly. Top with nuts just before serving. Yield: 6 to 8 servings.

Marjorie La Fever, Preceptor Alpha Psi
Menlo Park, California

SUMI SALAD

2   3-ounce packages
    ramen noodles
¼ cup slivered almonds
¼ cup sesame seed
2 tablespoons peanut oil
8 to 10 green onions,
  chopped
1 head cabbage, shredded
¼ to ½ cup sugar
1 teaspoon pepper
1 teaspoon salt
1 cup peanut oil
10 tablespoons rice
  vinegar

Cook broken noodles in boiling water in saucepan for 3 minutes; drain and rinse with cold water. Sauté almonds and sesame seed in oil in skillet until light brown. Combine with green onions, cabbage and noodles in bowl. Add mixture of remaining ingredients; mix well. Chill, covered, for several hours. Yield: 6 to 8 servings.

Jackie Hansen, Xi Upsilon Sigma
Solvang, California

Mary Ellen Tetrault, Preceptor Eta, Iowa City, Iowa,
suggests using prepackaged shredded cabbage. Not only is it easy, but the package often includes carrots and red cabbage which are good and pretty too.

TABBOULI

2 cups bulgur
½ cup finely chopped
  green onions
2 cups finely chopped
  fresh parsley
½ cup finely chopped
  fresh mint
½ cup lemon juice
½ cup olive oil
½ teaspoon allspice
Salt and pepper to taste
4 tomatoes, chopped
Romaine lettuce leaves

Soak bulgur in 4 to 6 cups water in bowl for 1 or 2 hours or until tender; drain well. Mix in green onions, next 4 ingredients and seasonings. Chill overnight if desired. Add tomatoes just before serving. Serve in romaine-lined salad bowl. Garnish with mint, black olives, strips of sweet red pepper, strips of cucumber or lemon rind twists. Use additional romaine leaves as edible spoons to scoop out salad. Yield: 12 servings.

Judith Edling, Delta Theta
Blue Earth, Minnesota

LUNCHEON SALAD

1 cup tomato soup
1 envelope unflavored
  gelatin
½ cup cold water
1 cup mayonnaise-style
  salad dressing
½ cup chopped celery
8 ounces cream cheese,
  softened
½ cup chopped nuts
1 teaspoon minced onion
Stuffed olives, chopped

Heat soup in saucepan. Soften gelatin in cold water. Stir into hot soup. Cool. Combine salad dressing, celery, cream cheese, nuts, onion and olives in shallow dish. Add to soup. Chill until set. Yield: 6 servings.

Hazel L. Smith
Maywood, California

FRESH TOMATO PLATE

½ cup sour cream
¼ teaspoon onion salt
¼ teaspoon garlic salt
2 medium tomatoes,
  thinly sliced
1 medium Bermuda
  onion, sliced
1 small cucumber,
  sliced
Leaf lettuce

Combine first 3 ingredients in bowl; mix well. Alternate tomatoes, onion and cucumber on lettuce-lined serving plate. Spoon dressing over vegetables. Yield: 4 servings.

Diane Spitzer, Delta Sigma
Monmouth, Illinois

MARINATED TOMATOES

2   4-ounce cans
    mushrooms
5 or 6 tomatoes, sliced
¼ cup wine vinegar
¾ cup safflower oil
1 tablespoon chopped
  parsley
1 clove of garlic, minced
½ teaspoon salt
Dash of pepper

Place mushrooms and tomatoes in dish. Combine remaining ingredients in bowl. Pour over vegetables. Marinate in refrigerator for 1 hour or longer.
Yield: 6 servings.

Sherry Johnson, Preceptor Alpha Pi
Glenwood, Iowa

TOMATO AND MOZZARELLA SALAD

6 tablespoons extra virgin olive oil
2 tablespoons balsamic vinegar
8 large Roma tomatoes, sliced
6 ounces fresh mozzarella cheese, thinly sliced
8 thin slices red onion
Salt and pepper to taste

Combine olive oil and vinegar in jar. Chill in refrigerator. Arrange slices of tomato, cheese and onion on salad plates. Mix oil and vinegar well; drizzle over salad. Season to taste. Yield: 4 servings.

Jo Roper, Preceptor Zeta Gamma
Tampa, Florida

TOMATO AND COTTAGE CHEESE SALAD

1 4-ounce package lemon gelatin
1½ cups hot tomato juice
1 tablespoon vinegar
2 tablespoons cold water
1¼ cups cottage cheese
2 tablespoons chopped green bell pepper
½ cup finely diced celery
2 cups shredded cabbage
⅓ cup mayonnaise
1 teaspoon (scant) salt

Dissolve gelatin in hot tomato juice in saucepan. Stir in vinegar. Combine ½ cup tomato mixture with cold water in ring mold. Chill until firm. Chill remaining gelatin until thickened. Fold in remaining ingredients. Pour over congealed layer. Chill until firm. Yield: 6 servings.

Dolores Sandusky, Preceptor Alpha Epsilon
Tucson, Arizona

TOMATO ASPIC

1 3-ounce package lemon gelatin
1¼ cups boiling water
1 8-ounce can tomato sauce
1½ tablespoons vinegar
½ teaspoon salt
⅛ teaspoon Tabasco sauce
¼ cup chopped green onions
Dash of cloves
⅛ teaspoon Worcestershire sauce
4 ounces cooked shrimp
1 cup diced celery

Dissolve gelatin in boiling water in bowl. Stir in next 7 ingredients. Chill until slightly thickened. Stir in shrimp and celery. Pour into 9x9-inch dish. Chill until firm. Yield: 6 servings.

Azile Goss, Preceptor Kappa Alpha
Willows, California

OREGANO TOMATOES

4 or 5 ripe tomatoes
1 cup corn oil
⅓ cup apple cider vinegar
½ teaspoon dry mustard
2 teaspoons oregano
1 teaspoon salt
1 clove of garlic, finely chopped

Peel tomatoes; slice 1 inch thick. Place in 9-inch square glass dish. Pour mixture of remaining ingredients over tomatoes. Chill, covered, for 2 to 3 hours. Yield: 4 servings.

Kathy Weber, Preceptor Beta Phi
Toledo, Ohio

MARINATED VEGETABLE SALAD

1 16-ounce can Shoe Peg corn, drained
1 16-ounce can large peas, drained
1 16-ounce can French-style green beans, drained
1 cup chopped celery
1 2-ounce jar pimento
1 cup chopped green onions
1 cup chopped green bell pepper
¾ cup sugar
½ cup corn oil
½ cup white vinegar
1 teaspoon salt
1 teaspoon pepper

Combine vegetables in bowl. Combine sugar and remaining ingredients in saucepan. Bring to a boil. Cool. Pour over vegetables. Chill for 12 hours to 1 week. Yield: 10 servings.

Gyl Dalrymple, Omega Preceptor
West Monroe, Louisiana

MIXED VEGETABLE SALAD

1 16-ounce can French-style green beans
1 16-ounce can wax beans
1 16-ounce can red kidney beans
1 16-ounce can white Shoe Peg corn
1 16-ounce can chopped carrots
1 16-ounce can peas
1 medium onion, chopped
6 stalks celery, chopped
1 4-ounce jar chopped pimento, drained
1½ cups sugar
1 cup vinegar
½ cup corn oil
1 teaspoon salt
Dash of pepper

Drain canned vegetables. Combine all vegetables in bowl. Combine sugar, vinegar, oil, salt and pepper in jar; shake well. Pour over vegetables. Marinate for 12 hours. Yield: 15 servings.

Maurine Glantz, Xi Gamma Zeta
Harvard, Nebraska

SEVEN-LAYER SALAD

1 head lettuce, shredded
½ cup chopped green bell pepper
½ cup chopped celery
1 small red onion, chopped
1 9-ounce package frozen peas, cooked
2 cups mayonnaise
1 tablespoon sugar
1 cup shredded Cheddar cheese
1 pound bacon, crisp-fried, crumbled

Fill salad bowl half full with lettuce. Add layers of green pepper, celery, onion and peas. Spread mayonnaise over peas, sealing to edge of bowl. Sprinkle sugar, cheese and bacon on top. Chill, tightly covered, for 8 hours to overnight. Toss before serving. Yield: 8 to 12 servings.

Anne M. MacNealy, Xi Eta Lambda
Reynoldsburg, Ohio

A plate of ripe tomato slices and cucumber slices sprinkled with dill makes a delicious salad when **Sally Ireland, Xi Kappa, Chaplin, Connecticut,** *has a summer cookout.*

TOSSED SALAD WITH ORANGE DRESSING

Lettuce, torn
Tomatoes, sliced
Hard-cooked eggs,
 chopped
Carrots, chopped
Celery, chopped
Red onion rings
Mandarin oranges,
 drained
Black olives
Watercress

Green bell pepper,
 chopped
Cucumber, chopped
Frozen green peas,
 thawed
½ cup corn oil
¼ cup lemon juice
¼ cup orange juice
½ teaspoon salt
Cayenne pepper to taste
1 tablespoon sugar

Mix desired amounts of first 12 ingredients in salad bowl. Combine oil, lemon juice, orange juice, salt, cayenne pepper and sugar in jar; shake well. Pour over salad; toss to mix. Yield: 4 servings.

Mary Perroni, Epsilon Kappa
Fairfax, Virginia

FIESTA TOSSED SALAD

1 large head lettuce,
 torn
1 12-ounce can white
 whole kernel corn,
 drained
½ cup Parmesan cheese

1 cup cherry tomato
 halves
1 3-ounce can French-
 fried onions
Creamy garlic salad
 dressing

Combine lettuce, corn, cheese, tomatoes and onions in salad bowl. Add enough salad dressing to moisten; toss lightly. Yield: 6 servings.

Julie Haldeman, Preceptor Epsilon Lambda
Wellington, Ohio

VEGETABLE SALAD

1 16-ounce can white
 corn
1 16-ounce can peas
2 4-ounce cans
 mushrooms
2 4-ounce cans water
 chestnuts
1 16-ounce can bean
 sprouts
1 4-ounce jar chopped
 pimento

½ cup chopped celery
½ cup chopped green
 onions
½ cup chopped green
 bell pepper
½ cup vinegar
1 cup corn oil
1 cup water
1 cup sugar
Salt and pepper to taste

Drain vegetables. Combine in bowl. Blend vinegar, oil, water, sugar, salt and pepper in bowl; mix well. Pour over vegetables. Marinate in refrigerator overnight. Drain before serving. Yield: 14 servings.

Karen Webb, Xi Beta Zeta
Johnson City, Tennessee

Betty Braw, Laureate Beta Epsilon, Port Angeles, Washington, *makes an easy salad by combining ½ chopped red bell pepper, 2 or 3 sliced zucchini, 3 chopped green onions, 2 finely chopped stalks celery and 1 bottle of italian salad dressing. Chill for 2 hours, and mix in 1 small can cocktail peanuts before serving.*

MARINATED VEGETABLE SALAD

¾ cup vinegar
½ cup sugar
⅓ to ½ cup corn oil
1 teaspoon salt
1 teaspoon pepper
1 16-ounce can
 tiny green peas
1 16-ounce can French-
 style green beans

1 16-ounce can Shoe Peg
 corn
1 large green bell pepper,
 chopped
1 cup chopped celery
1 bunch green onions,
 chopped

Heat first 5 ingredients in saucepan until sugar dissolves. Cool. Drain canned vegetables. Combine all vegetables in bowl. Pour vinegar mixture over vegetables. Chill overnight. Yield: 12 servings.

Karla Riskind, Theta Phi
Temple, Texas

VEGETABLE SALAD MEDLEY

3½ cups sliced
 cauliflower
3 cups thinly sliced
 carrots
1 10-ounce package
 frozen peas
1 8-ounce can sliced
 water chestnuts,
 drained
¼ cup chopped green
 bell pepper
2 tablespoons chopped
 green onion

½ cup corn oil
½ cup vinegar
1 tablespoon sugar
½ teaspoon salt
¼ teaspoon dried basil
¼ teaspoon dried
 dillweed
⅛ teaspoon pepper
1 cup shredded Cheddar
 cheese

Cook cauliflower and carrots in boiling salted water in covered saucepan for 4 minutes. Add peas. Cook for 2 minutes longer; drain. Cool. Combine cooked vegetables, water chestnuts, green pepper and onion in bowl. Combine oil, vinegar, sugar, salt, basil, dillweed and pepper in covered jar; shake well. Pour over vegetables; toss to mix. Chill, covered, in refrigerator. Add cheese just before serving. Yield: 10 to 12 servings.

Pat Le Sueur, Gamma Mu
Tulsa, Oklahoma

VEGETABLES WITH DRESSING

1 10-ounce package
 frozen small limas
1 10-ounce package
 frozen peas
1 10-ounce package
 frozen green beans
1½ cups mayonnaise

¼ cup corn oil
1 teaspoon
 Worcestershire sauce
Dash of Tabasco sauce
1 small onion, grated
3 hard-cooked eggs,
 grated

Cook vegetables using package directions; drain well. Mix mayonnaise and remaining ingredients in bowl. Add desired amount of mayonnaise mixture to vegetables in bowl; mix gently. Garnish with dollop of mayonnaise mixture. Yield: 8 servings.

Connie A. Miller, Zi Alpha Zeta
Shelbyville, Tennessee

Party
Main
Dishes

BARBECUED BRISKET

1 beef brisket	1 cup water
½ 3-ounce bottle of	½ cup packed light brown
liquid smoke	sugar
1 teaspoon celery salt	1 cup catsup
1 teaspoon onion salt	2 tablespoons all-purpose
1 teaspoon garlic salt	flour

Marinate brisket in mixture of first 5 ingredients in roaster overnight. Preheat oven to 250 degrees. Bake, covered, for 5 hours. Cool in refrigerator. Blend drippings, brown sugar, catsup and flour in saucepan. Bring to a boil, stirring constantly. Slice brisket thinly across grain. Cover with sauce. Bake at 300 degrees for 1 hour. Yield: 6 to 8 servings.

Beverly Taylor, Rho Chi
Liberty, Missouri

PEPPERED BEEF BRISKET

¼ cup coarsely ground	½ cup vinegar
pepper	1 tablespoon tomato paste
1 4 to 5-pound beef	1 teaspoon paprika
brisket	1 clove of garlic, crushed
⅔ cup soy sauce	

Press pepper firmly into brisket with waxed paper and heel of hand. Place in shallow dish. Combine soy sauce and remaining ingredients in bowl; mix well. Pour over brisket. Chill overnight, turning occasionally. Drain. Preheat oven to 200 degrees. Wrap brisket tightly in heavy foil. Place in shallow baking pan. Bake for 6 hours to overnight. Yield: 20 servings.

Mildred Northington, Preceptor Kappa Rho
Hilltop Lakes, Texas

SCRUMPTIOUS BEEF BRISKET

1 envelope dry onion soup	2 tablespoons orange
mix	marmalade
1 2-pound beef brisket	1 tablespoon Brandy
1 teaspoon cinnamon	1 teaspoon Worcestershire
2 tablespoons light brown	sauce
sugar	1 8-ounce package dried
1 teaspoon pepper	apricots, chopped
¾ teaspoon ginger	1 cup chopped pitted
1 tablespoon grated lemon	prunes
rind	1 12-ounce can beer
¼ cup clover honey	

Preheat oven to 350 degrees. Sprinkle half the soup mix in bottom of foil-lined roaster. Add brisket. Sprinkle with remaining soup mix; rub into brisket. Seal foil. Bake for 3 hours. Combine remaining ingredients in large bowl. Open foil carefully. Pour fruit mixture over brisket; reseal foil. Bake for 1 hour longer or until brisket is tender. Serve on hot cooked noodles. Yield: 4 servings.

Susan L. Miller, Xi Alpha Lambda
Mechanicsburg, Pennsylvania

SMOKED BEEF BRISKET WITH BUNS

1 3 to 4 pound brisket	2 teaspoons celery salt
2 tablespoons liquid	2 teaspoons pepper
smoke	2 teaspoons
1 teaspoon garlic salt	Worcestershire sauce
2 teaspoons onion powder	1 cup barbecue sauce

Rub brisket with mixture of next 6 ingredients. Wrap in heavy foil; seal tightly. Place in 9x13-inch pan. Refrigerate overnight. Preheat oven to 250 degrees. Bake for 5 hours. Open foil; shred brisket. Pour barbecue sauce over top. Serve with sesame seed buns. Yield: 6 servings.

Janet Staton Nesbitt, Alpha Upsilon
Danville, Illinois

ITALIAN BEEF

1 6-pound rump roast	½ teaspoon oregano
3 large onions, sliced	½ teaspoon Italian
1 teaspoon salt	seasoning
¼ teaspoon pepper	1 teaspoon MSG
½ teaspoon onion salt	¼ teaspoon basil
½ teaspoon garlic salt	

Preheat oven to 325 degrees. Place roast in roaster ¾ filled with water. Add onions, salt and pepper. Roast, covered, for 2 to 3 hours or until tender. Cool. Store overnight in refrigerator. Preheat oven to 350 degrees. Trim fat from roast; slice very thinly. Strain broth into saucepan; add remaining seasonings. Bring to a boil; remove from heat. Pour over sliced roast. Bake for 30 minutes. Serve as entrée or on freshly baked buns with broth for dipping. Yield: 12 servings.

Phyllis Paine, Preceptor Gamma Alpha
Mount Pleasant, Iowa

ROAST BEEF SUPREME

1 standing prime rib roast,	Seasonings to taste
at room temperature	

Preheat oven to 375 degrees. Place roast in shallow roasting pan; season to taste. Do not cover or add water. Place roast in oven. Bake for 1 hour. Turn off oven; do not open door until ready to serve. Turn oven on to 300 degrees 30 to 40 minutes before serving. Roast will warm to serving temperature and will be pink all the way through. Yield: 4 servings.

Note: For a 5 to 6-pound roast, let stand in closed oven for 4 hours. For an 8 to 10-pound roast, let stand in closed oven for 5 to 6 hours. Allow at least 8 hours for roast weighing 15 pounds or more.

Louise Goode
Sedan, Kansas

GRANDMA'S BARBECUED BEEF RIBS

¾ cup packed light brown sugar	¾ cup vinegar
2 tablespoons cornstarch	½ cup catsup
2 teaspoons dry mustard	½ cup water
1 cup crushed pineapple, drained	¼ cup chopped onion
	2 tablespoons soy sauce
	12 beef ribs

Preheat oven to 350 degrees. Mix together first 9 ingredients in 3-quart saucepan. Bring to a boil. Simmer over medium heat until thickened. Place ribs on rack in broiler pan. Broil until brown on all sides, turning as necessary. Dip ribs, 1 at a time, into thickened sauce; place in 9x13-inch baking dish. Pour remaining sauce over ribs. Bake, covered, for 1½ hours. Yield: 6 servings.

Cindy Horner, Kappa Sigma
Ackley, Iowa

MOM'S BARBECUED BEEF SANDWICHES

8 slices bacon, chopped	½ teaspoon meat tenderizer
1 large onion, chopped	1 teaspoon garlic salt
2 tablespoons corn oil	1 teaspoon salt
1 3 to 4-pound rump roast	1 teaspoon pepper
2 cups tomato juice	½ cup barbecue sauce
2 bay leaves	

Brown bacon and onion in oil in saucepan. Remove with slotted spoon. Add roast. Brown on all sides. Add tomato juice, next 5 ingredients and onion and bacon. Bring to a boil; cover and reduce heat. Simmer for 4 to 5 hours or until roast pulls apart with fork. Skim pan juices. Stir in barbecue sauce. Serve on buns. Yield: 4 servings.

Vickie Wolfe, Iota Delta
Oskaloosa, Iowa

CHEF'S DELIGHT TENDERLOIN

1 beef tenderloin	Garlic salt and lemon pepper to taste
Mayonnaise	

Preheat oven to 500 degrees. Coat cold tenderloin with mayonnaise; sprinkle generously with garlic salt and lemon pepper. Place on baking sheet; do not cover. Bake for 15 minutes for rare, 20 minutes for medium-rare, 25 minutes for medium or 30 minutes for well-done. Turn off oven. Let tenderloin stand in closed oven for 1 hour; do not open oven door. Yield: 4 to 6 servings.

Cathy Helleny, Xi Rho
Energy, Illinois

GRILLED BEEF TENDERLOIN

1 3 to 5-pound beef tenderloin	1 cup dry Sherry
½ cup finely chopped onion	3 tablespoons soy sauce
	2 teaspoons dry mustard
1½ tablespoons butter, melted	⅛ teaspoon salt
	⅛ teaspoon pepper
	1 teaspoon minced garlic

Trim excess fat from tenderloin. Place in shallow baking dish. Sauté onion in butter in skillet until tender. Add remaining ingredients. Bring to a boil; pour over tenderloin. Marinate for 12 to 24 hours, turning tenderloin several times. Drain, reserving marinade. Grill over hot coals to desired degree of doneness. Let stand on serving plate for several minutes before slicing. Serve with remaining marinade. Yield: 10 to 15 servings.

Melvye Cooper, Xi Beta Zeta
Decatur, Alabama

ALL-AMERICAN PEPPER STEAK

2 pounds beef tenderloin, well trimmed	2 tablespoons corn oil
	½ teaspoon salt
½ cup finely chopped green onions	¼ teaspoon pepper
	½ cup hot beef bouillon
3 cloves of garlic, minced	½ cup dry Sherry
1 green bell pepper, chopped	1 teaspoon soy sauce
	2 tablespoons cornstarch
1 red bell pepper, chopped	1 tablespoon chopped fresh parsley

Cut tenderloin into ¼x½-inch strips. Sauté green onions, garlic and bell peppers in 1 tablespoon oil in heavy skillet for 1 minute. Drain on paper towels. Add remaining tablespoon oil to skillet; heat. Sauté tenderloin strips over high heat until light brown. Add salt and pepper; reduce heat. Stir in hot bouillon and sautéed vegetables. Bring to simmer. Blend Sherry, soy sauce and cornstarch in small bowl. Pour over simmering pepper steak. Cook for 1 minute or until thickened, stirring constantly. Spoon into deep serving platter; sprinkle with chopped parsley. Serve with steamed white or brown rice or wild rice. Yield: 6 to 8 servings.

Karen Johnston, Xi Delta Alpha
Cairo, Illinois

BRONCO STEAK

1 1 to 1½-pound thinly sliced round steak	1 pound sausage
	8 slices bacon
Salt, pepper and garlic powder to taste	1 onion, finely chopped

Preheat oven to 350 degrees. Sprinkle steak with salt, pepper and garlic powder. Place steak on waxed paper. Spread sausage over steak, spreading to edge. Arrange bacon over sausage; sprinkle with onion. Roll as for jelly roll. Place seam side down in shallow baking pan. Bake for 1½ hours; cover with foil if necessary to prevent over-browning. Slice diagonally 1 inch thick. Yield: 6 to 8 servings.

Annette Ransdell, Delta Omega
Danville, Kentucky

CUBE STEAK AND ZUCCHINI ROLL-UPS

1 zucchini	1 teaspoon shortening
4 cube steaks	1 10-ounce can onion
½ cup Romano cheese	soup
2 teaspoons parsley	2 teaspoons all-purpose
Salt and pepper to taste	flour
4 slices bacon	1 cup water

Cut zucchini into 4 spears; place on steaks. Sprinkle with cheese, parsley, salt and pepper. Roll up; wrap with bacon and secure with toothpicks. Brown lightly in shortening in skillet. Add soup. Simmer, covered, for 20 minutes or until tender. Stir in flour mixed with water. Cook until thickened, stirring constantly. Yield: 4 servings.

Penny Oliver, Xi Psi
Spokane, Washington

ITALIAN BRAISED BEEF

2 tablespoons all-purpose	1 can mushrooms, drained
flour	1 beef bouillon cube
1 teaspoon salt	1 cup boiling water
¼ teaspoon pepper	1 8-ounce can tomato
¼ teaspoon garlic powder	sauce
1 to 2 pounds stew beef,	¼ to ½ cup dry red wine
cut into cubes	1 teaspoon seasoned salt
2 tablespoons olive oil	¼ teaspoon oregano
1 medium onion, finely	¼ teaspoon basil
chopped	

Combine flour, salt, pepper and garlic powder in paper bag. Add beef; toss to coat. Brown in olive oil in skillet. Stir in onion and mushrooms. Cook until onion is light brown. Add bouillon dissolved in boiling water and tomato sauce; stir until sauce is smooth. Add wine, seasoned salt, oregano and basil. Simmer, covered, for 2 hours or until beef is very tender, stirring frequently. Add small amounts of hot water if necessary to make sauce of desired consistency. Garnish with chopped parsley. Yield: 6 servings.

Marlene Perhot, Gamma Theta
Midway Park, North Carolina

BARBECUED STEAK

4 to 6 minute steaks	1 tablespoon
Corn oil	Worcestershire sauce
1 8-ounce can tomato	1 medium onion, chopped
sauce	2 teaspoons chili powder
2 tablespoons light brown	¼ teaspoon onion salt
sugar	¼ teaspoon garlic salt
2 tablespoons vinegar	

Preheat oven to 350 degrees. Brown steaks in a small amount of oil in 10-inch ovenproof skillet. Mix remaining ingredients in bowl; pour over steaks. Bake for 1 hour. Add a small amount of water or tomato juice if necessary. Bake for 1 hour longer. Yield: 4 to 6 servings.

Mildred Caughran, Preceptor Mu
Neosho, Missouri

PARTY STEAK DIANE

1 5-pound sirloin steak,	2 teaspoons dry mustard
2 inches thick	½ cup butter
1 teaspoon freshly ground	1 tablespoon lemon juice
pepper	1 tablespoon
12 ounces fresh	Worcestershire sauce
mushrooms, sliced	1 teaspoon salt
1½ cups sliced green	¼ cup chopped parsley
onions	

Let steak stand at room temperature for 1 hour. Trim excess fat; score edge at 1-inch intervals. Rub pepper into both sides. Sauté vegetables and mustard in butter in skillet on grill over hot coals for 10 minutes or until onions are tender. Stir in remaining ingredients; remove from heat. Rub hot grill with fat trimmings to prevent sticking. Place steak on grill 6 inches above hot coals. Grill for 15 minutes. Brush lightly with butter mixture. Grill for 5 minutes longer; turn steak. Grill for 20 minutes; brush lightly with butter mixture. Yield: 8 servings.

Brenda J. Broome, Preceptor Zeta Gamma
Tampa, Florida

FAJITAS

1 to 1¼-pounds skirt steak	1 small onion, chopped
1 8-ounce bottle of	Vegetable oil
Italian salad dressing	2 teaspoons
4 slices bacon, cut into	Worcestershire sauce
1-inch squares	½ teaspoon garlic salt
1 green bell pepper,	Flour tortillas
chopped	

Marinate steak overnight in salad dressing; drain. Cut into strips. Sprinkle steak, bacon, green pepper and onion with mixture of next 3 ingredients. Sauté in heavy skillet over high heat for 4 minutes. Spoon onto flour tortillas. Serve with shredded cheese, chopped tomatoes, taco sauce and onion for toppings. Yield: 14 servings.

FLOUR TORTILLAS

4 cups all-purpose flour	½ cup shortening
1½ teaspoons salt	

Sift flour and salt into bowl. Cut in shortening until crumbly. Add enough warm water to make soft dough. Knead several times on lightly floured surface. Divide into 14 portions. Let rest, covered, for 20 minutes. Roll each into circle. Cook in ungreased skillet over medium heat until light brown, turning once.

Harriett Laws, Preceptor Beta Psi
Cherokee, Iowa

FLANK STEAK FAJITAS

1 2-pound flank steak	2 cups shredded lettuce
½ cup soy sauce	2 cups diced tomatoes
¼ cup Worcestershire	2 cups shredded American
sauce	cheese
½ cup teriyaki marinade	2 cups mashed avocado
¼ cup white cooking	2 cups hot refried beans
Sherry	1 cup sour cream
Seasoned salt, pepper and	1 cup picante sauce
garlic powder to taste	3 packages flour tortillas

Pound steak several times. Marinate in mixture of next 4 ingredients and seasonings overnight. Drain, reserving marinade. Grill over very low coals for 1 to 1½ hours. Slice very thinly. Reheat in reserved marinade in saucepan when ready to serve. Arrange steak and remaining ingredients for buffet service. Fill flour tortilla with selected ingredients; roll up. Yield: 6 to 8 servings.
Note: Heat refried beans by mixing bacon drippings and 1 16-ounce can refried beans in hot skillet. Add 1 tablespoon chili powder.

Susie Harbers, Xi Upsilon Psi
Yoakum, Texas

FLUTES

2 pounds round steak, cubed	2 tomatoes, chopped
Shortening	Salt and pepper to taste
4 large potatoes, diced	12 to 14 large thin flour tortillas, warmed
1 4-ounce can chopped green chilles	Butter
	Hot Salsa

Brown steak in a small amount of shortening in skillet for several minutes. Add potatoes. Cook for several minutes. Add green chilies. Cook until steak and potatoes are tender, stirring occasionally. Stir in tomatoes. Season with salt and pepper. Place 2 tablespoons on each tortilla. Fold in sides; roll as for jelly roll. Heat 2 inches shortening in heavy skillet over medium-high heat. Fry rolled tortillas in hot shortening until crisp and lightly brown; drain on paper towel. Spread with butter. Keep warm in oven. Serve with Hot Salsa. Yield: 12 to 14 servings.

HOT SALSA

1 16-ounce can tomatoes	½ teaspoon leaf oregano
1 onion, chopped	1 teaspoon red chili seed
1 clove of garlic	Salt and pepper to taste

Combine tomatoes and remaining ingredients in blender container. Process to desired consistency. Pour into saucepan. Heat over low heat until bubbly; do not boil.

Verna Sorrels, Preceptor Beta
Pagosa Springs, Colorado

STUFFED MINUTE STEAK

¼ cup honey	2 cups stuffing mix
2 tablespoons soy sauce	1 green bell pepper, chopped
1 cup hot water	
2 tablespoons margarine	4 4-ounce minute steaks

Preheat oven to 375 degrees. Mix honey and soy sauce in small bowl. Stir hot water and margarine in bowl until margarine melts. Stir in stuffing mix and green pepper. Pound steaks. Spoon ½ cup stuffing onto each steak; roll to enclose stuffing and secure with toothpicks. Place steaks in baking pan. Spoon honey mixture over steaks. Bake for 20 minutes. Yield: 4 servings.

Sue Moak, Xi Psi
Ocean Springs, Mississippi

GRILLED BEEF WITH RED BUTTER SAUCE

1 2-pound boneless sirloin steak, 1½ inches thick	6 tablespoons finely chopped shallots
	1½ cups red Burgundy
2 tablespoons peanut oil	12 tablespoons butter
Salt and freshly ground pepper to taste	Salt and freshly ground pepper to taste

Preheat broiler. Rub steak on both sides with oil; sprinkle with salt and pepper. Place on rack in broiler pan. Broil 4 to 5 inches from heat for 3 to 5 minutes; turn. Broil for 3 to 5 minutes longer or to desired degree of doneness. Place on hot platter; cover loosely with foil. Let stand for 5 minutes. Slice steak diagonally cross-grain. Boil shallots in wine in saucepan until liquid is reduced to ⅓ cup. Add butter. Season to taste. Cook just until butter melts. Serve with steak. Yield: 4 servings.

Deborah Ann Hulse, Xi Gamma Theta
Casa Grande, Arizona

GRILLED FLANK STEAK

1 2-pound flank steak	½ cup corn oil
Garlic powder and seasoned pepper to taste	Several dashes of Worcestershire sauce
	Several dashes of A-1 sauce
1 cup picante sauce	
¼ cup lemon juice	Flour Tortillas (page 40)

Place steak and seasonings in plastic bag. Add mixture of picante sauce, lemon juice, oil, Worcestershire and A-1 sauces. Marinate in refrigerator for 24 hours. Drain, reserving marinade. Grill over hot coals for 7 minutes on each side or to desired degree of doneness, basting with reserved marinade. Slide diagonally cross-grain. Serve on warm tortillas. Serve with guacamole, shredded cheese, onions, tomatoes, sour cream, olives and salsa. Yield: 8 to 10 servings.

Gail M. Plache, Alpha Psi
Scottsdale, Arizona

STUFFED FLANK STEAK

1 2-pound flank steak	¼ teaspoon pepper
½ cup chopped onion	1 beef bouillon cube
¼ cup butter	1 cup water
1½ cups cooked rice	2 tablespoons snipped parsley
½ cup chopped parsley	
½ cup Parmesan cheese	1 tablespoon sugar
½ teaspoon salt	½ teaspoon dried thyme

Preheat oven to 350 degrees. Cut pocket in steak; set aside. Sauté onion in butter in skillet until golden. Stir in rice, ½ cup parsley, cheese, salt and pepper. Spoon into pocket in steak; secure. Place in baking pan. Pour mixture of bouillon cube dissolved in water, 2 tablespoons parsley, sugar and thyme over steak. Bake, covered, for 1½ hours. Yield: 4 to 6 servings.

Arlene Brown, Iota
Lima, New York

BEEF PARMIGIANA

1 1½-pound tenderized round steak	1 teaspoon salt
1 egg, beaten	¼ teaspoon pepper
⅓ cup Parmesan cheese	½ teaspoon sugar
⅓ cup Italian bread crumbs	½ teaspoon marjoram
⅓ cup corn oil	1 12-ounce can tomato paste
1 medium onion, minced	3 cups hot water
2 cloves of garlic, minced	8 ounces mozzarella cheese, sliced

Preheat oven to 350 degrees. Cut steak into 2 to 3-inch pieces. Dip in egg; coat with mixture of Parmesan cheese and bread crumbs. Heat oil in skillet. Brown steak on both sides in oil. Arrange in shallow baking dish. Sauté onion and garlic in drippings in same skillet until tender. Stir in seasonings and tomato paste. Stir in hot water gradually. Boil for 5 minutes, stirring to deglaze skillet. Pour ¾ of the sauce over steak. Top with cheese slices and remaining sauce. Bake for 1 hour. Serve with spaghetti. Yield: 4 to 6 servings.

Cyril Hennum, Pi Upsilon
San Diego, California

TEXAS-STYLE NO-BEAN CHILI

1 pound round steak	Salt to taste
Vegetable oil	4 to 5 teaspoons chili powder
4 or 5 cloves of garlic	
2 to 3 teaspoons cumin	

Cut round steak into bite-sized pieces. Brown in oil in saucepan; drain. Add seasonings and enough water to cover. Simmer for 30 minutes to 1 hour or until of desired consistency. Serve with rice. Yield: 4 servings.

Frances Shamhart Ferraro, Preceptor Pi
Phoenix, Arizona

THE VERY BEST CHILI

8 ounces dried pinto beans, washed	2½ pounds beef chuck roast, cut into ½-inch pieces
6 large onions, chopped	1½ pounds lean pork butt, cut into ½-inch pieces
4 large green bell peppers, chopped	2 tablespoons chopped seeded green chilies
4 cloves of garlic, minced	
¼ cup corn oil	1 tablespoon salt
½ cup chopped fresh parsley	1½ teaspoons freshly ground pepper
1 28-ounce can tomatoes, drained	2 tablespoons cumin
⅓ cup chili powder	

Cook beans in water to cover in 1-quart saucepan for 1 hour or until tender, adding additional water if necessary. Sauté onions, green peppers and garlic in oil in heavy kettle until onions are transparent. Add remaining ingredients. Simmer, covered, for 1 hour. Cook, uncovered, for 30 minutes longer or until thick. May be frozen and reheated. Yield: 8 servings.

Florence Anderson, Xi Alpha Delta
St. Simons Island, Georgia

AFRICAN CHOP

2 pounds beef, cubed	Chopped cucumber
2 10-ounce cans cream of mushroom soup	Sliced bananas
	Mandarin oranges
2 teaspoons curry powder	Pineapple chunks
Cooked rice	Spanish peanuts
Chopped onion	Coconut
Chopped tomato	

Preheat oven to 300 degrees. Place beef in 2-quart casserole. Mix soup and curry powder. Pour over beef; mix well. Bake for 3 hours. Serve hot over rice with choice of remaining ingredients. Yield: 6 servings.

Mary Eastman, Xi Beta Eta
Couer d' Alene, Idaho

BEEF BOURGUIGNON

8 ounces bacon, cut into 1-inch pieces	2 teaspoons salt
20 small white onions	½ teaspoon thyme leaves
3 pounds beef bottom round roast	¼ teaspoon pepper
	1 bay leaf
3 tablespoons all-purpose flour	2 cups Burgundy
1 large carrot, chopped	1 cup water
1 large onion, chopped	1 pound mushrooms, sliced
¼ cup Brandy	¼ cup butter, softened
2 cloves of garlic, crushed	2 tablespoons all-purpose flour

Preheat oven to 325 degrees. Fry bacon in Dutch oven over medium-high heat. Drain, reserving 3 tablespoons drippings. Sauté small onions in drippings until light brown. Set aside. Cut beef into 2-inch cubes. Coat with 3 tablespoons flour. Brown several cubes at a time in drippings; remove after browning. Sauté carrot and chopped onion in drippings for 5 minutes. Return beef cubes to Dutch oven. Drizzle Brandy over beef; ignite. Add bacon, seasonings, Burgundy and water when flames die. Bake, covered, for 2½ hours. Sauté mushrooms in 2 tablespoons butter in skillet over medium heat for 7 minutes. Blend remaining butter and flour in small bowl. Stir ½ teaspoon at a time into pan juices in Dutch oven. Add small onions and mushrooms. Bake, covered, for 1 hour longer. Yield: 10 servings.

Vicky Bothman, Lambda Psi
Edwardsville, Illinois

BEEF BURGUNDY

3 pounds beef stew meat	1 envelope dry onion soup mix
1 cup Burgundy	Canned mushrooms
3 10-ounce cans cream of mushroom soup	

Preheat oven to 325 degrees. Place beef in roaster. Add mixture of wine, canned soup and soup mix. Bake, covered, for 3 hours. Add desired amount of mushrooms near end of cooking time. Serve over buttered noodles or rice. Yield: 12 servings.

Billie Brazil, Iota Eta
Ennis, Texas

SLOW-COOKER BEEF BOURGUIGNON

2½ pounds sirloin, cubed
1 large carrot, peeled,
 sliced
2 medium onions, sliced
1 clove of garlic
1½ teaspoons salt
¼ teaspoon pepper
2 bay leaves
1 tablespoon chopped
 parsley

½ teaspoon thyme
1 10-ounce can
 condensed beef broth
1 tablespoon tomato paste
2½ cups Burgundy
8 ounces fresh
 mushrooms, sliced
2 to 4 tablespoons
 all-purpose flour
¾ cup cold water

Combine first 12 ingredients in slow cooker. Cook on Low for 7 hours. Add mushrooms. Cook for 1 hour longer. Blend flour with water. Stir into cooker. Cook until thickened, stirring frequently. Serve with wild rice and French bread. Yield: 5 servings.

Mary C. Henchon, Laureate Beta
Trenton, New Jersey

BEEF EN BROCHETTE

1 13-ounce can
 pineapple chunks
½ cup steak sauce
2 tablespoons dry white
 wine
1 tablespoon corn oil

½ teaspoon salt
Dash of pepper
2 pounds beef sirloin tips,
 cut into 1-inch cubes
Salt and pepper to taste

Drain pineapple, reserving 2 cups juice. Chill pineapple chunks. Combine reserved liquid with steak sauce and next 4 ingredients in small bowl; pour over beef in large bowl. Marinate in refrigerator for 2 to 3 hours, turning occasionally. Thread beef and pineapple alternately onto six 12-inch skewers, allowing 4 to 5 pieces beef and 5 to 6 chunks of pineapple for each skewer. Brush with marinade; season lightly with salt and pepper. Grill or broil 3 inches from heat source for 5 minutes on each side for medium rare. Yield: 6 servings.

R. Evelyn Bartlett, Chi Xi
Whittier, California

BEEF PYRENEES

2 pounds beef cubes
¼ cup all-purpose flour
1 teaspoon salt
Dash of pepper
3 medium onions,
 quartered
1 8-ounce bottle of
 Catalina salad dressing

1 16-ounce can tiny
 whole carrots, drained
1 cup water
2 cups mushroom caps
Hot cooked rice
Parsley

Coat beef with mixture of flour, salt and pepper. Sauté beef and onions in ⅓ cup salad dressing in skillet until brown. Add remaining dressing, carrots and water. Simmer for 50 minutes. Add mushrooms. Simmer for 10 minutes longer. Serve with hot cooked rice. Garnish with parsley. Yield: 6 servings.

Patti Hipp, Xi Delta
Owings Mills, Maryland

CARBONADES À LA FLAMANDE

2 pounds lean sirloin tips
Salt and pepper to taste
½ cup melted butter
5 large onions, minced
¼ cup melted butter

1 12-ounce bottle of
 dark beer
3 tablespoons dark brown
 sugar

Sprinkle sirloin tips with salt and pepper. Brown in ½ cup butter in skillet. Place in slow cooker. Sauté minced onions in ¼ cup butter in skillet. Spoon over sirloin tips. Add beer; sprinkle with brown sugar. Cook on Low for 3 hours or until tender. Yield: 3 servings.

Rita Mulders, Chi Xi
La Puente, California

HUNGARIAN GOULASH WITH NOODLES

1 pound beef cubes
2 medium onions, minced
¼ teaspoon dry mustard
1¼ teaspoons paprika
2 tablespoons light brown
 sugar
1¼ teaspoons salt
¾ teaspoon cider vinegar
3 tablespoons
 Worcestershire sauce

6 tablespoons catsup
1 cup water
3 tablespoons all-purpose
 flour
½ cup water
1 6-ounce package
 noodles, cooked

Brown beef on all sides in a small amount of oil in heavy skillet. Add onions and mixture of mustard, paprika, brown sugar, salt, vinegar, Worcestershire sauce and catsup; mix well. Stir in 1 cup water. Cook, covered, over low heat for 2½ hours or until very tender. Blend flour with ½ cup water. Stir into skillet. Cook until thickened, stirring constantly. Serve over hot cooked noodles. Yield: 8 servings.

Marilyn Kelly, Xi Gamma Upsilon
Dunedin, Florida

FIESTA BEEF KABOBS

¼ cup dry onion soup mix
2 tablespoons sugar
½ cup catsup
¼ cup corn oil
1 tablespoon prepared
 mustard
½ cup water
¼ cup vinegar
¼ teaspoon salt
1 beef sirloin tip, cut
 into 1-inch cubes

1 green bell pepper,
 chopped
1 red bell pepper,
 chopped
Mushrooms
Cherry tomatoes
Small onions, slightly
 cooked

Combine first 8 ingredients in saucepan. Bring to a boil; reduce heat. Simmer for 20 minutes. Cool. Add beef; toss to coat. Refrigerate overnight. Let stand at room temperature for 1 hour. Drain, reserving marinade. Thread beef and vegetables alternately onto 4 skewers. Broil over medium coals to desired degree of doneness, brushing frequently with reserved marinade. Yield: 4 servings.

Bernice L. Brown, Preceptor Nu
Trenton, Missouri

PINEAPPLE AND BEEF TERIYAKI KABOBS

1½ pounds beef sirloin
2 cups 1-inch fresh
   pineapple cubes
½ cup soy sauce
½ teaspoon salt
¼ cup packed light brown
   sugar
2 tablespoons lemon juice
1 clove of garlic, minced
1 tablespoon corn oil

Cut beef into 1-inch squares. Marinate in mixture of remaining ingredients in bowl for 1 hour or longer, stirring twice. Drain, reserving marinade. Thread beef and pineapple alternately onto skewers. Cook 2 to 4 inches from hot coals for 5 to 10 minutes, turning frequently and basting with reserved marinade. Garnish with flower on tip of each skewer. Yield: 4 to 6 servings.

Jo Evelyn Hannah, Exempler Eta Kappa
Graham, Texas

CORNISH PASTY

2 cups all-purpose flour
½ teaspoon baking
   powder
¼ teaspoon salt
½ cup lard
½ cup finely ground suet
Water
1½ pounds round steak,
   cubed
3 cups chopped potatoes
1 large onion, chopped
Salt and pepper to taste

Preheat oven to 400 degrees. Sift flour, baking powder and salt in bowl. Cut in lard and suet until crumbly. Add water 1 tablespoon at a time until pastry forms ball. Divide into 4 portions; roll each into circle. Place mixture of ½ cup steak, ¾ cup potato, onion and seasonings on each pastry round. Moisten edge. Fold in half; seal. Fold edge again; seal. Place on baking sheet. Bake for 15 minutes. Reduce temperature to 350 degrees. Bake for 40 minutes. Yield: 4 servings.

Bernadine Gerving, Xi Lambda
Deadwood, South Dakota

SAUERBRATEN OVER NOODLES

3 lemons
3 pounds beef chuck
   roast, cubed
2 cups cider vinegar
2 cups sugar
2 tablespoons pickling
   spice
2 large onions, chopped
2 quarts water
1 tablespoon salt
2 teaspoons pepper
10 gingersnaps, crushed
½ cup water
¼ cup browned
   all-purpose flour
1 tablespoon cornstarch
1 8-ounce package
   noodles, cooked

Cut lemons into fourths; discard seed. Marinate beef cubes in mixture of vinegar, lemons, sugar, spice, onions, 2 quarts water, salt and pepper in large saucepan overnight. Cook beef in marinade for 1½ hours or until tender enough to pull apart. Moisten gingersnaps with ½ cup water to make paste. Add browned flour and cornstarch. Bring beef mixture to a boil. Stir in gingersnap mixture. Simmer for 5 minutes, stirring constantly. Let stand until cool. Serve on hot cooked noodles. Yield: 8 servings.

Elizabeth Thompson, Preceptor Beta Eta
West Bradenton, Florida

BARBECUED BEEF FOR SANDWICHES

1 6-pound beef roast
6 stalks celery, chopped
3 onions, chopped
1 14-ounce bottle of
   catsup
1 large green bell pepper,
   chopped
2 tablespoons barbecue
   sauce
1 tablespoon salt
3 tablespoons vinegar
1 teaspoon hot pepper
   sauce
2 tablespoons chili
   powder
1 teaspoon pepper
1½ cups water
Sandwich buns

Preheat oven to 300 degrees. Place roast in roaster. Add next 11 ingredients. Roast, covered, for 6 hours. Discard fat and bone; skim sauce. Shred beef with fork. Serve on sandwich buns. Yield: 20 servings.

Anne M. MacNealy, Xi Eta Lambda
Reynoldsburg, Ohio

OVEN STROGANOFF

1 3-pound round steak,
   cubed
1 cup red wine
1 envelope dry onion
   soup mix
2 8-ounce jars sliced
   mushrooms
1 10-ounce can cream of
   chicken soup
1 10-ounce can cream of
   celery soup
1 10-ounce can cream of
   mushroom soup
1 teaspoon salt
½ teaspoon pepper
2 cups sour cream
1 pound wide noodles,
   cooked

Preheat oven to 300 degrees. Combine steak with next 8 ingredients in roaster. Bake for 3 to 4 hours or until steak is tender. Stir in sour cream just before serving. Yield: 10 servings.

 Pat Van Dootingh, Xi Zeta Epsilon
Sandusky, Ohio

BARBECUED SPARERIBS

6 pounds beef spareribs
6 to 8 large cloves of
   garlic, minced
½ cup chicken broth
½ cup orange marmalade
¼ cup wine vinegar
¼ cup catsup
¼ cup honey
¼ cup dry Sherry

Leave ribs whole for easier handling during cooking. Combine remaining ingredients in saucepan. Bring to a simmer. Simmer for 5 minutes; cool. Marinate ribs in mixture overnight. Drain, reserving marinade. Weave whole ribs onto barbeque spit. Cook over low coals for 1 to 1½ hours until fork-tender, basting frequently with reserved marinade. Cut into serving pieces. Yield: 6 servings.

Joan Smith, Lambda Mu
Morgan Hill, California

BEST EASY BEEF STEW

2 pounds stew beef
1 7-ounce can mushroom
   pieces and stems,
   drained
1 envelope dry onion soup
   mix
1 10-ounce can cream of
   mushroom soup
3 carrots, cut into 2-inch
   pieces
1 14-ounce can whole
   new potatoes, drained

Preheat oven to 300 degrees. Place beef in casserole. Layer mushrooms, soup mix and mushroom soup on top. Arrange carrots around stew. Bake for 2 hours. Arrange potatoes around edge. Bake for 1 hour longer. Yield: 4 to 6 servings.

Opal Cressy, Preceptor Lambda Phi
Desert Shores, California

WELSH CAWL

2½ cups coarsely chopped
   onions
6 cups chopped leeks
¼ cup butter
2½ pounds cubed beef
2 medium turnips,
   peeled, chopped
3 medium red potatoes,
   peeled, chopped

3 medium carrots, peeled
   chopped
8 cups water
8 beef bouillon cubes
1 small head cabbage,
   shredded
1 5-ounce package
   frozen Brussels sprouts
Salt and pepper to taste

Sauté onions and leeks in butter in skillet until brown. Add beef. Cook until brown. Add turnips, potatoes, carrots, water and bouillon; mix well. Reduce heat. Simmer for 45 minutes. Add cabbage. Simmer for 15 minutes or until beef is tender. Add Brussels sprouts. Simmer for 10 minutes. Season with salt and pepper. Yield: 10 servings.

Phyllis E. Gump, Xi Epsilon
Moberly, Missouri

FAJITA-STYLE STIR-FRY

2 tablespoons corn oil
1 pound sirloin steak,
   cut into thin strips
1 medium onion, cut into
   wedges
1 clove of garlic, minced

1 green bell pepper,
   cut into thin strips
⅔ cup picante salsa
8 flour tortillas, warmed
Avocado slices
Sour cream

Heat vegetable oil in wok or large skillet until hot. Add steak, onion, garlic and green pepper. Stir-fry for 3 to 4 minutes or until vegetables are tender-crisp. Add picante salsa. Stir-fry for 1 minute or until sauce is heated. Spoon ½ cup mixture onto each tortilla; top with avocado slices, sour cream and additional salsa. Yield: 4 servings.

Sue Troyer, Xi Beta Sigma
Dumfries, Virginia

TEX-MEX DELIGHT

1 envelope all-purpose
   meat marinade
1 16-ounce can tomatoes,
   chopped
1½ pounds round steak,
   thinly sliced
1 4-ounce can chopped
   green chilies
1 teaspoon ground cumin
1 teaspoon sugar
1 clove of garlic, minced

1 15-ounce can refried
   beans
2 cups cooked rice
Tortilla chips
½ cup sour cream
1 small tomato, seeded,
   chopped
1 cup shredded sharp
   Cheddar cheese
Shredded lettuce
Salsa

Combine dry meat marinade and undrained tomatoes in bowl. Add steak. Let stand for 10 to 15 minutes. Stir in

chilies, cumin, sugar and garlic. Simmer for 15 minutes, stirring occasionally. Stir in beans and rice. Cook until heated through. Serve over tortilla chips. Top with sour cream. Arrange tomatoes, Cheddar cheese and lettuce in rings around chips. Serve with salsa. Yield: 6 servings.

Sharon Fordahl, Preceptor Laureate Alpha Tau
Bremerton, Washington

THAT STUFF

2½ pounds stew beef
2 10-ounce cans
   mushroom soup
½ envelope dry onion
   soup mix

¾ cup dry vermouth
1 large onion, chopped
1 8-ounce can
   mushrooms, drained

Preheat oven to 325 degrees. Combine first 5 ingredients in large casserole; mix well. Top with mushrooms. Bake, covered, for 3 hours. Serve over rice, noodles or mashed potatoes. Yield: 6 to 8 servings.

Marion Mahalak, Xi Beta Xi
Alpena, Michigan

CHIPPED BEEF AND EGG CASSEROLE

8 ounces dried beef
3 slices bacon
1 4-ounce can
   mushrooms
¼ cup margarine
½ cup all-purpose flour

1 quart milk
¼ teaspoon pepper
16 eggs, beaten
¼ teaspoon salt
1 cup evaporated milk
¼ cup margarine

Sauté dried beef, bacon and mushrooms in ¼ cup margarine in skillet. Add next 3 ingredients. Stir until thickened. Scramble mixture of eggs, salt and evaporated milk in ¼ cup margarine in skillet. Alternate layers of sauce and eggs in buttered casserole, ending with sauce. Chill in refrigerator. Let stand at room temperature for 1 hour. Preheat oven to 300 degrees. Bake until bubbly. Yield: 10 servings.

Patty Murphy, Xi Alpha Alpha
Greensboro, North Carolina

CORNED BEEF AND VEGETABLES

½ cup wine vinegar
½ cup white vinegar
1 cup water
¼ cup sugar
1 tablespoon pickling
   spice
1 tablespoon whole cloves
2 teaspoons minced garlic

2 bay leaves
1 5-pound boneless beef
   brisket
2 heads cabbage, cut into
   halves
10 medium potatoes,
   peeled
10 carrots, peeled

Combine first 8 ingredients in bowl. Add brisket. Marinate in refrigerator for 8 hours, turning frequently. Place brisket in 8-quart saucepan. Add enough water to cover. Simmer for 4 hours or until tender. Remove to heatproof platter; cover with foil. Add vegetables to saucepan. Cook until vegetables are tender. Slice beef. Serve with vegetables. Yield: 10 servings.

Ruth Pendergraft, Xi Iota Eta
Aurora, Missouri

HOT AND SWEET CORNED BEEF

1 large piece corned beef
4 cloves of garlic
10 peppercorns
6 whole cloves
2 bay leaves
2 teaspoons pickling
  spice
½ bottle of maraschino
  cherry syrup (not juice)
Beer
½ to ¾ cup packed light
  brown sugar
Mustard

Preheat oven to 300 degrees. Place corned beef in roaster. Add next 6 ingredients and enough beer to cover. Roast, covered, for 3 to 4 hours or until tender, turning several times; drain and discard cooking liquid. Return beef to pan. Blend brown sugar and mustard to consistency of paste. Spoon over beef. Bake for 20 minutes. Let stand for 5 minutes before slicing. Serve with hot mustard, boiled potatoes and cabbage. Yield: 4 to 6 servings.

Dee Weybright, Xi Rho Eta
Santa Cruz, California

VEAL CUTLETS WITH MUSTARD SAUCE

8 2-ounce veal cutlets
⅓ cup all-purpose flour
2 eggs, slightly beaten
¾ cup dry bread crumbs
2 tablespoons butter
2 tablespoons corn oil
1 small onion, sliced
⅓ cup beef broth
1 tablespoon all-purpose
  flour
1 tablespoon Dijon-style
  mustard
½ teaspoon sugar
½ teaspoon salt
¼ teaspoon pepper
1 cup light cream

Flatten cutlets to ¼ inch between 2 sheets of waxed paper. Coat cutlets 1 at a time with ⅓ cup flour. Dip into eggs and coat with crumbs. Brown several at a time on both sides in mixture of butter and oil in skillet. Remove to serving platter; cover. Keep warm. Sauté onion in remaining butter and oil in skillet for 5 minutes or until tender. Stir in mixture of broth and 1 tablespoon flour and next 4 ingredients. Cook until thickened, stirring constantly. Stir in cream. Heat for 1 minute, stirring constantly. Pour over cutlets. Yield: 4 servings.

Delilah A. Ryan, Preceptor Pi
Laurel, Maryland

VEAL PARMESAN

1 package breaded veal
  cutlets
1 onion, chopped
1 green bell pepper,
  chopped
2 tablespoons olive oil
1 14-ounce can tomatoes,
  chopped
1 8-ounce can tomato
  sauce
½ teaspoon Italian
  seasoning
1 16-ounce package
  shredded mozzarella
  cheese

Preheat oven to 350 degrees. Prepare veal cutlets in microwave oven according to package directions. Sauté onion and green pepper in olive oil in skillet. Add tomatoes, tomato sauce and Italian seasoning. Layer cutlets, sauce mixture and cheese in 9x13-inch baking dish. Bake for 30 minutes. Yield: 5 to 6 servings.

Elizabeth Ann Dietz, Xi Mu
Louisville, Kentucky

VEAL SCALLOPINI

1½ pounds veal
All-purpose flour
2 tablespoons butter
2 tablespoons olive oil
1 clove of garlic, cut into
  halves
1 onion, sliced
8 ounces mushrooms
1 cup chicken broth
¼ cup dry white wine
½ cup tomato juice
1 tablespoon parsley
Dash of nutmeg

Dredge veal in flour. Melt butter and oil in skillet. Add garlic and veal. Cook until brown; remove from skillet. Add onion and mushrooms. Sauté for 5 minutes. Return veal to skillet. Add broth, wine, tomato juice, parsley and nutmeg. Simmer, covered, for 40 minutes. Serve with rice or noodles. Yield: 4 to 6 servings.

Carol S. Zumpano, Preceptor Gamma Nu
McMurray, Pennsylvania

WIENER SCHNITZEL

2 eggs
½ cup milk
4 veal steaks
½ cup all-purpose flour
½ cup cracker crumbs
Shortening
Salt and pepper to taste

Combine eggs and milk in bowl; mix well. Coat veal with flour. Dip in egg and milk mixture, then cracker crumbs. Brown in shortening in skillet. Season with salt and pepper. Yield: 4 servings.

Jane O'Mara, Xi Eta Lambda
Burlington, Kansas

A COMPLETE MEAL

1¼ pounds ground beef
Salt and pepper to taste
4 medium potatoes, sliced
5 carrots, chopped
1 medium onion, chopped
1 medium head cabbage,
  sliced
1 10-ounce can cream of
  chicken soup
6 to 8 slices cheese

Place ground beef in greased electric skillet. Season with salt and pepper. Layer potatoes, carrots, onion, cabbage and soup over ground beef. Arrange cheese on top. Cook, covered, on medium heat for 1½ hours. Yield: 6 to 8 servings.

Virginia Kesner, Gamma Nu
Romney, West Virginia

DINNER IN A CAN

4 slices bacon, cut into
  halves
2 pounds ground beef
Salt and pepper to taste
Barbecue sauce
2 stalks celery, cut into
  2-inch pieces
4 carrots, cut into 2-inch
  chunks
2 onions, cut into quarters
2 ears corn, cut into halves
Seasoned salt to taste
2 tablespoons butter

Arrange two pieces bacon in bottom of each of four 1-pound coffee cans. Pat ground beef to fit bottoms of cans. Season with salt and pepper. Place over bacon and brush with barbecue sauce. Top each with 2 pieces celery, carrots and onions; add piece of corn. Sprinkle with seasoned salt and dot with butter. Seal cans with foil. Cook on hot coals for 1 hour. May vary vegetables. Eat directly from can; throw cans away. Yield: 4 servings.

Betty M. Jumper, Preceptor Gamma Eta
Merritt Island, Florida

CREAMY BEEF TURNOVERS

8 ounces lean ground beef	Dash of pepper
½ cup finely chopped onion	4 ounces cream cheese, softened
1 hard-cooked egg, chopped	½ cup butter
½ teaspoon salt	1¾ cups all-purpose flour

Preheat oven to 400 degrees. Cook ground beef and onion in skillet until brown. Add egg, salt and pepper. Cut cream cheese and butter into flour in bowl until crumbly. Roll ½ at a time to ⅛-inch thickness. Cut into 2¾-inch rounds. Place 1 teaspoon ground beef mixture on each. Moisten edges with water; fold over and press with floured tines of fork to seal. Place on ungreased baking sheet. Bake for 12 to 15 minutes or until golden brown. Yield: 3 dozen.

Doris Daley Bartlett, Preceptor Eta
Chadron, Nebraska

BEEF IN COSTUME

1 4-pound pumpkin	1 teaspoon salt
1 pound lean ground beef	¼ teaspoon thyme
1 cup chopped onions	¼ teaspoon pepper
1 tablespoon corn oil	1 7-ounce can pitted
⅓ cup chopped red bell pepper	ripe olives
⅓ cup chopped green bell pepper	1 8-ounce can tomato sauce
1 clove of garlic, minced	2 eggs, beaten
	1 tablespoon corn oil

Preheat oven to 350 degrees. Cut top from pumpkin; remove seed and fibers. Wash pumpkin inside and out. Simmer in salted water to cover in large saucepan for 25 minutes or until almost tender; drain. Set pumpkin aside. Brown ground beef with onions in 1 tablespoon oil in skillet, stirring frequently; drain. Add peppers and garlic. Cook for 1 minute; remove from heat. Stir in next 5 ingredients. Spoon into pumpkin; replace pumpkin lid. Place in baking pan. Brush pumpkin with 1 tablespoon oil. Bake for 1 hour. Let stand for 10 minutes. Cut into wedges. Yield: 8 servings.

Loretta Hanft, Xi Theta
Pocatello, Idaho

BIEROCKS

2 pounds cabbage, chopped	2 tablespoons shortening
2 large onions, finely chopped	1 pound ground beef
	Salt and pepper to taste
	1 package hot roll mix

Preheat oven to 350 degrees. Simmer cabbage and onions in shortening in covered saucepan until tender. Brown ground beef in skillet, stirring until crumbly. Mix into cabbage mixture. Prepare hot roll mix according to package directions. Roll to ¼-inch thickness on floured surface. Cut into 6-inch squares. Place 1 tablespoon filling on each square. Fold corners to center; seal. Place seam side down on greased baking sheet. Let rise for 15 minutes. Bake for 25 minutes or until golden brown. Yield: 4 to 6 servings.

Leafa V. Blount, Preceptor Omicron
Dallas, Texas

BROCCOLI AND BEEF WELLINGTON

1 pound ground beef	¼ teaspoon salt
1 9-ounce package chopped broccoli, thawed, drained	¼ teaspoon pepper
	2 8-ounce packages refrigerator crescent rolls
1 cup shredded mozzarella cheese	1 egg, beaten
½ cup chopped onion	Poppy seed to taste
½ cup sour cream	

Preheat oven to 375 degrees. Brown ground beef in skillet, stirring until crumbly; drain. Add broccoli, cheese, onion, sour cream, salt and pepper. Simmer for 10 minutes. Separate roll dough into 4 long rectangles. Place 2 rectangles on ungreased baking sheet overlapping long sides ½ inch; seal edge and perforations. Press to 7x13-inch rectangle. Spoon half the ground beef mixture in 3-inch strip down center of rectangle. Fold sides over to enclose filling; seal edge and ends. Repeat with remaining ingredients. Brush with egg; sprinkle with poppy seed. Bake for 18 to 22 minutes or until deep golden brown. Yield: 6 to 8 servings.

Linda Nulf, Xi Alpha Beta
LaPorte, Indiana

STUFFED CABBAGE ROLLS

1 pound ground beef	¼ teaspoon pepper
8 ounces ground pork	1 head cabbage, cored
3 cups cooked rice	1 tablespoon butter
1 teaspoon sugar	1 cup hot water
1 onion, chopped	1 10-ounce can cream of tomato soup
1 teaspoon salt	

Preheat oven to 350 degrees. Combine first 7 ingredients in bowl; mix well. Parboil cabbage for several minutes. Separate leaves. Place about ½ cup ground beef mixture on each cabbage leaf; roll up. Place in baking dish. Dot each with butter. Combine water and soup in bowl. Pour over rolls. Bake for 1 hour. Yield: 6 servings.

Beverly Winans, Preceptor Gamma Omicron
McClure, Illinois

Frances Kucera, Laureate Omicron, Eugene, Oregon keeps hot dishes hot when going to a potluck, by wrapping in newspapers, sliding into a grocery bag and folding and taping down ends of the bag.

CAVATINI

1 to 2 pounds ground beef
1 onion, chopped
½ cup chopped green bell pepper
1 32-ounce jar garden-style spaghetti sauce
1 4-ounce package pepperoni, chopped
1 4-ounce can mushrooms
1 cup large shell macaroni
1 cup curly macaroni
½ cup mostaccioli
½ cup rigotoni
1 pound mozzarella cheese, shredded
Parmesan cheese to taste

Brown ground beef and onion in skillet, stirring until crumbly; drain. Mix in spaghetti sauce, pepperoni and mushrooms. Cook pastas using package directions; drain. Layer pastas, mozzarella cheese and sauce ½ at a time in greased 9x13-inch baking pan. Top with Parmesan cheese. Bake for 30 minutes. Yield: 6 to 8 servings.

Joan Koster, Xi Gamma Pi
Carroll, Iowa

SKIER'S CHILI

3 pounds ground beef
1 cup chopped green bell pepper
1 cup chopped onion
2 cloves of garlic, crushed
2 teaspoons salt
1 teaspoon red pepper flakes
1 tablespoon sugar
3 to 4 tablespoons chili powder
1 tablespoon oregano
3 16-ounce cans tomatoes
2 16-ounce cans red kidney beans

Brown ground beef with green pepper, onion and garlic in skillet, stirring until crumbly; drain. Add seasonings and tomatoes. Simmer, covered, for 1 hour. Stir in beans. Simmer for 10 to 15 minutes longer. Serve with corn bread. Yield: 12 servings.

Mary Alma Shook, Iota Chi
Wagoner, Oklahoma

SOUR CREAM CHILI BAKE

1 pound ground beef
1 15-ounce can pinto beans
1 10-ounce can hot enchilada sauce
1 8-ounce can tomato sauce
1 tablespoon onion flakes
1 cup shredded Cheddar cheese
1 6-ounce package corn chips
1 cup sour cream
½ cup shredded cheese

Preheat oven to 375 degrees. Brown ground beef in skillet until crumbly; drain. Stir in beans, enchilada sauce, tomato sauce, cheese and onion. Reserve 1 cup corn chips. Crush remaining chips; stir into ground beef mixture. Spoon into 1½-quart baking dish. Bake for 30 minutes. Spoon sour cream over casserole; sprinkle reserved chips and cheese around edge. Bake for 2 to 3 minutes longer. Yield: 6 servings.

Juanita Norwood, Laureate Alpha Nu
Lee's Summit, Missouri

UPSILON OMEGA CHILI COOK-OFF

1 pound pinto beans
1 pound coarsely ground beef
1 pound ground venison
2½ cups chopped yellow onion
3 12-ounce cans beer
3 tablespoons ground cumin
¼ cup chili powder
7 cups V-8 juice
1 cup instant mashed potato flakes

Soak beans in water to cover overnight; drain. Brown ground beef and venison in skillet, stirring until crumbly; drain. Add onion. Cook until transparent. Add beans and remaining ingredients. Simmer for 5 hours. Yield: 8 to 10 servings.

Teresa A. Long, Upsilon Omega
Sikeston, Missouri

CORN BREAD SKILLET CASSEROLE

2 eggs, slightly beaten
1 cup yellow cornmeal
2 teaspoons soda
1 teaspoon salt
1 17-ounce can cream-style corn
1 cup milk
¼ cup corn oil
1 pound ground beef
2 cups shredded Cheddar cheese
1 large onion, chopped
2 to 4 jalapeño peppers, finely chopped

Preheat oven to 350 degrees. Combine first 7 ingredients in bowl; mix well. Brown ground beef in skillet, stirring frequently; drain well. Pour half the cornmeal mixture into greased 10½-inch cast iron skillet. Layer with ground beef, cheese, onion, peppers and remaining batter. Bake for 45 to 50 minutes. Let stand for 5 minutes before serving. Yield: 8 servings.

Carole J. Hollifield, Xi
Sullivan, Indiana

EASY DINNER CASSEROLE

1 pound ground sirloin
1 envelope onion soup mix
1 green bell pepper, chopped
Dash of pepper
1 cup shredded Cheddar cheese
1 cup uncooked rice
1 cup shredded Cheddar cheese
1 16-ounce can stewed tomatoes
1½ cups water

Preheat oven to 350 degrees. Mix ground sirloin and soup mix in bowl. Press lightly into 9x13-inch baking dish. Layer remaining ingredients in order listed over top. Bake for 1½ hours. Yield: 6 to 8 servings.

Donna Jean Martin, Preceptor Alpha
Peoria, Illinois

SKILLET ENCHILADA

1 pound ground beef
1 4-ounce can chopped green chilies
1 10-ounce can cream of mushroom soup
1 16-ounce can enchilada sauce
12 tortillas
1 cup shredded longhorn cheese
1 8-ounce can black olives, drained

Combine first 4 ingredients in electric skillet in order listed. Simmer for 20 minutes. Roll tortillas and place under sauce. Sprinkle cheese over top. Let melt and serve. Sprinkle with black olives if desired.
Yield: 8 to 12 servings.

Karen Foutz, Xi Beta Iota
Cortez, Colorado

EGGPLANT PARMIGIANA

½ cup chopped onion
1 clove of garlic, crushed
8 ounces ground chuck
2 tablespoons olive oil
1 35-ounce can Italian tomatoes
1 8-ounce can tomato paste
2 teaspoons dried oregano leaves
1 teaspoon dried basil leaves
1½ teaspoons salt
¼ teaspoon pepper
1 tablespoon light brown sugar
1 1½-pound eggplant
2 eggs, slightly beaten
1 tablespoon water
½ cup Italian-flavored dry bread crumbs
½ cup Parmesan cheese
⅓ cup olive oil
8 ounces mozzarella cheese, sliced
¾ cup Parmesan cheese

Preheat oven to 350 degrees. Sauté onion, garlic and ground chuck in olive oil in large skillet for 15 minutes. Add next 7 ingredients. Bring to a boil, stirring constantly; reduce heat. Simmer, covered, for 45 minutes, stirring occasionally. Wash eggplant; do not peel. Cut crosswise into ¼-inch slices. Beat eggs and water in pie plate with fork. Combine bread crumbs with Parmesan cheese on waxed paper. Dip eggplant slices into egg mixture; coat with crumb mixture. Cook several slices at a time in 1 tablespoon olive oil in skillet until golden brown and crisp, adding oil as necessary. Drain on paper towels. Layer eggplant, mozzarella cheese and ¾ cup Parmesan cheese ½ at a time in greased 9x13-inch baking dish. Bake for 25 minutes. Yield: 8 servings.

Dorris Gronquist, Laureate Alpha Alpha
Pueblo, Colorado

GIANT EMPAÑADAS

1 pound lean ground beef
1 cup chopped onion
1 cup chopped green bell pepper
1 14-ounce can tomatoes
1 tablespoon chili powder
1 teaspoon cumin
1 teaspoon salt
1 teaspoon pepper
2 refrigerated ready-to-use pie crusts
1 egg yolk, beaten
1 tablespoon water

Preheat oven to 400 degrees. Sauté ground beef, onion and green pepper in skillet for 5 minutes; drain. Stir in tomatoes and spices. Simmer, uncovered, for 15 minutes, stirring occasionally. Place 1 unfolded pie crust at 1 end of greased baking sheet. Spoon half the ground beef mixture on half the pastry round, leaving 1-inch border. Fold pastry over filling; press edge to seal. Brush with mixture of egg yolk and water. Repeat with remaining crust and ground beef mixture at other end of baking sheet. Bake for 20 minutes or until golden. Yield: 4 servings.

Bertie Farabee, Preceptor Alpha Tau
Haysville, Kansas

FIASCO

2 pounds ground beef
2 8-ounce cans tomato sauce
1 envelope chili seasoning mix
1 8-ounce can whole kernel corn
1 cup minute rice
1 10-ounce can Cheddar cheese soup
1 can Ro-Tel tomatoes
1 pound Velveeta cheese
1 2-pound package corn chips, crushed
1 medium head lettuce, shredded
3 medium tomatoes, chopped
1 bunch green onions, chopped
1 4-ounce can black olives, chopped
1 cup chopped pecans

Brown ground beef in skillet, stirring until crumbly; drain. Add tomato sauce, seasoning mix, corn, rice and 2 tomato sauce cans water. Simmer for 30 minutes or until water is absorbed. Heat soup, Ro-Tel tomatoes and Velveeta cheese in saucepan until smooth. Layer chips, chili mixture, lettuce, tomatoes, green onions, soup mixture, black olives and pecans on serving plate.
Yield: 8 to 10 servings.

Cher Wigley, Theta Mu
Chickasha, Oklahoma

GROUND BEEF AND NOODLE CASSEROLE

1 pound ground beef
½ cup chopped celery
½ cup chopped onions
1 4-ounce can green chilies
1 16-ounce can mixed vegetables
Salt and pepper to taste
1 10-ounce can mushroom soup
1 8-ounce package noodles, cooked
Bread crumbs
Butter

Preheat oven to 350 degrees. Brown ground beef in skillet, stirring frequently; drain. Add vegetables and seasonings; mix well. Combine with soup and noodles in 9x13-inch casserole. Sprinkle with crumbs; dot with butter. Bake for 30 minutes. Yield: 10 servings.

Ethel E. Courier, Preceptor Delta Lambda
El Paso, Texas

GROUND BEEF CASSEROLE SUPREME

1½ pounds ground beef
1 medium onion, finely chopped
1 cup chopped celery
1 small package stove-top stuffing mix
¾ cup margarine
1⅓ cups hot water
1 10-ounce can cream of celery soup
¼ cup water
½ to 1 cup shredded cheese

Preheat oven to 350 degrees. Brown ground beef with onion and celery in skillet. Combine stuffing mix, margarine and 1⅓ cups hot water in bowl; mix well. Layer ½ the ground beef mixture, all the stuffing and remaining ground beef in 2-quart casserole. Blend soup with ¼ cup water in bowl; pour over casserole. Sprinkle cheese over top. Bake for 30 minutes. Yield: 8 servings.

Gladys Kozisek, Preceptor Alpha
Lincoln, Nebraska

KEFTETHAKIA

3 thick slices white bread	3 tablespoons mint leaves
Milk	3 tablespoons parsley
2½ pounds ground beef	⅛ teaspoon dill
1 cup finely chopped	Salt and pepper to taste
onions	All-purpose flour
2 eggs	Vegetable oil
¼ teaspoon oregano	

Combine bread and enough milk to moisten in bowl; drain and squeeze dry. Combine with ground beef, onions, eggs and seasonings; mix well. Shape into small balls. Coat with flour. Brown in a small amount of oil in skillet; drain. Yield: 10 servings.

Anna J. Floyd, Laureate Alpha Alpha
Pueblo, Colorado

AMERICANIZATION OF LASAGNA

1 pound ground chuck	¼ teaspoon pepper
2 cloves of garlic	½ teaspoon sugar
2 tablespoons olive oil	1 teaspoon oregano
1 envelope dry onion soup	8 ounces lasagna noodles
mix	1 tablespoon olive oil
1½ cups water	1 pound ricotta cheese
1 16-ounce can tomato	12 ounces mozzarella
sauce	cheese, shredded
1 12-ounce can tomato	2 tablespoons Parmesan
paste	cheese
½ teaspoon salt	

Preheat oven to 350 degrees. Brown ground chuck with garlic in 2 tablespoons hot olive oil in skillet. Stir in soup mix, 1½ cups water, tomato sauce, tomato paste, salt, pepper, sugar and oregano. Simmer, covered, for 30 minutes. Cook lasagna noodles using package directions; drain. Place in cold water with 1 tablespoon olive oil to prevent sticking. Spoon 2 tablespoons sauce into 8x12-inch baking pan. Alternate layers of noodles, sauce, ricotta cheese and mozzarella cheese ⅓ at a time in prepared dish. Sprinkle with Parmesan cheese. Bake for 30 minutes. Let stand for several minutes before serving. Yield: 8 to 10 servings.

Pat Duffield, Preceptor Nu
Orlando, Florida

MAKE-AHEAD LASAGNA ROLLS

16 lasagna noodles	2 tablespoons dried
¾ pound ground beef	parsley
¾ pound ground turkey	1 teaspoon dried basil
1 large onion, chopped	1 cup shredded
1 egg, beaten	mozzarella cheese
1 12-ounce container	2 cups spaghetti sauce
small curd cottage	¼ cup dry red wine
cheese	Basil and oregano to taste
½ cup Parmesan cheese	

Cook lasagna noodles in boiling, salted water for 10 to 12 minutes or until tender; drain and rinse with cold water. Cook ground beef and turkey with onion in skillet until brown; drain. Combine egg, cottage cheese, Parmesan cheese, parsley and 1 teaspoon basil in large bowl; stir in ground beef mixture. Spread each lasagna noodle with ¼ cup mixture; roll as for jelly roll. Place seam side down on baking sheet. May freeze until firm and store in freezer bag. Preheat oven to 400 degrees. Arrange in greased 9x13-inch baking pan. Sprinkle with mozzarella cheese. Pour mixture of spaghetti sauce, red wine, basil and oregano over roll-ups. Bake for 1 hour. Yield: 8 servings.

Priscilla Culkowski, Xi Omicron
Alexandria, Virginia

MICROWAVE LASAGNA

1 pound ground beef	1 teaspoon basil
1 medium onion, chopped	1 teaspoon oregano
1 clove of garlic, minced	½ cup chopped celery
2 6-ounce cans tomato	½ cup sliced mushrooms
paste	8 lasagna noodles
1 14-ounce can tomatoes	2 cups dry-curd cottage
1 teaspoon salt	cheese
⅛ teaspoon pepper	2 cups shredded
1 bay leaf	mozzarella cheese
1 tablespoon parsley	½ cup Parmesan cheese

Combine ground beef, onion and garlic in casserole. Microwave on High for 3 to 5 minutes, stirring 2 to 3 times to break up ground beef; drain. Add tomato paste, tomatoes, seasonings, celery and mushrooms. Microwave, uncovered, on Medium-High for 10 minutes. Cook the noodles using package directions. Layer ⅓ of the sauce, half the noodles, half the cottage cheese, half the mozzarella cheese and ⅓ of the Parmesan cheese in 8x12-inch baking dish. Repeat layers. Top with remaining sauce and Parmesan cheese. Cover with waxed paper. Microwave on Medium-High for 10 to 12 minutes. Let stand for 10 minutes. Yield: 6 to 8 servings.

Kathy Walls, Theta Theta
Fayetteville, Georgia

WHITE LASAGNA

1 pound ground beef	½ teaspoon pepper
3 tablespoons margarine	¼ teaspoon nutmeg
½ cup chopped onion	2 eggs, slightly beaten
1 clove of garlic, minced	3 cups ricotta cheese
1 pound mushrooms	1 cup shredded
⅓ cup parsley flakes	mozzarella cheese
¼ cup melted margarine	4 ounces blue cheese,
6 tablespoons all-purpose	crumbled
flour	½ cup Parmesan cheese
2 cups half and half	Paprika
2 cups milk	1 8-ounce package
½ cup dry white wine	lasagna noodles
1 teaspoon salt	

Preheat oven to 375 degrees. Brown ground beef in 3 tablespoons margarine in skillet, stirring until crumbly. Add onion and garlic. Sauté for 5 minutes. Add mushrooms and parsley. Cook for 5 minutes. Set aside. Blend ¼ cup melted margarine and flour in saucepan. Cook for 5 minutes, stirring constantly. Stir in half and half, milk and wine. Cook until thickened, stirring constantly. Stir in seasonings and ground beef mixture. Combine eggs, ricotta, mozzarella and blue cheeses in bowl. Add half the Parmesan cheese; mix well. Spoon a small amount of sauce into 9x13-inch baking pan. Layer noodles, cheese mixture and sauce ½ at a time in prepared pan. Sprinkle with remaining Parmesan cheese and paprika. Bake for 35 to 40 minutes. Let stand for 10 minutes before cutting. Yield: 8 servings.

Catherine Kiritsy, Gamma Omega
Spencer, Massachusetts

MACARONI BAKE

1 pound ground beef	¼ cup all-purpose flour
1 tablespoon butter	2½ cups milk
1 cup sliced mushrooms	1½ cups shredded
1 medium onion, chopped	Jarlsberg cheese
½ cup chopped red bell	3 cups cooked rotelle
pepper	pasta
1 teaspoon salt	1 8-ounce can tomato
⅛ teaspoon pepper	sauce
1 16-ounce can tomatoes,	½ cup shredded Jarlsberg
chopped	cheese
¼ cup butter, melted	

Preheat oven to 350 degrees. Brown ground beef in 1 tablespoon butter in skillet. Add next 6 ingredients. Cook until tender, stirring frequently. Set aside. Blend melted butter and flour in saucepan. Cook for several minutes, stirring constantly; remove from heat. Stir in milk gradually. Cook until thickened, stirring constantly. Add 1½ cups cheese. Cook until cheese melts, stirring constantly. Stir in pasta. Alternate layers of pasta and ground beef mixtures in buttered 2-quart baking dish. Pour tomato sauce over top. Bake for 35 minutes. Top with ½ cup cheese. Bake for 5 minutes longer. Yield: 6 to 8 servings.

Mendy Ritzman, Zeta Iota
Creston, Iowa

CRANBERRY MEATBALLS

2 pounds ground beef	1 16-ounce can jellied
1 cup cornflake crumbs	cranberry sauce
⅓ cup parsley flakes	1 12-ounce bottle of
2 eggs	chili sauce
2 tablespoons soy sauce	⅓ cup catsup
½ teaspoon pepper	2 tablespoons light brown
½ teaspoon garlic powder	sugar
2 tablespoons instant	1 tablespoon lemon juice
minced onion	

Preheat oven to 350 degrees. Combine first 8 ingredients in bowl; mix well. Shape into meatballs; arrange in 9x13-inch baking pan. Mix cranberry sauce, chili sauce, catsup, brown sugar and lemon juice in saucepan. Heat until blended, stirring constantly. Pour over meatballs. Bake, uncovered, for 30 minutes. Yield: 6 servings.

Maurine McManamy, Alpha
Council Bluffs, Iowa

FONDUE MEATBALLS

1 to 1½ pounds ground	1 teaspoon Italian
beef	seasoning
¾ cup oats	2 10-count packages
1 egg	refrigerator biscuits
¼ cup finely chopped	Oil for frying
onion	Spaghetti sauce
Salt and pepper to taste	Grated Parmesan cheese

Combine first 4 ingredients and seasonings in bowl; mix well. Shape into small meatballs. Separate each biscuit into thirds. Wrap each meatball in biscuit dough. Place on fondue fork. Fry in hot oil in fondue pot until golden brown. Dip into hot spaghetti sauce. Sprinkle with Parmesan cheese. Yield: 60 meatballs.

Sharon E. Race, Xi Beta Tau
Little Valley, New York

MEATBALLS AND YORKSHIRE PUDDING

1½ pounds ground beef	1 tablespoon water
1 envelope dry onion soup	1½ cups sifted
mix	all-purpose flour
2 tablespoons chopped	1½ teaspoons baking
parsley	powder
⅛ teaspoon pepper	1 teaspoon salt
¼ teaspoon poultry	4 eggs, beaten
seasoning	1½ cups milk
¼ cup chili sauce	3 tablespoons melted
1 egg, slightly beaten	butter or margarine

Preheat oven to 350 degrees. Combine first 6 ingredients in bowl; mix well. Add mixture of 1 egg and water; mix well. Shape into 24 balls. Place in greased 9x13-inch baking dish. Sift dry ingredients together. Combine eggs, milk and margarine in bowl; mix well. Add flour; beat until blended. Pour over meatballs. Bake for 50 minutes or until golden. Yield: 8 to 12 servings.

Mary Jo Pittsenbager, Xi Iota Theta
Gallatin, Missouri

GREEN CHILI MEAT LOAF

1½ pounds ground beef	3 tablespoons dried onion
1 cup undrained canned	flakes
tomatoes	1 4-ounce can green
1 cup soft bread crumbs	chilies, drained
1¼ teaspoons salt	¼ teaspoon garlic salt

Preheat oven to 375 degrees. Combine all ingredients in bowl; mix well. Shape into loaf in 5x9-inch loaf pan. Bake for 1 hour. Yield: 6 to 8 servings.

Dixie Short, Xi Beta Iota
Cortez, Colorado

GROUND BEEF ROLL

2 pounds ground beef	1 onion, chopped
1 onion, chopped	3 stalks celery, finely
½ cup catsup	chopped
1 teaspoon salt	1 teaspoon poultry
1 egg	seasoning
3 cups bread cubes	Salt and pepper to taste

Preheat oven to 350 degrees. Combine first 5 ingredients in bowl; mix well. Pat into 12x15-inch rectangle on foil-lined surface. Mix bread cubes and remaining ingredients in bowl. Layer over ground beef. Roll as for jelly roll. Place in large baking pan. Bake for 1 hour.
Yield: 8 servings.

Judy Sullivan, Preceptor Xi
Phillips, Nebraksa

LEMONY BARBECUED MEAT LOAF

1½ pounds ground chuck	⅓ cup packed light brown
4 slices day-old bread,	sugar
cubed	½ cup catsup
¼ cup lemon juice	1 teaspoon dry mustard
¼ cup minced onion	¼ teaspoon allspice
1 egg, slightly beaten	¼ teaspoon cloves
2 teaspoons seasoned salt	6 thin lemon slices

Preheat oven to 350 degrees. Combine first 6 ingredients in large bowl; mix well. Shape into 6 small loaves. Place in greased baking pan. Bake for 15 minutes. Combine brown sugar, catsup and spices in saucepan. Heat until brown sugar dissolves. Place lemon slice on each loaf. Pour sauce over top. Bake for 30 minutes.
Yield: 6 servings.

Janet Jensen, Preceptor Delta
Belle Fourche, South Dakota

MINI MEAT LOAVES AND VEGETABLES

1½ pounds ground beef	6 small potatoes, thinly
½ teaspoon salt	sliced
1 egg	1 16-ounce package
1 8-ounce can tomato	frozen mixed broccoli,
sauce	corn and red pepper,
½ teaspoon Italian	thawed, drained
seasoning	Salt and pepper to taste
1 3-ounce can	
French-fried onions	

Preheat oven to 375 degrees. Combine ground beef, salt, egg, ½ can tomato sauce, Italian seasoning and ½ can French-fried onions; mix well. Shape into loaves; place in 9x13-inch baking dish. Place potatoes around loaves. Bake, covered, for 35 minutes. Place broccoli mixture around loaves; mix with potatoes. Season with salt and pepper. Top loaves with remaining tomato sauce. Bake, uncovered, for 15 minutes. Top loaves with remaining French-fried onions. Bake, uncovered, for 5 minutes longer. Yield: 3 to 6 servings.

Tracy Lynn Hillman, Beta Phi
Perryton, Texas

MEAT LOAF ROLL

1 10-ounce package	¼ teaspoon pepper
frozen chopped broccoli	¼ teaspoon oregano
2 pounds ground beef	leaves
2 eggs	1 teaspoon salt
¾ cup soft bread crumbs	1 3-ounce package
¼ cup catsup	sliced ham
¼ cup milk	3 3x3-inch slices
½ teaspoon salt	mozzarella cheese

Preheat oven to 350 degrees. Rinse broccoli under cold running water to separate; drain. Combine ground beef, eggs, bread crumbs, catsup, milk, ½ teaspoon salt, pepper and oregano in bowl; mix well. Pat into 10x12-inch rectangle on 15x18-inch foil. Spread broccoli on ground beef to within ½ inch of edges. Sprinkle with 1 teaspoon salt. Arrange ham on broccoli. Roll as for jelly roll from 10-inch side. Press edge and ends to seal. Place on rack in shallow roasting pan. Bake, uncovered, for 1¼ hours. Overlap cheese on top. Bake until cheese begins to melt.
Yield: 6 to 8 servings.

Janis Nicholson, Gamma Nu
Springfield, West Virginia

PIZZA BEEF ROLLS

1 pound ground beef	1 small onion, chopped
¼ cup fine bread crumbs	1 6-ounce can tomato
1 egg	paste
2 tablespoons Parmesan	2 cups tomato juice
cheese	2 teaspoons Italian
½ cup tomato juice	seasoning
Salt and pepper	Salt and pepper to taste
6 lasagna noodles, cooked	1 cup shredded
3 tablespoons corn oil	mozzarella cheese

Preheat oven to 350 degrees. Combine first 7 ingredients in bowl; mix well. Shape into 12 balls. Cut lasagna noodles into halves; wrap around meatballs. Place in buttered baking dish. Combine oil, onion, tomato paste, juice and seasonings in bowl; mix well. Pour over rolls. Bake, covered, for 40 minutes. Sprinkle with cheese. Bake for 5 minutes longer. Yield: 4 to 6 servings.

Pat Jacoby, Rho Chi
Highland, Illinois

SICILIAN MEAT ROLL

2 eggs, beaten	2 pounds lean ground
¾ cup soft bread crumbs	beef
½ cup tomato juice	8 thin slices boiled ham
2 tablespoons parsley	6 ounces mozzarella
½ teaspoon oregano	cheese, shredded
¼ teaspoon salt	3 slices mozzarella cheese,
¼ teaspoon pepper	cut into wedges
1 clove of garlic, minced	

Preheat oven to 350 degrees. Combine first 9 ingredients in bowl; mix well. Pat into 10×12-inch rectangle on waxed paper. Layer ham and shredded cheese on top. Roll up meat from short end, using paper to lift; seal edges and ends. Place roll seam side down in baking pan. Bake at 350 degrees for 1¼ hours until done. Place cheese wedges over top of roll; return to oven for about 5 minutes or until cheese melts. Yield: 8 servings.

Pat Nelson, Beta
Springfield, Missouri

TACO MEAT LOAF

1½ pounds ground beef	1 envelope dry taco
1 onion, chopped	seasoning mix
1 cup tortilla chips	1 4-ounce package
1 32-ounce jar spaghetti	shredded Cheddar
sauce	cheese

Preheat oven to 350 degrees. Combine first 3 ingredients in bowl; mix well. Add enough spaghetti sauce to make of desired consistency. Pat ¼ inch thick on waxed paper. Sprinkle with taco seasoning and cheese. Roll as for jelly roll. Place in shallow baking dish. Pour remaining spaghetti sauce on top. Bake for 1 hour. Yield: 6 servings.

Devera D. Gladfelter, Mu Beta
Huntingdon, Pennsylvania

EASY MEXICAN CASSEROLE

1 pound ground beef	1 12-ounce package corn
1 8-ounce can tomato	chips
sauce	1 4-ounce package
1 envelope dry taco	shredded Cheddar
seasoning mix	cheese
1 16-ounce can refried	Taco sauce
beans	Sour cream

Preheat oven to 350 degrees. Brown ground beef in 10-inch skillet, stirring frequently; drain. Stir in ½ cup tomato sauce and taco seasoning; set aside. Combine refried beans with remaining tomato sauce in bowl. Line 2-quart casserole with ¾ of the corn chips. Layer ground beef mixture and bean mixture on top. Bake for 25 minutes. Sprinkle cheese and remaining crushed corn chips on top. Bake for 5 minutes longer. Serve with taco sauce and sour cream. Yield: 6 servings.

Eileen Peitsch, Epsilon Beta
Palm Bay, Florida

BINDERBURGERS

3 pounds ground beef	¼ cup butter
2 eggs, slightly beaten	2 10-ounce cans cream of
3 slices bread, crumbled	mushroom soup
20 slices bacon	2 4-ounce cans sliced
10 slices onion	mushrooms
10 slices tomato	

Preheat oven to 375 degrees. Combine ground beef, eggs and bread in bowl; mix well. Shape into 20 patties. Cross 2 slices bacon on 10 patties; add onion and tomato slices. Top with remaining patties; seal edges together. Fold

ends of crossed bacon strips over top patties; secure with toothpicks. Brown in butter in skillet. Place in baking pan. Top with soup and mushrooms. Bake until bubbly. Yield: 10 servings.

Donetta M. Robben, Theta Sigma
Hays, Kansas

BRATENBURGERS

3 slices dry bread	1 tablespoon butter
½ cup hot water	½ cup cider vinegar
1 pound ground beef	1½ cups water
2 tablespoons finely	12 whole cloves
chopped onion	6 bay leaves
1 egg	8 gingersnaps
2 teaspoons salt	

Soften bread in hot water in bowl. Add next 4 ingredients; mix well. Shape into patties. Brown in butter in skillet. Pour mixture of remaining ingredients over patties. Simmer, covered, for 1 hour. Remove bay leaf. Yield: 4 servings.

Dorothy E. Carstens, Laureate Alpha Beta
Colorado Springs, Colorado

HOBO BURGERS

1½ pounds ground beef	1 4-ounce can sliced
Salt and pepper to taste	mushrooms, drained
½ cup shredded Cheddar	4 slices bacon
cheese	Sandwich buns
½ cup shredded Swiss	
cheese	

Preheat coals. Combine ground beef, salt and pepper in bowl. Roll into 8 patties between waxed paper. Place cheese and mushrooms in center of 4 patties. Top with remaining patties. Press around edges to seal. Wrap each patty with bacon; secure with toothpick. Grill over hot coals for 14 minutes or to desired degree of doneness. Serve on buns. Yield: 4 servings.

Anna M. Handsake, Omicron Omega
Bettendorf, Iowa

MEAT LOAF PATTIES

1½ pounds ground beef	½ cup milk
1 stack crackers, crushed	8 slices bacon, cut into
2 eggs	halves
½ cup finely chopped	¼ cup (or more) catsup
celery	1 package Rice-A-Roni,
¼ cup chopped onion	cooked
Salt and pepper to taste	1 to 2 cups long grain
	rice, cooked

Preheat oven to 325 degrees. Mix first 7 ingredients in bowl. Shape into 16 patties. Wrap each with ½ slice bacon; secure with toothpick. Place in greased baking dish. Brush with catsup. Add a small amount of water; cover with foil. Bake for 2 hours. Serve over mixture of Rice-A-Roni and rice. Yield: 15 to 16 servings.

Verdell Monson, Xi Zeta Kappa
Rock Rapids, Iowa

STUFFED PLANTATION PEPPERS

1 pound ground beef
1 cup chopped onion
⅛ teaspoon minced garlic
2 teaspoons chili powder
1 teaspoon salt
½ teaspoon pepper
1 16-ounce can corn
2 10-ounce cans tomato
   soup
8 ounces Velveeta cheese
1½ cups cooked long
   grain white rice
8 medium green bell
   peppers

Preheat oven to 350 degrees. Cook ground beef with onion and garlic in skillet, stirring until crumbly. Add seasonings, undrained corn and soup. Simmer, covered, for 10 minutes. Add chopped cheese. Cook over low heat until cheese melts, stirring frequently. Stir in rice. Cool. Cut green peppers into quarters. Remove membrane. Cook in boiling, salted water in large saucepan for 3 minutes or until tender. Drain and cool. Place peppers in 9x13-inch baking dish. Pour ground beef mixture over top. Bake, uncovered, for 30 to 40 minutes.
Yield: 8 to 10 servings.

Phyllis Peterson, Preceptor Gamma Epsilon
Topeka, Kansas

GROUND BEEF CORN PONE PIE

1 pound ground beef
⅓ cup chopped onion
1 tablespoon shortening
¾ teaspoon salt
1 teaspoon Worcestershire
   sauce
1 to 2 cups canned
   tomatoes
1 to 2 cups canned kidney
   beans, drained
1 cup corn bread batter

Preheat oven to 425 degrees. Brown ground beef with onion in shortening in skillet, stirring until crumbly. Add seasonings and tomatoes. Simmer, covered, for 15 minutes. Add kidney beans. Pour into greased 1½-quart casserole. Top with corn bread batter; spread evenly with knife. Bake for 20 minutes. Yield: 6 to 8 servings.

Edith E. Heckler, Xi Theta Zeta
Panama City, Florida

MEXICAN PIZZA

1 pound ground beef
1 medium onion, chopped
2 cloves of garlic, minced
1 8-ounce jar picante
   sauce
6 flour tortillas
2 tablespoons melted
   butter
1 16-ounce can refried
   beans with green chilies
2 cups shredded Cheddar
   cheese
2 cups shredded Monterey
   Jack cheese
1 avocado, sliced

Preheat broiler. Brown ground beef with onion in skillet, stirring until crumbly; drain. Add garlic and picante sauce. Brush tortillas on both sides with butter. Place in 12-inch pizza pan, overlapping to cover bottom. Broil until lightly browned and crisp. Spread with beans; top with ground beef and cheeses. Reduce temperature to 450 degrees. Bake for 10 minutes. Garnish with avocado slices. Serve with sour cream, guacamole or taco sauce. Yield: 8 servings.

Gail M. Copa, Delta Mu
Miami, Florida

MEXICAN SOMBRERO PIE

1⅓ cups all-purpose flour
¼ cup yellow cornmeal
½ teaspoon salt
½ cup shortening
¼ cup cold water
1 pound lean ground beef
1 4-ounce jar pimento,
   chopped, drained
1 4-ounce can chopped
   green chilies, drained
3 tablespoons onion
   flakes
2 teaspoons instant beef
   bouillon
1 to 2 tablespoons chili
   powder
½ teaspoon basil
¼ teaspoon pepper
¼ teaspoon cayenne
   pepper
⅛ teaspoon garlic powder
1 16-ounce can whole
   tomatoes, chopped
1½ cups shredded
   Cheddar cheese
3 eggs, slightly beaten
1½ cups half and half
½ teaspoon salt

Combine flour, cornmeal and ½ teaspoon salt in mixer bowl. Cut in shortening until crumbly. Sprinkle in water 1 tablespoon at a time, mixing with fork until mixture clings together. Roll into 13-inch circle. Fit into deep 11-inch pie plate; crimp edges. Chill for 1 hour. Brown ground beef in large skillet, stirring until crumbly; drain. Add next 10 ingredients; mix well. Simmer, for 15 to 20 minutes or until moisture has evaporated. Layer cheese and ground beef mixture in prepared pie shell. Combine eggs, half and half and ½ teaspoon salt in bowl; beat until mixed well but not frothy. Pour over layers. Preheat oven to 375 degrees. Bake for 45 minutes or until knife inserted near center comes out clean. Let stand for 10 minutes. Yield: 10 servings.

Joyce Alexander, Theta Iota
Granite City, Iowa

MICROWAVE PIZZA CASSEROLE

1 pound ground beef
⅓ cup chopped green bell
   pepper
1 small onion, chopped
½ teaspoon garlic salt
1 16-ounce can pizza
   sauce
2 cups uncooked noodles
1 4-ounce can
   mushrooms, drained
1 3½-ounce package
   sliced pepperoni
1 cup water
1 cup shredded
   mozzarella cheese

Combine ground beef, green pepper and onion in 2-quart casserole. Microwave, covered, on High for 5 minutes, stirring once; drain. Add next 6 ingredients; mix well. Microwave, covered, on High for 15 to 17 minutes, stirring at 5 minute intervals. Top with cheese. Let stand, covered, for 10 minutes. Yield: 6 servings.

Mary Sandholdt, Beta Omega
Oskaloosa, Iowa

PIZZA CASSEROLE

2 pounds ground beef
2 cups uncooked egg
   noodles
1 teaspoon dried leaf
   oregano
2 teaspoons garlic salt
2 cups milk
2 cups shredded
   mozzarella cheese
2 10-ounce cans pizza
   sauce
1 8-ounce can sliced
   mushrooms, drained
Black olives, sliced

Brown ground beef in skillet, stirring until crumbly; drain. Combine all ingredients in 9x13-inch baking pan. Chill, covered, for 3 to 4 hours. Preheat oven to 350 degrees. Remove cover; stir to mix well. Bake for 1 hour or until almost set. Let stand for 10 minutes. Yield: 8 servings.

Susan Ellingsen, Delta Theta
Blue Earth, Minnesota

CHEESY BAKED SPAGHETTI

1 pound ground beef	½ teaspoon basil
½ cup minced onion	1½ cups broken spaghetti,
1 6-ounce can tomato	cooked
paste	2 cups cottage cheese
3 tablespoons light brown	2 cups shredded
sugar	mozzarella cheese
¾ teaspoon garlic salt	6 tablespoons Parmesan
½ teaspoon oregano	cheese
1½ teaspoon chili powder	

Preheat oven to 350 degrees. Brown ground beef with onion in skillet, stirring until crumbly. Stir in tomato paste, brown sugar and seasonings. Simmer for 30 minutes or until thickened. Toss spaghetti with cottage cheese in bowl. Spread in 9x13-inch baking dish. Spoon ground beef mixture over spaghetti. Top with cheeses. Bake for 45 minutes. Yield: 12 servings.

Shirley Eberhard, Xi Alpha Lambda
Spokane, Washington

SPAGHETTI PIZZA

1 pound ground beef	1 cup shredded
1 16-ounce package	mozzarella cheese
spaghetti	1 6-ounce can sliced
2 eggs, well beaten	black olives
½ cup milk	1 cup sliced green pepper
¾ teaspoon garlic powder	1 cup sliced mushrooms
½ teaspoon salt	1½ teaspoons oregano
1 32-ounce jar spaghetti	3 cups shredded
sauce	mozzarella cheese

Preheat oven to 400 degrees. Cook ground beef in skillet until brown and crumbly; drain. Cook spaghetti using package directions. Beat eggs with milk, garlic powder and salt in large bowl. Stir in spaghetti. Pour into greased 10x15-inch baking pan. Bake for 15 minutes. Reduce temperature to 350 degrees. Layer spaghetti sauce, ground beef, 1 cup mozzarella cheese, olives, green pepper, mushrooms and oregano over spaghetti. Top with 3 cups mozzarella cheese. Bake for 30 minutes. Let stand for 5 minutes. Cut into squares. Yield: 15 to 18 servings.

Betty J. Miller, Eta Lambda
Clarksville, Arkansas

MOCK SWISS STEAK

2 pounds ground beef	1 10-ounce can
2 eggs, beaten	mushroom soup
½ cup milk	1 10-ounce can beefy
⅔ cup cracker crumbs	mushroom soup
½ teaspoon seasoned salt	1 package onion gravy mix
All-purpose flour	¾ cup tomato juice

Mix first 5 ingredients in bowl. Spread in 9x13-inch dish. Chill for several hours to overnight. Preheat oven to 350 degrees. Cut beef mixture into 12 pieces. Coat with flour. Brown in skillet. Place in baking dish. Pour mixture of remaining ingredients over top. Bake for 45 minutes. Yield: 6 servings.

Janet Thompson, Preceptor Delta Alpha
Paxton, Illinois

SPAGHETTI AMORÉ

¼ cup chopped green bell	1 soup can milk
pepper	Dash of garlic powder
1 onion, chopped	Salt and pepper to taste
1 pound ground beef	1 cup shredded Velveeta
1 10-ounce can tomato	cheese
soup	8 ounces spaghetti,
1 10-ounce can	cooked
mushroom soup	

Preheat oven to 325 degrees. Sauté green pepper and onion in skillet. Add ground beef. Cook until light brown and crumbly. Mix soups with milk in bowl. Add ground beef mixture, garlic, salt and pepper. Simmer for 10 minutes. Add ½ cup Velveeta; stir until melted. Add spaghetti. Pour into greased 2-quart casserole. Sprinkle remaining cheese on top. Bake until bubbly. Yield: 6 servings.

Gail Saad, Preceptor Eta Delta
Houston, Texas

SPAGHETTI SAUCE

1 pound ground beef	2 15-ounce cans tomato
1 medium onion, chopped	paste
1 8-ounce can chopped	1 teaspoon sugar
mushrooms	1 teaspoon salt
1 medium bell pepper,	1 teaspoon pepper
chopped	1 bay leaf, crumbled
2 15-ounce cans whole	Oregano to taste
tomatoes	

Brown ground beef in skillet, stirring until crumbly; drain. Add onion, mushrooms and bell pepper. Simmer until tender; drain. Combine with remaining ingredients in saucepan. Cook over medium heat for 1 hour, stirring frequently. May cook in Crock•Pot on High for 1½ hours and on Low for 1 hour longer. Yield: 6 to 8 cups.

Marsha Kaye H. Jolley, Zeta Kappa
Forest City, North Carolina

SUPER HAMBURGERS

1 pound ground chuck	½ teaspoon dry mustard
1 cup chopped celery	¾ cup catsup
½ cup chopped onion	2 tablespoons all-purpose
1 tablespoon light brown	flour
sugar	6 hamburger buns,
2 tablespoons vinegar	toasted

Brown ground chuck with celery and onion in skillet, stirring frequently. Add next 5 ingredients; mix well. Simmer for 20 minutes. Serve on bun halves. Yield: 6 servings.

Ann N. Purser, Preceptor Beta
Macon, Georgia

POTLUCK CASSEROLE

2 tablespoons butter	1 8-ounce package
1 pound ground beef	noodles
1 clove of garlic, crushed	6 scallions, chopped
1 teaspoon salt	1 3-ounce package
Dash of pepper	cream cheese, softened
1 teaspoon sugar	1 cup sour cream
2 8-ounce cans tomato	½ cup shredded Cheddar
sauce	cheese

Preheat oven to 350 degrees. Melt butter in skillet. Add ground beef. Cook until brown and crumbly. Mix in garlic, salt, pepper, sugar and tomato sauce. Cook, covered, for 15 to 20 minutes. Cook noodles according to package directions; drain. Mix scallions with cream cheese and sour cream in bowl. Layer noodles, sour cream mixture and ground beef mixture ⅓ at a time in 1-quart casserole. Sprinkle with Cheddar cheese. Bake for 30 minutes or until bubbly. Yield: 6 to 8 servings.

Pat Wilson, Delta Gamma Xi
San Ramon, California

INSIDE-OUT RAVIOLI

1 pound ground beef	½ cup shredded American
½ cup chopped onion	cheese
1 clove of garlic, minced	½ cup Parmesan cheese
4 cups spaghetti sauce	1 cup seasoned Italian
with mushrooms	bread crumbs
1 10-ounce package	2 eggs, well beaten
frozen chopped spinach	¼ cup olive oil
2 cups small shell	1 cup shredded
macaroni	mozzarella cheese

Cook first 3 ingredients in large skillet until brown and crumbly. Add sauce. Cook for 1 hour. Cook spinach using package directions; drain. Cook macaroni using package directions; drain. Combine macaroni, spinach, American cheese, Parmesan cheese, bread crumbs, eggs and oil in bowl; mix well. Spread in oiled 9x13-inch baking pan. Top with ground beef mixture and mozzarella cheese. Cover with foil. Preheat oven to 350 degrees. Bake for 30 minutes. Let stand for 10 minutes before serving. Yield: 10 to 12 servings.

Michaelene Campana, Preceptor Gamma Epsilon
Monessen, Pennsylvania

TAMALE PIE

1 pound ground beef	1 clove of garlic, minced
1 cup chopped onion	1 tablespoons sugar
¼ cup chopped green bell	1 teaspoon salt
pepper	2 to 3 teaspoons chili
2 8-ounce cans tomato	powder
sauce	Dash of pepper
1 12-ounce can whole	8 ounces Cheddar cheese,
kernel corn, drained	shredded
1 12-ounce can pitted	1 6-ounce package corn
ripe olives, chopped	muffin mix

Preheat oven to 375 degrees. Brown ground beef, onion and green pepper in skillet, stirring frequently; drain.

Stir in next 8 ingredients. Simmer for 20 to 25 minutes. Add cheese. Cook until melted, stirring constantly. Pour into 9x13-inch baking dish. Prepare muffin mix according to package directions using twice the milk. Pour over ground beef mixture. Bake for 40 minutes.
Yield: 10 to 12 servings.

Sharon Howard, Epsilon Nu
St. Charles, Illinois

TACO QUICHE

1 cup whipping cream	8 ounces Cheddar cheese,
3 egg yolks	shredded
1 whole egg	1 unbaked 9-inch deep-
1 pound ground beef	dish pie shell
1 envelope dry taco	
seasoning mix	

Preheat oven to 375 degrees. Combine whipping cream egg yolks and egg in bowl; mix well with wire whisk. Set aside. Brown ground beef in skillet, stirring until crumbly; drain. Add taco seasoning mix and half the cheese; mix well. Spoon into pie shell. Pour cream mixture on top. Bake for 40 minutes. Remove from oven; top with remaining cheese. Bake for 15 minutes longer or until cheese melts. Cool for 5 minutes before serving.
Yield: 4 to 6 servings.

Marilyn Palmer, Alpha Theta Mu
Kingwood, Texas

TEXAS HASH

1½ pounds ground beef	½ teaspoon garlic powder
2 cups chopped onions	½ teaspoon pepper
2 cups chopped green bell	3 cups cooked rice
peppers	1 16-ounce can tomatoes,
1 to 2 tablespoons chili	chopped
powder	4 or 5 slices Velveeta
1 teaspoon salt	cheese

Preheat oven to 350 degrees. Cook ground beef with onions, green peppers and seasonings in skillet until vegetables are tender, stirring frequently; drain. Add rice and tomatoes. Spoon into 2-quart baking dish. Bake for 15 minutes. Arrange cheese over casserole. Bake for 10 minutes longer. Yield: 6 to 8 servings.

Doris Freeman, Zi Sigma Beta
White Deer, Texas

PORK ROAST WITH WALNUT DRESSING

1 7-pound pork crown	1 large onion, chopped
roast	3 cups butter
½ teaspoon dried thyme	2¼ cups chopped walnuts
leaves	½ cup chopped fresh
½ teaspoon dried sage	parsley
leaves	1¼ teaspoons salt
1 teaspoon salt	¼ teaspoon pepper
¼ teaspoon pepper	¼ cup dry white wine
1½ cups minute rice	2 tablespoons all-purpose
4 large stalks celery,	flour
sliced	½ teaspoon salt

Preheat oven to 325 degrees. Rub roast with thyme, sage, salt and pepper. Place rib end down in roasting pan. Roast for 2 hours. Prepare rice according to package directions, omitting salt and butter. Sauté celery and onion in butter in skillet until tender; remove from heat. Stir in rice, walnuts, chopped parsley, 1¼ teaspoons salt and ¼ teaspoon pepper. Turn roast rib end up. Spoon dressing into center. Roast for 2 hours longer or to 170 degrees on meat thermometer. Bake remaining dressing in greased 2-quart casserole during final 30 minutes of roasting time. Place roast on serving platter; keep warm. Pour pan juices into 2-cup measure. Let stand until fat rises to top. Reserve 3 tablespoons fat; discard remaining fat. Deglaze roaster with wine. Add to pan juices. Add enough water to measure 2 cups. Blend reserved fat with flour and ½ teaspoon salt in saucepan. Cook for 1 minute, stirring constantly. Stir in pan juices. Cook until thickened, stirring constantly. Serve with roast. Yield: 14 servings.

Cheryl Neeley, Nu Gamma
Abilene, Texas

ROAST PORK WITH TANGY SAUCE

1 4-pound rolled top loin pork roast	1 cup apple jelly
½ teaspoon salt	1 cup catsup
½ teaspoon chili powder	2 tablespoons vinegar
	2 teaspoons chili powder

Preheat oven to 325 degrees. Rub roast with mixture of seasonings. Place fat side up on rack in shallow roasting pan. Roast for 1¾ hours. Blend jelly, catsup, vinegar and 2 teaspoons chili powder in saucepan. Bring to a boil; reduce heat. Simmer for 1 minute. Brush over roast. Roast to 170 degrees on meat thermometer. Let stand for 10 minutes before carving. Blend ½ cup pan drippings with remaining jelly mixture. Heat to serving temperature. Serve with roast. Yield: 12 servings.

Margaret J. McDaniel, Laureate Gamma
Anchorage, Alaska

QUICK AND EASY PORK BARBECUE

1 pork butt roast	1 cup honey
½ cup barbecue sauce	2 teaspoons mustard

Cook pork with barbecue sauce in Crock•Pot on High for 6 hours. Bone and shred pork; place in foil-lined pan. Pour mixture of honey and mustard over pork. Broil until brown. Serve over rice. Yield: 6 to 8 servings.

Jo-Ann Gunn, Pi Eta
Titusville, Florida

ORIENTAL GRILLED PORK CHOPS

½ cup teriyaki sauce	4 cloves of garlic, minced
¼ cup minced green onions with tops	2 teaspoons crushed red pepper
¼ cup lemon juice	4 ¾-inch pork chops, trimmed
2 tablespoons peanut oil	

Mix first 6 ingredients in bowl. Pour over pork chops in dish. Chill, covered, for 4 hours or longer, turning occasionally. Drain, reserving marinade. Preheat grill. Grill 6

to 8 inches from hot coals for 30 to 45 minutes, turning and basting frequently with marinade. Yield: 6 servings.

JoAnne Murphy, Zeta Kappa
Virginia Beach, Virginia

PIZZA PORK CHOPS

8 thick chops with pocket	1 16-ounce can stewed tomatoes
8 1-inch cubes mozzarella cheese	1 6-ounce can tomato paste
Seasoned salt to taste	1 medium onion, chopped
2 tablespoons corn oil	8 ounces Cheddar cheese, shredded
2 envelopes spaghetti sauce mix	

Preheat oven to 350 degrees. Place mozzarella cubes in pork chop pockets; fasten with toothpick. Rub with seasoned salt. Brown in oil in skillet; place in baking pan. Bring next 4 ingredients to a boil in saucepan. Pour over chops. Bake for 30 minutes. Top with Cheddar cheese. Bake for 30 minutes. Yield: 8 servings.

Sally Hayes, Laureate Pi
Grand Blanc, Michigan

ORIENTAL PORK KABOBS

2 pounds boneless pork loin, cubed	Dash of garlic powder
¼ cup soy sauce	4 cups hot cooked rice
¼ cup peanut butter	½ cup soy sauce
1 tablespoon light brown sugar	1 tablespoon light brown sugar
1 tablespoon curry powder	2 tablespoons peanut butter
2 tablespoons lemon juice	½ teaspoon cayenne pepper

Mix pork with next 6 ingredients in bowl. Marinate in refrigerator overnight. Preheat broiler. Thread pork onto skewers; place on rack in broiler pan. Broil 6 to 8 inches from heat for 20 minutes, turning frequently. Serve over rice with mixture of remaining ingredients. Yield: 6 servings.

C. K. Vugteveen, Kappa
Sioux City, Iowa

GREEN CHILI STEW

1½ pounds pork steak, chopped	1 16-ounce can tomato juice
¼ cup corn oil	Garlic salt to taste
¼ cup all-purpose flour	Pepper to taste
2 cups water	1 onion, chopped
2 16-ounce cans stewed tomatoes	1 teaspoon cilantro
2 4-ounce cans green chilies	

Cook pork in oil in skillet until brown, stirring frequently. Sprinkle with flour. Pour into Crock•Pot. Add remaining ingredients; mix well. Cook on Low for 4 hours or longer. Serve with flour tortillas filled with melted cheese. Yield: 6 to 8 servings.

Paula L. Miller, Alpha Beta
Rocky Ford, Colorado

GREEN CHILI

3 pounds pork steak	3 cups water
2 quarts tomato juice	4 4-ounce cans sliced
Garlic salt to taste	green chilies
Salt, onion salt and	3 tablespoons all-purpose
pepper to taste	flour
2 teaspoons Tabasco sauce	Taco chips

Fry pork steak in skillet until tender; cool. Cut into bite-sized pieces; return to skillet. Bring tomato juice and seasonings to a boil in saucepan over medium heat. Add water and green chilies. Simmer for several minutes. Sprinkle flour over pork in skillet; stir until coated. Add tomato juice mixture. Simmer for 20 minutes. Serve over crushed taco chips. Yield: 12 servings.

Darlis Spiers, Lambda Nu
Pattonsburg, Missouri

PORK AU VIN

1 pound boneless pork	½ cup medium dry white
1 tablespoon corn oil	wine
1 small onion, chopped	1 tablespoon Grey
1 small clove of garlic,	Poupon mustard
crushed	1 tablespoon parsley
8 ounces mushrooms,	flakes
thinly sliced	1 teaspoon cornstarch
½ 10-ounce can chicken	1 tablespoon water
broth	

Preheat oven to 325 degrees. Trim fat from pork; slice ½ inch thick. Brown pork in oil in large skillet over medium-high heat. Place pork in baking dish. Sauté onion, garlic and mushrooms in pan drippings until light brown. Add broth, wine, mustard and parsley flakes. Bring to a boil; reduce heat. Simmer, covered, for 15 minutes. Dissolve cornstarch in water. Whisk into broth mixture. Pour over pork. Bake, covered, for 1 hour. Yield: 4 to 6 servings.

Molly Fatale, Preceptor Zeta Chi
Moraga, California

BARBECUED SPARERIBS

6 pounds spareribs	¼ teaspoon chili powder
Lemon juice to taste	2 tablespoons
Onions, sliced	Worcestershire sauce
2 tablespoons light brown	¼ cup vinegar
sugar	1 cup tomato juice
1 tablespoon paprika	¼ cup catsup
1 teaspoon salt	½ cup water
1 teaspoon dry mustard	

Preheat oven to 300 degrees. Bake ribs in roaster for 2 hours; drain. Sprinkle with lemon juice; cover with onions. Combine brown sugar and remaining ingredients in saucepan. Simmer for 15 minutes. Bake ribs for 2 hours longer, basting with sauce every 20 minutes. Yield: 6 servings.

Charmaine Evans, Xi Zeta
Chadron, Nebraska

OPEN HOUSE RIBS

6 pounds baby back ribs	3 tablespoons finely
1 cup CocoRibe coconut	chopped fresh
rum	gingerroot
½ cup Chinese barbecue	1 tablespoon minced
sauce	garlic
½ cup catsup	Hot pepper sauce to taste
⅔ cup chopped scallions	

Preheat oven to 375 degrees. Arrange ribs in single layer on wire racks in shallow baking pans. Cover loosely with foil. Bake for 1 hour. Combine remaining ingredients in bowl; mix well. Turn ribs bony side up. Brush with sauce. Bake for 15 minutes, basting frequently. Turn ribs. Bake for 15 minutes longer, basting frequently.
Yield: 8 servings.

Photograph for this recipe on page 2.

CHIMICHANGAS

2 pounds pork shoulder,	½ teaspoon oregano leaves
trimmed	1 tablespoon dry
2 medium onions,	coriander leaves
chopped	1 4-ounce can diced
2 cloves of garlic, minced	green chilies
1 large green bell pepper,	2 tablespoons water
chopped	1 package flour tortillas
½ teaspoon salt	Oil for frying

Cut pork into ½-inch cubes. Cook in skillet until light brown. Add onions, garlic and green pepper. Cook until onion is transparent. Add seasonings, green chilies and water. Simmer, covered, for 35 minutes or until pork is tender. Cool. Place about ¼ cup filling in center of each tortilla. Fold sides to overlap at center; secure with toothpicks. Fry in ¾-inch hot oil until tortilla is light brown. Drain on paper towels. Yield: 8 to 10 servings.

Karen Vondemkamp, Nu Upsilon
Council Grove, Kansas

SWEET AND SOUR PORK

1½ pounds pork	½ teaspoon salt
tenderloin, cubed	Oil for deep frying
2 cups water	⅔ cup pineapple chunks
¾ cup soy sauce	2 medium tomatoes,
2 tablespoons sugar	chopped
1 egg, beaten	1 small green bell pepper,
⅔ cup milk	chopped
1 cup all-purpose flour	½ cup chopped green
2 teaspoons baking	onions
powder	¾ cup butter

Cook pork in mixture of water, soy sauce and sugar in saucepan for 50 minutes; drain. Beat egg with milk in bowl. Add mixture of flour, baking powder and salt; beat until smooth. Dip pork cubes into batter. Deep-fry until brown. Sauté pineapple chunks and vegetables in butter in skillet until tender-crisp. Serve pork and vegetable mixture with Sweet and Sour Sauce.
Yield: 4 to 6 servings.

SWEET AND SOUR SAUCE

1 teaspoon instant coffee powder	¼ teaspoon salt
½ cup water	¼ teaspoon pepper
½ cup sugar	¼ cup cornstarch
¼ cup packed light brown sugar	½ cup pineapple juice
	2 tablespoons catsup

Dissolve coffee powder in water. Mix next 5 ingredients in saucepan. Add coffee, pineapple juice and catsup, stirring constantly over medium heat until thickened.

Nan Gough, Alpha Sigma
Flagstaff, Arizona

BREAKFAST ON THE RUN

1 pound bacon	¾ cup quick-cooking oats
⅓ cup butter, softened	3 ounces cream cheese, softened
⅓ cup packed light brown sugar	¼ cup milk
¾ cup all-purpose flour	8 eggs, beaten
½ teaspoon salt	

Preheat oven to 400 degrees. Cut bacon into 1-inch pieces. Sauté in skillet until crisp; drain, reserving 1 tablespoon drippings. Cream butter and brown sugar in bowl. Mix in flour, salt and oats. Press half the mixture into buttered 8x8-inch baking pan. Beat cream cheese with milk in mixer bowl. Add eggs; beat well. Cook in reserved drippings in skillet over low heat until consistency of pudding. Mix in bacon. Spoon into prepared baking pan. Top with remaining crumb mixture. Bake for 20 minutes. Cool. Cut into squares. Yield: 4 servings.

Sugar Carpenter, Preceptor Beta
Gresham, Oregon

CANADIAN BACON BAKE

¼ cup butter, melted	8 eggs, beaten
¼ cup all-purpose flour	2 ounces sharp cheese, shredded
½ teaspoon salt	8 ounces frozen hashed brown potatoes, thawed
⅛ teaspoon pepper	1 pound Canadian bacon
2 cups milk	
1 cup sour cream	
2 tablespoons parsley	

Blend butter, flour, salt and pepper in 3-quart saucepan. Stir in milk. Cook until thickened, stirring constantly. Stir in next 5 ingredients. Pour into 9x13-inch baking pan. Arrange overlapping slices of Canadian bacon on top. Bake, uncovered, for 40 minutes. Yield: 8 servings.

Dixie McGinley, Eta Psi
Albany, Missouri

LINGUINI MADALENA

12 ounces bacon, chopped	1 cup Romano cheese
6 cloves of garlic, minced	1½ cups half and half
6 quarts water	⅛ teaspoon pepper
1 tablespoon salt	⅛ teaspoon nutmeg
3 tablespoons corn oil	3 tablespoons minced fresh parsley
12 ounces linguini	
3 eggs	

Sauté bacon with garlic in large skillet until crisp. Combine water, salt and oil in large saucepan. Bring to a boil. Add linguini. Cook just until tender; drain. Add to bacon mixture; mix well. Heat over medium heat; push linguini to edge. Break eggs into center. Scramble eggs; stir into linguini. Toss with cheese. Pour in half and half. Cook until liquid is absorbed, stirring constantly. Add pepper and nutmeg. Sprinkle with parsley. Yield: 6 servings.

Margaret Nieberding, Preceptor Zeta
Marysville, Kansas

OMELET SUPREME

12 eggs, beaten	1 8-ounce can mushrooms
¾ cup half and half	⅔ cup half and half
1 pound bacon, chopped	1 10-ounce can mushroom soup
8 ounces Cheddar cheese, shredded	

Preheat oven to 325 degrees. Beat eggs with ¾ cup half and half in bowl; do not season. Scramble in skillet. Fry bacon; drain. Layer eggs, bacon, cheese, mushrooms and mixture of ⅔ cup half and half and soup in 9x13-inch baking pan. Bake for 40 minutes. Let stand for 5 minutes before serving. Yield: 6 to 10 servings.

Mary Ellen Hardy, Preceptor Alpha Kappa
San Antonio, Texas

HAM WITH NUTTY APRICOT STUFFING

1 10 to 12-pound fully cooked ham	¼ cup packed light brown sugar
½ cup chopped dried apricots	1 tablespoon Dijon-style mustard
1½ cups finely chopped pecans	2 egg whites
1 8-ounce can crushed pineapple	1 teaspoon thyme
½ cup fresh white bread crumbs	1 cup apple juice
	1 cup light brown sugar
	1 cup fine fresh white bread crumbs

Bone ham to make cavity. Remove about ½ pound ham from cavity; grind. Soak apricots in warm water for 30 minutes; drain. Preheat oven to 325 degrees. Combine ground ham, apricots, pecans, undrained pineapple, ½ cup bread crumbs, ¼ cup brown sugar, mustard, egg whites and thyme in bowl; mix well. Spoon into ham cavity; secure ham with poultry strings. Place ham in foil-lined shallow baking pan; insert meat thermometer. Add apple juice. Seal foil. Bake for 2 hours. Remove foil, string and rind from ham. Pat with mixture of 1 cup brown sugar and 1 cup crumbs. Increase temperature to 375 degrees. Bake for 40 minutes or until golden brown. Yield: 12 to 15 servings.

Norma E. Hall, Xi Gamma Nu
Cherokee Village, Arkansas

BAKED HAM WITH HORSERADISH GLAZE

5½ to 6 pounds fully cooked boneless ham	Whole cloves to taste
1 cup packed light brown sugar	⅓ cup horseradish
	¼ cup lemon juice

Preheat oven to 325 degrees. Have butcher slice ham ¼ inch thick, reassemble and tie with cord. Place ham on rack in shallow baking dish. Bake for 1½ hours. Mix remaining ingredients in small saucepan. Bring to a boil. Pour over ham. Increase oven temperature to 400 degrees. Bake for 15 minutes longer, basting occasionally with glaze. Yield: 10 servings.

Frances V. Scofield, Laureate Eta
Clarksville, Tennessee

STUFFED EASTER HAM

1 5-pound canned ham	⅓ cup raisins
¾ cup chopped onion	1 cup chicken broth
¾ cup chopped celery	2 tablespoons minced
6 tablespoons butter	fresh parsley
4½ cups ¼-inch soft bread cubes	½ teaspoon ground cinnamon
1½ cups chopped peeled apples	1 10-ounce jar pineapple preserves

Preheat oven to 350 degrees. Cut ham into twenty ⅜-inch slices using electric or sharp knife. Place ham slices upright in original shape in foil-lined shallow roasting pan. Sauté onion and celery in butter in skillet until tender; do not brown. Combine sautéed vegetables, bread crumbs, apples, raisins, chicken broth, parsley and cinnamon in bowl; mix lightly. Place stuffing between ham slices, leaving 2 ham slices between stuffing layers. Tie ham securely with string. Cover loosely with foil. Bake for 1 hour. Melt pineapple preserves in small saucepan over low heat. Remove foil. Bake for 1 hour longer, basting several times with melted preserves. Yield: 12 servings.

Michele M. Rauser, Alpha Alpha
Glasgow, Montana

ROSY HAM RING

3 pounds ground ham	1 10-ounce can tomato soup
1 pound ground pork	
2 eggs	½ cup packed light brown sugar
1¾ cups graham cracker crumbs	
1½ cups milk	1½ cups prepared mustard
½ teaspoon allspice	

Preheat oven to 350 degrees. Combine first 6 ingredients in bowl; mix well. Shape as for loaf in ring pan. Mix soup, brown sugar and mustard in bowl. Pour half the mixture over ham ring. Bake for 45 minutes. Pour remaining sauce over ring. Bake for another 45 minutes. Turn onto serving plate. Fill center of ring with cooked vegetable if desired. Yield: 12 to 14 servings.

Dorothy Zientarski, Preceptor Kappa
New Britain, Connecticut

GRILLED HAM STEAKS

¼ cup prepared mustard	6 ½-inch thick ham steaks
½ cup packed light brown sugar	
⅛ teaspoon ground cloves	1 20-ounce can pineapple slices
2 tablespoons pineapple juice	

Preheat coals. Mix mustard, brown sugar, cloves and pineapple juice in bowl. Place ham steaks on grill over hot coals. Baste with mustard mixture. Grill for 6 minutes. Turn ham over; baste with mustard mixture. Place 2 pineapples on each steak. Grill for 6 minutes longer. Yield: 8 to 12 servings.

Sally A. Ireland, Xi Kappa
Chaplin, Connecticut

CHEESY HAM TOWERS

1 chicken bouillon cube	2 cups ham, cubed
¼ cup margarine	1 3-ounce can sliced black olives, drained
¼ cup all-purpose flour	
1½ cups milk	2 tablespoons chopped pimento
1 teaspoon prepared mustard	
1 teaspoon Worcestershire sauce	2 tablespoons chopped parsley
1 cup Velveeta cheese, cubed	

Melt bouillon cube and margarine in 2-quart saucepan. Whisk in flour. Add milk, whisking constantly. Cook over medium heat until thickened, whisking constantly. Add mustard, Worcestershire and cheese. Stir until cheese melts. Add remaining ingredients. Serve in patty shells or over baked potatoes. Yield: 6 servings.

Pamela G. Becker, Epsilon Sigma
Alliance, Nebraska

HAM IN TOAST CUPS

¼ cup minced green pepper	¾ teaspoon Worcestershire sauce
2 tablespoons minced onion	1½ cups diced cooked ham
1½ tablespoons butter	¼ teaspoon salt
2½ tablespoons all-purpose flour	⅛ teaspoon pepper
¾ cup hot water	1½ tablespoons lemon juice
1 5-ounce can evaporated milk	8 slices white bread
2 tablespoons mustard	2 tablespoons melted butter

Preheat oven to 500 degrees. Sauté green pepper and onion in 1½ tablespoons butter in skillet until tender. Blend in flour. Stir in water gradually. Cook until thickened, stirring constantly. Add evaporated milk, stirring constantly until slightly thickened. Mix in next 6 ingredients. Keep warm. Press each bread slice into muffin cup. Brush with butter. Bake until brown and crisp. Fill cups with ham sauce. Bake for 10 minutes or until heated. Yield: 4 servings.

Crystal Richard, Iota Kappa
Ruston, Louisiana

HAM AND BROCCOLI STRATA

1 20-ounce package frozen chopped broccoli, cooked, drained	3 cups cubed cooked ham
	6 eggs, beaten
	3½ cups milk
12 bread slices, trimmed	½ teaspoon salt
3 cups shredded Cheddar cheese	¼ teaspoon dry mustard
	Onion flakes to taste

Preheat oven to 325 degrees. Cook broccoli using package directions; drain. Layer 6 bread slices, 1 cup cheese, remaining bread, 1 cup cheese, broccoli, ham and remaining cheese in greased 9x13-inch baking dish. Mix eggs, milk, salt and mustard in bowl. Pour over layers. Sprinkle with onion flakes. Refrigerate, covered, if desired. Remove from refrigerator 1 hour before baking. Bake for 1 hour. Let stand for 10 minutes before serving. Yield: 10 to 12 servings.

Melissa Stults, Alpha Tau
Wichita Falls, Texas

HAM AND CHEESE CASSEROLE

½ cup sliced celery	½ teaspoon salt
¼ cup chopped green pepper	½ teaspoon garlic salt
½ cup boiling water	2 cups diced cooked ham
1 cup milk	½ cup Parmesan cheese
8 ounces cream cheese, softened	8 ounces medium noodles, cooked

Preheat oven to 350 degrees. Cook celery and pepper in water in saucepan for 5 minutes; drain. Heat milk and cream cheese in saucepan over low heat until smooth, stirring constantly. Add seasonings, ham, cooked vegetables and half the Parmesan cheese; mix well. Toss sauce lightly with noodles. Place in buttered, 1½-quart casserole. Sprinkle with remaining Parmesan cheese. Bake, covered, for 30 to 35 minutes. Yield: 8 servings.

Claire Cowart, Eta Rho
Covington, Louisiana

CORN AND MUSHROOM SQUARES

2 8-count packages refrigerator crescent rolls	1½ cups shredded Swiss cheese
2 cups chopped ham	1 4½-ounce jar sliced mushrooms, drained
1 12-ounce can Mexicorn	6 eggs
1½ cups shredded Monterey Jack cheese	1 cup milk
	¼ to ½ teaspoon pepper

Preheat oven to 375 degrees. Separate roll dough into 4 long rectangles. Press over bottom and ¾ inch up side of 10x15-inch baking dish; seal perforations. Sprinkle next 5 ingredients evenly over crust. Beat eggs, milk and pepper in medium bowl. Pour over ham, cheese and vegetables. Bake for 35 minutes or until knife inserted in center comes out clean. Yield: 12 to 15 servings.

Marion F. Bierl, Alpha Lambda
Carroll, Iowa

MICROWAVE MACARONI AND HAM DISH

¼ cup margarine, sliced	5 cups cooked macaroni
6 ounces Parmesan cheese	3 cups shredded mozzarella cheese
1½-pound ham, slivered	
2 cups shredded Swiss cheese	Pepper to taste

Place margarine slices in 2-quart glass baking dish. Layer remaining ingredients ⅓ at a time in prepared dish. Cover with plastic wrap. Microwave on High for 20 minutes. Yield: 8 to 10 servings.

Joni A. Wood, Phi Alpha Epsilon
Great Bend, Kansas

GLAZED HAM LOAF

1 pound lean ground ham	½ cup packed brown sugar
1 pound lean ground pork	¼ cup cider vinegar
¾ cup cracker crumbs	¾ teaspoon dry mustard
3 tablespoons chopped onion	¼ cup mayonnaise
¾ teaspoon salt	¼ cup sour cream
2 eggs, well beaten	1 tablespoon horseradish
1 cup milk	¼ cup sugar
1 teaspoon chopped parsley	1 tablespoon lemon juice

Preheat oven to 350 degrees. Mix first 8 ingredients in bowl in order given, mixing well after each addition. Shape into loaf. Place in greased loaf pan. Bake for 30 minutes. Blend brown sugar, vinegar and dry mustard in saucepan. Boil for 1 minute. Pour over ham loaf. Bake for 1 hour longer. Blend mayonnaise and remaining ingredients in small bowl. Serve with ham loaf. Yield: 6 servings.

Patricia Hurst, Xi Zeta Lambda
Cocoa, Florida

HAM AND RICE QUICHE

1 6-ounce package Spanish rice mix	2 tablespoons chopped pimento
6 to 8 ounces cooked ham, cubed	4 eggs, beaten
	1¼ cups milk
1½ cups shredded Swiss cheese	¼ teaspoon salt
⅓ cup chopped onions	¼ teaspoon hot pepper sauce
⅓ cup chopped green pepper	

Preheat oven to 350 degrees. Cook rice mix using package directions. Cool. Press over bottom and side of buttered 10-inch pie plate, shaping rim. Layer ham, cheese, onion, green pepper and pimento in prepared pie plate. Pour mixture of eggs and remaining ingredients over layers. Bake for 50 minutes or until set. Yield: 6 servings.

Donna Faxon, Preceptor Alpha Epsilon
Tucson, Arizona

HAM AND SIX-CHEESE QUICHE

1 recipe 2-crust pie pastry	2 cups shredded Cheddar
12 eggs, beaten	cheese
8 ounces cream cheese,	2 cups shredded Swiss
softened	cheese
4 cups cream	2 cups shredded American
1 pound ham, finely	cheese
chopped	1/4 to 1/2 cup melted butter
2 cups ricotta cheese	1 medium onion, finely
3 cups shredded	chopped
mozzarella cheese	Salt and pepper to taste

Preheat oven to 350 degrees. Line 9x13-inch baking dish with pie pastry. Beat eggs with cream cheese and cream in bowl. Stir in remaining ingredients. Pour into prepared baking dish. Bake for 35 to 40 minutes or until knife inserted in center comes out clean.
Yield: 15 to 20 servings.

Geraldine Aldi, Xi Chi
Wolcott, Connecticut

VEGETABLE AND HAM CASSEROLE

1 10-ounce package	1/4 teaspoon salt
frozen corn	1 3-ounce can broiled,
1 10-ounce package	sliced mushrooms,
frozen baby limas	drained
1 cup sour cream	1/2 cup fresh bread crumbs
1 4 1/2-ounce can deviled	1 tablespoon melted
ham	butter
2 tablespoons minced	Paprika
onion	

Preheat oven to 350 degrees. Cook frozen vegetables using package directions; drain. Mix vegetables with next 5 ingredients in bowl. Pour into 6x10-inch baking dish. Top with crumbs tossed with butter; sprinkle with paprika. Bake for 25 to 30 minutes or until heated through. Yield: 6 servings.

Helen A. Heath, Preceptor Upsilon
Muncie, Indiana

QUICK BREAKFAST PIZZA

1 pound sausage	1/2 teaspoon salt
1 1/2 8-count packages	1/8 teaspoon pepper
refrigerator crescent	1 cup shredded sharp
rolls	Cheddar cheese
1 cup frozen hashed	1 cup shredded
brown potatoes, thawed	mozzarella cheese
5 eggs, beaten	2 tablespoons Parmesan
1/4 cup milk	cheese

Preheat oven to 375 degrees. Cook sausage in skillet until brown and crumbly; drain. Fit crescent roll dough into pizza pan, forming crust and sealing perforations. Layer sausage and potatoes over roll dough. Mix eggs, milk, salt and pepper. Pour over potatoes. Sprinkle with cheeses. Bake for 25 to 30 minutes.
Yield: 10 to 12 servings.

Bonnie Bottoms, Lambda Phi
Monroe City, Indiana

SAUSAGE CALZONE

2 1-pound loaves frozen	1/2 cup shredded
bread dough	mozzarella cheese
8 ounces sweet Italian	1/2 cup cottage cheese
sausage	2 tablespoons Parmesan
1/2 cup chopped onion	cheese
2 cloves of garlic, minced	1 egg, slightly beaten
1 8-ounce can tomato	2 egg whites, slightly
sauce	beaten
1/2 teaspoon basil	2 egg yolks
1 teaspoon oregano	1 tablespoon milk

Thaw bread dough, loosely wrapped in plastic wrap, in refrigerator overnight. Let stand at room temperature for 1 hour. Preheat oven to 425 degrees. Cook sausage in skillet until brown and crumbly; drain. Add onion and garlic. Cook until tender. Stir in tomato sauce, basil and oregano. Simmer for 5 minutes. Cool. Stir in cheeses and whole egg. Divide dough into 8 portions. Roll each into 6-inch circle on lightly floured surface. Place 1/3 cup filling on each. Brush edge of circle with beaten egg whites, fold over and press to seal. Place on baking sheet. Brush with egg yolks beaten with milk. Bake for 12 to 15 minutes or until golden brown. Yield: 8 servings.

Donna Ramsey, Preceptor Alpha Kappa
Fort Collins, Colorado

JAMBALAYA

4 slices bacon, chopped	1 bunch green onions,
1 pound bulk sausage	chopped
1 pound sausage, sliced	2 cups uncooked rice
1 pound chicken	4 cups hot water
3 tablespoons (about)	1 1/2 teaspoons Tony's
all-purpose flour	seasoning
2 stalks celery, chopped	1 teaspoon thyme
1 large onion, chopped	1 teaspoon parsley
1 green pepper, chopped	Tabasco sauce to taste
4 cloves of garlic, chopped	

Preheat oven to 350 degrees. Cook bacon, sausages and chicken in skillet; remove to large baking pan. Add enough flour to pan drippings to make roux. Add celery, onion, green pepper and garlic. Cook until tender, stirring frequently. Add green onions, rice, water and seasonings. Bring to a boil. Stir into baking pan. Bake, covered, with foil, for 50 minutes. Bake, uncovered, for 5 minutes longer. Yield: 8 to 10 servings.

Isabelle Bahan, Eta Rho
Mandeville, Louisiana

HASHED BROWN PIE

3 cups frozen hashed	2 tablespoons minced
brown potatoes, thawed	onion
3 tablespoons corn oil	2 eggs, beaten
1 cup shredded Cheddar	1 cup evaporated milk
cheese	
1 cup crumbled cooked	
sausage	

Preheat oven to 475 degrees. Mix hashed brown potatoes and oil in bowl. Press over bottom and side of 10-inch pie plate, forming crust. Bake for 15 minutes. Add layers of cheese, sausage, onion and eggs beaten with evaporated milk. Reduce temperature to 350 degrees. Bake for 30 minutes or until set. Yield: 6 to 8 servings.

Pat Gillett, Kappa Omega
Fredonia, Kansas

SHERRIED EGGS

1 pound ground sausage	½ teaspoon dry mustard
4 to 6 slices bread, cubed	1 10-ounce can
1¼ cups shredded	mushroom soup
Cheddar cheese	1 2-ounce can pimento
4 eggs, beaten	1 cup sliced fresh
2 cups milk	mushrooms
½ teaspoon salt	¼ cup cooking Sherry
½ teaspoon pepper	¼ cup cream

Cook sausage in skillet until brown and crumbly; drain. Layer bread cubes, sausage and cheese in 9x13-inch baking pan. Combine eggs and next 4 ingredients; mix well. Pour over layers. Chill, covered, for 2 to 24 hours. Preheat oven to 350 degrees. Bake eggs for 1 hour. Cut into squares. Combine soup, pimento, mushrooms and Sherry in saucepan. Heat until well blended, stirring constantly. Add cream. Heat to serving temperature; do not boil. Serve eggs with Sherry sauce.
Yield: 9 to 12 servings.

Diana Dee Fink, Preceptor Beta
Anchorage, Alaska

STUFFED FRENCH TOAST

½ cup chopped onion	½ teaspoon pepper
8 ounces hot sausage	4 ounces bacon,
2 tablespoons butter	crisp-fried, crumbled
4 ounces cream cheese,	1 loaf unsliced bread
softened	6 eggs, beaten
¼ teaspoon salt	½ cup (about) milk

Sauté onion and sausage in butter in skillet, stirring until sausage is brown and crumbly; drain. Combine with cream cheese, salt, pepper and bacon in bowl; mix well. Cut bread into slices, making every other cut to but not through bottom to form pockets. Spoon 2½ tablespoons sausage mixture into each pocket. Dip filled slices into mixture of eggs and milk as for French toast. Cook in a small amount of oil on grill until brown on both sides. Garnish with sprinkle of paprika. Serve with warm maple syrup. Yield: 6 to 8 servings.

 Jo Scott, Xi Lambda Theta
Buffalo Grove, Illinois

VENETIAN PASTA ROLLS

1 pound Italian sausage	½ cup Parmesan cheese
½ cup finely chopped	Pepperoni to taste, sliced
onion	8 lasagna noodles, cooked
1 16-ounce jar spaghetti	1 cup shredded
sauce	mozzarella cheese

Preheat oven to 350 degrees. Remove casing from sausage; crumble into skillet. Cook until brown and crumbly; drain. Add onion. Cook until tender. Stir in ½ cup spaghetti sauce, ⅓ cup Parmesan cheese and pepperoni. Spread ⅓ cup mixture on each noodle and roll as for jelly roll. Place seam side down in 8x12-inch baking pan. Spoon remaining sauce over rolls; top with mozzarella cheese. Sprinkle with remaining Parmesan cheese. Bake, covered, for 30 minutes. Yield: 8 servings.

Sharon Slaughter, Tau Theta
Flora, Illinois

ZUCCHINI AND SAUSAGE

2 pounds Italian sausage	1 teaspoon garlic salt
2 large onions, sliced	2 medium zucchini, sliced
1 large green bell pepper,	2 16-ounce cans tomato
sliced	purée
1 tablespoon corn oil	1 16-ounce can sliced
1 teaspoon oregano	mushrooms
1 teaspoon pepper	

Brown sausage in skillet; drain and set aside. Sauté onions and green pepper in oil in 5-quart Dutch oven until tender. Add sausage and remaining ingredients. Bring to a boil; reduce heat to low. Cook, covered, for 1 hour or longer, stirring occasionally. Yield: 8 servings.

Diane Smith Heaphy, Preceptor Alpha Xi
Syracuse, New York

SAUSAGES AND APPLES

2 large tart apples	1 cup long grain rice
¾ cup packed light brown	1 pound link sausages
sugar	¼ cup catsup

Preheat oven to 350 degrees. Core and slice apples; do not peel. Layer apples and brown sugar in 2-quart casserole. Cook rice using package directions. Spoon into casserole. Pour boiling water over sausages. Let stand for 3 minutes; drain well. Arrange sausages over rice. Spread catsup over top. Bake, covered, for 30 minutes. Bake, uncovered, for 15 to 30 minutes longer. Yield: 6 servings.

Marjorie LaFever, Preceptor Alpha Psi
Menlo Park, California

MUSHROOM STEW

1 bunch celery, chopped	12 ounces ground beef
4 onions, chopped	1 pound hot sausage links
8 to 12 ounces pork, cubed	2 20-ounce cans tomatoes
Mushrooms to taste	1 6-ounce can tomato
2 large green peppers	paste
3 tablespoons corn oil	Salt and pepper to taste

Sauté first 5 ingredients in oil in skillet. Cook ground beef in skillet until brown and crumbly; drain. Cook sausage in skillet; drain and slice. Combine sautéed vegetables, ground beef, sausage and remaining ingredients in large saucepan. Cook for 2 hours. Yield: 6 servings.

Karen Freytag, Xi Delta Epsilon
Whitesboro, New York

PINEAPPLE AND SAUSAGE OMELET

1 15-ounce can juice-pack pineapple slices	⅛ teaspoon white pepper
4 eggs, separated	1 tablespoon butter
1 teaspoon baking powder	12 ounces pork sausage links
½ teaspoon salt	½ cup packed light brown sugar

Preheat oven to 350 degrees. Drain pineapple, reserving juice. Beat egg yolks, ¼ cup reserved juice, baking powder, salt and pepper in small bowl. Beat egg whites in large mixer bowl until stiff but not dry. Stir ¼ of the egg whites into yolks; fold yolk mixture into whites. Heat butter in medium ovenproof skillet until bubbly; pour in egg mixture. Cook over low heat for 5 minutes or until bottom of omelet is golden. Bake for 15 minutes or until set. Cook sausages in medium skillet over low heat until cooked through; drain. Add ½ cup reserved pineapple juice and brown sugar to skillet. Bring to a boil; reduce heat. Simmer for 10 to 12 minutes or until thickened. Add pineapple slices. Cook for 2 to 3 minutes or until heated through. Slide omelet onto large platter; surround with glazed sausages and pineapple. Yield: 4 servings.

Nan Bazemore, Delta Pi
Montgomery, Alabama

GARBAGE CAN DINNER

10 to 20 pounds potatoes	5 heads cabbage, quartered
2 to 3 pounds carrots	1 pound onions, peeled, thinly sliced
20 to 25 pounds assorted kielbasa, knackwurst, bratwurst, and smoked Italian sausages	Wine and beer
4 pounds onions, peeled, cut into halves	

Build fire pits in suitable backyard location; start fire 2 hours before serving time. Scrub brand new 20 to 30 gallon galvanized garbage can; rinse well and place over fire. Place 5 beer cans filled with water in bottom of garbage can. Scrub potatoes and carrots; do not peel. Layer potatoes and carrots in can. Add sausages, 4 pounds onions and cabbages. Top with sliced onions. Pour desired amounts of wine and beer over top. Add lid. Cook for 2 hours or until vegetabes are tender, uncovering only to add liquid of choice or to serve hungry guests. Yield: 35 to 50 servings.

Anna Lawson Pitts, Xi Gamma Gamma
Sierra Vista, Arizona

SWEET AND SOUR KIELBASA

1 2-pound kielbasa	1 tablespoon honey
1 20-ounce can pineapple chunks	1 tablespoon dry mustard
1 10-ounce jar red currant jelly	2 tablespoons cornstarch
1 teaspoon ginger	2 tablespoons water
1 tablespoon vinegar	1 green bell pepper
	1 sweet red bell pepper

Preheat oven to 375 degrees. Bake kielbasa in baking dish for 20 to 30 minutes. Drain pineapple, reserving juice. Mix reserved juice and next 5 ingredients in saucepan. Heat until jelly melts. Add cornstarch mixed with water. Cook until thickened and clear, stirring constantly. Slice kielbasa and peppers ½-inch thick. Add to sauce. Heat for 10 to 15 minutes over low heat. Add pineapple. Heat to serving temperature. Serve over hot cooked rice. Yield: 4 to 6 servings.

Mary Lou Kowalewski, Eta Xi
Sterling Heights, Michigan

GERMAN SAUSAGE DISH

2½ to 3 pounds beef sausage	9 to 10 potatoes, peeled, halved
3 16-ounce cans sauerkraut	4 apples, cut into wedges
2 large onions, thickly sliced	3 cups apple juice

Cut sausage into chunks. Brown in electric skillet; remove from skillet. Layer sauerkraut, onion slices, potato halves and apple wedges in skillet. Place sausage chunks into mixture. Drizzle apple juice over top. Simmer, covered, at 220 to 240 degrees for 45 minutes or until apples and potatoes are tender but firm. Yield: 12 servings.

Lou Alexander, Xi Xi Rho
Arlington, Texas

BARBECUED RACK OF LAMB

1 1½-pound rack of lamb	1 teaspoon lemon pepper
2 teaspoons salt	1 teaspoon garlic salt
	1 teaspoon rosemary

Preheat oven to 350 degrees. Rub lamb on all sides with mixture of seasonings 6 hours or longer before cooking. Cook over indirect heat in covered barbecue for 1 hour. Yield: 4 servings.

Lynette Hibler, Laureate Epsilon Alpha
Arcata, California

ROAST LEG OF LAMB

1 5 to 7-pound leg of lamb	1 clove of garlic, slivered
	Salt and pepper to taste

Preheat oven to 325 degrees. Make 4 or 5 slits in lamb with tip of knife; insert garlic slivers into slits. Sprinkle lamb with salt and pepper. Place lamb fat side up on rack in shallow roasting pan. Insert meat thermometer so tip is in center of thickest part of lamb and does not touch bone or rest in fat. Do not add water. Roast, uncovered, for 2½ hours for 5 pound roast, 3½ hours for 7 pound roast or 140 degrees on meat thermometer for rare, 160 degrees for medium or 170 degrees for well-done. Let stand for 15 to 20 minutes before carving for easier slicing. Lamb may be cooked to 5 degrees lower than indicated and will continue to cook while standing. Yield: 8 servings.

Jeanette Azar, Preceptor Beta Zeta
Mount Clemens, Michigan

Poultry

CHICKEN ALBERGHETTI

6 chicken breast filets
Salt and pepper to taste
2 eggs, slightly beaten
¾ cup dry bread crumbs
½ cup butter
8 ounces prepared
  Italian cooking sauce
1 cup half and half
6 slices mozzarella cheese
6 slices Swiss cheese
Butter
Parmesan cheese

Preheat oven to 350 degrees. Season chicken with salt and pepper. Dip in egg, roll in crumbs. Sauté in ½ cup butter until browned. Dilute spaghetti sauce with half and half. Reserve 2 tablespoons. Pour sauce in casserole. Add chicken. Top each chicken breast with 1 slice of mozzarella and Swiss cheese. Spoon reserved sauce on top. Dot with butter, sprinkle with Parmesan cheese. Bake, covered, for 45 to 50 minutes. Yield: 6 servings.

Colleen B. Miller, Xi Delta Nu
Lamon, Oklahoma

COLD BROILED CHICKEN

½ cup soy sauce
1 cup Sherry
1 tablespoon paprika
2 cloves of garlic,
  minced
Dash of hot pepper sauce
6 whole chicken
  breasts, split
½ cup corn oil

Combine soy sauce, Sherry, paprika, garlic and hot pepper sauce in bowl. Add chicken. Marinate for 1 to 2 hours, turning occasionally. Preheat broiler. Remove chicken from marinade. Brush with oil. Place bone side up on rack in broiler pan. Broil for 13 minutes. Baste with marinade. Broil for 3 minutes longer. Turn chicken; move a little further from heat source to avoid blistering. Baste skin side with marinade. Broil for 12 minutes. Baste again. Broil until tender. Cool. Wrap in foil. Chill until serving time. Yield: 12 servings.

Pam Myers, Iota Epsilon
Fayetteville, Georgia

CHICKEN BREASTS IN CREAM

3 pounds chicken breasts
2 or 3 tablespoons corn oil
½ cup chopped onion
1 clove of garlic, minced
1 cup cream
1 cup chicken broth
2 teaspoons salt
⅛ teaspoon pepper
1 tablespoon
  Worcestershire sauce
2 tablespoons all-purpose
  flour
½ cup water

Preheat oven to 300 degrees. Brown chicken in oil in Dutch oven. Add next 7 ingredients. Bake, tightly covered, for 2 hours. Remove chicken to heated platter. Blend mixture of flour and water into pan drippings. Cook until thickened, stirring constantly. Pour over chicken. Serve over rice. Yield: 4 servings.

Karyn Wood, Xi Pi Kappa
Midland, Texas

ALMOND CHICKEN

1 pound chicken breasts	4 Chinese mushrooms,
2 teaspoons cooking	sliced
Sherry	3 ounces pea pods
2 teaspoons cornstarch	3 cups bean sprouts
1 egg white	2 tablespoons peanut oil
Salt and pepper to taste	½ teaspoon salt
2 tablespoons peanut oil	1 tablespoon soy sauce
½ teaspoon salt	¼ teaspoon MSG
1 medium onion, sliced	1 tablespoon cornstarch
2 stalks celery, sliced	¼ cup water
12 water chestnuts, sliced	Almonds

Bone, skin and slice chicken breasts. Mix Sherry, cornstarch, egg white and salt and pepper in bowl. Add chicken; stir to coat. Heat 2 tablespoons oil in wok; add ½ teaspoon salt. Stir-fry onion, celery, water chestnuts, mushrooms, pea pods and bean sprouts for 3 minutes; remove vegetables. Heat 2 tablespoons oil in wok; add ½ teaspoon salt. Stir-fry chicken until cooked through. Add soy sauce and MSG. Add cooked vegetables; mix well. Stir in cornstarch dissolved in water. Cook until thickened, stirring constantly. Sprinkle with almonds. Serve with rice. Yield: 4 servings.

Lisa Melcher, Alpha Nu
Havre, Montana

CHICKEN BREASTS AMANDINE

4 chicken breast filets	1 tablespoon (heaping)
¼ cup butter	all-purpose flour
½ teaspoon garlic powder	1 beef bouillon cube
¼ cup all-purpose flour	1 10-ounce can
½ cup milk	chicken broth
¾ cup bread crumbs	Salt and pepper to taste
½ cup butter	½ cup white wine
1 small package	½ cup Sherry
slivered almonds	

Preheat oven to 325 degrees. Pound chicken flat. Spread 1 tablespoon butter on each; sprinkle with garlic powder. Roll up, tucking in edges. Coat with ¼ cup flour; dip into milk. Coat with bread crumbs. Cook in ½ cup butter in skillet over low heat until brown. Place in baking dish. Sauté almonds in pan drippings until light brown. Sprinkle with 1 tablespoon flour. Add bouillon cube, chicken broth, additional garlic powder and salt and pepper. Cook over low heat for 20 minutes, stirring constantly. Stir in white wine and Sherry. Pour over chicken. Bake for 1 hour. Yield: 4 servings.

Donna Morse, Xi Alpha Epsilon
Louisville, Kentucky

BEER CHICKEN

2 to 4 chicken breasts	1½ tablespoons soy
¼ cup melted butter	sauce
1 10-ounce can cream	1 4-ounce can
of mushroom soup	mushrooms, drained
¾ cup beer	

Preheat oven to 350 derees. Arrange chicken in baking dish. Add mixture of remaining ingredients. Bake for 30 minutes. Baste. Bake for 30 minutes longer. Serve over rice. Yield: 2 to 4 servings.

Robette Gail Brier, Alpha Upsilon
Mobile, Alabama

CHICKEN SUPREME

6 chicken breast filets	½ cup white wine
6 slices Monterey Jack	1 4-ounce jar sliced
cheese	mushrooms, drained
1 recipe white sauce	

Preheat oven to 350 degrees. Parboil chicken in a small amount of water in skillet; drain. Place in greased 9x13-inch baking pan. Place slice of cheese on each. Combine white sauce, wine and mushrooms in bowl. Pour over chicken. Bake for 45 minutes or until tender. Serve with broccoli, new potatoes and scalloped apples. Yield: 6 servings.

Cynthia Sue Bair, Epsilon Phi
Farmington, Missouri

CHICKEN CACCIATORE

8 chicken breast filets	8 ounces mushrooms,
Salt and pepper to taste	sliced
All-purpose flour	1 4-ounce jar whole
⅓ cup olive oil	pimentos, undrained,
1 large onion, chopped	sliced
3 or 4 cloves of garlic,	3 bay leaves
minced	1 teaspoon thyme
2 16-ounce cans whole	1 teaspoon dried oregano
tomatoes, undrained,	2 medium green bell
quartered	peppers, cut into strips

Sprinkle chicken with salt and pepper; coat with flour. Heat olive oil in heavy saucepan over medium-high heat. Add chicken. Sauté for 4 to 5 minutes on each side or until golden brown. Drain on paper towels. Add onion and garlic. Sauté over medium heat for 5 minutes. Stir in tomatoes, mushrooms, pimentos and seasonings. Add chicken. Bring to a boil; reduce heat. Simmer for 30 minutes, stirring occasionally. Stir in green pepper. Cook for 30 minutes; stirring occasionally. Remove bay leaves. Serve with hot cooked spaghetti. Yield: 8 servings.

Helen Mornhill, Theta
Overland Park, Kansas

CHICKEN ELEGANT

8 chicken breast filets	1 10-ounce can
8 slices bacon	mushroom soup
4 ounces chipped beef	Paprika
1 cup sour cream	

Preheat oven to 275 degrees. Wrap chicken breasts with bacon. Place chipped beef in greased 9x12-inch baking dish. Arrange chicken on top. Pour mixture of sour cream and soup over chicken. Sprinkle with paprika. Bake for 3 hours. Yield: 8 servings.

Jean Shirey, Laureate Mu
Fort Collins, Colorado

CASHEW CHICKEN

1 teaspoon salt
1 teaspoon sugar
1 tablespoon soy sauce
3 tablespoons Sherry
2 chicken breast filets, cubed
3 tablespoons cornstarch
1 egg, beaten

2 tablespoons peanut oil
2 cloves of garlic, minced
½ teaspoon ginger
½ cup boiling water
1 teaspoon MSG
½ cup cashews
½ green onion, chopped

Combine salt, sugar, soy sauce and Sherry in bowl. Add chicken. Marinate for 30 minutes or longer. Drain, reserving marinade. Coat chicken with cornstarch; dip into beaten egg. Heat oil in wok. Add chicken. Cook, covered, for 15 minutes or until water has evaporated from batter. Cook, uncovered, for 1 minute for crispness. Remove chicken to serving dish. Add garlic, ginger, boiling water, MSG and reserved marinade to wok; mix well. Pour over chicken. Sprinkle with cashews and green onion. Yield: 4 servings.

Cynthia S. Gromer, Zeta Theta
Lee's Summit, Missouri

CHICKEN CORDON BLEU

6 chicken breast filets
6 thin slices ham
6 thin slices Swiss cheese
1 envelope Shake and Bake coating mix
¼ cup Parmesan cheese

½ 10-ounce can cream of mushroom soup
½ cup sour cream
¼ cup mayonnaise
1 egg yolk, beaten

Pound chicken flat. Top with ham and cheese. Roll up; secure with toothpick. Coat with Shake and Bake. Refrigerate, covered with plastic wrap, for 2 to 4 hours. Let stand at room temperature for 15 to 30 minutes. Preheat oven to 375 degrees. Place chicken in shallow 9x13-inch baking dish. Sprinkle with Parmesan cheese. Bake for 30 minutes. Mix soup, sour cream, mayonnaise and egg yolk in bowl; spoon over chicken. Bake for 15 minutes longer. Yield: 6 servings.

Sandra Smith, Eta Theta
Plant City, Florida

MICROWAVE CHICKEN CORDON BLEU

½ cup fine dry bread crumbs
1 tablespoon Parmesan cheese
1 teaspoon snipped chives
1 teaspoon dried parsley flakes
⅛ teaspoon poultry seasoning
⅛ teaspoon celery seed
4 large whole chicken breasts, skinned, boned
2 tablespoons butter, melted

4 thin slices fully cooked ham
4 thin slices Swiss cheese
2 tablespoons butter, melted
2 tablespoons all-purpose flour
1 teaspoon instant chicken bouillon
1 teaspoon dried parsley flakes
¼ teaspoon garlic powder
¼ teaspoon pepper
1 cup milk
¼ cup dry white wine

Combine first 6 ingredients in shallow plate. Flatten chicken breasts with meat mallet. Brush insides of chicken breasts with melted butter. Place 1 slice ham and 1 slice Swiss cheese on buttered side of each chicken breast; fold or roll to enclose filling. Brush with remaining melted butter; roll in crumb mixture to coat. Place in 7x12-inch baking dish. Sprinkle with half the remaining crumbs. Microwave, uncovered, on Medium (50% power) for 10 minutes. Turn breasts over; sprinkle with remaining crumbs. Microwave for 10 to 15 minutes or until fork-tender, rotating dish ½ turn after 6 minutes. Keep warm. Blend 2 tablespoons melted butter and flour in saucepan. Add bouillon, 1 teaspoon parsley and pepper. Stir in milk and wine gradually. Cook until thickened, stirring constantly. Serve over chicken. Yield: 4 servings.

Joanne Gardner, Preceptor Beta Alpha
Sedalia, Missouri

CHICKEN CURRY OVER RICE

1 large onion, minced
¼ cup butter
5 tablespoons all-purpose flour
2 to 3 cups chicken broth
Pinch of cayenne pepper

2 teaspoons curry powder
Salt and pepper to taste
4 chicken breasts, cooked, boned
2 hard-cooked eggs, chopped

Sauté onion in butter in skillet. Add flour and broth alternately, mixing well. Add enough broth to make of desired consistency. Add seasonings. Cook over low heat for 10 minutes. Add chicken. Pour into serving dish. Garnish with eggs. Serve with small bowls of chopped green pepper, tomato, oranges, grapefruit, pineapple, toasted coconut, raisins, roasted peanuts and sliced bananas. Yield: 8 to 10 servings.

Cindy Gurecky, Alpha Omega Eta
Richmond, Texas

CHICKEN BREASTS DELUXE

2 whole chicken breasts
½ teaspoon salt
½ teaspoon Accent pepper
2 eggs, beaten
Dry bread crumbs
½ cup margarine

2 3-ounce cans sliced mushrooms, drained
4 or 5 slices Muenster cheese
2 cups chicken stock
Juice of 1 lemon

Season chicken with salt and Accent. Cut into large pieces. Marinate in eggs in refrigerator for 3 hours. Drain. Roll in dry bread crumbs. Brown in margarine in skillet. Preheat oven to 350 degrees. Place chicken in single layer in 9x13-inch baking dish. Layer mushrooms and cheese over chicken. Bake for 30 minutes, basting every 5 minutes with chicken stock. Pour lemon juice over chicken. Yield: 5 servings.

Olivia Sholley, Laureate Lambda
Selinsgrove, Pennsylvania

CHICKEN DIJON

4 chicken breast filets
3 tablespoons butter
3 tablespoons all-purpose
  flour
1 cup chicken broth

1 cup half and half
2 tablespoons Dijon-
  style mustard
Hot cooked rice

Cut chicken into strips. Cook in butter in large skillet over medium heat for 20 minutes or until tender. Remove to warm serving platter. Blend flour into drippings. Stir in chicken broth and half and half gradually. Cook until thickened, stirring constantly. Stir in mustard; add chicken. Cook, covered, for 10 minutes. Spoon rice into ring around outer edge of platter. Spoon chicken pieces into center. Serve remaining sauce in gravy boat. Yield: 4 servings.

Georgia Lammert, Zeta Lambda
Havelock, North Carolina

CHICKEN BREASTS FLORENTINE

2 10-ounce packages
   frozen chopped spinach
6 large chicken breast
   filets
1 stalk celery, chopped
½ medium onion,
   chopped
½ teaspoon salt

1 cup water
¼ cup melted butter
¼ cup all-purpose flour
Dash of pepper
1 cup light cream
Dash of nutmeg
½ cup Parmesan cheese

Cook spinach using package directions; drain well. Combine chicken, celery, onion, salt and 1 cup water in saucepan. Bring to a boil; reduce heat. Simmer for 20 minutes or until tender. Drain, reserving 1 cup broth; discard vegetables. Blend butter, flour and pepper in saucepan. Stir in reserved broth and cream. Cook until thickened and bubbly, stirring constantly; remove from heat. Stir ½ cup sauce, nutmeg and half the cheese into drained spinach. Spread in 6x10-inch baking dish. Arrange chicken over top. Pour remaining sauce over top. Sprinkle with remaining cheese and additional nutmeg if desired. Cover with plastic wrap. Chill until ready to bake. Preheat oven to 375 degrees. Bake, uncovered, for 30 to 35 minutes or until light brown. Yield: 6 servings.

Isabelle Henry, Xi Beta Omicrom
Springfield, New Jersey

CHICKEN À LA GETCHER

3 chicken breasts
Vegetable oil
2 stalks celery, chopped
8 ounces mushrooms, or
   1 medium can sliced
   mushrooms
½ cup chopped onion
3 cups wild rice, cooked

2 10-ounce cans cream of
   chicken soup
¼ cup milk
1 teaspoon lemon juice
1 cup mayonnaise
1½ cups shredded cheese
¾ cup soft bread crumbs

Preheat oven to 350 degrees. Brush chicken with oil. Wrap in foil. Bake for 1½ hours. Remove skin. Sauté celery, mushrooms and onion in a small amount of oil in skillet. Add wild rice. Blend soup, milk, lemon juice and mayonnaise in bowl. Layer wild rice, chicken, soup mixture, cheese and bread crumbs in casserole. Bake for 45 minutes or until brown. Yield: 8 servings.

Beverly M. Smith, Laureate Delta Alpha
Oceanside, California

CHICKEN GRAND-MÈRE

8 chicken breasts
Salt and pepper to taste
1 cup all-purpose flour
½ cup margarine
5 green onions, chopped
3 stalks celery, chopped
½ cup chopped parsley
2 bouillon cubes

1 4-ounce jar sliced
   mushrooms
1 tablespoon
   Worcestershire sauce
1 tablespoon Kitchen
   Bouquet
1 cup white wine

Season chicken breasts with salt and pepper; coat with flour. Place in 9x13-inch baking dish. Combine remaining ingredients in saucepan. Cook over medium heat for 10 minutes. Pour over chicken. Marinate in refrigerator overnight. Preheat oven to 350 degrees. Bake for 45 minutes. Yield: 6 to 8 servings.

Sheron Gray Stickler, Kappa Kappa
Baytown, Texas

HAWAIIAN CHICKEN

1 teaspoon salt
⅛ teaspoon nutmeg
⅓ cup all-purpose flour
3 pounds chicken breasts,
   skinned
¼ cup shortening

1 20-ounce can sliced
   pineapple
¼ cup soy sauce
1 tablespoon cornstarch
2 tablespoons sugar
½ teaspoon celery salt

Preheat oven to 350 degreeds. Mix salt, nutmeg and flour in plastic bag. Shake chicken in flour mixture. Brown in shortening in skillet. Arrange in 9x-13-inch baking pan. Drain pineapple, reserving juice. Arrange pineapple over chicken. Blend reserved juice and soy sauce with mixture of cornstach, sugar and celery salt in saucepan. Bring to a boil, stirring constantly. Pour over chicken. Bake, covered, for 1¼ hours. Serve with hot cooked rice. Yield: 4 to 6 servings.

Edna Pearce, Laureate Delta Beta
Forestville, California

GLAZED CHICKEN

4 chicken breasts
Salt and pepper to taste
Garlic powder to taste
2 to 3 tablespoons
   apricot preserves

1 tablespoon
   Worcestershire sauce
Dash of tarragon vinegar
Sesame seed
Onion flakes

Preheat oven to 350 degrees. Season chicken breasts with salt, pepper and garlic powder. Place in baking pan. Combine preserves, Worcestershire sauce and vinegar in bowl. Spread over chicken. Sprinkle sesame seed and onion flakes on top. Bake for 1 hour. Yield: 4 servings.

Phyllis Johnson, Xi Eta Lamda
Tampa, Florida

ITALIAN CHICKEN BREASTS

6 chicken breasts
¾ cup Italian-seasoned
    bread crumbs
¼ cup Parmesan cheese
½ cup sliced green onions
2 tablespoons margarine
2 tablespoons all-purpose
    flour
1 cup milk

Preheat oven to 350 degrees. Coat chicken breasts with mixture of bread crumbs and cheese. Place in 9x13-inch baking pan. Sauté green onions in margarine in skillet. Add flour; mix well. Stir in milk. Cook until thickened, stirring constantly. Pour over chicken. Bake for 45 minutes or until chicken is tender. Yield: 6 servings.

Theresa Nipper, Xi Iota Phi
West Frankfort, Illinois

CHICKEN JERUSALEM

12 chicken breast filets
½ cup butter
2 green onions, chopped
½ cup white wine
½ cup water
1 cup sliced mushrooms
2 teaspoons salt
2   14-ounce cans
    artichoke hearts
Hot cooked noodles
Chopped parsley
Parmesan cheese

Brown chicken in butter in skillet. Add green onions, wine and water. Simmer for 45 minutes. Add mushrooms, salt and artichoke hearts. Cook over low heat for 15 minutes. Serve with noodles sprinkled with parsley. Top with Parmesan cheese. Yield: 12 servings.

Lennie Bates, Preceptor Mu
Neosho, Missouri

CHICKEN KABOBS

6 chicken breast filets
24 squares of green bell
    pepper
2 tomatoes, cut into
    wedges
1   12-ounce package
    mushroom caps
1 cup soy sauce
½ cup corn oil
¼ cup sugar
4 teaspoons lemon juice
1 teaspoon meat
    tenderizer
2 cloves of garlic

Preheat grill. Cut chicken into 2-inch pieces. Thread chicken and vegetables on skewers. Combine soy sauce and remaining ingredients in bowl; mix well. Place skewers on foil over hot coals. Grill for 30 minutes, basting frequently. Yield: 6 servings.

Cindy L. Spear, Omega
Valdosta, Georgia

KAWI CHICKEN

3 pounds chicken breast
    filets
1 teaspoon garlic salt
¼ teaspoon pepper
1 teaspoon paprika
2 tablespoons olive oil
1½ green bell peppers,
    thinly sliced
1 cup diagonally sliced
    celery
2 medium onions, sliced
8 ounces mushrooms,
    sliced
1¼ cups chicken broth
2 tablespoons cornstarch
3 tablespoons soy sauce
2 fresh tomatoes,
    cut into eights
3 cups cooked rice

Cut chicken into long strips. Sprinkle with garlic salt, pepper and paprika. Let stand for several minutes. Brown chicken in olive oil in skillet for 5 minutes. Add green peppers, celery, onions, mushrooms and half the chicken broth. Steam, covered, for 3 minuters. Blend remaining broth, cornstarch and soy sauce in bowl. Stir into chicken mixture. Cook until thickened, stirring constantly. Add tomatoes. Serve over rice. Yield: 6 servings.

Rita Bertler, Chi Nu
Englewood, Florida

POLLO DE KIEV CON SALSA

8 chicken breast filets
1   7-ounce can chopped
    green chilies
4 ounces Monterey Jack
    cheese, cut into strips
¾ cup melted butter
½ cup bread crumbs
¼ cup Parmesan cheese
1 tablespoon chili powder
½ teaspoon salt
¼ teaspoon cumin
¼ teaspoon pepper

Pound chicken to ¼-inch thickness. Place 2 tablespoons green chilies and 1 strip of Monterey Jack cheese in center of each piece; roll up and tuck ends under. Dip into melted butter; coat with mixture of crumbs and remaining ingredients. Place in baking dish. Drizzle with any remaining butter. Chill, covered, for 4 hours or longer. Preheat oven to 400 degrees. Bake for 25 minutes or until tender. Serve with Salsa Sauce. (See page 46.) Yield: 8 servings.

Bonnie Wakefield, Xi Delta Pi
Del Norte, Colorado

LEMON PEPPER CHICKEN

1 cup melted butter
1 cup sweet and sour mix
2 tablespoons garlic salt
¼ cup lemon-pepper
    seasoning
1 pound chicken breasts

Preheat grill. Combine first 4 ingredients in bowl. Add chicken. Marinate for 30 minutes. Grill over hot coals until brown on 1 side. Dip in marinade. Grill until brown and tender. Yield: 2 servings.

Debbie Yates, Xi Kappa Omega
Pickerington, Ohio

MELT-IN-YOUR-MOUTH CHICKEN

4 chicken breasts
2 cups chicken broth
1   10-ounce can cream of
    chicken soup
½ cup melted margarine
1 cup self-rising flour
1 cup buttermilk
½ teaspoon salt
Pepper to taste

Preheat oven to 425 degrees. Cook chicken as desired until tender. Bone and chop; place in 9x12-inch baking dish. Mix chicken broth and soup in saucepan. Bring to a boil. Pour over chicken. Combine remaining ingredients in bowl; mix well. Spoon over chicken. Bake for 25 to 30 minutes or until brown. Yield: 6 to 8 servings.

Lois M. Stephens, Xi Alpha Nu
Atlanta, Georgia

CHICKEN MACADAMIA

3 whole chicken breasts, boned	Oil for deep frying
Salt to taste	1 tablespoon cornstarch
2 eggs	½ cup packed light brown sugar
½ cup all-purpose flour	⅓ cup vinegar
¼ cup cornstarch	6 tablespoons pineapple juice
½ cup cold water	2 tablespoons soy sauce
1 tablespoon fresh ginger, minced	¼ cup chopped green bell pepper
1 medium onion, grated	1 small can macadamia nuts, chopped
¼ teaspoon pepper	Coconut
2 tablespoons corn oil	
2 tablespoons soy sauce	
2 tablespoons Brandy	

Sprinkle chicken lightly with salt. Let stand for 30 minutes. Combine eggs and next 9 ingredients in bowl; beat until smooth. Marinate chicken in batter for 20 minutes. Deep-fry in hot oil until golden brown; drain. Keep warm in oven. Mix 1 tablespoon cornstarch, brown sugar, vinegar, pineapple juice and 2 tablespoons soy sauce in saucepan. Cook until thickened, stirring constantly. Add additional pineapple juice if necessary to make of desired consistency. Stir in green pepper. Pour over chicken. Top with chopped macadamia nuts; sprinkle with coconut. Serve immediately. Yield: 6 servings.

Debbie Kubik, Xi Alpha Iota
Auburn, Nebraska

CHICKEN BREASTS MADEIRA

⅔ cup minced onion	Salt and pepper to taste
1 tablespoon sweet paprika	¼ cup canned beef broth
5 tablespoons unsalted butter	¼ cup Madeira
4 chicken breast filets	1 cup heavy cream
½ teaspoon lemon juice	2 tablespoons minced fresh parsley leaves

Preheat oven to 400 degrees. Blanch onion in boiling water in saucepan for 1 minute; drain and pat dry. Cook onion with paprika in butter in large ovenproof covered skillet over low heat for 8 minutes, stirring occasionally. Sprinkle chicken with lemon juice and salt and pepper. Arrange over onion in skillet. Cover with circle of buttered waxed paper. Bake for 10 minutes or until chicken is just springy to the touch. Remove chicken to heated platter with slotted spatula; cover and keep warm. Stir broth and Madeira into skillet. Bring to a boil over medium heat. Cook for 2 to 3 minutes or until liquid is reduced to about ½ cup, stirring constantly. Strain mixture through fine sieve into small skillet, pressing onion firmly. Stir ¼ cup cream into mixture. Bring to a boil. Stir in remaining cream ¼ cup at a time. Cook for 4 minutes or until thickened, stirring constantly. Remove from heat. Season with salt, pepper and additional lemon juice to taste. Spoon over chicken; sprinkle with parsley. Yield: 4 servings.

Sonnet Youstra Severson, Gamma Iota
Aurora, Colorado

CHICKEN BREASTS NEPTUNE

1½ to 2 pounds chicken breast filets	2 shallots, minced
½ teaspoon salt	½ cup chopped green bell pepper
¼ teaspoon pepper	1 tablespoon all-purpose flour
1 6-ounce package king crab meat	½ cup white wine
1 tablespoon lemon juice	½ cup whipping cream
¼ cup cornstarch	Chopped parsley
3 tablespoons butter	

Pound chicken to ¼-inch thickness between plastic wrap. Sprinkle with salt and pepper. Place crab meat at end of each; sprinkle with lemon juice. Roll to enclose filling. Coat generously with cornstarch. Brown evenly in butter in skillet over medium heat. Remove and keep warm. Sauté shallots and green pepper in pan drippings for 1 minute. Mix in flour. Add wine, stirring to deglaze skillet. Stir in cream. Cook until thickened, stirring constantly. Add chicken. Simmer for 5 minutes. Garnish with parsley. Yield: 4 servings.

Sandra Guidici, Preceptor Kappa Theta
Clio, California

CHICKEN BREASTS IN ORANGE SAUCE

6 chicken breast filets	½ cup orange juice
½ cup all-purpose flour	½ cup dry white wine
½ teaspoon salt	¼ teaspoon nutmeg or mace
½ teaspoon paprika	2 teaspoons light brown sugar
Dash of pepper	
Dash of garlic powder	4 to 8 ounces fresh mushrooms, sliced
6 tablespoons corn oil	2 cups sliced carrots
1 10-ounce can cream of mushroom soup	
½ cup chicken broth	

Preheat oven to 225 degrees. Coat chicken with mixture of flour, salt, paprika, pepper and garlic powder. Brown chicken in oil in electric skillet; drain. Blend soup, chicken broth, orange juice, wine, nutmeg and brown sugar in bowl. Pour over chicken. Add mushrooms and carrots. Cook, covered, for 1 hour or until chicken is tender. Yield: 6 servings.

Ann Davis, Preceptor Kappa Nu
San Antonio, Texas

CHICKEN BREASTS ORIENTAL

1 4-ounce jar sweet and sour sauce	1 16-ounce can whole cranberry sauce
1 envelope dry onion soup mix	8 chicken breast filets

Preheat oven to 325 degrees. Mix sweet and sour sauce, onion soup mix and cranberry sauce in bowl. Pour over chicken breasts in 7x11-inch baking dish. Bake, covered, for 30 minutes. Bake, uncovered, for 30 minutes longer. Yield: 8 servings.

Jane Schlusemeyer, Laureate Alpha Alpha
Evansville, Indiana

CHICKEN PARMESAN

6 chicken breast filets
3 eggs, lightly beaten
1 teaspoon salt
½ teaspoon pepper
¾ cup fine dry bread crumbs
½ cup corn oil
1 16-ounce can tomato sauce
¼ teaspoon basil leaves
⅛ teaspoon garlic powder
¼ teaspoon oregano
1 tablespoon butter
½ cup Parmesan cheese
16 ounces mozzarella cheese, shredded

Preheat oven to 350 degrees. Dip chicken into mixture of eggs, salt and pepper; coat with bread crumbs. Heat oil until very hot in large skillet. Brown chicken quickly on both sides; remove to shallow baking dish. Pour excess oil from skillet. Stir tomato sauce, basil, oregano and garlic powder into skillet. Simmer for 10 minutes or until thickened. Stir in butter. Pour over chicken; sprinkle with Parmesan cheese. Bake, uncovered, for 30 to 35 minutes. Top with mozzarella cheese. Bake for 10 minutes longer or until cheese melts. Yield: 6 servings.

Melanie Ann Rowe, Epsilon Psi
Holliday, Missouri

POPPY SEED CHICKEN

8 chicken breasts, cooked
1 cup sour cream
2 10-ounce cans cream of chicken soup
3 tablespoons poppy seed
2 cups crushed Ritz crackers
¾ cup melted margarine

Preheat oven to 350 degrees. Bone and chop chicken breasts. Place in casserole. Heat sour cream and soup in saucepan. Pour over chicken. Sprinkle mixture of poppyseed and crackers on top. Drizzle with margarine. Bake for 30 minutes. Yield: 10 to 12 servings.

Sharon Grotlisch, Xi Beta Zeta
Decatur, Alabama

PARTY-GOING CHICKEN

8 chicken breast filets
1 10-ounce can cream of chicken soup
2 tablespoons Brandy
⅓ cup sour cream
2 green onions, chopped
½ teaspoon paprika
½ teaspoon pepper
¼ cup cashews
Parsley

Preheat oven to 400 degrees. Rinse chicken breasts; pierce with fork. Place in single layer in 2½-quart baking dish. Bake for 35 minutes. Combine chicken soup, Brandy, sour cream, onions, paprika and pepper; mix well. Pour over chicken. Bake, covered, for 20 minutes. Garnish with cashews and parsley. Yield: 8 servings.

Maxine McGuire, Preceptor Kappa
Clearwater, Florida

For a delicious teriyaki, **Bonnie Keltz, Alpha Nu, Stillwater, Oklahoma**, marinates 8 boned chicken breasts in mixture of ½ cup soy sauce, minced clove of garlic, ¾ teaspoon ginger, 2 tablespoons sugar and 1 ounce Sherry for 4 to 6 hours. Grill for 15 minutes.

BAKED CHICKEN REUBEN

8 chicken breast filets
¼ teaspoon salt
⅛ teaspoon pepper
1 16-ounce can sauerkraut
4 slices Swiss cheese
1¼ cups Thousand Island salad dressing
1 tablespoon chopped fresh parsley

Preheat oven to 325 degrees. Arrange chicken in greased baking pan. Sprinkle with salt and pepper. Drain sauerkraut; squeeze dry. Spread over chicken; top with Swiss cheese. Pour salad dressing evenly over cheese. Cover with foil. Bake for about 1½ hours. Sprinkle with parsley. Yield: 4 servings.

Carol Young, Theta Beta
Peachtree City, Georgia

CHICKEN SARANNO

6 baked patty shells
6 chicken breast filets
Salt to taste
Pepper to taste
Garlic powder to taste
Curry powder to taste
All-purpose flour
¼ cup clarified butter
¼ cup Amaretto
8 ounces fresh mushrooms, thickly sliced
Grated rind and juice of 1 lemon
1½ cups chicken broth
1 tablespoon cornstarch
Chopped tomato and parsley

Keep patty shells warm. Cut chicken into 1-inch strips. Sprinkle with salt, pepper, garlic powder and curry powder. Coat with flour. Brown chicken in butter in skillet. Do not overcook chicken. Add Amaretto, mushrooms, lemon rind and juice. Simmer for 5 minutes. Add mixture of chicken broth and cornstarch. Cook until thickened, stirring constantly. Spoon into patty shells. Garnish with chopped tomato and parsley. Yield: 6 servings.

Kathy McReynolds, Xi Nu
Springfield, Missouri

SAUCY CHICKEN BREASTS

4 chicken breast filets
½ cup dry white wine
¼ cup lemon juice
2 tablespoons olive oil
¼ teaspoon pepper
½ teaspoon salt
¼ cup Parmesan cheese
½ cup fine Italian bread crumbs
¼ teaspoon oregano
Grated rind of 1 lemon
2 eggs, beaten
1 tablespoon olive oil
1 tablespoon butter

Flatten chicken breasts between waxed paper with meat mallet. Combine next 5 ingredients in bowl; mix well. Add chicken. Marinate, covered, in refrigerator for 2 hours or longer. Drain, reserving marinade; pat dry. Preheat oven to 350 degrees. Combine cheese, bread crumbs, oregano and lemon rind in bowl. Dip chicken in eggs; coat with crumbs. Brown in mixture of oil and butter in skillet. Remove to 8x12-inch baking dish. Bake for 30 minutes. Add reserved marinade to pan drippings. Cook over medium heat until slightly thickened, stirring frequently. Serve over chicken. Yield: 4 servings.

Roxane I. Fort, Zeta Sigma
Fairfield Bay, Arkansas

SESAME CHICKEN

1 teaspoon salt	1¼ cups all-purpose flour
½ teaspoon pepper	6 tablespoons sesame seed
¼ cup all-purpose flour	½ cup fine dry bread
8 chicken breast filets	crumbs
4 eggs, beaten	Oil for frying
¼ cup milk	Supreme Cream Sauce

Combine salt, pepper and ¼ cup flour in bag. Cut each chicken breast into 5 pieces. Add to flour mixture; shake to coat. Combine eggs and milk in small bowl; set aside. Combine 1¼ cups flour, sesame seed and bread crumbs in small bowl. Dip each chicken piece in egg mixture, then in flour mixture. Heat oil to 350 degrees. Add chicken. Sauté for 10 to 15 minutes or until golden brown. Serve with Supreme Cream Sauce. Yield: 10 servings.

SUPREME CREAM SAUCE

7 tablespoons melted	3 cups chicken broth
butter	2 egg yolks, beaten
5 tablespoons all-purpose	1½ cups half and half
flour	

Blend butter and flour in saucepan. Add broth gradually. Cook until thickened, stirring constantly. Stir ½ cup hot mixture into egg yolks; stir egg yolks into hot mixture. Add half and half. Cook until thickened, stirring constantly. Yield: 4½ cups.

Linda J. Watson, Xi Beta Beta
Birmingham, Alabama

SIMON AND GARFUNKLE CHICKEN

6 chicken breast filets	Bread crumbs
2 tablespoons butter,	1 cup melted butter
softened	2 tablespoons parsley
6 ounces mozzarella	¼ teaspoon sage
cheese, sliced	¼ teaspoon rosemary
Salt and pepper to taste	¼ teaspoon thyme
2 cups all-purpose flour	½ cup white wine
2 eggs, beaten	

Preheat oven to 350 degrees. Pound chicken breasts on both sides with meat mallet. Spread with butter; add ½ slice cheese. Season with salt and pepper. Tuck in ends and roll up, securing with toothpicks. Coat chicken rolls with flour, dip into eggs and roll in bread crumbs. Place in greased baking dish. Mix melted butter and herbs. Pour over chicken. Bake for 30 minutes, basting with butter mixture every 15 minutes. Pour wine over top. Bake for 30 minutes longer, basting every 15 minutes. Yield: 6 servings.

Shirlee Ingram-Butts, Sigma Delta
Kearney, Missouri

CHICKEN SUPREME

20 Ritz crackers, crushed	¾ cup Parmesan cheese
½ to 1 teaspoon garlic	6 chicken breast filets
powder	2 tablespoons melted
1 tablespoon parsley	butter
flakes	

Preheat oven to 350 degrees. Combine cracker crumbs, garlic powder, parsley flakes and cheese in bowl. Dip chicken in butter; coat with crumbs. Place in 9x13-inch baking dish. Bake, covered, for 45 minutes. Bake, uncovered, for 15 minutes longer. Yield: 6 servings.

Lois VanDeSompele, Xi Phi Iota
Apple Valley, California

SWEET AND SOUR CHICKEN BREASTS

6 chicken breasts	½ cup sugar
2 eggs, beaten	1 cup vinegar
1 teaspoon garlic salt	2 tablespoons soy sauce
1 cup cornstarch	2 teaspoons salt
Oil for frying	1 teaspoon MSG
2 cups chicken broth	

Preheat oven to 375 degrees. Dip chicken in eggs; roll in mixture of garlic salt and cornstarch. Brown in oil in skillet. Place in 9x13-inch baking dish. Bring mixture of lremaining ingredients to a boil in saucepan. Pour over chicken. Bake, covered, for 1½ hours. Yield: 6 servings.

Darlene Ingebritsen, Xi Alpha Eta
Payette, Idaho

CHICKEN TACO AND RICE

1 pound chicken breast	1 12-ounce can corn,
filets, cut into strips	drained
2 tablespoons corn oil	1 medium red bell
1 13-ounce can	pepper, cut into strips
chicken broth	1½ cups uncooked
1 8-ounce can tomato	minute rice
sauce	½ cup shredded
1 envelope dry taco	Cheddar cheese
seasoning mix	Tortilla chips

Sauté chicken in oil in skillet for 2 minutes. Add broth, tomato sauce and seasoning mix. Bring to a boil; reduce heat. Simmer, covered, for 5 minutes, stirring occasionally. Add corn and red pepper. Bring to a boil; stir in rice. Cover; remove from heat. Let stand for 5 minutes. Fluff with fork. Serve with cheese and tortilla chips.
Yield: 4 servings.

Elaine Tekippe, Theta Theta
Story City, Iowa

TARRAGON CHICKEN

2 pounds chicken breast	⅓ cup Parmesan cheese
filets	Oil for frying
2 tablespoons all-purpose	3 tablespoons melted
flour	butter or margarine
1 egg	1 tablespoon lemon juice
1 tablespoon milk	1 tablespoon tarragon
1 cup bread crumbs	

Coat chicken with flour, mixture of egg and milk, then mixture of crumbs and cheese. Brown chicken in oil in large skillet for 4 to 5 minutes on each side; drain. Heat butter, lemon juice and tarragon in saucepan. Pour over chicken. Yield: 4 servings.

Michelle Maginity, Xi Lambda Mu
Hanover Park, Illinois

VIVA LA CHICKEN TORTILLA CASSEROLE

4 chicken breasts
1 onion, grated
1 10-ounce can cream of
    mushroom soup
1 10-ounce can cream of
    chicken soup
1 cup sour cream
1 7-ounce can green
    chili salsa

½ teaspoon garlic salt
1 7-ounce package
    tortilla chips
1 cup sliced olives
8 ounces sharp Cheddar
    cheese, shredded
8 ounces Monterey
    Jack cheese, shredded

Preheat oven to 400 degrees. Wrap chicken breasts in aluminum foil. Bake for 1 hour. Cool. Bone and cut into large bite-sized pieces. Combine onion, soups, sour cream, chili salsa and garlic salt in bowl; stir until well blended. Layer tortilla chips, chicken, soup mixture, olives and cheeses ½ at a time in buttered 9x13-inch baking dish. Cover with foil. Refrigerate overnight. Preheat oven to 350 degrees. Bake for 1 hour.
Yield: 10 to 12 servings.

Frances Galyen, Xi Alpha Rho
Kanarraville, Utah

WALNUT CHICKEN

2 chicken breast filets
1 medium onion
½ pound broccoli
1 red bell pepper
1 tablespoon oil
2 teaspoons soy sauce
1 teaspoon cornstarch
½ cup chicken broth

½ teaspoon ginger
3 teaspoons soy sauce
2 teaspoons cornstarch
Dried red pepper
    to taste
¼ cup corn oil
1 clove of garlic, minced
½ cup chopped walnuts

Cut chicken and vegetables into 1-inch pieces. Mix 1 tablespoon oil, 2 teaspoons soy sauce and 1 teaspoon cornstarch in small bowl. Stir in chicken to coat. Chill, covered, for 30 minutes. Mix broth, ginger, 3 teaspoons soy sauce and 2 teaspoons cornstarch in bowl. Set aside. Stir-fry chicken mixture and dried red pepper in ¼ cup oil in large skillet over medium heat until chicken is no longer pink. Remove chicken from skillet. Stir-fry onion, red bell pepper and garlic in skillet until onion is tender. Add broccoli. Stir-fry until tender. Add chicken and broth. Cook until thickened, stirring constantly. Stir in walnuts. Serve over hot cooked rice. Yield: 4 servings.

Sherri Herrick, Alpha Omega
Centerville, Ohio

GEORGIA BARBECUED CHICKEN

¼ cup vinegar
½ cup water
½ teaspoon salt
¼ teaspoon cayenne
    pepper
1 clove of garlic, minced
Juice of 1 lemon
1 large onion, sliced
2 tablespoons light
    brown sugar

1 tablespoon prepared
    mustard
½ teaspoon pepper
¼ cup butter
½ cup catsup
2 tablespoons
    Worcestershire sauce
1½ teaspoons liquid
    smoke
6 to 8 chicken pieces

Preheat oven to 325 degrees. Combine first 11 ingredients in saucepan. Cook for 20 minutes. Add catsup and next 2 ingredients; mix well. Place chicken in roasting pan. Pour half the sauce over chicken. Bake for 1½ hours, turning and basting frequently. Yield: 4 servings.

Doris Ohe, Xi Tau Theta
Oakdale, California

CHERRY CHICKEN

2½ pounds chicken pieces
½ teaspoon salt
¼ teaspoon pepper
2 to 3 tablespoons corn oil
1 21-ounce can cherry
    pie filling
½ cup dry white wine

½ cup orange juice
¼ cup packed light
    brown sugar
½ teaspoon salt
¼ teaspoon allspice
¼ teaspoon nutmeg
¼ teaspoon cloves

Brown chicken seasoned with salt and pepper in oil in large skillet for 10 minutes on each side; drain. Pour mixture of remaining ingredients over chicken. Simmer, covered, for 20 to 25 minutes or until chicken is tender. Serve with rice. Yield: 4 servings.

Cindy Christensen, Xi Alpha Theta
Scottsdale, Arizona

CHICKEN CASSEROLE

6 to 8 chicken pieces
5 tablespoons cracker
    meal
1 teaspoon salt
½ teaspoon paprika
2 teaspoons dry mustard

2 tablespoons melted
    margarine
1 10-ounce can cream of
    chicken soup
1 soup can milk
2 teaspoons wine

Preheat oven to 425 degrees. Coat chicken with mixture of next 4 ingredients. Place in margarine in 8x11-inch baking pan. Bake for 35 minutes. Turn chicken. Pour mixture of soup, milk and wine over chicken. Bake for 20 minutes. Yield: 4 servings.

Brenda Johnson, Epsilon Psi
Nutter Fort, West Virginia

DEEP-FRIED SPICED CHICKEN

1 tablespoon brown
    peppercorns
3 tablespoons salt
1¼ pounds chicken
1 green onion, chopped
3 slices ginger
1 star anise

¼ cup soy sauce
1 tablespoon wine
½ egg white
1 tablespoon cornstarch
6 cups corn oil
1 teaspoon sesame oil

Combine peppercorns and salt in skillet. Cook over low heat for 1 minute. Cool. Grind and sift until fine. Cut chicken into halves; cut each half into 4 pieces. Marinate in mixture of next 7 ingredients for 30 minutes. Heat oil in deep frying pan. Add chicken. Deep-fry in corn oil for 3 minutes. Remove chicken and drain. Reheat oil. Add chicken. Fry for about 1 minute or until brown. Remove chicken; drain. Place on serving plate. Sprinkle with sesame oil. Serve with peppercorn salt. Yield: 4 servings.

Tracy Chvilicek, Alpha Nu
Havre, Montana

ELEGANT STUFFED CHICKEN QUARTERS

2 medium zucchini, shredded	1 egg
3 tablespoons butter or margarine	⅛ teaspoon pepper
	½ teaspoon salt
3 slices white bread, torn	1 2½ to 3-pound broiler-fryer, cut into quarters
½ cup shredded Swiss cheese	2 tablespoons honey

Preheat oven to 400 degrees. Sauté zucchini in butter in saucepan over medium heat for 2 minutes, stirring frequently. Remove from heat. Add bread, cheese, egg, pepper and salt. Loosen skin on each chicken quarter by pushing fingers between skin and meat to form pocket. Spoon stuffing into pockets. Place chicken in 9x13-inch glass baking dish. Bake for 50 minutes or until tender. Remove chicken to warm platter. Brush with honey; sprinkle with additional salt. Yield: 4 servings.

Casey Gonzolez, Xi Gamma Tau
Gilbert, Arizona

COMPANY HERBED CHICKEN

1 2½ to 3-pound chicken, cut up	1 clove of garlic
2 tablespoons corn oil	1 cup Sauterne
Salt and pepper to taste	2 tablespoons chopped parsley
1 8-ounce can small whole onions, drained	¼ teaspoon thyme
½ cup coarsely chopped carrots	1 4-ounce can sliced mushrooms
½ cup chopped celery	2 bay leaves

Preheat oven to 350 degrees. Brown chicken in hot oil in skillet. Season with salt and pepper. Place in deep 2-quart casserole. Add onions. Drain excess pan drippings from skillet. Add carrots, celery, garlic and Sauterne to skillet. Simmer until tender. Add parsley, thyme, mushrooms and bay leaves; mix well. Pour over chicken. Bake, covered, for 1 hour and 20 minutes. Remove bay leaves. Yield: 4 to 6 servings.

Beverly Austin, Preceptor Phi
Flowery Branch, Georgia

OVEN-FRIED HERBED CHICKEN

½ cup melted butter	½ teaspoon paprika
2 chickens, cut up	½ teaspoon thyme
⅓ cup water	2 teaspoons salt
1½ cups all-purpose flour	½ teaspoon lemon herb

Preheat oven to 425 degrees. Pour butter into foil-lined baking pan. Dip chicken into water. Coat with mixture of flour and seasonings. Place skin side down in butter. Bake for 25 minutes. Turn. Bake for 20 minutes. Serve with rice or mashed potatoes, any type vegetable or salad. Yield: 12 servings.

Marilyn Baumberger, Xi Alpha Rho
Kanarraville, Utah

ITALIAN BAKED CHICKEN

1 chicken, cut up	⅛ teaspoon garlic powder
½ cup olive oil	⅛ teaspoon red pepper
2 teaspoons salt	1 cup all-purpose flour
¼ teaspoon pepper	1 teaspoon paprika
¼ teaspoon oregano	

Arrange chicken in 9x13-inch baking pan. Mix oil, salt, pepper, oregano, garlic powder and red pepper in bowl; pour over chicken. Chill, covered, for 4 hours or longer, turning occasionally. Preheat oven to 425 degrees. Mix flour and paprika. Drain chicken, reserving marinade. Coat with flour mixture; dip into marinade. Bake for 1 hour or until tender. Yield: 4 servings.

Sue Radel, Gamma Omega
Evan, Minnesota

MAN-PLEASING CHICKEN

8 to 10 chicken thighs, skinned	1 10-ounce can cream of mushroom soup
1 teaspoon garlic powder	1 teaspoon salt
Butter or margarine	1 tablespoon parsley flakes
1 cup milk	

Preheat oven to 325 degrees. Place chicken in 9x13-inch baking pan; sprinkle with garlic powder. Dot with butter. Bake for 15 minutes; turn pieces. Bake for 15 minutes; drain. Add mixture of remaining ingredients. Bake for 15 minutes or until bubbly. Yield: 4 to 5 servings.

Savannah L. Silva, Xi Upsilon Iota
Modesto, California

MARINATED CHICKEN

2 cups 7-Up	1 tablespoon horseradish
2 cups corn oil	1 tablespoon garlic salt
1 cup soy sauce	2 or 3 chickens, cut up

Combine first 5 ingredients in large bowl. Add chicken. Marinate, covered, in refrigerator for 24 hours. Preheat grill. Grill over hot coals until tender, basting frequently with marinade. Yield: 6 servings.

Monica Johnston, Mu Kappa
Ellinwood, Kansas

FAMILY-SECRET MARINATED CHICKEN

1 cup corn oil	1 tablespoon garlic salt
½ cup cider vinegar	1 teaspoon garlic powder
¼ cup Worcestershire sauce	1 tablespoon salt
3 tablespoons lime juice	½ teaspoon pepper
1 teaspoon Tabasco sauce	1 tablespoon sugar
1 tablespoon paprika	2 chickens, cut up

Combine first 11 ingredients in blender container. Process on High for 4 to 5 minutes. Pour over chicken in large bowl. Marinate in refrigerator for 24 hours. Preheat grill. Cook chicken over medium coals for 45 to 60 minutes, turning and basting constantly. Yield: 8 servings.

Charlene Santivasci, Xi Beta Mu
San Bernardino, California

CHICKEN IN ONION AND THYME SAUCE

¼ cup corn oil	3 cups grated onions
1 3-pound chicken,	¼ cup orange juice
cut up	3 tablespoons all-purpose
1¼ teaspoons salt	flour
¼ teaspoon pepper	½ cup water
1 teaspoon thyme	

Preheat oven to 350 degrees. Heat oil in 6-quart saucepan. Add chicken. Brown over medium heat for 10 minutes, turning chicken frequently. Add salt, pepper and thyme; mix well. Add onions and orange juice; mix well. Simmer, covered, for 25 minutes, stirring occasionally. Brown flour in pie plate in oven for 10 minutes, stirring occasionally. Blend with water. Add to chicken. Simmer, covered, for 10 minutes. Add additional water if necessary to make sauce of desired consistency. Yield: 4 servings.

Carla Weinstock, Xi Sigma
Frederick, Maryland

SMOTHERED ONION CHICKEN

1 3-pound chicken,	⅛ teaspoon rosemary
cut up	⅛ teaspoon thyme
¾ cup olive oil	1 small piece fresh
3 or 4 large onions, sliced	ginger, grated
3 or 4 bay leaves	3 or 4 new potatoes,
1 teaspoon pepper	quartered
1 teaspoon oregano	1 cup cooking Sherry

Brown chicken in oil in skillet. Add remaining ingredients. Cook over high heat for 1 minute, stirring constantly; reduce heat. Simmer for 45 minutes or until chicken is tender. Yield: 4 servings.

Luz A. Stevenson, Preceptor Gamma Psi
Vacaville, California

GREAT OVEN-FRIED CHICKEN

1 cup bread crumbs	⅛ teaspoon pepper
¼ cup Parmesan cheese	½ cup butter
2 tablespoons chopped	1 clove of garlic, crushed
parsley	2½ pounds frying
1 teaspoon salt	chicken pieces
¼ teaspoon thyme	

Preheat oven to 400 degrees. Combine bread crumbs, cheese, parsley, salt, thyme and pepper. Melt butter with garlic in shallow baking pan. Dip chicken into butter mixture; coat with crumb mixture. Arrange in baking pan. Bake for 45 minutes; do not turn. Yield: 4 to 6 servings.

Florence Schaefer, Delta Psi
Lincroft, New Jersey

OVEN-CRISP CHICKEN

1 cup all-purpose flour	¼ teaspoon thyme
2 teaspoons salt	1 teaspoon instant onion
¼ teaspoon pepper	1 fryer, cut up
2 teaspoons paprika	½ cup buttermilk

Preheat oven to 400 degrees. Combine first 6 ingredients in bowl. Dip chicken in buttermilk. Coat with flour mixture. Place in greased 9x9-inch baking pan. Bake for 30 minutes on each side. Yield: 4 servings.

Doris Lane, Xi Alpha Omega
Paducah, Kentucky

PICANTE CHICKEN

1 2-pound chicken,	2 cups shredded
cut up	Cheddar cheese
1 egg, beaten	1 6-ounce package
1 cup cornmeal	taco chips, crushed
1 cup picante sauce	

Preheat oven to 375 degrees. Coat chicken with egg, then with cornmeal. Place in 9x13-inch baking pan. Cover with picante sauce. Bake, covered, for 1 hour. Sprinkle with shredded cheese and taco chips. Bake until cheese is melted. Yield: 4 servings.

Jan Peel, Epsilon Psi
Farmington, New Mexico

CHICKEN FRIED RICE

2 tablespoons peanut oil	¼ cup mashed Chinese
2 or 3 cloves of garlic,	black beans
finely chopped	Soy sauce to taste
2 slices fresh gingerroot,	½ to ¾ cup sliced
minced	mushrooms
4 green onions with tops,	1 16-ounce can Chinese
chopped	vegetables
2 stalks celery, sliced	2 to 3 cups cooked rice
2 cups marinated boned	1 or 2 eggs, slightly beaten
chicken pieces, drained	

Heat peanut oil in wok until drops of water sizzle on the side. Add garlic, ginger, green onions and celery. Cook until warm. Add chicken, black beans and soy sauce. Stir-fry until chicken is cooked through. Add remaining vegetables. Cook for several minutes until vegetables are hot. Stir in rice and eggs. Cook until eggs are set, stirring constantly. Yield: 4 servings.

Joan Marshall, Preceptor Alpha Omega
Oklahoma City, Oklahoma

SAUCY CHICKEN WITH RICE

1½ cups rice	1 10-ounce can cream of
1¾ cups milk	chicken soup
1 10-ounce can cream of	8 to 10 pieces chicken
mushroom soup	1 envelope dry onion
1 10-ounce can cream of	soup mix
celery soup	

Preheat oven to 325 degrees. Spread rice in well-greased 9x13-inch baking pan. Blend milk and soups in saucepan. Heat over medium heat. Pour over rice. Place chicken skin side up on top of rice-soup mixture. Sprinkle with onion soup mix. Cover tightly with foil. Bake for 2 hours. Yield: 10 servings.

Norma Gibson, Xi Eta
La Grande, Oregon

CHICKEN AND RICE

1 cup long grain rice	4 cups boiling water
1 fryer, cut up	2 teaspoons chicken
1 envelope dry onion	bouillon
soup mix	

Preheat oven to 375 degrees. Sprinkle rice evenly in bottom of greased 12x16-inch baking pan; arrange chicken over rice. Sprinkle onion mix on top. Pour mixture of boiling water and bouillon over chicken and rice. Bake for 1 hour. Yield: 4 to 6 servings.

Vickie Thomas, Xi Nu
Weiser, Idaho

ROAST CHICKEN

2 3-pound fryers	6 medium potatoes,
1 teaspoon salt	peeled, cut into wedges
1 teaspoon freshly	2 medium onions, peeled,
ground pepper	cut into wedges
2 cloves of garlic, crushed	1/3 cup fresh lemon juice
5 tablespoons melted	1/2 cup water
butter	

Preheat oven to 425 degrees. Rub chicken with salt, pepper and garlic. Place breast-side up in large roasting pan. Brush with 3 tablespoons butter. Coat potatoes with remaining 2 tablespoons butter. Arrange with onions over chicken. Roast for 25 minutes. Reduce heat to 325 degrees. Roast for 45 to 50 minutes or until tender. Pour lemon juice over chicken. Remove chicken, potatoes and onion to warm serving platter. Skim pan juices. Add water; bring to a boil. Slice chicken. Serve with gravy. Yield: 6 servings.

L. Maxine Mitchell, Xi Xi Epsilon
Boerne, Texas

SHERRIED CHICKEN AND MUSHROOMS

3 pounds chicken	3 tablespoons all-purpose
(breasts and thighs)	flour
Salt and pepper to taste	1 1/2 cups canned chicken
Paprika	broth
1/4 cup butter	1/2 cup dry Sherry
3/4 cup finely chopped	1 1/4 teaspoons crumbled
onions	dried rosemary
1 pound sliced fresh	
mushrooms	

Preheat oven to 375 degrees. Sprinkle chicken generously with salt, pepper and paprika. Brown chicken in butter in large skillet over medium heat. Remove to a 3-quart shallow casserole. Sauté onions and mushrooms in pan drippings in skillet. Sprinkle with flour; mix well. Add chicken broth, Sherry and rosemary. Cook until slightly thickened, stirring constantly. Pour over chicken. Bake, covered, for 45 minutes or until chicken is tender. Yield: 6 servings.

Julia Kay Cervantes, Xi Rho Omicron
Humble, Texas

SOUTH SEAS CHICKEN

1/2 cup all-purpose flour	1/2 cup chopped carrots
1 1/2 teaspoons salt	1 3-ounce can
1/4 teaspoon pepper	mushrooms
1 tablespoon paprika	1 tablespoon light
1 2 1/2 to 3-pound	brown sugar
chicken, cut up	1/4 teaspoon ginger
1/4 cup corn oil	1/2 6-ounce can frozen
1 8-ounce can whole	orange juice concentrate
onions, drained	3/4 cup water

Preheat oven to 350 degrees. Combine first 4 ingredients in paper bag. Add chicken; shake to coat. Reserve 2 tablespoons flour mixture for gravy. Brown chicken in oil in skillet. Place chicken in 9x13-inch casserole. Add onions, carrots and mushrooms. Blend reserved flour mixture, brown sugar and ginger into pan drippings; stir to make smooth paste. Add orange juice concentrate and 3/4 cup water. Cook and stir until bubbly. Pour over chicken. Bake, covered, for 1 1/2 hours. Yield: 4 servings.

Elizabeth Miller, Preceptor Pi
Polson, Montana

CHICKEN TARRAGON IN SOUR CREAM

1/4 cup butter	1/4 teaspoon pepper
1 broiler-fryer, cut up	2 cups sliced fresh
1/2 teaspoon salt	mushrooms
1/2 teaspoon tarragon	3/4 cup sour cream
leaves	Parmesan cheese

Preheat oven to 375 degrees. Melt butter in 9x13-inch baking dish in oven. Dip both sides of chicken in butter; place skin side up in pan. Sprinkle with salt, tarragon and pepper. Bake for 1 hour or until tender. Remove chicken to ovenproof platter. Sauté mushrooms in pan drippings; spoon over chicken. Spoon sour cream over chicken; sprinkle with cheese. Bake until sour cream is glazed. Yield: 4 servings.

Nancy Buck, Xi Gamma
Anchorage, Alaska

TERIYAKI CHICKEN

2 cups soy sauce	Cornstarch
1 1/2 cups unsweetened	1 4-ounce bottle of
pineapple juice	maraschino cherries
1 cup pancake syrup	1 16-ounce can
3/4 teaspoon ground ginger	pineapple chunks,
1 clove of garlic, chopped	drained
1 chicken, skinned,	1 11-ounce can mandarin
cut up	oranges, drained

Combine first 5 ingredients in bowl. Add chicken. Marinate for 2 hours or longer. Preheat oven to 350 degrees. Place chicken and sauce in baking pan. Bake for 1 hour. Drain, reserving marinade. Thicken marinade with cornstarch in saucepan. Add drained maraschino cherries, pineapple and mandarin oranges. Serve over rice with sauce. Yield: 6 servings.

Joni L. Dudley, Xi Alpha Eta
Torrington, Wyoming

CHICKEN-ARTICHOKE CASSEROLE

6 chicken breasts, cooked,
  boned, chopped
1 pound ham, cubed
2 cups mayonnaise
2 cups half and half
2 10-ounce cans
  artichoke hearts

1 loaf French bread, torn
2 dozen pimento-stuffed
  green olives, sliced
1 bell pepper, chopped
1 teaspoon minced onion
1 8-ounce package
  corn chips, crushed

Preheat oven to 350 degrees. Combine first 9 ingredients in bowl; mix well. Pour into greased 9x13-inch baking dish. Chill overnight. Sprinkle ¾ of the corn chips over top. Bake, covered, for 50 minutes. Add remaining chips. Bake, uncovered, for 15 minutes longer.
Yield: 9 to 12 servings.

Cammy Morgan, Iota Lambda
Auburn, California

BISCUIT-TOPPED CHICKEN

2 cups chopped cooked
  chicken
1 cup chopped cooked
  broccoli, drained
1 10-ounce can cream
  of chicken soup
¼ cup chopped onion
¼ cup mayonnaise
1½ teaspoon
  Worcestershire sauce

Dash of curry powder
½ cup shredded
  Cheddar cheese
1 10-count can
  refrigerator biscuits
¼ cup sour cream
1 egg
1 teaspoon celery seed
½ teaspoon salt

Preheat oven to 375 degrees. Combine chicken, broccoli, soup, onion, mayonnaise, Worcestershire sauce and curry powder in 1½-quart casserole; mix well. Bake for 20 to 25 minutes or until bubbly. Sprinkle with cheese. Separate biscuits; cut into halves. Arrange cut side down around edge of casserole. Combine sour cream, egg, celery seed and salt in bowl; blend well. Spread over biscuits. Bake for 25 to 30 minutes or until golden brown.
Yield: 6 servings.

Marilyn M. Kenjura, Alpha Iota Rho
Brenham, Texas

BROCCOLI-CHICKEN CASSEROLE

1 pound chopped
  broccoli, cooked
1 10-ounce can cream
  of mushroom soup
1 3-pound chicken,
  cooked, boned

Salt and pepper to taste
1 8-ounce package
  herb-seasoned
  stuffing mix
3 cups chicken broth

Preheat oven to 350 degrees. Layer broccoli, soup, chicken, salt, pepper, stuffing mix and broth in greased 9x13-inch casserole. Bake for 30 minutes.
Yield: 12 servings.

Jane Ann Tappendorf, Tau Omega
Altamont, Illinois

CHICKEN-BROCCOLI CASSEROLE

6 cups uncooked rice
2 pounds Velveeta
  cheese
2 10-ounce packages
  frozen chopped
  broccoli, cooked
1 10-ounce can cream of
  mushroom soup

1 10-ounce can cream of
  chicken soup
6 chicken breasts, cooked,
  boned, chopped
2 6-ounce cans sliced
  mushrooms
2 tablespoons pepper

Preheat oven to 375 degrees. Cook rice using package directions. Slice cheese thinly; reserve some for topping. Combine remaining cheese with rice and next 5 ingredients in large bowl; mix well. Pour into 9x13-inch baking dish. Top with reserved cheese and pepper. Bake for 40 minutes Yield: 8 servings.

Louise S. Shipe, Psi
Little Rock, Arkansas

BROCCOLI AND CHICKEN CASSEROLE

1 medium chicken
Salt and pepper to taste
Lemon slices
2 10-ounce packages
  frozen broccoli
2 cups cream of
  chicken soup
1 cup mayonnaise

1 tablespoon lemon juice
1 tablespoon curry
  powder
½ cup shredded sharp
  Colby cheese
1 cup soft bread crumbs
2 tablespoons melted
  butter

Preheat oven to 350 degrees. Cook chicken in water to cover in saucepan, adding salt, pepper and lemon slices. Drain and bone. Cook broccoli using package directions for half the time. Layer chicken and broccoli in 9x13-inch baking dish. Bring soup to a simmer in saucepan. Add mayonnaise, lemon juice, curry powder and cheese; stir until blended. Pour over chicken and broccoli. Toss crumbs with butter; sprinkle over casserole. Bake for 25 to 30 minutes. Yield: 6 to 8 servings.

Betty Allgood, Xi Mu Delta
Argyle, Texas

CHICKEN AND CHEESE CRÊPES

8 ounces sausage
3 tablespoons butter
3 tablespoons all-purpose
  flour
1½ cups milk
1 cup finely chopped
  cooked chicken

1 10-ounce package
  frozen chopped
  spinach, thawed
¾ cup Parmesan cheese
⅛ teaspoon oregano
⅛ teaspoon pepper
12 Crêpes (page 128)

Brown sausage in skillet, stirring until crumbly; drain. Melt butter in saucepan. Blend in flour. Add milk. Cook until thickened, stirring constantly. Add sausage, chicken, spinach, cheese and seasonings. Cook until heated through. Spoon into warm Crêpes; roll to enclose filling. Yield: 12 crêpes.

Deborah Blaz, Xi Delta Xi
Angola, Indiana

ROYAL CHICKEN CRÊPES

1 10-ounce can cream of chicken soup	1 cup cooked peas
1 cup sour cream	12 to 14 Crêpes (this page)
2 cups chopped cooked chicken	8 ounces fresh mushrooms, sliced
6 slices dried beef, chopped	1/4 cup butter
	1/4 teaspoon seasoned salt

Combine soup and sour cream in saucepan. Stir in chicken, dried beef and peas. Cook until heated through; do not boil. Fill Crêpes with hot mixture; fold over. Keep warm. Sauté mushrooms in butter in skillet. Sprinkle with seasoned salt. Spoon over filled crêpes; serve immediately. Yield: 12 to 14 servings.

Garland Wahl, Preceptor Beta Psi
Akron, Colorado

CHICKEN AND GREEN CHILI CRÊPES

1/2 cup chopped onion	1 teaspoon salt
8 ounces fresh mushrooms, sliced	1/4 teaspoon pepper
2 tablespoons corn oil	3 cups skim milk
6 tablespoons all-purpose flour	1/3 cup dry white wine
1 chicken bouillon cube	1 cup chopped cooked chicken
3 tablespoons chopped parsley	1/2 cup chopped mild green chilies
	12 Crêpes (this page)

Preheat oven to 350 degrees. Sauté onion and mushrooms in oil in saucepan for 5 minutes. Sprinkle with flour; mix well. Add bouillon cube, parsley, salt and pepper. Stir in milk gradually. Cook over medium heat until thickened, stirring constantly. Stir in wine. Cook for 5 minutes longer. Combine chicken, 1 3/4 cups sauce and chilies in bowl; mix well. Spoon onto Crêpes. Roll to enclose filling. Place seam side down in 9x13-inch baking dish. Top with remaining sauce. Bake, covered, for 20 to 30 minutes. Yield: 6 servings.

Frances A. Myers, Preceptor Iota
Albuquerque, New Mexico

COMPANY CHICKEN IN CRÊPES

3 chicken breasts	6 tablespoons butter
1 chicken bouillon cube	1/3 cup all-purpose flour
1 cup water	1 teaspoon salt
1 cup finely chopped celery	1 cup half and half
1/2 cup diced onion	16 Crêpes
	1/4 cup slivered almonds

Preheat oven to 350 degrees. Place chicken, bouillon cube and water in medium saucepan. Simmer, covered, for 40 minutes, or until chicken is tender. Remove chicken; bone and chop. Add enough water to broth to measure 1 1/2 cups. Add celery and onion. Simmer for 10 minutes. Melt butter in saucepan. Stir in flour and salt. Add broth mixture and half and half. Cook until sauce thickens, stirring constantly. Stir in chicken. Spoon chicken mixture onto Crêpes; roll to enclose filling. Place crêpes seam side down in 9x13-inch baking pan. Spoon any remaining chicken mixture over top. Sprinkle with almonds. Bake for 20 minutes. Yield: 8 servings.

CRÊPES

1 cup milk	3/4 cup sifted all-purpose flour
3 eggs, well beaten	
1 tablespoon sugar	1/4 teaspoon salt

Blend milk and eggs in mixer bowl; sift in sugar, flour and salt. Beat until smooth. Preheat lightly buttered 8-inch skillet over medium heat. Pour in 3 to 4 tablespoons batter, rotating pan to spread batter evenly. Bake until light golden brown on both sides. Repeat with remaining batter. Stack between layers of waxed paper.

Chelle Watson, Tau
Worland, Wyoming

CHICKEN ENCHILADA CASSEROLE

1 10-ounce can cream of mushroom soup	1 medium onion, chopped
	12 corn tortillas
1 10-ounce can cream of chicken soup	1 chicken, cooked, boned, chopped
1 cup chicken broth	2 cups shredded sharp Cheddar cheese
1 8-ounce can chopped green chilies	

Preheat oven to 350 degrees. Combine soups, broth, chilies and onion in bowl; mix well. Alternate layers of tortillas, chicken, soup mixture and cheese in casserole. Bake for 30 minutes. Yield: 8 to 12 servings.

Pearlie Chadwick, Xi Beta Iota
Cortez, Colorado

WHITE CHILI

2 pounds large white beans	4 teaspoons ground cumin
12 cups chicken broth	1 tablespoon oregano
4 cloves of garlic, minced	1/2 teaspoon cloves
4 medium onions, chopped	1/2 teaspoon cayenne pepper
2 tablespoons corn oil	8 cups chopped cooked chicken breasts
4 4-ounce cans chopped green chilies	6 cups shredded Monterey Jack cheese

Soak beans in water to cover in stockpot overnight. Drain. Add chicken broth, garlic and half the onion. Bring to a boil; reduce heat. Simmer for 3 hours or until beans are very soft. Add additional broth if necessary. Sauté remaining onion in oil in skillet until tender. Add chilies and seasonings; mix well. Add to bean mixture with chicken. Simmer for 1 hour. Serve topped with shredded cheese. Yield: 16 to 20 servings.

Patricia Dewey, Xi Gamma Tau
Nacagdoches, Texas

---

*An easy chicken fajita comes from **Judith Foret, Gamma Lambda, Houma, Louisiana**, who sautés 3 to 4 cups boned chicken breast strips with 1/2 teaspoon seasoned salt and 1 tablespoon liquid smoke. Serve with flour tortillas, lettuce, tomato, green onions, picante sauce and sour cream.*

CHICKEN FETTUCINI

½ 12-ounce package
  extra-long fettucini
1 39-ounce can
  chicken broth
4 chicken breasts, cooked,
  boned, chopped
1 10-ounce can
  mushroom soup
¼ teaspoon celery salt
½ teaspoon parsley
¼ teaspoon poultry
  seasoning
¼ teaspoon pepper
¼ cup ground almonds
½ cup chopped
  white onion
5 ounces seasoned
  croutons
2 tablespoons butter

Preheat oven to 350 degrees. Cook fettucini in chicken broth in saucepan until tender. Drain, reserving broth. Combine chicken, half of reserved broth and soup in bowl; mix well. Mix with fettucini. Add celery salt, parsley, poultry seasoning, pepper, almonds and onion; mix well. Pour into 9x9-inch baking dish. Top with seasoned croutons; dot with butter. Pour remaining broth over top. Bake, covered, for 40 minutes. Yield: 8 servings.

Linda Faye Lemon, Preceptor Chi
Douglas, Arizona

KING RANCH CHICKEN

1 2½-pound chicken,
  cooked
1 small onion, chopped
1 small green bell pepper,
  chopped
½ cup butter
2 cups medium
  white sauce
  made with broth
1 can Ro-Tel tomatoes
1 10-ounce can cream of
  chicken soup
1 10-ounce can cream of
  mushroom soup
1 large package taco-
  flavored tortilla chips
1 4-ounce can sliced
  black olives
⅔ pound Cheddar
  cheese, shredded

Preheat oven to 350 degrees. Bone chicken in large pieces. Sauté onion and green pepper in melted butter in saucepan. Add white sauce, Ro-Tel, soups and chicken. Place half the tortilla chips in 10x13-inch baking dish. Cover with half the chicken mixture, half the olives and half the cheese. Repeat layers. Bake for 35 to 40 minutes. Yield: 8 servings.

Margaret Little, Preceptor Gamma Omicron
Cape Girardeau, Missouri

LUAU CHICKEN CASSEROLE

2 fryers, cooked,
  boned, chopped
½ cup soy sauce
½ cup water
½ cup vinegar
¾ cup packed light
  brown sugar
1 teaspoon ginger
½ teaspoon pepper
1 teaspoon garlic salt
2 tablespoons cornstarch
2 tablespoons water
1 cup pineapple chunks
½ cup pineapple juice
1 8-ounce package rice,
  cooked

Preheat oven to 300 degrees. Place chicken in 9x12-inch casserole. Combine next 7 ingredients in saucepan. Bring to a boil. Add mixture of cornstarch and 2 tablespoons water. Cook until slightly thickened, stirring constantly. Pour over chicken. Arrange pineapple chunks on top;

pour pineapple juice over all. Cover with foil. Bake for 30 minutes. Increase temperature to 350 degrees. Bake for 30 minutes longer. Serve with hot cooked rice. Yield: 4 to 6 servings.

Elizabeth A. Payne, Laureate Theta
New Albany, Indiana

CHICKEN SALAD CASSEROLE

5 cups chopped cooked
  chicken
4 cups cooked rice
1 cup chopped celery
1 cup chopped onion
1½ teaspoons salt
½ teaspoon pepper
1 10-ounce can cream
  of mushroom soup
1 cup mayonnaise-type
  salad dressing
2 tablespoons lemon
  juice
½ cup slivered almonds

Combine first 9 ingredients in order listed in 4-quart baking dish, mixing well after each addition. Sprinkle with almonds. Refrigerate, covered, for 24 hours. Let stand at room temperature for 1 hour. Preheat oven to 350 degrees. Bake for 1 hour. Yield: 6 to 8 servings.

Ruth E. Kirkpatrick, Preceptor Lambda Omicron
Burbank, California

HOT CHICKEN SALAD

4 cups chopped cooked
  chicken
4 hard-cooked eggs,
  chopped
1 cup sliced celery
1 cup sliced water
  chestnuts
1 tablespoon pimento
1 teaspoon minced onion
¾ cup mayonnaise
1 cup shredded
  Cheddar cheese
1 10-ounce can cream
  of mushroom soup
2 tablespoons lemon
  juice
1 teaspoon salt
1½ cups chow mein
  noodles
⅔ cup toasted almonds

Preheat oven to 325 degrees. Combine first 11 ingredients in bowl in order listed; mix well. Spoon into 2-quart casserole. Top with mixture of noodles and almonds. Bake for 30 minutes. Yield: 6 to 8 servings.

Marlys Montz, Xi Epsilon Theta
Marshalltown, Iowa

BAKED CURRIED CHICKEN SALAD

3 cups chopped cooked
  chicken
½ cup slivered almonds
⅔ cup mayonnaise
5 tablespoons sour cream
¼ cup chopped green
  bell pepper
¼ cup chopped celery
1 8-ounce can water
  chestnuts, drained,
  chopped
¼ cup chopped mild
  onion
1 2-ounce jar chopped
  pimento, drained
1 tablespoon lemon juice
⅛ teaspoon pepper
¼ teaspoon curry powder
1¼ cups soft bread
  crumbs
¾ cup shredded Cheddar
  cheese

Preheat oven to 350 degrees. Combine first 12 ingredients in bowl; mix well. Spoon into 2-quart casserole. Top with mixture of crumbs and cheese. Bake for 35 to 45 minutes. Yield: 6 servings.

Phyllis Johnson, Beta Iota
Custer, South Dakota

CHICKEN SALAD TWIST

2 cups chopped cooked
  chicken
½ cup thinly sliced
  celery
½ cup toasted slivered
  almonds
½ cup mayonnaise
2 tablespoons lemon
  juice
⅛ teaspoon salt

1 tablespoon finely
  chopped onion
2 cups buttermilk
  baking mix
½ cup cold water
1 egg yolk
1 teaspoon water
8 ounces process cheese
  spread, cubed
⅔ cup milk

Preheat oven to 425 degrees. Mix first 7 ingredients in bowl. Combine baking mix and ½ cup water in bowl until soft dough forms. Beat vigorously. Knead on floured surface 5 times. Roll into 11x14-inch rectangle. Place on ungreased baking sheet. Spoon chicken mixture lengthwise down center. Make cuts 2½ inches long at 1-inch intervals on long sides of rectangle. Fold strips over filling. Brush with mixture of egg yolk and 1 teaspoon water. Bake for 15 to 28 minutes or until brown. Combine cheese spread and milk in glass bowl. Microwave on HIGH until cheese melts; mix well. Serve with sliced Twist. Yield: 10 to 12 servings.

Merline McCoy, Laureate Beta Psi
Port Neches, Texas

CHICKEN WITH CREAM SAUCE

3 cups chopped cooked
  chicken
1 cup sliced celery
4 ounces fresh
  mushrooms, quartered
2 cups chicken broth
½ cup sliced green onions
2 cups cooked rice
¼ cup diced pimento
2 cups soft bread crumbs
2 tablespoons minced
  fresh parsley
4 eggs, slightly beaten
½ teaspoon salt
½ teaspoon freshly
  ground pepper

¼ teaspoon paprika
½ cup slivered almonds
¼ cup butter
2 cups croutons
4 ounces fresh
  mushrooms, slivered
¼ cup butter
¼ cup all-purpose flour
2 cups chicken broth
2 egg yolks
¼ cup half and half
¼ teaspoon salt
1 tablespoon lemon juice
Hot pepper sauce to taste
1 tablespoon minced fresh
  parsley

Preheat oven to 350 degrees. Mix first 13 ingredients in bowl. Pour into greased 9x13-inch baking dish. Sauté almonds in ¼ cup butter in skillet. Add croutons; stir until well coated. Sprinkle over casserole. Bake for 30 to 40 minutes. Sauté mushrooms in ¼ cup butter in saucepan for 3 to 5 minutes. Blend in flour. Stir in 2 cups chicken broth gradually. Simmer for 10 to 15 minutes or until thickened. Beat egg yolks with half and half, ¼ teaspoon salt, lemon juice and hot pepper sauce in bowl. Stir a small amount of hot mixture into egg mixture. Stir egg mixture into hot mixture. Cook over low heat for 3 to 5 minutes, stirring constantly. Stir in parsley. Serve with chicken. Yield: 6 servings.

Sharon Ayres, Tau
Caldwell, Idaho

CHICKEN SPAGHETTI

1 chicken
1 16-ounce package
  spaghetti
1 cup chopped onion
½ cup chopped celery
½ cup margarine
¼ cup all-purpose flour
1 10-ounce can cream of
  mushroom soup

¾ teaspoon garlic salt
1 2-ounce can chopped
  pimento
1 4-ounce can chopped
  black olives
Salt and pepper to taste
1 pound Velveeta cheese,
  shredded

Preheat oven to 350 degrees. Cook chicken in water to cover generously until tender; bone and chop. Strain chicken stock. Cook spaghetti in chicken stock until tender; drain and reserve stock. Sauté onion and celery in margarine in skillet until brown. Mix in flour. Add soup, garlic salt, 1 cup reserved stock, pimento, olives, chicken, spaghetti, salt and pepper; mix well. Pour into large baking dish. Sprinkle with cheese. Bake for 30 minutes. Yield: 10 servings.

Cheryl Hudson, Alpha Phi Tau
San Angelo, Texas

CHICKEN AND SQUASH CASSEROLE

½ cup melted margarine
4 ounces herb-seasoned
  stuffing mix
1 16-ounce can sliced
  yellow squash
1 carrot, grated

1 10-ounce can cream of
  chicken soup
½ cup chopped onion
1 cup sour cream
2 cups chopped cooked
  chicken

Preheat oven to 350 degrees. Mix margarine with stuffing mix in bowl. Spread half the mixture in 8x10-inch baking dish. Combine undrained squash and remaining ingredients in bowl; mix well. Spoon into prepared casserole. Top with remaining stuffing mixture. Bake for 30 minutes or until bubbly. Yield: 8 servings.

Betty Conrad, Laureate Alphi Phi
Houston, Texas

CHICKEN STRATA

2 teaspoons butter
6 slices day-old
  white bread
2 to 3 cups chopped
  cooked chicken
½ cup chopped onion
½ cup chopped celery
¼ cup chopped green
  bell pepper

½ cup mayonnaise
¾ teaspoon salt
Dash of pepper
2 eggs, slightly beaten
1½ cups milk
1 10-ounce can cream of
  mushroom soup
½ cup shredded
  American cheese

Preheat oven to 325 degrees. Butter 2 slices bread; cut into cubes and set aside. Cube 4 slices unbuttered bread; place in 9x13-inch baking pan. Combine chicken, onion, celery, green pepper, mayonnaise, salt, pepper and eggs in bowl. Add milk and soup; mix well. Spoon into prepared baking dish. Chill overnight. Top with cheese and reserved buttered bread cubes. Bake for 1 hour. Yield: 6 to 10 servings.

Joni L. Condon, Xi Delta Sigma
Adrian, Michigan

ZESTY CHICKEN TETRAZZINI

10 to 12 pounds chicken	1 teaspoon pepper
2 pounds vermicelli	1 teaspoon paprika
1 large onion, chopped	1 4-ounce jar chopped
2 cups chopped celery	pimento
1 medium green bell	2 cups shredded
pepper, chopped	Velveeta cheese
6 tablespoons margarine	2 10-ounce cans cream of
¼ cup all-purpose flour	mushroom soup
2 cups milk	1 8-ounce can
½ teaspoon cayenne	mushrooms
pepper	6 hard-cooked eggs,
1 teaspoon salt	chopped

Preheat oven to 300 degrees. Cook chicken in water to cover in stockpot until tender; bone and chop. Reserve 2½ cups broth. Cook vermicelli in remaining broth. Sauté onion, celery and green pepper in margarine in skillet. Add flour; mix well. Stir in milk. Cook until thickened, stirring constantly. Add seasonings and remaining ingredients; mix well. Mix with vermicelli, chicken and enough reserved broth to make of desired consistency in large roasting pan. Bake for 45 minutes to 1 hour or until heated through. Yield: 30 servings.

Estelline Mikeworth, Beta Omega
Bellevue, Texas

CHICKEN TORTELLINI

2 5-ounce cans chunky	⅛ teaspoon garlic powder
chicken	1 tablespoon dried
1½ cups water	minced onion
1 tablespoon all-purpose	1 9-ounce package
flour	spinach and cheese
2 tablespoons dried	tortellini, cooked
parsley	Salt and pepper to taste

Preheat oven to 350 degrees. Drain chicken, reserving broth. Combine broth, water and flour in saucepan. Bring to a simmer, stirring constantly. Cook until mixture thickens, stirring constantly. Add parsley, garlic powder and onion. Mix chicken, tortellini, sauce, salt and pepper in 1½-quart casserole. Bake, covered, for 25 minutes. Yield: 4 servings.

Ellen Winchell, Alpha Eta
Steamboat Springs, Colorado

CHICKEN TURNOVERS

1 pound chicken breasts	2 8-count packages
8 ounces cream cheese,	refrigerator
softened	crescent rolls
1 teaspoon seasoned salt	1 tablespoon melted
1 teaspoon chives	butter
½ cup chopped pecans	Bread crumbs

Preheat oven to 350 degrees. Cook chicken in water to cover in saucepan for 1 hour. Drain; bone and chop. Combine cream cheese, seasoned salt, chives and pecans in bowl; mix well. Stir in chicken. Place 2 crescent rolls with long sides together; seal seam. Spoon mixture into center. Fold in half to make triangular turnover; seal seams. Repeat for each turnover. Dip in melted butter; coat with crumbs. Place on baking sheet. Bake until golden brown. Serve with gravy. Yield: 8 servings.

Joyce Short, Preceptor Delta
Salt Lake City, Utah

GRILLED TURKEY BREAST

1 pound turkey breast	1 tablespoon minced
⅓ cup corn oil	onion
¼ cup white wine vinegar	½ teaspoon rosemary
¼ cup lemon juice	¼ teaspoon garlic powder

Cut turkey into ½-inch pieces. Place in shallow pan. Marinate in mixture of remaining ingredients for 4 hours to overnight in refrigerator. Drain. Grill 3 to 4 inches from hot coals for about 10 minutes, turning once. Yield: 4 servings.

Mary Dyck, Theta Sigam
Hays, Kansas

CURRIED TURKEY

6 tablespoons melted	2 cups chopped cooked
butter	turkey
6 tablespoons all-purpose	2 tablespoons Sherry
flour	2 tablespoons curry
1 teaspoon salt	powder
¼ teaspoon pepper	1 cup sautéed mushrooms
1½ cups chicken stock	½ cup slivered green
1 cup cream	bell pepper

Blend butter, flour, salt and pepper in saucepan. Stir in chicken stock and cream. Cook until thickened, stirring constantly. Add remaining ingredients. Heat to serving temperature. Yield: 4 to 6 servings.

Bettie Bogarte, Laureate Beta
Salt Lake City, Utah

SMOKED TURKEY

1 cup Tender-Quick	1 gallon water
8 teaspoons liquid smoke	1 10 to 14-pound turkey
½ cup non-iodinized salt	1 oven-cooking bag

Combine first 5 ingredients in large bowl. Marinate for 24 hours. Drain. Place turkey in cooking bag in roasting pan. Seal and cut steam vents. Preheat oven to 275 degrees. Bake for 6 to 12 hours or until turkey is tender. Yield: 15 to 20 servings.

Karen O'Brien, Laureate Upsilon
Prescott, Arizona

SMOKED TURKEY TERRIFIC

1 10 to 15-pound turkey	2 medium onions
1 tablespoon salt	4 stalks celery with leaves

Preheat smoker to 185 degrees. Rinse turkey inside and out with cold water. Rub inside and out with salt. Cut onion into quarters and celery into chunks. Place in turkey. Place turkey in smoker. Smoke for 5 to 7 hours or until leg moves easily in joint. Yield: 15 to 20 servings.

Lois Lynne Miller, Epsilon, Omega
Thornton, Colorado

TURKEY ENCHILADAS

1 10-ounce can cream of
   chicken soup
4 ounces Velveeta cheese
1 8-ounce can green
   chilies
¾ cup milk
1 envelope ranch salad
   dressing mix
1 small onion, chopped

1 tablespoon corn oil
2 cups chopped cooked
   turkey
1 envelope dry taco
   seasoning mix
2 cups shredded Cheddar
   cheese
1 cup chicken broth
12 to 14 corn tortillas

Preheat oven to 375 degrees. Mix soup, Velveeta cheese, chilies, milk and salad dressing mix in medium saucepan. Cook over medium heat just until cheese is melted, stirring constantly. Sauté onion in corn oil in skillet. Add turkey, dry taco seasoning and Cheddar cheese. Heat chicken broth in shallow saucepan. Dip corn tortillas into hot broth to soften. Remove from broth. Add spoonful turkey mixture; roll to enclose filling. Place in 9x13-inch baking pan sprayed with nonstick cooking spray. Pour soup mixture over top; cover with foil. Bake for 20 to 25 minutes. Yield: 4 to 6 servings.

Bea Glassco, Xi Rho Zeta
Deer Park, Texas

TURKEY ROLL-UPS

1 package stuffing mix
8 slices turkey breast
   luncheon meat
1 10-ounce can cream of
   mushroom soup
1 cup (about) evaporated
   milk

1 10-ounce package
   frozen broccoli
1 cup shredded
   Cheddar cheese
1 can onion rings

Preheat oven to 350 degrees. Prepare stuffing mix using package directions. Place 2 tablespoons stuffing on each turkey slice; roll to enclose filling. Place in buttered 8x8-inch baking dish. Mix soup with milk; pour over roll-ups. Cook broccoli using package directions for half the time. Arrange over roll-ups. Sprinkle cheese and onion rings on top. Bake for 30 to 40 minutes or until cheese is melted. Yield: 8 servings.

Judith A. Hanam, Preceptor Gamma Epsilon
Monessen, Pennsylvania

GREAT CRESCENT ROLL-UPS

1 8-count package
   refrigerator crescent
   rolls
2 cups chopped cooked
   turkey
1 cup sour cream

1 10 ounce can cream of
   chicken soup
1 10-ounce can Cheddar
   cheese soup
2 cups shredded
   Cheddar cheese

Preheat oven to 350 degrees. Separate crescent rolls. Spoon turkey onto rolls; roll to enclose filling. Place in 9x12-inch baking dish. Mix sour cream and soups in bowl. Pour over roll-ups; sprinkle with Cheddar cheese. Bake for 20 to 30 minutes or until light brown. Yield: 4 servings.

Lorraine Bennett, Xi Gamma Rho
Fulton, Illinois

CORNISH HENS WITH LEMON BUTTER

6 Rock Cornish
   game hens
Salt

¾ cup butter, melted
3 tablespoons lemon juice

Wash hens; dry thoroughly. Sprinkle cavities with salt. Place on spit; tie securely with string. Brush with mixture of butter, lemon juice and ½ teaspoon salt. Place on rotisserie over hot coals. Grill for 1 to 1½ hours or until tender, brushing with lemon butter every 15 minutes. Yield: 6 servings.

Judy Kutcher, Xi Zeta Mu
Eldridge, Iowa

TANDOORI CORNISH HENS

4 22-ounce Rock
   Cornish game hens
½ cup nonfat yogurt
½ cup lemon juice
3 cloves of garlic
1 tablespoon paprika

1 teaspoon ground
   cardamom
½ teaspoon ground ginger
½ teaspoon red pepper
Fresh cilantro

Remove giblets from hens; reserve for another purpose. Rinse hens with cold water; pat dry. Split hens lengthwise, using electric knife. Remove and discard skin. Place hens cavity side up in shallow dish. Combine yogurt and next 6 ingredients in blender container; process until smooth. Pour over hens. Marinate, covered, in refrigerator for 8 hours to overnight, turning occasionally. Preheat broiler. Arrange hens cavity side down on rack in broiler pans coated with nonstick cooking spray; brush with yogurt mixture. Broil 6 inches from heat source for 7 minutes; turn over. Broil for 5 minutes or until tender. Place on serving platter. Garnish with cilantro. Serve immediately. Yield: 8 servings.

Kathy Kaufman, Alpha Pi
Jeanie Waugh, Alpha Pi
Missoula, Montana

BRAISED DUCK WITH PLUM SAUCE

1 8-ounce can pitted
   plums
1 10-ounce jar plum
   jelly
½ cup tarragon vinegar
4 wild duck breasts

6 tablespoons butter
1 medium onion, chopped
1½ cups sauerkraut
1 Bouquet Garni
½ cup wine
½ cup chopped pecans

Drain plums, reserving syrup. Blend syrup with jelly and vinegar. Rinse duck breasts; pat dry. Brown in butter in skillet. Add onion, sauerkraut, Bouquet Garni and wine. Cook over low heat for 35 minutes or until tender. Add half the jelly mixture and plums. Simmer for 10 minutes. Remove duck and plums to serving plate; discard drippings. Spoon remaining jelly mixture over duck; sprinkle with pecans. Yield: 4 servings.
Note: The Bouquet Garni is made of 2 stalks celery, 3 or 4 sprigs of parsley, 1 bay leaf, ½ teaspoon thyme and 2 whole cloves wrapped in cheesecloth.

Jennifer S. Thompson, Kappa Sigma
Richmond, Missouri

Seafood

BRITISH FISH FRY

1 12-ounce can beer
Juice of ¼ to ½ lemon
Several slices onion
3 or 4 peppercorns
Dash of Old Bay
   seasoning
Perch or haddock fillets,
   cut into bite-sized
   pieces

1 cup buttermilk
1 egg
1 to 2 cups buttermilk
   baking mix
Oil for frying
Salt and pepper to taste

Combine first 5 ingredients in bowl. Add fish. Marinate for several hours; drain. Add fish to mixture of buttermilk and egg in bowl. Marinate for 15 to 30 minutes; drain. Coat with baking mix. Deep-fry in hot oil for 2 to 5 minutes until golden brown. Season with salt and pepper. Yield: 8 servings.

Marlene Koenig, Xi Theta Nu
Ironton, Ohio

CEVICHE

3 pounds frozen flounder
   fillets
Juice of 25 limes
1 teaspoon salt
1 teaspoon pepper
1 teaspoon garlic salt
3 large tomatoes, chopped

½ large onion, chopped
5 or 6 large jalapeños,
   chopped
½ bunch cilantro,
   chopped
½ small bottle of olive oil
¼ cup white vinegar

Chop fish into tiny cubes while still partially frozen; place in glass bowl. Pour lime juice over fish. Add salt, pepper and garlic salt; cover tightly. Chill overnight. Drain fish well, reserving marinade. Add mixture of remaining ingredients. Add reserved marinade to taste. Yield: 12 servings.

Jeanette Felger, Laureate Upsilon
New Braunfels, Texas

COUNTRY TRACE FISH

3 green onions, chopped
1 cup sliced fresh
   mushrooms
Garlic powder to taste
Juice of ½ lemon
¼ cup butter or margarine
2 or 3 Mexican tomatoes,
   chopped

½ cup white wine
2 pounds fresh fish fillets
1 egg, beaten
1 tablespoon water
All-purpose flour
¼ cup butter or margarine
1 pound fresh asparagus

Sauté green onions, mushrooms, garlic powder and lemon juice in ¼ cup butter in skillet. Add tomatoes. Sauté for several minutes. Add wine; set aside. Dip fillets in mixture of egg and water. Coat with flour. Sauté in remaining ¼ cup butter in skillet. Steam fresh asparagus. Arrange fish and asparagus on serving plate; top with sautéed mixture. Yield: 4 servings.

Vikki Pippin, Theta Beta
Fayetteville, Georgia

CREOLE FISH FILLETS

1 medium onion, sliced	2 or 3 slices lemon
½ cup chopped celery	1 tablespoon
½ cup chopped green	Worcestershire sauce
bell pepper	1 bay leaf
1 clove of garlic, minced	1 tablespoon paprika
2 tablespoons butter	¼ teaspoon thyme
1 28-ounce can tomatoes,	2 pounds fish fillets
chopped	1 to 1¼ cups raisins

Sauté first 4 ingredients in butter in electric skillet. Add tomatoes with juice, lemon slices and remaining seasonings. Simmer for 15 minutes, stirring occasionally. Add fillets. Simmer, covered, for 20 minutes. Add raisins. Simmer for 15 minutes longer. Yield: 6 servings.

Karen Lloyd, Beta Kappa
Meeteetse, Wyoming

SEAFOOD AND CHEESE ENCHILADAS

2 cups shredded Cheddar	⅓ cup butter
cheese	⅓ cup margarine
2 cups shredded Monterey	⅔ cup all-purpose flour
Jack cheese	3 cups chicken broth
½ cup chopped green	1 cup sour cream
onions	2 7-ounce cans crab meat
8 8-inch flour tortillas	1 6-ounce can shrimp

Preheat oven to 350 degrees. Combine cheeses. Place ½ cup cheese and 1 tablespoon onion in each tortilla; roll up. Place in 9x13-inch baking pan. Melt butter and margarine in saucepan. Add flour; mix well. Add chicken broth. Cook until thick, stirring constantly. Remove from heat. Add sour cream, crab meat and shrimp. Pour over tortillas. Bake for 25 minutes. Yield: 8 servings.

Pam Allen, Theta Iota
Aurelia, Iowa

FILLETS IN CREAM

1 teaspoon lemon juice	¼ teaspoon tarragon
1 scallion, chopped	6 tablespoons butter
⅓ cup dry white wine	3 tablespoons all-purpose
5 or 6 fish fillets	flour
¼ pound mushrooms,	½ cup milk
sliced	½ cup cream
1 clove of garlic, minced	Salt and pepper to taste
1 tablespoon chopped	⅓ cup shredded Swiss
parsley	cheese

Preheat oven to 350 degrees. Combine lemon juice, scallion and wine in buttered 9x13-inch baking dish. Place fillets in dish; cover with foil. Bake for 12 minutes. Remove fillets to ovenproof platter; keep warm. Strain pan juices. Sauté mushrooms, garlic, parsley and tarragon in butter in skillet for 3 to 4 minutes. Remove from heat. Stir in flour. Cook for 1 minute; remove from heat. Stir in milk, cream and half the pan juices. Cook until thickened, stirring constantly. Add salt and pepper. Stir in cheese. Cook until cheese melts. Pour over fillets. Broil until brown. Yield: 5 to 6 servings.

Jo Evelyn Hannah, Exempler Eta Kappa
Graham, Texas

FISH FILLETS ITALIAN

6 to 8 fresh sole fillets	1 teaspoon Italian herbs
½ teaspoon salt	1 8-ounce can tomato
⅛ teaspoon pepper	sauce
4 fresh mushrooms, thinly	¼ cup Parmesan cheese
sliced	¾ cup shredded
4 green onions, thinly	mozzarella cheese
sliced	

Preheat oven to 425 degrees. Spray baking dish with nonstick cooking spray. Arrange fillets in 9x14-inch dish; do not overlap. Sprinkle evenly with next 5 ingredients. Pour tomato sauce over fish. Sprinkle with cheeses. Bake for 20 minutes or until fish flakes easily. Serve immediately. Yield: 4 to 6 servings.

Jeanette Morris, Xi Rho Sigma
Templeton, California

FISH AND VEGETABLE STEW

1 cup chopped onion	⅛ teaspoon salt
½ cup chopped celery	½ teaspoon dried whole
1 large clove of garlic,	basil
minced	⅔ cup water
1 16-ounce can tomatoes,	1 cup sliced carrots
chopped	1 cup frozen whole kernel
2 tablespoons malt	corn
vinegar	1 cup frozen lima beans
1 tablespoon reduced-	1 pound orange roughy
sodium Worcestershire	fillets or other lean
sauce	white fillets, cut into
½ teaspoon pepper	bite-sized pieces

Coat heavy saucepan with nonstick cooking spray. Preheat over medium-high heat. Add onion, celery and garlic. Sauté until tender. Add remaining ingredients. Cover; reduce heat. Simmer for 20 minutes, stirring occasionally. Yield: 7 cups.

Karen Menard, Preceptor Gamma Omicron
Cape Girardeau, Missouri

BAKED ORANGE ROUGHY

½ cup margarine	⅛ teaspoon minced garlic
1½ pounds orange roughy	½ teaspoon cayenne
fillets	pepper
½ teaspoon MSG	1 tablespoon paprika
1 teaspoon salt	1½ tablespoons parsley
½ teaspoon onion flakes	flakes

Preheat oven to 375 degrees. Melt margarine in 9x12-inch baking dish. Coat fillets in margarine on both sides. Sprinkle remaining ingredients over fish in order listed. Bake for 45 minutes. Yield: 4 servings.

Suzi McDaniel, Preceptor Alpha Omega
Oklahoma City, Oklahoma

Linda Ragsdale, Xi Delta, Viburnum, Missouri, seasons her deep-fried catfish with lemon-pepper seasoning for added spicy flavor.

BASIL ORANGE ROUGHY

3 tablespoons olive oil	1½ pounds orange roughy
1 medium onion, sliced	fillets
2 small zucchini, thinly	Salt and pepper to taste
sliced	2 fresh tomatoes, peeled,
1 pound mushrooms,	sliced
sliced	½ cup Parmesan cheese
½ cup chopped fresh basil	

Heat oil in large skillet. Add onion, zucchini, mushrooms and basil. Sauté over medium heat for 4 minutes, stirring frequently. Season fillets with salt and pepper. Place over vegetables. Arrange tomato slices over fillets. Simmer, covered, for 8 minutes or until fish flakes easily. Sprinkle cheese over tomatoes. Simmer, covered, until cheese melts. Serve immediately. Yield: 4 servings.

Jamie Hilbig, Alpha Upsilon Psi
The Colony, Texas

SALMON CHAMPAGNE CREAM SAUCE

2 cups Champagne	Salt and pepper to taste
2 cups water	Red Pepper Pasta
1 teaspoon whole allspice	(page 160)
1 bay leaf	½ cup minced green
1 pound salmon fillets	onions
2½ cups whipping cream	

Bring Champagne to a boil in skillet with water, allspice and bay leaf. Add salmon. Simmer, covered, for 7 to 10 minutes or until salmon is opaque in the thickest part. Lift out salmon; flake. Strain liquid; return to skillet. Add cream. Boil rapidly until reduced to 2½ cups, stirring occasionally. Add salmon to reduced mixture; season with salt and pepper to taste. Serve over hot Red Pepper Pasta. Garnish with green onions.

Diane Runo, Xi Beta
Peoria, Arizona

SALMON STUFFED WITH CRAB

1½ pounds crab meat	½ cup finely chopped
½ cup melted butter	onion
¼ cup parsley flakes	Juice of 2 lemons
½ cup chicken stock	1 8-pound salmon
2 cups bread cubes	
1 cup finely chopped	
celery	

Preheat oven to 350 degrees. Combine first 8 ingredients in bowl; mix well. Stuff salmon; tie salmon together. Wrap in foil. Bake for 1 hour and 45 minutes. Uncover. Bake for 15 to 20 minutes or until salmon is browned. Serve with melted butter, lemon and caper sauce. Yield: 10 to 12 servings.

Carol Brenckle, Xi Nu
Kenai, Alaska

SALMON CROQUETTES

2 tablespoons melted	Salt and pepper to taste
margarine	1 15-ounce can salmon
3 tablespoons all-purpose	2 eggs, beaten
flour	1 7-ounce package
1 teaspoon cider vinegar	potato chips, crushed
¾ cup milk	Oil for frying

Blend margarine, flour and vinegar in saucepan. Add milk. Cook over low heat until thickened, stirring constantly. Add seasonings. Set aside to cool. Flake salmon with fork in large mixing bowl. Add white sauce; mix well. Shape into patties. Dip in eggs; coat with potato chips. Brown in oil in skillet. Yield: 8 croquettes.

Maribeth V. Dottore, Pi
Hockessin, Delaware

TERIYAKI SALMON

¼ cup soy sauce	2 tablespoons minced
2 tablespoons light brown	fresh ginger
sugar	1 pound salmon steaks

Combine soy sauce, brown sugar and ginger in plastic bag. Place salmon steaks in bag. Marinate salmon for 2 hours. Preheat grill. Grill over hot coals for 10 minutes per inch of thickness or until salmon flakes easily. Yield: 4 servings.

Donna Schmidt, Xi Mu
Knoxville, Tennessee

STEGT RODSPAETTE

4 8-ounce flounder	2 tablespoons vegetable
fillets	oil
Salt to taste	¼ cup butter
All-purpose flour	8 ounces small cooked
½ cup dried bread crumbs	shrimp
2 eggs	¼ cup butter
2 tablespoons water	Lemon wedges

Rinse fish with cold water. Pat dry. Season with salt; coat with flour. Shake off excess. Spread bread crumbs on waxed paper. Beat eggs with water in bowl. Dip each fillet into egg; coat with bread crumbs. Let stand for 10 minutes. Heat 2 tablespoons oil and 2 tablespoons butter in heavy skillet over moderate heat until foam subsides. Sauté fillets for 3 to 4 minutes on each side. Place on warm platter. Melt 2 tablespoons butter in saucepan over moderate heat. Add shrimp. Stir-fry for 2 to 3 minutes or until well coated. Arrange shrimp down each fillet. Heat remaining ¼ cup butter in saucepan over low heat until nutty brown; pour over fillets. Garnish with lemon wedge. Yield: 4 servings.

Barbara Hanson, Xi Gamma Xi
Ames, Iowa

BROILED TUNA MELT

2 tablespoons mayonnaise
1 teaspoon lemon juice
Several drops red pepper
  sauce
1 7-ounce can water-
  pack tuna
¼ cup chopped onion
3 tablespoons chopped
  cucumber
2 tablespoons chopped
  sweet pickle
2 English muffins, split,
  toasted
½ avocado, sliced
½ cup alfalfa sprouts
2 slices Cheddar cheese,
  cut into triangles

Preheat broiler. Blend first 3 ingredients in bowl. Add tuna, onion, cucumber and pickle; toss gently. Place English muffins on cookie sheet, overlapping sides slightly. Place avocado slices and alfalfa sprouts over each pair, dividing evenly. Spoon tuna mixture over top. Arrange cheese over top. Broil for 2 minutes or until cheese melts. Serve immediately. Yield: 2 servings.

Vera Roberts, Xi Epsilon
Edmond, Oklahoma

TUNA RING

1 egg, slightly beaten
2 7-ounce cans tuna,
  drained
½ cup shredded sharp
  Cheddar cheese
¼ cup chopped onion
½ cup chopped parsley
1 teaspoon celery salt
¼ teaspoon pepper
1 recipe biscuit dough
1 recipe cheese sauce

Preheat oven to 375 degrees. Reserve about 2 tablespoons egg. Mix remaining egg with tuna, cheese, onion, parsley, celery salt and pepper. Roll biscuit dough into large rectangle. Spread with tuna mixture. Roll as for jelly roll from long edge. Shape into circle on greased baking sheet. Cut 12 slices ¾-inch through roll. Fan each slice back and to side. Brush with reserved egg. Bake for 25 minutes. Serve with hot cheese sauce. Yield: 6 servings.

Charlene A. Bickler, Xi Upsilon
Salem, Oregon

TUNA AND RICE MUFFINLETTS

2 cups cooked brown rice
1 7-ounce can water-pack
  chunk-style tuna,
  drained
1 cup shredded Cheddar
  cheese
½ cup sliced pitted ripe
  olives
2 tablespoons minced
  onion
2 tablespoons minced
  parsley
1 teaspoon seasoned salt
⅛ teaspoon pepper
2 eggs, slightly beaten
2 tablespoons milk
1 tablespoon capers
¼ cup melted butter
Parsley sprigs
Lemon wedges

Preheat oven to 375 degrees. Combine first 10 ingredients in bowl; mix well. Pack into 12 well greased muffin cups. Bake for 15 minutes or until brown. Let stand for 5 minutes; remove from pans. Invert on hot platter. Add capers to melted butter. Pour butter over muffinletts. Garnish with parsley and lemon wedges. Yield: 4 servings.

Maryann Ream-Carnes
Springfield, Illinois

FOR THE SEAFOOD LOVER IN YOU

1 clove of garlic
2 tablespoons butter
½ cup Chablis
½ cup chicken broth
¼ cup finely chopped
  parsley
¼ teaspoon basil
¼ teaspoon oregano
1 7-ounce can crab meat,
  drained
1 6-ounce can lobster,
  drained
8 ounces cooked peeled
  shrimp, chopped
½ cup butter
½ cup flour
1 pound linguine, cooked

Sauté garlic in 2 tablespoons butter in skillet until garlic is brown; discard garlic. Add Chablis, broth, parsley, basil and oregano. Bring to the simmering point over low heat. Add crab meat, lobster and shrimp. Melt ½ cup butter in saucepan. Stir in flour until blended into roux. Add small amounts of roux at a time to seafood mixture, cooking until thickened to desired consistency. Serve over linguine. Yield: 4 servings.

Debbie Alvis, Lambda Pi
Sarasota, Florida

CONEY ISLAND CLAM CHOWDER

2 medium potatoes,
  chopped
1 cup water
1 onion, chopped
½ cup chopped celery
1 tablespoon butter
1 tablespoon all-purpose
  flour
2 cups clam juice
1 cup canned tomatoes,
  chopped
2 7-ounce cans clams
Salt and pepper to taste
½ teaspoon
  Worcestershire sauce

Cook potatoes in water in saucepan until almost tender. Sauté onion and celery in butter in skillet until tender; do not brown. Add flour. Cook for several minutes, stirring frequently. Add to potato mixture. Cook until slightly thickened, stirring constantly. Add with remaining ingredients. Cook until potatoes are tender. Yield: 8 to 10 servings.

Leona Arnold, Preceptor Gamma Psi
Vacaville, California

MANHATTAN CLAM CHOWDER

3 slices bacon, chopped
1 cup chopped onion
1 cup chopped celery
4 cups clam juice
4 cups chopped clams
3 16-ounce cans stewed
  tomatoes
1 10-ounce package
  frozen mixed
  vegetables
Salt and pepper to taste
1 teaspoon oregano
1 teaspoon sweet basil
2 tablespoons parsley

Brown bacon with onion and celery in skillet; drain. Add next 4 ingredients in order listed; mix well. Stir in seasonings. Cook until clams are tender. Yield: 3½ quarts.

Jeanne Hegner, Iota Omega
Fort Myers, Florida

LINGUINI WITH CLAM SAUCE

8 ounces linguini	1/8 teaspoon pepper
2 6-ounce cans clams, minced	2 tablespoons chopped parsley
1/4 cup chopped onion	1 teaspoon grated lemon rind
3 cloves of garlic, minced	1 to 2 tablespoons fresh lemon juice
1/3 cup olive oil	
2 tablespoons butter	
1 tablespoon oregano	Parmesan cheese
1/2 teaspoon salt	

Cook linguini using package directions; drain and keep warm. Drain clams, reserving juice. Sauté onion and garlic in olive oil and butter in skillet; do not brown. Add reserved clam juice, oregano, salt and pepper. Bring to a boil over high heat. Cook for 5 minutes. Reduce heat. Add clams, parsley, lemon rind and juice. Cook until heated through. Combine with linguini; toss to mix. Serve with Parmesan cheese. Yield: 4 servings.

Carol Faquinto, Beta Tau
Price, Utah

AVOCADO CRAB MORNAY

1/4 cup melted butter	Dash of nutmeg
1/4 cup all-purpose flour	Dash of cayenne pepper
1 cup light cream	Dash of salt
1/2 cup chicken broth	6 scallions, minced
1/2 cup Sherry	1/4 cup butter
1/4 cup Parmesan cheese	3 avocados, chopped
2 tablespoons shredded Swiss cheese	1 1/2 pounds crab meat

Preheat oven to 500 degrees. Blend 1/4 cup butter and flour in saucepan. Add cream and chicken broth. Cook until thickened, stirring until smooth. Blend in Sherry, cheeses and seasonings; remove from heat. Sauté scallions in 1/4 cup butter in skillet until tender-crisp. Add to sauce. Cook until heated through, stirring gently; do not boil. Fold in avocados and crab meat. Mound the crab meat mixture in scallop shells; sprinkle with additional cheese. Bake for 5 minutes. Serve immediately. Yield: 8 servings.

Cecile Loudat, Xi Eta Nu
Bryan, Texas

BAKED CRAB DISH

1 6-ounce can crab meat	4 Holland rusks
8 ounces cream cheese, softened	1/2 cup mayonnaise
	1 tomato, sliced
Dash of seasoned salt	1 avocado, sliced

Preheat oven to 350 degrees. Mix crab meat, cream cheese and seasoned salt in bowl. Arrange 4 Holland rusks on baking sheet. Layer mayonnaise, tomato, avocado and crab meat mixture on each. Sprinkle with rusk crumbs. Bake for 45 minutes. Yield: 4 servings.

Helen E. Blanchard, Preceptor Eta
Arcadia, California

CAJUN CRAB GUMBO

2 tablespoons margarine	1/4 teaspoon dried thyme
2 tablespoons all-purpose flour	1/2 teaspoon cayenne pepper
4 small zucchini, sliced	1 clove of garlic, minced
1 large onion, chopped	1 1/2 pounds crab meat
1 19-ounce can tomatoes	2 cups boiling water
1 bay leaf, crushed	1 teaspoon salt
2 tablespoons chopped parsley	3 cups cooked rice

Melt margarine in heavy kettle. Blend in flour. Add zucchini, onion, tomatoes with juice, bay leaf, parsley, thyme, cayenne pepper, garlic and crab meat. Simmer for 10 minutes, stirring frequently. Add water and salt. Simmer, covered, for 1 hour. Uncover. Simmer until consistency of thick soup, stirring frequently. Serve over rice. Yield: 6 servings.

Mary A. Gruss, Preceptor Nu
Waterford, Connecticut

CORN AND CRAB MEAT BISQUE

1/2 cup melted butter	1/2 teaspoon Worcestershire sauce
2 tablespoons all-purpose flour	1/2 teaspoon Tabasco sauce
1/2 cup chopped onion	1/4 cup shredded cheese
1 pound white crab meat	1/4 cup chopped parsley
1 16-ounce can cream-style corn	1/4 cup chopped shallots
1 10-ounce can cream of potato soup	1 tablespoon Konriko seasoning

Blend butter and flour in 5-quart soup pot. Add onion. Cook over low heat for 10 minutes, stirring frequently. Add crab meat and next 4 ingredients. Cook over low heat for 15 to 20 minutes. Stir in cheese, parsley, shallots and seasoning just before serving. Yield: 15 to 20 servings.

Diana Fromdahl, Kappa
New Iberia, Louisiana

CRAB AND ASPARAGUS BELMONT

2 tablespoons melted butter	1/2 teaspoon dry mustard
2 tablespoons all-purpose flour	1/8 teaspoon cayenne pepper
1 1/2 cups milk	1/8 teaspoon paprika
1 cup shredded Cheddar cheese	1 pound asparagus, cooked
1/2 teaspoon salt	1 pound back-fin crab meat

Preheat broiler. Blend butter and flour in saucepan. Stir in milk. Cook until thickened, stirring constantly; reduce heat. Add cheese and seasonings. Cook until cheese melts, stirring constantly. Arrange asparagus in ramekins. Sprinkle with crab meat. Pour sauce over crab meat. Broil until bubbly. Yield: 4 servings.

Lenna L. Riddlebarger, Preceptor Alpha Kappa
Waynesboro, Virginia

CRAB MEAT MORNAY

1 small bunch green onions, chopped	8 ounces Swiss cheese, shredded
½ cup finely chopped parsley	1 tablespoon Sherry
½ cup melted butter	1 tablespoon Worcestershire sauce
2 tablespoons all-purpose flour	Salt and red pepper to taste
2 cups half and half	1 pound lump crab meat

Sauté onions and parsley in butter in heavy saucepan. Blend in flour, half and half and cheese. Cook until cheese is melted, stirring constantly. Add Sherry, Worcestershire sauce, salt and red pepper. Fold in crab meat gently. Serve in chafing dish. Yield: 5 cups.

Mary Jo Wartelle, Tau Omega
Apple Valley, California

CRAB-SAUCED BRUNCH EGGS

6 hard-cooked eggs	3 English muffins, split, toasted
⅛ teaspoon salt	
1 teaspoon prepared mustard	1 6-ounce package frozen crab meat
½ cup mayonnaise	1 10-ounce can cream of celery soup
½ cup finely chopped celery	⅓ cup milk
2 tablespoons chopped green onions	1 tablespoon chopped parsley
⅛ teaspoon salt	

Preheat oven to 350 degrees. Cut eggs into halves. Remove yolks. Mash yolks with ⅛ teaspoon salt, mustard and 2 tablespoons mayonnaise in bowl. Fill egg white halves with yolk mixture. Combine remaining 6 tablespoons mayonnaise with celery, green onions and remaining ⅛ teaspoon salt. Spread over toasted muffins on baking sheet. Place 2 egg halves on each muffin half. Bake for 5 to 7 minutes or until heated through. Drain. Slice crab meat. Combine with soup, milk and parsley in saucepan. Cook until heated through. Serve over warm eggs and muffins. Yield: 6 servings.

Esther Hobson, Preceptor Alpha Upsilon
Lake Havasu City, Arizona

CRAB THERMIDOR

5 ounces sliced mushrooms	2 to 3 tablespoons dry Sherry
¼ cup butter	Salt and pepper to taste
3 tablespoons all-purpose flour	½ teaspoon dry mustard
1¼ cups half and half	2 tablespoons Parmesan cheese
1 pound crab meat	Paprika

Preheat broiler. Sauté mushrooms in 2 tablespoons butter in medium saucepan over medium heat for 3 minutes. Melt remaining 2 tablespoons butter in saucepan; remove from heat. Add flour; mix well. Add half and half gradually. Heat to the boiling point or until thickened, stirring constantly. Turn off heat. Add sautéed mushrooms, crab meat, Sherry, salt, pepper and mustard; mix well. Spread in greased 9-inch baking dish; sprinkle with Parmesan cheese and paprika. Broil until brown and bubbly. Serve very hot with rice and fresh vegetables. Yield: 4 servings.

Melanie Mastin, Preceptor Zeta Phi
Morgan Hill, California

EASY CRAWFISH CASSEROLE

1½ cups Sherry	2 pounds crawfish tails
¾ cup butter	1 cup chopped green onions and tops
3 cloves of garlic, crushed	
1½ teaspoons tarragon	3 tablespoons chopped white onions
2 tablespoons chopped parsley	1 teaspoon salt
2 cups French bread cubes	½ teaspoon red pepper
	½ teaspoon black pepper

Preheat oven to 400 degrees. Combine Sherry, butter, garlic, tarragon and parsley in blender container. Process until smooth. Add French bread gradually, processing to make thick paste. Arrange crawfish tails in bottom of large casserole. Sprinkle green and white onions on top. Season with salt and peppers. Spread bread mixture on top. Bake for 20 minutes or until golden brown. Yield: 6 servings.

Mary Louise Bell, Preceptor Alpha Gamma
New Iberia, Louisiana

CRAWFISH PIES

1 pound crawfish, chopped	1 10-ounce can condensed celery soup
⅓ cup chopped green bell pepper	3 hard-cooked eggs, chopped
⅓ cup chopped parsley	Salt and pepper to taste
⅓ cup chopped celery	1 teaspoon Worcestershire sauce
½ cup chopped green onions	½ teaspoon Tabasco sauce
½ cup butter	1 cup bread crumbs
1 16-ounce can stewed tomatoes, chopped	2 unbaked 9-inch pie shells

Preheat oven to 350 degrees. Sauté crawfish and first 4 vegetables in butter in skillet. Add tomatoes. Simmer for 20 minutes. Add soup gradually; mix well. Add eggs. Simmer for several minutes longer. Stir in seasonings. Remove from heat; stir in bread crumbs. Add additional liquid if necessary. Spoon into pie shells. Bake for 30 minutes or until browned. Yield: 16 servings.

Gloria M. Firmin, Preceptor Alpha Delta
Albuquerque, New Mexico

FLORIDA LOBSTER FONDUE

2 pounds lobster tails	2 dashes of soy sauce
1 recipe white sauce	8 ounces Cheddar cheese, shredded
1 jigger white wine	
Dash of Worcestershire sauce	Herb-flavored cracker crumbs

Preheat oven to 350 degrees. Steam lobster tails in water in saucepan until shells turn red. Remove meat from the shells; cut into 1-inch cubes. Combine white sauce, wine, Worcestershire sauce and soy sauce in saucepan. Add cheese. Cook until cheese melts. Place lobster in 2-quart baking dish; pour sauce over top. Sprinkle with cracker crumbs. Bake for 20 to 30 minutes or until brown. Yield: 6 servings.

Theresa Nyre, Laureate Epsilon
Minot, North Dakota

LOBSTER NEWBURG

1 pound lobster	Salt and pepper to taste
½ cup butter	2 cups half and half
¼ cup all-purpose flour	Sherry to taste

Sauté lobster in butter in saucepan. Sprinkle flour over lobster. Cook until lobster is red, stirring constantly. Add salt, pepper and half and half. Cook until thickened, stirring constantly. Add Sherry to taste. Serve over pastry puffs or toast points. Yield: 4 servings.

Pat Hansen, Laureate Beta
Westbrook, Maine

LOBSTER CASSEROLE

2 10-ounce cans cream of mushroom soup	2 5-ounce cans sliced water chestnuts, drained
1 cup mayonnaise	½ cup minced green onions
¼ cup dry Sherry	
½ cup milk	1 cup shredded Cheddar cheese
1½ pounds lobster chunks	
3 cups seasoned croutons	

Preheat oven to 350 degrees. Mix soup, mayonnaise and Sherry in bowl. Stir in milk. Combine with remaining ingredients except cheese. Spoon into 3-quart baking dish; top with cheese. Bake for 1 hour. Yield: 4 servings.

Wanda Combs, Beta Rho
Independence, Missouri

LOLLIE'S SCALLOPED OYSTERS

Margarine	1 pint oysters
Saltine crackers, crumbled	Salt and pepper to taste
	Milk

Preheat oven to 350 degrees. Grease casserole with margarine. Layer crackers, oysters, dot of margarine, salt and pepper alternately in casserole, ending with crackers. Add enough milk to layers to fill casserole. Let stand for 30 minutes. Pour additional milk over mixture if needed. Bake for 1 hour. Yield: 6 servings.

Nancy C. Whitworth, Xi Alpha Rho
Elberton, Georgia

OYSTER STEW

4 pints small oysters	Seafood seasoning to taste
½ cup butter or margarine	Salt and pepper to taste
1 gallon milk, scalded	

Sauté oysters in margarine in heavy saucepan until oysters curl. Add milk to oysters. Season to taste. Yield: 16 to 20 servings.

Helene Lewis, Laureate Alpha Beta
Oak Harbor, Washington

SCALLOPS IN SEAFOOD SAUCE

1 pound bay scallops	Bread crumbs
1 10-ounce can cream of shrimp soup	Margarine

Preheat oven to 350 degrees. Combine scallops and soup in casserole. Top with bread crumbs; dot with margarine. Bake for 15 to 20 minutes or until scallops are tender. Serve over rice. Yield: 4 servings.

Caroline Redpath, Lambda Phi
West Palm Beach, Florida

BARBECUED SHRIMP

5 pounds unpeeled medium shrimp	2 cups Italian salad dressing
2 cups melted margarine	1 2-ounce can pepper
Juice of 5 lemons	

Preheat oven to 350 degrees. Combine all ingredients in roasting pan. Bake, tightly covered, for 30 minutes, stirring once. Chill in refrigerator. Yield: 16 servings.

Mariam Ramey, Iota Epsilon
Fayetteville, Georgia

FETTUCINI WITH SCAMPI

1 cup butter	½ teaspoon dill
⅛ cup grated Romano cheese	1 cup heavy cream
	2 cups cooked fettucini
2 tablespoons Parmesan cheese	6 shrimp, cooked, chopped
Pinch of garlic salt	

Melt butter in skillet. Add cheeses, garlic salt and dill. Cook until cheese begins to melt, stirring constantly. Blend in cream gradually, stirring constantly. Add fettucini; toss to mix. Cook just until heated through. Add shrimp just before serving. Yield: 2 servings.

Joyce Hoffman, Sigma
Nashville, Tennessee

SHRIMP SCAMPI

¼ cup chopped scallions	1 tablespoon white wine
2 tablespoons minced garlic	½ teaspoon salt
	Coarsely ground pepper
1 cup butter	1 teaspoon dillweed
¼ cup olive oil	2 tablespoons parsley
2 pounds shrimp, peeled	2 tablespoons sesame seed
1 tablespoon lemon juice	

Sauté scallions and garlic in butter and olive oil in skillet. Add shrimp, lemon juice, wine, salt and pepper. Cook for 4 minutes, stirring occasionally. Add dillweed, parsley and sesame seed. Serve over rice. Yield: 6 servings.

Bettye Parker, Beta Beta Rho
Winnsboro, Texas

CAJUN SHRIMP

1 tablespoon corn oil	1 small red bell pepper,
1 pound large shrimp,	finely chopped
peeled	1 tablespoon finely
1/4 cup corn oil	chopped fresh basil
1/3 cup all-purpose flour	1/4 to 1/2 teaspoon cayenne
1 medium onion, finely	pepper
chopped	3/4 cup water
1 stalk celery, chopped	Salt to taste

Heat heavy 10-inch skillet over medium-high heat. Add 1 tablespoon oil and shrimp. Cook until shrimp are pink, stirring frequently. Remove shrimp to bowl; wipe skillet. Add 1/4 cup oil to skillet. Stir in flour. Cook for 5 minutes or until dark golden brown, stirring constantly. Stir in vegetables, basil, cayenne pepper and water. Bring to a boil. Cook over low heat until vegetables are tender. Add shrimp. Cook until heated through. Season with salt to taste. Serve over rice. Yield: 4 servings.

Denise L. Messier, Epsilon Xi
Manassas, Virginia

CASHEW SHRIMP

1 pound medium shrimp	1/2 cup chicken broth
1/2 teaspoon salt	Dash of salt
1 teaspoon lemon juice	3 tablespoons sesame oil
1 8-ounce can water	4 slices gingerroot
chestnuts	2 green onions, cut into
1 teaspoon cornstarch	pieces
1 teaspoon dry Sherry	1/2 cup roasted cashews
1/2 teaspoon sesame oil	

Peel, devein and rinse shrimp. Sprinkle with 1/2 teaspoon salt and lemon juice. Chill for 30 minutes. Cut water chestnuts into quarters. Mix next 5 ingredients in small bowl; set aside. Heat 3 tablespoons oil in wok over high heat. Add gingerroot, green onions, shrimp and water chestnuts. Stir-fry for 3 to 4 minutes or until shrimp turn pink. Discard gingerroot. Add cornstarch mixture. Cook until thickened, stirring constantly. Spoon onto serving dish; sprinkle cashews over top. Yield: 4 servings.

Jackie Vogler, Preceptor Kappa Rho
Hilltop Lakes, Texas

PASTA SHRIMP

2 tablespoons chopped	1 pound sea sticks,
garlic	chopped
1/2 cup butter	1/2 cup chopped parsley
1/4 cup olive oil	1 tablespoon lemon juice
8 ounces cooked medium	1 pound fettucini, cooked
shrimp	

Sauté garlic in butter and olive oil in skillet. Add shrimp. Cook until well coated with butter. Add sea sticks. Cook until heated through. Add parsley and lemon juice. Place pasta on platter. Spoon seafood mixture over pasta. Yield: 6 servings.

Laura Babcock, Preceptor Laureate
Athens, Pennsylvania

PEA PODS AND SHRIMP

2 eggs, beaten	3/4 cup sugar
1/2 cup all-purpose flour	1/4 cup vinegar
3/4 teaspoon salt	1/2 cup canned pineapple
1/4 cup water	chunks
1 1/2 cups peanut oil	1 medium green or red
1 pound large shrimp,	bell pepper, chopped
peeled, drained	1 6-ounce package
2 tablespoons cornstarch	frozen pea pods
3/4 cup water	1 tablespoon soy sauce

Combine eggs, flour, salt and 1/4 cup water in bowl; beat until smooth. Heat oil in wok or skillet to 375 degrees. Dip shrimp in batter. Cook 5 or 6 at a time in hot oil for 5 minutes or until golden brown; drain. Blend cornstarch with 3/4 cup cold water in saucepan. Add sugar and vinegar. Cook until thickened and bubbly. Add remaining ingredients. Heat for 2 to 4 minutes longer. Serve with shrimp over rice. Yield: 4 servings.

Geraldine E. Sowards, Laureate Beta Delta
Columbus, Ohio

RAGIN' CAJUN SHRIMP

4 pounds shrimp, peeled	1/2 teaspoon dried red
1 cup corn oil	pepper flakes
1/2 cup chopped green	1/2 teaspoon dried thyme
onions	1/2 teaspoon dried
2 cloves of garlic, minced	rosemary
1 teaspoon cayenne	1/4 teaspoon dried oregano
pepper	Bamboo skewers
1 teaspoon black pepper	

Combine shrimp with next 9 ingredients in large bowl, stirring to coat shrimp. Refrigerate, covered, for 2 hours, stirring occasionally. Soak bamboo skewers in ice water for 2 hours. Preheat grill. Drain shrimp, reserving marinade. Thread shrimp on skewers. Grill just until pink, basting with marinade. Serve immediately. Yield: 8 servings.

 Brittany M. Kollmann, Alpha Phi Nu
Lewisville, Texas

SHERMAN'S SHRIMP CASSEROLE

1 5-ounce package	1/2 teaspoon
saffron rice mix	Worcestershire sauce
1 10-ounce can cream of	1 teaspoon prepared
mushroom soup	mustard
3 tablespoons melted	1 16-ounce package
margarine	frozen uncooked
2 tablespoons chopped	shrimp
green bell pepper	Salt and pepper to taste
2 tablespoons finely	1/2 cup shredded mild
chopped onion	cheese

Preheat oven to 350 degrees. Cook saffron rice using package directions. Add remaining ingredients, reserving a small amount of cheese. Spoon into 2-quart casserole sprayed with nonstick cooking spray. Sprinkle reserved cheese over top. Bake for 30 minutes. Yield: 4 to 6 servings.

Trisha Winship, Delta Kappa
Ellisville, Mississippi

SHRIMP AND SAUSAGE JAMBALAYA

*1 pound smoked sausage,
  sliced
3 large onions, chopped
2 cloves of garlic, minced
1¼ cups chopped green
  bell pepper
2 stalks celery, chopped
1½ cups canned tomatoes
3 tablespoons tomato
  paste
1 bay leaf*

*1 tablespoon chopped
  parsley
½ teaspoon thyme
1 cup uncooked rice
1 teaspoon salt
¼ teaspoon cayenne
  pepper
1½ cups water
2 pounds medium
  shrimp, peeled*

Sauté sausage and onions in stockpot until onions are soft. Add garlic, green pepper and celery. Sauté until vegetables are soft. Add tomatoes, tomato paste, bay leaf, parsley, thyme and rice. Season with salt and cayenne pepper. Add water. Bring to a boil; add shrimp. Reduce heat. Cook over very low heat for 30 to 45 minutes.
Yield: 8 servings
Note: May add 1 dozen oysters, 1 pound chopped smoked ham or 1 teaspoon Creole seasoning.

*Virginia Fitzgerald, Laureate Iota
Raleigh, North Carolina*

NASI GORENG

*6 cups uncooked rice
12 cups boiling water
5 teaspoons salt
1 teaspoon minced dried
  red pepper
1½ cups finely chopped
  salted peanuts*

*1 cup finely chopped
  onion
2 cups butter
3 cups ½-inch cooked ham
  cubes
2 pounds medium
  prawns, cooked, peeled*

Cook rice in boiling water with salt in large saucepan until tender but firm. Sauté red pepper, peanuts and onion in butter in saucepan for 5 minutes. Pour over rice in large bowl. Add ham and prawns; toss carefully with 2 forks. Let stand to season and blend flavors. Store in refrigerator. Reheat over low heat, tossing occasionally. Yield: 16 to 20 servings.

*Betty L. Thomas, Preceptor Laureate Beta Tau
Twenty-Nine Palms, California*

BAYOU BOUNTY SEAFOOD CASSEROLE

*8 ounces cream cheese,
  softened
¾ cup margarine
2 large onions, chopped
1 green bell pepper,
  chopped
2 stalks celery, chopped
8 ounces mushrooms,
  sliced
1 pound shrimp, peeled,
  deveined*

*1 10-ounce can
  mushroom soup
1 pound fresh white
  crab meat
1½ cups cooked rice
1 tablespoon garlic salt
1 teaspoon Tabasco sauce
½ teaspoon red pepper
Cheddar cheese, shredded
Ritz crackers, crushed*

Preheat oven to 350 degrees. Melt cream cheese and ½ cup margarine together in saucepan. Sauté onions, green pepper, celery and mushrooms in remaining ¼ cup margarine in skillet. Add shrimp. Sauté until shrimp turn pink. Add soup, crab meat, rice and seasonings; mix well. Spoon into shallow 3-quart casserole. Top with mixture of Cheddar cheese and cracker crumbs. Bake for 30 minutes. Yield: 8 servings.

*Shirley B. Griffin, Preceptor Upsilon
Crowley, Louisiana*

CIOPPINO

*3 cups dry Chablis
2 cups fish stock
2 teaspoons basil
1½ teaspoons oregano
½ teaspoon thyme
½ teaspoon sage
1 teaspoon pepper
6 bay leaves
12 cherrystone clams
24 mussels
2 cups butter
¼ cup all-purpose flour
1 green bell pepper, sliced
1 bunch green onions,
  sliced
2 medium carrots, finely
  chopped*

*2 stalks celery, chopped
2 zucchini, sliced
2 cloves of garlic
2 pounds scallops
2 pounds unpeeled
  shrimp
2 dungeness crabs,
  cracked
1½ cups firm whitefish
1 16-ounce can pear
  tomatoes, chopped
1 15-ounce can tomato
  purée
1 18-ounce can tomato
  sauce
½ cup Worcestershire
  sauce*

Combine first 8 ingredients in stockpot. Add clams and mussels. Simmer for 15 to 20 minutes or until shells open. Remove shellfish. Keep stock at the simmering point. Melt butter in stockpot. Blend in flour. Cook for several minutes, stirring constantly. Add next 6 ingredients. Cook until vegetables are tender-crisp. Add scallops, shrimp, crabs, whitefish, simmering stock, tomatoes, purée, tomato sauce and Worcestershire sauce. Simmer for 8 to 10 minutes. Add clams and mussels. Cook until heated through. Yield: 12 servings.

*Sandy Miller, Preceptor Beta Lambda
Lakewood, Colorado*

SEAFOOD FETTUCINI

*1 pound shrimp
1 clove of garlic, crushed
6 tablespoons butter
1 pound scallops
2 to 3 tablespoons
  cornstarch*

*2 cups whipping cream
¼ teaspoon dillweed
½ cup Parmesan cheese
12 ounces fettucini,
  cooked*

Rinse shrimp; pat dry. Sauté shrimp and garlic in butter in skillet for 5 minutes. Add scallops. Sauté for 5 minutes. Remove seafood. Stir mixture of cornstarch and whipping cream into pan juices. Cook until thickened, stirring frequently. Add dillweed and cheese; mix well. Add seafood. Cook until heated through. Serve over fettucini. Yield: 4 servings.

*Hannah Tipper, Preceptor Eta
Ladson, South Carolina*

SEAFOOD LASAGNA

8 large lasagna noodles	2 10-ounce cans cream
1 cup chopped onion	of mushroom soup
2 tablespoons butter	1/3 cup milk
8 ounces cream cheese,	1/3 cup dry white wine
softened	1 pound shrimp, cooked,
1½ cups cream-style	split
cottage cheese	1 7-ounce can crab meat
1 egg, beaten	1/4 cup Parmesan cheese
2 teaspoons basil	1/2 cup shredded sharp
1/2 teaspoon salt	cheese
1/8 teaspoon pepper	

Preheat oven to 350 degrees. Cook lasagna noodles using package directions; drain well. Arrange 4 noodles in bottom of greased 9x13-inch baking dish. Sauté onion in butter in skillet. Blend in cream cheese. Stir in cottage cheese, egg, basil, salt and pepper. Spread half the mixture over noodles. Combine soup, milk and wine in bowl. Stir in shrimp and crab meat. Spread half the mixture over cottage cheese layer. Repeat layers. Sprinkle with Parmesan cheese. Bake for 45 minutes. Top with shredded cheese. Bake for 2 to 3 minutes or until cheese melts. Let stand for 15 minutes before serving.
Yield: 12 servings.

Janine Marples, Preceptor Laureate Gamma
Marysville, Kansas

SEAFOOD PIE

1 medium onion, chopped	2 slices American cheese
1 medium green bell	2 teaspoons
pepper, chopped	Worcestershire sauce
2 stalks celery, chopped	1 teaspoon Tabasco sauce
2 cloves of garlic, minced	Salt to taste
1/2 cup margarine	1 pound crab meat
1 10-ounce can golden	1 pound shrimp, chopped
mushroom soup	1 recipe 2-crust pie pastry
1/2 10-ounce can cream	
of mushroom soup	

Preheat oven to 425 degrees. Sauté vegetables and garlic in margarine in skillet. Add soups, cheese, seasonings and seafood. Cook over low heat until shrimp are pink. Spoon into pastry-lined pie plate. Top with remaining pie pastry. Bake until golden brown. Yield: 1 pie.

Denise B. Minvielle, Beta Lambda
Abbeville, Louisiana

SEAFOOD POTPOURRI

2 4-ounce cans sliced	2 7-ounce cans tuna,
mushrooms	drained
3 to 4 cups thin white	2 7-ounce cans crab
sauce	meat, drained
2 cups shredded Cheddar	2 5-ounce cans shrimp
cheese	3 to 6 hard-cooked eggs,
3 to 6 tablespoons	sliced
chopped chives	Potato chips, crushed
1 4-ounce can black	
olives, sliced	

Preheat oven to 350 degrees. Drain mushrooms, reserving liquid. Prepare white sauce using mushroom liquid for part of milk; cool slightly. Add cheese; stir until melted. Blend in chives and olives. Combine half the seafood in greased 9x13-inch casserole. Arrange half the egg slices on top. Add mushrooms and half the sauce. Repeat with remaining seafood, eggs and sauce. Top with potato chips. Bake for 30 minutes. Yield: 10 servings.

Marceline Cliver, Preceptor Omega
Sundance, Wyoming

SHRIMP AND CRAB QUICHE

4 ounces crab meat,	1 unbaked 9-inch pie shell
drained	4 eggs, slightly beaten
4 ounces tiny shrimp,	1½ cups half and half
drained	1/8 teaspoon cayenne
4 ounces shredded	pepper
natural Swiss cheese	1 teaspoon salt
1/3 onion, finely chopped	1/4 teaspoon pepper

Preheat oven to 425 degrees. Sprinkle crab meat, shrimp, cheese and onion in pie shell. Combine eggs and remaining ingredients in bowl. Pour into pie shell. Bake for 15 minutes. Reduce temperature to 300 degrees. Bake for 30 minutes or until knife inserted in center comes out clean. Cool for 10 minutes or longer before serving.
Yield: 8 servings.

Helen Murphy, Preceptor Eta Theta
Lewisville, Texas

SEAFOOD SUPREME

1 green bell pepper,	8 ounces Velveeta cheese,
chopped	cubed
1¼ pounds scallops	8 ounces Mexican
Vegetable oil	Velveeta cheese, cubed
6 tablespoons margarine	12 ounces lobster
3 to 4 tablespoons	1½ pounds shrimp,
all-purpose flour	cooked, peeled
2½ cups milk	1/4 cup white wine

Sauté green pepper and scallops in small amount of oil in saucepan. Melt margarine in skillet. Stir in flour. Add milk. Cook until thickened, stirring constantly. Add cheeses. Cook until melted, stirring constantly. Add green pepper, scallops, lobster, shrimp and wine. Cook until heated through. Serve over rice. Yield: 6 servings.

Georgeann E. Ireton, Xi Delta
Baltimore, Maryland

WILD RICE AND SEAFOOD CASSEROLE

2 6-ounce packages	1/3 cup grated onion
wild and white rice mix	1 cup chopped green bell
2 7-ounce cans crab meat	pepper
4 4½-ounce cans shrimp	1 cup chopped pimento
3 10-ounce cans	1 cup chopped celery
mushroom soup	2 teaspoons lemon juice

Preheat oven to 350 degrees. Prepare rice mix using package directions. Combine all ingredients in greased 4-quart casserole. Bake for 1 hour. Yield: 4 to 6 servings.

Rebecca C. Minke, Xi Omicron
Wiley Ford, West Virginia

Party
Vegetables
and Side Dishes

ARTICHOKES AND GREEN BEANS

1   16-ounce can
artichoke hearts
1   16-ounce can French-
style green beans,
drained
½ cup Parmesan cheese

½ cup Italian bread
crumbs
¼ cup olive oil
2 teaspoons garlic powder
Bread crumbs

Preheat oven to 350 degrees. Drain and chop artichoke hearts. Mix with green beans, cheese, ½ cup crumbs, olive oil and garlic powder in bowl. Place in greased 1-quart casserole. Top with additional bread crumbs. Bake for 30 minutes. Yield: 6 to 8 servings.

Aimee Klimezak, Eta Rho
Covington, Louisiana

ASPARAGUS SOUFFLÉ

1   16-ounce can cut
asparagus, drained
1 cup milk
4 eggs

¾ cup mayonnaise
1 cup shredded sharp
cheese

Preheat oven to 325 degrees. Combine first 4 ingredients and ¾ cup cheese in blender container. Process until smooth. Pour into greased 1½-quart casserole. Sprinkle remaining ¼ cup cheese on top. Place in larger pan with about 1 inch water. Bake for 1 hour or until slightly browned and puffed. Serve immediately. Yield: 8 servings.

Remine Moss, Xi Beta Eta
Earl, North Carolina

HOPPIN' JOHN

1 cup dried black-eyed
peas
6 cups water
6 slices bacon, cut up
4 cups water
¾ cup chopped onion

1 stalk celery, chopped
1½ teaspoons salt
½ to ¾ teaspoon ground
red pepper
1 cup long grain rice

Rinse peas. Combine with 6 cups water in large saucepan. Bring to a boil; reduce heat. Simmer for 2 minutes; remove from heat. Let stand, covered, for 1 hour. Drain and rinse. Cook bacon in saucepan until crisp. Drain, reserving 3 tablespoons drippings. Add peas, 4 cups water, onion, celery, salt and red pepper. Bring to a boil; reduce heat. Simmer, covered, for 30 minutes. Add uncooked rice. Simmer, covered, for 20 minutes or until peas and rice are tender, stirring occasionally. Yield: 10 servings.

Patricia Hudson, Xi Alpha Psi
Superior, Wisconsin

BARBECUED GREEN BEANS

3 slices bacon, chopped
¼ cup chopped onion
2 tablespoons all-purpose
flour
1   10-ounce can tomato
soup

1 cup packed light
brown sugar
4   16-ounce cans cut
green beans, drained

Preheat oven to 325 degrees. Brown bacon and onion in skillet. Add flour, soup and brown sugar; mix well. Pour over green beans in 8x8-inch baking dish. Bake for 45 minutes. Yield: 6 to 8 servings.

Denise Barber, Kappa
South Sioux City, Nebraska

CROCK•POT BEAN SUPREME

1   15-ounce can
pinto beans, drained
1   15-ounce can black-
eyed peas, drained
1   15-ounce can lima
beans, drained
1   15-ounce can kidney
beans, drained
1   31-ounce can pork
and beans
2 pounds ground beef

1 large onion, chopped
1 green bell pepper,
chopped
2 cups catsup
1 cup dry red wine
½ cup packed light
brown sugar
1 tablespoon dry mustard
1 tablespoon
Worcestershire sauce

Combine drained beans and undrained pork and beans in Crock•Pot. Brown ground beef with onion and green pepper in skillet, stirring until crumbly; drain. Stir into bean mixture. Add catsup and remaining ingredients; mix well. Cook on Low for 8 hours. Yield: 12 servings.

Betty Kennedy, Preceptor Beta Omega
Littleton, Colorado

CHEESY GRITS AND BEAN BAKE

3 cups water
1 teaspoon salt
¾ cup yellow grits
¼ pound bacon, crisp-
fried, crumbled
8 ounces pepper cheese,
cubed
2 tablespoons butter
2 eggs, beaten
½ cup milk
1 cup shredded
Cheddar cheese
1   15-ounce can
garbanzo beans

1   15-ounce can kidney
beans
1 cup chopped celery
¾ cup chopped green
bell pepper
¾ cup tomato juice
¼ cup corn oil
¼ cup vinegar
1   1⅜-ounce envelope
chili seasoning mix
1 cup cherry tomato
halves

Preheat oven to 350 degrees. Bring water and salt to a boil in saucepan; stir in grits. Return to a boil; reduce heat. Cook for 5 minutes, stirring frequently. Remove from heat. Stir in bacon, pepper cheese and butter until cheese melts. Combine eggs and milk in bowl. Stir a small amount of grits into eggs; add remaining grits. Spoon into buttered 7x12-inch baking dish. Bake for 35 minutes, or until knife inserted in center comes out clean. Sprinkle with Cheddar cheese. Bake for 3 minutes longer. Let stand for 5 minutes. Drain and rinse garbanzo and kidney beans. Combine with next 6 ingredients in saucepan. Cook until heated through, stirring frequently. Stir in cherry tomatoes. Heat to serving temperature. Spoon around edge of casserole. Serve remaining bean mixture with casserole. Yield: 12 servings.

Maxine Allgood, Preceptor Beta Kappa
Webster, Florida

SOUTH OF THE BORDER BEANS

1 pound dried red kidney beans	3 tablespoons corn oil
1 medium yellow onion, coarsely chopped	½ teaspoon oregano
	2 teaspoons minced parsley
1 clove of garlic, crushed	1 tablespoon honey
½ cup minced green pepper	2 teaspoon vinegar
Salt and pepper to taste	¼ teaspoon crushed jalapeño peppers
1 28-ounce can tomatoes	

Rinse beans. Soak in cold water to cover overnight. Drain; rinse under cold running water. Preheat oven to 275 degrees. Place beans in ungreased 2½-quart bean pot. Mix in remaining ingredients. Bake, uncovered, for 2½ hours, stirring every hour. Bake, covered, for 2 to 2½ hours longer or until beans are tender, stirring every hour and adding a small amount of hot water if beans become too dry. Yield: 15 servings.

Kathi Moss, Xi Beta Iota
Cortez, Colorado

FIVE BAKED BEANS

1 16-ounce can lima beans	9 slices crisp-fried bacon, crumbled
1 16-ounce can green beans	1 onion, chopped
1 16-ounce can yellow wax beans	2 tablespoons Worcestershire sauce
1 16-ounce can kidney beans	½ cup catsup
	1½ cups packed dark brown sugar
1 16-ounce can baked beans	1 teaspoon dry mustard

Preheat oven to 350 degrees. Drain beans. Combine with remaining ingredients in large baking dish; mix well. Bake for 1 hour. Yield: 12 servings.

Joyce A. Vosteen, Xi Beta
Lincoln, Nebraska

GREEN BEAN BUNDLES

1½ pounds fresh green beans	½ teaspoon salt
4 or 5 slices bacon	1 teaspoon paprika
3 tablespoons butter, melted	1 tablespoon parsley
	1 teaspoon finely chopped onion
3 tablespoons vinegar	

Snip ends from beans; leave whole. Cook in a small amount of boiling water in saucepan until tender-crisp; drain. Divide into 8 to 10 bundles. Cut bacon into halves. Wrap 1 piece bacon around each bundle; secure with toothpick. Place on rack in broiler pan. Broil until bacon is crisp. Remove to warm serving platter. Combine butter and remaining ingredients in saucepan. Simmer for 1 to 2 minutes. Pour over hot green bean bundles. Yield: 8 to 10 servings.

Angela Galen, Xi Epsilon Epsilon
Herndon, Virginia

FRENCH BEANS

2 tablespoons butter	2 16-ounce cans sliced green beans, drained
1 tablespoon sugar	
2 tablespoons all-purpose flour	2 cups shredded Cheddar cheese
¼ teaspoon pepper	⅔ cup crushed cornflakes
⅛ teaspoon salt	2 tablespoons melted butter
1 cup sour cream	

Preheat oven to 350 degrees. Combine first 5 ingredients in 1½-quart saucepan. Cook over medium heat until butter melts, stirring constantly. Add sour cream and beans; mix well. Mix in beans. Pour into 1½-quart baking dish; top with cheese. Sprinkle with mixture of cornflake crumbs and melted butter. Bake for 30 minutes. Yield: 4 to 6 servings.

Ruth Boitz, Epsilon Xi
Independence, Oregon

GREEN BEANS ITALIENNE

2 16-ounce cans cut green beans, drained	2 teaspoons dry oregano
	1 teaspoon garlic salt
2 tablespoons wine vinegar	2 tablespoons olive or corn oil

Combine green beans with remaining ingredients in saucepan. Heat for 5 to 7 minutes. Yield: 6 servings.

Pauline Bourdon, Laureate Beta
Claremont, New Hampshire

GREEN BEANS WITH MUSHROOMS

2 10-ounce packages frozen French-style green beans	2 tablespoons chopped parsley
	⅛ teaspoon pepper
½ cup boiling water	½ cup toasted slivered almonds
¼ teaspoon salt	
2 4-ounce cans mushrooms	⅓ cup dry vermouth
	Salt to taste
¼ cup butter	

Cook green beans in boiling salted water in saucepan until tender. Add remaining ingredients; stir gently. Heat to serving temperature over low heat. Yield: 8 servings.

Beverly Lubeski, Xi Gamma Pi
Merriam, Kansas

GREEN BEANS AND CORN SUPREME

2 16-ounce cans seasoned French-style green beans, drained	Salt to taste
	1 10-ounce can cream of celery soup
1 16-ounce can Shoe Peg corn, drained	2 tablespoons mayonnaise
	2 cups sour cream
1 7-ounce can water chestnuts, drained	1 cup chopped onions
	Ritz crackers, crumbled

Preheat oven to 350 degrees. Mix first 4 ingredients in 4-quart casserole. Pour mixture of soup, mayonnaise, sour cream and onions over top. Sprinkle with cracker crumbs. Bake for 30 minutes. Yield: 6 to 8 servings.

Chris Benoit, Gamma Theta
Dothan, Alabama

BROCCOLI CASSEROLE

2 tablespoons melted butter	1 cup milk
2 tablespoons all-purpose flour	2 10-ounce packages frozen chopped broccoli, cooked, drained
3 ounces cream cheese, softened	
¼ cup crumbled blue cheese	⅓ cup crushed rich round crackers

Preheat oven to 350 degrees. Blend butter and flour in a saucepan. Add cheeses and milk. Cook until thickened, stirring constantly. Stir in broccoli. Place in 1-quart casserole; top with cracker crumbs. Bake for 30 minutes. Yield: 8 to 10 servings.

Suzette K. Sample, Chi Xi
Key Largo, Florida

BROCCOLI AND CHEESE CASSEROLE

3 10-ounce packages frozen broccoli, cooked	8 ounces Velveeta cheese, cubed
6 eggs, beaten	8 ounces cream cheese, cubed
1 tablespoon all-purpose flour	½ cup butter, sliced

Preheat oven to 350 degrees. Cut broccoli into bite-sized pieces; place in greased 10x12-inch baking pan. Beat eggs and flour in bowl until smooth. Layer cheeses and butter over broccoli. Pour egg mixture over top. Bake for 35 to 45 minutes or until egg mixture has consistency of cooked eggs. Let stand for several minutes before serving. Yield: 10 to 16 servings.

Deborah L. Walters, Xi Beta Delta
Elkridge, Maryland

BROCCOLI AND CORN CASSEROLE

1 10-ounce package frozen chopped broccoli, cooked, drained	1 tablespoon instant minced onion
1 16-ounce can cream-style corn	2 tablespoons melted margarine
	Dash of pepper
1 egg, beaten	¼ cup cracker crumbs
½ cup cracker crumbs	1 tablespoon melted margarine
½ teaspoon salt	

Preheat oven to 350 degrees. Combine broccoli, corn, egg, ½ cup cracker crumbs, salt, onion, 2 tablespoons melted margarine and pepper in bowl; mix well. Pour into 1-quart caserrole. Combine remaining ¼ cup cracker crumbs and 1 tablespoon melted margarine in bowl. Sprinkle over casserole. Bake for 35 minutes or until bubbly. Yield: 6 servings.

Kendra Meadows, Epsilon Kappa
Beckley, West Virginia

BROCCOLI WITH CHOWDER SAUCE

2 10-ounce packages frozen broccoli spears	½ cup sour cream
	½ teaspoon salt
1 10-ounce can New England clam chowder	4 slices American cheese, chopped

Preheat oven to 325 degrees. Cook broccoli using package directions; drain. Arrange in 8x8-inch baking dish. Combine clam chowder, sour cream and salt in saucepan. Cook over low heat, stirring constantly. Spoon over broccoli. Bake for 20 minutes. Sprinkle with cheese. Bake until cheese melts. Yield 6 to 7 servings.

Marjorie Harms, Preceptor Psi
Fremont, Nebraska

PARTY BROCCOLI

2 tablespoons minced onion	½ teaspoon paprika
	¼ teaspoon salt
2 tablespoons butter	2 10-ounce packages frozen chopped broccoli
1½ cups sour cream	
2 teaspoons sugar	Cashews
1 teaspoon cider vinegar	Cayenne pepper to taste
½ teaspoon poppy seed	

Preheat oven to 325 degrees. Sauté onion in butter in saucepan until brown; remove from heat. Stir in sour cream and next 5 ingredients. Cook broccoli using package directions; drain and place in serving bowl. Spoon sour cream sauce over top. Sprinkle with cashews and cayenne pepper. Yield: 6 to 8 servings.

Velda Koch, Preceptor Alpha Eta
Lincoln, Nebraska

RICE AND BROCCOLI CASSEROLE

2 10-ounce packages frozen broccoli	2 8-ounce jars jalapeño Cheez Whiz
4 cups minute rice, cooked	1 8-ounce jar plain Cheez Whiz
1 cup melted margarine	1 8-ounce can sliced water chestnuts, drained
Chopped onion to taste	
1 10-ounce can cream of chicken soup	1 4½-ounce jar sliced mushrooms, drained
1 10-ounce can cream of mushroom soup	

Preheat oven to 350 degrees. Cook broccoli using package directions; drain. Combine with remaining ingredients in large bowl; mix well. Spread in 9x13-inch baking pan. Bake for 20 minutes or until bubbly. Yield: 18 servings.

LaWanda Henry, Zeta Nu
Sherman, Texas

LOVE THAT BROCCOLI SAUCE

1 tablespoon dried onion	1 tablespoon wine vinegar
1 tablespoon dried parsley	½ cup mayonnaise
2 tablespoons white wine	2 cups steamed broccoli

Mix first 5 ingredients in bowl. Let stand for 30 minutes. Pour over hot broccoli. Yield: 4 servings.

Gail Booth, Xi Beta
Lincoln, Nebraska

CABBAGE AU GRATIN

1 medium cabbage, cooked, chopped	2 cups white sauce
¾ cup shredded Cheddar cheese	½ cup cracker crumbs
	3 tablespoons melted butter
Salt and paprika to taste	

Preheat oven to 400 degrees. Layer cabbage, cheese, seasonings and white sauce ½ at a time in buttered casserole. Mix cracker crumbs with melted butter; sprinkle over top. Bake for 15 to 20 minutes or until brown. Yield: 8 to 10 servings.

Elizabeth Hertelendy, Laureate Zeta
Louisville, Kentucky

CHEESY CARROT CASSEROLE

2 pounds carrots, peeled, sliced	¼ cup melted butter
1 cup shredded Velveeta cheese	1½ cups buttered croutons

Preheat oven to 350 degrees. Cook carrots in a small amount of water until tender; drain. Place in 2-quart casserole. Cover with cheese and butter. Bake, covered, for 20 minutes. Stir in croutons. Bake for 10 minutes longer. Yield: 6 to 8 servings.

Dodie Grachek, Gamma
Omaha, Nebraska

CARROTS IN CHAMPAGNE

2 pounds carrots, peeled	2 tablespoons lemon juice
½ cup beef stock	2 teaspoons dillweed
1 cup champagne	

Cut carrots into matchsticks. Sauté in butter in skillet over medium heat until beginning to brown. Add beef stock and champagne. Cook, covered, just until tender. Cook, uncovered, over high heat until liquid is almost gone. Add lemon juice and dillweed. Serve immediately. Yield: 10 servings.

Diane Runo, Xi Beta
Peoria, Arizona

LEMONY BUTTERED CARROTS

24 small carrots	2 teaspoons grated lemon rind
½ cup butter	
½ cup sugar	1 tablespoon lemon juice

Cook carrots in a small amount of water in saucepan. Melt butter and sugar in saucepan; stir in lemon rind and lemon juice. Add carrots. Simmer until glazed, turning carrots frequently. Garnish with parsley. Yield: 8 servings.

Dorothy Locatelli, Xi Rho Eta
Santa Cruz, California

ORANGE-GLAZED CARROTS

5 medium carrots	¼ teaspoon salt
¼ cup boiling salted water	¼ to ½ teaspoon ginger
	¼ cup orange juice
1 tablespoon sugar	2 tablespoons butter
1 teaspoon cornstarch	

Slice carrots diagonally about 1 inch thick. Cook, covered, in boiling salted water in saucepan for 15 minutes or just until tender. Mix sugar, cornstarch, salt, ginger, orange juice and butter in bowl. Pour over carrots. Cook, for about 5 minutes stirring occasionally. Yield: 4 servings.

Georgiana Van Istendal, Laureate Alpha Gamma
Hollywood, Florida

CARROTS VICHY

2 cups thinly sliced carrots	¼ cup butter
	Light brown sugar to taste
3 cups club soda	

Cook carrots in club soda in saucepan until tender-crisp; drain. Add butter and brown sugar. Cook for 2 to 3 minutes longer. Yield: 5 to 6 servings.

Elaine Smith, Delta Omicron
Lexington, South Carolina

ZESTY CARROTS

6 to 8 medium carrots	½ cup mayonnaise
2 tablespoons grated onion	Salt and pepper to taste
	¼ cup bread crumbs
2 tablespoons grated horseradish	1 tablespoon butter
	Pinch of paprika

Preheat oven to 375 degrees. Cut carrots into long strips. Cook in a small amount of boiling water in saucepan until tender; drain, reserving liquid. Place carrot strips in shallow baking dish. Mix reserved liquid, grated onion, horseradish, mayonnaise, salt and pepper in bowl. Pour over carrots. Sprinkle bread crumbs on top; dot with butter. Sprinkle with paprika. Bake for 20 minutes. Garnish with minced parsley. Yield: 4 to 6 servings.

Marlene Koenig, Xi Theta Nu
Ironton, Ohio

CORN CASSEROLE

1 17-ounce can cream-style corn	2 tablespoons chopped onion
1 17-ounce can whole kernel corn	½ cup margarine, sliced
	1 cup curly macaroni, cooked
1 cup shredded Cheddar cheese	

Preheat oven to 350 degrees. Combine all ingredients in bowl; mix well. Pour into 9x13-inch baking pan. Bake for 30 minutes; stir. Bake for 30 minutes longer. Yield: 20 servings.

Patty Day, Preceptor Zeta
Marysville, Kansas

CORN CHOWDER

2 stalks celery, chopped
2 large potatoes,
  peeled, chopped
1 16-ounce can whole
  kernel corn
1 2-ounce jar
  pimento strips

1 10-ounce can cream of
  mushroom soup
1 10-ounce can cream of
  chicken soup
1 medium onion,
  chopped
2 soup cans milk

Cook celery, potatoes and onion in water to cover in large saucepan until tender. Add remaining ingredients; mix well. Heat to serving temperature, stirring frequently; do not boil. Yield: 10 servings.

Cecile Loudat, Xi Eta Nu
Bryan, Texas

GULLIVER'S CORN

2 10-ounce packages
  frozen corn
1 cup milk
1 cup whipping cream
1 teaspoon salt
1 teaspoon MSG
7 teaspoons sugar

Pinch of white pepper
2 tablespoons melted
  butter
2 tablespoons all-purpose
  flour
Parmesan cheese

Combine first 7 ingredients in saucepan; mix well. Bring to a simmer, stirring frequently. Blend butter and flour in small bowl. Stir into corn mixture; mix well. Pour into 1½-quart casserole. Sprinkle with Parmesan cheese. Broil until brown and bubbly. Yield: 6 to 8 servings.

 Billie J. Smith, Iota Lambda
Monument, Colorado

CORN PUDDING

2 16-ounce cans cream-
  style corn
¼ cup sugar
¼ cup all-purpose flour

¼ cup melted butter
4 eggs, beaten
Salt to taste
Grated cheese

Preheat oven to 350 degrees. Combine all ingredients in bowl; mix well. Pour into buttered baking dish. Bake, uncovered, for 1 hour. Yield: 6 servings.

Rebecca C. Longanacre, Preceptor Alpha
Fort Spring, West Virginia

AMERICAN CORN SOUFFLÉ

Parmesan cheese
¼ cup melted butter
¼ cup all-purpose flour
¼ teaspoon salt
⅛ teaspoon pepper
1 cup milk
1 cup shredded Colby
  cheese

4 eggs, separated
1 10-ounce package
  frozen whole kernel
  corn, cooked, drained
6 slices bacon, crisp-
  fried, crumbled
¼ teaspoon cream of tartar

Preheat oven to 350 degrees. Sprinkle Parmesan cheese to coat bottom and side of well-buttered 1½-quart soufflé dish. Blend butter, flour, salt and pepper in medium saucepan over medium heat. Whisk in milk gradually.

Cook until mixture thickens, stirring constantly. Cook for 1 minute longer; remove from heat. Stir in Colby cheese until melted. Whisk half the hot mixture into beaten egg yolks; whisk egg yolk mixture into hot mixture. Stir in corn and bacon. Beat egg whites with cream of tartar until stiff peaks form. Fold in corn mixture gently. Pour into prepared soufflé dish. Bake for 45 to 50 minutes or until puffed and brown. Serve immediately. Yield: 6 servings.

Sherry Sorenson, Preceptor Beta Lambda
Garden City, Kansas

MEXICAN CORN SCRAMBLE

1 cup chopped onion
¼ cup margarine
10 eggs, beaten
1 12-ounce can Mexicorn
1 2½-ounce can sliced
  ripe olives, drained

1 cup shredded Monterey
  Jack cheese
4 ounces dry salami,
  sliced
Tortilla chips
Taco sauce

Sauté onion in margarine in large skillet over medium heat until tender-crisp. Add eggs, corn and olives; stir gently until eggs begin to set. Stir in cheese and salami. Cook until eggs are set and cheese is melted, stirring frequently. Stand tortilla chips around edge of skillet; top with taco sauce. Yield: 10 to 12 servings.

Beverly Phillips, Xi Beta Omicron
Excelsior Springs, Missouri

TAMALE CORN

1 16-ounce can tamales
3 16-ounce cans whole
  kernel corn
1 green bell pepper,
  chopped

1 large onion, chopped
A small amount of
  chopped chili peppers
4 slices American cheese

Remove husks from tamales; chop. Combine with undrained corn, green pepper, onion and chili peppers in large skillet. Bring to a boil. Simmer for 45 minutes or until thickened. Cut cheese into triangles; place on top of corn. Cook until cheese melts. Yield: 6 servings.

Margaret Bell, Xi Psi
Oklahoma City, Oklahoma

MEXI-CORN

2 16-ounce cans cream-
  style corn
2 cups soft bread crumbs
½ cup chopped green
  onions
½ cup chopped green
  bell pepper

½ cup chopped pimento
2 12-ounce cans whole
  kernel corn
2 teaspoons salt
½ teaspoon pepper
2 eggs, beaten

Preheat oven to 350 degrees. Combine all ingredients in bowl; mix well. Pour into greased 9x13-inch baking dish. Bake for 45 to 60 minutes or until set. Yield: 25 servings.

Erma Sinor, Xi Alpha Omicron
Forest Park, Georgia

CORN AND RICE CASSEROLE

½ medium onion, chopped	1 16-ounce can cream-style corn
½ green bell pepper, chopped	1 tablespoon sugar
½ cup chopped celery	1 egg, beaten
½ cup butter	1 cup minute rice
1 2-ounce jar chopped pimento	Salt and pepper to taste
	1 cup shredded Cheddar cheese

Preheat oven to 325 degrees. Sauté onion, green pepper and celery in butter in skillet until brown. Add pimento, corn and sugar. Beat egg with rice in bowl. Add to corn mixture; mix well. Pour into buttered 2-quart casserole. Bake for 30 minutes. Yield: 6 servings.

Janet Thompson, Preceptor Delta Alpha
Paxton, Illinois

SPECIAL EGGPLANT CASSEROLE

1 large eggplant	8 Cheddar-flavored Ritz crackers, crushed
2 eggs	1 small onion, chopped
½ cup melted butter	Dash of Worcestershire sauce
2 cups shredded Cheddar cheese	
3 ounces cream cheese, softened	Dash of Tabasco sauce
	Salt and pepper to taste

Preheat oven to 350 degrees. Peel eggplant; cut into ½-inch cubes. Cook in a small amount of boiling salted water in saucepan for 5 to 8 minutes or until tender; drain. Mix with remaining ingredients in bowl. Pour into 10x12-inch baking dish. Bake for 30 minutes.
Yield: 4 servings.

Debbi Sanchez, Xi Epsilon Mu
Vero Beach, Florida

EGGPLANT PARMESAN

2 medium eggplant	1 pound lean ground beef
½ cup fine dry bread crumbs	½ cup minced onion
¼ teaspoon oregano	1 clove of garlic, pressed
¼ teaspoon basil	2 8-ounce cans tomato sauce
1 teaspoon salt	¼ teaspoon salt
⅛ teaspoon pepper	⅛ teaspoon pepper
1 egg, beaten	8 ounces mozzarella cheese, sliced
1 tablespoon water	8 ounces ricotta cheese
¼ cup fine-grade olive oil	¼ cup Parmesan cheese

Preheat oven to 350 degrees. Peel and slice eggplant into ½-inch slices. Combine bread crumbs with oregano, basil, 1 teaspoon salt and ⅛ teaspoon pepper. Beat egg with water in bowl. Dip eggplant slices into egg mixture; coat with seasoned crumbs. Brown lightly on both sides in 2 tablespoons hot olive oil in skillet; drain on absorbent paper. Add remaining 2 tablespoons oil to skillet. Add ground beef, onion and garlic. Sauté until ground beef is brown. Add tomato sauce, ½ teaspoon salt and ⅛ teaspoon pepper. Simmer for 5 minutes. Spoon half the sauce mixture into greased baking dish. Layer eggplant, ricotta and mozzarella cheese ½ at a time in prepared dish. Sprinkle with Parmesan cheese. Bake for 30 minutes or until golden. Serve piping hot. Yield: 6 servings.

Jamie Hilbig, Alpha Upsilon Psi
The Colony, Texas

EGGPLANT TIMBALE

1 large eggplant	1 cup red wine
All-purpose flour	2 cups tomato sauce
2 eggs, well beaten	Salt and pepper to taste
Bread crumbs	4 cups cooked ziti macaroni
2 cloves of garlic	
½ cup chopped onion	1 cup imported Romano cheese
1 cup sliced mushrooms	
1 cup ground veal	½ cup shredded mozzarella cheese
1 cup ground pork	
2 tablespoons olive oil	

Preheat oven to 400 degrees. Peel eggplant; cut lengthwise into paper thin slices. Roll eggplant slices in flour. Dip in beaten eggs; coat with bread crumbs. Fry in oil in skillet; drain well. Butter bundt pan generously. Line pan with overlapping eggplant slices; reserve several slices for top. Sauté garlic, onion, mushrooms, veal and pork in olive oil in skillet. Cook red wine in saucepan until reduced to ½ cup. Stir wine and tomato sauce into meat and vegetable mixture. Season with salt and pepper. Combine sauce with ziti macaroni and cheese in bowl; mix well. Spoon into eggplant-lined pan; press gently. Cover with reserved eggplant slices. Bake for 30 minutes. Cool for 15 minutes. Unmold onto serving plate.
Yield: 12 to 16 servings.

Virginia L. Exter, Laureate Delta Omicron
Roseville, California

MUSHROOM CASSEROLE

6 slices bread, buttered, cubed	½ cup chopped onion
1 pound fresh mushrooms, sliced	½ cup mayonnaise
	2 eggs, slightly beaten
¾ cup chopped celery	¼ cup milk
½ cup chopped green bell pepper	1 10-ounce can cream of mushroom soup
	Cheddar cheese, shredded

Preheat oven to 350 degrees. Spread half the bread cubes in 2-quart casserole. Combine mushrooms, celery, green pepper, onion and mayonnaise in bowl; mix well. Layer vegetable mixture and remaining bread cubes in casserole. Beat eggs with milk and soup in bowl. Pour over layers. Bake for 50 minutes; top with cheese. Bake for 10 minutes longer. Yield: 6 servings.

Virginia Grafft, Eta Kappa
Graham, Texas

MARINATED MUSHROOMS

⅓ cup red wine vinegar
½ cup corn oil
1 small onion, thinly sliced into rings
1 teaspoon prepared mustard
1 teaspoon salt
2 teaspoons parsley flakes
1 tablespoon light brown sugar
1½ pounds fresh mushrooms

Bring first 7 ingredients to a boil in saucepan. Add mushrooms. Simmer, uncovered, for 5 to 6 minutes. Pour into glass bowl. Chill, covered, for several hours, stirring occasionally. Drain and serve. Yield: 8 to 10 servings.

Margaret M. Parker, Laureate Alpha Zeta
Raton, New Mexico

SPINACH-STUFFED MUSHROOMS

1 12-ounce package frozen spinach soufflé
1 cup soft bread crumbs, lightly toasted
1 teaspoon dried minced onion
¼ teaspoon salt
2 teaspoons lemon juice
24 large fresh mushrooms
1 tablespoon melted butter
1½ tablespoons grated Parmesan cheese
Leaf spinach
Fresh parsley sprigs
Pimento rose

Preheat oven to 350 degrees. Uncover soufflé. Bake for 15 to 18 minutes or until slightly warmed. Combine with bread crumbs, onion, salt and lemon juice in bowl; mix well. Clean mushrooms with damp paper towels. Remove mushroom stems; reserve for another purpose. Place mushrooms stem side up in shallow baking pan; brush with melted butter. Spoon spinach mixture into mushroom caps; sprinkle with Parmesan cheese. Bake for 15 minutes. Arrange mushrooms on spinach-lined serving plate; garnish with parsley and pimento rose. Yield: 2 dozen.

 Emily Mullis, Laureate Iota
Rome, Georgia

OKRA AND RICE CASSEROLE

1 16-ounce package long grain brown rice
1 to 1½-pounds bacon, finely chopped
6 large onions, chopped
2 10-ounce packages frozen cut okra, thawed

Preheat oven to 350 degrees. Cook brown rice according to package directions; rinse in cold water. Chill in refrigerator. Fry bacon in skillet until crisp; remove with slotted spoon. Cook onions in bacon drippings until golden brown. Add okra and bacon. Cook until okra is tender. Mix with rice. Spoon into two 9x12-inch baking dishes. Bake for 1½ to 2 hours. Yield: 24 servings.

Sandra Miller, Preceptor Beta Lambda
Lakewood, Colorado

BARBECUED ONIONS

1 cup catsup
¾ cup water
¼ cup cider vinegar
2 cloves of garlic, minced
1 tablespoon Worcestershire sauce
1 tablespoon sugar
1 teaspoon salt
1 teaspoon celery seed
¼ teaspoon hot sauce
3 cups sliced yellow onions

Combine first 9 ingredients in large saucepan. Bring to a boil, stirring occasionally. Cover; reduce heat. Simmer for 4 to 5 minutes. Stir in onions. Simmer, covered, for 3 minutes. Chill, covered, in refrigerator. Serve with vegetables or barbecued meats. Yield: 4 cups.

Lois Nurnberg, Xi Gamma Gamma
Washington, Missouri

ONION CASSEROLE

2 large sweet onions, sliced
2 tablespoons butter
1 cup sour cream
1 10-ounce can celery soup
1½ cups crumbled corn bread

Preheat oven to 350 degrees. Sauté onions in butter in skillet. Combine with remaining ingredients in bowl; mix well. Pour into 1½-quart casserole. Sprinkle top with additional crumbled corn bread. Bake for 35 minutes. Yield: 6 to 8 servings.

Janet B. Turner, Xi Gamma Epsilon
Lewisburg, West Virginia

CURRIED ONIONS

2 16-ounce jars tiny whole onions, drained
1 10-ounce can cream of mushroom soup
2 tablespoons mayonnaise
¼ teaspoon curry powder
½ cup bread crumbs
2 tablespoons melted butter
2 tablespoons chopped parsley

Preheat oven to 350 degrees. Place drained onions in casserole. Combine soup, mayonnaise and curry powder in bowl; mix well. Spoon over onions. Toss bread crumbs with melted butter and chopped parsley. Sprinkle on casserole. Bake for 30 minutes. Yield: 6 servings.

Frances V. Scofield, Laureate Eta
Clarksville, Tennessee

VIDALIA ONION CASSEROLE

5 large Vidalia onions
½ cup margarine
Parmesan cheese
Crispy butter crackers

Preheat oven to 325 degrees. Peel and slice onions into thin rings. Sauté in margarine in skillet until tender. Place half the onions into 1½-quart casserole. Cover with Parmesan cheese and crushed crackers. Repeat layers. Bake for 30 minutes or until golden brown. Yield: 6 servings.

Nancy Jessee, Beta Nu
Kingsport, Tennessee

ONION-STUFFED ONIONS

2 large yellow onions
4 ounces saltine crackers,
 crumbled
4 cloves of garlic, minced
1¾ cups shredded
 Cheddar cheese
1 tablespoon paprika
½ cup melted butter
¼ cup shredded
 Cheddar cheese
¼ teaspoon paprika

Preheat oven to 375 degrees. Peel onions; cut into halves crosswise. Remove center, leaving 2 or 3 layers to form cups. Chop half the centers; reserve remainder for another purpose. Combine with crackers, garlic, 1¾ cups cheese, 1 tablespoon paprika and melted butter in bowl; mix well. Pack into onion cups. Top with ¼ cup cheese and ¼ teaspoon paprika. Place in 9x9-inch baking pan. Bake for 30 minutes. Yield: 4 servings.

Patricia Crawford, Preceptor Kappa Kappa
Fairfield, California

CHEESY ONION TART

1¼ cups flavored
 bread crumbs
¼ cup melted butter
4 medium onions, thinly
 sliced
2 tablespoons butter
¼ cup melted butter
¼ cup all-purpose flour
1 cup milk
½ cup water
1 tablespoon instant
 chicken bouillon
½ cup sour cream
1 egg yolk, beaten
Salt and pepper to taste
1½ cups shredded
 Cheddar cheese
Cherry tomato halves

Preheat oven to 350 degrees. Toss crumbs with ¼ cup butter in bowl until well mixed. Press over bottom and side of greased 9-inch pie plate. Sauté onions in 2 tablespoons butter in large skillet until tender. Blend ¼ cup melted butter and flour in saucepan. Cook for 1 minute, stirring constantly; remove from heat. Stir in milk, water and bouillon. Cook until thickened, stirring constantly. Combine sour cream and egg yolk in bowl; add to sauce. Season with salt and pepper. Combine sauce with onions in pie plate. Sprinkle cheese over top. Bake for 30 to 45 minutes or until set. Garnish with cherry tomato halves. Yield: 6 to 8 servings.

Gail Jasionowski, Xi Epsilon Eta
Centreville, Virginia

SPINACH DELIGHT

2 10-ounce packages
 frozen spinach
1 5-ounce can sliced
 water chestnuts
4 slices crisp-fried
 bacon, crumbled
1 10-ounce can Cheddar
 cheese soup
1 3-ounce can French-
 fried onions

Preheat oven to 350 degrees. Cook spinach using package directions; drain and cut into pieces with scissors. Place in 7x10-inch baking dish. Top with water chestnuts and bacon. Spread soup evenly over top. Top with onions. Bake for 20 to 25 minutes. Yield: 8 to 10 servings.

Dorothy Jane Murphy, International
Overland Park, Kansas

MOCK SPINACH SOUFFLÉ

1 10-ounce package
 frozen spinach, thawed
3 eggs, slightly beaten
1 tablespoon all-purpose
 flour
1 cup shredded cheese
12 ounces small curd
 cottage cheese
Pepper to taste
¼ cup melted butter

Preheat oven to 350 degrees. Drain spinach; squeeze dry. Combine eggs, flour, cheese, cottage cheese and pepper in bowl or blender container; mix until smooth. Stir in spinach. Pour into 2-quart casserole. Top with melted butter. Bake, uncovered, for 1 hour. Yield: 6 to 8 servings.

Susan L. Miller, Xi Alpha Lambda
Mechanicsburg, Pennsylvania

PORTUGUESE GREEN SOUP

2 medium onions,
 coarsely chopped
2 cloves of garlic, minced
1 tablespoon olive oil
6 cups chicken broth
2 large potatoes,
 peeled, sliced
2 10-ounce packages
 frozen chopped
 spinach, thawed
1 teaspoon salt
¼ teaspoon freshly
 ground pepper

Sauté onions and garlic in oil in large saucepan until tender. Add broth and potatoes. Simmer, covered, for 45 minutes. Mash potatoes slightly with masher. Stir in spinach, salt and pepper. Bring to a boil; reduce heat. Simmer, covered, for 20 minutes longer or until spinach is tender. Yield: 6 to 8 servings.

Susan H. Davis, Xi Delta Zeta
Richmond, Virginia

GRILLED TOMATOES

2 medium tomatoes
Salt to taste
Pepper to taste
Cayenne pepper to taste
Butter
Bread crumbs

Cut tomatoes into halves. Sprinkle with salt, pepper and cayenne pepper; dot with butter and sprinkle with bread crumbs. Arrange cut side up on barbecue rack. Cook until crumbs are brown and tomatoes are tender. Yield: 2 to 4 servings.

Jo Anne Murphy, Zeta Kappa
Virginia Beach, Virginia

SCALLOPED TOMATOES

6 medium tomatoes
¾ cup water
2 slices toast, buttered,
 chopped
6 soda crackers, broken
1 teaspoon butter
½ teaspoon parsley
Salt and pepper to taste
2 soda crackers, broken

Peel and quarter tomatoes. Combine with water in saucepan. Cook until very tender. Add toast, 6 crackers, butter, parsley and salt and pepper; mix well. Heat to serving temperature. Sprinkle remaining crackers on top. Yield: 4 servings.

Jackie Hostetler, Lambda Nu
Pattonsburg, Missouri

BAKED POTATO CASSEROLE

8 medium potatoes
2 bay leaves
1/4 cup melted margarine
1 1/2 cups sour cream
1/2 teaspoon salt

1/4 teaspoon white pepper
3 green onions, chopped
2 cups shredded
Cheddar cheese

Preheat oven to 350 degrees. Parboil unpeeled potatoes in saucepan in water to cover with bay leaves. Mix margarine with sour cream in bowl until blended. Add salt, pepper, green onions and 1 1/2 cups cheese; mix well. Peel and grate potatoes finely. Add to sour cream mixture; mix well. Pour into casserole. Bake, uncovered, for 30 minutes. Sprinkle remaining 1/2 cup cheese on top. Bake, covered, for 15 minutes longer. Yield: 12 to 15 servings.

Sherrie Bedlan, Delta Phi
North Platte, Nebraska

POTATO CASSEROLE

5 pounds potatoes, peeled
8 ounces cream cheese,
  softened
1/2 cup margarine
1 cup half and half

1 teaspoon seasoned salt
1 teaspoon onion powder
1/4 teaspoon seasoned
  pepper

Preheat oven to 350 degrees. Boil potatoes in water to cover in large saucepan until tender; drain. Mash potatoes; add remaining ingredients. Spoon into greased 9x12-inch casserole; cover. Dot with additional margarine. Bake for 30 minutes. May store unbaked casserole in refrigerator for up to 1 week if desired. Yield: 14 to 16 servings.

Lorraine Risch, Xi Gamma Xi
Ames, Iowa

SOUR CREAM POTATO CASSEROLE

1 2-pound package
   frozen hashed brown
   potatoes, thawed
1/2 cup melted butter
1/4 cup chopped onions
1 10-ounce can cream of
   chicken soup

2 cups sour cream
2 cups shredded
  Cheddar cheese
1 teaspoon salt
1/4 teaspoon pepper
2 cups cornflake crumbs

Preheat oven to 350 degrees. Combine potatoes and next 7 ingredients in large bowl; mix well. Spoon into buttered 9x13-inch baking dish. Cover with cornflake crumbs. Bake for 1 hour. May chill unbaked casserole overnight if desired. Bake for 1 hour. Yield: 6 servings.

Jodie Newton, Xi Mu Epsilon
Englewood, Florida

To prepare easy make-ahead potatoes, Jean Ann Casey, Upsilon Psi, Mercer, Missouri, scoops out 8 baked potatoes, adds 1 cup sour cream, 1/4 cup butter, 2 teaspoons salt and 1/4 teaspoon pepper, and spoons into potato shells. Bake potatoes at 400 degrees for 10 minutes just before serving.

MICROWAVE POTATO CASSEROLE

2 cups frozen shredded
  hashed brown
  potatoes, thawed
1 tablespoon butter
1 cup cottage cheese
1/2 cup yogurt
2 tablespoons chopped
  scallions

2 tablesppons chopped
  parsley
1 clove of garlic, minced
1/2 teaspoon salt
2 tablespoons dry bread
  crumbs
Butter
Pepper to taste

Place potatoes in greased casserole. Microwave, covered, on High for 3 minutes; stir. Microwave for 3 minutes longer. Add cottage cheese, yogurt, scallions, parsley, garlic and salt; mix well. Sprinkle crumbs over top. Dot with butter; sprinkle with pepper. Microwave, covered, on High for 4 to 6 minutes. Let stand for 5 minutes. Yield: 4 servings.

Norma Jo Speroff, Preceptor Alpha Eta
Kokomo, Indiana

CHANTILLY POTATOES

6 to 8 medium potatoes
1/2 pint whipping cream
2 tablespoons butter
1/2 cup Parmesan cheese

Salt and pepper to taste
2 tablespoons parsley
  flakes

Preheat oven to 350 degrees. Peel potatoes; cut into 2-inch cubes. Place in casserole. Pour whipping cream over potatoes. Dot with butter; sprinkle with Parmesan cheese, salt and pepper. Sprinkle parsley over all. Bake, covered, for 1 hour or until potatoes are tender. Yield: 6 to 8 servings.

Judy Harold, Xi Theta
Pocatello, Idaho

MASHED POTATOES CHANTILLY

4 cups seasoned mashed
  potatoes
1/2 cup whipping cream,
  whipped

1/4 cup Parmesan cheese

Preheat oven to 300 degrees. Spoon mashed potatoes into greased 1 1/2-quart casserole. Top with whipped cream. Sprinkle with cheese. Bake for 30 to 35 minutes or until brown. Yield: 6 to 8 servings.

Carolyn J. Ferry, Omicron
Greenwood, South Carolina

CROCK•POT POTATOES

20 small red potatoes
1 cup sour cream
1 cup crumbled bacon bits
1/2 cup chopped chives

1/2 cup minced green
  onions
1/2 cup butter
Salt and pepper

Place washed potatoes in Crock•Pot. Cover. Cook on Low for 8 to 10 hours. Serve remaining ingredients in individual serving dishes for guests to serve themselves. Yield: 20 servings.

Kathy Steinsberger, Alpha Zeta
Raleigh, North Carolina

EASY OVEN POTATOES

5 or 6 baking potatoes, scrubbed	*1 teaspoon crushed basil*
1 medium onion, sliced	*1 teaspoon garlic salt*
	½ teaspoon coarsely ground pepper
1 teaspoon crushed oregano	*¼ cup butter*

Preheat oven to 350 degrees. Cut unpeeled potatoes into bite-sized chunks. Layer potatoes and onion in 9x13-inch baking dish. Sprinkle with seasonings; dot with butter. Bake for 45 minutes or until potatoes are tender; stirring occasionally. May microwave on High for 18 to 20 minutes if preferred. Yield: 5 servings.

Kathleen Hess, Alpha Gamma
Lawrence, Kansas

FLUFFY POTATOES

10 potatoes	*1 tablespoon grated onion*
½ cup butter	*1 cup milk, scalded*
1 teaspoon salt	*8 ounces cream cheese, softened*
¼ teaspoon pepper	

Preheat oven to 325 degrees. Peel, cook and mash potatoes. Add butter; beat until blended. Add remaining ingredients; beat until fluffy. Spoon into buttered casserole. Bake for 25 minutes. Yield: 8 to 10 servings.

Peggy Frances Hunt, Gamma Delta
Mt. Sterling, Kentucky

FRENCH-FRIED POTATO CASSEROLE

¾ cup chopped green bell pepper	*¾ cup coarsely shredded carrots*
¾ cup chopped celery	*⅓ cup chopped pimento*
⅓ cup margarine	*¾ cup shredded American cheese*
⅓ cup all-purpose flour	
½ teaspoon salt	*1 32-ounce package frozen French-fried potatoes*
⅛ teaspoon pepper	
3 cups milk	

Preheat oven to 375 degrees. Sauté green pepper and celery in margarine in large saucepan until tender but not brown. Stir in flour, salt and pepper. Add milk all at once. Cook until bubbly, stirring constantly. Cook for 1 minute longer, stirring constantly. Add carrots, pimento and half the cheese, stirring until cheese is melted. Combine potatoes and cheese sauce in 9x13-inch baking dish. Bake for 30 minutes. Sprinkle remaining cheese on top. Bake for 5 minutes longer. Garnish with additional chopped green pepper. Yield: 12 servings.

Doris L. Plahn, Beta Nu
Webster Groves, Missouri

SORORITY POTATOES

8 large unpeeled potatoes, boiled	*2 tablespoons chopped parsley*
1½ pounds Cheddar cheese, shredded	*2 cups sour cream*
	Paprika to taste
2 bunches green onions, chopped	

Preheat oven to 350 degrees. Peel and grate potatoes. Reserve 1 cup cheese. Mix remaining ingredients in bowl. Pour into 9x12-inch baking dish. Sprinkle with reserved cheese. Dust with paprika. Bake for 30 to 40 minutes. Yield: 8 servings.

Georgine Wasley, Xi Alpha Eta
Nevada City, California

OVERNIGHT POTATOES

8 or 9 medium unpeeled potatoes	*1 cup milk*
	1 teaspoon dry mustard
5⅓ ounces Cheddar cheese, shredded	*1½ teaspoons salt*
	Dash each of pepper and nutmeg
½ cup whipping cream	

Cook potatoes in boiling water in saucepan until tender. Cool, peel and shred into buttered 3-quart casserole. Melt cheese in saucepan over low heat. Add remaining ingredients. Pour over potatoes. Chill overnight. Preheat oven to 350 degrees. Bake for 1 hour. Yield: 6 to 8 servings.

Linda Robinson, Beta Alpha
Mt. Vernon, Ohio

OVERNIGHT POTATOES ROMANOFF

6 large unpeeled potatoes	*¼ teaspoon pepper*
2 cups sour cream	*1½ cups shredded Cheddar cheese*
1 bunch green onions, chopped	*Paprika to taste*
1½ teaspoons salt	

Cook potatoes in boiling water in saucepan until tender. Peel and shred into large bowl. Stir in next 4 ingredients and 1 cup cheese. Spoon into greased 2-quart casserole. Top with remaining ½ cup cheese and paprika. Chill for several hours. Preheat oven to 350 degrees. Bake casserole for 30 minutes or until bubbly. Yield: 8 to 10 servings.

Dawn Price, Phi
Moscow, Idaho

MICROWAVE PARTY POTATOES

8 to 10 medium potatoes, peeled, chopped	*1 8-ounce carton French onion dip*
½ cup water	*1½ teaspoons salt*
8 ounces cream cheese, softened	*½ teaspoon garlic salt*
	Butter to taste
Dash of pepper	*½ teaspoon paprika*

Place potatoes in 3-quart glass casserole. Add water. Microwave, covered, on High for 15 minutes or until potatoes are tender; drain. Beat cream cheese, pepper, onion dip, salt and garlic salt in large bowl until blended. Add hot potatoes gradually, beating until light and fluffy after each addition. Spoon into 2-quart casserole. Top with butter. Microwave on Medium for 5 minutes or until heated through. Sprinkle with paprika. Yield: 8 servings.

Peg Hinkle, Lambda Phi
Monroe City, Indiana

SPINACH POTATOES

6 to 8 large potatoes, peeled	½ cup chopped onion
1 cup sour cream	1 tablespoon sugar
½ cup margarine	2 teaspoons salt
1 10-ounce package frozen spinach, thawed	¼ teaspoon pepper
	1½ cups shredded Cheddar cheese

Preheat oven to 400 degrees. Cook potatoes in boiling water in saucepan until tender; drain. Mash with sour cream and margarine in bowl. Add spinach, onion, sugar, salt and pepper; mix well. Spoon into 2-quart baking dish. Sprinkle with cheese. Bake for 20 minutes or until lightly browned and cheese is melted.
Yield: 8 servings.

Sandi Dalton, Preceptor Delta
Ashland, Ohio

SWEET POTATO AND PINEAPPLE BAKE

2 1-pound cans sweet potatoes	1 teaspoon vanilla extract
1 tablespoon butter	1 cup miniature marshmallows
1 8-ounce can crushed pineapple, drained	½ cup broken walnuts

Preheat oven to 350 degrees. Heat sweet potatoes in saucepan; drain. Mash with butter. Add pineapple and vanilla. Spread in 8x8-inch baking dish. Top with marshmallows and walnuts. Bake for 35 minutes or until marshmallows are golden brown. Yield: 6 to 8 servings.

June Swart, Xi Theta Psi
Anaheim Hills, California

SHERRIED SWEET POTATO CASSEROLE

8 medium sweet potatoes	2 cups orange juice
1 cup packed light brown sugar	½ cup raisins
2 tablespoons cornstarch	6 tablespoons butter
½ teaspoon salt	⅓ cup dry Sherry
½ teaspoon grated orange rind	¼ cup chopped walnuts

Preheat oven to 325 degrees. Cook sweet potatoes in boiling water to cover in saucepan just until tender. Arrange sweet potatoes in 9x13-inch baking dish. Combine brown sugar, cornstarch and salt in saucepan. Blend in orange rind and juice. Add raisins. Cook over medium heat until thickened, stirring constantly. Cook for 1 minute longer. Add butter, Sherry and walnuts. Pour over sweet potatoes. Bake for 30 minutes, basting occasionally. Yield: 8 servings.

Sarah E. Ferrara, Preceptor Alpha Xi
Syracuse, New York

SWEET POTATO CASSEROLE

1 29-ounce can sweet potatoes, drained	2 eggs, beaten
1 cup sugar	1 cup broken pecans
6 tablespoons butter	6 tablespoons butter
1 teaspon salt	½ cup packed light brown sugar
1 teaspoon vanilla extract	¾ cup cornflakes, crushed

Preheat oven to 350 degrees. Mash sweet potatoes with next 5 ingredients in large bowl. Spoon into 2-quart casserole. Mix pecans, 6 tablespoons butter, brown sugar and cornflakes in small bowl. Sprinkle over sweet potatoes. Bake for 45 minutes. Yield: 6 to 8 servings.

Arlene E. Keffer, Gamma Iota
Berlin, Maryland

BAKED YAMS AND CHESTNUTS

6 medium yams	Mace to taste
3 small cans chestnuts	Butter
4 large tart apples	½ cup apple cider
1½ cups packed light brown sugar	

Preheat oven to 350 degrees. Cook yams in water to cover in saucepan until almost tender. Peel and slice. Drain and slice chestnuts. Peel, core and slice apples. Layer half the apples, yams, chestnuts and brown sugar in buttered 3-quart casserole. Sprinkle with mace; dot generously with butter. Repeat layers. Pour cider over top. Bake for 1 hour. Yield: 15 servings.

Bessie Konishi, Laureate Epsilon
Alamosa, Colorado

ZUCCHINI CASSEROLE

6 cups chopped zucchini	1½ cups shredded carrots
½ cup chopped onion	1 8-ounce package herb-seasoned stuffing mix
1 cup sour cream	½ cup butter, melted
1 10-ounce can cream of mushroom soup	

Preheat oven to 350 degrees. Cook zucchini and chopped onion in a small amount of water in saucepan for 10 minutes; squeeze dry. Combine with sour cream, soup and carrots in bowl; mix well. Toss stuffing mix with butter. Spread half the stuffing mixture in greased casserole. Add zucchini mixture and remaining stuffing mixture. Bake for 30 minutes. Yield: 12 servings.

Connie Novak, Xi Alpha
South Burlington, Vermont

FAVORITE ZUCCHINI CHEESE CASSEROLE

1½ pounds zucchini	¼ teaspoon pepper
1 small onion, chopped	1½ cups shredded Monterey Jack cheese
2 tablespoons butter	1 egg
1 4-ounce can chopped green chilies, drained	1 cup small curd cottage cheese
3 tablespoons all-purpose flour	2 tablespoons parsley
½ teaspoon salt	½ cup Parmesan cheese

Preheat oven to 400 degrees. Chop zucchini. Sauté with onion in butter in skillet. Add chilies, flour, salt and pepper. Spoon into shallow 1½-quart baking dish. Sprinkle with Monterey Jack cheese. Mix egg with cottage cheese and parsley. Spoon over top. Sprinkle with Parmesan cheese. Bake for 20 minutes. Yield: 4 servings.

Helen Prince, Preceptor Theta Sigma
Los Angeles, California

ZUCCHINI CRESCENT PIE

4 cups thinly sliced
  unpeeled zucchini
1 cup coarsely chopped
  onion
½ cup margarine
½ cup chopped parsley
½ teaspoon salt
½ teaspoon pepper
¼ teaspoon garlic powder
¼ teaspoon sweet
  basil leaves

¼ teaspoon oregano
  leaves
2 eggs, well beaten
2 cups shredded
  Muenster cheese
1 8-count package
  refrigerator crescent
  rolls
2 tablespoons Dijon-style
  mustard

Preheat oven to 375 degrees. Sauté zucchini and onion in margarine in 10-inch skillet for 10 minutes or until tender. Stir in parsley and seasonings. Beat eggs with cheese in bowl. Stir in vegetable mixture. Separate dough into 8 triangles. Press over bottom and side of ungreased 10-inch pie plate to form crust. Spread with mustard. Pour in vegetable mixture. Bake for 18 to 20 minutes or until knife inserted in center comes out clean. Let stand for 10 minutes. Yield: 6 servings.

Inga Dickson, Laureate Nu
Mesa, Arizona

ALMOND AND VEGETABLE SAUTÉ

1 cup water
2 teaspoons cornstarch
2 tablespoons soy sauce
2 teaspoons instant
  chicken bouillon
1 clove of garlic, crushed
1 cup thinly sliced carrots

1 cup cut green beans
2 tablespoons vegetable
  oil
1 cup sliced cauliflower
1 onion, sliced
1 cup cubed tofu
½ cup roasted almonds

Combine water, cornstarch, soy sauce, chicken bouillon and garlic in small bowl; set aside. Stir-fry carrots and beans in oil in skillet over medium-high heat for 2 minutes. Add cauliflower and onion. Stir-fry for 2 minutes. Add soy sauce mixture. Cook until thickened, stirring constantly. Add tofu. Stir-fry for 2 minutes. Sprinkle almonds over top. Serve with brown rice. Yield: 4 servings.

Lillian M. Gillingham, Preceptor Theta Epsilon
Laguna Hills, California

CHEESY VEGETABLE CASSEROLE

1 20-ounce package
  frozen mixed
  vegetables, thawed
1 cup mayonnaise
½ cup chopped onion

1 cup shredded
  Cheddar cheese
1½ cups bread crumbs
¼ cup melted butter

Preheat oven to 350 degrees. Combine mixed vegetables, mayonnaise, onion and cheese in bowl. Toss bread crumbs with butter. Layer vegetable mixture and crumb mixture in casserole. Bake for 30 to 45 minutes or until golden. Yield: 10 to 12 servings.

Gloria Roth, Xi Delta Nu
Rome, New York

CRUNCHY VEGETABLE CASSEROLE

1 7-ounce can sliced
  water chestnuts
1 6-ounce can Shoe
  Peg corn
1 16-ounce can green
  beans
1 16-ounce can cream of
  celery soup
1 cup chopped celery
1 cup chopped onion

1 cup chopped green
  bell pepper
1 cup shredded
  Cheddar cheese
1 cup sour cream
4 cups Ritz cracker
  crumbs
1 2-ounce package
  sliced almonds
½ cup melted butter

Preheat oven to 350 degrees. Combine first 9 ingredients in large casserole; mix well. Toss crumbs with almonds and butter. Sprinkle over vegetable mixture. Bake for 30 to 40 minutes. Yield: 16 servings.

Mary Seffert, Preceptor Kappa Rho
Hilltop Lakes, Texas

HEALTHY VEGETABLE BAKE

1 20-ounce package
  frozen cauliflower
1 10-ounce package
  frozen cut broccoli
1 17-ounce can cream-
  style corn
1 17-ounce can whole
  kernel corn, drained
2 cups shredded
  Swiss cheese

1 10-ounce can cream of
  celery soup
1 4-ounce can sliced
  mushrooms, drained
1½ cups soft rye
  bread crumbs
2 tablespoons melted
  butter

Preheat oven to 375 degrees. Cook frozen vegetables according to package directions; drain. Combine corn, cheese and soup in large bowl. Stir in cooked vegetables and mushrooms. Spoon into buttered 9x13-inch baking dish. Toss bread crumbs with melted butter; sprinkle over vegetable mixture. Bake, uncovered, for 30 to 35 minutes or until golden. Let stand for 10 minutes before serving. Yield: 12 to 15 servings.

Blanche Elliott, Xi Eta Beta
Madrid, Iowa

VEGETABLES WITH PUMPKIN SEED

8 ounces fresh
  mushrooms
2 tablespoons butter
5 medium zucchini,
  peeled, sliced
1 20-ounce can petit pois
  peas, drained

1 10-ounce can cream of
  mushroom soup
1 6-ounce jar salted
  pumpkin seed

Preheat oven to 350 degrees. Sauté mushrooms in butter in skillet. Layer zucchini, peas and sautéed mushrooms in large casserole. Spread desired amount of soup over top. Bake for 30 minutes. Sprinkle generously with pumpkin seed. Bake for 15 minutes longer. Yield: 8 to 10 servings.

Marcy Ballew, Preceptor Kappa Rho
Hilltop Lakes, Texas

Side Dishes

BREAKFAST DEVILS

8 hard-cooked eggs
1 tablespoon mayonnaise
1 tablespoon mustard
2 tablespoons all-purpose
  flour
2 tablespoons margarine
1 cup milk
8 ounces Cheddar cheese,
  shredded
2 slices bread, crumbled

Preheat oven to 350 degrees. Cut eggs in half; remove yolks. Combine with mayonnaise and mustard in bowl; mix well. Spoon into egg whites. Place in ovenproof serving dish. Blend flour and margarine in saucepan. Add milk and cheese. Cook until thickened, stirring constantly. Pour sauce over eggs. Top with bread crumbs. Bake for 30 minutes. Yield: 10 servings.

LaNita Cloninger, Alpha Kappa
Weaverville, North Carolina

SIS'S COUNTRY BAKE

4 eggs
2 tablespoons margarine
2 tablespoons all-purpose
  flour
1 cup milk
1 teaspoon salt
½ teaspoon pepper
¼ teaspoon dry mustard
⅓ cup shredded cheese
1 teaspoon butter
  flavoring
½ cup bread crumbs

Preheat oven to 350 degrees. Break eggs into greased 8 x 8-inch baking pan. Melt margarine in saucepan. Stir in flour; add milk. Cook until thickened, stirring constantly. Add salt, pepper, mustard, cheese and flavoring; mix well. Pour over eggs. Top with additional cheese and bread crumbs. Bake for 15 minutes. Yield: 4 to 6 servings.

Velda Kloke, Xi Gamma Zeta
Harvard, Nebraska

THREE-CHEESE DISH

3 eggs, beaten
¼ cup (about) milk
½ teaspoon salt
¼ teaspoon pepper
1 teaspoon parsley flakes
½ teaspoon
  Worcestershire sauce
2 tablespoons
  Parmesan cheese
¼ teaspoon dry mustard
2 slices process Swiss
  cheese, slivered
1¼ cups shredded
  Cheddar cheese
1 4-ounce can mushroom
  pieces, drained
1½ green onions, chopped

Preheat oven to 350 degrees. Combine eggs, milk, salt, pepper, parsley, Worcestershire sauce, Parmesan cheese and mustard in bowl; beat well. Stir in Swiss and Cheddar cheeses, mushrooms and green onions. Pour into buttered 9-inch pie plate. Bake for 25 to 30 minutes or until set. Yield: 4 servings.

Nancy Jo Reed, Laureate Rho
Richmond, Virginia

SPECIAL EGG BAKE

2 10-ounce cans cream of chicken soup	1 cup milk
1 tablespoon instant minced onion	2 cups shredded Swiss cheese
1 teaspoon prepared mustard	12 eggs
	French bread, sliced, buttered

Preheat oven to 350 degrees. Heat soup, onion, mustard and milk in saucepan, stirring constantly. Remove from heat. Add cheese; stir until melted. Pour into 10x15-inch casserole. Break eggs on top of sauce, spacing evenly. Stand French bread slices around edge of casserole. Bake for 20 minutes. Yield: 6 servings.

Patricia Hancock, Preceptor Epsilon Alpha
Winter Haven, Florida

CHILIES RELLENOS CASSEROLE

2 7-ounce cans whole green chilies, rinsed, seeded	½ teaspoon dry mustard
	¼ teaspoon pepper
8 ounces sharp Cheddar cheese, cut into sticks	Dash of Worcestershire sauce
4 eggs, slightly beaten	1 pound Monterey Jack cheese, shredded
1 cup evaporated milk	
2 tablespoons all-purpose flour	

Preheat oven to 350 degrees. Stuff each chili with Cheddar cheese stick. Arrange in single layer in greased 7x11-inch casserole. Combine remaining ingredients in bowl; mix well. Pour over chilies. Bake for 30 minutes or until set and golden. Cool for 5 minutes before serving. Yield: 6 to 8 servings.

Carol Hurley, Xi Beta Iota
Cortez, Colorado

SCRAMBLED EGG CASSEROLE

3 tablespoons all-purpose flour	1 pound bacon, crisp-fried, crumbled
2 tablespoons butter	12 eggs, scrambled
2 cups milk	1 4-ounce jar button mushrooms
¼ cup chopped green onions	Salt and pepper to taste
3 tablespoons butter	½ cup buttered bread crumbs
1 cup shredded Cheddar cheese	Paprika

Combine flour and 2 tablespoons butter in saucepan. Stir in milk. Cook until thickened, stirring constantly. Sauté green onions in 3 tablespoons butter in skillet. Add cheese. Stir until melted. Add bacon, eggs, mushrooms, salt and pepper; mix well. Pour into buttered 9x12-inch casserole. Top with bread crumbs; sprinkle with paprika. Refrigerate overnight. Preheat oven to 350 degrees. Bake for 30 minutes. Yield: 8 to 10 servings.

Carole Cox, Xi Zeta Iota
Lake Alfred, Florida

MEXICAN STRATA

4 cups cheese-flavored tortilla chips	4 ounces green chilies, chopped
2 cups shredded Monterey Jack cheese	1 cup chopped onion
6 eggs, beaten	3 tablespoons catsup
2½ cups milk	½ teaspoon salt
	¼ teaspoon Tabasco sauce

Preheat oven to 325 degrees. Layer tortilla chips, cheese and mixture of remaining ingredients in greased 7x12-inch baking pan. Refrigerate overnight. Bake for 50 minutes or until set. Yield: 4 servings.

Joyce Steele, Alpha Zeta
Los Alamos, New Mexico

CONFETTI OMELET

½ cup chopped onion	1 tablespoon chopped parsley
1 tablespoon bacon drippings	¾ teaspoon salt
6 slices bacon, crisp-fried, crumbled	1 cup shredded Cheddar cheese
8 eggs, slightly beaten	1 cup shredded Swiss cheese
1 cup milk	1 tablespoon all-purpose flour
3 tablespoons chopped pimento	

Preheat oven to 350 degrees. Sauté onion in bacon drippings in skillet until tender. Combine sautéed onion, bacon, eggs, milk, pimento, parsley and salt in bowl; mix well. Combine cheeses and flour in bowl; toss to mix. Add to egg mixture. Pour into greased 1½-quart casserole. Bake for 40 minutes. Serve hot. Yield: 10 servings.

Elizabeth Buchine, Theta Iota
Satellite Beach, Florida

ONION OMELET

¼ cup butter	2 teaspoons salt
18 eggs	¼ cup chopped green onions
1 cup sour cream	
1 cup milk	

Preheat oven to 325 degrees. Melt butter in 9x13-inch baking dish in oven. Beat next 4 ingredients in bowl until blended. Stir in onions. Pour into prepared dish. Bake for 35 minutes or until set but moist. Yield: 12 servings.

Helen C. Cochrane, Laureate Gamma
South Williamson, Kentucky

OVEN OMELET

1 cup left over mashed potatoes	½ teaspoon nutmeg
	1 cup chopped ham
8 eggs	

Preheat oven to 350 degrees. Preheat well-greased iron skillet. Combine all ingredients in bowl; mix well. Pour into hot skillet. Cook over medium heat until almost set. Bake for 15 minutes or until top is firm. Yield: 4 servings.

Georgia Brazil, Xi Beta Kappa
Santa Rosa, New Mexico

GREEN CHILI QUICHE

2 cups all-purpose flour	½ teaspoon salt
2 teaspoons sugar	¼ teaspoon pepper
1 teaspoon salt	¼ teaspoon garlic powder
¾ cup shortening	¼ teaspoon cilantro
1 egg	¾ cup chopped mild
¼ cup cold water	green chilies
¾ teaspoon apple cider	¾ cup medium-hot
vinegar	thick salsa
4 eggs	1½ cups shredded mild
¾ cup evaporated milk	Cheddar cheese

Preheat oven to 375 degrees. Combine flour, sugar and salt in bowl. Cut in shortening until crumbly. Add mixture of egg, water and vinegar; mix well. Roll on floured surface into 14-inch circle. Fit into pie plate; flute edges. Combine 4 eggs and evaporated milk in bowl. Stir in remaining ingredients. Pour into pie shell. Bake for 30 minutes. Cover edges with foil. Increase temperature to 400 degrees. Bake for 15 minutes longer or until knife inserted near center comes out clean. Let stand for 10 minutes before serving. Yield: 10 servings.

Laura Jarvinen, Alpha Zeta
Los Alamos, New Mexico

SPINACH AND MUSHROOM QUICHE

1 recipe 2-crust	1½ cups whipping cream
pie pastry	1 cup milk
8 ounces mushrooms,	2 tablespoons all-purpose
thinly sliced	flour
¼ cup chopped onion	1 teaspoon salt
2 tablespoons butter	⅛ teaspoon cayenne
2 10-ounce packages	⅛ teaspoon nutmeg
frozen chopped	¼ cup melted butter
spinach, thawed,	8 ounces Swiss cheese,
well drained	shredded
6 eggs	

Preheat oven to 425 degrees. Roll pie pastry to fit 9x13-inch baking dish. Sauté mushrooms and onion in 2 tablespoons butter in skillet for 10 minutes, stirring occasionally. Remove from heat. Stir in spinach; set aside. Beat eggs with cream, milk, flour, salt, cayenne and nutmeg in bowl. Add melted butter; mix well. Layer spinach mixture, cheese and egg mixture in pastry-lined dish. Bake for 15 minutes. Reduce temperature to 325 degrees. Bake for 40 minutes. Yield: 12 servings.

Shirley Ayers, Preceptor Alpha Chi
Federal Way, Washington

SIMPLY SUPER QUICHE

½ cup chopped onion	2 eggs
2 tablespoons margarine	2 cartons egg substitute
2 tablespoons Sherry	1 package leek soup mix
2 unbaked 9-inch	2 cups buttermilk
pie shells	½ cup shredded Monterey
2 tablespoons melted	Jack cheese
margarine	½ cup bacon bits

Preheat oven to 375 degrees. Sauté onion in margarine in skillet. Stir in Sherry. Brush pie shells with melted margarine. Spoon onion into pie shells. Beat eggs, egg substitute, soup mix, buttermilk and cheese in bowl. Pour over onions. Top with bacon bits. Bake for 40 minutes or until set. Let stand for several minutes before serving. Yield: 12 servings.

Flora Simay, Laureate Beta Alpha
Palm Desert, California

SWISS AND BACON QUICHE

1 cup shredded	4 eggs, slightly beaten
Swiss cheese	2 cups whipping cream
12 slices crisp-fried	¾ teaspoon salt
bacon, crumbled	¼ teaspoon sugar
⅓ cup minced onion	⅛ teaspoon pepper
1 unbaked 9-inch pie shell	

Preheat oven to 425 degrees. Combine cheese, bacon and onion in pie shell. Mix eggs and remaining ingredients in bowl. Pour into pie shell. Bake for 15 minutes. Reduce temperature to 300 degrees. Bake for 30 minutes longer or until knife inserted in center comes out clean. Let stand for 10 minutes before serving. Yield: 6 servings.

Millie Bickle, Theta Sigma
Hays, Kansas

TOMATO AND SQUASH QUICHE

2 cups sliced zucchini	¾ cup buttermilk
1 cup chopped tomato	baking mix
½ cup chopped onion	3 eggs, beaten
⅓ cup Parmesan cheese	½ teaspoon salt
1½ cups milk	¼ teaspoon pepper

Preheat oven to 400 degrees. Grease 10-inch quiche dish. Sprinkle zucchini, tomato, onion and cheese in dish. Beat remaining ingredients in bowl until smooth. Pour into dish. Cook for 10 to 15 minutes or until knife inserted near center comes out clean. Yield: 6 servings.

Jauneta Harman, Laureate Alpha Kappa
Escondido, California

ZUCCHINI FRITTATA CASSEROLE

4 eggs, beaten	2 teaspoons garlic powder
1 pound Cheddar cheese,	1 tablespoon chopped
shredded	parsley
2 4-ounce cans chopped	5 zucchini, sliced
green chili peppers	1 medium onion, minced
2 teaspoons baking	7 or 8 mushrooms, sliced
powder	1½ cups melted butter
2 tablespoons all-purpose	1 cup crushed cornflakes
flour	

Preheat oven to 350 degrees. Combine eggs, cheese, chili peppers, baking powder, flour, garlic powder and parsley in bowl; mix well. Add zucchini, onion and mushrooms. Layer half the butter, half the cornflakes and all the zucchini mixture into 9x13-inch baking dish. Sprinkle remaining butter and crumbs over top. Bake for 45 to 50 minutes. Yield: 4 to 6 servings.

B.J. O'Donnell, Xi Lambda
Merrimack, New Hampshire

SOUTHERN HOT CHEESY GARLIC GRITS

1 cup white quick-cooking grits	2 eggs, well beaten
4 cups boiling water	1 small clove of garlic, minced
½ teaspoon salt	½ cup chopped black olives
1½ cups shredded mild Cheddar cheese	
½ cup butter	½ cup chopped jalapeño peppers
½ cup milk	

Preheat oven to 350 degrees. Stir grits into salted boiling water in heavy saucepan gradually. Return to a boil; reduce heat. Cook for 2½ to 5 minutes or until thickened, stirring occasionally. Stir in cheese, butter, milk, eggs, garlic, olives and peppers. Cook over low heat until cheese is melted. Pour into greased 2-quart casserole. Bake for 1 hour. Yield: 6 servings.

Jayne Ross Manasco, Epsilon Omega
Broomfield, Colorado

BASIL FETTUCINI IN TOMATO CUPS

1 8-ounce package fettucini	2 tablespoons olive oil
¼ cup whipping cream	Dash of pepper
¼ cup minced fresh basil	1 cup grated Parmesan cheese
2 tablespoons melted butter	10 tomatoes
	Salt to taste

Cook fettucini according to package directions, omitting salt. Rinse in cold water; drain. Combine with next 5 ingredients in bowl. Toss until noodles are well coated. Add Parmesan cheese, toss gently. Chill overnight. Slice off top of each tomato; scoop out pulp. Sprinkle inside of each tomato shell lightly with salt. Invert on paper towel to drain. Chill, covered, for 1 hour or longer. Spoon fettucini mixture into tomato shells. Yield: 10 servings.

Connie Beuder, Xi Epsilon Nu
Cedar Rapids, Iowa

SPINACH LASAGNA

1 6-ounce can tomato paste	2 eggs, beaten
1 8-ounce can tomato sauce	½ teaspoon salt
	¼ cup Parmesan cheese
1¾ cups water	1 10-ounce package frozen chopped spinach, thawed, drained
⅛ teaspoon garlic powder	
Italian seasoning to taste	
1½ teaspoons salt	
1 4-ounce can mushrooms	1 8-ounce package lasagna noodles
1 16-ounce carton cottage cheese	1 pound mozzarella cheese, sliced

Preheat oven to 350 degrees. Combine first 7 ingredients in medium saucepan. Bring to a boil over low heat; set aside. Combine cottage cheese, eggs, ½ teaspoon salt, Parmesan cheese and spinach in bowl; mix well. Spread ½ cup tomato sauce in 9x13-inch baking dish. Layer noodles, spinach-cheese mixture, sauce mixture and mozzarella cheese ½ at a time in prepared pan. Cover with foil. Bake for 1 hour. Let stand for 10 minutes before serving. Yield: 8 to 10 servings.

Anna C. Walker, Mu Omega
Houstonia, Missouri

LINGUINE WITH ASPARAGUS

2 pounds asparagus	1½ teaspoons anchovy paste
3 tablespoons grainy mustard	2 tablespoons minced parsley
3 tablespoons olive oil	1 pound linguine
1 onion, chopped	Salt and pepper to taste
1 clove of garlic, minced	
Pinch of thyme	

Cook asparagus in a small amount of water in saucepan for 3 minutes. Drain; rinse under cold water. Combine mustard, olive oil, onion, garlic, thyme, anchovy paste and parsley in bowl; mix well. Cook linguine using package directions for 7 to 10 minutes; drain well. Combine linguine with dressing and asparagus in serving bowl. Season with salt and pepper. Serve warm or at room temperature. Yield: 4 servings.

Marcia Donini, Xi Lambda Xi
Highland, Illinois

PASTA PRIMAVERA

1 pound thin asparagus	1 cup whipping cream
1 medium onion, minced	½ cup chicken stock
1 large clove of garlic, minced	2 teaspoons basil
	½ cup finely chopped ham
½ cup unsalted butter	
8 ounces mushrooms, sliced	1 bunch green onions, chopped
6 ounces cauliflowerets	Salt and pepper to taste
1 large carrot, cut into julienne strips	1 pound fettucini, cooked
	1¼ cups Parmesan cheese
½ 6-ounce package frozen Chinese pea pods	Pine nuts
	Basil sprigs

Cut asparagus diagonally into ¼-inch slices. Sauté onion and garlic in butter in skillet. Add vegetables. Stir-fry for 2 minutes. Remove vegetables; keep warm. Increase heat to high. Add cream, stock and basil. Boil for 3 minutes. Stir in ham and green onions. Cook for 1 minute. Season with salt and pepper. Add fettucini and Parmesan cheese; toss to mix. Spoon into serving dish. Garnish with pine nuts and fresh basil. Yield: 6 to 8 servings.

Janet Miller, Preceptor Kappa
Ludington, Michigan

For an easy and delicious pasta dish, **Mari Jo Tenski, Alpha Nu, Farmington, New Mexico,** *sautées ½ clove of garlic and 1 bunch of chopped cooked broccoli in a mixture of olive oil and vegetable oil, adds 1 pound of cooked spaghetti, and serves with cheese.*

RED PEPPER PASTA

2 tablespoons boiling water	½ teaspoon salt
2 teaspoons dried hot pepper flakes	1 tablespoon corn oil
	1 tablespoon tomato paste
1 cup semolina flour	2 eggs, slightly beaten
1 cup all-purpose flour	1 tablespoon olive oil

Combine red pepper flakes and boiling water in small bowl. Let steep for 15 minutes. Combine flours and salt in food processor container. Add pepper flakes, tomato paste and eggs, processing constantly until mixture forms ball. Let rest, wrapped in plastic wrap, for 20 minutes. Roll out; cut into strips by hand or with pasta machine. Place in boiling water in saucepan with 1 tablespoon olive oil added. Cook for 2 minutes; drain. Yield: 4 servings.

Diane Runo, Xi Beta
Peoria, Arizona

STUFFED SHELLS FLORENTINE

1 16-ounce package jumbo pasta shells	1 egg
1 10-ounce package frozen chopped spinach	1 32-ounce jar spaghetti sauce
2 pounds ricotta cheese	1 cup shredded mozzarella cheese
2 tablespoons Parmesan cheese	Parmesan cheese

Preheat oven to 350 degrees. Bring 5 quarts salted water to a boil in saucepan. Add shells. Parboil for 9 minutes. Drain immediately. Arrange on baking sheet. Cook spinach using package directions; drain. Add ricotta cheese, 2 tablespoons Parmesan cheese and egg. Spoon into shells. Spread half the spaghetti sauce in bottoms of two 2-quart baking dishes. Arrange filled shells on sauce. Pour the remaining sauce on top of shells. Sprinkle with mozzarella cheese and additional Parmesan cheese. Bake for 15 to 20 minutes. Yield: 6 servings.

Rose Duszkin, Eta Eta
Titusville, Florida

GOOD FRIDAY CASSEROLE

1 7-ounce package elbow macaroni	1 egg, slightly beaten
2 cups small curd cream-style cottage cheese	¾ teaspoon salt
	Dash of pepper
	2 cups shredded sharp American cheese
1 cup sour cream	Paprika

Preheat oven to 350 degrees. Cook macaroni using package directions; drain well. Combine cottage cheese, sour cream, egg, salt and pepper in bowl. Add American cheese; mix well. Add macaroni. Spoon into greased baking dish. Sprinkle with paprika. Bake for 45 minutes. Yield: 4 servings.

Susan E. Banton, Preceptor Alpha Lambda
Caldwell, West Virginia

PINEAPPLE CASSEROLE

5 tablespoons cornstarch	1½ cups shredded sharp cheese
1 cup sugar	
2 20-ounce cans pineapple tidbits	1 stack Ritz crackers, crushed
½ cup melted margarine	

Preheat oven to 350 degrees. Combine cornstarch, sugar, and pineapple in bowl; mix well. Pour into 3-quart baking dish. Mix margarine, cheese and crackers in bowl. Sprinkle over pineapple. Bake for 30 to 40 minutes. Yield: 12 servings.

Ann N. Purser, Preceptor Beta
Macon, Georgia

COUSCOUS

¼ to ⅓ cup chopped green onions	⅛ teaspoon cayenne pepper
1 teaspoon butter	¼ cup water
⅛ teaspoon garlic	⅓ cup tomato juice
¾ cup chicken stock	1 cup cracked wheat

Sauté onions in butter in skillet over low he;at until golden brown. Add garlic, chicken stock, pepper, water and tomato juice. Bring to a boil. Add wheat; cover. Remove from heat. Let stand for 6 minutes until liquid is absorbed. Yield: 4 servings.

Bridgette Fincher, Lambda Sigma
Houston, Texas

ALMOND PILAF

1½ cups rice	⅛ teaspoon pepper
1 medium onion, chopped	1 tablespoon instant chicken bouillon
¼ cup margarine	
½ teaspoon salt	3 cups hot water
½ teaspoon allspice	¼ cup slivered blanched almonds
½ teaspoon turmeric	
¼ teaspoon curry powder	

Preheat oven to 325 degrees. Sauté rice and onion in margarine in skillet until onion is tender. Stir in salt, allspice, turmeric, curry powder and pepper. Pour into 2-quart casserole. Stir in instant bouillon and water. Bake, covered, for 40 minutes or until rice is tender. Yield: 6 servings.

Jeanette Azar, Preceptor Beta Zeta
Mt. Clemens, Michigan

ALMOND AND BACON BROWN RICE

6 slices bacon	1 cup brown rice, cooked
¼ cup slivered almonds	1 to 2 tablespoons soy sauce
½ cup sliced onions	
1 cup mushrooms	

Fry bacon in skillet until crisp. Remove bacon. Add almonds, onions and mushrooms. Sauté for 5 minutes. Add rice and soy sauce; mix well. Cook until heated through. Spoon onto serving dish. Top with bacon. Yield: 3 to 4 servings.

Jan Semsak, Preceptor Alpha Chi
Federal Way, Washington

HERB AND BUTTER RICE

1 cup rice	1 tablespoon tarragon
1 tablespoon thyme	1 teaspoon rosemary
1 tablespoon summer savory	2 tablespoons parsley
1 tablespoon basil	3 tablespoons butter or margarine

Cook rice using package directions. Add remaining ingredients; toss to coat. Serve hot. Yield: 4 to 6 servings.

Colleen Rucker, Omega Xi
San Marcos, California

RICE JARDIN

¾ cup chopped onion	1 16-ounce can whole kernel corn, drained
1½ pounds zucchini, thinly sliced	1½ teaspoons salt
3 tablespoons margarine	¼ teaspoon pepper
3 cups cooked rice	½ teaspoon oregano
1 16-ounce can tomatoes	

Sauté onion and zucchini in margarine in skillet until tender. Add remaining ingredients. Simmer, covered, for 15 minutes. Yield: 8 servings.

Linda Jackson, Xi Alpha Alpha
Jacksonville, Florida

SKILLET SPANISH RICE

2 medium onions, chopped	4 8-ounce cans tomato sauce
1 medium green bell pepper, chopped	2 teaspoons prepared mustard
2 cups rice	2 teaspoons salt
½ cup corn oil	Dash of pepper
3½ cups hot water	

Sauté onions, green pepper and rice in oil in skillet over high heat until lightly browned, stirring constantly. Add hot water and remaining ingredients; mix well. Bring to a boil; cover tightly. Simmer for 25 minutes. Yield: 4 to 6 servings.

Linda Gardner, Xi Beta Iota
Dolores, Colorado

WILD RICE CASSEROLE

½ cup wild rice	1 8-ounce can chopped mushrooms
½ cup butter or margarine	1 cup butter
⅔ cup white rice	1 10-ounce can mushroom soup
1 cup chopped onion	
⅔ cup chopped celery	Salt and pepper to taste

Preheat oven to 325 degrees. Parboil wild rice for 15 minutes; drain. Add ½ cup butter. Parboil white rice for 10 to 15 minutes; drain. Add to wild rice. Sauté onion, celery and mushrooms in 1 cup butter in saucepan. Add soup, sautéed vegetables and seasonings to rice; mix well. Pour into large casserole. Bake for 1½ hours. Yield: 4 to 6 servings.

Shirley Ugland, Xi Mu
Byron, Minnesota

CORN BREAD DRESSING

6 cups corn bread crumbs	1 cup chopped celery
6 cups biscuit or bread crumbs	6 tablespoons melted margarine
1 tablespoon sage	8 cups hot chicken broth
1 teaspoon pepper	6 eggs, well beaten
1 cup chopped onion	

Preheat oven to 350 degrees. Combine crumbs, sage and pepper in large bowl. Sauté onion and celery in margarine in skillet. Add to crumbs; mix well. Add 6 cups hot broth; mix well. Add enough remaining broth to make the mixture soupy. Let stand, covered, for 15 minutes. Add eggs; mix well. Pour into 9x13-inch baking pan. Bake for 30 minutes or until knife inserted near center comes out clean. Yield: 15 servings.

Martha Hallman, Mu
Jackson, Tennessee

PECAN AND RICE DRESSING

1 cup long grain rice	1 cup butter
1 package wild rice with mushrooms	1 cup chopped pecans
	½ cup dried parsley
1 cup finely chopped onion	1 teaspoon salt
	1 teaspoon pepper
1 cup finely chopped celery	2 tablespoons soy sauce

Preheat oven to 325 degrees. Cook long grain rice using package directions; set aside. Cook wild rice using package directions. Sauté onions and celery in butter in skillet until translucent. Add pecans and parsley. Sauté for 5 minutes. Combine rices, vegetables, salt, pepper and soy sauce in large bowl. Toss until well mixed. Pour into shallow 10-inch baking dish. Bake for 25 minutes. Yield: 10 servings.

Lynn Bright, Epsilon Psi
San Angelo, Texas

WILD RICE DRESSING SUPREME

1 cup wild rice	1 10-ounce can mushroom pieces and stems
8 ounces bacon, chopped	
2 cups chopped celery tops and leaves	
2 cups chopped onions	1 16-ounce can chop suey vegetables
1 or 2 carrots, chopped	Salt, pepper, seasoned salt, garlic and herbs to taste
½ cup chopped fresh parsley	
1 8-ounce can water chestnuts, chopped	

Preheat oven to 350 degrees. Wash rice until water runs clear; drain. Steam using package directions. Sauté bacon, celery, onions, carrots, parsley, water chestnuts, mushrooms, chop suey vegetables and seasonings in skillet over low heat for 30 minutes. Add rice; mix well. Serve as side dish or use as stuffing. Yield: 12 servings.

Annetta M. Henry, Preceptor Beta
Davenport, Iowa

MUSTARD RING

1 envelope unflavored gelatin	¾ cup sugar
¼ cup water	1 tablespoon dry mustard
4 eggs, beaten	1 cup whipping cream, whipped
1 cup vinegar	1 teaspoon horseradish

Soften gelatin in water. Combine with eggs, vinegar, sugar and dry mustard in double boiler. Cook until smooth and creamy, stirring constantly. Cool. Add cream and horseradish. Grease mold with mayonnaise. Pour mustard mixture into prepared mold. Chill for 24 hours. Serve with baked ham. Yield: 12 to 16 servings.

Cleo H. Wickham, Laureate Mu
Idaho Falls, Idaho

APRYL'S CRANBERRY CHUTNEY

1 pound fresh cranberries	1 very firm pear, chopped
2 cups sugar	1 apple, chopped
1 cup water	1 tablespoon grated orange rind
1 envelope unflavored gelatin	2½ teaspoons ginger
¼ cup water	1 cup golden raisins
1 cup orange juice	1 cup chopped pecans
1 cup chopped celery	

Combine cranberries with sugar and 1 cup water in saucepan. Bring to slow boil. Cook until sugar is dissolved, stirring constantly. Simmer for 15 minutes, stirring occasionally. Remove from heat; cool. Soften gelatin in ¼ cup water. Add to mixture with remaining ingredients. Refrigerate, covered, for 3 hours. Stir in pecans. Yield: 6 to 8 servings.

Mary Ann Anthony, Xi Psi
Ocean Springs, Mississippi

MANGO CHUTNEY

24 firm not ripe mangoes	2 teaspoons allspice
1 pound raisins	2 teaspoons cinnamon
1 pound dates, chopped	6 cups vinegar
3 cloves of garlic, minced	½ cup packed light brown sugar
½ cup dried red pepper	10 cups sugar
2 teaspoons salt	Juice of 3 limes
1 tablespoon ginger	
2 teaspoons ground cloves	

Peel mangoes; slice ¼ inch thick. Place in bowl. Add raisins, dates, spices and vinegar; mix well. Let stand for 3 days, stirring 3 times each day. Mix with sugars in large heavy saucepan. Bring to a boil, stirring until sugars dissolve. Add lime juice. Simmer for 2 hours or until mangoes appear clear around edges. Ladle into hot sterilized jelly jars; seal and cool. Let stand for 1 day. Reseal with plastic wrap or paraffin. Serve over cream cheese. Yield: Several gallons.

Maureen M. Humphreys, Xi Alpha Zeta
Virginia Beach, Virginia

PEAR MARMALADE

3 cups chopped pears	2 3-ounce packages strawberry gelatin
3 cups sugar	

Purée pears in blender container. Add sugar and gelatin. Pour into saucepan. Bring to a boil, stirring constantly. Cook for 5 minutes. Pour into jars; seal with wax. Store in refrigerator. Yield: 4 cups.

Marjie M. Norcutt, Xi Alpha Upsilon
Gretna, Virginia

FRESH KIWIFRUIT JAM

1 pound kiwifruit, peeled	5 tablespoons liquid pectin
2½ cups sugar	
1 tablespoon lemon juice	

Purée kiwifruit in blender. Pour into bowl. Add sugar and lemon juice. Stir until dissolved. Let stand, covered, for 20 minutes. Add pectin. Stir for 2 minutes. Let stand, covered, for 24 hours. Pour into jars; seal with paraffin. Store in refrigerator for up to 5 weeks or in freezer for 1 year. Yield: 6 to 8 six-ounce jars.

Jeanne Stringer, Preceptor Kappa Xi
Orange Cove, California

PEPPER JELLY

6 large green or red bell peppers	1 teaspoon cayenne pepper
1½ cup cider vinegar	1 bottle of Certo
6 cups sugar	Food coloring
½ teaspoon salt	

Purée peppers with vinegar ½ at a time in blender container. Pour into saucepan. Add sugar, salt and cayenne pepper. Bring to a full rolling boil. Cook for 10 minutes. Add Certo and food coloring. Pour into hot sterilized jars; seal. Cool. Store in refrigerator. Serve over cream cheese or triscuits. Yield: 4 cups.

Rosemarie Campbell, Preceptor Beta Tau
Escanaba, Michigan

ZUCCHINI RELISH

12 cups peeled grated zucchini	1 teaspoon celery seed
4 cups chopped onions	1 tablespoon cornstarch
2 large green bell peppers, chopped	1 teaspoon nutmeg
	1 teaspoon dry mustard
5 tablespoons canning salt	1 teaspoon turmeric
2¼ cups white vinegar	1 4-ounce jar chopped pimento
2½ cups sugar	

Marinate zucchini, onions and peppers in salt in covered container in refrigerator overnight. Drain. Rinse with cold water; drain well. Combine with remaining ingredients in saucepan. Cook for 30 minutes. Pack hot relish in hot sterilized jars; seal. Yield: 4 quarts.

Cathy Severin, Gamma Gamma
Belle Fourche, South Dakota

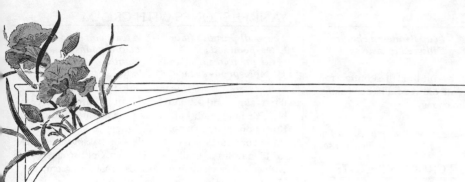

Party
Breads

PARMESAN BISCUITS

2 8-ounce packages refrigerator biscuits ½ cup melted butter	1 cup Parmesan cheese Dillweed to taste

Separate biscuits. Dip each biscuit in melted butter; roll in cheese. Sprinkle lightly with dillweed. Place in baking pan. Bake using package directions.
Yield: 12 to 16 servings.

Rosalie Stone, Preceptor Alpha Tau
Wichita, Kansas

SAUSAGE AND SOUR CREAM BISCUITS

1 8-ounce package
    brown and serve
    sausage links
	1 cup melted margarine
	1 cup sour cream
	2 cups self-rising flour

Preheat oven to 450 degrees. Cook sausages using package directions for about half the time. Slice ¼ inch thick. Blend margarine and sour cream in large bowl. Add flour; mix well. Drop by teaspoonfuls into ungreased miniature muffin cups. Press sausage slices lightly into dough. Bake for 15 minutes. Yield: 2½ dozen.

Gyl Dalrymple, Omega Preceptor
West Monroe, Louisiana

SAVORY BISCUITS

1 10-ounce package refrigerator biscuits	⅓ cup melted butter 3 tablespoons blue cheese

Preheat oven to 400 degrees. Cut biscuits in quarters. Arrange in 11 x 17-inch baking pan. Mix butter and cheese in bowl; mix well. Pour over biscuits. Bake for 15 minutes.

Kay Van Metre, Honorary Member Laureate Zeta
Martinsburg, West Virginia

SWEET POTATO BISCUITS

1 egg, slightly beaten
1 cup mashed cooked
    sweet potatoes
¼ to ½ cup sugar
3 tablespoons shortening
	2 tablespoons butter,
	    softened
	2 cups (about) self-rising
	    flour

Preheat oven to 350 degrees. Combine egg, sweet potatoes, sugar, shortening and butter in bowl; mix well. Stir in enough flour to make soft dough. Knead lightly several times on floured surface. Roll to ¼-inch thickness; cut with 2-inch biscuit cutter. Place on greased baking sheet. Bake for 15 minutes. Yield: 17 biscuits.

Mary Louise Bell, Preceptor Alpha Gamma
New Iberia, Louisiana

*An old family favorite, says **Linda Annette Thompson, Xi Beta Beta, Birmingham, Alabama**, is a chocolate gravy to serve over buttered biscuits. Just cook 1 cup sugar, 1 tablespoon cocoa, 2 heaping tablespoons cornstarch, 1 cup water and a pinch of salt in saucepan over medium heat until thickened, stirring constantly. Stir in 2 tablespoons margarine.*

YANKEE SCONES WITH CREAM

2 cups all-purpose flour ½ teaspoon soda ½ teaspoon cream of tartar 1½ tablespoons sugar	½ teaspoon salt 2 tablespoons unsalted butter ¾ to 1 cup buttermilk

Preheat oven to 475 degrees. Sift flour, soda, cream of tartar, sugar and salt into bowl. Cut in butter until crumbly. Stir in enough buttermilk to make medium dough. Knead on floured surface 2 or 3 times. Roll about ½ inch thick; cut with 2-inch cutter. Place on baking sheet. Bake for 15 minutes or until golden brown. Split scones. Serve with strawberry jam and Mock Devonshire Cream.
Yield: 10 servings.

MOCK DEVONSHIRE CREAM

3 ounces cream cheese,
    softened
¼ cup sour cream
	2½ tablespoons
	    confectioners' sugar
	¼ cup whipping cream

Blend cream cheese and sour cream in bowl until light. Beat in confectioners' sugar and cream. Chill for 1 hour.

 Zeilla Smith, Chi Xi
Whittier, California

CREAM CHEESE BRUNCH GOODIE

½ cup margarine,
    softened
1¼ cups sugar
8 ounces cream cheese,
    softened
2 eggs
1 teaspoon vanilla extract
2 cups all-purpose flour
1 teaspoon baking powder
	½ teaspoon soda
	¼ teaspoon salt
	¼ cup milk
	⅓ cup packed light brown
	    sugar
	2 tablespoons margarine
	½ teaspoon cinnamon
	⅓ cup all-purpose flour

Preheat oven to 350 degrees. Cream first 5 ingredients in mixer bowl. Add mixture of next 4 dry ingredients alternately with milk, mixing well after each addition. Pour into greased and floured 9x13-inch glass baking dish. Mix brown sugar, 2 tablespoons margarine, cinnamon and ⅓ cup flour in bowl. Sprinkle over batter. Bake for 35 to 40 minutes. Yield: 16 servings.

Lodema Erbacher, Preceptor Zeta
Williamsville, New York

MONKEY BREAD

3 10-count packages refrigerator biscuits 1 cup sugar 1 tablespoon cinnamon	½ cup margarine 1 cup sugar 1 teaspoon cinnamon 1 cup chopped nuts

Preheat oven to 375 degrees. Cut biscuits into quarters. Combine 1 cup sugar and 1 teaspoon cinnamon in bag. Add biscuits; shake well. Layer biscuits, margarine, remaining 1 cup sugar, remaining 1 teaspoon cinnamon and nuts in greased bundt pan ½ at a time. Bake for 25 minutes or until golden brown. Yield: 12 servings.

Susie Jones, Delta Phi
Hoxie, Arkansas

CHERRY COFFEE CAKE

2 cups sugar
1 cup margarine, softened
4 eggs
2 cups all-purpose flour
1½ teaspoons baking
  powder

1 teaspoon almond extract
2 20-ounce cans cherry
  pie filling
1 to 2 cups confectioners'
  sugar
Milk

Preheat oven to 350 degrees. Cream sugar and margarine in mixer bowl. Beat in eggs, flour, baking powder and almond extract. Spread ⅔ of the batter in greased 11x15-inch baking pan. Dot with pie filling. Spoon remaining batter over top. Bake for 25 minutes. Blend confectioners' sugar with enough milk to make of desired consistency. Drizzle over warm coffee cake. Yield: 12 to 15 servings.

Bernice Lowdon, Preceptor Alpha Beta
St. Joseph, Missouri

NIGHT BEFORE COFFEE CAKE

¾ cup margarine,
  softened
1 cup sugar
½ cup packed light brown
  sugar
2 eggs
2 cups all-purpose flour
1 teaspoon baking powder
1 teaspoon soda

1 teaspoon cinnamon
½ teaspoon salt
1 cup buttermilk
½ cup dates
½ cup packed light brown
  sugar
¼ teaspoon nutmeg
½ teaspoon cinnamon
½ cup chopped nuts

Cream the first 4 ingredients in mixer bowl. Add mixture of next 5 dry ingredients alternately with buttermilk, mixing well after each addition. Add dates. Pour into greased 9x16-inch baking pan. Sprinkle with mixture of ½ cup brown sugar, nutmeg, ½ teaspoon cinnamon and nuts. Cover tightly with foil. Refrigerate overnight. Preheat oven to 350 degrees. Bake for 35 to 40 minutes or until coffee cake tests done. Yield: 15 servings.

Ruth M. Burgess, Preceptor Alpha Nu
Muskogee, Oklahoma

OVERNIGHT COFFEE CAKE

1 cup packed light brown
  sugar
½ cup coconut
½ cup pecans
1 teaspoon cinnamon
2 cups all-purpose flour
1 cup sugar
2 teaspoons baking
  powder

1 teaspoon salt
2 4-ounce packages
  vanilla instant pudding
  mix
1 cup water
¾ cup corn oil
1 teaspoon vanilla extract
4 eggs

Mix first 4 ingredients in bowl; set aside. Combine flour and remaining ingredients in mixer bowl. Beat at low speed for 30 seconds. Beat at medium speed for 2 minutes. Layer batter and coconut mixture ½ at a time in greased and floured 9x13-inch baking pan. Refrigerate overnight if desired. Preheat oven to 325 degrees. Bake for 40 to 60 minutes or until coffee cake tests done. Yield: 12 to 15 servings.

Veronica Filipek, Preceptor Eta
Minot, North Dakota

POPPY SEED COFFEE CAKE

¼ cup poppy seed
1 cup buttermilk
1 teaspoon almond extract
1 cup margarine, softened
1½ cups sugar
4 egg yolks
2½ cups all-purpose flour

1 teaspoon soda
1 teaspoon baking powder
Dash of salt
4 egg whites, stiffly
  beaten
½ cup sugar
1 teaspoon cinnamon

Preheat oven to 350 degrees. Mix first 3 ingredients in bowl. Let stand for several minutes. Cream margarine, 1½ cups sugar and egg yolks in mixer bowl. Add sifted dry ingredients alternately with poppy seed mixture, mixing well after each addition. Fold in stiffly beaten egg whites. Layer batter and mixture of ½ cup sugar and cinnamon ½ at a time in greased bundt pan. Cut through with knife to marbleize. Bake for 1 hour or until cake tests done. Cool for 10 minutes before serving. Yield: 16 servings.

Erma Erickson, Laureate Psi
Ames, Iowa

SOUR CREAM-PUMPKIN COFFEE CAKE

½ cup butter, softened
¾ cup sugar
1 teaspoon vanilla extract
3 eggs
2 cups all-purpose flour
1 teaspoon baking powder
1 teaspoon soda
1 cup sour cream
1¾ cups canned solid-
  pack pumpkin

1 egg, slightly beaten
⅓ cup sugar
1 teaspoon pumpkin pie
  spice
1 cup packed light brown
  sugar
⅓ cup butter
2 teaspoons cinnamon
1 cup chopped nuts

Preheat oven to 325 degrees. Cream butter, ¾ cup sugar and vanilla in mixer bowl. Add 3 eggs; beat well. Add mixture of flour, baking powder and soda alternately with sour cream, mixing well after each addition. Combine pumpkin, 1 egg, ⅓ cup sugar and pie spice in bowl. Mix brown sugar and remaining ingredients in bowl until crumbly. Layer half the coffee cake batter, half the nut mixture, all the pumpkin mixture and remaining batter and nut mixture in 9x13-inch baking dish. Bake for 50 minutes or until cake tests done. Yield: 12 servings.

Dortha L. Parker, Xi Eta Tau
Wakeman, Ohio

TWIN MOUNTAIN COFFEE CAKE

2 cups all-purpose flour
1 tablespoon baking
  powder
¼ teaspoon salt
1 cup sugar

½ cup shortening
2 eggs, beaten
1 cup milk
1½ cups blueberries
1⅓ cups flaked coconut

Preheat oven to 375 degrees. Sift dry ingredients into bowl. Cut in shortening until crumbly. Beat eggs with milk. Stir into dry ingredients. Fold in blueberries. Pour into 2 greased 8-inch round cake pans. Sprinkle flaked coconut over top. Bake for 25 minutes. Yield: 16 servings.

Muriel Buchino, Preceptor Laureate Alpha Gamma
Hollywood, Florida

FILLED STREUSEL COFFEE CAKE

¾ cup sugar
¼ cup shortening
1 egg
½ cup milk
1½ cups all-purpose flour
2 teaspoons baking
   powder
½ teaspoon salt
2 tablespoons butter
½ cup packed light brown
   sugar

2 tablespoons all-purpose
   flour
2 teaspoons cinnamon
½ cup chopped nuts
½ cup milk
2½ tablespoons
   all-purpose flour
½ cup sugar
½ cup butter, softened
Dash of salt
1 teaspoon vanilla extract

Preheat oven to 375 degrees. Cream first 3 ingredients in bowl. Blend in ½ cup milk. Add 1½ cups flour, baking powder and salt; mix well. Batter will be thick. Pour into greased and floured 9-inch baking pan. Top with mixture of 2 tablespoons butter, brown sugar, 2 tablespoons flour, cinnamon and nuts. Bake for 25 to 35 minutes or until coffee cake tests done. Cool. Blend ½ cup milk and 2½ tablespoons flour in saucepan. Cook until thickened, stirring constantly. Cool slightly. Combine ½ cup sugar, ½ cup butter, dash of salt and vanilla in mixer bowl. Beat until fluffy. Add cooked mixture; beat until creamy. Split coffee cake into 2 layers. Spread filling between layers. Yield: 8 servings.

Elizabeth E. Zall, Alpha Omicron
Findlay, Ohio

BEST CORN BREAD

¾ cup sugar
2 cups buttermilk baking
   mix
¾ cup yellow cornmeal
½ teaspoon baking
   powder

1 cup milk
2 eggs, slightly beaten
1 teaspoon vanilla extract
¾ cup melted butter

Preheat oven to 350 degrees. Combine all ingredients in bowl in order listed, mixing well after each addition. Pour into greased and floured 8x8-inch baking pan. Bake for 35 to 40 minutes or until golden brown. Serve warm with butter and honey. Yield: 9 servings.

Ruth Casteel, Laureate Gamma Theta
Diamond Bar, California

BROCCOLI CORN BREAD

1 10-ounce package
   frozen chopped broccoli
1 7-ounce package
   corn bread mix
4 eggs

1 24-ounce carton
   cottage cheese
1 medium onion, chopped
¼ cup corn oil

Preheat oven to 350 degrees. Cook broccoli using package directions; drain well. Combine with remaining ingredients in bowl; mix well. Pour into greased 9x9-inch baking pan. Bake for 35 to 40 minutes or until golden brown. Yield: 9 servings.

Lisa M. Grimsley, Xi Beta Pi
Boonville, Missouri

SUE'S UNBELIEVABLE CORN BREAD

1 large sweet onion,
   chopped
¼ cup butter
1 12-ounce package corn
   muffin mix
1 16-ounce can cream-
   style corn

1 egg, beaten
5 drops of hot pepper
   sauce
Salt and pepper to taste
1 cup sour cream
1¼ cups shredded sharp
   cheese

Preheat oven to 425 degrees. Sauté onion in butter in skillet. Combine muffin mix, corn, egg, hot sauce and seasonings in bowl; mix well. Spoon into buttered 8x8-inch baking pan. Mix sour cream and ½ of the cheese with sautéed onion. Spread over batter. Sprinkle with remaining cheese. Bake for 25 to 30 minutes or until corn bread tests done. Yield: 8 servings.

Janet Edmonds, Omicron Lambda
Sarasota, Florida

CORNMEAL CRISPS

2 cups yellow cornmeal
¼ teaspoon salt
⅛ teaspoon seasoned salt
Pepper to taste

Dash of cayenne pepper
2½ cups boiling water
3 to 4 teaspoons butter

Preheat oven to 375 degrees. Mix cornmeal and seasonings in bowl. Add boiling water; stir until smooth. Melt butter in large heavy iron skillet. Pour into batter; mix well. Drop by tablespoonfuls into 2½ to 3-inch circles in hot skillet; circles may touch. Bake for 45 minutes. Turn crisps over. Decrease temperature to 250 degrees. Bake for 15 minutes longer. Turn off oven. Let stand in warm oven for 15 minutes. Yield: 20 crisps.

Nancy E. Carpenter, Xi Gamma Eta
Paris, Tennessee

JALAPEÑO CORN BREAD

3 cups corn bread mix
2 large onions, grated
1 cup cream-style corn
1½ cups shredded
   longhorn cheese
2 tablespoons sugar
Garlic to taste

3 eggs, beaten
½ cup corn oil
2 cups milk
1 pound bacon,
   crisp-fried, crumbled
1 cup chopped jalapeño
   peppers

Combine first 9 ingredients in bowl; mix well. Stir in bacon and jalapeño peppers. Pour into well-greased 9x13-inch baking pan. Bake for 35 to 40 minutes or until golden brown. Yield: 12 to 15 servings.

Connie Carder, Lambda Alpha
Cameron, Missouri

MEXICAN CORN MUFFINS

2 cups self-rising
   cornmeal
2 eggs, beaten
⅔ cup corn oil
1 onion, chopped

1 green bell pepper,
   chopped
1 cup sour cream
1 8-ounce can cream-
   style corn

Preheat oven to 350 degrees. Combine all ingredients in bowl; mix well. Fill muffin cups sprayed with nonstick cooking spray ⅔ full. Bake for 30 to 35 minutes or until golden brown. Yield: 1 to 1½ dozen.

Barbara Brown, Omega
Jonesboro, Arkansas

CORN BREAD STICKS

1 cup yellow cornmeal	½ teaspoon salt
1 cup all-purpose flour	1 cup milk
¼ cup sugar	1 egg
4 teaspoons baking powder	¼ cup melted shortening

Preheat oven to 400 degrees. Combine dry ingredients in bowl. Add milk, egg and shortening; beat until smooth. Spoon into well-greased corn stick pans. Bake for 15 to 20 minutes or until golden brown. Yield: 1 dozen.

Kay Kratzer, Epsilon Tau
El Dorado, Kansas

CAKE DOUGHNUTS

2½ cups sugar	7½ cups all-purpose flour
6 eggs	1 teaspoon salt
1 cup cold unseasoned mashed potatoes	1 tablespoon vanilla extract
2 tablespoons shortening	1¼ cups milk
8 teaspoons baking powder	Oil for deep frying

Beat sugar and eggs in mixer bowl until thick and foamy. Add potatoes and shortening; beat until smooth. Sift dry ingredients together. Add vanilla to milk. Add dry ingredients to egg mixture alternately with milk mixture, mixing well after each addition. Batter will be very stiff. Chill for 2 hours to overnight. Roll about ½ inch thick on lightly floured surface; cut with doughnut cutter. Deep-fry at 365 to 370 degrees. Drain on paper towels. Roll in additional sugar. Yield: 4½ dozen.

Karlene Scofied, Xi Gamma Sigma
Rocky Ford, Colorado

APPLE BREAD

2 cups sugar	1 teaspoon soda
1¼ cups vegetable oil	1 teaspoon cinnamon
2 eggs	1 cup raisins
1 teaspoon vanilla extract	3 large apples, peeled, chopped
3 cups sifted all-purpose flour	1½ cups chopped pecans
1 teaspoon salt	

Preheat oven to 350 degrees. Combine sugar, oil, eggs and vanilla in bowl; mix well. Add mixture of flour, salt, soda and cinnamon; mix well. Stir in raisins, apples and pecans.Pour into 2 greased and floured loaf pans. Bake for 1 hour and 15 minutes or until loaves test done. Yield: 2 loaves.

Melissa Stroud, Eta Rho
Covington, Louisiana

WHOLE WHEAT APPLE AND NUT BREAD

2 cups sugar	1 teaspoon salt
1 cup vegetable oil	1 teaspoon cinnamon
3 eggs	¼ cup wheat germ
1½ cups all-purpose flour	¼ cup sesame seed
1½ cups whole wheat flour	3 cups chopped unpeeled apples
1 teaspoon soda	1 cup walnuts

Preheat oven to 375 degrees. Blend sugar and oil in bowl. Add eggs 1 at a time, mixing well after each addition. Add mixture of dry ingredients; mix well. Stir in apples and walnuts. Pour into 2 greased loaf pans. Bake for 1 hour or until loaves test done. Yield: 2 loaves.

Nancy Curtis, Xi Delta Lambda
Flint, Michigan

APRICOT BREAD

1½ cups boiling water	½ teaspoon baking powder
1 cup chopped dried apricots	2 teaspoons soda
1½ cups sugar	1 cup chopped walnuts
1 egg, beaten	1 tablespoon melted shortening
2½ cups sifted all-purpose flour	1 teaspoon vanilla extract
½ teaspoon salt	

Preheat oven to 350 degrees. Pour boiling water over apricots in bowl; let stand for 10 minutes. Beat sugar gradually into egg with spoon. Sift flour, salt, baking powder and soda together in bowl. Stir in walnuts. Add dry ingredients alternately with sugar mixture to apricots, mixing well after each addition. Stir in shortening and vanilla. Pour into greased loaf pan. Bake for 1 hour or until loaf tests done. Yield: 1 loaf.

Phyllis Tschabrun, Laureate Chi
Spring Arbor, Michigan

AVOCADO BREAD

2⅔ cups sifted all-purpose flour	1¾ cups plus 2 tablespoons sugar
¾ teaspoon cinnamon	¾ cup buttermilk
¾ teaspoon allspice	1½ cups mashed avocados
¾ teaspoon salt	¾ cup nuts
1½ teaspoons soda	½ cup raisins
1 teaspoon baking powder	⅓ cup sugar
½ cup butter, softened	1 teaspoon cinnamon
3 eggs	

Preheat oven to 350 degrees. Sift first 6 dry ingredients together. Combine butter, eggs and 1¾ cup plus 2 tablespoons sugar in mixer bowl. Beat for 2 minutes. Add buttermilk and avocados; mix well. Add dry ingredients. Beat for 2 minutes. Stir in nuts and raisins. Pour into 2 greased loaf pans. Sprinkle with mixture of ⅓ cup sugar and 1 teaspoon cinnamon. Bake for 1 hour or until loaves tests done. Yield: 2 loaves.

Judi Davis, Xi Beta Theta
Broken Arrow, Oklahoma

BANANA BREAD

2 cups sifted all-purpose flour	½ cup butter, softened
1½ teaspoons baking powder	2 eggs
	1 cup sugar
½ teaspoon salt	3 tablespoons sour cream
½ teaspoon soda	1 teaspoon lemon juice
¼ teaspoon nutmeg	1½ cups sliced bananas
	½ to 1 cup pecans

Preheat oven to 350 degrees. Sift first 5 dry ingredients into large bowl. Set aside. Combine butter, eggs, sugar, sour cream and lemon juice in blender or food processor; process until smooth and creamy. Add bananas; process until smooth. Add pecans; process just until pecans are broken. Pour banana mixture into flour mixture; mix well. Pour into greased loaf pan. Bake for 50 minutes or until bread tests done. Cool slightly before removing from pan. Yield: 1 loaf.

Carol Julian, Preceptor Pi
Columbia, Missouri

ALOHA BANANA BREAD

2 cups all-purpose flour	1 tablespoon grated orange rind
1 cup sugar	
1 teaspoon soda	1 teaspoon vanilla extract
½ teaspoon salt	½ teaspoon almond extract
½ cup butter, softened	
2 eggs	1 cup flaked coconut
¼ cup milk	½ cup chopped walnuts
1 cup mashed banana	½ cup crushed pineapple

Preheat oven to 350 degrees. Combine first 11 ingredients in mixer bowl. Beat at low speed until moistened. Beat at medium speed for 3 minutes. Stir in coconut, walnuts and pineapple. Grease bottom of 5x9-inch loaf pan. Pour mixture into pan. Bake for 60 to 70 minutes or until toothpick inserted in center comes out clean. Remove from pan immediately. Cool completely before slicing. Yield: 1 loaf.

Ellen Christine Colflesh
Granville, West Virginia

BROWN BREAD

1 cup milk	1 teaspoon soda
1 cup sour milk	1 cup molasses
1 cup cornmeal	½ teaspoon salt
1 cup all-purpose flour	1 cup raisins

Combine all ingredients in bowl; mix well. Fill mold or coffee can ⅔ full. Place mold on trivet in large kettle. Add enough boiling water to come halfway up side of mold. Cover mold and kettle tightly. Steam for 3 hours, adding additional water if necessary. Remove bread from mold. Cool on wire rack. Wrap and store overnight. Yield: 8 to 10 servings.

Cheryl Turner, Beta Theta
Fort Mill, South Carolina

NANTUCKET CRANBERRY BREAD

3 eggs	1 teaspoon soda
1½ cups corn oil	1 teaspoon cinnamon
2 cups sugar	1½ cups chopped walnuts
2 teaspoons vanilla extract	1 16-ounce package cranberries
3 cups all-purpose flour	
1 teaspoon salt	

Preheat oven to 350 degrees. Combine eggs, oil, sugar and vanilla in bowl; mix well. Sift in dry ingredients; mix well. Fold in walnuts and cranberries. Pour into 2 greased and floured loaf pans. Bake for 1 hour or until loaves test done. Yield: 2 loaves.

Linda Mihlmester, Theta Eta
Oak Ridge, Tennessee

DATE NUT BREAD

8 ounces dates, pitted	2 tablespoons butter
2 teaspoons soda	2 teaspoons vanilla extract
2 cups boiling water	½ cup chopped nuts
4 cups all-purpose flour	2 cups sugar
2 eggs	1 teaspoon salt

Preheat oven to 350 degrees. Combine first 3 ingredients in bowl. Let stand until cool. Mix in flour, eggs, butter, vanilla, nuts, sugar and salt. Pour into 5 greased 16-ounce cans. Bake for 1 hour. Cool in cans for 5 minutes. Remove to wire rack to cool completely. Yield: 5 loaves.

Lee Sanders, Laureate Alpha Gamma
Hollywood, Florida

ORANGE AND DATE BREAD

Juice and grated rind of 1 orange	1 teaspoon vanilla extract
	1 egg, beaten
1 cup boiling water	2 cups all-purpose flour
1 cup dates	1 teaspoon baking powder
1 teaspoon soda	¼ teaspoon salt
1 cup sugar	½ cup chopped nuts
2 tablespoons butter, softened	

Preheat oven to 350 degrees. Add enough boiling water to orange juice to measure 1 cup. Process orange rind in food processor until grated. Add enough dates to measure 1 cup; process until smooth. Place orange mixture in bowl; add orange juice. Stir in soda, sugar, butter and vanilla. Add egg, flour, baking powder and salt; beat well. Fold in nuts. Pour into greased loaf pan. Bake for 50 to 60 minutes or until loaf tests done. Cool on wire rack. Yield: 1 loaf.

Joyce Martin, Xi Alpha Mu
Minneapolis, Minnesota

SWEET GRAPE NUTS BREAD

½ cup sugar	2 cups all-purpose flour
1 egg	½ teaspoon soda
1 cup milk	½ cup Grape Nuts
½ teaspoon baking powder	½ teaspoon salt
	½ teaspoon vanilla extract

Preheat oven to 375 degrees. Combine all ingredients in bowl; mix well. Pour into greased loaf pan. Bake for 40 minutes or until bread tests done. Yield: 1 loaf.

Terri Shifflett, Gamma Theta
Cedar Rapids, Iowa

LEMONY PECAN BREAD

3 tablespoons fresh lemon juice	1½ cups sifted all-purpose flour
¼ cup sugar	1 teaspoon baking powder
½ cup melted butter	½ teaspoon salt
1 cup sugar	½ cup milk
2 eggs	1 tablespoon freshly grated lemon rind
½ teaspoon almond extract	½ cup pecans

Preheat oven to 325 degrees. Mix lemon juice with ¼ cup sugar; set aside. Beat butter and 1 cup sugar in mixer bowl. Beat in eggs 1 at a time. Add almond extract. Sift dry ingredients together. Add to egg mixture alternately with milk, stirring just enough to blend. Fold in remaining ingredients. Pour into greased 5x9-inch loaf pan. Bake for 1 hour or until loaf tests done. Pour lemon juice mixture over hot loaf. Cool in pan. Let stand, wrapped in plastic wrap, for 24 hours. Yield: 1 loaf.

Norma J. Berger, Preceptor Alpha Lambda
Peoria Heights, Illinois

ORANGE AND NUT HONEY BREAD

2 tablespoons shortening	2¼ cups sifted all-purpose flour
1 cup honey	2½ teaspoons baking powder
1 egg, beaten	
1¼ tablespoons grated orange rind	¼ cup orange juice
½ teaspoon salt	½ cup chopped pecans

Preheat oven to 325 degrees. Cream shortening and honey in bowl. Add egg and orange rind; mix well. Add sifted dry ingredients alternately with juice, mixing well after each addition. Stir in pecans. Pour into greased loaf pan. Bake for 1 hour and 10 minutes. Serve with cream cheese blended with honey. Yield: 1 loaf.

Sharon Carter, Alpha Omicron Sigma
Plano, Texas

PEAR AND NUT BREAD

4 or 5 fresh pears	¼ teaspoon baking powder
3 eggs	
1 cup vegetable oil	1½ teaspoons cinnamon
1½ cups sugar	⅔ cup chopped nuts
½ teaspoon grated lemon rind	½ cup oats
1 teaspoon vanilla extract	¼ cup all-purpose flour
3 cups sifted all-purpose flour	¾ cup packed light brown sugar
1 teaspoon salt	3 tablespoons melted margarine
1 teaspoon soda	

Preheat oven to 325 degrees. Grate pears. Beat eggs in mixer bowl until light and fluffy. Add oil, sugar, lemon rind, vanilla and grated pear; mix well. Sift dry ingredients together. Add to pear mixture; mix just until blended. Stir in nuts. Pour into 3 well-greased 4x7-inch loaf pans. Sprinkle mixture of oats and remaining ingredients on top. Bake for 50 to 60 minutes or until loaves test done. Yield: 3 loaves.

Linda Rogers, Eta
Orlando, Florida

POPPY SEED BREAD

1½ teaspoon salt	1½ cups milk
3 eggs	1½ teaspoons vanilla extract
2¼ cups sugar	
1½ teaspoons almond extract	1½ teaspoons poppy seed
	½ cup orange juice
1½ teaspoons butter extract	¾ cup sugar
3 cups all-purpose flour	1½ teaspoons butter extract
1½ teaspoons baking powder	1 teaspoon almond extract
1 cup plus 2 tablespoons corn oil	1½ teaspoons vanilla extract

Preheat oven to 350 degrees. Combine first 11 ingredients in mixer bowl. Beat for 2 minutes. Pour into 2 greased loaf pans. Bake for 1 hour. Cool in pans for 10 minutes. Remove to wire rack to cool completely. Mix orange juice and remaining ingredients in bowl. Let stand for 10 minutes. Place loaves on foil. Pierce with fork. Pour orange juice mixture over loaves. Seal foil. Yield: 2 loaves.

Cathy Heacox, Xi Epsilon Zeta
Sikeston, Missouri

PORK AND BEAN BREAD

1 cup raisins	1 teaspoon cinnamon
1 cup boiling water	½ teaspoon baking powder
3 eggs	
1 cup vegetable oil	1 teaspoon soda
2 cups sugar	½ teaspoon salt
1 16-ounce can pork and beans	1 cup nuts
	1 teaspoon vanilla extract
3 cups all-purpose flour	

Preheat oven to 325 degrees. Mix raisins with boiling water in bowl. Set aside. Beat eggs, oil, sugar and beans in mixer bowl until well mixed. Add dry ingredients; mix well. Add nuts and vanilla. Drain raisins; stir into batter. Pour into 3 well-greased loaf pans. Bake for 50 to 60 minutes or until loaves test done. Yield: 3 loaves.

Sheila A. Pearson, Beta Mu
Lawrence, Kansas

Parmesan bread adds to an Italian menu according to Laura Shunn, Xi Alpha Eta, Fruitland, Idaho. She spreads a mixture of 1 cup mayonnaise and ½ cup Parmesan cheese on bread slices, sprinkles bread with Salad Supreme and broils until bubbly.

PUMPKIN BREAD

1 cup sugar	1 teaspoon soda
½ cup packed light brown sugar	½ teaspoon salt
	½ teaspoon nutmeg
1 cup pumpkin	1½ teaspoons cinnamon
½ cup corn oil	¼ teaspoon ginger
2 eggs	1 cup raisins
2 cups sifted all-purpose flour	½ cup chopped nuts
	¼ cup water

Preheat oven to 350 degrees. Combine sugars, pumpkin, oil and eggs in bowl; mix well. Add sifted dry ingredients; mix well. Stir in raisins, nuts and water. Pour into well-oiled 5x9-inch loaf pan. Bake for 60 to 70 minutes or until loaf tests done. Remove to wire rack to cool. Yield: 1 loaf.

Anne Pierce, Delta Sigma
Statesboro, Georgia

CHOCOLATE CHIP-ZUCCHINI BREAD

3 eggs	1 cup chopped walnuts
2 cups sugar	3 cups sifted all-purpose flour
1 cup corn oil	
2 teaspoons vanilla extract	¼ teaspoon baking powder
2 cups grated unpeeled zucchini	
	1 teaspoon soda
1 cup miniature chocolate chips	1 teaspoon salt
	1 teaspoon cinnamon
1 tablespoon grated orange rind	1 teaspoon nutmeg

Preheat oven to 350 degrees. Beat eggs in mixer bowl until light and fluffy. Beat in sugar. Stir in oil and vanilla. Add zucchini, chocolate chips, orange rind, walnuts and sifted dry ingredients; mix well. Spoon into 2 greased 5x9-inch loaf pans. Bake for 50 to 60 minutes or until bread tests done. Remove from pans. Cool on wire rack. Chill before slicing. Yield: 2 loaves.

Ada Anderson, Laureate Delta
Spokane, Washington

PINEAPPLE AND ZUCCHINI BREAD

3 eggs, beaten	3 cups all-purpose flour
1 cup corn oil	2 teaspoons soda
2 cups sugar	1 teaspoon salt
2 teaspoons vanilla extract	½ teaspoon baking powder
2 cups coarsely shredded zucchini	
	1½ teaspoons cinnamon
1 8-ounce can crushed pineapple, drained	¾ teaspoon nutmeg
	1 cup nuts

Preheat oven to 350 degrees. Beat eggs with oil, sugar and vanilla in mixer bowl until thick. Stir in zucchini and pineapple. Mix flour, soda, salt, baking powder, cinnamon, nutmeg and nuts. Add to zucchini mixture; stir just until blended. Spoon into 2 greased and floured 5x9-inch pans. Bake for 1 hour or until loaves test done. Cool in pans for 10 minutes. Remove to wire racks to cool completely. Yield: 2 loaves.

Judy Woltz, Preceptor Lambda Theta
Simi Valley, California

STRAWBERRY BREAD

3 cups all-purpose flour	1¼ cups vegetable oil
1 teaspoon soda	½ cup chopped pecans
1 teaspoon salt	3 ounces cream cheese, softened
1 tablespoon cinnamon	
2 cups sugar	1 cup sifted confectioners' sugar
4 eggs	
2 10-ounce packages frozen strawberries	¼ teaspoon vanilla extract

Preheat oven to 350 degrees. Combine first 9 ingredients in bowl; mix well. Pour into 2 greased 5x9-inch loaf pans. Bake for 1 hour. Remove to wire rack to cool. Cut into thin slices. Combine cream cheese, confectioners' sugar and vanilla in bowl. Beat until smooth. Spread between slices of strawberry bread. Yield: 30 servings.

Melissa Stults, Alpha Tau
Wichita Falls, Texas

CHEESE BREAD

8 slices bacon, chopped	Dash of cayenne pepper
¼ cup mayonnaise	2 tablespoons melted butter
2 cups grated Cheddar cheese	
	1 loaf French bread, sliced
1 tablespoon grated onion	

Preheat oven to 350 degrees. Fry bacon in skillet until crisp. Combine mayonnaise, cheese, onion, cayenne pepper and butter in bowl; mix well. Spread mixture on both sides of bread. Top with bacon. Place on baking sheet. Bake for 10 to 15 minutes. Yield: 8 servings.

Louise Rada, Chi Delta
Blue Springs, Missouri

CHEESE HERB BREAD

2 tablespoons grated onion	¾ teaspoon prepared mustard
2 teaspoons lemon juice	1 tablespoon poppy seed
1 teaspoon Beau Monde seasoning	8 slices Swiss cheese
	1 long loaf French bread
1 cup margarine, softened	

Preheat oven to 325 degrees. Combine first 6 ingredients in bowl; mix well. Cut cheese slices in half diagonally. Cut bread in ½-inch slices, to but not through bottom. Spread each slice with margarine mixture. Place cheese between slices. Wrap in foil. Bake for 25 minutes. Yield: 10 servings.

Epsilon Omicron
Portage, Michigan

GARLIC AND CHEESE BREAD

4 ounces mozzarella cheese, shredded	2 tablespoons chopped parsley
¾ cup margarine	1 loaf French bread
⅓ cup chopped onion	Garlic salt to taste

Preheat oven to 375 degrees. Combine first 4 ingredients in bowl; mix well. Slice French bread. Spread each slice with margarine mixture; sprinkle with garlic salt. Reassemble loaf; wrap in foil. Bake for 15 minutes. Yield: 10 servings.

Jan Frank, Iota
Devils Lake, North Dakota

HICKORY CHEESE BREAD

1 16-ounce loaf French bread	1 tablespoon snipped parsley
½ cup butter or margarine, softened	½ teaspoon hickory-smoked salt
1 cup shredded sharp Cheddar cheese	2 teaspoons Worcestershire sauce

Preheat grill. Cut bread diagonally into 1-inch slices, to but not through bottom of loaf. Combine remaining ingredients in bowl; mix well. Spread between slices of bread. Wrap in heavy foil. Grill bread 5 to 6 inches from medium coals for 15 to 20 minutes or until heated through, turning once. Yield: 24 servings.

Judy Kutcher, Xi Zeta Mu
Eldridge, Iowa

SAVORY BREAD

½ cup melted butter	⅛ teaspoon thyme
¼ cup chopped parsley	⅛ teaspoon marjoram
¼ cup chopped green onions	Dash of garlic salt
	1 loaf French bread

Preheat oven to 400 degrees. Combine first 6 ingredients in bowl; mix well. Chill until thick. Slice bread to but not through bottom. Spread with butter mixture. Wrap in foil. Bake for 10 to 15 minutes. Yield: 3 to 4 servings.

Val Tyska, Xi Lambda Mu
Bartlett, Illinois

APPLESAUCE PUFFS

2 cups buttermilk baking mix	1 egg, slightly beaten
¼ cup sugar	2 teaspoons corn oil
1 teaspoon cinnamon	Melted margarine
½ cup applesauce	¼ cup sugar
¼ cup milk	¼ teaspoon cinnamon

Preheat oven to 400 degrees. Combine baking mix, ¼ cup sugar and 1 teaspoon cinnamon in bowl. Add applesauce, milk, egg and oil. Beat vigorously for 30 seconds. Fill greased muffin cups ⅔ full. Bake for 12 minutes or until golden. Cool slightly. Dip muffin tops into melted margarine, then into mixture of ¼ cup sugar and ¼ teaspoon cinnamon. Yield: 2 dozen.

Eleanore B. Lewnfield, Chi Nu
Englewood, Florida

BEST-EVER BANANA MUFFINS

3 large bananas, mashed	1 teaspoon soda
¾ cup sugar	1 teaspoon baking powder
1 egg, slightly beaten	½ teaspoon salt
⅓ cup melted butter	1½ cups all-purpose flour

Preheat oven to 375 degrees. Combine bananas, sugar, egg and butter in mixer bowl; beat until mixed. Add dry ingredients; mix well. Spoon into greased muffin cups. Bake for 20 minutes. Yield: 2 dozen.

Michelle Schuch, Mu Gamma
Brooklyn, Michigan

BLUEBERRY MUFFINS

2 eggs	⅓ cup sugar
¼ cup melted butter	1 tablespoon baking powder
¾ cup milk	
1 cup blueberries, drained	1 teaspoon grated orange rind
3¾ cups all-purpose flour	
¾ teaspoon salt	

Preheat oven to 425 degrees. Beat eggs in bowl. Blend in butter and milk. Coat blueberries with a small amount of sifted dry ingredients. Fold into egg mixture with rind. Stir in flour mixture quickly. Batter can be lumpy. Fill greased muffin cups ⅓ full. Bake for 15 minutes or until golden. Yield: 2½ to 3 dozen.

Marilynn Jossy, Preceptor Theta Rho
Thousand Oaks, California

BROWN SUGAR MUFFINS

2 cups all-purpose flour	½ cup butter
1 cup packed light brown sugar	1 cup chopped walnuts
	1 egg
1 teaspoon cinnamon	1 cup milk
1 teaspoon soda	2 teaspoons vanilla extract

Preheat oven to 400 degrees. Mix dry ingredients in large bowl. Cut in butter until crumbly. Add walnuts; mix well. Make well in center. Beat egg with milk and vanilla in bowl. Add to well in dry ingredients; mix just until moistened. Spoon into greased or paper-lined muffin cups. Bake for 12 to 15 minutes or until golden brown. Yield: 1½ to 2 dozen.

Loretta Hantt, Xi Theta
Pocatello, Idaho

OATMEAL MUFFINS

1 cup quick-cooking oats	1 cup all-purpose flour
1 cup buttermilk	1 teaspoon salt
1 egg, beaten	1 teaspoon baking powder
½ cup packed light brown sugar	½ teaspoon soda
	⅓ cup melted shortening

Preheat oven to 400 degrees. Mix oats and buttermilk in bowl. Let stand for 1 hour. Add egg, brown sugar, sifted dry ingredients and shortening, mixing well after each addition. Fill greased muffin cups ⅔ full. Bake for 20 minutes. Yield: 1 dozen.

Virginia DeMarais, Xi Upsilon Delta
Borrego Springs, California

ICEBOX GINGERBREAD MUFFINS

1 cup margarine, softened
1 cup sugar
4 eggs
1 cup molasses
½ cup raisins
½ cup chopped nuts
4 cups all-purpose flour
Pinch of salt
2 teaspoons ginger
½ teaspoon cinnamon
¼ teaspoon allspice
2 teaspoons soda
1 cup sour milk

Cream margarine and sugar in bowl. Add eggs and molasses; mix well. Coat raisins and nuts with a small amount of flour. Sift remaining flour with salt and spices. Stir soda into sour milk. Add flour mixture and milk to batter alternately, mixing well after each addition. Stir in nuts and raisins. Store in refrigerator for up to 1 month. Preheat oven to 400 degrees. Spoon into greased muffin cups. Bake for 15 to 18 minutes or until muffins test done. Yield: 4 dozen.

Elisabeth Ann Daniels, Preceptor Eta
Carrollton, Missouri

FRESH STRAWBERRY MUFFINS

1 cup chopped
   strawberries
1 tablespoon sugar
2 cups all-purpose flour
¾ cup sugar
2 teaspoons baking
   powder
1 teaspoon salt
3 eggs
¼ cup vegetable oil
½ cup milk
1 teaspoon grated orange
   rind
8 ounces cream cheese
¼ cup crushed
   strawberries

Preheat oven to 400 degrees. Sprinkle chopped strawberries with 1 tablespoon sugar; set aside. Sift dry ingredients into large bowl. Beat eggs in small bowl until light. Blend in oil, milk and orange rind. Add to flour mixture; stir for 10 to 15 strokes until mixed. Drain chopped berries; fold into batter. Fill paper-lined muffin cups ⅔ full. Bake for 15 minutes. Serve warm with cream cheese mixed with crushed strawberries. Yield: 1 dozen.

Linda Keef, Preceptor Iota Mu
Huntington Beach, California

SWEET POTATO MUFFINS

½ cup butter
1¼ cups sugar
1¼ cups mashed sweet
   potatoes
2 eggs
1½ cups all-purpose flour
2 teaspoons baking
   powder
1 teaspoon cinnamon
¼ tablespoon nutmeg
¼ teaspoon salt
1 cup milk
¼ cup chopped pecans
½ cup chopped raisins
Cinnamon-sugar

Preheat oven to 400 degrees. Have all ingredients at room temperature. Cream butter, sugar and sweet potatoes in bowl until smooth. Add eggs; blend well. Add sifted dry ingredients alternately with milk; do not overmix. Fold in pecans and raisins. Spoon into greased muffin cups; sprinkle cinnamon-sugar on top. Bake for 25 minutes. Yield: 2 dozen.

Martha Donaldson, Xi Gamma Rho
Columbus, Georgia

APPLE PANCAKES

4 cups all-purpose flour,
   sifted
¼ cup sugar
2 tablespoons baking
   powder
2 teaspoons salt
4 eggs, beaten
2 cups cottage cheese
½ cup yogurt
1 cup milk
3 tablespoons melted
   margarine
2 cups finely chopped
   apples

Sift dry ingredients into bowl. Mix eggs with cottage cheese, yogurt and milk in bowl. Pour into dry ingredients; mix well. Stir in margarine and apples. Ladle ¼ cup batter for each pancake onto hot greased griddle. Bake until brown on both sides, turning once. Yield: 3 dozen.

Sara Lovell, Gamma Epsilon
Henderson, Kentucky

BAKED APPLE PANCAKES

3 cups sliced peeled tart
   apples
3 tablespoons butter
⅓ cup sugar
1 teaspoon cinnamon
¾ cup buttermilk pancake
   mix
½ cup milk
3 eggs
1 teaspoon sugar

Preheat oven to 450 degrees. Sauté apple slices in butter in large skillet over low heat for 5 minutes or until tender. Pour into 10-inch pie plate. Mix sugar and cinnamon. Sprinkle half the mixture over apples. Combine pancake mix, milk, eggs and 1 teaspoon sugar in bowl; mix until smooth. Pour over apples; top with remaining cinnamon mixture. Bake for 12 to 15 minutes or until golden and set in center. Serve hot. Yield: 6 servings.

Karen Rudisill, Xi Delta
Reisterstown, Maryland

HOOTENANY PANCAKE

6 eggs
1 cup milk
1 cup all-purpose flour
1 teaspoon salt
½ cup margarine

Preheat oven to 425 degrees. Combine eggs and milk in mixer bowl. Beat for 3 to 5 minutes. Sift in flour and salt. Beat for 3 to 5 minutes longer. Melt margarine in 9x13-inch baking pan in oven. Pour batter into pan. Bake for 20 to 25 minutes or until golden. Cut into squares. Yield: 8 to 10 servings.

Pam Lopp, Xi Beta Zeta
Spokane, Washington

RICE PANCAKES

3 cups cooked rice
⅓ cup Parmesan cheese
¼ cup grated onion
3 eggs, slightly beaten
1 teaspoon salt
¼ teaspoon pepper

Combine all ingredients in bowl; mix well. Spoon ¼ cup portions onto hot greased griddle; flatten. Cook until golden brown. Serve with applesauce and sour cream. Yield: 6 to 8 servings.

Florence Shaw, Alpha Gamma
Aurora, Illinois

ANGEL WAFFLES

2⅓ cups all-purpose flour	1½ tablespoons sugar
4 teaspoons baking powder	2 eggs, beaten
¾ teaspoon salt	2¼ cups milk
	¾ cup corn oil

Sift dry ingredients into bowl. Beat eggs with milk and oil. Add to dry ingredients; mix just until moistened. Batter will be thin. Bake in preheated waffle iron.
Yield: 10 to 12 servings.

Vicky Dean, Delta Beta
Bessemer, Alabama

GERMAN WAFFLES

8 eggs, beaten	1 tablespoon honey
¾ cup butter, softened	1 teaspoon salt
1 cup sour cream	1 teaspoon vanilla extract
1½ cups all-purpose flour	½ cup (or more) milk

Mix eggs and butter in bowl. Add sour cream and ½ cup flour; mix well. Add remaining flour, honey, salt and vanilla. Add milk; beat until smooth. Bake in hot waffle iron. Serve with whipped cream and peaches, blueberries and strawberries. Yield: 5 servings.

Maxine Wegner, Omega
Sundance, Wyoming

MEXICAN WAFFLES

2 cups buttermilk baking mix	1⅓ cups milk
1 egg	1 cup Mexicorn
2 tablespoons corn oil	⅛ teaspoon red pepper

Combine first 4 ingredients in mixer bowl; beat until smooth. Fold in corn and pepper. Bake in hot waffle iron. Serve with Dutch Honey. Yield: 4 waffles.

DUTCH HONEY

1 cup packed light brown sugar	1 cup dark corn syrup
	1 cup sour cream

Mix all ingredients in saucepan. Bring mixture to a boil, stirring constantly; reduce heat. Simmer for 5 minutes. Serve hot or cold on waffles, pancakes or ice cream. Store in refrigerator.

Janice Venrick, Preceptor Beta Psi
Akron, Colorado

COTTAGE CHEESE ROLLS

½ cup whipping cream	¼ cup sugar
1 cup packed light brown sugar	1 cup cottage cheese
¼ cup chopped pecans	1 egg
1¾ cups all-purpose flour	¼ cup margarine, softened
⅛ teaspoon salt	¼ cup sugar
1½ teaspoons baking powder	1 teaspoon cinnamon
⅛ teaspoon soda	

Preheat oven to 375 degrees. Mix whipping cream, brown sugar and pecans in bowl. Pour into 9-inch round cake pan. Mix next 5 dry ingredients in bowl. Add cottage cheese and egg; mix well. Shape into ball. Roll on floured surface. Spread with margarine. Sprinkle with mixture of ¼ cup sugar and cinnamon. Roll as for jelly roll. Cut into 12 slices. Place cut side down in prepared pan. Bake for 20 to 25 minutes or until golden brown.
Yield: 1 dozen.

Tami Brown, Mu Epsilon
Colby, Kansas

QUICK BREAD STICKS

12 day-old hot dog buns	1 teaspoon dried dillweed, crushed
1 cup butter, softened	¼ teaspoon garlic powder
1 teaspoon sweet basil leaves	

Preheat oven to 250 degrees. Cut buns into quarters lengthwise. Combine remaining ingredients in small bowl; mix well. Spread on cut sides of buns. Place on baking sheets. Bake for 1 to 1½ hours or until crisp.
Yield: 4 dozen.

Vicki G. Prescott, Xi Zeta Eta
St. John, Kansas

SWEDISH ALMOND RUSKS

1 cup sugar	3 cups all-purpose flour
1 cup butter, softened	1 teaspoon baking powder
3 tablespoons milk	⅛ teaspoon soda
2 eggs, beaten	¼ teaspoon salt
1 teaspoon almond extract	½ cup chopped almonds

Preheat oven to 350 degrees. Cream sugar and butter in mixer bowl. Add milk, eggs and almond extract; mix well. Add dry ingredients and almonds; mix well. Pat into 2 loaf pans. Bake for 30 to 35 minutes or until golden. Cool and slice. Reduce temperature to 325 degrees. Arrange slices on baking sheet. Bake for several minutes; turn slices over. Turn off oven. Let stand in closed oven until dry. Yield: 1½ dozen.

Sally Finch Nelson, Xi Iota Zeta
Galva, Illinois

SOPAIPILLAS

1 cup all-purpose flour	¼ cup buttermilk
1 teaspoon baking powder	¼ cup water
½ teaspoon salt	Oil for deep frying
1 teaspoon shortening	

Mix dry ingredients and shortening in bowl. Add buttermilk and water; mix well. Roll to ¼-inch or less thickness on floured surface. Cut into 3-inch triangles and squares. Deep-fry in hot oil until brown, basting with hot oil. Drain on paper towels. Serve warm with honey.
Yield: 20 sopaipillas.

Julie Guyer, Xi Beta Iota
Cortez, Colorado

TORTILLAS DE HARINA

4 cups all-purpose flour
2 teaspoons salt
2 teaspoons baking
  powder
¼ cup shortening
1½ cups (about) warm
  water

Combine dry ingredients in bowl. Cut in shortening until crumbly. Make well in center. Add water gradually, mixing until medium dough forms. Knead until smooth. Let rest, covered, for 10 minutes. Shape into egg-sized balls. Roll each into 6-inch circle. Heat griddle or skillet over medium-high heat. Cook tortillas 1 at a time for about 1 minute on each side or until lightly speckled. Yield: 1 dozen.

Cleo B. Valdez, Xi Beta Lambda
Los Ojos, New Mexico

COMPANY FRENCH TOAST

½ cup margarine
1 cup packed light brown
  sugar
1 teaspoon cinnamon
12 slices white bread
3 or 4 eggs
1½ cups milk

Melt margarine in 9x13-inch baking pan. Stir in brown sugar and cinnamon. Place bread slices in double layer over sugar mixture. Beat eggs and milk in bowl. Pour over bread slices. Chill, covered, in refrigerator overnight. Preheat oven to 350 degrees. Bake, uncovered, for 45 minutes. Cut into squares. Invert onto serving plate. Serve with warm syrup, fresh fruit or sprinkle of confectioners' sugar. Yield: 12 servings.

Virginia R. Matlock, Preceptor Beta Mu
Indianapolis, Indiana

COLORADO CRUNCH

3 eggs
¼ cup milk
½ teaspoon vanilla extract
8 to 10 pieces Texas Toast
2 teaspoons
  cinnamon-sugar
½ cup butter
Strawberry preserves
Syrup
¼ cup confectioners'
  sugar

Preheat griddle. Combine eggs, milk and vanilla in bowl; mix well. Dip Texas toast into egg mixture. Place on hot greased griddle. Sprinkle with cinnamon-sugar. Cook until golden brown on both sides. Serve with butter, strawberry preserves, syrup or sprinkle of confectioners' sugar. Yield: 8 to 10 servings.

Zeta Epsilon
Carbondale, Colorado

YORKSHIRE PUDDING

1¼ cups milk
1¼ cups all-purpose flour
½ teaspoon salt
3 eggs

Preheat oven to 450 degrees. Grease popover cups generously with shortening. Beat milk, flour and salt in medium bowl with wire whisk until well blended; do not overbeat. Add eggs, 1 at a time, beating just until blended after each addition. Preheat popover cups in oven until shortening melts but does not smoke. Pour batter into hot cups, filling ⅔ full; do not scrape bowl. Bake for 20 minutes. Reduce temperature to 350 degrees. Bake for 15 to 20 minutes or until brown. Serve immediately with roast beef and gravy. Yield: 6 to 8 servings.

Judy Guthrie, Gamma Delta
Edmond, Oklahoma

YEAST BISCUITS

1 package dry yeast
½ cup (115-degree) water
5 cups self-rising flour
½ teaspoon soda
1 tablespoon sugar
2 cups buttermilk
¾ cup vegetable oil

Dissolve yeast in warm water in bowl. Sift flour and soda together into bowl. Add yeast mixture and sugar; mix well. Add buttermilk and oil; mix well. Roll out and cut on floured surface; cut with biscuit cutter. Place on baking sheet. Let rise for 2 hours. Preheat oven to 400 degrees. Bake for 7 minutes or until golden brown. Yield: 12 servings.

Cindy Levens, Epsilon Beta
Palm Bay, Florida

FREEZER CHEESE DANISH

16 ounces cream cheese,
  softened
½ cup sugar
1 tablespoon grated lemon
  rind
2 egg whites
1½ cups all-purpose flour
⅓ cup sugar
1 teaspoon salt
2 packages dry yeast
1 cup margarine, softened
1⅓ cups (120-degree)
  water
2 eggs, at room
  temperature
¾ to 1¼ cups all-purpose
  flour

Blend first 3 ingredients in bowl. Add 2 egg whites gradually; mix well. Set aside. Combine 1½ cups flour, sugar, salt and dry yeast in mixer bowl. Add margarine; mix well. Add water gradually. Beat at medium speed for 2 minutes. Add eggs and ½ cup flour. Beat at high speed for 2 minutes. Stir in enough remaining flour to make soft dough. Let rest, covered, for 20 minutes. Divide into 24 balls. Roll each ball into 8-inch rope. Coil on greased baking sheet. Make wide indentation in center of coil. Spoon 2 tablespoons prepared filling into indentations. Freeze until firm if desired. Store in plastic bag in freezer for up to 4 weeks. Thaw for 1¾ hours before second rising. Let rise, loosely covered, in warm place for 45 minutes or until more than doubled in bulk. Preheat oven to 375 degrees. Bake for 15 to 20 minutes or until golden. Cool on wire racks. Drizzle with confectioners' sugar glaze or dust with confectioners' sugar. Yield: 2 dozen.

Barbara A. Scherer, Nu Xi
Lansing, Kansas

AFRICAN HONEY BREAD

1 package dry yeast	¼ teaspoon cloves
¼ cup (110-degree) water	1 teaspoon salt
1 egg	1 cup lukewarm milk
½ cup honey	¼ cup melted butter
1 tablespoon coriander	4 to 5 cups all-purpose
½ teaspoon cinnamon	flour

Dissolve yeast in lukewarm water. Let stand in warm place for 5 minutes or until bubbly. Combine egg, honey, coriander, cinnamon, cloves and salt in deep bowl; mix with wire whisk. Add yeast mixture, milk and melted butter; beat until well blended. Stir in flour, ½ cup at a time, until dough forms soft ball. Knead on lightly floured surface for 10 minutes or until smooth and elastic. Place in large lightly greased bowl. Let rise, covered, with towel, until doubled in bulk. Spread melted butter over the bottom and side of 3-quart soufflé dish. Punch dough down. Knead lightly for about 2 minutes. Shape into ball. Place in prepared dish, pressing gently to cover bottom of dish completely. Let rise, covered with towel, until doubled in bulk. Dough rises very slowly; rising time may vary up to 2½ hours. Preheat oven to 300 degrees. Bake for 50 to 60 minutes or until top is crusty and golden brown. Yield: 1 loaf.

Jill Spears, Alpha Upsilon Psi
The Colony, Texas

BULGUR WHEAT BREAD

2 packages dry yeast	1 tablespoon salt
½ cup (115-degree) water	½ cup honey
1 cup dry bulgur wheat	6 to 7 cups unbleached
3 cups boiling water	white flour
2 tablespoons corn oil	Butter

Dissolve yeast in warm water in bowl; mix well. Combine bulgur, boiling water, oil, salt and honey in bowl. Cool to lukewarm. Add yeast and flour; mix well. Knead on lightly floured surface until dough is smooth and elastic. Place in greased bowl. Let rise until doubled in bulk. Place in 3 well-greased loaf pans. Let rise until doubled in bulk. Preheat oven to 350 degrees. Bake for 45 minutes. Remove from pans. Brush tops with butter. Yield: 3 loaves.

Lana Smith, Xi Gamma Zeta
Stanberry, Missouri

CAKE BREAD

1 package dry yeast	2 eggs, beaten
¼ cup (115-degree) water	2 teaspoons vanilla extract
1 cup milk, scalded	1 teaspoon salt
½ cup butter or margarine	4 to 4½ cups all-purpose
½ cup sugar	flour

Dissolve yeast in warm water. Combine milk, butter and sugar in large bowl. Cool to lukewarm. Reserve 1 tablespoon egg. Add remaining eggs, vanilla, salt and yeast mixture to milk mixture. Add flour gradually, beating well after each addition. Let rise, covered, for 1 hour or until doubled in bulk. Stir dough down. Let rise for 45 minutes or until doubled in bulk. Pour into 2 well-greased loaf pans. Let rise for 45 minutes or until light. Preheat oven to 350 degrees. Brush with reserved egg. Bake for 25 to 30 minutes or until golden. Wrap in foil to store. Yield: 1 loaf.

Blanche Elliott, Xi Eta Beta
Madrid, Iowa

EGG TWIST BREAD

1 cup whole wheat flour	½ cup water
1 cup all-purpose flour	½ cup milk
2 packages instant dry	2 tablespoons shortening
yeast	3 eggs, slightly beaten
2 tablespoons sugar	2 to 2½ cups all-purpose
2 teaspoons salt	flour

Combine first 5 ingredients in large mixer bowl; mix well. Heat water, milk and shortening in saucepan. Add to flour mixture. Reserve 1 tablespoon egg for glaze. Beat in remaining eggs at low speed until moistened. Beat at medium speed for 3 minutes. Stir in enough remaining flour gradually to make firm dough. Knead on floured surface for 5 minutes or until smooth and elastic. Place in greased bowl, turning to grease surface. Let rise, covered, in warm place for 1 hour or until doubled in bulk. Punch dough down. Divide into three 15-inch rope-like portions. Braid loosely on greased baking sheet; tuck ends under. Let rise, covered, for 30 minutes or until doubled in bulk. Brush with reserved egg. Preheat oven to 400 degrees. Bake for 25 minutes or until golden. Yield: 1 braid.

Elizabeth Bellanti, Preceptor Theta
Milwaukee, Wisconsin

FOOD PROCESSOR FRENCH BREAD

1½ cups (115-degree)	⅓ cup chopped fresh
water	herbs
1½ packages dry yeast	3½ cups all-purpose flour
2 teaspoons sugar	1 egg, beaten
2 teaspoons salt	

Combine water, yeast and sugar in bowl. Let stand for 5 minutes or until foamy. Combine salt, fresh herbs and flour in food processor fitted with steel blade. Process for 5 seconds. Add yeast mixture and additional flour if mixture is too soft, processing constantly. Knead on floured surface until smooth and elastic. Shape into 2 long loaves on greased baking sheet. Make slashes in top. Let rise until doubled in bulk. Preheat oven to 350 degrees. Brush tops of loaves with egg. Bake for 15 to 20 minutes or until loaves test done. Cool on wire rack. Yield: 2 loaves.

Pam Allen, Theta Iota
Aurelia, Iowa

MOM'S MONKEY BREAD

1¼ packages dry yeast
2 cups (115-degree) water
6 tablespoons (heaping) shortening
½ cup sugar
6 cups all-purpose flour
1½ tablespoons salt
¾ cup melted butter

Dissolve yeast in water in bowl. Add next 4 ingredients; mix well. Knead on floured surface, adding enough flour to make stiff dough. Roll out to ½-inch thickness. Cut into 2 or 3-inch triangles. Dip triangles into butter. Place in large tube pan, overlapping triangles. Let rise for 1½ hours. Preheat oven to 350 degrees. Bake for 40 to 45 minutes or until bread tests done. Invert onto plate. Brush with butter. Yield: 12 servings.

Cindy Phillips, Eta Rho
Clarksville, Arkansas

ONION-HERB BREAD

2 loaves frozen bread dough, thawed
2 tablespoons parsley flakes
½ cup melted butter
1 small onion, chopped
2 teaspoons garlic salt

Slice bread dough. Combine parsley flakes, butter, onion and garlic salt in bowl. Dip bread dough into butter mixture; place in bundt pan. Let rise for 1½ hours. Preheat oven to 350 degrees. Bake for 30 minutes. Invert onto serving plate. Yield: 18 to 20 servings.

Carol McDowell, Beta Rho
Ankeny, Iowa

OVERNIGHT OATMEAL BREAD

2 packages dry yeast
¼ cup sugar
½ cup (115-degree) water
1¾ cups scalded milk, cooled
3 tablespoons margarine
2 tablespoons molasses
2 teaspoons salt (optional)
5 to 6 cups all-purpose flour
1 cup quick-cooking oats
Vegetable oil

Dissolve yeast and 1 teaspoon sugar in warm water in mixer bowl. Let stand until bubbly. Add remaining sugar, milk, margarine, molasses, salt and 2 cups flour. Beat at medium speed until smooth. Add 1 cup flour and oats. Beat until smooth. Mix in enough additional flour to make soft dough. Knead on floured surface for about 10 minutes or until smooth and elastic for about 10 minutes. Cover with plastic wrap and towel. Let rest for 10 minutes. Shape into 2 loaves; place in loaf pans. Brush tops with oil; cover with plastic wrap. Chill for 2 to 24 hours. Preheat oven to 375 degrees. Let dough stand at room temperature for 10 minutes. Puncture any large bubbles with toothpick. Bake for 30 to 40 minutes or until brown. Cover with foil to prevent overbrowning if necessary. Yield: 2 loaves.

 Helen Robinson, Gamma Delta
Yale, Iowa

PEPPERONI LOAVES

2 1-pound loaves frozen bread dough
¼ cup Italian salad dressing
4 ounces pepperoni, sliced
8 ounces mozzarella cheese, grated

Thaw bread dough in package in refrigerator overnight. Divide into 2 portions. Place each portion in greased bowl. Let rise for 2 to 3 hours or until doubled in bulk. Preheat oven to 350 degrees. Roll each portion into 5x9-inch rectangle on floured surface. Brush with Italian salad dressing. Arrange pepperoni on each rectangle. Sprinkle mozzarella cheese over pepperoni. Roll each rectangle as for jelly roll from long edge. Place rolls, seam side down, on baking sheet. Bake for 30 minutes. Let stand for 10 minutes. Cut into thin slices. Yield: 4 loaves.

Janice Vogt, Rho Chi
Highland, Illinois

HJORDIS' SWEDISH RYE BREAD

2 packages compressed yeast
1 tablespoon salt
2 cups lukewarm milk
2 cups lukewarm water
1 egg, beaten
½ cup corn syrup
3 cups (scant) rye flour
9 cups (or less) all-purpose flour

Combine yeast, salt, milk, water, egg and corn syrup in large bowl; mix well. Stir in rye flour. Add all-purpose flour gradually; mix well. Let rise, covered, until doubled in bulk. Divide into 8 to 10 portions. Roll each to size of dinner plate and about 1 inch thick. Prick with fork on both sides. Cut out center with 2-inch cutter. Place on greased baking sheets. Let rise until doubled in bulk. Preheat oven to 425 degrees. Prick loaves with fork if necessary. Bake for 10 minutes. Cut into wedges. Yield: 8 to 10 loaves.

Betty Lou Lindstrom, Laureate Beta Epsilon
Port Angeles, Washington

WHOLE WHEAT BREAD

¼ cup molasses
½ cup hot water
3 tablespoons yeast
2 tablespoons honey
1 cup (115-degree) water
1½ cups whole wheat flour
1 tablespoon (or less) salt
2 cups water

Mix molasses and ½ cup hot water; cool. Dissolve yeast and honey in 1 cup warm water; set aside. Combine whole wheat flour and salt in large glass bowl. Microwave on Low until warm. Mix cooled molasses and yeast mixtures together. Add to warm flour mixture; mix well. Add 2 cups water; mix well. Spoon into 2 greased loaf pans. Dough will be sticky. Let rise for 1 hour. Preheat oven to 350 degrees. Bake for 40 minutes. Yield: 2 loaves.

Sheila Powell, Xi Eta
Spearfish, South Dakota

MAID SERVICE PANCAKES

6 eggs, beaten
4 cups buttermilk
1/4 cup vegetable oil
1 package dry yeast
1 cup cream
4 cups all-purpose flour

2 tablespoons baking
   powder
2 tablespoons soda
2 tablespoons sugar
1 teaspoon salt

Combine first 5 ingredients in bowl; mix well. Add flour, baking powder, soda, sugar and salt; mix well. Refrigerate, in covered container, overnight to 1 week. Bake on hot griddle as needed. Serve with ice cream and honey. Yield: 2 dozen.

JoAnn Williamson, Xi Epsilon Chi
Fulton, Missouri

PRETZELS

1 package dry yeast
1 teaspoon sugar
1/4 cup (115-degree) water
2 1/2 cups all-purpose flour
1/4 teaspoon salt

10 tablespoons milk
1 tablespoon butter
2 tablespoons soda
2 cups water
Coarse salt

Preheat oven to 400 degrees. Dissolve yeast and 1 teaspoon sugar in warm water in bowl. Combine flour and salt in bowl. Add yeast mixture, milk and butter; mix well. Knead for 10 minutes. Let rise until doubled in bulk. Cut dough into 8 or 10 pieces. Shape into pretzels. Let rise for 20 to 30 minutes. Mix soda and water in saucepan. Bring to a boil. Cook pretzels, 1 at a time, in boiling water for 10 seconds on each side. Place on baking sheet. Sprinkle with salt. Bake for 10 to 12 minutes or until golden. Yield: 8 to 12 pretzels.

Waltraud Jewett, Xi Lambda
Deadwood, South Dakota

AUNT WILMA'S ICEBOX ROLLS

1 package dry yeast
1/2 teaspoon sugar
1 cup (115-degree) water
2 eggs
3/4 cup sugar
2 teaspoons salt

1/2 cup margarine,
   sliced
1 cup boiling water
5 1/2 cups all-purpose flour
Melted butter

Dissolve yeast and 1/2 teaspoon sugar in warm water in bowl. Beat eggs very lightly in mixer bowl. Add 3/4 cup sugar, salt and margarine. Stir in boiling water. Cool to lukewarm. Add yeast mixture and flour; mix well. Let stand at room temperature for 30 minutes. Refrigerate, covered, for several hours to overnight. Knead on lightly floured surface. Roll out and cut as desired. Place in pan with melted butter; brush with butter. Let rise for 3 hours. Preheat oven to 375 degrees. Bake for 15 minutes. Yield: 4 dozen.

Judith Meier, Eta Pi
Pocahontas, Arkansas

BASIC ROLLS

2 packages dry yeast
1/3 cup (115-degree) water
1 cup shortening
3 cups milk, scalded
1 cup sugar

2 eggs, slightly beaten
8 to 9 cups all-purpose
   flour
1 teaspoon soda
1 teaspoon baking powder

Dissolve yeast in water. Melt shortening in milk in bowl. Add sugar. Cool to lukewarm. Mix in remaining ingredients. Let rise, covered, until doubled in bulk. Punch dough down. Store, covered, in refrigerator for up to 1 week. Preheat oven to 350 degrees. Roll dough on floured surface. Cut with biscuit cutter; fold in half. Place in greased baking pan. Bake for 15 to 20 minutes. Yield: 5 dozen.

CARAMEL NUT ROLLS

1 recipe Basic Rolls
Melted butter
Cinnamon-sugar
1/2 cup packed light brown
   sugar

1/3 cup melted margarine
1 tablespoon dark corn
   syrup
2/3 cup pecans

Roll basic dough into 1/4-inch thick rectangles. Brush with butter; sprinkle with cinnamon-sugar. Roll as for jelly roll; slice 1 inch thick. Combine remaining ingredients in baking pan. Arrange rolls on top. Let rise until doubled in bulk. Bake as for rolls.

CARAMEL NUT RING

Roll basic dough into rectangle. Brush with butter; sprinkle with cinnamon-sugar. Roll as for jelly roll. Shape into ring on greased baking sheet. Make cuts every 3/4 inch to within 1/2 inch of bottom. Twist slices alternately to inside and outside of ring. Insert generous amount of mixed nuts into dough. Let rise until doubled in bulk. Preheat oven to 350 degrees. Bake until golden brown. Cool slightly. Drizzle caramel icing over ring.

FRUIT CRUMB COFFEE CAKE

1/2 cup margarine, softened
1 cup confectioners' sugar
Pinch of salt
1 egg, beaten

2 cups all-purpose flour
1 recipe Basic Rolls
1 21-ounce can fruit pie
   filling

Beat margarine and confectioners' sugar in mixer bowl until smooth. Mix in salt, egg and enough flour to make dry crumbly mixture. Crumble onto towel. Let dry for 4 hours to overnight. Roll basic dough into large rectangle; fit into greased baking pan. Spoon fruit filling in lengthwise strips 2 inches from each long edge; fold dough over filling from each side. Spoon filling down middle. Brush with margarine; sprinkle generously with crumb mixture. Let rise until doubled in bulk. Preheat oven to 350 degrees. Bake for 15 minutes or until golden brown. Cool. Drizzle with vanilla icing.

Jini Rosenstengel, Preceptor Alpha Omega
Desloge, Missouri

CINNAMON AND NUT ROLLS

2 packages dry yeast
¼ cup (115-degree) water
2 cups milk, scalded
½ cup shortening
½ cup sugar
2 teaspoons salt
2 eggs, well beaten
7 cups all-purpose flour, sifted
Softened butter

2 teaspoons cinnamon
1 cup sugar
1½ cups margarine
1½ cups packed light brown sugar
¼ cup milk
2 tablespoons light corn syrup
1½ cups chopped nuts

Dissolve yeast in water. Combine milk, shortening, ½ cup sugar, salt and eggs in large bowl. Add yeast. Add 4 cups flour, 2 cups at a time, mixing well with electric mixer after each addition. Stir in 1¼ cups flour with wooden spoon. Knead in 1½ cups flour on floured board. Knead until smooth and elastic. Place in greased bowl, turning to grease surface. Let rise for 1 hour or until doubled in bulk. Punch dough down. Let rise again. Roll into rectangle. Spread with softened butter; sprinkle with mixture of cinnamon and 1 cup sugar. Roll as for jelly roll; slice. Melt ¾ cup margarine in each of two 9x13-inch baking pans. Add ¾ cup brown sugar, 2 tablespoons milk, 1 tablespoon corn syrup and ¾ cup nuts to each; mix well. Arrange rolls in prepared pans. Let rise until doubled in bulk. Preheat oven to 375 degrees. Bake for 25 to 30 minutes or until golden brown. Invert onto plates. Yield: 4 dozen.

Patricia J. Austin, Xi Beta Lambda
Derby, Kansas

CINNAMON TWIST ROLLS

1¾ cups all-purpose flour
¾ cup sugar
1 teaspoon salt
2 packages dry yeast
1 cup milk
⅔ cup water
¼ cup margarine
½ cup all-purpose flour

2 eggs, at room temperature
3¾ to 4¾ cups all-purpose flour
¾ cup raisins
Butter, softened
¾ cup sugar
2 teaspoons cinnamon

Combine first 4 ingredients in large mixer bowl; set aside. Heat milk, water and margarine in saucepan until very warm, 120 to 130 degrees. Add to flour mixture. Beat at medium speed for 2 minutes. Add ½ cup flour and eggs. Beat at high speed for 2 minutes. Stir in raisins. Add enough remaining flour to make stiff dough. Knead on floured surface for 8 to 10 minutes or until smooth and elastic. Cover with plastic wrap and towel. Let rest for 20 minutes. Divide into 2 portions. Roll each portion, ¼ inch thick. Brush center with butter. Sprinkle with mixture of ¾ cup sugar and cinnamon. Fold left side over center to cover filling; fold right side over top. Seal edges. Cut crosswise into 1-inch strips. Twist and place in greased baking pan. Cover with oiled waxed paper. Chill for 2 to 24 hours. Let stand for 15 minutes. Preheat oven to 375 degrees. Bake for 25 to 30 minutes. Yield: 2 dozen.

Connie Sprague, Xi Alpha Theta
Kennedy, New York

FAMOUS CINNAMON ROLLS

2 packages dry yeast
1 tablespoon sugar
½ cup (115-degree) water
1 cup mashed potatoes
1 cup shortening
1 cup (115-degree) potato water
2 eggs, beaten
¼ cup sugar
2 teaspoons salt

1 cup (115-degree) water
7 to 8 cups all-purpose flour
Butter, melted
Cinnamon-sugar
Raisins
Chopped nuts
1 recipe confectioners' sugar icing

Dissolve yeast and 1 tablespoon sugar in ½ cup water. Combine next 6 ingredients in bowl; mix well. Add yeast; mix well. Add remaining 1 cup water; mix well. Stir in flour. Knead on floured surface until smooth and elastic. Place in greased bowl, turning to grease surface. Let rise for 1½ hours or until doubled in bulk. Divide into 3 portions. Roll each portion into 9x13-inch rectangle. Spread with melted butter. Sprinkle with cinnamon-sugar. Sprinkle with raisins and nuts; roll as for jelly roll. Cut into 1½-inch thick slices. Place cut side up in 9x13-inch baking pans. Let rise for 1 hour or until doubled in bulk. Preheat oven to 350 degrees. Bake for 20 to 25 minutes. Glaze with favorite confectioners' sugar icing. Yield: 40 rolls.

Diana Dee Fink, Preceptor Beta
Anchorage, Alaska

MOM'S HOMEMADE CINNAMON ROLLS

4 packages dry yeast
2⅔ cups (110-degree) water
1 cup sugar
⅓ cup shortening
½ cup nonfat dry milk powder

4 eggs
8 cups all-purpose flour
1 tablespoon salt
1 cup melted margarine
½ cup sugar
¼ cup cinnamon

Dissolve yeast in water in bowl. Add 1 cup sugar, shortening, milk powder and eggs. Add 4 cups flour and salt; mix well. Add remaining flour; mix well. Let rise, covered, for 1 hour or until doubled in bulk. Roll on floured surface. Sprinkle with margarine, ½ cup sugar and cinnamon. Roll as for jelly roll; slice. Place on baking sheet. Let rise for 30 minutes. Preheat oven to 350 degrees. Bake for 10 to 15 minutes or until golden. Yield: 2½ dozen.

Denise Karst, Epsilon Tau
Towanda, Kansas

COTTAGE CHEESE CINNAMON ROLLS

¼ cup margarine
½ cup packed light brown sugar
¼ cup chopped pecans
1¾ cups all-purpose flour
⅛ teaspoon salt
1½ teaspoons baking powder

⅛ teaspoon soda
¼ cup sugar
1 cup cottage cheese
1 egg
¼ cup margarine, softened
¼ cup sugar
1 teaspoon cinnamon

Preheat oven to 375 degrees. Melt margarine with brown sugar in saucepan and spread in 8-inch baking pan. Sprinkle with pecans. Combine dry ingredients in bowl. Add cottage cheese and egg; mix well. Knead to form ball. Flour surface of dough. Roll out on floured surface. Brush with ¼ cup softened margarine. Sprinkle with ¼ cup sugar and 1 teaspoon cinnamon. Roll as for jell roll. Cut into 12 pieces with a sharp knife and place in pan. Bake for 20 minutes or until golden brown. Invert onto serving plate. Yield: 12 servings.

Susan Volkland, Omicron
Pawnee Rock, Kansas

CREAM CHEESE ROLLS

1 cup sour cream	*¾ cup sugar*
2 packages dry yeast	*1 egg, beaten*
½ cup (115-degree) water	*⅛ teaspoon salt*
½ cup sugar	*2 teaspoons vanilla extract*
1 teaspoon salt	*2 cups confectioners'*
½ cup melted butter	*sugar*
2 eggs, beaten	*¼ cup milk*
4 cups all-purpose flour	*2 teaspoons vanilla extract*
16 ounces cream cheese, softened	

Heat sour cream in saucepan. Dissolve yeast in water. Combine sour cream, yeast and next 5 ingredients in bowl; mix well. Chill, tightly covered, overnight. Combine cream cheese, ¾ cup sugar, 1 egg, ⅛ teaspoon salt and 2 teaspoons vanilla in mixer bowl. Beat until light and fluffy. Divide dough into 4 portions. Roll each portion into 8x12-inch rectangle on floured surface. Spread cream cheese mixture down center of rectangle, spreading to ends. Roll as for jelly roll; seal edges. Place on baking sheet. Shape into ring if desired. Let rise for 1 hour. Preheat oven to 375 degrees. Bake for 12 minutes or until golden. Drizzle mixture of remaining ingredients over warm rolls. Cut into slices. Yield: 4 dozen.

Kathy Drake, Nu Chi
Bolivar, Missouri

CRESCENT ROLLS

1 package dry yeast	*1 teaspoon salt*
¼ cup (115-degree) water	*½ teaspoon soda*
1 cup milk, scalded	*2 eggs*
½ cup corn oil	*4 cups all-purpose flour*
½ cup sugar	

Dissolve yeast in water in bowl. Combine milk, oil, sugar, salt, soda, eggs, yeast and flour in bowl in order listed, mixing well after each addition. Cover with plastic wrap. Let stand at room temperature overnight. Knead lightly on floured surface. Divide into 3 portions. Roll each portion into circle. Cut each circle into 12 wedges. Roll up from wide edge; shape into crescents. Place 1 inch apart on greased baking sheet. Let rise, covered, for 2 hours. Preheat oven to 350 degrees. Bake until golden. Yield: 3 dozen.

Carol Bosch, Xi Gamma Eta
Clay Center, Kansas

CRUSTY ROLLS

1 loaf frozen bread dough	*1 teaspoon poppy seed*
⅓ cup seasoned bread crumbs	*2 tablespoons melted butter*

Thaw dough. Divide into 12 portions. Shape into rolls. Combine crumbs and seed. Coat rolls with butter; roll in crumb mixture. Place 3 inches apart on greased baking sheet. Let rise, covered, for 1½ hours or until doubled in bulk. Preheat oven to 375 degrees. Bake for 15 to 20 minutes or until brown. Yield: 1 dozen.

Mary Perroni, Epsilon Kappa
Fairfax, Virginia

HUNGARIAN BUTTERHORNS

4 cups sifted all-purpose flour	*½ cup sour cream*
½ teaspoon salt	*1 teaspoon vanilla extract*
2 cakes yeast, crumbled	*3 egg whites*
1¼ cups butter	*1 cup sugar*
4 egg yolks, beaten	*1 pound pecans, chopped*
	1 teaspoon vanilla extract

Combine first 3 ingredients in bowl. Cut in butter until crumbly. Add egg yolks, sour cream and 1 teaspoon vanilla; mix well. Shape into roll; wrap in waxed paper. Chill in refrigerator. Beat egg whites in bowl until stiff peaks form. Add sugar gradually, beating until very stiff peaks form. Fold in pecans and 1 teaspoon vanilla. Preheat oven to 400 degrees. Divide dough into 8 portions. Roll each portion into 9-inch circle on surface sprinkled with confectioners' sugar. Cut each circle into 12 wedges. Spread 1 teaspoon filling on each wedge. Roll up from wide edge. Place on baking sheet. Bake for 15 to 18 minutes or until golden. Cool on wire rack. Yield: 6 dozen.

Peggy Switzer, Rho Chi
Highland, Illinois

MORMON ROLLS

7 cups all-purpose flour	*½ cup sugar*
½ teaspoon soda	*2 packages dry yeast*
2 teaspoons baking powder	*4 cups milk, scalded*
2 teaspoons salt	*½ cup vegetable oil*

Mix flour, soda, baking powder, salt, sugar and yeast in large bowl. Add warm milk and oil; mix well. Pour into large wide-mouthed jar; cover with cloth. Chill for 4 hours or longer. Preheat oven to 450 degrees. Pour desired amount of dough onto floured surface. Pat to desired thickness; cut with biscuit cutter. Brush with oil; fold over. Place on baking sheet. Bake for 15 to 20 minutes. Store remaining dough in refrigerator for up to 2 weeks. Yield: 3 to 4 dozen.

Juanita B. Hardin, Laureate Iota
Jonesboro, Arkansas

OVERNIGHT REFRIGERATOR ROLLS

2 packages dry yeast
2½ cups (115-degree) water
¾ cup shortening
¾ cup sugar
2 eggs, beaten
8 to 8½ cups all-purpose flour
2½ teaspoons salt

Dissolve yeast in water in bowl. Add shortening, sugar, eggs, 4 cups flour and salt. Beat until smooth. Add remaining flour; mix well. Chill, covered, overnight. Shape into rolls; place in greased baking pan. Let rise, covered, for 1 hour. Preheat oven to 400 degrees. Bake for 15 to 20 minutes or until brown. Yield: 3 dozen.

JoAnn Williamson, Xi Epsilon Chi
Fulton, Missouri

SOUR CREAM AND PECAN TEA RING

2 packages dry yeast
¾ cup warm (115-degree) water
½ cup melted margarine
1 cup sour cream
½ cup sugar
1½ teaspoons salt
1 egg
5½ to 6½ cups flour
Melted margarine
1 cup chopped pecans
½ cup packed light brown sugar
½ teaspoon cinnamon

Dissolve yeast in warm water. Combine margarine, sour cream, sugar and salt in large bowl. Add yeast, egg and 3 cups flour; beat until smooth. Add enough remaining flour to make stiff dough. Knead on floured surface for 8 to 10 minutes. Place in greased bowl, turning to grease surface. Let rise, covered, for 1¼ hours until doubled in bulk. Punch dough down. Let rest, covered, for 15 minutes. Roll into two 9x16-inch rectangles. Brush with melted margarine. Sprinkle with mixture of pecans, brown sugar and cinnamon. Roll as for jelly roll; seal edge. Shape into rings on greased baking sheets; seal ends. Slice at 1-inch intervals ⅔ through ring from outer edge; turn slices cut side up. Let rise, covered, for 1 hour or until doubled in bulk. Preheat oven to 375 degrees. Bake for 25 minutes. Frost with confectioners' sugar frosting. Yield: 20 servings.

Mary C. Oestreich, Tau Theta
Flora, Illinois

SPOON ROLLS

1 package dry yeast
2 cups (115-degree) water
¾ cup melted margarine
¼ cup sugar
1 egg
4 cups self-rising flour, sifted
⅓ cup water
⅓ cup butter, softened
⅓ cup corn oil

Dissolve yeast in warm water in bowl. Combine margarine and sugar in large bowl. Add egg and yeast. Add self-rising flour 1 cup at a time, mixing well after each addition. Cover with foil. Refrigerate overnight. Preheat oven to 400 degrees. Drop by spoonfuls into greased muffin cups. Bake for 20 minutes. Combine ⅓ cup water, butter and corn oil in mixer bowl. Beat until light and fluffy. Serve with hot rolls. Yield: 2 dozen.

Gina Morgan, Alpha Theta
Douglas, Georgia

SWIRLED CHOCOLATE SWEET ROLLS

1 package hot roll mix
1 tablespoon sugar
¼ cup unsweetened baking cocoa
1¼ cups (120-degree) water
2 tablespoons margarine
1 egg
2 tablespoons margarine
2 tablespoons sugar
½ cup miniature chocolate chips
Confectioners' sugar
¼ cup miniature chocolate chips
1 teaspoon shortening

Combine yeast and flour from roll mix, 1 tablespoon sugar and cocoa in bowl. Stir in water, 2 tablespoons margarine and egg until dough pulls from side of bowl. Knead on floured surface until smooth. Cover with large bowl. Let rest for 5 minutes. Roll into 12x15-inch rectangle; spread with 2 tablespoons margarine. Sprinkle with 2 tablespoons sugar and ½ cup chocolate chips. Roll up from short end; press edges to seal. Cut into 12 slices. Arrange in greased 9x13-inch pan. Let rise, covered, for 30 minutes on wire rack over hot water. Preheat oven to 375 degrees. Bake for 15 to 20 minutes. Sprinkle with confectioners' sugar. Melt remaining ingredients in saucepan over low heat. Drizzle over rolls. Yield: 1 dozen.

Jennifer Marsh, Xi Epsilon Pi
Abilene, Kansas

SOPAIPILLAS (MEXICAN FRIED BREAD)

1 cake yeast
2 cups (115-degree) water
1 teaspoon salt
¼ cup sugar
1 egg
1 cup evaporated milk
1 teaspoon baking powder
5 to 6 cups all-purpose flour, sifted
Oil for deep-frying
Confectioners' sugar

Combine first 7 ingredients in bowl. Add enough flour to make easily handled dough. Let rise until doubled in bulk. Roll ¼ inch thick on floured surface. Cut into pieces. Let rise for 30 minutes. Deep-fry in hot oil until golden. Sprinkle with confectioners' sugar.

Sherie Bargar, Eta Xi
Casselburg, Florida

CHEESE-FILLED CRESCENTS

2 8-count packages refrigerator crescent rolls
16 ounces cream cheese, softened
¾ cup sugar
1 teaspoon lemon juice
½ teaspoon vanilla extract
1 egg yolk, beaten
1 egg white, beaten
½ cup chopped walnuts
Confectioners' sugar

Preheat oven to 325 degrees. Separate crescent rolls into rectangles; place in greased 9x13-inch baking pan, sealing edges and perforations. Blend cream cheese, sugar, lemon juice, vanilla and egg yolk in bowl. Spread over rolls. Separate remaining rolls. Place rectangles together; seal edges and perforations. Place over cream cheese mixture. Brush with beaten egg white; sprinkle with walnuts. Bake for 25 minutes or until brown. Sprinkle with confectioners' sugar. Cut into squares. Yield: 12 servings.

Mary Perroni, Epsilon Kappa
Fairfax, Virginia

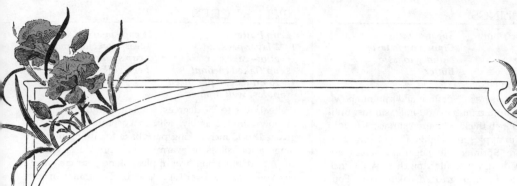

Party
Desserts

APPLE DUMPLINGS

2 cups all-purpose flour
1 teaspoon salt
⅔ cup shortening
½ cup milk
6 cooking apples, peeled

Sugar to taste
Cinnamon to taste
Nutmeg to taste
Butter

Preheat oven to 350 degrees. Sift flour and salt into bowl. Cut in shortening until crumbly. Add milk; stir just until moistened. Roll ¼ inch thick on floured surface. Cut into 5-inch squares. Cut apples into eights. Place 6 pieces on each dough square. Sprinkle with sugar and spices; dot with butter. Fold dough to center; pinch to seal. Prick with fork. Arrange in large greased baking pan. Pour Pineapple Sauce over top. Bake until pastry is brown and apples are tender. Yield: 6 to 8 servings.

PINEAPPLE SAUCE

3 cups sugar
2 cups unsweetened
  pineapple juice
½ cup butter

1 teaspoon cinnamon
1 teaspoon nutmeg
½ cup broken nuts

Combine first 5 ingredients in saucepan. Cook until thickened, stirring constantly. Stir in nuts.

Virginia L. DeMarais, Xi Upsilon Delta
Borrego Springs, California

FRESH APPLE PASTRY SQUARES

2½ cups all-purpose flour
1 teaspoon salt
1 cup plus 2 tablespoons
  butter
1 egg yolk
Milk
1 cup crushed cornflakes
8 cups peeled, sliced
  tart apples

⅔ cup sugar
½ teaspoon ginger
½ teaspoon cinnamon
1 egg white, stiffly beaten
1 cup sifted confectioners'
  sugar
½ teaspoon vanilla extract
1 to 2 tablespoons water

Preheat oven to 400 degrees. Mix flour and salt in large bowl. Cut in butter until crumbly. Beat egg yolk lightly with fork in 1 cup measure. Add enough milk to measure ⅔ cup. Stir into flour mixture; mix with fork until mixture forms ball. Divide into two portions. Roll half the dough to fit 10x15-inch baking pan. Sprinkle with cornflakes. Mix apples, sugar, ginger and cinnamon in large bowl. Spread in prepared pan. Top with remaining dough; seal edges. Brush stiffly beaten egg white over top. Bake for 50 to 60 minutes or until golden brown. Cool. Frost with mixture of confectioners' sugar, vanilla and water. Cut into squares. Yield: 16 servings.

Dorothy E. Carstens, Laureate Alpha Beta
Colorado Springs, Colorado

---

*For an unusual Mexican dessert, **Lisa Bruhn, Alpha Delta Kappa, Sulphur Springs, Texas,** makes Apple Empañadas by filling flour tortillas with a mixture of 1 can apple pie filling, ¼ cup melted butter and 2 teaspoons cinnamon. Fold and secure with toothpicks, deep-fry and sprinkle with cinnamon-sugar.*

APPLE KUCHEN

½ cup butter
1 2-layer package
   yellow cake mix
½ cup flaked coconut
1 20-ounce can pie sliced
   apples, well drained

½ cup sugar
1 teaspoon cinnamon
1 cup sour cream
2 egg yolks

Preheat oven to 350 degrees. Cut butter into dry cake mix in bowl until crumbly. Mix in coconut. Pat into ungreased 9x13-inch baking pan. Bake for 10 minutes. Arrange apple slices on warm crust. Sprinkle mixture of sugar and cinnamon over apples. Blend sour cream and egg yolks; drizzle over top. Bake for 25 minutes or until edges are light brown; do not overbake. Serve warm. Yield: 12 to 15 servings.

Becky Tichy, Xi Alpha Sigma
Vienna, West Virginia

TROPICAL APPLE CRISP

8 cups peeled, sliced
  sweet apples
1 cup chopped dried
  apricots
⅔ cup flaked coconut
2 tablespoons sugar
½ cup all-purpose flour

⅓ cup oats
2 teaspoons allspice
⅛ teaspoon salt
½ cup sugar
6 tablespoons butter,
  softened

Preheat oven to 375 degrees. Combine apples, apricots, coconut and 2 tablespoons sugar in 9x9-inch baking dish. Combine flour, oats, allspice, salt and ½ cup sugar in medium bowl. Cut in butter until crumbly. Sprinkle evenly over apple slices. Bake for 30 minutes or until apples are tender. Serve warm or cold. Yield: 8 servings.

Arlene M. Rothberger, Preceptor Theta
Topeka, Kansas

ANGELIC APRICOT AMBROSIA

1½ cups sugar
7 tablespoons cornstarch
1 46-ounce can apricot
   nectar
1 28-ounce can apricot
   halves

1 cup pecan pieces
1 large angel food cake
1 8-ounce container
   extra creamy
   whipped topping

Combine sugar and cornstarch in 2-quart saucepan. Stir in apricot nectar gradually. Bring to a boil over medium heat, stirring constantly. Cook until mixture is thickened and clear, stirring constantly. Remove from heat. Drain apricots. Reserve 12 halves for decoration; chop remaining apricots. Stir chopped apricots into cooked mixture. Add pecans. Tear angel food cake into bite-sized pieces. Add to cooked mixture. Pour into 9x13-inch dish. Refrigerate overnight. Top each serving with whipped topping. Place reserved apricot half cut side down on each. Yield: 12 servings.

Alberta Crary, Laureate Gamma
Deadwood, South Dakota

BANANA SPLIT DESSERT

3 cups graham cracker
  crumbs
½ cup melted butter
3 cups confectioners'
  sugar
2 eggs
1 cup butter, softened
4 bananas, sliced

1 16-ounce can crushed
   pineapple, drained
1 16-ounce container
   whipped topping
1 cup maraschino
  cherries
1 cup chopped pecans

Combine graham cracker crumbs and melted butter in bowl. Press into 9x13-inch dish. Cream confectioners' sugar, eggs and softened butter in mixer bowl for 15 minutes. Spread over crust. Arrange bananas over creamed mixture. Spoon pineapple evenly over bananas. Layer whipped topping, cherries and pecans over top. Chill for 4 hours before serving. Yield: 16 to 20 servings.

Gail Drake, Xi Gamma Eta
Tonganoxie, Kansas

AMARETTO CHEESECAKE

1½ cups graham cracker
  crumbs
2 tablespoons sugar
1 teaspoon cinnamon
6 tablespoons melted
  margarine
24 ounces cream cheese,
  softened
1 cup sugar

4 eggs
⅓ cup Amaretto
1 cup sour cream
4 teaspoons sugar
1 tablespoon Amaretto
¼ cup toasted almonds
1 12-ounce milk
   chocolate bar, grated

Preheat oven to 375 degrees. Mix first 4 ingredients in bowl. Press over bottom and halfway up side of springform pan. Beat cream cheese in mixer bowl until light and fluffy. Add 1 cup sugar gradually, beating constantly. Add eggs 1 at a time, beating well after each addition. Stir in ⅓ cup Amaretto. Pour into prepared pan. Bake for 45 to 50 minutes or until set. Blend sour cream, 4 teaspoons sugar and 1 tablespoon Amaretto in bowl. Spoon over hot cheesecake. Increase temperature to 500 degrees. Bake for 5 minutes longer. Turn off oven. Let cheesecake stand in oven with door ajar until cool. Refrigerate for 24 hours. Place on serving plate; remove side of pan. Garnish with toasted almonds and grated milk chocolate. Yield: 10 servings.

Marian Ramey, Iota Epsilon
Fayetteville, Georgia

NO-BAKE BLUEBERRY CHEESECAKE

4 ounces fine graham
  cracker crumbs
½ cup melted butter
½ cup sugar
2 envelopes whipped
  topping mix

16 ounces cream cheese,
   softened
1 cup sugar
1 21-ounce can
   blueberry pie filling

Mix crumbs, butter and ½ cup sugar in bowl. Press over bottom of 9x13-inch dish. Prepare whipped topping mix using package directions. Beat cream cheese with 1 cup sugar in mixer bowl. Fold into whipped topping. Pour into prepared dish. Chill until firm. Top with blueberry pie filling. Chill until serving time. Yield: 12 servings.

Gladys I. Clark, Beta Theta
Hulett, West Virginia

EASY BLUEBERRY CHEESECAKE

1½ cups graham cracker
  crumbs
½ cup margarine
½ cup sugar
8 ounces cream cheese,
  softened

½ cup sugar
2 eggs
1 21-ounce can
   blueberry pie filling
1 8-ounce container
   whipped topping

Preheat oven to 350 degrees. Mix first 3 ingredients in bowl. Press into 9x12-inch pan. Beat cream cheese, sugar and eggs in mixer bowl until smooth. Spread over crumb layer. Bake for 20 minutes. Cool. Cover with pie filling; top with whipped topping. Yield: 15 servings.

Berneida M. Ritter, Alpha Omicron
North Baltimore, Ohio

EASY CHEESECAKE

8 ounces cream cheese,
  softened
⅓ cup sugar
1 cup sour cream
1 teaspoon vanilla extract

1 8-ounce container
   whipped topping
1 graham cracker
  pie shell

Blend cream cheese and sugar in bowl. Add sour cream and vanilla. Fold in whipped topping. Pour into pie shell. Chill for 3 to 4 hours. Top with fruit. Yield: 6 servings.

Mary Lewis Ward, Pi Eta
Titusville, Florida

CHOCOLATE CHEESECAKE

⅓ cup melted margarine
1½ cups graham cracker
  crumbs
¼ cup sugar
24 ounces cream cheese,
  softened
1 14-ounce can
   sweetened condensed
   milk

1 cup chocolate chips,
  melted
4 eggs
1 teaspoon vanilla extract
2 cups whipping cream
⅔ cup sugar

Preheat oven to 350 degrees. Combine margarine, graham cracker crumbs and ¼ cup sugar in bowl; mix well. Press over bottom of 10-inch springform pan. Beat cream cheese with condensed milk in mixer bowl. Blend in chocolate. Add eggs and vanilla. Beat for 2 minutes. Pour into springform pan. Bake for 65 minutes. Cool. Chill until serving time. Place on serving plate; remove side of pan. Whip cream in bowl with ⅔ cup sugar until soft peaks form. Serve with cheesecake.
Yield: 12 servings.

Gina Griffis Morgan, Alpha Beta
Douglas, Georgia

GERMAN CHOCOLATE CHEESECAKE

1¼ cups chocolate wafer crumbs (about 18)
2 tablespoons sugar
3 tablespoons butter, melted
19 ounces cream cheese, softened
1 cup sugar
¼ cup unsweetened baking cocoa
2 teaspoons vanilla extract
3 eggs
2 tablespoons butter
⅓ cup cream
2 tablespoons light brown sugar
1 egg
½ teaspoon vanilla extract
½ cup chopped pecans
½ cup flaked coconut

Preheat oven to 350 degrees. Mix crumbs and 2 tablespoons sugar in bowl, mix in melted butter. Press evenly over bottom of ungreased springform pan. Bake for 10 minutes. Cool. Reduce temperature to 300 degrees. Beat cream cheese in large mixer bowl. Add 1 cup sugar and cocoa gradually, beating until fluffy. Add 2 teaspoons vanilla. Beat in eggs 1 at a time. Pour into prepared pan. Bake for 1 hour or until firm in center. Cool. Combine 2 tablespoons butter, cream, brown sugar and 1 egg in saucepan. Cook over low heat until thickened, stirring constantly. Remove from heat. Stir in vanilla, pecans and coconut. Cool. Spoon over cooled cheesecake. Yield: 12 servings.

Janice Justis, Delta Tau
Petoskey, Michigan

CHOCOLATE VELVET CHEESECAKE

1 to 2 tablespoons unsalted butter, softened
1 8½-ounce package chocolate wafers, finely ground
Pinch each of salt and cinnamon
⅓ cup melted unsalted butter
12 ounces semisweet chocolate, broken
2 tablespoons unsalted butter
24 ounces cream cheese, softened
1½ cups whipping cream
1 teaspoon vanilla extract
1 cup sugar
3 eggs, slightly beaten
2 tablespoons unsweetened baking cocoa
Confectioners' sugar

Preheat oven to 350 degrees. Coat bottom and side of 9-inch springform pan with softened butter. Mix crumbs, salt, cinnamon and melted butter in bowl. Press over bottom and side of pan. Chill for 30 minutes. Melt semisweet chocolate and 2 tablespoons butter in double boiler; blend well. Cut cream cheese into 1-inch cubes. Beat in mixer bowl until smooth. Add chocolate mixture, whipping cream and vanilla. Add sugar gradually, beating constantly. Add eggs ¼ cup at a time, beating well after each addition. Sift cocoa over batter; beat at low speed until blended. Pour into prepared pan; smooth top. Bake for 30 minutes. Reduce temperature to 325 degrees. Bake for 30 minutes longer. Turn off oven. Let stand in oven with door ajar for 30 minutes. Place on wire rack to cool completely. Remove side of pan. Chill, uncovered, for 8 hours to overnight. Chill, loosely covered with plastic wrap, until serving time. Sift confectioners' sugar lightly over cheesecake just before serving. Serve with fresh strawberries. Yield: 12 servings.

Gayle Bloom, Omicron Omicron
Pensacola, Florida

CHOCOLATE RASPBERRY CHEESECAKE

2½ cups graham cracker crumbs
½ cup sugar
½ cup melted butter
24 ounces cream cheese, softened
1 cup sugar
2 eggs, beaten
6 ounces semisweet chocolate
2 tablespoons heavy cream
1 cup sour cream
¼ cup strong coffee
¼ cup raspberry liqueur
1 teaspoon vanilla extract
Whipped cream
Chocolate curls

Preheat oven to 350 degrees. Mix first 3 ingredients in bowl. Press over bottom of lightly greased 9-inch springform pan. Beat cream cheese with sugar and eggs in mixer bowl. Melt chocolate with cream in double boiler. Add to cream cheese mixture with remaining ingredients; blend well. Pour into prepared pan. Bake for 45 minutes. Cool. Chill until serving time. Place on serving plate; remove side of pan. Garnish with whipped cream and chocolate curls. Yield: 12 servings.

Donna Faxon, Preceptor Alpha Epsilon
Tucson, Arizona

MOCHA CHOCOLATE CHIP CHEESECAKE

3 tablespoons butter
½ cup ground walnuts
½ cup fine dry bread crumbs
¼ cup sugar
1 teaspoon cinnamon
½ teaspoon nutmeg
32 ounces cream cheese, softened
¼ cup sour cream
1½ cups sugar
1½ tablespoons instant coffee powder
1 tablespoon vanilla extract
6 eggs
1⅓ cups semisweet chocolate chips

Preheat oven to 350 degrees. Butter 10-inch springform pan with 3 tablespoons butter. Chill. Combine walnuts and next 4 ingredients in bowl; mix well. Pat evenly over bottom and side of pan. Beat cream cheese and sour cream in mixer bowl until fluffy. Add sugar and coffee powder dissolved in vanilla; blend well. Add eggs 1 at a time, beating well after each addition. Fold in chocolate chips. Pour into prepared pan. Bake for 15 minutes. Reduce temperature to 250 degrees. Bake for 1¼ hours longer. Cool in oven for 1 hour or longer. Remove from oven. Cool to room temperature. Refrigerate for 12 hours or longer. Place on serving plate; remove side of pan. Cut with thin knife dipped in hot water. Yield: 12 to 16 servings.

Carolyn Kamor, Preceptor Alpha Phi
Mishawaka, Indiana

THREE-LAYER CHOCOLATE CHEESECAKE

2 cups chocolate wafer crumbs	1 egg
¼ cup sugar	½ teaspoon vanilla extract
5 tablespoons melted butter	¼ cup chopped pecans
8 ounces cream cheese, softened	5 ounces cream cheese, softened
¼ cup sugar	¼ cup sugar
1 egg	1 egg
¼ teaspoon vanilla extract	1 cup sour cream
2 ounces semisweet baking chocolate, melted	¼ teaspoon vanilla extract
	¼ teaspoon almond extract
⅓ cup sour cream	6 ounces semisweet baking chocolate
8 ounces cream cheese, softened	¼ cup butter
⅓ cup packed dark brown sugar	¾ cup sifted confectioners' sugar
1 tablespoon all-purpose flour	2 tablespoons water
	1 teaspoon vanilla extract

Preheat oven to 325 degrees. Mix first 3 ingredients in bowl. Press over bottom and 2 inches up side of 9-inch springform pan. Beat 8 ounces cream cheese and ¼ cup sugar in bowl until fluffy. Blend in 1 egg, ¼ teaspoon vanilla, melted chocolate and ⅓ cup sour cream. Pour into prepared pan. Beat 8 ounces cream cheese, brown sugar and flour in bowl until fluffy. Beat in 1 egg and ½ teaspoon vanilla. Stir in pecans. Spoon over chocolate layer. Beat 5 ounces cream cheese and ¼ cup sugar in bowl until fluffy. Blend in 1 egg, 1 cup sour cream, ¼ teaspoon vanilla and almond extract. Spoon over pecan layer. Bake for 1 hour. Turn off oven. Let stand in closed oven for 1 hour. Open oven door. Let stand in open oven for 30 minutes. Cool completely. Chill for 8 hours. Remove side of pan. Melt 6 ounces chocolate and ¼ cup butter in double boiler; remove from heat. Add confectioners' sugar, water and 1 teaspoon vanilla; stir until smooth. Spread warm glaze over cheesecake. Yield: 10 to 12 servings.

Pam Kirk, Xi Beta Eta
Grand Bay, Alabama

WHITE CHOCOLATE CHEESECAKE

1½ cups graham cracker crumbs	10 ounces white chocolate, melted
5 tablespoons melted butter	4½ teaspoons vanilla extract
1 tablespoon sugar	1 cup sugar
32 ounces cream cheese, softened	1 cup sour cream
½ cup butter, softened	¼ cup sugar
4 eggs	1 teaspoon vanilla extract
	Strawberries

Preheat oven to 350 degrees. Mix first 3 ingredients in bowl. Press into 9-inch springform pan. Chill for several hours. Beat cream cheese with softened butter in mixer bowl until smooth. Add eggs 1 at a time, beating well after each addition. Beat in chocolate, 4½ teaspoons vanilla and 1 cup sugar. Beat for 2 minutes. Pour into prepared pan. Bake for 1 hour. Mix sour cream, ¼ cup sugar

and 1 teaspoon vanilla in bowl. Spread over baked layer. Bake for 10 to 15 minutes longer or until glaze is set. Turn off oven. Let stand in closed oven for 2 hours. Chill overnight. Place on serving plate; remove side of pan. Garnish with fresh strawberries. Yield: 10 to 12 servings.

Janet Staton Nesbitt, Alpha Upsilon
Danville, Kentucky

COFFEE AND CREAM CHEESECAKE

1½ cups fine graham cracker crumbs	1 cup sour cream
	6 eggs
5 tablespoons melted butter	6 tablespoons all-purpose flour
3 tablespoons sugar	3 tablespoons instant coffee powder
1 teaspoon cinnamon	
24 ounces cream cheese, softened	¼ cup coffee-flavored liqueur
½ cup sugar	

Preheat oven to 350 degrees. Mix graham cracker crumbs, butter, 3 tablespoons sugar and cinnamon in bowl. Press evenly over bottom and about 1 inch up side of 11-inch springform pan. Bake for 15 minutes. Cool. Reduce temperature to 300 degrees. Beat cream cheese and ½ cup sugar in mixer bowl at high speed until blended. Beat in sour cream, eggs and flour. Dissolve coffee powder in coffee liqueur; stir into cream cheese mixture. Pour into cooled crust. Bake for 1 hour or until cheesecake is firm, except for 4-inch area in center, when shaken gently. Cool for 4 hours or longer. Garnish individual servings with drizzle of additional liqueur. Yield: 10 to 12 servings.

Sharon Carlile, Xi Eta
Walla Walla, Washington

LOW-FAT LEMON CHEESECAKE

1 cup graham cracker crumbs	½ cup low-fat evaporated milk
2 tablespoons butter, melted	⅓ cup sugar
	1 tablespoon grated lemon rind
2 cups low-fat cottage cheese	⅓ cup fresh lemon juice
2 egg whites	¼ cup all-purpose flour
2 whole eggs	Lemon slices

Preheat oven to 300 degrees. Combine crumbs and butter in small bowl. Press over bottom of greased 9-inch springform pan. Chill in freezer while preparing filling. Combine cottage cheese and next 6 ingredients in food processor or blender container. Process until smooth. Add flour; process until blended. Pour into chilled pan. Bake for 1 hour or until filling is set. Cool on wire rack. Loosen from side of pan with knife; remove side of pan. Garnish with lemon slices. Yield: 10 to 12 servings.

Elizabeth A. Brammer, Xi Gamma Theta
Salem, Oregon

CREAMY MINCEMEAT CHEESECAKE

¼ cup melted butter	1 envelope unflavored
1 cup graham cracker	gelatin
crumbs	¼ cup lemon juice
¼ cup sugar	1⅓ cups mincemeat
16 ounces cream cheese,	½ cup chopped nuts
softened	1 tablespoon grated
1 14-ounce can	lemon rind
sweetened condensed	1 cup whipping cream,
milk	whipped

Press mixture of butter, crumbs and sugar into 9-inch springform pan. Chill. Beat cream cheese in large mixer bowl until fluffy. Add condensed milk; beat until smooth. Soften gelatin in lemon juice in small saucepan. Heat until dissolved, stirring constantly. Add to creamed mixture with mincemeat, nuts and lemon rind; mix well. Fold in whipped cream. Pour into prepared pan. Chill for 3 hours or until set. Garnish with sour cream, additional nuts and candied cherries. May freeze without garnishes. Defrost in refrigerator overnight. Yield: 12 servings.

Arlene Wagner, Mu
Santa Monica, California

TEXAS CHEESECAKE

8 eggs	3 tablespoons sugar
2 cups sugar	3 tablespoons melted
3 pounds cream cheese,	butter
softened	1 pint sour cream
16 graham crackers,	2 tablespoons sugar
crushed	1 teaspoon vanilla extract
2 tablespoons cinnamon	

Preheat oven to 325 degrees. Combine eggs, 2 cups sugar and cream cheese in mixer bowl. Beat for 20 minutes. Mix graham cracker crumbs, cinnamon, 3 tablespoons sugar and 3 tablespoons melted butter in bowl. Press into large springform pan. Pour cream cheese mixture into prepared pan. Bake for 45 minutes. Mix sour cream with 2 tablespoons sugar and vanilla. Remove from oven. Let stand for 10 minutes. Pour sour cream mixture over top. Bake for 10 minutes longer. Turn off oven. Let stand in closed oven until cool enough to handle. Cool to room temperature. Chill for 8 hours or longer. Increase baking time to 1 hour when using gas oven. Yield: 24 servings.

Merilyn Smith, Preceptor Iota Omicron
San Angelo, Texas

CHERRY-BERRY ON-A-CLOUD

6 egg whites, at room	2 cups miniature
temperature	marshmallows
½ teaspoon cream of	6 ounces cream cheese,
tartar	softened
¼ teaspoon salt	1 20-ounce can cherry
1½ cups sugar	pie filling
2 cups whipping cream	2 cups sliced strawberries
1 cup sugar	1 teaspoon lemon juice

Preheat oven to 275 degrees. Beat egg whites in bowl until foamy. Add cream of tartar and salt. Beat until soft peaks form. Add 1½ cups sugar gradually, beating until very stiff peaks form. Spread in greased 9x13-inch baking pan. Bake for 1 hour. Turn off oven. Let stand in closed oven for 12 hours. Do not open oven during standing time. Whip cream in bowl until soft peaks form. Fold in 1 cup sugar, marshmallows and cream cheese gently. Spread over meringue. Chill for 12 hours. Combine remaining ingredients in bowl; mix well. Spoon over cream layer. Chill until serving time. Yield: 12 to 15 servings.

Cynthia Struve, Mu
Sioux City, Iowa

CHERRY CHOCOLATE SUPREME

½ cup all-purpose flour	1 3-ounce package
¼ cup confectioners'	vanilla instant
sugar	pudding mix
¼ cup margarine,	1½ cups milk
softened	1 20-ounce can cherry
1 egg yolk	pie filling
1 cup chocolate chips	2 cups whipped topping
2 tablespoons milk	Chocolate curls
1 egg yolk	

Preheat oven to 375 degrees. Combine flour and confectioners' sugar in bowl. Cut in margarine until crumbly. Stir in 1 egg yolk. Pat into greased 9x9-inch baking pan. Bake for 8 minutes or until light brown. Cool. Melt chocolate chips in 2 tablespoons milk in double boiler. Cool slightly. Blend in remaining egg yolk. Spread over cooled crust. Combine pudding mix and 1½ cups milk in bowl. Beat until thickened. Spread over chocolate layer. Spoon 1½ cups pie filling and whipped topping over pudding. Chill, covered, for several hours. Top with remaining pie filling and chocolate curls. Yield: 12 servings.

Marlene J. Baucum, Preceptor Omega
Phoenix, Arizona

CHERRY DELIGHTS

4 egg whites	1 cup confectioners'
1 cup sugar	sugar
½ teaspoon baking	1 teaspoon sugar
powder	1 8-ounce container
1 cup chopped nuts	whipped topping
40 Ritz crackers,	1 21-ounce can
finely crushed	cherry pie filling
8 ounces cream cheese,	
softened	

Preheat oven to 350 degrees. Beat egg whites in mixer bowl until soft peaks form. Add sugar gradually, beating until stiff. Fold in baking powder, nuts and crumbs. Press about ½ inch thick into bottoms of well-greased muffin cups. Bake for 10 to 12 minutes. Cool. Loosen from side of cup. Cool on wire rack. Beat cream cheese with next 3 ingredients until smooth. Drop by spoonfuls onto cups. Top with cherry pie filling. Chill until serving time. Yield: 2 dozen.

Pat Kaiser, Preceptor Beta Zeta
Chambersburg, Pennsylvania

CHERRY SPLIT DESSERT

3 cups graham cracker
  crumbs
¾ cup melted margarine
2 20-ounce cans cherry
  pie filling
½ gallon vanilla ice
  cream, sliced
1 cup chopped walnuts

2 cups chocolate chips
½ cup margarine
2 cups confectioners'
  sugar
1½ cups milk
1 teaspoon vanilla extract
2 cups whipping cream,
  whipped

Mix cracker crumbs with ¾ cup margarine in bowl. Layer 2 cups crumb mixture, pie filling and ice cream in 9x13-inch pan. Sprinkle with walnuts. Freeze for 1 to 2½ hours. Melt chocolate chips and ½ cup margarine in saucepan over low heat, stirring constantly. Add confectioners' sugar and milk. Bring to a boil, stirring constantly. Cook until thickened. Add vanilla. Cool. Spread over frozen mixture. Freeze for 1 to 2½ hours. Top with whipped cream and remaining crumb mixture. Freeze for 12 hours or longer. Let stand at room temperature for 5 to 10 minutes before serving. Yield: 15 servings.

Julie Nelson, Beta Tau
Pierre, South Dakota

DUMP CAKE

1 2-layer package
  banana cake mix
1 cup cherry pie filling
1 cup drained crushed
  pineapple

½ cup chopped pecans
½ cup coconut
1 cup butter, melted

Preheat oven to 325 degrees. Layer all ingredients in order listed in 8x11-inch baking pan. Bake for 1 hour. Serve with ice cream or whipped cream. Yield: 6 to 8 servings.

Edith Scott, Preceptor Epsilon Tau
Venice, Florida

HEAVENLY CHERRY DESSERT

½ cup margarine
1 cup all-purpose flour
1 cup chopped pecans
8 ounces cream cheese,
  softened
1 cup confectioners'
  sugar
2 cups whipped topping

1 20-ounce can cherry
  pie filling
1 3-ounce package
  vanilla instant
  pudding mix
2 cups whipped topping
Pecans, chopped

Preheat oven to 350 degrees. Cut margarine into flour in bowl until crumbly. Stir in 1 cup pecans. Pat into 9x12-inch baking pan. Bake for 20 minutes. Cool. Beat cream cheese with confectioners' sugar in bowl until light and fluffy. Add 2 cups whipped topping; mix gently. Spread on cooled crust. Spoon pie filling on top. Prepare pudding mix using package directions. Spread over pie filling. Top with remaining 2 cups whipped topping and additional pecans. Chill until serving time. Yield: 12 to 15 servings.

Vivian Neeley, Gamma Eta
Sherman, Texas

ANACAPA DELIGHT

2 tablespoons sugar
½ cup chopped almonds
½ cup melted margarine
8 ounces cream cheese,
  softened
1 16-ounce container
  whipped topping

1 cup confectioners' sugar
1 6-ounce package
  chocolate instant
  pudding mix
2½ cups milk
Almonds, chopped

Preheat oven to 350 degrees. Combine first 3 ingredients in 9x11-inch baking dish. Bake for 15 minutes. Cool. Blend cream cheese, 1 cup whipped topping and confectioners' sugar in bowl. Spread over cooled crust. Prepare pudding mix according to package directions using 2½ cups milk. Spread over cream cheese layer. Chill until firm. Top with remaining whipped topping and almonds. Chill until serving time. Yield: 8 to 10 servings.

Marge Beck, Delta Iota Psi
Ventura, California

CHOCOLATE ÉCLAIR CAKE

1 16-ounce package
  graham crackers
2 3-ounce packages
  vanilla instant
  pudding mix
3½ cups milk
1 9-ounce container
  whipped topping
2 squares unsweetened
  baking chocolate

1 teaspoon vanilla extract
1½ cups confectioners'
  sugar
3 tablespoons light
  corn syrup
3 tablespoons melted
  butter
3 tablespoons milk

Line 9x13-inch dish with graham crackers. Prepare pudding mix according to package directions using 3½ cups milk. Fold in whipped topping. Spread half the pudding mixture over crackers. Repeat layers, ending with crackers. Melt chocolate in saucepan over low heat. Add vanilla, confectioners' sugar, corn syrup, butter and 3 tablespoons milk; mix well. Spread over graham crackers. Chill for 3 days. Yield: 15 to 18 servings.

LaDonna M. Smith, Preceptor Kappa Xi
Schertz, Texas

CHOCOLATE ÉCLAIR CAKE

2 3-ounce packages
  French vanilla instant
  pudding mix
3 cups milk
1 8-ounce container
  whipped topping

1 16-ounce package
  graham crackers
1 can supreme chocolate
  fudge frosting

Combine pudding mix and milk in bowl. Beat for 1 to 2 minutes or until thickened. Fold in whipped topping. Layer graham crackers and pudding in 9x13-inch glass dish, ending with graham crackers. Chill until set. Spread frosting over crackers. Chill until serving time. Yield: 16 servings.

Lela R. Breger, Laureate Alpha
Phoenix, Arizona

ICEBOX PUDDING CAKE

1 6-ounce package chocolate pudding mix	1 cup heavy cream, whipped
1 6-ounce package vanilla pudding mix	1 4-ounce jar maraschino cherries
Milk	
1 16-ounce package graham crackers	

Prepare each pudding according to package directions using ¾ cup less milk. Place layer of graham crackers in bottom of 10x12-inch dish. Pour ⅓ of the chocolate pudding over the graham cracker layer; spread evenly. Place layer of graham crackers on top. Pour ½ of the vanilla pudding on top; spread evenly. Repeat layers with remaining ingredients, ending with chocolate pudding. Chill in refrigerator. Cut into squares. Spread whipped cream on top of each square. Top each square with cherry. Yield: 20 servings.

Ruth E. Kolb, Xi Beta Omega
Valdosta, Georgia

CHOCOLATE REFRIGERATOR CAKE

2 cups semisweet chocolate chips	2 teaspoons vanilla extract
2 cups milk	1 cup whipping cream, whipped
2 tablespoons unflavored gelatin	20 unfilled ladyfingers, split
¼ cup cold water	2 cups whipping cream
¼ cup sugar	1 tablespoon sugar

Combine chocolate chips and milk in double boiler. Cook until chocolate is melted, stirring occasionally. Soften gelatin in cold water for 5 minutes. Add softened gelatin and ¼ cup sugar to chocolate mixture. Cook until gelatin dissolves, stirring constantly; remove from heat. Beat with rotary beater until smooth. Add vanilla. Chill mixture until thickened. Fold whipped cream into chocolate mixture. Line bottom and side of springform pan with ladyfingers. Pour half the chocolate mixture over ladyfingers. Arrange remaining ladyfingers on top. Pour remaining chocolate over ladyfingers. Refrigerate until serving time. Remove side of pan. Whip 2 cups whipping cream with 1 tablespoon sugar in bowl until soft peaks form. Serve with cake. Yield: 8 to 10 servings.

Jeanne Clark, Xi Gamma Xi
Greenville, North Carolina

CHOCOLATE NUT CRUNCH

22 to 24 single graham crackers, crushed	6 egg yolks, beaten
1 cup chopped nuts	3 squares unsweetened chocolate, melted
½ cup melted butter	1 teaspoon vanilla extract
¼ cup sugar	6 egg whites, stiffly beaten
1 cup butter, softened	½ gallon vanilla ice cream, softened
2 cups confectioners' sugar	

Preheat oven to 325 degrees. Reserve a small amount of crumbs for garnish. Combine remaining crumbs, nuts, melted butter and sugar in bowl. Line 10x15-inch baking pan with half the mixture. Bake for 5 minutes. Cool. Cream softened butter and confectioners' sugar in bowl. Add egg yolks, chocolate and vanilla; mix well. Fold in stiffly beaten egg whites gently. Spread half the chocolate mixture over crumb crust. Chill for 1 hour. Add layers of ice cream and remaining chocolate mixture. Top with reserved crumbs. Freeze until firm. Store in freezer for up to 3 weeks. Let stand at room temperature for several minutes before serving. Yield: 20 servings.

Harriet L. Roberts, Preceptor Delta Tau
Farina, Illinois

CHOCOLATE FRANGOS

1 cup butter, softened	2 teaspoons vanilla extract
2 cups confectioners' sugar	1 cup crushed vanilla wafers
4 squares baking chocolate, melted	1 cup whipping cream, whipped
4 eggs	18 small maraschino cherries
¾ teaspoon peppermint extract	

Beat butter and confectioners' sugar in mixer bowl until light and fluffy. Add melted chocolate; beat well. Add eggs 1 at a time, beating well after each addition. Beat until fluffy. Beat in peppermint and vanilla. Sprinkle half the vanilla wafer crumbs into paper-lined muffin cups. Fill half full with chocolate mixture. Top with remaining crumbs. Freeze until serving time. Top with whipped cream and cherries. Yield: 18 servings.

Carol Tingley, Preceptor Pi
Albuquerque, New Mexico

CHOCOLATE TRUFFLE CAKE

1 pound semisweet chocolate chips	2 cups whipping cream
10 tablespoons unsalted butter	2 tablespoons sugar
5 egg yolks, beaten	½ teaspoon vanilla extract
5 egg whites, stiffly beaten	Grated chocolate

Preheat oven to 375 degrees. Melt chocolate and butter in double boiler; stir until smooth. Pour into large bowl. Cool slightly. Butter 9-inch springform pan. Stir egg yolks into chocolate mixture. Fold ¼ of the stiffly beaten egg whites into chocolate mixture to lighten. Fold in remaining egg whites. Pour into prepared pan. Bake for 12 minutes; do not overbake. Cool in pan overnight. Beat whipping cream, sugar and vanilla in mixer bowl until soft peaks form. Spread evenly over cake in pan. Remove side of pan. Store unfrosted cake in refrigerator for up to 2 weeks. Serve in thin slices. Cake is very rich although not very sweet. Yield: 10 to 12 servings.

Rosie Miller, Gamma Theta
Cedar Rapids, Iowa

BLENDER CHOCOLATE MOUSSE

1 12-ounce package semisweet chocolate chips	3 eggs
	1 cup hot milk
½ cup sugar	2 to 4 tablespoons Brandy
	Whipped cream

Combine chocolate, sugar and eggs in blender container. Add hot milk and Brandy. Process on medium speed until smooth. Pour into dessert dishes. Chill for 1 hour. Garnish with whipped cream. Yield: 6 servings.

Eddie Rae Lord, Xi Alpha Rho
East Wenatchee, Washington

FROZEN CHOCOLATE MOUSSE

Oreo cookies	1 cup semisweet chocolate chips, melted
⅓ cup melted margarine	
8 ounces cream cheese, softened	
	¼ cup sugar
¼ cup sugar	1 cup whipping cream, whipped
1 teaspoon vanilla extract	
2 eggs, separated	¾ cup chopped pecans

Preheat oven to 350 degrees. Separate Oreos; discard creamy filling. Crush enough to yield ½ cup fine crumbs. Mix with melted margarine in bowl. Press into bottom of 9-inch springform pan. Bake for 10 minutes. Combine cream cheese, ¼ cup sugar and vanilla in mixer bowl; beat until blended. Blend in well-beaten egg yolks and chocolate. Beat egg whites in mixer bowl until stiff peaks form. Beat in ¼ cup sugar gradually. Fold in chocolate mixture, whipped cream and pecans. Pour into prepared springform pan. Freeze until firm. Serve with Heavenly Hot Fudge Sauce. Yield: 10 servings.

HEAVENLY HOT FUDGE SAUCE

4 1-ounce squares unsweetened chocolate	3 cups sugar
	1⅔ cups evaporated milk
½ cup margarine	1 teaspoon vanilla extract
Dash of salt	

Melt chocolate and margarine in double boiler. Add salt. Stir in sugar gradually. Add evaporated milk very gradually, stirring constantly. Remove from heat. Add vanilla. Serve hot sauce over frozen mousse. Yield: 4 cups.

Kristina L. Adams, Xi Gamma Chi
Peachtree City, Georgia

TORTILLA TORTE

12 ounces milk chocolate chips	¼ cup sifted confectioners' sugar
2 cups sour cream	Chocolate curls
10 8-inch flour tortillas	Fresh strawberries
1 cup sour cream	

Melt chocolate in medium saucepan over low heat, stirring occasionally. Stir in 2 cups sour cream; remove from heat. Cool. Place 1 tortilla on serving plate. Spread about ⅓ cup of the chocolate mixture on top. Repeat layers with remaining tortillas and chocolate mixture, ending with tortilla. Combine remaining 1 cup sour cream and confectioners' sugar in bowl. Spread on top. Chill, covered, overnight. Garnish with chocolate curls and strawberries. Yield: 6 to 8 servings.

Margaret Rieckelman, Xi Iota
Clarkston, Washington

VERY SPECIAL ICE BOX CAKE

1 cup whipping cream	1 cup chopped pecans
1 teaspoon vanilla extract	
1 box thin chocolate wafers	

Whip cream in bowl until soft peaks form. Fold in vanilla. Alternate layers of wafers, whipped cream and pecans in 5x8-inch dish. Chill, covered, for 24 hours. Unmold onto serving plate. Slice very thin. Yield: 8 servings.

Wanda T. McMahon, Preceptor Epsilon Alpha
Winter Haven, Florida

HYDROX DESSERT

1 16-ounce package Hydrox cookies, crushed	1 cup milk
	2 cups whipped cream
	3 tablespoons melted butter
1 pound marshmallows	

Sprinkle half the cookie crumbs in 9x13-inch dish. Melt marshmallows in milk in double boiler. Cool slightly. Fold in whipped cream and butter. Pour into dish. Top with remaining crumbs. Chill for 4 hours or longer. Serve with additional whipped cream. Yield: 12 to 16 servings.

Darla Armstrong Munkel, Lambda Mu
Cresco, Iowa

COFFEE JELL-O

1 envelope unflavored gelatin	2 cups boiling strong coffee
½ cup cold coffee	½ to ¾ cup sugar

Dissolve gelatin in ½ cup cold coffee. Add boiling coffee and sugar; mix well. Pour into dessert dishes. Chill until set. Serve with whipped cream. Yield: 6 servings.

Rosabel S. Bannon, Preceptor Beta Eta
Gig Harbor, Washington

DUTCH BUTTERCREAM DESSERT

1 cup unsalted butter, softened	¼ to ½ cup very strong coffee
1½ cups sugar	1 package unfilled ladyfingers, split
4 egg yolks	

Cream butter and sugar in bowl until light and fluffy. Add egg yolks, 1 at a time, beating well after each addition. Add coffee 1 tablespoon at a time, beating until mixture appears to curdle. Place ladyfingers in 8x10-inch glass dish. Sprinkle ½ teaspoon coffee on each ladyfinger. Spread layer of creamed mixture on top. Repeat layers, ending with ladyfingers. Sprinkle with remaining coffee. Chill in refrigerator. Serve with whipped cream. Yield: 12 servings.

Suzanne Polkowske, Epsilon Kappa
Great Falls, Virginia

EASTER DESSERT

1 pint whipping cream	1 pint raspberry
3 or 4 tablespoons sugar	sherbet, softened
1 teaspoon vanilla extract	1 pint lime
18 to 20 coconut	sherbet, softened
macaroons, crushed	1 pint pineapple
1 cup chopped nuts	sherbet, softened

Whip cream in bowl, adding sugar and vanilla gradually. Spread half the macaroon crumbs in 9x13-inch pan. Add layers of half the whipping cream mixture and ¾ cup nuts. Arrange scoops of sherbet in alternating flavors in pan. Add remaining whipped cream mixture and half the remaining nuts. Top with remaining crushed macaroons and remaining nuts. Freeze until firm. Let stand at room temperature for several minutes. Cut into squares. Yield: 15 servings.

Thyra Strate, Iota Kamma
Lewis, Kansas

ENGLIGH TOFFEE DESSERT

1 cup butter, softened	½ cup chopped walnuts
2 cups confectioners'	1 teaspoon vanilla extract
sugar	3 egg whites, stiffly
3 egg yolks, beaten	beaten
2 ounces semisweet	8 ounces vanilla wafers,
chocolate, melted	crushed

Cream butter and sugar in bowl until light and fluffy. Add egg yolks, chocolate, walnuts and vanilla; mix well. Fold in egg whites. Sprinkle half the wafer crumbs in 6x6-inch dish. Add creamed mixture. Cover with remaining crumbs. Freeze until firm. Cut into squares. Yield: 12 servings.

Rita Rodoni
Butte, Montana

DEEP-FRIED ÉCLAIRS

3 frozen pastry shells,	1½ cups milk
thawed but still cold	¼ cup sour cream
Oil for deep frying	2 tablespoons Brandy
1 3-ounce package	Confectioners' sugar
vanilla pudding	
and pie filling mix	

Roll pastry shells into 5x8-inch recangles on floured surface; trim edges evenly with sharp knife. Cut each rectangle in half; each piece should be about 2½x8-inches. Heat 3 inches oil in wok to 375 degrees. Drop 2 or 3 cold pastry strips into hot oil. Fry until puffed and golden on both sides; drain on paper towels. Slit into halves horizontally. Place in single layer in shallow paper towel-lined dish; cover with paper towels. Let stand in dry place until ready to assemble. Combine pudding mix and milk in large saucepan. Bring to a boil over low heat, stirring constantly. Cool to lukewarm. Stir in sour cream and Brandy. Cover with plastic wrap. Chill for 2 to 3 hours or until very thick. Spoon chilled filling on bottom half of each pastry; cover with top. Dust with confectioners' sugar. Chill for up to 2 hours before serving. Yield: 6 servings.

Pat Smyth, Epsilon Beta
Palm Bay, Florida

FRESH FRUIT NAPOLEONS

1 large apple, chopped	1½ teaspoons lemon juice
1 large orange, peeled,	1 package frozen phyllo
chopped	dough, thawed
8 ounces seedless	¼ cup melted butter
grape halves	⅔ cup confectioners'
2 cups sliced fresh	sugar
strawberries	1 16-ounce container
1 large peach, peeled,	whipped topping
chopped	

Preheat oven to 375 degrees. Mix fruit and lemon juice in bowl. Chill in refrigeraor. Unfold 3 sheets phyllo according to package directions. Cut into halves. Keep unused phyllo covered loosely with foil to prevent drying. Brush between layers of 3-sheet section with butter; sprinkle with confectioners' sugar. Shape into cone around 2-inch long roll of aluminum foil. Brush with butter; sprinkle with confectioners' sugar. Place on baking sheet. Repeat with remaining phyllo. Bake for 8 minutes or until light brown. Cool. Spoon about ½ cup fruit mixture into each cone. Top with whipped topping. Yield: 14 Napoleons.

Jo Ann Brewer, Preceptor Alpha Beta
Senatobia, Mississippi

FROSTY FRUIT

2 cups sugar	Juice of 3 lemons
3 cups cold water	3 bananas, finely chopped
Juice of 3 oranges	

Dissolve sugar in water in large bowl. Add juices and bananas; mix well. Pour into freezer container. Freeze until firm. Chop until slushy. Refreeze. Spoon into dessert dishes. Garnish with peaches or apricots. Yield: 12 servings.

Margaret Walker, Alpha Zeta
Los Alamos, New Mexico

FROZEN FRUIT CUPS

1 17-ounce can apricot	1 6-ounce can frozen
halves, drained	orange juice
1 16-ounce can peach	concentrate, thawed
halves, drained	1 10-ounce package
1 6-ounce can crushed	frozen strawberries,
pineapple	thawed
2 bananas, sliced	¼ cup lemon juice

Cut apricots and peaches into bite-sized pieces. Mix with remaining ingredients in bowl. Spoon into paper-lined muffin cups. Freeze until firm. Store in plastic freezer bags. Let stand at room temperature for 30 minutes before serving. Yield: 12 to 18 servings.

Meryl Plummer, Upsilon
Pennsauken, New Jersey

FRUIT SOUP

3 tablespoons Minute tapioca	1 8-ounce can sliced peaches
½ cup sugar	1 8-ounce can pineapple tidbits
Pinch of salt	
2½ cups water	1 10-ounce package frozen strawberries, thawed
1 6-ounce can frozen orange juice concentrate	
	2 bananas, sliced
1 8-ounce can mandarin oranges, drained	

Combine tapioca, sugar, salt and 1 cup water in saucepan. Bring to a boil, stirring constantly. Cook for 6 to 8 mintues or until clear, stirring constantly. Stir in remaining 1½ cups water, orange juice and canned and frozen fruit. Chill for 6 hours to overnight. Stir in bananas just before serving. Yield: 12 servings.

Sonja Sturtz
Ogden, Iowa

MIXED FRUIT PIZZA

½ cup butter, softened	½ cup sugar
2¾ cups all-purpose flour	1 16-ounce can pineapple tidbits
½ cup shortening	1 10-ounce can mandarin oranges
2 teaspoons cream of tartar	
2 eggs	1 10-ounce package frozen strawberries
1½ cups sugar	
1 tablespoon soda	2 fresh peaches, peeled, sliced
8 ounces cream cheese, softened	2 fresh bananas, sliced
	Lemon juice
2 tablespoons fruit juice	2 tablespoons cornstarch

Preheat oven to 400 degrees. Combine first 7 ingredients in bowl; mix until crumbly. Press into two 12-inch pizza pans. Blend cream cheese, 2 tablespoons fruit juice and ½ cup sugar in bowl. Spread on cooled crust. Drain canned and frozen fruit, reserving juices. Brush peaches and bananas with lemon juice to prevent darkening. Arrange fruit on cream cheese mixture. Blend reserved juices with cornstarch in saucepan. Cook until thickened, stirring constantly. Drizzle over fruit. Yield: 12 servings.

Joan Warner, Xi Chi Beta
Lake Dallas, Texas

PIE FILLING PIZZA

1 2-layer package white or yellow cake mix	¼ cup quick-cooking oats
	½ cup chopped nuts
1 cup quick-cooking oats	¼ cup packed light brown sugar
6 tablespoons margarine, softened	
	½ teaspoon cinnamon
1 egg	1 21-ounce can fruit pie filling
2 tablespoons margarine, softened	

Preheat oven to 350 degrees. Combine cake mix, 1 cup oats and 6 tablespoons margarine in large mixer bowl. Beat a low speed until crumbly. Reserve 1 cup mixture for topping. Mix egg with remaining crumbs. Press into greased 12-inch pizza pan. Bake for 12 minutes. Combine reserved crumbs, 2 tablespoons margarine, ¼ cup oats, nuts, brown sugar and cinnamon in large mixer bowl; beat until well mixed. Spread pie filling over crust; sprinkle with crumbs. Bake for 15 to 20 minutes longer or until crumbs are light brown. Cool completely before cutting. Yield: 12 servings.

Glenda McMillan, Xi Zeta Eta
St. John, Kansas

SCHNITZ SOUP

1 8-ounce package dried mixed fruit	2 tablespoons sugar
	2 tablespoons all-purpose flour
1 cup white raisins	
2 quarts water	

Cut dried fruit into bite-sized pieces. Mix with raisins and water in saucepan. Cook over medium heat until tender; reduce heat. Simmer for 1 hour. Stir in mixture of sugar and flour. Cook until thickened, stirring constantly. Serve hot or cold. Garnish with whipped cream. Yield: 12 servings.

Barbara Vogel, Preceptor Phi
Mesa, Arizona

FRUIT FLUFF

8 ounces cream cheese, softened	1 16-ounce can pineapple chunks, drained
2 cups milk	
1 3-ounce package vanilla instant pudding mix	1 cup miniature marshmallows
1 11-ounce can mandarin oranges, drained	

Blend cream cheese and ½ cup milk in bowl. Add remaining milk and pudding; mix well. Add fruit and marshmallows. Chill until serving time. Yield: 12 servings.

Linda Pangburn, Alpha Lambda
Greybull, Wyoming

BISCUIT TORTONI

1 cup crushed almond macaroons	1 teaspoon almond extract
	3 pints vanilla ice cream, slightly softened
⅓ cup chopped toasted almonds	
	1 12-ounce jar apricot preserves
3 tablespoons unsalted butter, melted	

Line 8-inch square pan with aluminum foil. Mix first 4 ingredients in bowl. Reserve ¼ cup mixture for topping. Sprinkle half the remaining mixture in prepared pan. Spoon half the ice cream over crumbs. Drizzle with half the preserves and sprinkle with remaining crumb mixture. Repeat ice cream and preserve layers; top with reserved ¼ cup crumbs. Freeze for 1 hour. Cut into squares. Serve immediately. Yield: 6 servings.

Joyce Hoffman, Sigma
Nashville, Tennessee

COFFEE ICE CREAM

3 cups coffee ice cream	2 tablespoons Kahlua
1 tablespoon Crème de Cacao	1 teaspoon vanilla extract

Combine all ingredients in blender container. Process until smooth. Pour into dessert dishes. Freeze until firm. Let stand at room temperature for 15 minutes before serving. Serve with vanilla wafers. Yield: 4 servings.

Charlotte Greenwood, Preceptor Epsilon Upsilon
Eureka, California

CRANBERRY ICE

1 pound cranberries	¼ cup cold water
2 cups boiling water	2 cups sugar
1 teaspoon unflavored gelatin	2 cups ginger ale
	¼ cup cold water

Cook cranberries in 2 cups boiling water in saucepan until berries pop. Press through sieve. Dissolve gelatin in cold water. Stir gelatin and sugar into hot mixture until dissolved. Add ginger ale. Place in freezer container. Freeze until firm, stirring several times. Yield: 6 servings.

Mary Bieberle, Xi Zeta Eta
St. John, Kansas

MILKY WAY HOMEMADE ICE CREAM

5 eggs, separated	1 cup milk, scalded
2½ cups sugar	2 cups half and half
6 Milky Way candy bars, melted	1 cup whipping cream
	Milk

Beat egg whites in mixer bowl until stiff. Add beaten egg yolks and sugar; mix well. Mix candy into hot milk. Stir a small amount of hot mixture into egg mixture; stir egg mixture into hot mixture. Stir in half and half and whipping cream. Pour into ice cream freezer container. Add additional milk to fill line. Freeze, using manufacturer's instructions. Yield: 1 gallon.

Darlene Greenwell, Delta Pi
Adrian, Missouri

FRESH PEACH ICE CREAM

6 cups mashed peaches	½ cup milk
1 cup sugar	1 cup whipping cream, whipped
5 eggs	
2 cups sugar	1 cup half and half
¼ teaspoon salt	Milk
1 teaspoon vanilla extract	

Purée peaches in blender. Mix with 1 cup sugar in bowl. Let stand for several minutes. Beat eggs in mixer bowl until frothy. Add 2 cups sugar gradually, beating until thick. Add salt, vanilla and ½ cup milk; beat until sugar dissolves. Add whipped cream and half and half. Add peaches. Pour into 1-gallon ice cream freezer container. Add enough milk to fill ⅔ full. Freeze, using manufacturer's instructions. Let ripen for 1 hour. Yield: 1 gallon.

Della D. Reynolds, Tau Theta
Archie, Missouri

HOMEMADE VANILLA ICE CREAM

7 eggs	1¼ cups sugar
1 can sweetened condensed milk	1 teaspoon vanilla extract
	1 gallon warm milk

Mix eggs, condensed milk, sugar and vanilla in large bowl until blended. Stir in milk. Pour into 6-quart ice cream freezer container. Freeze, using manufacturer's instructions. Let ripen for 45 minutes. Yield: 20 to 24 servings.

Sheryl Gerberman, Theta Delta
El Campo, Texas

FREEZER-FRIED ICE CREAM

1 cup packed light brown sugar	½ cup chopped nuts
½ cup butter	½ cup flaked coconut
2½ cups cornflakes, crushed	1 quart vanilla ice cream, softened

Heat brown sugar and butter in saucepan until melted, stirring constantly. Mix in crumbs, nuts and coconut. Press half the mixture into 7x11-inch pan. Spread with ice cream. Top with remaining crumb mixture. Freeze until firm. Cut into squares. Yield: 8 to 10 servings.

Cindy Christensen, Xi Alpha Theta
Scottsdale, Arizona

ROCKY MOUNTAIN HIGH

1 15-ounce package pound cake mix	⅛ teaspoon cream of tartar
2 pints rocky road ice cream, slightly softened	6 tablespoons sugar
3 egg whites, at room temperature	

Prepare cake mix according to package directions using 5x9-inch loaf pan. Cool on wire rack. Line clean loaf pan with waxed paper. Spread ice cream in prepared pan. Freeze until firm. Slice cake in half horizontally. Place half the cake cut side up in center of foil sheet. Unmold ice cream onto cake layer. Reserve remaining cake layer for another purpose. Freeze, tightly wrapped, until firm. Preheat oven to 500 degrees. Beat egg whites and cream of tartar in bowl until soft peaks form. Add sugar 2 tablespoons at a time, beating until very stiff peaks form. Place ice cream cake, cake side down, on chilled cookie sheet. Spread meringue over entire surface, sealing to cookie sheet. Bake for 3 minutes or until meringue is lightly browned. Place on chilled platter. Serve immediately. Yield: 8 to 10 servings.

Dixie Norris, Xi Alpha Phi
Boulder, Colorado

*When serving ice cream to a group, **Verla Vaepel, Page, Arizona**, lines muffin cups with paper liners, adds scoops of ice cream and tops with colored sugar. Store in freezer and serve on doily-covered plates.*

ORANGE AND PINEAPPLE SHERBET

2 cups sugar
2 cups water
1 cup juice-pack
  crushed pineapple

1 bottle of orange
  crush
2 cups milk

Dissolve sugar in water in saucepan. Boil for 5 minutes. Add remaining ingredients; mix well. Pour into ice cream freezer. Freeze, using manufacturer's instructions. Yield: 2 quarts.

Judy Kutcher, Xi Zeta Mu
Eldridge, Iowa

ORANGY RUM SHERBET

2 teaspoons unflavored
  gelatin
3/4 cup cold water
3/4 cup sugar
1½ tablespoons lime
  juice

1 cup orange juice
½ cup light rum
1 tablespoon grated
  orange rind
Salt to taste

Soften gelatin in ¼ cup water. Combine ½ cup water and sugar in saucepan. Boil for 1 minute. Add gelatin; stir until dissolved. Add juices, rum, orange rind and salt. Strain and cool. Pour into freezer tray. Freeze until slushy. Place mixture in chilled bowl; beat with rotary beater until smooth. Return to freezer tray. Freeze until almost firm, stirring several times. Yield: 4 servings.

JoAnne, Murhly, Zeta Kappa
Virginia Beach, Virginia

SHERBET SURPRISE CUPS

½ cup semisweet
  chocolate chips
4 1-inch white chocolate
  truffles

1 cup favorite flavor
  sherbet
¼ cup Crème de Cacao

Heat chocolate chips in heavy 1-quart saucepan over low heat until melted, stirring constantly. Spread over bottom and sides of paper-lined muffin cups. Chill until firm. Peel off paper cups carefully. Place 1 truffle in each chocolate cup. Scoop ¼ cup sherbet into thin petals with tablespoon. Arrange sherbet over and around truffle. Pour 1 tablespoon Crème de Cacao over sherbet in each chocolate cup. Yield: 4 servings.

 D. Jean Colburn, Zeta Nu
Boardman, Oregon

FLOWERPOT SUNDAES

1 pint strawberry ice
  cream
1 pint chocolate ice
  cream
1 pint vanilla ice cream
8 marshmallows
8 round lollipops

1 tube pink frosting
  with writing tip
4 spearmint gumdrop
  leaves, split into
  halves
Green sugar crystals
Tiny multicolor mints

Fill 7-ounce paper cups nearly to top with assorted ice creams using ice cream scoop. Cover. Freeze until firm.

Cut marshmallows with scissors around edge to make petals; attach to lollipops with small amount of frosting. Make rosettes of frosting in center of lollipop flowers and attach gumdrop leaves with frosting. Insert flowers into ice cream cups. Sprinkle ice cream with sugar crystals and mints. Freeze until serving time. Yield: 8 servings.

Gail Miller, Preceptor Gamma Beta
Clarks Summit, Pennsylvania

APPLE CRUNCH OVER ICE CREAM

1 21-ounce can apple
  pie filling
1 9-ounce package white
  cake mix

3 tablespoons margarine
⅓ cup packed light
  brown sugar
Vanilla ice cream

Pour apple pie filling into 8x8-inch glass baking dish. Sprinkle cake mix over filling; dot with margarine. Sprinkle brown sugar over top. Microwave on High for 12 minutes. Let stand for 5 minutes. Serve warm over ice cream. Yield: 4 servings.

Sally Andres, Beta Pi
Clewiston, Florida

KAHLUA CARMELO SAUCE

3 cups miniature
  marshmallows
1¼ cups packed light
  brown sugar
1 cup whipping cream

¼ cup Kahlua
¼ cup butter
1½ teaspoons vanilla
  extract

Bring marshmallows, brown sugar, cream and Kahlua to a boil in heavy 1½-quart saucepan, stirring until sugar is dissolved. Cook to 224 degrees on candy thermometer, stirring occasionally; remove from heat. Add butter and vanilla. Cool. Serve warm or at room temperature on ice cream or in parfaits. Store in refrigerator. Yield: 2¼ cups.

Margaret Fleck, Delta Eta Gamma
Carson, California

LEMON LUSH

1 cup all-purpose flour
½ cup chopped nuts
½ cup margarine,
  softened
1 cup confectioners'
  sugar
8 ounces cream cheese,
  softened

1 8-ounce container
  whipped topping
1 6-ounce package
  lemon instant
  pudding mix
2⅔ cups milk
Nuts, chopped

Preheat oven to 375 degrees. Combine first 3 ingredients in bowl; mix well. Press into 8x11-inch glass baking dish. Bake for 15 minutes or until light brown. Cool. Cream confectioners' sugar and cream cheese in bowl until fluffy. Fold in 1 cup whipped topping. Spread over cooled crust. Combine pudding mix and milk in bowl. Beat until thickened. Spoon over creamed mixture. Top with remaining whipped topping. Sprinkle with nuts. Chill until serving time. Yield: 6 to 8 servings.

Penelope O. Soos, Xi Delta Zeta
Webster, New York

LEMON SOUFFLÉ

2 tablespoons margarine,
  softened
1 cup sugar
¼ cup all-purpose flour
¼ teaspoon salt
Grated rind of 1 lemon

5 or 6 tablespoons
  lemon juice
3 egg yolks, well beaten
1⅓ cups milk
3 egg whites, stiffly
  beaten

Preheat oven to 350 degrees. Cream margarine in bowl.
Add sugar, flour, salt, lemon rind and juice; mix well.
Add well-beaten egg yolks to milk; stir into lemon mixture. Fold in stiffly beaten egg whites gently. Pour into
greased 8x8-inch baking dish. Place in shallow pan of
hot water. Bake for 45 minutes until lightly browned.
Yield: 8 to 10 servings.

Frances Holda, Laureate Pi
Glendora, California

MICROWAVE LEMON PUDDING

1 cup sugar
⅓ cup cornstarch
⅛ teaspoon salt
2 cups cold water
2 drops of yellow
  food coloring
3 egg yolks

3 tablespoons butter
⅓ cup lemon juice
2 teaspoons grated
  lemon rind
3 egg whites
6 tablespoons sugar

Combine first 5 ingredients in casserole. Microwave on
High for 3 minutes; stir until smooth. Microwave for 3
minutes longer; stir. Beat egg yolks in small bowl. Stir a
small amount of hot mixture into egg yolks; stir egg yolks
into hot mixture. Microwave for 4 minutes or until thickened, stirring once. Stir in butter, lemon juice and rind.
Beat egg whites in mixer bowl until soft peaks form. Beat
in sugar, 1 tablespoon at a time, until stiff peaks form.
Fold into lemon mixture. Microwave for 3 to 4 minutes
longer. Yield: 8 servings.

Claudene Harland, Preceptor Kappa Xi
Dinuba, California

COTTON CANDY CAKE

9 egg whites
1 teaspoon vanilla extract
1 teaspoon white vinegar
1¾ cups confectioners'
  sugar

6 chocolate-covered
  toffee bars, crushed
1 16-ounce container
  whipped topping

Preheat oven to 275 degrees. Beat egg whites in large
mixer bowl until soft peaks form. Add vanilla and vinegar; beat until blended. Add sugar gradually, beating
constantly until very stiff peaks form. Spread evenly in 2
greased 9-inch baking pans. Bake for 1½ hours. Turn off
oven. Let stand in closed oven for 2 hours. Fold candy
into whipped topping. Spread candy mixture between
layers and on top. Chill until serving time.
Yield: 12 servings.

Gena Farrin, Eta Pi
Pocahontas, Arkansas

MAGIC SURPRISE CAKE

3 egg whites
½ teaspoon cream of tartar
¼ teaspoon baking
  powder
1 teaspoon vanilla extract
16 crackers, crushed

1 cup sugar
1 cup chopped nuts
1 cup whipping cream,
  whipped
1 cup flaked coconut

Preheat oven to 325 degrees. Beat egg whites in bowl
until foamy. Add cream of tartar. Beat until stiff peaks
form. Fold in next 5 ingredients in order listed. Spread in
well-buttered 18x20-inch baking dish. Bake for 28 minutes. Cool. Layer whipped cream and coconut on meringue just before serving. Yield: 10 to 12 servings.

Lola Bohannon, Xi Mu
Santa Fe, New Mexico

MANGO MERINGUES

6 egg whites
¼ teaspoon cream of tartar
1½ cups sugar
1 teaspoon vanilla extract
2 tablespoons lime juice

3 to 4 cups sliced fresh
  mangoes, puréed
1¾ cups sweetened
  condensed milk
½ cup whipped cream

Preheat oven to 250 degrees. Beat egg whites in mixer
bowl until foamy; add cream of tartar. Add sugar gradually, beating constantly until stiff peaks form. Add vanilla.
Cover 2 baking sheets with foil. Drop meringue by
spoonfuls into 2½-inch mounds. Bake for 1 hour. Turn
off oven. Let meringues stand in closed oven for several
hours. Combine lime juice, mango purée and condensed
milk in bowl; blend well. Chill for 3 hours. Fold in
whipped cream. Spoon into meringue shells.
Yield: 12 servings.

Patricia Dewey, Xi Gamma Tau
Nacogdoches, Texas

SPECIAL MERINGUES

3 egg whites
¼ teaspoon cream of
  tartar
¾ cup sugar
1½ teaspoons vanilla
  extract
½ cup chopped almonds

1 egg white
2 tablespoons sugar
1 cup whipping cream
1½ cups confectioners'
  sugar
1 10-ounce package
  frozen raspberries

Preheat oven to 275 degrees. Beat 3 egg whites and
cream of tartar in bowl until foamy. Add ¾ cup sugar 1
tablespoon at a time, beating until stiff and glossy. Add
vanilla. Swirl by heaping tablespoonfuls onto parch-
ment-lined baking sheet, making 16. Bake for 30 minutes. Turn off oven. Let stand in closed oven for 1 hour.
Mix almonds, 1 unbeaten egg white and 2 tablespoons
sugar in bowl. Spread on ungreased baking sheet. Bake
for 30 minutes. Cool and crumble. Whip cream with confectioners' sugar in bowl. Place flat sides of 2 meringues
together with 2 tablespoons whipped cream between.
Stand on side on dessert platter. Top with warm raspberries and additional almonds. Yield: 8 servings.

Dee A. McBride, Xi Eta Lambda
Burlington, Kansas

MERINGUE CRUNCH SUNDAE

4 egg whites, at room
   temperature
¼ teaspoon cream of
   tartar
¼ teaspoon vanilla extract
1 cup sugar
½ cup finely chopped
   blanched almonds

4 cups fresh raspberries
1 cup sugar
3 to 4 tablespoons
   Chambord
1 quart lemon, chocolate
   or vanilla ice cream
Chopped pistachio nuts

Preheat oven to 250 degrees. Draw two 8-inch circles on baking parchment. Place marked side down on greased baking sheet; grease parchment. Beat egg whites in mixer bowl until soft peaks form. Beat in cream of tartar, vanilla and 1 tablespoon sugar. Add remaining 1 cup sugar gradually, beating until stiff peaks form. Fold in almonds. Spread half the meringue evenly onto each marked circle. Bake for 1 hour. Turn off oven. Let stand in closed oven for 1 hour or until dry. Cool completely. Crush coarsely. May store in plastic bag in freezer for up to 1 month. Mix raspberries, 1 cup sugar and Chambord in bowl. Chill in refrigerator. Roll 1 scoop ice cream in frozen meringue crumbs. May freeze for up to 2 hours if desired. Place in dessert dishes. Top with raspberry sauce and nuts. Garnish with unsweetened whipped cream and additional fresh raspberries. Yield: 6 servings.

Julie St.Clair, Psi Chi
Los Altos, California

AUSTRALIAN PAVLOVA

3 egg whites
½ teaspoon cream of tartar
¾ cup sugar
1 cup whipping cream,
   chilled

3 tablespoons sugar
1½ cups sliced
   strawberries
Kiwifruit, peeled, sliced

Preheat oven to 225 degrees. Cover baking sheet with baking parchment. Beat egg whites and cream of tartar in small mixer bowl until foamy. Add ¾ cup sugar 1 tablespoon at a time, beating until stiff and glossy; do not underbeat. Drop by ½ cupfuls onto prepared baking sheet; shape into ovals. Bake for 1 hour. Turn off oven. Let stand in closed oven for 1 hour. Cool completely. Beat whipping cream and 3 tablespoons sugar in chilled bowl until soft peaks form. Fold in strawberries. Place baked meringue on serving plate. Spoon on whipped cream mixture. Arrange kiwifruit over top. Yield: 12 servings.

Jana M. Whitesell, Mu Beta
Waterville, Kansas

PAVLOVA WITH STRAWBERRIES

4 egg whites
3 tablespoons cold water
1 cup sugar
1 teaspoon cornstarch
1 teaspoon vanilla extract

1 teaspoon vinegar
1 20-ounce package
   frozen strawberries,
   thawed
Sugar to taste

Preheat oven to 320 degrees. Beat egg whites in mixer bowl until stiff. Add cold water; beat until stiff. Add sugar, beating until very stiff. Fold in cornstarch, vanilla and vinegar. Spread in 2-inch thick circle on waxed paper-lined baking sheet. Bake for 10 minutes. Turn off oven. Let stand in closed oven until oven is cold. Mash strawberries; add sugar. Cut pavlova into wedges; cover with strawberries. Garnish with whipped cream. Yield: 10 to 12 servings.

Nancy Andrade, Preceptor Delta
Kaneohe, Hawaii

SWEDISH ALMOND TORTE

7 tablespoons butter,
   softened
1¾ cups confectioners'
   sugar, sifted
2 tablespoons grated
   cooked potato

1½ cups ground blanched
   almonds
3 egg whites, stiffly
   beaten

Preheat oven to 350 degrees. Cream butter, confectioners' sugar and potato in mixer bowl until smooth. Add almonds. Fold in stiffly beaten egg whites. Spread in buttered 9-inch layer cake pan. Bake for 40 to 45 minutes. Slice torte; spoon Lemon Sauce over slices.
Yield: 8 to 12 servings.

LEMON SAUCE

1 cup sugar
Juice and grated rind
   of 1 lemon

6 egg yolks, slightly
   beaten
1 cup white wine

Mix sugar, lemon juice and rind and egg yolks in saucepan. Stir in white wine. Cook over medium heat until thickened, stirring constantly. Remove from heat. Stir until cool.

Linnea Wiese, Tau
Worland, Wyoming

MOON CAKE

1 cup water
½ cup butter
1 cup all-purpose flour
4 eggs
2 3-ounce packages
   vanilla instant
   pudding mix

8 ounces cream cheese,
   softened
1 16-ounce container
   whipped topping
Chocolate syrup
Walnuts

Preheat oven to 400 degrees. Bring water and butter to a boil in saucepan. Add flour; mix well. Add eggs 1 at a time, beating well after each addition. Spread in 10x15-inch cake pan. Bake for 30 minutes. Cool. Prepare pudding mix using package directions. Add cream cheese; mix well. Pour over puff layers. Chill for 20 minutes. Spread whipped topping over pudding. Drizzle with chocolate syrup. Chill until serving time. Sprinkle with walnuts. Yield: 20 servings.

Patricia A. Main, Preceptor Psi
Fremont, Nebraska

CROWNING GLORY

1 11-ounce can mandarin orange sections	2 cups marshmallows
1 envelope unflavored gelatin	1 pint orange sherbet
½ cup water	1 cup whipping cream, whipped
	1 angel food cake, cubed

Drain oranges, reserving syrup. Soften gelatin in water in saucepan. Add reserved syrup. Cook over low heat until gelatin dissolves, stirring constantly. Add marshmallows. Cook until melted, stirring constantly; remove from heat. Add sherbet. Stir until melted. Chill until partially set. Fold in whipped cream, cake cubes and orange sections. Pour into 2½-quart mold. Chill for 6 hours to overnight. Unmold onto serving plate. Yield: 8 to 10 servings.

Jean Heston, Iota Pi
Humeston, Iowa

SWEETLY SPICED ORANGES

8 large navel oranges	¼ cup confectioners' sugar
1 tablespoon orange flower water	¼ teaspoon cinnamon

Grate rind of 2 oranges; set aside. Remove and discard peel and pith of all oranges. Slice oranges crosswise ¼ inch thick; arrange on serving plate. Sprinkle with flower water; sift confectioners' sugar over top and sprinkle with orange rind. Refrigerate, covered, for 2 hours or longer. Sprinkle with cinnamon just before serving. Yield: 8 servings.

Jeanie Waugh, Alpha Pi
Kathy Kaufman, Alpha Pi
Missoula, Montana

NATILLAS

2 tablespoons all-purpose flour	1 egg yolk
2 cups milk	1 egg white
3 tablespoons sugar	2 tablespoons sugar
	¾ teaspoon vanilla extract

Blend flour with ¼ cup milk in small bowl; strain if necessary. Mix remaining 1¾ cups milk with 3 tablespoons sugar and egg yolk in saucepan. Stir in flour mixture gradually. Bring to a boil over medium heat, stirring constantly; reduce heat to low. Simmer for 5 minutes, stirring constantly. Set aside. Beat egg white in bowl until foamy. Add 2 tablespoons sugar, beating until soft peaks form. Add to cooked milk mixture gradually, stirring quickly just until blended. Stir in vanilla. Cool for 20 minutes; stir. Serve warm or chilled. Garnish with cinnamon or nutmeg. Yield: 5 servings.

Loyola Vigil, Xi Beta Lambda
Chama, New Mexico

PEACH COBBLER

½ cup melted butter	1 cup sugar
1 cup milk	1 28-ounce can peaches
¾ cup buttermilk baking mix	½ cup water

Preheat oven to 350 degrees. Pour butter into bottom of 9x12-inch baking dish. Mix milk, baking mix and sugar in bowl. Pour over butter. Spoon peaches and water over batter. Bake until brown. Yield: 6 servings.

Betty McGinty, Preceptor Mu
Neosho, Missouri

PEACHES AND CREAM

1 3-ounce package lemon gelatin	1 3-ounce package lemon gelatin
1 cup boiling water	1 cup boiling water
1 cup orange juice	1 21-ounce can peach pie filling
3 ounces cream cheese, softened	
1 12-ounce container whipped topping	

Dissolve 1 package gelatin in 1 cup boiling water in bowl. Add orange juice. Chill until partially set. Blend cream cheese into whipped topping. Fold into gelatin mixture. Pour into 9x13-inch dish. Chill until firm. Dissolve 1 package gelatin in 1 cup boiling water. Stir in pie filling. Pour over congealed layer. Chill until firm. Yield: 10 to 16 servings.

Pat Jacoby, Rho Chi
Highland, Illinois

PEACH CRISP

1 28-ounce can sliced peaches	1 cup flaked coconut
1 2-layer package butter brickle cake mix	1 cup chopped nuts
	½ cup melted margarine

Preheat oven to 325 degrees. Layer undrained peaches, cake mix and mixture of coconut and nuts in 9x13-inch baking pan. Drizzle melted margarine over all. Bake for 50 to 55 minutes or until brown. Serve with ice cream or whipped topping. Yield: 12 to 15 servings.

Dorothy Bobbitt, Xi Delta Nu
Lamont, Oklahoma

PEACH MOUSSE

⅓ cup sugar	1 29-ounce can sliced peaches, drained
2 envelopes unflavored gelatin	¼ cup Amaretto
4 eggs	2 cups whipping cream, whipped
3 egg yolks	

Mix sugar and gelatin in 2-quart saucepan. Beat eggs and egg yolks until thick and lemon-colored. Stir into gelatin mixture. Cook over medium heat just until mixture comes to a boil, stirring constantly. Remove from heat. Purée peaches in blender. Add peaches and Amaretto to cooked mixture. Chill until partially set. Fold in whipped cream gently. Pour into 8-cup mold. Refrigerate until firm. Unmold onto serving plate. Serve with Tortilla Crispas (page 230). Yield: 6 servings.

Pam Allen, Theta Iota
Aurelia, Iowa

BLUE RIBBON PERSIMMON ROLL

1 1-pound package graham crackers, finely crushed	20 marshmallows, chopped
1½ cups persimmon pulp	1 cup chopped nuts
1½ cups sugar	1½ teaspoons vanilla extract

Reserve ½ cup crumbs. Combine remaining crumbs and ingredients in bowl; mix well. Shape into roll. Roll in reserved crumbs. Chill, wrapped, overnight. Cut into slices. Serve with whipped topping, sauce or ice cream. Yield: 8 servings.

Pauline Scherschel, Alpha Beta
Bedford, Indiana

SUPER PINEAPPLE SPLIT

¼ cup butter, softened	¼ cup butter, softened
2 cups confectioners' sugar	1 20-ounce can crushed pineapple, drained
½ cup semisweet chocolate chips	2 large bananas
1½ cups evaporated milk	2 tablespoons lemon juice
1 12-ounce package vanilla wafers, crushed	½ cup coarsely chopped pecans
½ cup butter, softened	1 16-ounce container whipped topping
8 ounces cream cheese, softened	1 3-ounce jar maraschino cherries, drained

Combine first 4 ingredients in saucepan. Cook until thick and smooth, stirring constantly. Cool. Mix vanilla wafer crumbs and ½ cup butter in bowl. Press over bottom of 9x13-inch baking dish. Beat cream cheese and ¼ cup butter in bowl; blend well. Add ⅔ cup pineapple; mix well. Spread over crust. Slice bananas ½ inch thick. Drizzle with lemon juice; drain well. Arrange over cream cheese layer. Top with chocolate sauce. Sprinkle pecans over sauce. Spread whipped topping over all. Sprinkle with remaining pineapple and cherries. Chill for several hours. Yield: 12 servings.

Jane Moonen, Preceptor Kappa
Lilburn, Georgia

PRALINE CREME DESSERT

2 eggs	1 teaspoon soda
3 cups packed light brown sugar	1 cup chopped pecans
¾ cup all-purpose flour	2 cups whipping cream
	Sugar to taste

Preheat oven to 350 degrees. Beat eggs in bowl until frothy. Blend in brown sugar. Add flour, soda and pecans; mix well. Spread in buttered 9x13-inch baking pan. Bake for 35 to 40 minutes or until golden. This usually rises during baking but will fall. Cool completely. Cut or break into ¼ to ½-inch pieces. Whip cream in mixer bowl; sweeten to taste. Fold in crumbs. Spread in 9x13-inch pan. Freeze for 24 hours or longer. Cut into squares. Yield: 12 servings.

Ralph E. Williams, Alpha Alpha
Sapulpa, Oklahoma

PIÑA COLADA SQUARES

8 ounces cream cheese, softened	1 8-ounce can crushed pineapple with syrup
⅓ cup sugar	2⅔ cups flaked coconut
½ teaspoon rum extract	Pineapple
3½ cups whipped topping	Cherries

Beat cream cheese with sugar and rum extract in bowl until smooth. Fold in 2 cups whipped topping, pineapple with syrup and 2 cups coconut. Spread in 8-inch square pan lined with plastic wrap. Freeze for 2 hours or until firm. Invert onto serving dish; spread with remaining whipped topping; sprinkle with remaining ⅔ cup coconut. Cut into squares. Garnish with pineapple and cherries. Yield: 9 servings.

Norma Mae Ottmann, Laureate Lambda
Omaha, Nebraska

APPLE PUDDING

1 cup sugar	1 cup all-purpose flour
¼ cup margarine, softened	½ teaspoon soda
1 egg	1 teaspoon cinnamon
2 apples, peeled, sliced	½ cup ground nuts
	½ teaspoon vanilla extract

Preheat oven to 350 degrees. Cream sugar and margarine in bowl. Blend in egg. Add apples, dry ingredients, nuts and vanilla, mixing well after each addition. Pour into well-greased pie plate. Bake for 30 to 40 minutes or until golden. Cool. Garnish with whipped topping and cinnamon just before serving. Yield: 8 servings.

Ruth Casteel, Laureate Gamma Theta
Diamond Bar, California

COOL BANANA PUDDING

2 3-ounce packages banana instant pudding mix	1 12-ounce container whipped topping
3 cups cold milk	2 packages vanilla wafers
1 14-ounce can sweetened condensed milk	4 or 5 medium bananas, sliced

Prepare pudding mix according to package directions using 3 cups milk. Fold in sweetened condensed milk and 1 cup whipped topping. Layer vanilla wafers, bananas and pudding mixture ½ at a time in 9x13-inch dish. Top with remaining whipped topping. Chill, covered with plastic wrap, until serving time. Yield: 16 servings.

Marie E. Rice, Sigma
Northport, Alabama

A favorite party of **Sherry Smith, Omega, Owensboro, Kentucky,** *is a sundae party. She arranges scoops of different flavors of ice cream in a large bowl and serves crushed pineapple, coconut, nuts, mandarin orange slices and whipped cream in individual bowls for toppings.*

BREAD AND BUTTER PUDDING

3 tablespoons raisins
⅓ cup warm water
1 cup plus 3 tablespoons
   whipping cream
1 cup plus 2 tablespoons
   milk
1 vanilla bean,
   split lengthwise
Pinch of salt

4 eggs
¾ cup sugar
4 small croissants, cut
   into ½-inch slices
3 tablespoons butter,
   melted
3 tablespoons
   confectioners' sugar

Preheat oven to 375 degrees. Mix raisins and water in bowl. Let stand for 30 minutes; drain well. Bring cream, milk, vanilla bean and salt to a simmer in double boiler. Beat eggs and sugar in medium bowl. Whisk in cream mixture gradually. Remove vanilla bean; scrape seed from bean into cream mixture and mix well. Brush croissant slices lightly with melted butter. Arrange in 9-cup soufflé dish. Sprinkle with raisins. Strain custard over croissant slices. Press slices gently to absorb liquid. Sprinkle with 1 tablespoon confectioners' sugar. Place in large baking pan. Add enough hot water to large pan to come 1 inch up side of soufflé dish. Bake for 45 to 50 minutes or until tester inserted in center comes out clean. Spoon pudding onto plates. Sprinkle remaining confectioners' sugar over top. Serve hot. Yield: 4 servings.

Marie Martin, Preceptor Gamma Upsilon
Orlando, Florida

BREAD PUDDING WITH AMARETTO

1 loaf stale French bread
1 quart milk
4 jumbo eggs
2 cups sugar
1 cup raisins
2 tablespoons cinnamon

2 teaspoons vanilla extract
¾ cup sugar
½ cup butter
1 egg, slightly beaten
½ cup Amaretto

Preheat oven to 350 degrees. Soak bread in milk in large bowl for 1 hour. Mix in 4 eggs, 2 cups sugar, raisins, cinnamon and vanilla. Pour into 9x13-inch baking pan. Bake for 1 hour. Blend ¾ cup sugar and butter in saucepan over medium heat, stirring constantly. Stir in 1 egg. Cook for 1 minute, stirring constantly; remove from heat. Add Amaretto. Spoon over warm bread pudding.
Yield: 12 servings.

Dale St.Amant, Eta Rho
Mandeville, Louisiana

LOUISIANA BREAD PUDDING

4 eggs
4 cups low-fat milk
1 cup sugar
½ teaspoon salt

½ teaspoon cinnamon
½ teaspoon nutmeg
4 cups French bread cubes
1 cup raisins

Whisk eggs and milk in 2-quart casserole until blended. Stir in remaining ingredients. Let stand for several minutes. Microwave, uncovered, on High for 20 minutes or

until knife inserted in center comes out clean. Serve with Whiskey Sauce. Yield: 12 to 16 servings.

WHISKEY SAUCE

1 teaspoon cornstarch
1 cup sugar
1 cup low-fat milk

2 tablespoons margarine
¼ cup Bourbon

Whisk together first 4 ingredients in 1½-quart casserole. Microwave on High for 4 to 6 minutes or until sauce is thickened and smooth, stirring every 2 minutes. Stir in Bourbon. Yield: 1½ cups.

Flora Simay, Laureate Beta Alpha
Palm Desert, California

CHOCOLATE CREAM

8 ounces sweet cooking
   chocolate, chopped
⅓ cup butter

4 egg yolks, beaten
4 egg whites
2 tablespoons sugar

Melt chocolate and butter in small heavy saucepan over low heat, stirring constantly. Stir about half the mixture into beaten egg yolks; stir egg yolks into hot mixture. Cook over low heat for 2 minutes or until very thick and glossy, stirring constantly; remove from heat. Cool to room temperature. Beat egg whites in mixer bowl until soft peaks form. Add sugar gradually, beating until stiff peaks form. Fold a small amount of egg whites into chocolate mixture to lighten; fold chocolate mixture into remaining egg whites. Spoon about ¼ cup mixture into each dessert dish. Chill, covered, for several hours to overnight. Garnish with whipped cream and finely chopped orange rind. Yield: 10 servings.

Laraine Hopper, Xi Iota Mu
Crescent City, California

FLAN

¼ cup sugar
1 15-ounce can
   evaporated milk
1 14-ounce can
   sweetened condensed
   milk

1 teaspoon salt
1 tablespoon sugar
2 tablespoons vanilla
   extract
1 cup milk
4 eggs, beaten

Caramelize ¼ cup sugar in bottom of 1½-quart metal mold; tilt to coat all sides. Mix remaining ingredients except eggs in bowl. Strain beaten eggs into milk mixture. Pour into mold; cover with aluminum foil and secure with rubber band. Place in pressure cooker. Add water to ½ the depth of mold. Cover tightly. Cook at 10 pounds pressure for 10 minutes. Remove from pressure cooker. Cool. Invert onto serving plate. Yield: 10 to 12 servings.

Judith A. Miller, Eta Psi
Palm Harbor, Florida

*After the theater, **Billie Smith, Iota Lambda, Monument, Colorado,** feels it is especially nice to have people come over for desserts and cheese, sweet omelets or sweet crêpes.*

PEACH PUDDING DESSERT

1 cup all-purpose flour	1 16-ounce can sliced
¾ cup sugar	peaches, drained
2 teaspoons baking	1 cup packed light
powder	brown sugar
¼ teaspoon salt	¼ cup chopped nuts
½ cup milk	1 teaspoon cinnamon
3 tablespoons corn oil	1 cup boiling water

Preheat oven to 350 degrees. Mix flour, sugar, baking powder and salt in bowl. Add milk and oil; beat until smooth. Pour into ungreased 8x8-inch baking pan. Arrange peaches on top. Mix brown sugar, nuts and cinnamon in bowl. Sprinkle over peaches. Pour boiling water over top. Bake for 60 to 70 minutes or until toothpick inserted in center comes out clean. Garnish with whipped topping. Yield: 9 servings.

Marjorie Jurgensen, Mu Upsilon
Manilla, Iowa

RICE PUDDING WITH RASPBERRY SAUCE

2½ cups milk	½ cup whipping cream,
¼ teaspoon salt	whipped
½ cup uncooked rice	1 10-ounce package
1 teaspoon vanilla extract	frozen raspberries
1 teaspoon almond extract	4 teaspoons cornstarch
⅓ cup sugar	½ cup red currant jelly

Bring milk and salt to a boil in medium saucepan over medium heat. Stir in rice; reduce heat. Simmer for 5 minutes, stirring constantly; cover. Cook for 45 minutes or until milk is almost absorbed and rice is tender and creamy. Add vanilla, almond extract and sugar; stir until sugar dissolves. Pour into large bowl; cover. Refrigerate for 2 hours or until chilled. Fold in whipped cream. Refrigerate, covered, until ready to serve. Mix raspberries, cornstarch and jelly in small saucepan. Bring to a boil over medium heat, stirring constantly. Boil for 1 minute, stirring constantly. Cool. Serve over rice pudding. Yield: 6 servings.

Mary Taylor, Preceptor Delta
Salt Lake City, Utah

PUMPKIN CHIFFON

1¾ cups graham	2 3-ounce packages
cracker crumbs	vanilla instant
¼ cup sugar	pudding mix
½ cup melted butter	2 cups canned pumpkin
8 ounces cream cheese,	Cinnamon to taste
softened	1 8-ounce container
2 eggs	whipped topping
¾ cup sugar	¼ cup chopped pecans
¾ cup milk	

Preheat oven to 350 degrees. Combine first 3 ingredients in 9x13-inch dish. Press over bottom. Beat cream cheese, eggs and ¾ cup sugar in bowl until smooth. Pour over crust. Bake for 20 minutes. Cool. Combine milk with pudding mix in bowl. Beat for 2 minutes. Add pumpkin and cinnamon. Stir in 1 cup whipped topping. Spread over cooled cream cheese layer. Spread remaining whipped topping over pudding mixture. Sprinkle with pecans. Chill until serving time. Yield: 20 servings.

Mona G. Johnson, Sigma Xi
Harviell, Missouri

STRAWBERRY BUTTER TORTE

¼ cup melted butter	1½ cups sliced fresh
1 cup vanilla wafer	strawberries
crumbs	1 cup whipping cream
½ cup butter, softened	¼ cup sugar
2½ cups confectioners'	½ cup vanilla wafer
sugar	crumbs
2 eggs	

Combine melted butter and 1 cup crumbs in bowl; mix well. Press over bottom of 8x8-inch dish. Combine remaining softened butter and confectioners' sugar in mixer bowl. Beat until light and fluffy. Add eggs; beat well. Spread over crumbs. Spoon strawberries on top. Whip cream with sugar in bowl until soft peaks form. Spread over strawberries. Sprinkle remaining crumbs on top. Keep refrigerated. Yield: 8 to 10 servings.

Carol Deeds, Phi Alpha Xi
Goodland, Kansas

STRAWBERRIES CHANTILLY

⅓ cup whipping cream	1 pint fresh strawberries
2 teaspoons sugar	¼ cup Melba Sauce
¼ teaspoon vanilla extract	Kirsch to taste
Dash of salt	Whipped cream

Combine cream with sugar, vanilla and salt in chilled mixer bowl. Beat with chilled beaters until doubled in bulk. Rinse, drain and hull strawberries; drain on paper towels. Mix whole strawberries with ¼ cup Melba Sauce and Kirsch in bowl. Spoon into clear dessert dishes. Top with whipped cream. Yield: 4 servings.

MELBA SAUCE

1 10-ounce package	1 tablespoon lemon juice
frozen raspberries,	¼ teaspoon grated lemon
thawed	rind
½ cup red currant jelly	Dash of salt
¼ cup sugar	

Simmer raspberries in covered saucepan for 15 minutes. Press through fine strainer into 1 cup measure. Add enough water to measure ⅔ cup. Combine with remaining ingredients in saucepan. Simmer until smooth, stirring constantly. Store in airtight container in refrigerator. For thicker sauce, use additional jelly or reduce water. Yield: 1¼ cups.

Nancy K. Henry, Xi Beta Psi
Raleigh, North Carolina

FROZEN STRAWBERRY DELIGHT

1 cup all-purpose flour	3 egg whites
½ cup pecans	1 cup sugar
¼ cup packed light brown sugar	1 tablespoon lemon juice
½ cup melted butter	1 teaspoon salt
1 10-ounce package frozen strawberries	1 teaspoon vanilla extract
	1 16-ounce container whipped topping

Preheat oven to 350 degrees. Combine first 4 ingredients in bowl; mix well. Spread on baking sheet. Bake for 15 minutes, stirring frequently. Cool. Crumble into 9x13-inch pan, reserving a small amount for topping. Combine thawed strawberries, egg whites, sugar, lemon juice and salt in large mixer bowl. Beat until stiff peaks form. Fold in vanilla and whipped topping. Spoon into prepared pan. Top with reserved crumbs. Freeze overnight. Yield: 12 to 15 servings.

Kathy Dorson, Zeta Nu
Princeton, Missouri

STRAWBERRY DELIGHT

½ cup plus 6 tablespoons butter, softened	2 cups confectioners' sugar
1½ cups all-purpose flour	1 8-ounce container whipped topping
2 tablespoons sugar	1 20-ounce can strawberry pie filling
1 cup chopped pecans	
8 ounces cream cheese, softened	

Preheat oven to 350 degrees. Combine first 4 ingredients in bowl. Press into 9x13-inch baking dish. Bake for 20 minutes. Cool. Beat cream cheese, confectioners' sugar and whipped topping in bowl. Spread on cooled crust. Spoon pie filling on top. Chill until serving time. Yield: 12 servings.

Edna Dehart, Alpha Theta Psi
Elkhart, Texas

STRAWBERRY SOUP

2 10-ounce packages frozen strawberries, thawed	2 tablespoons cornstarch
	1 cup white wine
	1 tablespoon lemon juice
Sugar to taste	

Mix strawberries and sugar in saucepan. Dissolve cornstarch in ¼ cup wine. Stir into strawberries. Cook over low heat until mixture begins to thicken and bubble, stirring constantly. Stir in remaining ¾ cup wine and lemon juice. Cook for several minutes. Serve hot or cold, garnished with whipped cream or sour cream. Yield: 4 servings.

Frances Kucera, Laureate Omicron
Eugene, Oregon

STRAWBERRIES WITH LEMON CREME

8 ounces cream cheese, softened	1 teaspoon grated lemon rind
⅓ cup confectioners' sugar	1 tablespoon lemon juice
	42 fresh strawberries

Beat cream cheese, confectioners' sugar, lemon rind and juice in mixer bowl until smooth. Chill, covered, for several hours to overnight. Remove hulls from strawberries; place hulled end down on paper-lined trays. Cut shallow X in end of each strawberry with sharp knife. Spoon filling into pastry bag fitted with ½-inch star tip. Pipe heaping teaspoonful into center of each strawberry. Chill for up to 2 hours before serving. Place in paper bonbon cups. Yield: 3½ dozen.

Jill Spears, Alpha Upsilon Psi
The Colony, Texas

TWINKIE SURPRISE

1 10-ounce package Twinkies	1 8-ounce container whipped topping
2 3-ounce packages instant pudding mix	Chocolate-covered toffee bars, chopped
3 cups milk	

Cut twinkies into halves lengthwise. Place cream side up in 9x13-inch dish. Combine pudding mix and milk in bowl; beat until thick. Spread over Twinkies. Spoon whipped topping over pudding. Sprinkle toffee bar crumbs over top. Chill for 1 hour. Cut into squares. Chill until serving time. Yield: 16 servings.

Dorothy L. Kalissa, Laureate Gamma Zeta
Highland, California

WAIKIKI CRÊPES

1 8-ounce can crushed pineapple, well drained	1 8-ounce carton orange or pineapple yogurt
1 11-ounce can mandarin orange sections, drained	⅓ cup sliced maraschino cherries
	8 to 10 crêpes
½ cup flaked coconut	Confectioners' sugar

Combine pineapple, oranges, coconut and yogurt in bowl; mix well. Reserve several cherries for garnish. Stir remaining cherries into yogurt mixture. Fill crêpes with fruit mixture; fold to enclose filling. Place on serving plate. Sprinkle with confectioners' sugar; top with reserved cherry slices. Yield: 8 to 10 crêpes.

Garland Wahl, Preceptor Beta Psi
Akron, Colorado

YOGURT CREAM MOLD

4 teaspoons gelatin	½ cup sugar
¼ cup cold water	1 teaspoon vanilla extract
1½ cups whipping cream	3 cups yogurt

Soften gelatin in water in bowl. Heat whipping cream in saucepan over low heat. Add sugar and gelatin. Heat until sugar is dissolved, stirring constantly; remove from heat. Stir in vanilla and yogurt. Pour into 6-cup mold. Chill until set. Unmold onto serving plate. Serve with fruit. Yield: 8 to 10 servings.

Marilyn Tremper, Alpha Gamma
Fresno, California

Cakes

OLD-FASHIONED APPLESAUCE CAKE

2 cups sugar
½ cup shortening
2 cups unsweetened
   applesauce
2 eggs
3 cups all-purpose flour
2 cups raisins

1 cup chopped black
   walnuts
2 teaspoons soda
1 teaspoon salt
2 teaspoons cinnamon
1 teaspoon cloves
½ teaspoon nutmeg

Preheat oven to 350 degrees. Cream sugar and shortening in bowl. Add applesauce and eggs; mix well. Mix a small amount of flour with raisins and walnuts to coat. Add remaining flour, soda, salt and spices to applesauce mixture; mix well. Stir in raisins and walnuts. Pour into greased and floured tube pan. Bake for 1 hour. Store, tightly covered, for 2 days before serving for improved flavor. Yield: 12 to 16 servings.

Joyce M. McCord, Gamma Rho
Warner Robins, Georgia

FRESH APPLE CAKE

2 cups sugar
1¼ cups corn oil
2 eggs
1 teaspoon vanilla extract
3 cups all-purpose flour
1 teaspoon salt
1 teaspoon soda

1 teaspoon cinnamon
¼ teaspoon each ginger,
   nutmeg, cloves and
   allspice
3 large apples, finely
   chopped

Preheat oven to 350 degrees. Beat sugar, oil, eggs and vanilla in bowl. Add mixture of dry ingredients; mix well. Batter will be stiff. Stir in apples. Pour into greased 9x13-inch baking pan. Bake for 45 minutes. Yield: 12 servings.

Elaine Warden, Xi Delta Alpha
Woodland Park, Colorado

CHOCOLATE CHIP APPLESAUCE CAKE

2 cups all-purpose flour
1½ cups sugar
1½ teaspoons soda
1 tablespoon unsweetened
   baking cocoa
1½ teaspoons cinnamon
1½ teaspoons nutmeg
1½ teaspoons allspice
1½ teaspoons cloves
1 teaspoon salt

½ cup shortening
2 cups canned applesauce
2 eggs
½ cup chopped walnuts
½ cup chocolate chips
1 cup raisins
2 to 3 tablespoons light
   brown sugar
½ cup chopped walnuts
½ cup chocolate chips

Preheat oven to 350 degrees. Combine first 9 dry ingredients in large bowl; mix well. Cut in shortening until crumbly. Add applesauce, eggs, ½ cup walnuts, ½ cup chocolate chips and 1 cup raisins; beat well. Pour into greased 9x13-inch baking pan. Sprinkle batter with brown sugar, ½ cup walnuts and ½ cup chocolate chips. Bake for 45 to 50 minutes or until cake tests done. Yield: 10 to 12 servings.

Barbara Osborn, Xi Sigma
Holtville, California

APPLE DRAPPLE CAKE

3 eggs	1 cup nuts
2 cups sugar	2 cups finely chopped
1½ cups corn oil	apples
3 cups self-rising flour	1 cup packed light brown
1 teaspoon cinnamon	sugar
2 teaspoons vanilla extract	½ cup butter

Preheat oven to 325 degrees. Beat eggs, sugar and oil in large bowl. Add flour and cinnamon; mix well. Add vanilla, nuts and apples; mix well. Pour into greased and floured 9x13-inch cake pan. Bake for 1 hour or until toothpick inserted in center comes out clean. Combine brown sugar and butter in small saucepan. Boil for 2½ minutes. Pour over hot cake. Serve warm with whipped topping. Yield: 8 servings.

Lona Thompson, Epsilon Beta
Palm Bay, Florida

BANANA RIPPLE CAKE

½ cup semisweet	1 cup sugar
chocolate chips	2 egg yolks
¼ cup water	1 cup mashed bananas
2 cups all-purpose flour	⅓ cup sour cream
¾ teaspoon soda	1 teaspoon vanilla extract
½ teaspoon salt	⅓ cup chopped
¼ teaspoon baking	maraschino cherries
powder	2 egg whites
½ cup butter, softened	½ cup sugar

Preheat oven to 350 degrees. Grease and flour bottom of 9-inch tube pan. Melt chocolate chips in water in saucepan over low heat, stirring constantly. Cool. Combine flour, soda, salt and baking powder. Cream butter in large mixer bowl. Add 1 cup sugar gradually, beating at high speed until light and fluffy. Add egg yolks; beat well. Combine bananas, sour cream and vanilla in bowl. Add to egg mixture alternately with dry ingredients, beginning and ending with dry ingredients and beating at low speed until well blended after each addition. Stir in cherries. Beat egg whites in bowl until soft peaks form. Add ½ cup sugar gradually, beating until stiff. Fold into batter. Place ⅓ of the batter into prepared pan, drizzle with half the chocolate mixture. Repeat layers, ending with batter. Bake for 50 to 60 minutes or until cake springs back when lightly touched. Cool. Place on serving plate. Yield: 12 servings.

Sandra Duncan, Alpha Epsilon
Honolulu, Hawaii

BEET CAKE

1 cup vegetable oil	1 cup canned Harvard
2 cups sugar	beets
2½ cups all-purpose flour	1 cup drained crushed
2 teaspoons cinnamon	pineapple
2 teaspoons soda	1 cup cottage cheese
1 teaspoon salt	1 cup chopped walnuts
2 teaspoons vanilla extract	

Preheat oven to 370 degrees. Combine first 6 ingredients in large bowl; beat with spoon until well mixed. Beat in vanilla. Process beets, pineapple, cottage cheese and walnuts in a blender or food processor until smooth. Add to flour mixture; beat well. Pour into greased and floured bundt pan. Bake for 45 minutes or until cake tests done. Garnish with light dusting of confectioners' sugar or drizzle with confectioners' sugar glaze.
Yield: 16 to 20 servings.

Arlene Oakes, Xi Alpha Beta
Wellington, Nevada

BLACKBERRY SPICE CAKE

3 eggs	2 teaspoons soda
2 cups sugar	½ teaspoon salt
1 cup butter, softened	1 teaspoon each
2 cups blackberries	cinnamon, cloves,
2 cups all-purpose flour	allspice and nutmeg

Preheat oven to 375 degrees. Combine eggs, sugar and butter in bowl; mix until creamy. Add undrained blackberries; mix well. Sift in flour, soda, salt and spices; beat until smooth. Pour into 2 greased and floured 9-inch cake pans. Bake until cake springs back when lightly touched. Frost with favorite frosting or serve plain with ice cream. Yield: 12 servings.

Wanda Oliver, Laureate Sigma
New Whiteland, Indiana

A CAKE TO CELEBRATE!

2 2-layer packages	2 pints fresh strawberries
yellow cake mix	3 cups whipping cream
3 medium bananas, cut	⅓ cup confectioners'
into ¼-inch slices	sugar
¼ cup freshly squeezed	1½ cups fresh blueberries
lemon juice	

Preheat oven to 350 degrees. Prepare cake mixes 1 at a time using package directions. Pour each into greased 10x15-inch baking pan lined with greased waxed paper. Bake for 15 minutes or until cakes test done. Invert onto wire racks; peel off paper. Cool. Toss bananas with lemon juice in medium bowl. Pour off excess juice; set bananas aside. Rinse and hull strawberries; pat dry. Slice 24 well-shaped strawberries in half lengthwise; reserve for top of cake. Chop remaining strawberries coarsely; set aside. Beat whipping cream in mixer bowl until soft peaks form. Add confectioners' sugar gradually, beating until stiff. Fold chopped strawberries into half the whipped cream. Place 1 cake layer on large serving board; tuck strips of waxed paper under cake to keep board clean. Spread strawberry whipped cream over cake; top with second cake layer. Spread plain cream over top and sides of cake; remove waxed paper strips carefully. Mark 5x7½-inch rectangle in top left corner of cake using tip of sharp knife. Place blueberries in even rows in rectangle to form stars of flag. Alternate rows of strawberries and bananas to form stripes. Chill for up to 2 hours before serving. Yield: 50 servings.

Lori Zaiser, Xi Gamma Lambda
Burlington, Iowa

CARROT CAKE PLUS

1½ cups sugar
1½ cups vegetable oil
4 eggs
2 cups all-purpose flour
1½ teaspoons soda
1½ teaspoons baking
 powder
1 teaspoon cinnamon
1½ cups coarsely chopped
 pecans

1 pound carrots, shredded
1 cup green seedless
 grapes
½ cup margarine,
 softened
4 ounces cream cheese,
 softened
1 teaspoon vanilla extract
1 pound confectioners'
 sugar

Preheat oven to 325 degrees. Beat sugar and oil in large bowl. Add eggs; beat well. Add sifted dry ingredients; mix well. Add pecans, carrots and grapes; mix well. Pour into greased and floured 9x13-inch cake pan. Bake for 1 hour or until toothpick inserted in center comes out clean. Cool completely. Cream margarine and cream cheese in large bowl. Add vanilla; mix well. Add confectioners' sugar; beat until smooth and fluffy. Spread on cooled cake. Store in refrigerator. Yield: 12 servings.

Rose Mary Coakes, Preceptor Alpha Omicron
Marshall, Michigan

ALMOND JOY CAKE

2 cups sugar
1 cup water
1 cup margarine
¼ cup unsweetened
 baking cocoa
2 cups sifted all-purpose
 flour
1 teaspoon soda
2 eggs, beaten
½ cup buttermilk
1 teaspoon vanilla extract

1 cup evaporated milk
24 large marshmallows
1 14-ounce can coconut
1½ cups sugar
½ cup margarine
½ cup evaporated milk
12 ounces milk chocolate
 chips
2 2-ounce packages
 slivered almonds

Preheat oven to 350 degrees. Combine 2 cups sugar, water, 1 cup margarine and cocoa in saucepan. Bring to a boil. Add flour and soda; mix well. Add eggs, buttermilk and vanilla; mix well. Pour into greased and floured 9x13-inch baking pan. Bake for 13 minutes or until cake tests done. Bring 1 cup evaporated milk and marshmallows to a boil in saucepan. Add coconut. Pour over hot cake; spread to cover. Bring 1½ cups sugar, ½ cup margarine and ½ cup evaporated milk to a boil in saucepan; remove from heat. Add chocolate chips; stir until melted. Stir in almonds. Pour over cake. Yield: 15 to 20 servings.

Jolene Foshag, Epsilon Pi
Houston, Texas

TWO-LAYER ALMOND JOY CAKE

1 2-layer package
 chocolate cake mix with
 pudding
1 cup evaporated milk
1 cup sugar
24 large marshmallows
1 14-ounce package
 coconut

½ cup sugar
½ cup evaporated milk
½ cup margarine
12 ounces chocolate chips
Chopped almonds

Preheat oven to 350 degrees. Prepare cake mix using package directions. Pour into 2 greased and floured 9x13-inch baking pans. Bake for 15 to 20 minutes or until cake tests done. Bring 1 cup evaporated milk and 1 cup sugar to a boil in saucepan; remove from heat. Stir in marshmallows until melted. Add coconut. Spread half the mixture over 1 of the warm layers. Top with remaining layer and remaining coconut mixture. Bring ½ cup sugar, ½ cup evaporated milk and margarine to a boil in saucepan; remove from heat. Stir in chocolate chips until melted. Spread over top. Sprinkle with almonds. Store in refrigerator. Serve chilled. Yield: 15 to 20 servings.

Sue Elliott, Xi Epsilon Pi
Paris, Illinois

BETTER THAN SEX CHOCOLATE CAKE

1 2-layer package
 German chocolate cake
 mix
1 14-ounce can
 sweetened condensed
 milk

1 12-ounce jar caramel
 ice cream topping
1 12-ounce container
 whipped topping
3 Heath bars, finely
 chopped

Preheat oven to 350 degrees. Prepare and bake cake mix according to package directions for 9x13-inch cake. Poke holes in top of warm cake with end of wooden spoon. Pour sweetened condensed milk into holes. Pour ice cream topping into same holes. Spread with whipped topping. Sprinkle with candy. Store in refrigerator. Yield: 12 to 15 servings.

 Lea Ann Bishop, Xi Beta Upsilon
Belmond, Iowa

COCA-COLA CAKE

2 cups sugar
2 cups all-purpose flour
½ cup butter
½ cup shortening
3 tablespoons
 unsweetened baking
 cocoa
1 cup Coca-Cola
1 teaspoon soda
½ cup buttermilk
1 teaspoon vanilla extract

1½ cups miniature
 marshmallows
2 eggs, beaten
½ cup butter
3 tablespoons cocoa
6 tablespoons Coca-Cola
1 pound confectioners'
 sugar
1 teaspoon vanilla extract
1 cup chopped pecans

Preheat oven to 350 degrees. Sift sugar and flour into large bowl. Combine butter, shortening, 3 tablespoons cocoa and 1 cup Coca-Cola in saucepan. Bring to a boil, stirring constantly; remove from heat. Pour over dry ingredients; mix until well moistened. Add soda to buttermilk; stir into batter. Add vanilla, marshmallows and eggs; mix well. Pour into greased and floured 10x14-inch baking pan. Bake for 45 minutes. Bring ½ cup butter, 3 tablespoons cocoa and 6 tablespoons Coca-Cola to a boil in saucepan. Add confectioners' sugar, 1 teaspoon vanilla and pecans; mix well. Spread over warm cake. Yield: 15 to 18 servings.

Mary Beth Watson, Preceptor Zeta Mu
Rocklin, California

THE DARKEST CHOCOLATE CAKE

½ cup melted butter	1 teaspoon salt
2 cups sugar	1 teaspoon baking powder
2 cups all-purpose flour	1 teaspoon vanilla extract
1 cup unsweetened	2 teaspoons soda
baking cocoa	2 cups boiling water
2 eggs	

Preheat oven to 375 degrees. Combine first 8 ingredients in bowl; mix well. Dissolve soda in boiling water. Stir into batter; mixture will be thin. Grease 9x13-inch baking pan; coat with cocoa. Pour in batter. Bake for 35 minutes or until cake tests done. Frost with whipped cream or cream cheese frosting. Yield: 20 servings.

Loretta Peacock, Xi Alpha Zeta
Laurel, Maryland

HERSHEY BAR CAKE

1 cup butter, softened	2 5½-ounce cans
2 cups sugar	chocolate syrup
4 eggs	2 cups confectioners'
2¼ cups all-purpose flour	sugar
½ teaspoon soda	2 tablespoons
¼ teaspoon salt	unsweetened baking
1 cup buttermilk	cocoa
1½ teaspoons vanilla	¼ cup butter
extract	¼ cup buttermilk
5 1½-ounce milk	
chocolate candy bars	

Preheat oven to 350 degrees. Cream 1 cup butter and sugar in mixer bowl until fluffy. Add eggs 1 at a time, beating well after each addition. Add sifted dry ingredients alternately with 1 cup buttermilk and vanilla, mixing well after each addition. Melt candy bars with syrup in double boiler over hot water. Stir into batter. Pour into greased bundt pan. Bake for 1 hour. Cool. Invert onto serving plate. Sift confectioners' sugar and cocoa into bowl. Bring ¼ cup butter and ¼ cup buttermilk to a boil in saucepan. Pour into cocoa mixture; beat until creamy. Pour over cake. Yield: 16 servings.

Mary Nell Story, Xi Gamma
Paducah, Kentucky

CHOCOLATE MAYONNAISE CAKE

2 cups all-purpose flour	1 teaspoon vanilla extract
1 cup sugar	Confectioners' sugar
2 teaspoons soda	¼ cup shortening
4 teaspoons unsweetened	Water
baking cocoa	1 teaspoon almond
1 cup cold water	flavoring
1 cup mayonnaise	

Preheat oven to 350 degrees. Mix first 4 dry ingredients in bowl. Add water, mayonnaise and vanilla; beat until well mixed. Pour into 2 greased and floured 8 or 9-inch cake pans. Bake for 45 minutes. Cool. Combine remaining ingredients in bowl; mix well. Spread between layers and over cooled cake. Yield: 12 servings.

Kim Kincaid, Alpha Lambda
Salisbury, North Carolina

MILKY WAY CAKE

6 Milky Way candy bars	2½ cups sifted
1 cup butter, softened	all-purpose flour
2 cups sugar	1¼ cups buttermilk
4 eggs	1 teaspoon vanilla extract
½ teaspoon soda	1 cup chopped nuts

Preheat oven to 350 degrees. Melt candy bars and ½ cup butter in saucepan over low heat. Cream remaining ½ cup butter and sugar in mixer bowl until fluffy. Add eggs 1 at a time, beating well after each addition. Add soda and sifted flour alternately with buttermilk, beginning and ending with flour mixture and beating well after each addition. Stir in melted candy, vanilla and nuts. Pour into greased and floured 10-inch tube pan. Bake for 1 hour and 20 minutes. Cool. Invert onto serving plate. Yield: 12 to 24 servings.

Barbara Dillon, Theta Upsilon
Anawalt, West Virginia

MINNESOTA CHOCOLATE CAKE

2 cups all-purpose flour	1 teaspoon vanilla extract
1¾ cups sugar	1 cup sugar
½ cup unsweetened	3 tablespoons cornstarch
baking cocoa	½ teaspoon salt
1 teaspoon salt	2 1-ounce squares
1 tablespoon soda	unsweetened chocolate
1 cup buttermilk	1 cup boiling water
1 cup strong hot coffee	1 teaspoon vanilla extract
⅔ cup vegetable oil	3 tablespoons margarine
1 egg	

Preheat oven to 350 degrees. Mix first 5 dry ingredients in bowl. Mix in buttermilk, coffee, oil, egg and 1 teaspoon vanilla. Batter will be thin. Pour into greased and floured 9x13-inch baking pan. Bake for 30 minutes or until cake tests done. Cook remaining ingredients in saucepan over medium heat until thickened, stirring constantly. Frost cake. Yield: 12 to 15 servings.

Cheryl Hellyer, Delta Rho
Corydon, Iowa

MISSISSIPPI MUD CAKE

2 cups sugar	1 7-ounce jar
1 cup margarine, softened	marshmallow creme
¼ cup unsweetened	1 pound confectioners'
baking cocoa	sugar
Dash of salt	¼ cup unsweetened
1½ teaspoons vanilla	baking cocoa
extract	½ cup margarine,
4 eggs	softened
1½ cups all-purpose flour	1 teaspoon vanilla extract
1½ cups coconut	Milk
1½ cups walnuts	

Preheat oven to 350 degrees. Cream first 3 ingredients in bowl. Add salt, vanilla and eggs; mix well. Add flour, coconut and walnuts. Beat for 1 minute. Batter will be stiff. Pour into greased 11x15-inch baking pan. Bake for 30 minutes or until cake tests done. Spread marshmallow creme over hot cake. Mix next 4 ingredients and enough milk to make of spreading consistency in bowl. Spread over cooled cake. Yield: 20 to 25 servings.

Barbara Kabage, Xi Delta Omega
Sebastopol, California

PEANUT BUTTER FUDGE CAKE

1 cup butter	1 cup creamy peanut
1 cup water	butter
¼ cup unsweetened	1 tablespoon peanut oil
baking cocoa	½ cup butter
½ cup buttermilk	¼ cup unsweetened
2 eggs, beaten	baking cocoa
2 cups sugar	6 tablespoons buttermilk
2 cups all-purpose flour	1 pound confectioners'
1 teaspoon soda	sugar
1 teaspoon vanilla extract	1 teaspoon vanilla extract

Preheat oven to 350 degrees. Combine 1 cup butter, water, ¼ cup cocoa, ½ cup buttermilk and eggs in saucepan. Cook over low heat until bubbly, stirring constantly. Mix sugar, flour and soda in large bowl. Stir in hot mixture; beat until smooth. Stir in 1 teaspoon vanilla. Pour into greased and floured 9x13-inch baking pan. Bake for 25 minutes. Cool. Blend peanut butter and oil in bowl until smooth. Spread on cooled cake. Heat ½ cup butter, ¼ cup cocoa and 6 tablespoons buttermilk in saucepan until bubbly. Beat into confectioners' sugar in bowl until smooth. Stir in vanilla. Pour evenly over peanut butter mixture. Let stand until set. Yield: 12 to 16 servings.

Cathy Kusmaul, Nu Kappa
Harper, Kansas

NUTTY CHOCOLATE POTATO CAKE

1 cup butter, softened	1 teaspoon vanilla extract
2 cups sugar	2 cups English walnuts
4 egg yolks, beaten	4 egg whites, stiffly
2 1-ounce squares	beaten
chocolate, melted	1 pound confectioners'
1 cup mashed potatoes	sugar
1 cup chopped apples	1 cup butter, softened
2 cups all-purpose flour	3 1-ounce squares
1 teaspoon cinnamon	unsweetened chocolate,
1 teaspoon ginger	melted
1 teaspoon soda	1 teaspoon vanilla extract
½ teaspoon salt	Coffee
1 cup sour cream	

Cream butter and sugar in mixer bowl. Add egg yolks, chocolate, mashed potatoes and apples; mix well. Add dry ingredients alternately with sour cream, mixing well after each addition. Add vanilla and walnuts. Fold in stiffly beaten egg whites. Pour into 2 greased and floured 8-inch round cake pans. Bake for 25 to 30 minutes or until cake tests done. Cool. Combine confectioners' sugar, 1 cup butter, 3 ounces chocolate, 1 teaspoon vanilla and enough coffee to make of spreading consistency. Frost cooled cake. Garnish top of cake with crushed English walnuts. Yield: 12 servings.

Linda S. Naggie, Theta Upsilon
Bluefield, West Virginia

CHOCOLATE SWEETHEART CUPCAKES

2 cups butter	8 eggs
8 ounces semisweet	1 14-ounce package
chocolate	coconut
3½ cups sugar	2 teaspoons vanilla extract
2 cups all-purpose flour	1 cup pecans

Preheat oven to 350 degrees. Melt butter and chocolate in saucepan over medium heat. Add remaining ingredients. Spoon into paper-lined muffin cups. Bake for 35 minutes. Yield: 2 dozen.

Char Zimmerman, Preceptor Chi
Bellevue, Nebraska

CHOCOLATE PRALINE LAYER CAKE

½ cup butter	1 2-layer package devil's
¼ cup whipping cream	food cake mix with
1 cup packed light brown	pudding
sugar	3 eggs
¾ cup coarsely chopped	1¾ cups whipping cream
pecans	¼ cup confectioners'
1¼ cups water	sugar
⅓ cup vegetable oil	¼ teaspoon vanilla extract

Preheat oven to 325 degrees. Heat butter, ¼ cup whipping cream and brown sugar in small saucepan until butter melts, stirring occasionally. Pour into 2 greased and floured 8 or 9-inch cake pans; sprinkle with pecans. Combine water, oil, cake mix and eggs in mixer bowl. Beat at low speed until moistened. Beat at high speed for 2 minutes. Spoon batter over pecan mixture. Bake for 35 minutes or until cakes test done. Cool in pans for 5 minutes. Remove to wire rack to cool completely. Beat 1¾ cups whipping cream in mixer bowl until soft peaks form. Beat in confectioners' sugar and vanilla until stiff. Stack layers praline side up, spreading whipped cream between layers and over top. Garnish with pecan halves and chocolate curls. Store in refrigerator. Yield: 12 servings.

Tamara D. Cowan, Alpha Delta Zeta
Llano, Texas

TRIPLE CHOCOLATE CAKE

1 2-layer package	1 cup chocolate chips
chocolate cake mix	2 cups confectioners'
1 cup sour cream	sugar
1 3-ounce package	½ cup butter, softened
chocolate instant	2 tablespoons
pudding mix	unsweetened baking
4 eggs	cocoa
½ cup water	1 teaspoon vanilla extract
½ cup vegetable oil	¼ cup evaporated milk

Preheat oven to 350 degrees. Combine first 6 ingredients in mixer bowl. Beat for 2 minutes or longer. Stir in chocolate chips. Pour into lightly greased 9x13-inch baking pan. Bake for 30 to 40 minutes or until cake tests done. Cool. Combine confectioners' sugar, butter, cocoa, vanilla and evaporated milk in bowl; beat until of spreading consistency. Spread on cooled cake. Yield: 12 servings.

Betty Ohlin, Laureate Delta Delta
San Diego, California

THE RAMS WON! CAKE

1 2-layer package white cake mix	⅔ cup vodka
1 3-ounce package chocolate instant pudding mix	⅓ cup coffee liqueur
	¼ cup water
	¼ cup coffee liqueur
4 eggs	¼ cup confectioners' sugar
1 cup vegetable oil	

Preheat oven to 350 degrees. Combine first 7 ingredients in large bowl; beat until well-blended. Pour into greased and floured bundt pan. Bake for 50 to 60 minutes or until cake tests done. Cool in pan. Invert onto wire rack. Blend ¼ cup liqueur with confectioners' sugar in small bowl. Drizzle over cake. Yield: 12 to 15 servings.

Dorris Neal, Preceptor Gamma Nu
Rohnert Park, California

MYSTERY MOCHA CAKE

¾ cup sugar	1 teaspoon vanilla extract
1 cup all-purpose flour	½ cup packed light brown sugar
2 teaspoons baking powder	¼ cup sugar
⅛ teaspoon salt	¼ cup unsweetened baking cocoa
1 1-ounce square unsweetened chocolate	1 cup cold double-strength coffee
2 tablespoons butter	
½ cup milk	

Preheat oven to 350 degrees. Sift first 4 ingredients into bowl. Melt chocolate and butter in double boiler over hot water. Add to flour mixture; mix well. Add mixture of milk and vanilla; mix well. Pour into greased 8-inch square cake pan. Sprinkle with mixture of sugars and cocoa. Pour coffee over top. Bake for 35 to 40 minutes or until cake tests done. Serve warm. Yield: 6 servings.

Wanda E. Dudley, Preceptor Pi
Albuquerque, New Mexico

CHOCOLATE PECAN CUPCAKES

4 1-ounce squares semisweet chocolate	2 cups chopped pecans
1 cup margarine	1 cup all-purpose flour
1 teaspoon vanilla extract	1¾ cups sugar
	4 eggs

Melt chocolate and margarine in saucepan; add vanilla and pecans. Combine flour, sugar and eggs in mixer bowl. Add chocolate mixture; mix well. Spoon into paper-lined muffin cups. Bake for 15 minutes for miniature cupcakes or 30 minutes for large cupcakes. Yield: 5 dozen miniature or 2 dozen large cupcakes.

Gaynell Richey, Preceptor Beta Alpha
El Dorado, Kansas

CHRISTMAS SNOW CAKE

6 egg yolks	¼ cup sugar
½ teaspoon vanilla extract	Buttercream Filling
½ cup milk	1 cup whipping cream
¾ cup sugar	½ cup confectioners' sugar
1¼ cups sifted cake flour	
6 egg whites	

Preheat oven to 325 degrees. Beat egg yolks and vanilla at high speed in mixer bowl for 5 minutes. Beat in milk at low speed until blended. Beat in ¾ cup sugar at medium speed until sugar dissolves. Beat in flour ¼ cup at a time at low speed. Beat egg whites in large mixer bowl until soft peaks form. Add ¼ cup sugar, beating until stiff peaks form. Stir 1 cup egg whites into egg yolk mixture. Fold yolk mixture into remaining whites. Spread in 9-inch springform pan. Bake for 45 minutes. Invert to cool. Remove from pan. Slice horizontally into 4 layers. Spread Buttercream Filling between layers. Whip cream with confectioners' sugar until soft peaks form. Spread over cake. Chill until serving time.

BUTTERCREAM FILLING

½ orange, squeezed	3 egg yolks
1 cup unsalted butter	1 tablespoon orange liqueur
1 cup sifted confectioners' sugar	

Place orange half in food processor container; reserve juice for another purpose. Process until finely grated. Add remaining ingredients. Process until smooth.

Rose Knoebel, Delta Chi
Maquoketa, Iowa

CHRISTMAS TREE CAKE

4 ounces red food coloring	2 cups buttermilk
6 tablespoons cocoa drink mix	½ teaspoon salt
1 cup shortening	2 teaspoons soda
3 cups sugar	2 teaspoons vanilla extract
4 eggs	2 teaspoons vinegar
4½ cups all-purpose flour, sifted	2 recipes Frosting
	Silver dragées

Preheat oven to 350 degrees. Grease and flour 5-inch, 7-inch, 9-inch and 11-inch round cake pans. Combine food coloring with cocoa mix. Let stand for several minutes. Cream shortening and sugar in mixer bowl until fluffy. Mix in eggs and food coloring. Add flour, buttermilk, salt and soda; mix well. Beat in vanilla. Stir in vinegar. Fill prepared pans ⅔ full. Bake for 30 minutes. Cool. Cut each layer in shape of star. Stack graduated layers on cake plate, staggering points and spreading a small amount of frosting between layers. Frost layers. Use cut-out triangle from large star as tree top. Frost completely. Attach small ball decorations with toothpicks. Sprinkle with dragées. Yield: 20 servings.

FROSTING

3 tablespoons all-purpose flour	6 tablespoons shortening
¾ cup milk	1½ teaspoons vanilla extract
¾ cup sugar	Dash of salt
6 tablespoons butter, softened	Green food coloring

Cook flour and milk in saucepan until thickened, stirring constantly. Beat with mixer until smooth; set aside.

Cream next 5 ingredients in bowl. Add flour mixture; beat until mixture is fluffy and resembles whipped cream. Tint with food coloring. Do not double recipe.

Ruby J. Kelley, Preceptor Kappa Zeta
Redding, California

COCONUT CREAM CAKE

1 15-ounce package	1 cup cream of coconut
white cake mix with	1 14-ounce can
pudding	sweetened condensed
3 eggs	milk
1/3 cup vegetable oil	1 cup whipping cream
1 cup water	1 tablespoon sugar
1/2 teaspoon coconut	1 cup flaked coconut
flavoring	

Preheat oven to 350 degrees. Combine first 5 ingredients in mixer bowl. Beat at medium speed for 2 minutes. Pour into greased 9x13-inch cake pan. Bake for 30 minutes. Poke holes in warm cake with 2-prong serving fork. Pour mixture of cream of coconut and condensed milk into holes. Chill overnight. Whip cream in bowl until soft peaks form. Sprinkle with sugar. Beat until smooth and mixture holds shape. Frost cake; sprinkle with coconut. Chill until serving time. Yield: 12 servings.

Marie Peterson, Preceptor Gamma Gamma
Cypress, California

CRANBERRY CAKE

1 cup chopped nuts	1 teaspoon soda
1 cup chopped dates	Grated rind of 2 oranges
1 cup cranberries	2 eggs
2 1/2 cups all-purpose flour	1 cup buttermilk
1 cup sugar	3/4 cup vegetable oil
1/4 teaspoon salt	1 cup orange juice
1 teaspoon baking powder	1 cup sugar

Preheat oven to 350 degrees. Put nuts, dates and cranberries through food grinder. Sift dry ingredients into bowl. Stir in nuts, dates, cranberries and orange rind. Add mixture of eggs, buttermilk and oil; mix well. Pour into greased 10-inch tube pan. Bake for 1 hour. Cool to lukewarm; remove to cake plate. Spoon mixture of orange juice and 1 cup sugar over cake until absorbed. Yield: 12 to 16 servings.

Agnes Vaughan, Laureate Zeta
Lafayette, Indiana

CARAMEL-SAUCED CRANBERRY CAKE

2 cups sugar	4 cups cranberries
6 tablespoons butter,	1 cup butter
softened	1 cup sugar
4 cups all-purpose flour	1 cup packed light brown
4 teaspoons baking	sugar
powder	1 cup whipping cream
1/2 teaspoon salt	1 teaspoon vanilla extract
2 cups milk	Whipped topping

Preheat oven to 350 degrees. Cream 2 cups sugar and butter in bowl until fluffy. Add dry ingredients alternately with milk, mixing well after each addition. Fold in cranberries. Pour into 9x13-inch greased and floured

cake pan. Bake for 35 minutes. Combine next 4 ingredients in saucepan. Bring to a boil; remove from heat. Add vanilla. Serve warm sauce over cake. Top with whipped topping. Yield: 12 servings.

Pam Allen, Theta Iota
Aurelia, Iowa

CRÈME DE MENTHE BUNDT CAKE

1 18-ounce package	1/2 cup vegetable oil
white cake mix	1/4 cup water
4 eggs	1/4 cup green
1 3-ounce package	Crème de Menthe
vanilla instant pudding	1/4 teaspoon vanilla extract
mix	1 5-ounce can chocolate
1/2 cup orange juice	syrup

Preheat oven to 350 degrees. Mix all ingredients except chocolate syrup in bowl. Beat for 4 minutes. Pour 2/3 of the batter into greased and floured bundt pan. Pour mixture of chocolate syrup and remaining batter into pan; do not stir. Bake for 35 minutes. Cool in pan for 25 minutes. Invert onto cake plate. Yield: 12 servings.

Esther Adkins, Xi Delta Beta
Hartford City, Indiana

FIG CAKE

2 cups self-rising flour	1/2 cup butter
1 1/2 cups sugar	1 cup sugar
1 cup vegetable oil	1 tablespoon corn syrup
3 eggs	1/2 cup buttermilk
1 cup buttermilk	1/2 teaspoon soda
1 cup fig preserves	1 tablespoon vanilla
1 cup chopped pecans	extract
1 teaspoon vanilla extract	

Preheat oven to 350 degrees. Sift flour and 1 1/2 cups sugar into bowl. Add oil and eggs; mix well. Add next 4 ingredients; mix well. Pour into greased tube pan. Bake for 35 minutes or until cake tests done. Combine butter and remaining ingredients in saucepan. Boil for 3 minutes. Spread on warm cake. Yield: 10 servings.

Genny S. Mulry, Xi Gamma Beta
Beaumont, Texas

CHOCOLATE FRUITCAKE

1 cup chopped walnuts	4 cups all-purpose flour
2 cups hot water	4 teaspoons cinnamon
1 cup chopped raisins	2 teaspoons vanilla extract
1 cup chopped dates	1 1/2 cups mayonnaise
2 teaspoons soda	3/4 cup candied pineapple
2 cups sugar	1 1/2 cups mixed candied
6 tablespoons cocoa	red and green cherries

Preheat oven to 350 degrees. Combine first 5 ingredients in bowl. Let stand for several minutes. Sift sugar, cocoa, flour and cinnamon together. Add to fruit mixture; mix well. Add vanilla and mayonnaise; mix well. Add fruit. Spoon into 3 buttered and floured 4x8-inch loaf pans. Bake for 1 hour or until cake tests done. Yield: 3 cakes.

Betty J. Ault, Preceptor Eta
Whitefish, Montana

FRIENDSHIP CAKE

1 18-ounce package yellow cake mix	4 eggs
	1 cup raisins
1 6-ounce package vanilla instant pudding mix	1 cup coconut
	1 cup chopped pecans
	1½ cups Friendship Fruit
⅔ cup vegetable oil	

Preheat oven to 350 degrees. Combine first 4 ingredients in mixer bowl. Beat at medium speed for 4 minutes. Fold in raisins, coconut, pecans and Friendship Fruit. Pour into greased and floured bundt pan. Bake for 40 to 60 minutes or until cake tests done. Cool in pan for 10 minutes. Invert onto wire rack to cool completely. Yield: 16 servings.

FRIENDSHIP FRUIT

3½ cups sugar	3½ cups sugar
1½ cups Brandy or mixed fruit juices	1 20-ounce can fruit cocktail
1 28-ounce can sliced peaches	2 9-ounce jars maraschino cherries, drained
1 20-ounce can crushed pineapple	

Combine first 3 ingredients in glass bowl. Let stand, tightly covered, at room temperature for 10 days, stirring every 24 hours. Add pineapple, 3½ cups sugar and fruit cocktail. Let stand for 10 days, stirring every 24 hours. Add cherries. Let stand for 10 days longer, stirring every 24 hours. Drain fruit, reserving liquid. Use fruit in cake, over ice cream or as gifts for friends. Substitute reserved liquid for Brandy to make additional recipes of Friendship Fruit. Yield: 4½ cups fruit.

Melody Cook, Xi Beta Epsilon
Rock View, West Virginia

SPECIAL HOLIDAY FRUITCAKE

1¾ cups whole Brazil nuts	Pinch of salt
2¼ cups whole walnuts	1 3-ounce bottle of red maraschino cherries
3 cups whole dates	
1½ cups sugar	1 3-ounce bottle of green maraschino cherries
1½ cups all-purpose flour	
1 teaspoon baking powder	4 eggs, separated

Preheat oven to 325 degrees. Combine first 7 ingredients in bowl; mix well. Add cherries and juice and beaten egg yolks. Fold in stiffly beaten egg whites. Spoon into 2 greased and floured waxed paper-lined loaf pans. Bake for 1 hour and 10 minutes. Cool slightly. Remove from pan; peel off paper. Cool completely. Yield: 2 cakes.

Sandra L. Miller, Preceptor Beta Lambda
Lakewood, Colorado

---

*Glaze your fruitcake like **Megan Carter, Delta Mu, Murfreesboro, Tennessee**, does by combining 1 cup sugar, ½ cup buttermilk, ½ cup butter, 1 teaspoon corn syrup and ½ teaspoon soda in saucepan and boiling for 10 minutes. Pour over warm fruitcake.*

FRUIT COCKTAIL CAKE

1 16-ounce can fruit cocktail	½ teaspoon almond flavoring
1 cup all-purpose flour	1 tablespoon butter
1 cup sugar	1 egg
1 teaspoon baking powder	½ cup packed light brown sugar
½ teaspoon soda	
Pinch of salt	1 cup chopped nuts

Preheat oven to 350 degrees. Combine first 9 ingredients in bowl; mix well. Pour into 8x10-inch cake pan. Top with mixture of brown sugar and nuts. Bake for 30 to 35 minutes or until cake tests done. Serve warm or cool with whipped topping. Yield: 8 servings.

Eileen Barbito, Laureate Beta Epsilon
Garden Grove, California

FUZZY NAVEL DREAM

1 8-ounce container orange yogurt	1 8-ounce jar orange marmalade
1 8-ounce container peach yogurt	½ cup peach schnapps
	2 tablespoons sugar
1 2-layer package white cake mix	1 8-ounce container whipped topping
⅓ cup vegetable oil	4 ounces cream cheese, softened
2 eggs	
¾ cup peach schnapps	

Mix first 6 ingredients in large bowl. Beat at high speed for 3 minutes. Pour into 2 greased and floured 9-inch cake pans. Bake for 35 minutes or until cake tests done. Cool. Heat marmalade, ½ cup schnapps, and 2 tablespoons sugar in saucepan until bubbly. Cool until thickened. Spread between layers. Beat whipped topping and cream cheese in mixer bowl at high speed for 3 minutes. Spread over cake. Yield: 8 servings.

 Sally DySard, Preceptor Alpha Nu
Morehead City, North Carolina

HALF MOON CAKES

1 cup butter, softened	Grated rind of 1 lemon
1½ cups sugar	6 egg whites, stiffly beaten
6 egg yolks	
1½ cups all-purpose flour	½ cup ground walnuts
1 teaspoon baking powder	¼ cup sugar
Juice of ½ lemon	Confectioners' sugar

Preheat oven to 350 degrees. Cream butter and 1½ cups sugar in mixer bowl. Beat in egg yolks until fluffy. Sift in flour and baking powder. Mix in lemon juice and rind. Fold in stiffly beaten egg whites. Pour into greased and floured 9x13-inch baking pan. Sprinkle with walnuts and ¼ cup sugar. Bake for 25 minutes or until cake tests done. Cool. Cut circle with floured 2½-inch glass in 1 corner. Cut crescent shapes by moving glass down side of pan about 1¼ inches each cut, removing crescent after each cut. Dust on all sides with confectioners' sugar. Serve with coffee for dessert or brunch. Yield: 20 servings.

Helen L. Judge, Beta Omicron
Westland, Michigan

ITALIAN CASSATA

¾ cup sifted all-purpose flour	2 tablespoons water
½ teaspoon baking powder	1 teaspoon vanilla extract
¼ teaspoon salt	Ricotta Filling
4 eggs, separated	Buttercream Frosting
¾ cup sugar	Kiwifruit
2 tablespoons lemon juice	Strawberries
	Pistachio nuts

Preheat oven to 350 degrees. Sift flour, baking powder and salt together. Beat egg whites in mixer bowl at high speed until soft peaks form. Add half the sugar gradually, beating until stiff peaks form. Beat egg yolks in small bowl for 5 minutes. Add lemon juice, water and vanilla. Blend in flour mixture at low speed until completely blended. Fold gently into egg white mixture. Pour into 10-inch angel food cake pan with removable bottom; smooth top. Bake for 50 minutes. Invert on wire rack to cool completely. Remove from pan. Slice into 3 layers. Spread Ricotta Filling between layers. Frost with Buttercream Frosting. Pipe frosting rosettes around base. Decorate base with kiwifruit and strawberries. Sprinkle pistachio nuts over top. Yield: 16 servings.

FILLING AND FROSTING BASE

1 cup sugar	1¼ cups milk
5 tablespoons cornstarch	⅛ teaspoon salt

Combine all ingredients in saucepan; mix well. Cook over medium heat until thickened, stirring constantly. Let stand, covered, until cool.

RICOTTA FILLING

2 cups ricotta cheese	½ recipe Filling and Frosting Base
2 tablespoons orange liqueur	½ cup miniature chocolate chips
Grated rind of 1 orange	½ cup finely ground pistachio nuts
1½ teaspoons vanilla extract	

Beat ricotta in medium bowl until smooth. Add liqueur and flavorings; mix well. Add Filling and Frosting Base; beat well. Fold in chocolate chips and pistachio nuts.

BUTTERCREAM FROSTING

½ cup butter, softened	½ recipe Filling and Frosting
2 tablespoons shortening	
1 teaspoon vanilla extract	

Combine first 3 ingredients in small bowl. Add by spoonfuls to Filling and Frosting base, beating until fluffy after each addition.

Connie Painter, Preceptor Beta
Owl's Head, Maine

Regina Smith, Xi Eta Chi, Morton, Illinois, tops her apple or butter cake batter with a mixture of ½ cup nuts, ½ cup butterscotch chips and ½ cup brown sugar before baking.

CREAM-FILLED HAZELNUT CAKE

½ cup butter or margarine	3 egg whites, stiffly beaten
⅔ cup sugar	1½ cups whipping cream
3 egg yolks	¼ cup sugar
¼ cup all-purpose flour	½ cup finely ground hazelnuts
½ teaspoon baking powder	
¼ teaspoon cinnamon	
½ cup finely ground hazelnuts	

Preheat oven to 350 degrees. Cream butter in mixer bowl at medium speed for 30 seconds. Add ⅔ cup sugar; beat until fluffy. Beat in egg yolks. Add mixture of flour, baking powder and cinnamon; beat well. Stir in ½ cup hazelnuts. Fold in stiffly beaten egg whites. Pour into greased 8-inch round cake pan. Bake for 30 to 35 minutes or until cake tests done. Split into 2 layers. Whip cream with ¼ cup sugar until stiff peaks form. Add ½ cup hazelnuts. Spread whipped cream between layers and over top of cake. Yield: 12 to 16 servings.

Clella Rogers Minor, Preceptor Alpha Omega
Norton, Virginia

JELLY ROLL

3 eggs, beaten	1 teaspoon soda
1 cup sugar	1 teaspoon baking powder
3 tablespoons water	Confectioners' sugar
1 cup all-purpose flour	

Preheat oven to 375 degrees. Combine eggs with sugar, water, flour, soda and baking powder; mix well. Pour into 12x16-inch baking sheet lined with waxed paper. Bake for 10 minutes. Invert onto towel sprinkled generously with confectioners' sugar. Spread with any filling of choice such as pudding, jelly or sugar. Roll as for jelly roll. Slice to serve. Yield: 10 servings.

Carolynde S. Hodgson, Xi Gamma Kappa
Havelock, North Carolina

LADYFINGER LAYER CAKE

½ cup butter, softened	1½ teaspoons baking powder
1 cup sugar	¼ teaspoon salt
2 eggs	½ cup water
¼ teaspoon grated orange rind	Apricot or strawberry preserves
1 tablespoon orange juice	Whipped cream
1½ cups sifted cake flour	

Preheat oven to 350 degrees. Cream butter and sugar in mixer bowl until light. Add eggs 1 at a time, beating well after each addition. Beat in orange rind and juice. Add sifted flour, baking powder and salt alternately with water, beating until smooth after each addition. Pour into 2 greased and floured waxed paper-lined 9-inch pans. Bake for 25 minutes. Cool. Spread preserves and whipped cream between layers. Yield: 8 servings.

Barbara Donnelly, Preceptor Beta Eta
Tacoma, Washington

LEMON ANGEL DELIGHT

1 1-step angel food cake mix	½ cup margarine, softened
1 22-ounce can lemon pie filling	1 pound confectioners' sugar
8 ounces cream cheese, softened	1 teaspoon vanilla extract

Preheat oven to 350 degrees. Combine cake mix and pie filling in mixer bowl; beat until well blended. Spread in ungreased 10x15-inch baking pan. Bake for 20 to 25 minutes or until cake tests done. Cool. Beat cream cheese and margarine in bowl until light. Add confectioners' sugar and vanilla; beat until smooth. Spread on cake. Yield: 24 servings.

Mary Muninger, Xi Epsilon Eta
Independence, Kansas

LEMON FRUITCAKE

4 ounces candied red cherries	1 pound pecans, chopped
4 ounces candied green cherries	2 cups butter, softened
4 ounces candied red pineapple	2½ cups sugar
4 ounces candied green pineapple	6 eggs, beaten
4 ounces white raisins	1 3-ounce bottle of lemon extract
1 cup sifted all-purpose flour	4 cups sifted all-purpose flour
	1½ teaspoons baking powder

Preheat oven to 250 degrees. Cut up fruit. Combine with 1 cup flour in bowl; mix well. Add pecans; mix well. Cream butter, sugar and eggs in bowl until light and fluffy. Add lemon extract; blend well. Sift in remaining dry ingredients; mix well. Add fruit and nuts; mix well. Spoon into greased and floured 10-inch tube pan. Cover outside of pan with foil. Place pan of water on bottom oven rack. Bake for 2½ to 3 hours or until firm. Cool in pan. Remove to cake plate. Yield: 16 servings.

Lucille A. Spence, Preceptor Alpha Lambda
Lewisburg, West Virginia

LEMON CHIFFON CAKE

2¼ cups cake flour	¾ cup orange juice
1½ cups sugar	8 egg whites
1 teaspoon salt	½ teaspoon cream of tartar
1 tablespoon baking powder	1⅓ cups grated coconut
½ cup vegetable oil	Yellow food coloring
8 egg yolks, beaten	1 recipe seven-minute frosting
2 teaspoons grated lemon rind	

Preheat oven to 325 degrees. Sift dry ingredients into bowl; make well in center. Add oil, egg yolks, lemon rind and orange juice; beat until smooth. Beat egg whites with cream of tartar in bowl until stiff peaks form. Pour batter in thin stream over egg whites. Fold in several drops of yellow food coloring if desired. Fold in coconut.

Pour into ungreased 10-inch tube pan. Bake for 55 minutes. Invert to cool. Remove from pan. Frost with seven-minute frosting tinted with yellow food coloring. Sprinkle with additional coconut. Yield: 12 servings.

Della Marie Cothern, Preceptor Gamma Beta
Osceola, Iowa

CAKE MIX CHIFFON CAKE

1 2-layer package cake mix	Water
Vegetable oil	6 eggs, separated

Preheat oven to 350 degrees. Place cake mix in large bowl. Add oil and water as specified by package directions. Add egg yolks; beat until blended. Beat egg whites in bowl until very stiff peaks form. Fold into batter. Spoon into ungreased angel food cake pan. Bake until golden brown. Cool. Remove to serving plate. Frost cake with lemon frosting. Yield: 16 servings.
Note: Select cake mix that requires oil, water and 3 eggs to prepare; no other type cake mix will work.

La Verna J. Rodler, Preceptor Kappa Kappa
Fairfield, California

GRANDMOTHER FISHER'S CHEESE CAKE

1 cup butter, softened	¾ cup milk
2 cups sugar	6 egg whites, stiffly beaten
½ teaspoon lemon extract	1 recipe confectioners' sugar frosting
3 cups sifted cake flour	
1 tablespoon baking powder	

Preheat oven to 350 degrees. Cream butter and sugar in mixer bowl until light and fluffy. Add lemon extract. Add sifted flour and baking powder alternately with milk, mixing well after each addition. Fold in stiffly beaten egg whites. Pour into greased 9-inch cake pans. Bake for 25 to 30 minutes or until cake tests done. Cool. Spread Lemon Cheese Filling between layers and over top of cake. Frost side of cake with confectioners' sugar frosting.
Yield: 12 to 15 servings.

LEMON CHEESE FILLING

½ cup butter	Grated rind and juice of 2 lemons
1 cup sugar	
6 egg yolks	

Combine all ingredients in double boiler. Cook over hot water until thickened, stirring constantly. Cool.

Janice F. Nepita, Beta Lambda
Columbia, South Carolina

Sharon G. Crouse, Gamma Nu, Lexington, North Carolina,
splits a Swiss chocolate cake mix cake into 4 layers and fills
with a mixture of 16 ounces whipped topping, 8 ounces cream
cheese, 4 cups confectioners' sugar, 2 cups miniature choco-
late chips and ½ cup nuts.

MACAROON CAKE

⅓ cup butter, softened	½ teaspoon almond
½ cup sugar	extract
4 egg yolks	4 egg whites
1 cup sifted all-purpose	1 cup sugar
flour	½ teaspoon almond
1½ teaspoons baking	extract
powder	1 cup flaked coconut
½ cup milk	

Preheat oven to 325 degrees. Combine first 7 ingredients in bowl; mix well. Pour into greased 9x13-inch cake pan. Beat egg whites until very stiff peaks form. Add 1 cup sugar and ½ teaspoon almond extract gradually, beating constantly. Fold in coconut. Spread over batter. Bake for 30 minutes or until cake tests done. Yield: 15 servings.

Pearle Jesfjeld, Laureate Theta
Prairie City, South Dakota

ALL-AMERICAN OATMEAL CAKE

1½ cups boiling water	2 eggs, beaten
1 cup quick-cooking oats	1⅓ cups all-purpose flour
1 cup sugar	1 teaspoon soda
1 cup packed light brown	1 teaspoon cinnamon
sugar	½ teaspoon nutmeg
½ cup margarine, softened	½ teaspoon salt

Preheat oven to 350 degrees. Combine boiling water and oats in bowl. Let stand for 20 minutes. Cream sugars, margarine and beaten eggs in bowl. Add to oats mixture; mix well. Sift in dry ingredients; mix well. Pour into greased and floured 9x13-inch cake pan. Bake for 35 to 45 minutes or until cake tests done. Pour warm Coconut Topping over warm cake. Bake for 5 minutes longer or broil until topping is golden brown. Serve warm with whipped cream. Yield: 15 servings.

COCONUT TOPPING

1 cup packed light brown	1 cup coconut
sugar	1 cup nuts
6 tablespoons margarine	1 teaspoon vanilla extract
¼ cup milk or cream	

Combine sugar, margarine and milk in saucepan. Boil for 3 minutes. Add coconut, nuts and vanilla; mix well.

Cheryl Ann Jansen, Iota Delta
Oskaloosa, Iowa

PIÑA COLADA CAKE

1 14-ounce can crushed	1 4-ounce can coconut
pineapple	1 16-ounce can cream of
1 2-layer package yellow	coconut
or white cake mix	1 8-ounce container
1½ cups water	whipped topping
2 eggs, beaten	

Preheat oven to 350 degrees. Drain pineapple, reserving juice. Combine cake mix, water and eggs in bowl; mix well. Mix in pineapple and half the coconut. Pour into 9x13-inch cake pan. Bake for 30 minutes. Punch holes in top of hot cake. Pour mixture of cream of coconut and reserved pineapple juice over cake. Cool. Spread with whipped topping; sprinkle remaining coconut on top. Chill in refrigerator. Yield: 12 servings.

June Faut, Preceptor Gamma Rho
Dumas, Texas

PINEAPPLE COCONUT CAKE

1½ cups sugar	2 teaspoons soda
½ cup vegetable oil	½ teaspoon salt
2 eggs	1 20-ounce can crushed
2½ cups all-purpose flour	pineapple

Preheat oven to 350 degrees. Combine all ingredients in bowl; mix well with spoon. Pour into greased and floured 9x13-inch cake pan. Bake for 35 minutes. Cool. Pour Coconut Icing over cake. Yield: 10 to 12 servings.

COCONUT ICING

1¾ cups evaporated milk	1 cup nuts
1½ cups sugar	1 cup coconut
½ cup margarine	1 teaspoon vanilla extract

Bring mixture of evaporated milk, sugar and margarine to a boil in saucepan. Cook for 3½ minutes; remove from heat. Mix in remaining ingredients.

Ruby Eaton, Laureate Pi
Liberal, Kansas

PINEAPPLE MANDARIN CREAM CAKE

1 2-layer package lemon	½ cup vegetable oil
supreme cake mix	1 teaspoon vanilla extract
1 11-ounce can mandarin	1 teaspoon grated orange
oranges	rind
4 eggs	

Preheat oven to 325 degrees. Combine cake mix, undrained oranges and remaining ingredients in mixer bowl. Beat for 2 minutes or until blended. Pour into 3 greased and floured 8-inch cake pans. Bake for 20 to 24 minutes or until cake tests done. Cool in pans for several minutes; remove to wire racks to cool completely. Spread Icing between layers and over top and side of cake. Yield: 12 servings.

ICING

1 3-ounce package	1 9-ounce container
vanilla instant pudding	whipped topping
mix	1 tablespoon Amaretto
1 15-ounce can crushed	or 1 teaspoon vanilla
pineapple	extract

Combine dry pudding mix and undrained pineapple in bowl; mix well. Add whipped topping and Amaretto; beat until of spreading consistency.

Eleanore Peters, Omicron Nu
Sarasota, Florida

PINEAPPLE MERINGUE CAKE

4 egg whites	2 teaspoons baking
1 cup sugar	powder
1 teaspoon vanilla extract	1/8 teaspoon salt
1/2 cup shortening	5 tablespoons milk
1/2 cup sugar	1 teaspoon vanilla extract
4 egg yolks	3/4 cup finely chopped
1 cup sifted cake flour	pecans

Preheat oven to 350 degrees. Beat egg whites in mixer bowl until soft peaks form. Add 1 cup sugar gradually, beating until stiff peaks form. Fold in 1 teaspoon vanilla. Set aside. Cream shortening and 1/2 cup sugar in mixer bowl until light and fluffy. Beat in egg yolks. Sift flour, baking powder and salt together. Add to creamed mixture alternately with milk, mixing well after each addition. Add 1 teaspoon vanilla. Pour batter into 2 greased 8 or 9-inch cake pans. Spread meringue carefully over batter; sprinkle with pecans. Bake for 40 to 45 minutes or until cake tests done and meringue is light golden brown. Cool in pans. Loosen cake and meringue from edge of pan with spatula. Place 1 layer meringue side down on serving plate. Spread with Pineapple Cream Filling. Top with remaining layer meringue side up. Chill for several hours to overnight. Yield: 10 to 12 servings.

PINEAPPLE CREAM FILLING

1 13-ounce can crushed	1 1/2 teaspoons
pineapple	confectioners' sugar
1 cup whipping cream	1/4 teaspoon vanilla extract

Drain pineapple very well. Whip cream with confectioners' sugar and vanilla in mixer bowl until stiff peaks form. Fold in pineapple.

Kathy Swanson, Preceptor Beta Omicron
Winter Haven, Florida

HUMMINGBIRD CAKE

1 1/2 cups honey	1 teaspoon soda
3 eggs	1 teaspoon cinnamon
1 cup vegetable oil	1 8-ounce can
1 1/2 teaspoons vanilla	unsweetened crushed
extract	pineapple
1 1/2 cups whole wheat	2 ripe bananas, chopped
flour	1 cup coconut
1 1/2 cups all-purpose flour	1 cup chopped pecans

Preheat oven to 350 degrees. Combine honey, eggs, oil and vanilla in mixer bowl; beat until well blended. Sift dry ingredients into large bowl. Pour in honey mixture; mix well. Fold in pineapple, bananas, coconut and pecans. Spoon into buttered 9x13-inch cake pan. Bake for 45 minutes or until center springs back when lightly touched. Serve warm with whipped topping. Yield: 18 servings.

Elaine Cybul, Laureate Alpha Gamma
Union Lake, Michigan

PINEAPPLE SHEET CAKE

2 cups sugar	2 eggs
2 1/4 cups sifted	2 teaspoons soda
all-purpose flour	1 teaspoon vanilla extract
1/4 teaspoon salt	1 cup chopped pecans
1 20-ounce can crushed	
pineapple	

Preheat oven to 350 degrees. Combine all ingredients in order listed in large bowl, mixing well after each addition. Pour into greased and floured 11x17-inch cake pan. Bake for 25 minutes. Cool completely. Frost with Cream Cheese Frosting. Yield: 30 servings.

CREAM CHEESE FROSTING

8 ounces cream cheese,	1/2 cup chopped pecans
softened	1/2 teaspoon vanilla extract
1/2 cup margarine, softened	
1 pound confectioners'	
sugar	

Combine all ingredients in order listed in mixer bowl. Beat at medium speed until well mixed.

Frances Choate, Delta Eta
Charleston, Illinois

TEXAS YUM-YUM CAKE

2 cups sugar	2 cups all-purpose flour
1 20-ounce can crushed	1/2 to 1 cup chopped nuts
pineapple	1 cup sour cream
1 teaspoon soda	1/2 cup melted butter
1 teaspoon vanilla	3/4 cup sugar
extract	1/2 to 1 cup chopped nuts

Preheat oven to 350 degrees. Combine first 6 ingredients in bowl; mix well after each addition. Pour into ungreased 9x13-inch baking pan. Bake for 30 minutes or until cake tests done. Blend next 3 ingredients in bowl. Stir in nuts. Pour over cake. Cool. Yield: 12 servings.

Lynda L. Appelt, Xi Pi Psi
Eagle Lake, Texas

TOP ME TWICE CAKE

1 cup sugar	1/2 cup flaked coconut
2 eggs	1/2 cup packed light brown
1 teaspoon vanilla extract	sugar
2 cups sifted flour	1/2 cup chopped pecans
1 teaspoon soda	1/2 cup melted margarine
1 teaspoon salt	1/2 cup cream
1 13-ounce can crushed	1/2 cup sugar
pineapple, undrained	1/2 teaspoon vanilla extract

Preheat oven to 350 degrees. Beat first 3 ingredients in mixer bowl at medium speed for 2 minutes. Beat in flour and next 3 ingredients at low speed until well mixed. Pour into greased 8x12-inch baking pan. Sprinkle with mixture of coconut, brown sugar and pecans. Bake for 45 minutes or until cake tests done. Heat mixture of remaining ingredients in saucepan until well mixed. Pour over warm cake. Yield: 18 servings.

Lawana Lewis, Preceptor Rho
Chanhassen, Minnesota

PISTACHIO CAKE

1 2-layer package white cake mix	1 3-ounce package pistachio instant pudding mix
3 eggs	
1 cup vegetable oil	
1 cup club soda	Coconut

Preheat oven to 350 degrees. Beat first 5 ingredients in mixer bowl for 4 minutes. Pour into greased and floured bundt pan. Bake for 45 minutes. Cool. Spread Frosting over top; sprinkle with coconut. Chill. Yield: 8 servings.

FROSTING

1 envelope whipped topping mix	1 cup cold milk
1 3-ounce package pistachio instant pudding mix	1 4-ounce container whipped topping

Combine whipped topping mix, pudding mix, milk and whipped topping in mixer bowl. Beat until well blended.

Lynn Pence, Theta Upsilon
Princeton, West Virginia

POPPY SEED BUNDT CAKE

1/3 cup poppy seed	2 teaspoons baking powder
1 cup buttermilk	
1 cup shortening	1 teaspoon soda
1 1/2 cups sugar	4 egg whites, stiffly beaten
4 egg yolks	
1 teaspoon almond extract	1/2 cup sugar
1 teaspoon vanilla extract	1 tablespoon cinnamon
2 1/2 cups all-purpose flour	Confectioners' sugar glaze

Preheat oven to 350 degrees. Mix poppy seed and buttermilk in large bowl. Let stand for 15 minutes. Add next 3 ingredients. Mix almond and vanilla extracts, flour, baking powder and soda in small bowl. Blend into buttermilk mixture gradually. Fold in stiffly beaten egg whites. Pour half the batter into greased and floured bundt pan. Sprinkle with mixture of 1/2 cup sugar and cinnamon. Cover with remaining batter. Bake for 1 hour. Cool. Invert onto serving plate. Garnish with confectioners' sugar glaze. Yield: 12 to 16 servings.

Paula Seward, Mu Nu
New Providence, Iowa

APRICOT POUND CAKE

1 3/4 cups sugar	2 cups all-purpose flour
1 cup vegetable oil	1 teaspoon salt
3 eggs	2 teaspoons baking powder
1 7 3/4-ounce jar apricots with tapioca baby food	Confectioners' sugar glaze

Preheat oven to 350 degrees. Mix sugar and oil in bowl. Add eggs and baby food; mix well. Add dry ingredients; mix well. Pour into bundt pan sprayed with nonstick cooking spray. Bake for 40 minutes. Cool. Invert onto serving plate. Garnish with thin confectioners' sugar glaze. Yield: 12 to 15 servings.

Deena S. Foster, Beta
Springfield, Missouri

BROWN SUGAR POUND CAKE

1 pound light brown sugar	3 cups all-purpose flour
	1 teaspoon baking powder
1 cup sugar	1/2 teaspoon salt
1 1/2 cups shortening	1 cup milk
5 eggs	1 teaspoon vanilla extract

Preheat oven to 375 degrees. Cream sugars and shortening in mixer bowl. Add eggs 1 at a time, beating well after each addition. Sift flour, baking powder and salt 3 times. Add to creamed mixture alternately with milk, mixing well after each addition. Mix in vanilla. Pour into greased bundt pan. Bake for 1 hour. Cool. Invert onto serving plate. Garnish with lemon confectioners' sugar glaze. Yield: 12 servings.

Pat Gillett, Kappa Omega
Fredonia, Kansas

MOM'S CHOCOLATE POUND CAKE

1 1/2 cups butter, softened	1/4 teaspoon salt
3 cups sugar	1 1/4 cups milk
5 eggs	1/2 cup unsweetened baking cocoa
3 cups all-purpose flour	
1/2 teaspoon baking powder	1 teaspoon vanilla extract
	Confectioners' sugar

Preheat oven to 300 degrees. Cream butter in mixer bowl. Add sugar gradually, beating constantly until well blended. Blend in eggs 1 at a time. Add sifted flour, baking powder and salt alternately with milk, mixing well after each addition. Add cocoa; blend well. Blend in vanilla. Pour into greased and floured 10-cup bundt pan. Bake for 1 1/2 hours. Cool in pan for 15 minutes. Invert onto serving plate. Garnish with confectioners' sugar. Yield: 12 servings.

Betsy Radford, Beta Xi
Chesapeake, Virginia

CREAM CHEESE POUND CAKE

8 ounces glacéed cherries, chopped	1 1/2 cups sugar
	4 eggs
1/4 cup all-purpose flour	1/2 teaspoon vanilla extract
1 cup butter, softened	2 1/4 cups all-purpose flour
8 ounces cream cheese, softened	1/2 teaspoon baking powder

Preheat oven to 300 degrees. Toss cherries with 1/4 cup flour in bowl to coat well; set aside. Cream butter, cream cheese and sugar in mixer bowl until very smooth. Add eggs 1 at a time, beating well after each addition. Mix in vanilla. Sift in 2 1/4 cups flour and baking powder gradually, mixing well. Fold in cherries. Pour into greased and floured bundt pan. Bake for 70 minutes or until toothpick inserted in center comes out clean. Cool in pan for 5 minutes. Invert onto wire rack to cool completely. May decorate with confectioners' sugar glaze or top with glacéed fruit and slivered almonds. Yield: 12 to 15 servings.

Juanita McLeod, Xi Pi Chi
Costa Mesa, California

THREE-FLAVOR POUND CAKE

3 cups sugar
1 cup butter, softened
½ cup shortening
5 eggs
3 cups all-purpose flour
½ teaspoon baking
  powder
½ teaspoon salt
1 cup milk
1 teaspoon vanilla extract
1 teaspoon rum extract
1 teaspoon coconut extract
Confectioners' sugar

Preheat oven to 325 degrees. Cream first 3 ingredients in mixer bowl. Add eggs 1 at a time, beating well after each addition. Sift flour, baking powder and salt together. Add flour mixture and milk alternately ⅓ at a time, beating well after each addition. Mix in flavorings; do not overbeat. Pour in well greased and floured bundt pan. Bake for 1½ hours or until cake tests done. Cool in pan for 10 minutes. Invert onto serving plate. Cool. Garnish with sifted confectioners' sugar. Yield: 20 servings.

Helen R. Kadera, Laureate Alpha Kappa
St. Joseph, Missouri

SOUR CREAM POUND CAKE

1 cup butter, softened
3 cups sugar
6 egg yolks
3 cups all-purpose flour
¼ teaspoon soda
1 cup sour cream
6 egg whites, stiffly
  beaten

Preheat oven to 300 degrees. Cream butter and sugar in mixer bowl. Add egg yolks 1 at a time, beating well after each addition. Sift flour and soda together twice. Add to creamed mixture alternately with sour cream, mixing well after each addition. Fold in stiffly beaten egg whites. Pour into greased and floured angel food cake pan. Bake for 1½ hours or until brown. Invert onto serving plate immediately. Serve unfrosted cake with light lemon-flavored frosting, lemon ice cream or lemon sauce. Yield: 12 to 14 servings.

Thelma True Borger, Xi Alpha Kappa
Mason City, Iowa

ELVIS' FAVORITE POUND CAKE

3 cups sugar
1 cup butter, softened
7 eggs, at room
  temperature
3 cups cake flour, sifted
  twice
1 cup whipping cream
2 teaspoons vanilla extract

Cream sugar and butter in mixer bowl until light and fluffy. Add eggs 1 at a time, beating well after each addition. Mix in half the flour, whipping cream and remaining flour, mixing well after each addition. Add vanilla. Pour into buttered and floured 10-inch tube pan. Place in cold oven. Turn oven on to 350 degrees. Bake for 60 to 70 minutes or until sharp knife inserted in cake comes out clean. Cool in pan for 5 minutes. Invert onto serving plate. Cool completely. Store tightly wrapped. Yield: 14 to 16 servings.

Barbara A. Huseboe, Preceptor Mu Delta
Perris, California

PRUNE CAKE

1 pound seedless raisins
2 cups sugar
3 cups water
¼ cup shortening
1 cup prunes, cooked,
  chopped
4 cups all-purpose flour
2 teaspoons soda
1 teaspoon salt
2 teaspoons cinnamon
Pinch of allspice
1 cup chopped nuts

Preheat oven to 350 degrees. Bring first 5 ingredients to a boil in saucepan; reduce heat. Simmer for 15 minutes. Cool. Mix in sifted dry ingredients and nuts. Pour into greased 10-inch tube pan. Bake for 45 minutes. Cool on wire rack. Yield: 12 servings.

Beverly Beyeler, Laureate Alpha Rho
Fremont, California

RHUBARB UPSIDE-DOWN CAKE

1 2-layer package yellow
   cake mix
2 to 3 cups frozen chunk
   rhubarb
1 6-ounce package
   cherry gelatin
1 8-ounce container
   whipped topping

Preheat oven to 375 degrees. Prepare cake mix according to package directions. Place frozen rhubarb in 9x13-inch cake pan. Sprinkle dry gelatin over rhubarb. Pour cake mixture over top. Bake for 50 to 60 minutes or until brown and cake tests done. Serve with whipped topping. Yield: 12 servings.

Cheryl L. Conway, Xi Gamma Rho
Clinton, Iowa

CHOCOLATE FLUFF ROLL WITH CREAM

⅔ cup sifted all-purpose
  flour
1 teaspoon baking powder
½ teaspoon salt
4 eggs, separated
½ cup sugar
¼ cup sugar
2 tablespoons water
1 teaspoon vanilla extract
Confectioners' sugar

Sift together flour, baking powder and salt. Beat egg whites in mixer bowl until soft peaks form. Beat in ½ cup sugar 2 tablespoons at a time, until stiff peaks form. Beat egg yolks until thick lemon-colored in bowl. Add remaining ¼ cup sugar gradually. Beat in water and vanilla. Fold egg yolk mixture gently into egg whites. Sift dry ingredients over egg mixture; fold in gently. Spread batter evenly in greased waxed paper-lined 10x15-inch cake pan. Bake for 10 minutes or until golden. Invert onto towel sprinkled with confectioners' sugar. Remove paper; trim edges. Roll cake up in towel; cool. Unroll; fill with Chocolate Mint Cream. Yield: 10 servings.

CHOCOLATE MINT CREAM

½ cup sugar
¼ cup unsweetened
  baking cocoa
⅛ teaspoon salt
½ teaspoon vanilla extract
¼ teaspoon peppermint
  extract
1¼ cups whipping cream

Combine all ingredients in bowl; blend well. Refrigerate for 3 hours. Beat with rotary beater until stiff peaks form.

Katherine Krenitsky, Xi Zeta Psi
Stroudsberg, Pennsylvania

PEPPERMINT ICE CREAM ROLL

4 egg yolks	1 teaspoon baking powder
¼ cup sugar	¼ teaspoon salt
½ teaspoon vanilla extract	Confectioners' sugar
4 egg whites	1 quart peppermint ice
½ cup sugar	cream, softened
⅔ cup sifted cake flour	1 cup whipped topping
¼ cup unsweetened	¼ cup crushed
baking cocoa	peppermint candy

Preheat oven to 375 degrees. Beat egg yolks in small mixer bowl until thick. Beat in ¼ cup sugar gradually. Add vanilla. Beat egg whites in large mixer bowl until soft peaks form. Add ½ cup sugar gradually, beating until stiff peaks form. Fold egg yolk mixture into egg whites gently. Fold in sifted dry ingredients gently. Spread batter evenly in greased and floured 10x15-inch cake pan. Bake for 10 minutes. Loosen from side of pan; invert onto towel sprinkled with sifted confectioners' sugar. Roll in towel as for jelly roll. Cool. Unroll. Spread with ice cream; reroll. Freeze until firm. Frost with mixture of whipped topping and candy. Yield: 10 servings.

Carol McGarraugh, Delta Upsilon
Perryton, Texas

RHUBARB CAKE

1½ cups packed light	½ teaspoon salt
brown sugar	2 cups all-purpose flour
½ cup shortening	3 cups finely chopped
1 egg	rhubarb
1 teaspoon vanilla extract	1 teaspoon cinnamon
1 cup buttermilk	½ cup chopped nuts
1 teaspoon soda	½ cup sugar

Preheat oven to 350 degrees. Cream brown sugar, shortening and egg in mixer bowl. Add next 5 ingredients; mix well. Pour boiling water to cover over rhubarb in bowl; drain. Stir rhubarb into batter. Pour into greased 9x13-inch baking pan. Sprinkle with mixture of cinnamon, nuts and sugar. Bake for 45 minutes. Yield: 12 servings.

Peggy Callahan, Preceptor Laureate Gamma
Santa Ana, California

SHAMROCK DELIGHT CAKE

1 2-layer package white	3 to 4 tablespoons
cake mix	Crème de Menthe
3 tablespoons	1 8-ounce container
Crème de Menthe	whipped topping
1 16-ounce can chocolate	
fudge ice cream topping	

Preheat oven to 350 degrees. Prepare cake mix according to package directions, adding 3 tablespoons Crème de Menthe. Pour into greased and floured 9x13-inch cake pan. Bake for 30 minutes or until cake tests done. Cool. Spread with fudge topping. Blend 3 or 4 tablespoons Crème de Menthe with whipped topping. Spread over fudge topping. Refrigerate cooled cake overnight. Store in refrigerator for up to 4 days. Yield: 12 to 15 servings.

Sue Valentine, Pi Phi
Raymore, Missouri

STRAWBERRY CAKE

1 18-ounce package	½ cup milk
white cake mix	½ cup frozen strawberries,
1 3-ounce package	thawed, crushed
strawberry gelatin	½ cup flaked coconut
1 cup shortening	½ cup chopped pecans
4 eggs	

Preheat oven to 350 degrees. Combine all ingredients in mixer bowl. Beat for 2 minutes. Pour into 3 greased 9-inch layer pans. Bake until cake tests done. Cool in pans for 10 minutes. Remove to wire rack to cool completely. Frost with Strawberry Frosting. Yield: 8 servings.

STRAWBERRY FROSTING

1 16-ounce package	½ cup chopped pecans
confectioners' sugar	½ cup strawberry purée
⅓ cup melted margarine	½ cup coconut

Beat confectioners' sugar and margarine in bowl until light and fluffy. Add remaining ingredients; mix well.

Jan Trimble, Alpha Delta Kappa
Sulphur Springs, Texas

STRAWBERRY SHORTCAKE

1 18-ounce package	2 10-ounce packages
yellow cake mix	frozen strawberries
1 14-ounce can	2 12-ounce containers
sweetened condensed	whipped topping
milk	1 cup chopped pecans

Preheat oven to 350 degrees. Prepare cake mix using package directions for 9x13-inch cake pan. Cool. Cut into slices. Alternate layers of cake, condensed milk, strawberries, whipped topping and pecans on serving plate. Top with whipped topping. Garnish with strawberries. Yield: 15 servings.

Blanca Lozano, Eta Sigma
Odessa, Texas

STRAWBERRY SHORTCAKE DESSERT

1 10-inch angel food or	8 ounces cream cheese,
sponge cake without	softened
hole in center	¾ cup sugar
1½ quarts fresh	1 envelope unflavored
strawberries	gelatin
¼ cup sugar	1½ cups whipping cream
1 teaspoon vanilla extract	¼ cup sugar

Slice cake into 3 layers. Purée 2 cups strawberries with ¼ cup sugar in blender. Place 1 cake layer on serving plate. Top with strawberry purée and second cake layer. Beat next 3 ingredients in mixer bowl until thickened. Spread over cake. Slice 3 cups strawberries. Arrange over cream cheese. Top with remaining layer. Chill for 6 hours. Soften gelatin in whipping cream for 5 minutes. Whip until soft peaks form. Add ¼ cup sugar gradually. Whip until mixture holds shape. Frost top and sides of cake. Cut remaining 1 cup strawberries into halves. Arrange stem ends toward center on top of cake. Yield: 12 servings.

Lucie D. LaRocco, Laureate Gamma
Torrington, Connecticut

STRAWBERRY-CHOCOLATE SHORTCAKE

⅔ cup unsalted butter
1½ cups self-rising flour
½ cup sugar
3 tablespoons
   unsweetened baking
   cocoa
⅔ cup miniature
   semisweet chocolate
   chips

⅔ cup milk
2 cups whipping cream
2½ teaspoons
   confectioners' sugar
½ teaspoon vanilla extract
4 cups sliced strawberries

Preheat oven to 400 degrees. Cut butter into mixture of flour, sugar and cocoa in bowl until crumbly. Add chocolate chips and milk; stir just until moistened. Spread in greased 8-inch round baking pan. Bake for 20 to 22 minutes. Cool in pan for 10 minutes. Remove to wire rack to cool completely. Cut into 2 layers. Whip cream with confectioners' sugar and vanilla in bowl until soft peaks form. Spread 3½ cups strawberries on 1 layer of cake. Top with half of the whipped cream. Add top layer, remaining whipped cream and strawberries. Chill until serving time. Yield: 8 servings.

Jean Pessano, Preceptor Alpha Beta
Ocean City, New Jersey

STRAWBERRY CROWN CAKE

1 18-ounce package
   yellow cake mix
4 eggs
1 3-ounce package
   vanilla instant pudding
   mix
½ cup vegetable oil
1 cup water
3 tablespoons all-purpose
   flour

1½ cups milk
1 cup butter or margarine,
   softened
½ cup shortening
1½ cups sugar
1 tablespoon vanilla
   extract
2 quarts strawberries,
   sliced into halves

Preheat oven to 350 degrees. Combine first 5 ingredients in mixer bowl. Beat at medium speed for 2 minutes. Pour into 2 greased 9-inch cake pans. Bake for 20 minutes or until cake tests done. Cool in pans for 5 minutes. Remove to wire rack to cool completely. Combine flour and milk in saucepan. Cook until thickened, stirring constantly. Cool. Cream butter, shortening and sugar in mixer bowl until light. Add cooked mixture and vanilla. Split each cake layer into 2 layers. Spread frosting and strawberries between layers and over top and side of cake. Chill until serving time. Yield: 10 to 12 servings.

Beverly A. Englar, Preceptor Epsilon Psi
Brandon, Florida

TOMATO SOUP CAKE

½ cup butter, softened
1½ cups sugar
2 eggs
2 cups all-purpose flour
½ teaspoon cloves
½ teaspoon nutmeg
1 teaspoon cinnamon
2 tablespoons water

1 11-ounce can tomato
   soup
1 teaspoon baking powder
1 teaspoon soda
1½ cups raisins
1 cup chopped nuts
¼ cup all-purpose flour

Preheat oven to 350 degrees. Cream butter and sugar in bowl until fluffy. Blend in eggs. Sift in 2 cups flour and spices. Add water, soup, baking powder and soda; mix well. Combine raisins, nuts and ¼ cup flour in bowl. Fold into batter. Pour into 2 greased 8-inch cake pans. Bake for 1 hour. Cool in pans for 5 minutes. Remove to wire rack to cool completely. Frost with cream cheese frosting. Yield: 12 servings.

Kerri Weatherly, Alpha Epsilon Chi
Amarillo, Texas

TEXAS TORNADO CAKE

1½ cups sugar
2 eggs
2 cups fruit cocktail with
   syrup
2 teaspoons soda
2 cups all-purpose flour
1 cup chopped pecans

¼ cup packed light brown
   sugar
½ cup butter or margarine
½ cup evaporated milk
¾ cup packed light brown
   sugar
1 cup flaked coconut

Preheat oven to 325 degrees. Mix first 5 ingredients in bowl. Pour into greased 9x13-inch pan. Combine pecans and ¼ cup brown sugar. Sprinkle over batter. Bake for 40 minutes. Combine remaining ingredients in saucepan. Boil for 2 minutes, stirring occasionally. Spoon over warm cake. Cool. Cut into squares. Yield: 15 servings.

Patricia Lynch, Preceptor Upsilon
St. Petersburg, Florida

TWELFTH NIGHT CAKE

2½ cups all-purpose flour
1 teaspoon soda
1 teaspoon salt
½ teaspoon cinnamon
¾ cup butter or
   margarine, softened
1½ cups sugar
½ cup orange juice
½ cup milk
2 eggs

1 tablespoon grated
   orange rind
1 teaspoon vanilla extract
½ cup chopped walnuts
½ cup golden raisins
¼ cup currants
1 cup chopped almonds
1 whole almond
¼ cup sugar
¼ cup orange juice

Preheat oven to 350 degrees. Sift first 4 ingredients together; set aside. Cream butter and 1½ cups sugar in bowl until light and fluffy. Add ½ cup orange juice, milk, eggs, orange rind and vanilla; mix well. Add sifted ingredients ¼ at a time, beating well after each addition. Fold in walnuts, raisins, currants, chopped almonds and whole almond. Pour into greased 8-inch bundt pan. Bake for 55 minutes or until cake tests done. Cool in pan on wire rack for 15 minutes. Combine remaining ¼ cup sugar and ¼ cup orange juice in saucepan. Bring to a boil. Cool for several minutes. Prick top of cake with fork. Spoon orange juice mixture over cake until liquid is completely absorbed. Cool cake completely. Remove to cake plate. Wrap in plastic wrap. Let stand for 12 hours before slicing. Yield: 16 servings.
Note: Whoever has the whole almond in his serving is king or queen for the night and will have good luck for the new year.

Photograph for this recipe on page 1.

BLITZ TORTE

½ cup sugar
½ cup butter, softened
4 eggs, separated
¼ cup milk
½ cup all-purpose flour
1 teaspoon baking powder
1 teaspoon vanilla extract

1 cup sugar
1 teaspoon vanilla extract
½ cup chopped nuts
½ cup whipping cream, whipped
1 pint fresh strawberries, sliced

Preheat oven to 375 degrees. Cream ½ cup sugar with butter in bowl. Blend in beaten egg yolks. Add milk and flour alternately, mixing well after each addition. Add baking powder and 1 teaspoon vanilla. Pour into 2 buttered 8-inch cake pans. Beat egg whites in mixer bowl until stiff peaks form. Add 1 cup sugar gradually, beating until very stiff. Add 1 teaspoon vanilla and chopped nuts. Spread over cake batter. Bake for 25 minutes. Cool on wire rack. Spread whipped cream and strawberries between layers and on top. Yield: 8 servings.

Minnie Jackson, Delta Theta
Blue Earth, Minnesota

BROWNIE MINT TORTE

3 egg whites
Dash of salt
¾ cup sugar
½ teaspoon vanilla extract
¾ cup fine chocolate wafer crumbs

½ cup chopped walnuts
1 cup whipping cream
2 tablespoons confectioners' sugar
½ teaspoon mint extract

Preheat oven to 325 degrees. Beat egg whites and salt in mixer bowl until soft peaks form. Add sugar 1 tablespoon at a time, beating well until glossy. Beat in vanilla. Fold in crumbs and walnuts. Spread in buttered 9-inch pie pan, shaping high edge. Bake for 35 minutes. Cool. Whip cream in mixer bowl until stiff. Fold in confectioners' sugar and mint flavoring. Spoon into chocolate shell. Chill for 3 hours. Garnish with chocolate curls. Yield: 6 to 8 servings.

Martha A. Hawkins, Xi Delta Nu
Carrollton, Missouri

MERINGUE TORTE

8 egg whites
1 cup sugar
1 tablespoon vinegar
Dash of salt
1 teaspoon vanilla extract

12 dry macaroon cookies
1 pint whipping cream
1 tablespoon confectioners' sugar
½ teaspoon vanilla extract

Preheat oven to 250 degrees. Beat egg whites in mixer bowl until stiff peaks form. Beat in sugar gradually. Beat in vinegar, salt and 1 teaspoon vanilla. Pour into 2 greased and waxed paper-lined 8-inch cake pans. Bake for 1 hour. Chill in pans overnight. Crush macaroon cookies into crumbs. Whip cream, adding confectioners' sugar and ½ teaspoon vanilla. Fold in cookie crumbs. Spread whipped cream mixture between layers and over top and side of torte. Chill for 2 hours. Yield: 8 servings.

Chris Teubert, Preceptor Eta Rho
Huntington Beach, California

FRENCH WALNUT TORTE

1½ cups sugar
3 eggs
1 tablespoon vanilla extract
1¾ cups all-purpose flour
2 teaspoons baking powder
1 cup ground walnuts
1½ cups whipping cream, whipped

1 cup peach preserves
2 tablespoons sugar
½ cup margarine, softened
8 ounces cream cheese, softened
4 cups confectioners' sugar
1 teaspoon vanilla extract
1 cup ground walnuts

Preheat oven to 350 degrees. Beat 1½ cups sugar, eggs and 1 tablespoon vanilla in mixer bowl at high speed for 5 minutes. Mix flour, baking powder and 1 cup walnuts in bowl. Add walnut mixture and whipped cream alternately to sugar mixture, beginning and ending with walnut mixture and mixing well after each addition. Pour into 2 greased and floured 9-inch cake pans. Bake for 25 to 30 minutes or until toothpick inserted in center comes out clean. Cool in pans for 15 minutes. Heat preserves and 2 tablespoons sugar in saucepan until sugar is dissolved. Reserve ½ cup preserve mixture. Brush remaining glaze over warm layers. Chill layers and reserved preserve mixture for 30 minutes. Combine margarine, cream cheese, confectioners' sugar and 1 teaspoon vanilla in mixer bowl. Beat at medium speed for 2 minutes. Spread between layers and over top of cake. Sprinkle with ½ cup walnuts. Chill for 30 minutes. Spread reserved glaze over side of torte. Press remaining ½ cup walnuts into glaze. Store in refrigerator. Yield: 16 to 20 servings.

Rosemary L. Fisette, Preceptor Alpha Tau
Vienna, Virginia

CHRISTMAS ALMOND TORTE

¼ cup butter
½ cup sugar
4 egg yolks, beaten
⅞ cup all-purpose flour
2 teaspoons baking powder
¼ teaspoon salt
¼ cup half and half

Vanilla extract to taste
4 egg whites
3 tablespoons sugar
Sliced almonds
1 12-ounce container whipped topping
Green and red food coloring

Preheat oven to 350 degrees. Cream butter and ½ cup sugar in bowl. Blend in egg yolks. Add sifted flour, baking powder and salt alternately with half and half, mixing well after each addition. Add vanilla. Pour into 2 greased and floured 9-inch cake pans. Beat egg whites and 3 tablespoons sugar in mixer bowl until stiff peaks form. Spread over batter. Top with almond slices. Bake until brown. Remove from pans. Cool completely. Tint half the whipped topping with each color food coloring. Spread 1 color on each layer. Stack layers on serving plate. Swirl any remaining whipped topping together to garnish individual servings. Yield: 12 servings.

Marilys Bergquist, Xi Epsilon Phi
Gaylord, Michigan

CHOCOLATE CHIP BROWNIE TORTE

⅔ cup butter	1 teaspoon vanilla extract
1 cup miniature semisweet chocolate chips	2 cups whipping cream, chilled
1½ cups sugar	¼ cup confectioners' sugar
1½ cups all-purpose flour	1 teaspoon vanilla extract
1 teaspoon baking powder	1 cup miniature semisweet chocolate chips
½ teaspoon salt	
4 eggs	

Preheat oven to 350 degrees. Line 10x15-inch baking pan with greased waxed paper. Heat butter and 1 cup chocolate chips in 3-quart saucepan over medium heat until chocolate is melted. Add sugar and next 5 ingredients; mix well. Spread evenly in prepared pan. Bake for 20 to 25 minutes. Cool for 10 minutes. Invert onto work surface; remove waxed paper. Cool completely. Cut crosswise into four 3¾x10-inch pieces. Beat whipping cream, confectioners' sugar and 1 teaspoon vanilla in chilled bowl until stiff. Stir in ⅔ cup miniature chocolate chips. Spread between layers and over top and side of torte. Garnish with remaining ⅓ cup miniature chips. Yield: 10 to 20 servings.

Marcia Hayes, Xi Epsilon Pi
Abilene, Kansas

CHOCOLATE PECAN TORTE

¾ cup unsalted butter	¼ teaspoon salt
2 cups sugar	12 ounces semisweet chocolate, melted
8 eggs	
2 tablespoons vanilla extract	3½ cups finely ground pecans

Preheat oven to 375 degrees. Butter four 9-inch round cake pans; line bottoms with buttered baking parchment. Cream butter in mixer bowl until light. Add sugar; beat until light and fluffy. Beat in eggs 1 at a time. Add vanilla and salt. Fold in chocolate and pecans. Pour into prepared pans. Bake for 22 minutes or until tester inserted in center comes out fudgy but not wet. Cool in pans on wire rack for 5 minutes. Loosen from side of pan with knife. Invert onto wire racks to cool completely. Stack layers bottom side up on cake plate, spreading about ⅔ cup Strawberry Buttercream between each layer. Chill, covered, for 6 hours or longer. Spread Chocolate Glaze over top and side of torte. Let stand at room temperature for 1 hour before serving. Yield: 14 to 16 servings.

STRAWBERRY BUTTERCREAM FROSTING

1¼ cups unsalted butter, slightly softened	½ cup puréed strawberries
2 cups confectioners' sugar, sifted	3 tablespoons strawberry preserves
4 egg yolks	

Cream butter and sugar in mixer bowl until light and fluffy. Mix in egg yolks, puréed strawberries and preserves. Chill, covered tightly, until set. Let stand at room temperature until of spreading consistency.

EASY CHOCOLATE GLAZE

3 ounces semisweet chocolate, coarsely chopped	3 tablespoons vegetable oil
½ cup water	¾ cup unsweetened baking cocoa
6 tablespoons unsalted butter	½ cup plus 2 tablespoons sugar

Heat chocolate, water, butter and oil in double boiler over gently simmering water until chocolate melts; remove from heat. Add cocoa and sugar; stir until sugar dissolves and glaze is smooth. Cool until slightly thickened but pourable.

Cheryl Baker, Xi Alpha Theta
Jamestown, New York

TREASURE TOFFEE CAKE

¼ cup sugar	½ cup butter, softened
1 teaspoon cinnamon	2 eggs
2 cups all-purpose flour	¼ cup chopped nuts
1 cup sugar	3 1⅛-ounce chocolate toffee candy bars, crushed
1½ teaspoons soda	
¼ teaspoon salt	
1 teaspoon vanilla extract	¼ cup melted butter
1 cup sour cream	Confectioners' sugar

Preheat oven to 325 degrees. Combine ¼ cup sugar and cinnamon; set aside. Combine next 8 ingredients in mixer bowl. Beat at low speed until moistened. Beat at medium speed for 3 minutes. Pour half the batter into greased and floured tube pan. Sprinkle with 2 tablespoons cinnamon-sugar. Spoon remaining batter into pan. Top with remaining cinnamon-sugar, nuts and candy. Pour melted butter over top. Bake for 45 minutes. Cool in pan for 15 minutes. Remove to wire rack to cool completely. Dust with confectioners' sugar. Yield: 16 servings.

 Marilyn Borras, Xi Epsilon Alpha
Stafford, Virginia

GREEK WALNUT CAKE

2 cups buttermilk baking mix	¼ teaspoon nutmeg
1 cup chopped walnuts	1 teaspoon cinnamon
1 cup sugar	¼ teaspoon cloves
1 cup milk, at room temperature	1 teaspoon orange flavoring
1 cup corn oil	4 eggs
1½ teaspoons baking powder	1 cup sugar
½ teaspoon soda	1 cup water
	1 teaspoon orange flavoring

Preheat oven to 350 degrees. Combine first 12 ingredients in bowl with fork until well blended. Pour into greased 9x13-inch cake pan. Bake for 30 minutes. Combine 1 cup sugar, water and remaining 1 teaspoon orange flavoring in saucepan. Boil for 15 minutes. Cool. Drizzle over hot cake. Cool completely. Cut into diamond shapes. Place in paper cupcake liners. Yield: 12 servings.

Gloria S. Watkins, Preceptor Phi
Rochester, New York

WHITE FOREST CAKE

1 18-ounce package white cake mix	2 eggs, beaten
1 21-ounce can pie filling	1 cup sugar
	5 tablespoons margarine
1 teaspoon almond extract	½ cup milk
	6 ounces white chocolate

Preheat oven to 350 degrees. Combine first 4 ingredients in bowl with fork until moistened. Pour into greased 9x13-inch cake pan. Bake for 25 to 30 minutes or until cake tests done. Combine sugar, margarine and milk in saucepan. Bring to a boil. Cook for 1 minute. Add chocolate, stirring until melted. Spread over cake.

Linda Weingeroff, Xi Alpha Alpha
Jacksonville, Florida

TEDDY BEAR CAKES

3 bakery pound cakes	2 tablespoons margarine, softened
1 12-ounce jar grape jelly	½ teaspoon vanilla extract
3 cups confectioners' sugar	¼ teaspoon almond extract
2 tablespoons Amaretto	1 tube pink decorator icing
¼ cup water	
3 tablespoons light corn syrup	1 tube blue decorator icing

Slice pound cakes lengthwise. Spread jelly between 2 slices. Cut with cookie cutter in shape of teddy bear or other shape cookie cutters. Combine confectioners' sugar and next 6 ingredients in bowl; beat until smooth. Place each bear on wire rack over waxed paper. Pour icing on each bear slowly, allowing icing to trickle down sides; spread with knife if necessary. Let dry for 1 hour to 1 day before serving. Use decorator icing for eyes, nose and other detailing.

Kathy Hutchinson, Rho Lambda
Levelland, Texas

BRANDY ALEXANDER CAKE

1 baked angel food cake	1 tablespoon dark Crème de Cacao
½ cup dark Crème de Cacao	
1 tablespoon heavy cream	1 12-ounce container whipped topping

Prick top of cake halfway to center with ice pick in several places. Mix ½ cup Crème de Cacao with heavy cream in bowl. Pour half the mixture over top of cake gradually, allowing liquid to saturate cake. Let cake stand for 30 minutes. Invert onto serving plate. Prick cake; pour remaining Crème de Cacao mixture onto cake. Blend 1 tablespoon Crème de Cacao into half the whipped topping. Spoon into center of cake. Frost with remaining whipped topping. Chill, covered, until serving time. Must prepare and serve same day. Garnish each slice with strawberries. Yield: 12 servings.

Gail Ann Ditmore, Xi Gamma Mu
Indianapolis, Indiana

RUM AND ALMOND TORTE

1 large baked angel food cake	½ teaspoon salt
	1 teaspoon vanilla extract
3 to 4 tablespoons rum	2 teaspoons rum
1 cup sour cream	1 12-ounce container whipped topping
1 cup confectioners' sugar	
1 cup chocolate chips, melted	1 2-ounce milk chocolate candy bar, grated
1 tablespoon butter, melted	1 2-ounce package slivered almonds, toasted

Slice cake into 3 or 4 layers. Sprinkle with 3 to 4 tablespoons rum. Blend sour cream and next 6 ingredients in bowl. Spread between layers. Frost with whipped topping. Top with grated chocolate and almonds. Store in refrigerator. Yield: 12 servings.

Anne Fountaine, Theta Eta
Covington, Virginia

MEXICAN PARTY CAKE

¾ cup chocolate chips	1 teaspoon ground cinnamon
½ teaspoon instant coffee powder	¼ teaspoon ground cloves
2 tablespoons water	1 cup whipping cream, whipped
4 eggs, separated	
¼ cup sugar	1 baked angel food cake

Combine chocolate chips, coffee powder and water in double boiler. Heat over hot water until blended, stirring constantly; remove from heat. Cool slightly. Add egg yolks 1 at a time, beating well after each addition. Beat egg whites in large bowl until foamy. Add sugar and spices gradually, beating until stiff. Fold chocolate mixture into stiffly beaten egg whites gently. Fold in whipped cream. Cut cake into 3 layers. Spread chocolate mixture between layers and over top and side of cake. Chill for 4 hours or longer. Yield: 12 servings.

Billie Jo Sadler, Xi Alpha Mu
Little Rock, Arkansas

MOCHA DREAM CAKE

1 baked angel food cake	2 tablespoons sugar
2 4-ounce packages chocolate fudge instant pudding mix	1 cup chocolate chips
	¼ cup confectioners' sugar
3 cups milk	1 tablespoon water
2 tablespoons instant coffee powder	Pecans

Cut ¾-inch layer off top of cake; set aside. Scoop out cake, leaving ½ to ¾-inch shell. Tear scooped out cake into small pieces; set aside. Mix pudding mix with milk using package directions and adding coffee powder and sugar. Mix in torn cake. Spoon pudding into cake shell; replace top. Melt chocolate chips in double boiler. Blend in confectioners' sugar and water. Drizzle over top of cake. Chill until serving time. Garnish each serving with pecans. Yield: 12 to 15 servings.

Ruth Balzer, Preceptor Eta
Mobile, Alabama

Cookies

WHITE ALMOND BARS

4 eggs
2 cups sugar
¼ teaspoon salt
2 cups all-purpose flour
1 cup melted butter

2 teaspoons almond
   flavoring
¼ cup sugar
1 cup slivered almonds

Preheat oven to 325 degrees. Beat eggs, 2 cups sugar and salt in bowl until light. Add mixture of flour and butter. Add flavoring. Pour into greased and floured 9x13-inch baking pan. Sprinkle with ¼ cup sugar and almonds. Bake for 30 minutes. Yield: 3 dozen.

 Marilyn Mangelos, Gamma Alpha Omega
Ripon, California

ANISE SLICES

6 eggs
1½ cups sugar
1 cup vegetable oil
1 teaspoon vanilla extract
1 teaspoon anise extract

3 cups all-purpose flour
1 tablespoon baking
   powder
1 cup chopped nuts
Nonpareils

Preheat oven to 350 degrees. Beat first 5 ingredients in bowl. Mix in flour, baking powder and nuts. Fill greased and floured metal ice cube trays ½ full; sprinkle with nonpareils. Bake for 30 minutes. Slice diagonally. Place on baking sheet. Bake until brown. Yield: 30 slices.

Anna M. Greer, Beta Sigma Phi
Zwolle, Louisiana

ANISE SUGAR COOKIES

2 cups lard
1 cup sugar
1 tablespoon aniseed
1 teaspoon salt
3 eggs
6 cups all-purpose flour

1 tablespoon baking
   powder
¼ cup orange juice
½ cup sugar
1 teaspoon cinnamon

Preheat oven to 375 degrees. Cream first 4 ingredients in bowl until light and fluffy. Add eggs, flour, baking powder and juice; mix well. Roll ½ inch thick; cut with cookie cutter. Sprinkle mixture of ½ cup sugar and cinnamon on top. Place on baking sheet. Bake for 20 minutes.
Yield: 6 dozen.

Melissa Polaco, Xi Beta Lambda
Tierra Amarilla, New Mexico

CHEWY BARS

1 cup melted butter
1   16-ounce package
   light brown sugar
2 eggs, beaten

2 cups all-purpose flour
½ cup chopped pecans
2 teaspoons vanilla extract
1 teaspoon baking powder

Preheat oven to 350 degrees. Combine all ingredients in bowl; mix well. Spoon into greased 9x13-inch baking dish. Bake for 20 to 30 minutes or until golden brown. Cool. Cut into bars. Yield: 3 dozen.

Margaret Doherty, Xi Alpha Alpha Omicron
Ennis, Texas

DANISH APPLE BARS

2½ cups all-purpose
   flour, sifted
1 teaspoon salt
1 cup butter-flavored
   shortening
1 egg yolk
Milk
1 cup crushed cornflakes

5 large apples
1 cup sugar
1 teaspoon cinnamon
1 egg white, beaten
1 cup confectioners' sugar
1 tablespoon water
1 teaspoon vanilla extract

Preheat oven to 375 degrees. Sift flour and salt into bowl. Cut in shortening until crumbly. Combine egg yolk and enough milk to measure ⅔ cup; beat until blended. Add to flour mixture gradually; do not overmix. Divide into 2 portions. Roll half the dough on floured surface. Fit over bottom and sides of 10x15-inch baking pan. Sprinkle with crushed cornflakes. Peel and slice apples; arrange over cornflakes. Sprinkle with mixture of sugar and cinnamon. Roll remaining dough; fit over top. Moisten edges; seal. Brush with beaten egg white. Bake for 1 hour or until golden brown. Drizzle mixture of confectioners' sugar, water and vanilla over baked layer. Cut into bars. Yield: 12 to 15 servings.

Dorcas Snyder, Zi Iota Omicron
Hamilton, Missouri

BABY FOOD BARS

2 cups sugar
1 cup vegetable oil
2 eggs, well beaten
2 cups all-purpose flour
2 teaspoons soda
2 teaspoons cinnamon
1 teaspoon salt
1 4-ounce jar baby
   food carrots
1 4-ounce jar baby
   food applesauce

1 4-ounce jar baby
   food apricots
½ cup margarine,
   softened
3 ounces cream cheese,
   softened
3½ cups confectioners'
   sugar

Preheat oven to 350 degrees. Beat sugar and oil in bowl. Add eggs; mix well. Add next 4 dry ingredients; mix well. Stir in baby food. Pour into greased 12x18-inch baking pan. Bake for 20 to 25 minutes or until golden brown. Cool. Beat margarine, cream cheese and confectioners' sugar in bowl until creamy. Spread on cooled baked layer. Cut into bars. Yield: 4 to 5 dozen.

Cindy Bingheim, Rho Rho
Spring Valley, Illinois

BLONDE BROWNIES

2 cups all-purpose flour
1 teaspoon baking powder
¼ teaspoon soda
1 teaspoon salt
2 cups packed light
   brown sugar

⅔ cup vegetable oil
2 eggs, slightly beaten
2 teaspoons vanilla extract
1 cup chocolate chips
½ cup chopped pecans

Mix dry ingredients; set aside. Blend brown sugar and oil in bowl. Stir in eggs and vanilla. Add flour mixture gradually, mixing well after each addition. Spread in greased

9x13-inch glass baking pan. Sprinkle chocolate chips and pecans over top. Bake for 25 minutes; do not overbake. Cool in pan. Cut into squares. Yield: 2 dozen.

Peggy Spieckermann, Xi Eta Mu
Moberly, Missouri

BROWNIES

1 cup sugar
½ cup butter, softened
4 eggs
1 16-ounce can chocolate
   syrup
1 cup all-purpose flour

1½ cups sugar
6 tablespoons half and
   half
6 tablespoons butter
½ cup chocolate chips
1 teaspoon vanilla extract

Preheat oven to 350 degrees. Cream 1 cup sugar and butter in bowl. Add eggs 1 at a time, beating well after each addition. Add chocolate syrup alternately with flour, mixing well after each addition. Pour into greased 11x15-inch baking pan. Bake for 25 to 30 minutes. Bring 1½ cups sugar, half and half and butter to a boil in saucepan. Boil for 30 seconds; remove from heat. Add chocolate chips and vanilla; beat until of spreading consistency. Frost brownies. Yield: 2 to 3 dozen.

Irene N. Schwenker, Laureate Iota
Madison, Wisconsin

BUSY DAY BROWNIES

2 cups sugar
10 tablespoons
   unsweetened baking
   cocoa
1 teaspoon salt

1 cup shortening
4 eggs
2 teaspoons vanilla extract
1½ cups all-purpose flour

Preheat oven to 350 degrees. Combine all ingredients in bowl; mix well. Pour into greased 9x12-inch baking pan. Bake for 25 to 30 minutes or until brownies test done. Frost if desired. Cut into squares. Yield: 2 dozen.

Karen Davis, Xi Iota
Lewiston, Idaho

CARAMEL BROWNIES

50 caramels
⅓ cup evaporated milk
¾ cup margarine
⅓ cup evaporated milk
1 2-layer package
   chocolate cake mix

1 cup coarsely chopped
   pecans
1 cup chocolate chips

Preheat oven to 350 degrees. Melt caramels with ⅓ cup evaporated milk in saucepan; set aside. Melt margarine with ⅓ cup evaporated milk. Add to mixture of cake mix and pecans in bowl. Pat half the mixture into greased 9x13-inch baking pan. Bake for 6 minutes. Sprinkle with chocolate chips; spread melted caramel mixture over chips. Pat remaining cake mix over top. Bake for 15 to 18 minutes. Cool. Cut into squares. Yield: 2½ dozen.

Becky Goodin, Zeta Nu
Princeton, Missouri

CHOCOLATE CHIP BROWNIES

1 20-ounce roll chocolate 1 cup sugar
   chip refrigerator   24 ounces cream cheese,
   cookie dough   softened
3 eggs

Preheat oven to 375 degrees. Cut cookie dough roll into halves lengthwise. Slice each half. Place half the slices in bottom of greased and floured 9x13-inch baking pan. Beat eggs, sugar and cream cheese in bowl until smooth. Pour cream cheese mixture over sliced cookie dough. Top with remaining cookie dough. Slices will not overlap. Bake for 40 to 45 minutes or until golden brown. Cut into squares. Serve warm with vanilla ice cream. Yield: 16 servings.

Lou Ann Allison, Delta Gamma
Greensboro, North Carolina

COCOA BROWNIES

1 cup melted butter   1½ cups all-purpose flour
¼ cup unsweetened   1 cup nuts
   baking cocoa   ½ cup butter
4 eggs   1½ cups sugar
2 cups sugar   ⅓ cup milk
½ teaspoon salt   ½ cup chocolate or
2 teaspoons vanilla extract   peanut butter chips

Preheat oven to 350 degrees. Blend melted butter and cocoa in bowl. Add eggs, 2 cups sugar, salt and vanilla; mix well. Stir in flour and nuts; mix well. Pour into greased 9x13-inch baking pan. Bake for 30 minutes. Cool. Bring ½ cup butter, 1½ cups sugar and milk to a boil in saucepan. Boil for 1 minute. Add chips; beat until of spreading consistency. Spread on brownies. Cut into squares. Yield: 2 dozen.

Jennifer Uher, Omega
Cedar Falls, Iowa

DEATH BY CHOCOLATE

1 cup butter, softened   1 teaspoon soda
2 cups packed dark   ¾ teaspoon salt
   brown sugar   2 cups coarsely crushed
2 eggs   cornflakes
1 teaspoon vanilla extract 2 cups oats
1½ cups all-purpose flour 1 cup chopped pecans

Preheat oven to 350 degrees. Cream butter and brown sugar in large mixer bowl. Add eggs 1 at a time, beating well after each addition. Beat in vanilla. Add sifted flour, soda and salt; mix well. Stir in cornflakes, oats and pecans. Press half the mixture into greased 10x15-inch baking pan with floured fingers. Spread Filling evenly over top, dipping spatula in hot water as necessary. Top with remaining crumb mixture. Bake for 30 to 35 minutes or until layers pull slightly from side or pan. Let stand for

5 minutes. Cut into 1½-inch squares. Cool completely before removing from pan. Yield: 4½ dozen.

FILLING

2 cups semisweet   2 teaspoons vanilla extract
   chocolate chips   ½ teaspoon salt
2 tablespoons butter   1 cup finely chopped
¾ cup sweetened   pecans
   condensed milk

Melt chocolate chips and butter in double boiler over hot water; remove from heat. Stir in condensed milk, vanilla and salt; mix well. Stir in pecans.

Sarah Preston, Xi Beta Alpha
Bowling Green, Kentucky

MINT BROWNIE PETIT FOURS

1 cup sugar   2½ cups confectioners'
½ cup butter, softened   sugar
4 eggs   ½ cup butter, softened
1 teaspoon vanilla extract 1 teaspoon peppermint
1 cup all-purpose flour   extract
½ teaspoon salt   Green food coloring
1 16-ounce can   1½ cups chocolate chips
   chocolate syrup   6 tablespoons butter

Preheat oven to 350 degrees. Combine first 7 ingredients in bowl; mix well with spoon. Pour into greased and lightly floured 9x13-inch baking pan. Bake for 30 minutes. Cool. Blend confectioners' sugar, ½ cup butter, flavoring and food coloring in bowl. Spread over cooled brownies. Melt chocolate chips with 6 tablespoons butter in saucepan over low heat. Pour over frosting; shake pan to distribute chocolate evenly to edges of pan. Refrigerate for several hours to overnight. Cut cooled brownies into small squares with sharp knife. Serve at room temperature. Yield: 3 dozen.

Helen Jenkins, Epsilon Xi
Manassas, Virginia

DOUBLE CHOCOLATE BROWNIES

1 cup margarine   1 teaspoon vanilla extract
4 squares unsweetened   1 cup all-purpose flour
   baking chocolate   1½ cups chopped walnuts
2 cups sugar   1 cup semisweet chocolate
3 eggs   chips

Preheat oven to 350 degrees. Melt margarine and chocolate in saucepan; remove from heat. Beat in sugar gradually with wooden spoon until well mixed. Add eggs 1 at a time, beating well after each addition. Stir in vanilla. Add flour; mix well. Stir in 1 cup walnuts. Spread in greased 9x13-inch baking pan. Sprinkle mixture of ½ cup walnuts and chocolate chips over top; press in lightly. Bake for 35 minutes. Cool. Cut into bars. Yield: 2 to 3 dozen.

Sandra Casdorph, Xi Alpha Omicron
Elkview, West Virginia

HEAVENLY HASH BROWNIES

4 eggs
2 cups sugar
1½ cups all-purpose
  flour
1 teaspoon vanilla extract
1 cup melted margarine

⅓ cup unsweetened
  baking cocoa
1½ cups chopped pecans
1 7-ounce jar
  marshmallow creme

Preheat oven to 350 degrees. Combine eggs, sugar, flour and vanilla in bowl; mix well. Add mixture of margarine and cocoa; beat well. Mix in pecans. Pour into greased 9x13-inch baking pan. Bake for 25 to 30 minutes or until brownies test done. Spread with marshmallow creme. Cool. Spread with Frosting. Cut into squares.
Yield: 2 dozen.

FROSTING

½ cup melted margarine
3 tablespoons
  unsweetened baking
  cocoa

⅓ cup milk
1 teaspoon vanilla extract
1 pound confectioners'
  sugar

Blend margarine, cocoa and milk in bowl. Add vanilla and confectioners' sugar; mix until creamy.

Kay Faraldo, Preceptor Beta Xi
Key West, Florida

MARBLED BROWNIES

1 cup butter
4 ounces unsweetened
  baking chocolate
2 cups sugar
4 eggs
2 teaspoons vanilla extract
1½ cups all-purpose flour
½ teaspoon salt

1 cup chopped nuts
8 ounces cream cheese,
  softened
¼ cup sugar
1 teaspoon cinnamon
1 egg
1½ teaspoons vanilla
  extract

Preheat oven to 350 degrees. Heat butter and chocolate in saucepan over low heat until melted; cool. Combine chocolate mixture, sugar, eggs and 2 teaspoons vanilla in large mixer bowl. Beat a medium speed for 1 minute. Add flour and salt. Beat at medium speed for 1 minute. Stir in nuts. Spread half the batter in greased 9x9-inch baking pan. Combine remaining ingredients in mixer bowl. Beat until light and fluffy. Spread over batter. Spread remaining batter over cream cheese layer. Swirl through batter with spoon for marbled effect. Bake for 55 to 65 minutes or until brownies test done. Cool. Cut into bars. Yield: 3 dozen.

Libby Benson, Iota Epsilon
Fayetteville, Georgia

BUTTER NUT CHEWIES

½ cup butter-flavored
  shortening
2 eggs, beaten
2 cups packed light
  brown sugar
1 teaspoon vanilla extract

1½ cups all-purpose flour
2 teaspoons baking
  powder
½ teaspoon salt
1 cup chopped nuts

Preheat oven to 350 degrees. Combine all ingredients in bowl; mix well. Pour into greased 9x13-inch baking pan. Bake for 25 to 30 minutes. Cool. Cut into squares.
Yield: 2 dozen.

Jowahna Hill, Upsilon
Claremore, Oklahoma

CARAMEL BARS

1 14-ounce package
  caramels
¾ cup whipping cream
2 cups all-purpose flour
½ cup packed light
  brown sugar

1 teaspoon soda
2 cups oats
1 cup margarine
¼ cup whipping cream
½ cup chopped nuts

Preheat oven to 350 degrees. Melt caramels with ¾ cup whipping cream in double boiler. Mix flour, brown sugar, soda and oats in bowl. Cut in margarine until crumbly. Add ¼ cup whipping cream; mix well. Reserve 1 cup mixture; pat remaining mixture into greased 9x13-inch baking pan. Bake for 10 minutes. Pour caramel mixture over baked layer. Top with reserved mixture and nuts. Bake for 15 minutes. Cool. Cut into bars. Yield: 2 dozen.

Virginia Mae Ideker, Laureate Beta
Lakewood, Colorado

CARMELITAS

2 cups all-purpose flour
2 cups quick-cooking oats
1½ cups packed light
  brown sugar
1 teaspoon soda
1½ cups melted
  margarine

½ teaspoon salt
2 cups chocolate chips
1 cup chopped pecans
1½ cups caramel ice
  cream topping
5 tablespoons all-purpose
  flour

Preheat oven to 350 degrees. Mix first 6 ingredients in bowl until crumbly. Press half the mixture into 9x13-inch baking pan. Bake for 10 minutes. Layer with chocolate chips, pecans and mixture of caramel topping and 5 tablespoons flour. Top with remaining crumbs. Bake for 20 minutes. Chill before cutting. Yield: 2 to 4 dozen.

Sue Goodwin, Xi Alpha Sigma
Vienna, West Virginia

DELICIOUS CARAMEL CHOCOLATE BARS

⅓ cup evaporated milk
1 2-layer package
  German chocolate
  cake mix
¾ cup melted margarine

1 cup chocolate chips
1 14-ounce package
  caramels
⅓ cup evaporated milk

Preheat oven to 350 degrees. Mix first 3 ingredients in bowl. Press half the mixture into greased and floured 9x13-inch baking pan. Bake for 6 minutes. Sprinkle with chocolate chips. Melt caramels in ⅓ cup evaporated milk in saucepan. Pour over chips. Crumble remaining cake mixture on top. Bake for 15 to 18 minutes. Cool before cutting. Yield: 2 dozen.

Dorothy Garner, Omicron
Mobile, Alabama

CHOCOLATE MINT SQUARES

1 cup sugar
½ cup margarine, softened
4 eggs
1 teaspoon vanilla extract
1 cup all-purpose flour
½ teaspoon salt
1 16-ounce can chocolate syrup

1 cup chocolate chips
6 tablespoons margarine
2 cups confectioners' sugar
½ cup margarine, softened
2 tablespoons Crème de Menthe

Preheat oven to 350 degrees. Cream sugar and ½ cup margarine in bowl. Beat in eggs and vanilla. Add mixture of flour and salt; mix well. Add chocolate syrup; mix well. Pour into greased 9x13-inch baking pan. Bake for 30 minutes. Cool. Melt chocolate chips and 6 tablespoons margarine in saucepan over low heat, stirring constantly. Blend confectioners' sugar, ½ cup margarine and Crème de Menthe in bowl. Stir in chocolate mixture. Pour over warm baked layer. Chill for 20 minutes. Cut into squares. Store, covered, in refrigerator. Yield: 25 squares.

Kathleen L. Adams, Xi Theta
Dover, Delaware

CRÈME DE MENTHE SQUARES

½ cup butter
½ cup unsweetened baking cocoa
½ cup sifted confectioners' sugar
1 egg, beaten
1 teaspoon vanilla extract
2 cups graham cracker crumbs

½ cup melted butter
⅓ cup green Crème de Menthe
3 cups sifted confectioners' sugar
¼ cup butter
1½ cups semisweet chocolate chips

Combine ½ cup butter and cocoa in saucepan. Heat until well blended, stirring constantly; remove from heat. Add ½ cup confectioners' sugar, egg and vanilla. Stir in graham cracker crumbs. Press into bottom of 9x12-inch dish. Combine ½ cup melted butter and Crème de Menthe in mixer bowl. Add remaining 3 cups confectioners' sugar, beating at low speed until smooth. Spread over chocolate layer. Chill for 1 hour. Melt ¼ cup butter and chocolate chips in saucepan over low heat; blend well. Spread over mint layer. Chill for 2 hours. Cut into small squares. Store in refrigerator. Yield: 8 dozen.

Cynthia Potthoff, Xi Kappa Beta
Effingham, Illinois

PEANUT CREAM CHOCOLATE BARS

1 2-layer package devil's food cake mix
⅓ cup corn oil
1 egg
½ cup sugar

¾ cup peanut butter
8 ounces cream cheese, softened
1 egg
1 teaspoon vanilla extract

Preheat oven to 350 degrees. Combine cake mix, oil and egg in bowl; mix well. Reserve 1 cup for topping. Press remainder into 9x13-inch baking pan. Bake for 10 minutes. Cool. Mix sugar, peanut butter, cream cheese, egg and vanilla in bowl. Spread over baked layer. Sprinkle reserved cake mixture on top. Bake for 20 minutes. Chill for 1 hour. Cut into squares. Yield: 2 dozen.

Sharon G. Crouse, Gamma Nu
Lexington, North Carolina

SWISS CHOCOLATE SQUARES

1 cup water
½ cup margarine
1½ squares unsweetened baking chocolate
2 cups all-purpose flour
2 cups sugar
2 eggs
½ cup sour cream
1 teaspoon soda

½ teaspoon salt
½ cup margarine
6 tablespoons milk
1½ squares unsweetened baking chocolate
4½ cups confectioners' sugar
1 teaspoon vanilla extract
½ cup chopped nuts

Preheat oven to 375 degrees. Combine first 3 ingredients in saucepan. Bring to a boil; remove from heat. Stir in mixture of flour and sugar. Add eggs, sour cream, soda and salt; mix well. Pour into greased 10x15-inch baking pan. Bake for 20 to 25 minutes. Combine next 3 ingredients in saucepan. Bring to a boil. Cook for 1 minute. Stir in confectioners' sugar and vanilla. Spread on baked layer. Sprinkle with nuts. Cut into squares. Yield: 2 dozen.

Deb Espey, Xi Zeta
Maryville, Missouri

FUDGE NUT BARS

1 cup margarine
2 cups packed light brown sugar
2 eggs
2 teaspoons vanilla extract
2½ cups all-purpose flour
1 teaspoon soda
3 cups quick-cooking oats
2 tablespoons margarine

2 cups semisweet chocolate chips
1 cup sweetened condensed milk
½ teaspoon salt
1 cup chopped walnuts
2 tablespoons vanilla extract

Preheat oven to 350 degrees. Cream margarine and brown sugar in bowl. Add eggs and 2 teaspoons vanilla; beat until creamy. Sift flour and soda together; stir in oats. Mix dry ingredients into creamed mixture; set aside. Melt 2 tablespoons margarine and chocolate chips with condensed milk and salt in saucepan. Stir in walnuts and vanilla. Pat ⅔ of the oats mixture into greased 10x15-inch baking pan. Cover with melted chocolate mixture; top with remaining oats mixture. Bake for 25 to 30 minutes. Cool. Cut into bars. Yield: 15 to 20 bars.

Virginia Millholland, Xi Omicron
Cumberland, Maryland

CITY CLERK BARS

1 2-layer package
   yellow cake mix
½ cup margarine
4 eggs

1 16-ounce package
   confectioners' sugar
8 ounces cream cheese,
   softened

Preheat oven to 350 degrees. Cut margarine into cake mix in bowl until crumbly. Stir in 1 egg. Spread in sheet cake pan. Cream 3 eggs, confectioners' sugar and cream cheese in bowl until fluffy. Spread over cake layer. Bake for 30 minutes or until set. Cut into bars. Yield: 5 dozen.

June Blevins, Laureate Gamma
Williamson, West Virginia

COCONUT CHEESE BARS

1 2-layer package
   yellow cake mix
½ cup butter
1 egg
1 cup nuts
1 cup coconut

2 eggs
8 ounces cream cheese,
   softened
1 16-ounce package
   confectioners' sugar

Preheat oven to 350 degrees. Combine cake mix, butter and egg in bowl; mix well. Pat into 10x15-inch baking pan. Sprinkle nuts and coconut over dough. Cream eggs, cream cheese and confectioners' sugar in bowl until light and fluffy. Pour evenly over nuts and coconut. Bake for 40 minutes. Cool in pan. Cut into small bars. Sprinkle with additional confectioners' sugar. Yield: 3 dozen.

Sharon Wilson, Preceptor Omicron
Marion, Illinois

CRANBERRY DATE BARS

1 12-ounce package
   cranberries
1 8-ounce package
   dates, chopped
1 teaspoon vanilla extract
2 cups all-purpose flour
1½ cups packed light
   brown sugar

2 cups oats
½ teaspoon soda
¼ teaspoon salt
1 cup melted butter
2 cups sifted
   confectioners' sugar
½ teaspoon vanilla extract
Orange juice

Preheat oven to 350 degrees. Combine cranberries and dates in saucepan. Cook, covered, over low heat for 10 to 15 minutes or until cranberries pop, stirring frequently. Stir in 1 teaspoon vanilla. Set aside. Mix flour, brown sugar, oats, soda and salt in large bowl. Stir in butter. Pat half the mixture over bottom of 9x13-inch baking pan. Bake for 8 minutes. Spread cranberry mixture over baked layer. Top with remaining oats mixture; pat gently. Bake for 20 minutes. Cool on wire rack. Blend confectioners' sugar, ½ teaspoon vanilla and enough orange juice to make of drizzling consistency in bowl. Drizzle over cooled cookies. Cut into bars. Yield: 32 bars.

Edith A. Shirer, Preceptor Omega
Belmond, Iowa

CRANBERRY AND PEANUT BUTTER BARS

1 cup butter, softened
1¼ cups packed
   light brown sugar
2 cups all-purpose flour
2 cups oats
1 teaspoon soda
½ teaspoon salt

3 tablespoons water
⅓ cup chunky peanut
   butter
1 16-ounce can
   cranberry-raspberry
   sauce

Preheat oven to 375 degrees. Cream butter and brown sugar in mixer bowl. Add flour, oats, soda, salt and water. Mix at low speed until crumbly. Mix in peanut butter. Press half the mixture into greased 11x16-inch baking pan. Bake for 10 minutes. Mash cranberry sauce with fork. Spread evenly over warm crust. Sprinkle reserved crumb mixture over sauce. Bake for 30 minutes. Cool. Cut into bars. Yield: 2 to 3 dozen.

Maxine Wachenheim, Laureate Delta
Quincy, Illinois

HONEY BARS

¾ cup sugar
¼ cup honey
¾ cup oil
2 cups all-purpose flour
Dash of salt
1 teaspoon soda
1 teaspoon cinnamon

1 egg, beaten
1 cup pecans
½ cup confectioners'
   sugar
¼ teaspoon vanilla extract
1 tablespoon mayonnaise
½ tablespoon water

Preheat oven to 325 degrees. Combine first 9 ingredients in bowl in order listed, mixing well after each addition. Spread in ungreased 9x9-inch baking pan. Bake for 25 to 30 minutes or until golden brown. Combine confectioners' sugar, vanilla, mayonnaise and water in bowl; blend well. Spread glaze over warm layer. Cool. Cut into bars. Yield: 20 bars.

Celeste P. Litton, Alpha Theta Zeta
Houston, Texas

EASY CHEESY LEMON BARS

1 2-layer package
   lemon cake mix
½ cup margarine,
   softened
1 egg

8 ounces cream cheese,
   softened
1 16-ounce can lemon
   frosting
2 eggs

Preheat oven to 350 degrees. Combine cake mix, margarine and 1 egg in bowl; mix well. Press into bottom of greased 9x13-inch baking pan. Blend softened cream cheese and frosting in bowl. Reserve ½ cup for frosting. Add 2 eggs to remaining mixture. Beat for 3 to 5 minutes. Spread over mixture in pan. Bake for 30 to 40 minutes or until light golden brown. Cool. Frost with reserved cream cheese mixture. Cut into bars. Yield: 3 dozen.

Cathie Geier, Xi Eta
Salem, Illinois

SCRUMPTIOUS LEMON BARS

1 cup butter, softened
2 cups all-purpose flour
½ cup confectioners'
  sugar
2 cups sugar

¼ cup all-purpose flour
1 teaspoon baking powder
4 eggs, beaten
6 tablespoons lemon juice

Preheat oven to 350 degrees. Combine butter, 2 cups flour and confectioners' sugar in bowl; mix until crumbly. Pat into 9x13-inch baking pan. Bake for 15 minutes or until light golden brown. Mix sugar, ¼ cup flour and baking powder in bowl. Add eggs and lemon juice. Spread over baked layer. Bake for 25 to 30 minutes or until light golden brown. Cool. Sprinkle with additional confectioners' sugar. Cut into squares. Yield: 2 dozen.

Beverly Klein, Delta Alpha Beta
San Jose, California

LEMON SQUARES

1 cup melted butter
2 cups sifted all-purpose
  flour
½ cup confectioners'
  sugar
2 cups sugar

¼ cup all-purpose flour
1 teaspoon baking powder
4 eggs
6 tablespoons lemon juice
Pinch of salt
Confectioners' sugar

Preheat oven to 350. Combine butter, 2 cups flour and ½ cup confectioners' sugar in bowl; mix well. Pat into 9x13-inch baking pan. Bake for 15 minutes. Mix sugar, ¼ cup flour and baking powder in bowl. Add eggs 1 at a time, beating well after each addition. Add lemon juice and salt. Pour over baked layer. Bake for 25 to 30 minutes or until set. Cool. Cut into small squares. Sprinkle with additional confectioners' sugar. Yield: 4 dozen.

Doris Ramirez, Xi Alpha Rho
Sumter, South Carolina

MACADAMIA BAR COOKIES

½ cup butter, softened
¼ cup confectioners'
  sugar
1 cup plus 2 tablespoons
  all-purpose flour
2 eggs, slightly beaten
1 teaspoon vanilla extract
1 cup packed light
  brown sugar

2 tablespoons all-purpose
  flour
½ teaspoon salt
1 cup flaked coconut
¾ cup broken
  macadamia nuts

Preheat oven to 325 degrees. Cream butter and confectioners' sugar in bowl until light and fluffy. Stir in flour. Pat into 9x9-inch baking pan. Bake for 15 minutes or until lightly browned. Combine eggs and vanilla in bowl. Add brown sugar gradually. Add 2 tablespoons flour, salt, coconut and nuts; mix well. Pour over baked layer. Bake for 20 minutes or until toothpick inserted in center comes out clean. Cool. Cut into squares. Yield: 9 servings.

Grace Semple, Tau
Newark, Delaware

MAGIC COOKIE BARS

½ cup melted margarine
1½ cups graham cracker
  crumbs
1 14-ounce can
  sweetened condensed
  milk

1 cup semisweet
  chocolate chips
1 3½-ounce can
  flaked coconut
1 cup chopped nuts

Preheat oven to 350 degrees. Layer all ingredients in order listed in 9x13-inch baking pan; press gently. Bake for 25 minutes or until lightly browned. Cool. Chill if desired. Cut into bars. Store, loosely covered, at room temperature. Yield: 2 to 3 dozen.

Tracy Lynn Hillman, Beta Phi
Perryton, Texas

MINT BARS

1 cup margarine
1 cup water
¼ cup unsweetened
  baking cocoa
2 cups sugar
2 cups all-purpose flour
1 teaspoon soda

½ teaspoon salt
2 eggs, beaten
½ cup sour cream
1 teaspoon vanilla extract
½ cup margarine
1¼ cups chocolate chips

Preheat oven to 350 degrees. Combine margarine, water and cocoa in large saucepan. Bring to a boil; remove from heat. Add sugar, flour, soda, salt, eggs, sour cream and vanilla; mix well. Pour into 10x15-inch baking pan. Bake for 20 minutes. Cool completely. Spread with Mint Frosting. Chill until firm. Melt ½ cup margarine and chocolate chips in saucepan over low heat. Spread over Frosting. Chill. Store in refrigerator. Yield: 4 to 5 dozen.

MINT FROSTING

2 cups confectioners'
  sugar
¼ cup margarine,
  softened
2 tablespoons milk

1 teaspoon peppermint
  extract
4 to 6 drops green
  food coloring

Combine all ingredients in bowl; blend well.

Margaret Walker, Delta Beta
Apple Valley, Minnesota

NO-BAKE SCOTCHEROOS

1 cup light corn syrup
1 cup sugar
6 cups crisp rice cereal

1 cup peanut butter
1 cup chocolate chips
1 cup butterscotch chips

Combine corn syrup and sugar in saucepan. Bring to a boil . Add cereal and peanut butter. Press into 9x13-inch dish. Melt chocolate chips and butterscotch chips in saucepan. Spread on cookies. Refrigerate until firm. Cut into bars. Yield: 2 dozen.

Shari Burkett, Tau Theta
Flora, Illinois

OATMEAL COOKIE BARS

1 2½-cup package
  oatmeal cookie mix
2 eggs
½ cup vegetable oil
⅓ cup chopped nuts
  (optional)
⅓ cup raisins (optional)

⅓ cup sunflower seed
  (optional)
⅓ cup shredded coconut
  (optional)
⅓ cup chocolate chips
  (optional)

Preheat oven to 350 degrees. Combine first 3 ingredients in bowl; mix well. Stir in 1 or 2 of the optional ingredients. Spread in greased 7x11-inch baking pan. Bake for 20 to 25 minutes or until brown. Cool. Cut into bars. Yield: 2 dozen.

Mary McFie, Xi Beta Omicron
Anaheim, California

PEANUT BUTTER CUP BARS

1 cup margarine
2½ cups graham cracker
  crumbs
2½ cups confectioners'
  sugar

1 cup peanut butter
2 cups chocolate
  chips, melted

Melt margarine in saucepan. Add crumbs, confectioners' sugar and peanut butter; mix well. Spread evenly in buttered 9x13-inch pan. Spread melted chocolate over top. Chill until firm. Cut into bars. Yield: 2 dozen.

Marilyn Gross, Preceptor Delta Omicron
Moline, Illinois

PEANUT BUTTER FINGERS

½ cup margarine,
  softened
½ cup sugar
½ cup packed light
  brown sugar
⅓ cup peanut butter
1 cup oats
1 cup all-purpose flour
½ teaspoon soda

½ teaspoon vanilla extract
¼ teaspoon salt
1 cup chocolate chips
½ cup confectioners'
  sugar
¼ cup peanut butter
2 tablespoons margarine,
  softened

Preheat oven to 325 degrees. Cream ½ cup margarine and sugars in bowl. Add ⅓ cup peanut butter, oats, flour, soda, vanilla and salt; mix well. Spread in greased 9x13-inch baking pan. Bake for 20 minutes. Sprinkle with chocolate chips. Let stand until melted. Spread over top. Blend confectioners' sugar, ¼ cup peanut butter and 2 tablespoons margarine in small bowl. Swirl into warm chocolate. Cool. Cut into bars. Yield: 2 dozen.

Susan Rieder, Xi Beta Xi
Jefferson, Iowa

For an easy no-bake cookie, **Betty Jane Harrington, Preceptor Laureate, Carthage, Missouri,** combines ½ cup softened margarine, 4 cups confectioners' sugar, ½ cup chopped pecans, 6 ounces orange juice concentrate and 4 cups vanilla wafer crumbs. Shape into balls, and coat with additional crumbs.

RAISIN MUMBLES

2½ cups raisins
½ cup sugar
2 tablespoons cornstarch
¾ cup water
3 tablespoons lemon
  juice
¾ cup butter

1 cup packed light
  brown sugar
1¾ cups all-purpose flour
½ teaspoon salt
½ teaspoon soda
1½ cups oats

Preheat oven to 425 degrees. Combine first 5 ingredients in saucepan. Bring to a boil; set aside. Combine butter and dry ingredients in bowl until crumbly. Pat half the crumb mixture into 8x13-inch baking pan. Pour raisin mixture over crumbs; spreading evenly to edges. Pat remaining crumb mixture over top. Bake for 15 to 20 minutes. Cool. Cut into bars. Yield: 16 to 20 bars.

Elaine Trimmell, Xi Nu
Springfield, Missouri

SOUR CREAM RAISIN BARS

¾ cup oats
¾ cup all-purpose flour
½ teaspoon soda
½ cup packed light
  brown sugar
½ cup margarine,
  softened
4 egg yolks
1½ cups sugar

3 tablespoons
  cornstarch
2 cups raisins
2 cups sour cream
4 egg whites
½ teaspoon vanilla extract
¾ teaspoon cream of tartar
6 tablespoons sugar

Preheat oven to 350 degrees. Combine first 4 ingredients in bowl. Cut in margarine until crumbly. Pat into bottom of 9x13-inch baking pan. Bake for 15 minutes. Mix egg yolks, 1½ cups sugar and cornstarch in double boiler. Add raisins and sour cream. Cook over low heat until thick, stirring constantly. Pour over baked layer. Beat egg whites with vanilla and cream of tartar in bowl until soft peaks form. Add 6 tablespoons sugar gradually, beating until stiff peaks form. Spread over hot filling. Bake for 15 to 20 minutes. Yield: 15 servings.

Nancy Ann Stammer, Lambda Eta
Manning, Iowa

GLORIFIED SHORTBREAD

1 cup butter
2 cups all-purpose flour
½ cup confectioners'
  sugar
1½ teaspoons cornstarch
Pinch of salt
2 eggs, beaten

1 cup sugar
1 cup walnuts
1 cup coconut
1 tablespoon all-purpose
  flour
⅛ teaspoon baking
  powder

Preheat oven to 350 degrees. Cut butter into mixture of next 4 ingredients until crumbly. Press into 9x13-inch baking pan. Bake for 15 minutes. Spoon mixture of eggs and remaining ingredients on top of partially cooked shortbread. Bake for 15 minutes longer. Cool completely. Cut into bars. Yield: 2 dozen.

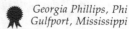

Georgia Phillips, Phi
Gulfport, Mississippi

BISCOCHITOS

1 cup sugar	1 tablespoon baking
1 pound lard	powder
2 eggs	1 tablespoon aniseed
1 teaspoon vinegar	½ cup orange juice
7 cups all-purpose flour	⅔ cup sugar
1 teaspoon salt	1 teaspoon cinnamon

Preheat oven to 350 degrees. Cream 1 cup sugar and lard in large bowl until fluffy. Add eggs and vinegar; beat well. Add mixture of flour, salt, baking powder and aniseed alternately with orange juice, mixing well after each addition. Divide into 4 portions. Chill for 30 minutes or longer. Roll and cut 1 portion at a time. Dip cookies into mixture of ⅔ cup sugar and cinnamon. Place on ungreased cookie sheet. Bake for 10 to 12 minutes or until golden brown. Yield: 12 dozen.

Patricia A. Castillo, Xi Mu
Santa Fe, New Mexico

BLOND BOMBERS

½ cup margarine,	1 teaspoon soda
softened	½ teaspoon salt
½ cup sugar	1 teaspoon vanilla extract
1 cup packed light	½ 10-ounce package
brown sugar	giant white chocolate
2 eggs	chips
2 cups all-purpose flour	

Preheat oven to 350 degrees. Cream margarine, sugars and eggs in bowl until light and fluffy. Sift in flour, soda and salt; mix well. Stir in vanilla and white chocolate chips. Drop by teaspoonfuls 2 inches apart onto cookie sheet. Bake for 10 minutes. Remove to wire rack to cool. Yield: 5 dozen.

Elle Plahn, Preceptor Beta Beta
Columbus, Indiana

COOKIES WHILE YOU SLEEP

2 egg whites, at room	1 teaspoon vanilla extract
temperature	1 cup chocolate chips
⅔ cup sugar	1 cup pecans
½ teaspoon almond	
extract	

Preheat oven to 350 degrees. Beat egg whites in mixer bowl until stiff peaks form. Add sugar gradually, beating until very stiff. Add flavorings. Mix in chocolate chips and pecans. Drop by teaspoonfuls onto foil-covered cookie sheet. Place in preheated oven; turn off oven. Let stand in closed oven overnight. Yield: 2 to 3 dozen.

Debra Hodges, Lambda
Eagle, Idaho

---

*Add a surprise to your chocolate chip cookies as **Pat Gillett, Kappa Omega, Freiedonia, Kansas,** does by stirring in 6 ounces brickle chips with the chocolate chips.*

CHERRY AND COCONUT TEA COOKIES

½ cup butter, softened	¼ teaspoon salt
½ cup sugar	¾ teaspoon cream of
¼ cup packed light	tartar
brown sugar	½ teaspoon soda
1 egg	12 maraschino cherries,
2 teaspoons milk	chopped
1½ cups sifted	½ cup chopped nuts
all-purpose flour	½ cup flaked coconut

Cream butter and sugars in bowl. Add egg and milk; mix well. Add sifted dry ingredients; mix well. Stir in cherries, nuts and coconut. Chill until easy to handle. Shape into log. Refrigerate overnight. Preheat oven to 325 degrees. Cut log into thin slices. Place on greased cookie sheet. Bake for 10 to 12 minutes or until golden brown. Yield: 3½ dozen.

Betty Spurgeon, Preceptor Beta Beta
Columbus, Indiana

PERFECT CHOCOLATE CHIP COOKIES

4½ cups all-purpose flour	2 teaspoons orange juice
2 teaspoons soda	4 eggs
1 teaspoon salt	Grated rind of 1 orange
1½ cups sugar	2 cups milk chocolate
1½ cups packed light	chips
brown sugar	2 cups chopped pecans
2 cups shortening	

Combine flour, soda and salt in bowl; set aside. Cream sugars, shortening and juice in bowl until light and fluffy. Add eggs 1 at a time, beating well after each addition. Add orange rind, chocolate chips and pecans. Stir in the flour, soda and salt mixture ½ cup at a time, mixing well after each addition. Chill for 2 hours to overnight. Preheat oven to 325 degrees. Drop dough by teaspoonfuls onto cookie sheet. Bake for 10 to 12 minutes or until light brown. Yield: 8 dozen.

Sylvia White, Nu Delta
Burlington, Kansas

CHOCOLATE CHIP COOKIES

2 cups butter, softened	2 teaspoons baking
2 cups sugar	powder
2 cups packed light	2 teaspoons soda
brown sugar	2 cups oats
4 eggs	4 cups semisweet
2 teaspoons vanilla extract	chocolate chips
4 cups all-purpose flour	1 cup milk chocolate
1 teaspoon salt	chips

Preheat oven to 350 degrees. Cream butter and sugars in bowl. Add eggs and vanilla; beat well. Add mixture of flour, salt, baking powder and soda gradually. Stir in oats and chocolate chips. Drop by teaspoonfuls onto lightly greased cookie sheet. Bake for 10 to 15 minutes or until light brown. Cool. Yield: 17 dozen.

Sherrie Bostick, Xi Alpha Gamma
Hobbs, New Mexico

HEAVENLY CHOCOLATE CHIP COOKIES

½ cup margarine, softened	1 teaspoon salt
⅔ cup shortening	3 cups sifted all-purpose flour
1 cup sugar	12 ounces white chocolate discs, quartered
1 cup packed light brown sugar	
2 eggs	½ cup oats
2 teaspoons vanilla extract	1 cup pecans
1 teaspoon soda	

Preheat oven to 375 degrees. Cream margarine and shortening in mixer bowl until smooth. Add sugars, eggs and vanilla; beat until well blended. Add mixture of soda, salt and flour gradually, mixing well after each addition. Add chocolate, oats and pecans; mix well. Drop by rounded teaspoonfuls onto ungreased cookie sheet. Bake for 8 to 10 minutes or until golden brown. Yield: 6 dozen.

Sherry Schroder, Xi Gamma Xi
Logansport, Indiana

GERMAN CHOCOLATE COOKIES

1 2-layer package German chocolate cake mix with pudding	1 egg
	½ cup chopped nuts
½ cup instant mashed potato flakes	¼ to ½ cup sugar
	1 cup confectioners' sugar
1 teaspoon cream of tartar	2 teaspoons unsweetened baking cocoa
1 teaspoon cinnamon	1 tablespoon margarine
¾ cup melted margarine	2 tablespoons milk
3 tablespoons milk	

Preheat oven to 350 degrees. Combine first 7 ingredients in bowl; mix well. Stir in nuts. Let stand for 5 minutes. Drop by teaspoonfuls into sugar. Gently toss until coated. Place 2 inches apart on cookie sheet. Bake for 8 to 10 minutes. Cool for 5 minutes; remove from pans. Combine confectioners' sugar, cocoa, 1 tablespoon margarine and 2 tablespoons milk in bowl. Blend until smooth. Spread on cooled cookies. Yield: 3 dozen.

Wanda Combs, Beta Rho
Independence, Missouri

CHOCOLATE-COVERED RAISIN COOKIES

1 cup butter, softened	2¼ cups all-purpose flour
¾ cup sugar	
¾ cup packed light brown sugar	1 teaspoon soda
	½ teaspoon salt
2 eggs	2 cups chocolate-covered raisins
1 teaspoon vanilla extract	

Preheat oven to 375 degrees. Cream butter, sugar and brown sugar in bowl until light and fluffy. Add eggs and vanilla; beat well. Add mixture of flour, soda and salt gradually, mixing well after each addition. Stir in raisins. Drop by rounded teaspoonfuls onto cookie sheet. Bake for 8 to 10 minutes. Cool slightly on cookie sheet.
Yield: 4 to 4½ dozen.

Della Sorensen, Preceptor Delta
Salt Lake City, Utah

CREAM WAFER COOKIES

1 cup butter, softened	¾ cup confectioners' sugar
½ cup whipping cream	
2 cups all-purpose flour	1 egg yolk
Sugar	1 teaspoon vanilla extract
¼ cup butter, softened	Food coloring

Combine butter, cream and flour in bowl; mix well. Chill. Preheat oven to 375 degrees. Divide dough into 3 portions. Roll ⅛ inch thick on floured board. Cut with round cookie cutter. Place on waxed paper. Coat both sides with sugar. Place on cookie sheet. Prick 4 times with fork. Bake for 7 minutes or until light brown. Cool on wire rack. Spread mixture of remaining ingredients between wafers. Yield: 5 dozen.

Elizabeth Oligmueller, Alpha Psi Theta
Fort Worth, Texas

ICE CREAM KOLACKY

2 cups butter or margarine, softened	1 pint vanilla ice cream
	Confectioners' sugar
4 cups all-purpose flour	Fruit filling

Cut butter into flour in bowl until crumbly. Mix in ice cream. Chill overnight. Preheat oven to 350 degrees. Roll dough on surface sprinkled with ¼ inch confectioners' sugar; cut as desired. Make indentation in center; fill with fruit filling. Place on cookie sheet. Bake for 15 minutes or until edges start to brown. Cool on wire rack. Dust with confectioners' sugar. Yield: 6 dozen.

Judy Addleman, Theta
Burnsville, Minnesota

MAIDS OF HONOR

½ 11-ounce package pie crust mix	½ cup ground blanched almonds
1 egg white	¼ teaspoon almond extract
Dash of salt	
½ cup confectioners' sugar	½ cup raspberry jam
	Sliced blanched almonds

Prepare pastry using package directions. Press by teaspoonfuls into 2-inch tart molds. Chill in refrigerator. Preheat oven to 375 degrees. Beat egg white with salt in small mixer bowl until soft peaks form. Add confectioners' sugar 2 tablespoons at a time, beating until thick. Stir in ground almonds and flavoring. Spoon 1 teaspoon raspberry jam and 1 teaspoon almond topping into each pastry shell. Decorate with sliced almonds. Bake for 25 to 30 minutes or until topping is puffy and golden.
Yield: 26 tarts.

Zeilla Smith, Chi Xi
Whittier, California

Janet Weises, Xi Alpha Gamma, Mountain Home, Idaho,
varies the filling for Maids of Honor by creaming ½ cup
butter and ½ cup sugar in bowl, adding 1 egg, ½ teaspoon
vanilla and 1 cup self-rising flour and spooning over jam in
tart shells. She bakes them at 400 degrees for 15 minutes.

TEA TASSIES

1 cup all-purpose flour	Pinch of salt
3 ounces cream cheese, softened	1 egg
	1 tablespoon butter
7 tablespoons butter, softened	1 teaspoon vanilla extract
	2 tablespoons light
¾ cup sugar	corn syrup
¾ cup chopped nuts	

Preheat oven to 350 degrees. Mix flour, cream cheese and 7 tablespoons butter in bowl. Shape into 24 balls; press into miniature muffin cups. Mix sugar, nuts, salt, egg, 1 tablespoon butter, vanilla and corn syrup in bowl. Pour into prepared muffin cups. Bake for 15 to 20 minutes or until brown. Yield: 2 dozen.

Pat Savage, Delta Mu
Monticello, Arkansas

OATMEAL COOKIES

1 cup margarine, softened	½ teaspoon salt
	1 teaspoon cinnamon
1½ cups packed light brown sugar	1 teaspoon nutmeg
	½ cup milk
2 eggs	2 cups quick-cooking oats
2¼ cups all-purpose flour	1 cup raisins
2 teaspoons baking powder	1 cup chopped dates
	½ cup walnuts
¼ teaspoon soda	

Preheat oven to 375 degrees. Cream margarine and brown sugar in bowl. Beat in eggs. Sift dry ingredients together. Add sifted dry ingredients alternately with milk, beginning and ending with dry ingredients and mixing well after each addition. Stir in oats, raisins, dates and walnuts. Drop by spoonfuls onto cookie sheet. Bake for 12 to 15 minutes or until brown. Yield: 4 to 5 dozen.

Betty Wilde, Preceptor Laureate Delta
Phoenix, Arizona

ORANGE BLOSSOMS

3 eggs	1 teaspoon vanilla extract
½ cup water	1 16-ounce package
1½ cups all-purpose flour	confectioners' sugar
1⅓ cups sugar	Juice of 2 lemons
1½ teaspoons baking powder	Juice and grated rind of 2 oranges
½ teaspoon salt	Grated rind of 1 lemon

Preheat oven to 350 degrees. Combine first 7 ingredients in bowl; mix well. Fill greased small teacake molds ⅔ full. Bake for 12 minutes. Combine confectioners' sugar, juices and rinds in bowl; mix well. Spoon over hot teacakes. Yield: 2 dozen.

Judy Klein, Xi Tau Pi
Linden, California

PIÑON FINGERS

1 cup butter, softened	2 cups all-purpose flour
¼ cup confectioners' sugar	1 cup pine nuts
	2 cups confectioners'
2 teaspoons vanilla extract	sugar

Preheat oven to 275 degrees. Cream butter, ¼ cup confectioners' sugar and vanilla in bowl until light and fluffy. Stir in flour and pine nuts. Roll by 2 tablespoonfuls into ½-inch thick ropes on lightly floured surface. Cut ropes into 2-inch lengths. Place 1 inch apart on baking sheet. Bake for 25 to 30 minutes or until edges are light brown. Sift remaining 2 cups confectioners' sugar over warm cookies. Cool. Yield: 5 to 6 dozen.

 Lora Hill, Laureate Epsilon
Alamosa, Colorado

SACHERTORTE COOKIES

1 cup butter, softened	3 tablespoons sugar
1 3-ounce package chocolate instant pudding mix	½ cup preserves
	½ cup semisweet chocolate chips
1 egg	3 tablespoons butter
2 cups all-purpose flour	

Preheat oven to 325 degrees. Cream 1 cup butter and pudding mix in mixer bowl until light and fluffy. Add egg, flour and sugar gradually, mixing well after each addition. Shape into 1-inch balls; roll in additional sugar. Place on lightly greased cookie sheet. Make indentation with thumb in center of each. Bake for 12 to 15 minutes or until firm and light brown. Remove to wire rack to cool. Fill each indentation with preserves. Melt chocolate chips and 3 tablespoons butter in saucepan. Drizzle over cookies. Yield: 4 dozen.

Becky Clayton, Xi Theta
Durham, North Carolina

SUGAR COOKIES

3 cups all-purpose flour	½ teaspoon soda
1 cup butter, softened	2 eggs, well beaten
½ teaspoon baking powder	1 cup sugar
	1 teaspoon vanilla extract

Preheat oven to 375 degrees. Combine flour, butter, baking powder and soda in food processor. Process until well mixed. Beat eggs with sugar and vanilla. Add to flour mixture; mix well. Roll thin on floured surface. Cut with cookie cutters. Place on cookie sheet. Bake for 8 to 10 minutes or until golden brown. May decorate with colored sugar or frosting if desired. Yield: 5 to 6 dozen.

Claudia M. Epstein, Preceptor Beta Eta
Richardson, Texas

TORTILLA CRISPAS

12 10-inch flour tortillas	2 tablespoons cinnamon
	1 cup sugar
¾ cup corn oil	

Cut tortillas into quarters. Cook several at a time in hot oil in skillet until puffed and brown, turning once or twice. Drain on paper towels. Mix cinnamon and sugar in bag. Add tortilla puffs. Shake until coated. Serve warm or cool. Yield: 4 dozen.

Barbara A. Kuykendall, Mu Delta
Beaver, Oklahoma

Pies

APPLEBERRY PIE

1   15-ounce package
    2-crust refrigerator pie
    pastry
3 cups chopped peeled
    apples
½ cup sugar
¼ cup chopped pecans
¼ cup raisins

3 tablespoons all-purpose
    flour
½ teaspoon cinnamon
¼ teaspoon nutmeg
⅛ teaspoon cloves
2 tablespoons margarine
1   16-ounce can whole
    cranberry sauce

Preheat oven to 425 degrees. Line 9-inch pie plate with
pastry. Cut remaining pastry into 8 wedges; set aside.
Mix remaining ingredients in bowl. Spoon into pie shell.
Arrange pastry wedges over berry mixture with points
meeting in the center; do not overlap. Turn back center
points to form petals. Flute edges. Bake for 40 minutes or
until apples are tender. Yield: 8 servings.

Bonnie Gray, Laureate Lambda
Salmon, Idaho

STREUSEL-TOPPED APPLE CUSTARD PIE

3 cups sliced apples
1 unbaked 9-inch pie shell
2 eggs, beaten
1   14-ounce can
    sweetened condensed
    milk
¼ cup melted butter

½ teaspoon cinnamon
Dash of nutmeg
¼ cup cold butter
½ cup packed light brown
    sugar
½ cup all-purpose flour
½ cup chopped nuts

Preheat oven to 425 degrees. Arrange apples in pie shell.
Add mixture of next 5 ingredients. Cut cold butter into
brown sugar and flour in bowl until crumbly. Stir in nuts.
Sprinkle over apples. Bake for 10 minutes. Reduce temperature to 375 degrees. Bake for 35 minutes. Chill in refrigerator. Yield: 6 servings.

Rosemary Scheiben, Xi Phi
Montgomery, Alabama

UPSIDE-DOWN APPLE PECAN PIE

2 tablespoons butter,
    softened
30 pecan halves
⅓ cup packed light brown
    sugar
1 recipe 2-crust pie pastry
6 cups sliced apples

¾ cup sugar
2 tablespoons all-purpose
    flour
1 teaspoon cinnamon
½ teaspoon nutmeg
Milk

Preheat oven to 450 degrees. Line 9-inch pie plate with
13-inch foil circle, leaving 1-inch overhang. Spread with
butter. Press pecans round side down in butter. Pat
brown sugar into butter. Roll half the pastry into 11-inch
circle; fit into pie plate. Mound mixture of next 5 ingredients in pastry. Top with remaining pastry; seal and flute.
Prick with fork. Brush lightly with milk. Bake for 10 minutes. Bake at 375 degrees for 35 minutes. Let stand for 5
minutes. Invert onto plate. Serve warm. Yield: 8 servings.

 *Elizabeth Aimo, Xi Epsilon*
Albany, New York

BANANA CREAM PIE

3 cups milk
4½ tablespoons (heaping) all-purpose flour
1½ tablespoons (heaping) cornstarch
¾ cup sugar
¼ teaspoon salt
2 eggs, slightly beaten
1 teaspoon vanilla extract
2 to 4 bananas, sliced
1 baked 9-inch pie shell
1 8-ounce container whipped topping

Scald milk in top of double boiler. Combine flour, cornstarch, sugar and salt; mix well. Add to scalded milk. Cook for 15 minutes, stirring constantly. Stir a small amount of hot mixture into beaten eggs; stir eggs into hot mixture. Cook for several minutes longer. Cool. Stir in vanilla. Layer pudding and bananas ½ at a time in pie shell. Spread whipped topping over pie. Chill in refrigerator. Yield: 6 to 8 servings.

Shirley Maher, Xi Delta Zeta
King City, Missouri

BROWNIE PIES

2 cups chocolate chips
1 cup margarine
¾ cup all-purpose flour
2 cups sugar
4 eggs
½ teaspoon vanilla extract
½ cup milk
2 cups chopped nuts
2 unbaked 9-inch deep-dish pie shells

Preheat oven to 350 degrees. Melt chocolate chips and margarine in saucepan over low heat. Combine flour and sugar in bowl. Beat eggs, vanilla and milk in bowl. Add flour mixture and chocolate mixture; mix well. Add nuts; mix well. Pour into pie shells. Bake for 45 minutes. Serve warm with vanilla ice cream. Yield: 2 pies.

Nancy Carol Mann, Xi Alpha Gamma
Beckley, West Virginia

GRANDMA'S BURNT SUGAR PIE

½ cup sugar
½ cup boiling water
1 cup milk
1 cup half and half
1 tablespoon butter
½ cup plus 1 tablespoon sugar
¼ teaspoon salt
3 tablespoons cornstarch
2 egg yolks
½ teaspoon vanilla extract
1 baked 9-inch pie shell
1 recipe meringue

Preheat oven to 425 degrees. Cook ½ cup sugar in heavy skillet until rich brown, stirring constantly; remove from heat. Stir in boiling water. Cook until sugar dissolves. Cool. Add milk, half and half and butter; stir until well blended. Add remaining ½ cup plus 1 tablespoon sugar, salt and cornstarch; mix well. Add egg yolks and vanilla; mix well. Bring to a boil, stirring constantly. Cool. Pour into baked pie shell. Spread meringue over top, sealing to edge. Bake until light brown. Yield: 6 to 8 servings.

Liz Wilson, Eta Psi
Albany, Missouri

BUTTERSCOTCH PIE

1¾ cups packed light brown sugar
3 tablespoons (heaping) all-purpose flour
3 egg yolks
Pinch of salt
1½ cups milk
3 tablespoons butter
1½ teaspoons vanilla extract
1 baked 9-inch pie shell
3 egg whites
¼ teaspoon cream of tartar
6 tablespoons sugar

Preheat oven to 400 degrees. Combine first 5 ingredients in double boiler. Cook until thickened, stirring constantly. Add butter and vanilla. Pour into pie shell. Beat egg whites with cream of tartar until soft peaks form. Add sugar gradually, beating until stiff. Spread over pie, sealing to edge. Bake until golden. Yield: 6 servings.

Ernestine Stewart, Preceptor Iota
Atlanta, Georgia

OLD-FASHIONED BUTTERSCOTCH PIE

¾ cup packed dark brown sugar
5 tablespoons instant flour
¼ teaspoon salt
1 cup evaporated milk
1 cup water
2 egg yolks
2 tablespoons butter
1 teaspoon vanilla extract
1 baked 9-inch pie shell
1 recipe meringue

Preheat oven to 400 degrees. Mix first 5 ingredients in double boiler. Cook until mixture thickens, stirring constantly. Cook, covered, for 7 minutes, stirring frequently. Add a small amount of hot mixture to egg yolks; add egg yolks to hot mixture. Cook, covered, for 1 to 2 minutes longer. Remove from heat. Add butter and vanilla; mix well. Cool. Pour into pie shell. Top with meringue, sealing to edge. Bake until brown. Yield: 6 to 7 servings.

Wanda R. Bell, Xi Beta Theta
Northfork, West Virginia

CALYPSO PIE

18 Oreos, crushed
⅓ cup melted margarine
1 quart coffee ice cream, softened
1½ ounces semisweet chocolate
1 tablespoon margarine
½ cup sugar
⅔ cup evaporated milk
1 8-ounce container whipped topping
Pecans

Combine Oreos and ⅓ cup margarine in bowl; press into 10-inch pie plate. Spread ice cream over cookies. Freeze until firm. Melt chocolate and 1 tablespoon margarine in saucepan. Add sugar and evaporated milk. Cook until thick, stirring constantly. Cool. Pour over ice cream. Top with whipped topping. Sprinkle pecans on top. Freeze until firm. Yield: 6 to 8 servings.

Norma M. Johnson, Xi Phi
Elmore, Alabama

CHEESECAKE PIES

8 ounces cream cheese,
  softened
1 cup sour cream
1 3½-ounce package
  vanilla instant pudding
  mix
2 cups milk
1 teaspoon vanilla extract
2 graham cracker pie
  shells
1 21-ounce can cherry
  pie filling
1 21-ounce can blueberry
  pie filling

Beat cream cheese in mixer bowl. Add sour cream, pudding mix and milk, beating constantly. Beat in vanilla. Pour into pie shells. Top each with 1 can pie filling. Chill until serving time. Yield: 2 pies.

Melody J. Stevens, Alpha Alpha Eta
West Columbia, Texas

EASY PUMPKIN CHEESECAKE PIE

1 16-ounce can pumpkin
8 ounces cream cheese,
  softened
¼ teaspoon vanilla extract
3 eggs
¾ cup sugar
½ cup buttermilk baking
  mix
1½ teaspoons pumpkin
  pie spice
¾ cup whipping cream
3 tablespoons
  confectioners' sugar
1 teaspoon grated orange
  rind

Preheat oven to 350 degrees. Combine first 7 ingredients in blender container. Process for 2 minutes, scraping sides of container occasionally. Pour into greased 9-inch pie plate. Bake for 45 minutes or just until puffed and center is dry; do not overbake. Cool. Whip cream with confectioners' sugar and orange rind in bowl. Spread over baked layer. Yield: 6 servings.

Shirley Hannon, Xi Beta Theta
North Little Rock, Arkansas

SOUR CREAM CHERRY PIE

1 16-ounce can sour
  cherries, drained
1 8-inch unbaked pie
  shell
1 cup sugar
3 tablespoons cherry juice
½ teaspoon vanilla extract
2 cups sour cream
3 tablespoons all-purpose
  flour

Preheat oven to 325 degrees. Place cherries in unbaked pie shell. Sprinkle 1 tablespoon sugar over cherries. Combine remaining sugar and remaining ingredients in bowl; mix well. Pour over cherries. Bake for 1 hour or until brown and crusty on top. Yield: 6 to 8 servings.

Donna Borstad, Xi Beta Omicron
Anaheim, California

CHOCOLATE ANGEL STRATA PIE

2 egg whites
½ teaspoon white vinegar
¼ teaspoon salt
¼ teaspoon cinnamon
½ cup sugar
1 baked 9-inch pie shell
1 cup semisweet
  chocolate chips
2 egg yolks, beaten
¼ cup water
¼ teaspoon cinnamon
1 cup whipping cream
¼ cup sugar

Preheat oven to 425 degrees. Beat egg whites with vinegar, salt and ¼ teaspoon cinnamon until soft peaks form. Add ½ cup sugar gradually, beating until stiff peaks form. Spread over bottom and side of baked pie shell. Bake for 15 minutes or until light brown. Cool. Melt chocolate in double boiler. Add egg yolks and water. Spread 3 tablespoons over cooled meringue. Chill remaining chocolate mixture. Combine ¼ teaspoon cinnamon and whipping cream in bowl. Beat until thick. Add ¼ cup sugar gradually, beating until soft peaks form. Spread half the mixture in pie shell. Fold remaining whipped cream into chocolate mixture. Spread over whipped cream in pie shell. Chill for 4 hours or longer. Yield: 6 to 8 servings.

Barbara J. Jones, Gamma Eta
Columbus, Kansas

CHOCOLATE CHEESE PIE

6 ounces cream cheese,
  softened
1 cup sugar
¼ to ½ cup milk
1⅓ cups semisweet
  chocolate chips, melted
¼ cup chopped pecans
1 graham cracker pie shell
1 16-ounce container
  whipped topping
1 2-ounce milk chocolate
  candy bar, shaved

Beat cream cheese, sugar and milk in bowl. Stir in chocolate and pecans. Spoon into pie shell. Freeze until firm. Thaw for 15 minutes. Garnish with whipped topping and shaved chocolate. Yield: 6 to 9 servings.

Joan E. Powers, Laureate Lambda
Wichita, Kansas

CHOCOLATE CHIP PIE

2 eggs, beaten
½ cup all-purpose flour
½ cup packed light brown
  sugar
½ cup sugar
1 cup melted butter
1 cup chocolate chips
1 unbaked 9-inch pie shell

Preheat oven to 325 degrees. Beat first 4 ingredients in bowl until well blended. Blend in butter; stir in chocolate chips. Pour into pie shell. Bake for 1 hour. Serve with ice cream or whipped cream. Yield: 8 servings.

Sherrilyn Tatum, Tau Theta
Flora, Illinois

CHOCOLATE PIES

30 large marshmallows
1 12-ounce milk
  chocolate and almond
  candy bar
¾ cup milk
1 16-ounce container
  whipped topping
2 8-inch chocolate wafer
  pie shells
Sliced almonds
1 2-ounce milk chocolate
  bar, shaved

Melt marshmallows and almond candy bar in milk in double boiler, stirring constantly. Chill in freezer for 10 minutes. Fold in 1½ cups whipped topping. Chill for 10 minutes. Pour into pie shells. Top with remaining ingredients. Freeze until firm. Remove from freezer 10 minutes before serving. Yield: 12 servings.

Bonnie Bruckman, Preceptor Kappa Xi
Porterville, California

HEAVENLY CHOCOLATE-BERRY PIE

1¼ cups graham cracker crumbs
3 tablespoons sugar
⅓ cup melted butter or margarine
½ cup semisweet chocolate chips
8 ounces cream cheese, softened
¼ cup packed light brown sugar
½ teaspoon vanilla extract
1 cup whipping cream, whipped
1 pint fresh strawberries
1 teaspoon shortening
2 tablespoons chocolate chips, melted

Preheat oven to 325 degrees. Mix first 3 ingredients in bowl. Press over bottom and side of lightly greased 9-inch pie plate. Bake for 10 minutes. Cool. Melt ½ cup chocolate chips in double boiler. Cool slightly. Beat cream cheese in mixer bowl until fluffy. Mix in brown sugar, vanilla and chocolate. Fold in whipped cream gently. Spoon into crust. Chill for 8 hours. Reserve 1 strawberry. Slice remaining strawberries. Arrange over filling; place whole strawberry in center. Combine shortening and melted chocolate chips in bowl. Drizzle over strawberries. Yield: 8 servings.

Teresa Edmison, Xi Phi Alpha
Pampa, Texas

CINNAMON PIE

2 egg yolks
¾ cup sugar
2 tablespoons all-purpose flour
1 tablespoon cinnamon
1½ cups milk
2 egg whites, beaten
1 unbaked 9-inch pie shell

Preheat oven to 350 degrees. Combine egg yolks, sugar, flour and cinnamon in saucepan. Add milk. Heat to 110 degrees, stirring constantly. Beat egg whites until stiff peaks form. Fold into warm mixture. Pour into pie shell. Bake for 35 minutes or until set. Yield: 6 servings.

Tammy Rollins, Upsilon Psi
Mercer, Missouri

CLOUD PIES

1 14-ounce can sweetened condensed milk
5 tablespoons lemon juice
1 16-ounce can crushed pineapple, drained
1 8-ounce container whipped topping
1¼ cups chopped nuts
2 8-inch graham cracker pie shells

Combine condensed milk and lemon juice in mixer bowl; mix well. Mix in next 3 ingredients. Pour into pie shells. Chill until 10 minutes before serving. Yield: 2 pies.

Billie Fitts, Chi Zeta
Palestine, Texas

COCONUT CHRISTMAS PIES

½ cup sugar
¼ cup self-rising flour
1 envelope unflavored gelatin
½ teaspoon salt
1¾ cups milk
¾ teaspoon vanilla extract
3 egg whites
¼ teaspoon cream of tartar
½ cup sugar
½ cup whipping cream, whipped
1 cup shredded coconut
2 baked 9-inch pie shells

Combine first 4 ingredients in saucepan. Stir in milk gradually. Bring to a simmer over medium heat, stirring constantly. Simmer for 1 minute. Place pan in cold water. Let stand until mixture mounds slightly when dropped from spoon. Add vanilla. Beat egg whites in bowl until frothy. Add cream of tartar. Beat in ½ cup sugar gradually until stiff peaks form. Fold in cooked mixture gently. Fold in whipped cream and shredded coconut. Spoon into pie shells. Sprinkle with additional coconut. Chill in refrigerator. Yield: 2 pies.

Frances V. Scofield, Laureate Eta
Clarksville, Tennessee

EASY CREAM PIE

1 cup (scant) sugar
3 tablespoons all-purpose flour
Pinch of salt
1 cup whipping cream
¼ cup milk
2 tablespoons melted margarine
1½ teaspoons vanilla extract
1 unbaked 8-inch pie shell
Cinnamon to taste

Preheat oven to 325 degrees. Combine first 7 ingredients in bowl; mix well. Pour into pie shell. Sprinkle with cinnamon. Bake for 1 hour. Yield: 6 servings.

Barbara M. McFadden, Alpha Beta
Bedford, Indiana

CRANBERRY CREAM PIE

1¼ cups graham cracker crumbs
2 tablespoons sugar
⅓ cup chopped pecans
6 tablespoons melted margarine
8 ounces cream cheese, softened
⅓ cup confectioners' sugar
2 tablespoons orange juice
1 teaspoon vanilla extract
1 cup whipping cream, whipped
1 cup sugar
1 tablespoon water
2½ cups fresh cranberries
3 tablespoons cornstarch
2 teaspoons water

Preheat oven to 350 degrees. Combine first 4 ingredients in bowl. Press over bottom and side of 9-inch pie plate. Bake for 8 minutes or until light brown. Cool on wire rack. Beat cream cheese and confectioners' sugar in mixer bowl for 3 minutes or until fluffy. Add orange juice and vanilla. Fold in whipped cream. Spoon into pie shell. Chill for 2 hours. Cook 1 cup sugar, water and cranberries in medium saucepan over high heat until mixture comes to a full boil and berries pop, stirring constantly. Stir in cornstarch dissolved in 2 teaspoons water. Cook until thickened, stirring constantly. Cool. Spread over cream cheese filling; cover with plastic wrap. Chill in refrigerator. Garnish with whipped cream. Yield: 8 servings.

Linda Snape, Beta Delta
Lincoln, Maine

DIRT PIES

1 1-pound package Oreo cookies, crushed	1 cup confectioners' sugar
¼ cup melted margarine	2 3-ounce packages vanilla instant pudding mix
8 ounces cream cheese, softened	
¼ cup margarine, softened	3 cups milk
	1 8-ounce container whipped topping

Mix ¾ of the cookie crumbs and melted margarine in bowl. Press in bottoms of two 8-inch pie plates. Mix cream cheese, softened margarine and confectioners' sugar in bowl. Combine pudding mix and milk in bowl; beat until thick. Add to cream cheese mixture. Fold in whipped topping. Pour into pie shells. Sprinkle with remaining cookie crumbs. Freeze until firm. Remove from freezer several minutes before serving. Yield: 12 servings.

Brenda Williamson, Xi Epsilon Chi
Fulton, Missouri

FUDGE PECAN PIE

½ cup margarine	½ cup all-purpose flour
¼ cup unsweetened baking cocoa	1 teaspoon vanilla extract
1 cup sugar	1 cup pecans
2 eggs	1 unbaked 9-inch pie shell

Preheat oven to 325 degrees. Melt margarine with cocoa in heavy saucepan over medium heat; remove from heat. Add sugar; beat well. Add eggs, beat until blended. Add flour, vanilla and pecans; mix well. Pour into pie shell. Bake for 20 minutes. Let stand until slightly cooled. Serve with vanilla ice cream. Yield: 8 servings.

Sharon Carter, Alpha Omicron Sigma
Plano, Texas

KENTUCKY BOURBON PIE

¼ cup butter, softened	½ cup light corn syrup
½ cup sugar	¼ cup Bourbon
¼ cup packed light brown sugar	Dash of salt
2 tablespoons all-purpose flour	1 cup chopped walnuts
3 eggs	1 cup semisweet chocolate chips
	1 unbaked 9-inch pie shell

Preheat oven to 375 degrees. Cream butter and sugars in bowl until fluffy. Add flour; mix well. Add eggs 1 at a time, beating well after each addition. Mix in corn syrup, Bourbon and salt. Fold in walnuts and chocolate chips. Pour into pie shell. Bake for 35 minutes or until golden. Cool for 30 minutes before serving. Yield: 8 servings.

Ivy Jean Summers, Xi Gamma
Paducah, Kentucky

GRAPE TART

1 15-ounce package 2-crust refrigerator pie pastry	1 cup sour cream
	2 eggs
2½ pounds seedless grapes	½ cup sugar
	¼ cup all-purpose flour

Preheat oven to 400 degrees. Fit 1 pastry into 9-inch springform pan. Cut leaf shapes from remaining pastry. Chill in refrigerator. Bake shell for 5 minutes. Place grapes in baked shell. Pour mixture of remaining ingredients over grapes. Arrange pastry leaves on top. Bake for 1 hour or until pastry is golden and custard is set. Cool on wire rack. Chill until serving time. Remove side of pan. Yield: 8 servings.

Alyce Davis, Preceptor Zeta
Grand Junction, Colorado

KONA KRUNCH PIE

¾ cup chopped macadamia nuts	3 ounces cream cheese, softened
½ 11-ounce package pie crust mix	¼ cup sugar
¼ cup packed light brown sugar	2 tablespoons whipping cream
1 tablespoon water	¼ cup coffee-flavored liqueur
1 teaspoon vanilla extract	1½ cups plus 3 tablespoons whipping cream
4 ounces sweet baking chocolate	
3 tablespoons whipping cream	¼ cup sifted confectioners' sugar

Preheat oven to 350 degrees. Rub macadamia nuts in tea towel to remove excess salt; place on baking sheet. Bake for 8 minutes, stirring occasionally. Cool. Increase oven temperature to 375 degrees. Combine nuts with next 4 ingredients in bowl; mix with fork until blended. Press into greased 9-inch pie plate. Bake for 15 minutes. Cool. Heat chocolate and 3 tablespoons cream in heavy saucepan over low heat until chocolate melts. Beat cream cheese in mixer bowl. Mix in sugar, 2 tablespoons cream and chocolate mixture. Add coffee liqueur gradually; set aside. Whip remaining cream in mixer bowl at high speed until soft peaks form. Add confectioners' sugar. Blend chocolate mixture into whipped cream until smooth. Spoon into pie shell. Chill until firm. Yield: 6 servings.

Nancy Wilson, Xi Beta Omicron
Medford, Oklahoma

TWO-CRUST LEMON PIE

1¼ cups sugar	1 lemon
2½ tablespoons all-purpose flour	1 teaspoon grated lemon rind
¼ cup margarine	½ cup water
¼ teaspoon salt	1 recipe 2-crust pie pastry
3 eggs	Cinnamon-sugar

Preheat oven to 425 degrees. Cream first 4 ingredients in bowl until fluffy. Reserve 1 teaspoon egg white for top crust. Beat eggs in bowl. Peel lemon; cut into paper-thin slices. Add to eggs with lemon rind and water. Add to creamed mixture; mix well. Pour into pastry-lined pie plate. Top with remaining pastry. Brush top crust with egg white. Sprinkle with cinnamon-sugar. Bake for 35 minutes. Yield: 6 to 8 servings.

Alice C. Galbraith, Laureate Beta
Waukegan, Illinois

LEMON MERINGUE PIE

1½ cups sugar
⅓ cup plus 1 tablespoon
  cornstarch
1½ cups water
3 egg yolks, slightly
  beaten
3 tablespoons butter or
  margarine

2 teaspoons grated lemon
  rind
½ cup lemon juice
2 drops of yellow food
  coloring
1 baked 9-inch pie shell
1 recipe meringue

Preheat oven to 400 degrees. Mix sugar and cornstarch in medium saucepan. Stir in water gradually. Cook over medium heat until mixture thickens and boils, stirring constantly. Boil for 1 minute, stirring constantly. Stir half the hot mixture into egg yolks; stir egg yolks into hot mixture. Cook for 1 minute, stirring constantly; remove from heat. Stir in butter, lemon rind, lemon juice and food coloring. Pour into pie shell. Heap meringue onto pie filling; seal meringue to edge. Bake for 10 minutes or until delicate brown. Cool. Yield: 6 to 8 servings.

Carmen S. Alldritt, Nu Kappa
Harper, Kansas

QUICK KEY LIME PIE

Ritz crackers
1 14-ounce can
  sweetened condensed
  milk

¼ cup Key lime juice
1 8-ounce container
  whipped topping

Line 9-inch pie plate with whole crackers. Combine condensed milk and lime juice in bowl; mix well. Fold in whipped topping. Spoon into prepared pie plate. Freeze until firm. Yield: 6 servings.

Dolores Sandusky, Preceptor Alpha Epsilon
Tucson, Arizona

FROZEN MARGARITA PIE

10 tablespoons butter or
  margarine
1 5-ounce package salted
  pretzels, finely crushed
½ cup sugar
1 14-ounce can
  sweetened condensed
  milk

1½ tablespoons lime juice
1½ tablespoons tequila
1 tablespoon plus 1
  teaspoon Triple Sec
1 drop of green food
  coloring
2½ cups whipping cream,
  whipped

Microwave butter in greased 9-inch pie plate on High for 30 seconds or until melted. Stir in pretzels and sugar. Press firmly over bottom and side of pie plate, forming rim above edge. Freeze until firm. Combine condensed milk, lime juice, liquors and food coloring in small bowl; mix well. Fold into whipped cream gently. Pour into prepared crust. Freeze for 8 hours or longer. Let stand at room temperature for 15 minutes before serving. Garnish with pretzels. Yield: 10 servings.

Note: May omit liquors and increase lime juice to ⅔ cup.

 Bev McConaughey, Kappa Pi
Atchison, Kansas

MILLIONAIRE PIES

1 14-ounce can
  sweetened condensed
  milk
Juice of 2 lemons
1 cup chopped pecans
1 can crushed pineapple,
  drained

10 to 15 maraschino
  cherries, chopped
1 8-ounce container
  whipped topping
2 baked 9-inch pie shells

Combine first 6 ingredients in bowl; mix well. Pour into pie shells. Refrigerate until set. Yield: 2 pies.

Rosa M. Eaches, Epsilon Rho
U.S. Air Force Academy, Colorado

ORANGE PEACH PIE

1 cup sugar
3 tablespoons cornstarch
¼ teaspoon salt
1 cup water

¼ cup orange gelatin
5 cups diced fresh peaches
1 baked 9-inch pie shell

Mix sugar, cornstarch and salt in saucepan. Add water; mix well. Bring to a boil. Cook until thickened, stirring constantly. Add gelatin; mix well. Cool. Fold in peaches. Pour into pie shell. Chill until serving time. Serve with whipped cream or ice cream. Yield: 6 servings.

Karen Harmon, Preceptor Xi
Winnemucca, Nevada

PEANUT BUTTER PIES

8 ounces cream cheese,
  softened
½ cup chunky peanut
  butter
1 cup confectioners' sugar
½ cup milk

1 8-ounce container
  whipped topping
2 graham cracker pie
  shells
½ cup chopped peanuts

Beat first 3 ingredients in bowl until fluffy. Mix in milk. Fold in whipped topping. Spoon into pie shells. Sprinkle with peanuts. Cover with plastic wrap. Freeze until firm. Remove from freezer 15 minutes before serving. Yield: 2 pies.

Lucille Morris, Xi Eta Rho
Camdenton, Missouri

PEANUT PIE

1 cup sugar
½ teaspoon salt
1 cup creamy peanut
  butter
½ cup dark corn syrup
3 eggs
1 cup dry-roasted peanuts

1 unbaked 9-inch pie shell
1 cup semisweet chocolate
  chips
2 tablespoons
  butter-flavored
  shortening

Preheat oven to 375 degrees. Cream first 3 ingredients in bowl until fluffy. Add corn syrup and eggs. Stir in peanuts. Pour into pie shell. Cover loosely with foil. Bake for 30 minutes. Remove foil. Bake for 10 minutes longer or until crust is golden. Cool completely. Melt chocolate chips and shortening in double boiler. Spread over filling. Cool completely. Chill. Yield: 16 servings.

Pat Reagan, Eta Beta
Mount Vernon, Illinois

COUNTRY PEAR PIE

1 29-ounce can Bartlett pears	½ teaspoon cinnamon
½ cup packed light brown sugar	¼ teaspoon nutmeg
2 tablespoons all-purpose flour	1 tablespoon lemon juice
⅛ teaspoon salt	1 recipe 2-crust pie pastry
3 tablespoons butter	¼ cup chopped pecans
	Milk
	Sugar

Preheat oven to 400 degrees. Drain pears, reserving ½ cup syrup. Slice pears. Combine brown sugar, flour, salt and reserved pear syrup in saucepan. Add butter. Cook over medium heat until thick and smooth, stirring constantly. Remove from heat; add spices and lemon juice. Place sliced pears in pastry-lined 8-inch pie plate. Sprinkle with pecans. Pour syrup over pears. Top with remaining pastry; flute edge. Brush with milk. Sprinkle with sugar. Bake for 30 minutes. Yield: 6 to 8 servings.

Lynda Veihl, Xi Gamma Eta
Grand Rapids, Michigan

BUTTERMILK PECAN PIES

½ cup chopped pecans	2 teaspoons vanilla extract
2 unbaked 9-inch pie shells	3 tablespoons all-purpose flour
½ cup margarine, softened	¼ teaspoon salt
2 cups sugar	1 cup buttermilk
3 eggs	

Preheat oven to 300 degrees. Sprinkle pecans into pie shells. Cream margarine in bowl until light and fluffy. Add sugar ½ cup at a time beating constantly. Add eggs 1 at a time, beating well after each addition. Blend in vanilla. Add mixture of flour and salt. Add buttermilk; mix well. Pour custard over pecans. Bake for 1 hour and 15 minutes. Serve at room temperature. Yield: 8 servings.

Doris St. Clair, Laureate Beta Nu
El Campo, Texas

MYSTERY PECAN PIE

8 ounces cream cheese, softened	1 unbaked 9-inch pie shell
⅓ cup sugar	1 cup pecans
¼ teaspoon salt	3 eggs
1 teaspoon vanilla extract	¼ cup sugar
1 egg	1 teaspoon vanilla extract
	1 cup light corn syrup

Preheat oven to 350 degrees. Combine cream cheese, ⅓ cup sugar, salt, vanilla and 1 egg in bowl. Beat until well blended; pour into pie shell. Sprinkle with pecans. Combine 3 eggs, ¼ cup sugar, 1 teaspoon vanilla and corn syrup in bowl; blend well. Pour over pecans. Bake for 35 to 40 minutes or until center is firm. Yield: 8 servings.

Shirley A. Willard, Xi Iota Eta
Aurora, Missouri

PECAN PIE

¼ cup melted margarine	½ cup light corn syrup
3 eggs, beaten	1 cup chopped pecans
1 cup sugar	1 unbaked 9-inch pie shell

Preheat oven to 350 degrees. Beat margarine and eggs in bowl. Mix in next 3 ingredients. Pour into pie shell. Bake for 40 minutes or until firm. Yield: 6 servings.

Anita Foley, Xi Alpha
Catlin, Illinois

RITZY PECAN PIE

6 egg whites	46 Ritz crackers, crushed
1 teaspoon baking powder	1 8-ounce container whipped topping
2 cups sugar	
2 teaspoons vanilla extract	1 milk chocolate candy bar, grated
2 cups chopped pecans	

Preheat oven to 350 degrees. Beat egg whites until soft peaks form. Add baking powder and 2 cups sugar, beating gradually until very stiff peaks form. Fold in vanilla, pecans and cracker crumbs. Pour into buttered pie plate. Bake for 45 minutes. Cool. Cover with whipped topping. Sprinkle grated chocolate on top. Chill in refrigerator. Yield: 8 servings.

Janet K. Mather, Xi Kappa Alpha
Drexel, Missouri

PECANISH PIE

3 eggs, beaten	1 teaspoon vanilla extract
¾ cup pancake syrup	½ cup coconut
¾ cup quick-cooking oats	¼ cup chopped pecans
¼ cup margarine	1 unbaked 9-inch pie shell
¾ cup sugar	

Preheat oven to 350 degrees. Combine first 8 ingredients in bowl; mix well. Pour into pie shell. Bake for 40 minutes. Yield: 6 servings.

Vera Hunt, Laureate Eta
Dunedin, Florida

PEPPERMINT CHRISTMAS PIE

1 cup chocolate chips	1¼ cups milk
1 cup butter	¼ teaspoon salt
2 cups crisp rice cereal	4 to 5 drops red food coloring
½ cup crushed peppermint candy	
	¼ cup sugar
¼ cup sugar	3 egg whites
1 envelope unflavored gelatin	½ cup whipping cream, whipped

Melt chocolate chips and butter in double boiler. Add cereal; mix well. Spread in 10-inch pie plate. Chill until firm. Combine next 5 ingredients in saucepan. Cook over low heat until gelatin dissolves and candy melts, stirring constantly. Tint mixture red. Chill until almost set. Add ¼ cup sugar to egg whites. Beat until stiff peaks form. Fold into chilled mixture. Fold in whipped cream gently. Pour into pie shell. Chill until firm. Yield: 6 servings.

Linda Baron, Iota Alpha
Independence, Louisiana

PUMPKIN PECAN PIE

4 eggs, slightly beaten	½ cup dark corn syrup
¾ cup sugar	¼ teaspoon salt
1 teaspoon cinnamon	1 unbaked 9-inch pie shell
1 16-ounce can pumpkin	1 cup pecan halves

Preheat oven to 350 degrees. Combine first 6 ingredients in bowl; mix well. Pour into pie shell. Arrange pecan halves on top. Bake for 45 to 55 minutes or until knife inserted in center comes out clean. Cool on wire rack. Serve with whipped cream. Yield: 8 servings.

Marcia Veltri, Phi Alpha Chi
Salida, Colorado

SOUR CREAM PUMPKIN PIE

1 unbaked 9-inch pie shell	¼ teaspoon ginger
1 envelope unflavored	¼ teaspoon cloves
gelatin	¼ teaspoon nutmeg
¼ cup cold water	3 egg whites, at room
3 egg yolks	temperature
⅓ cup sugar	¼ cup sugar
¼ cup canned pumpkin	2 cups whipping cream
½ cup sour cream	1 cup confectioners' sugar
½ teaspoon salt	2 teaspoons vanilla extract
½ teaspoon cinnamon	½ cup chopped nuts

Preheat oven to 375 degrees. Pierce pie shell with fork. Line with foil. Fill with dried beans. Bake for 10 minutes. Remove beans and foil. Bake for 20 minutes or until pie shell is golden. Cool. Soften gelatin in water; set aside. Cook egg yolks and ⅓ cup sugar in double boiler over simmering water for 5 minutes, stirring constantly. Whisk in gelatin mixture. Remove from heat; whisk until gelatin has completely dissolved. Transfer to large bowl. Whisk in next 7 ingredients. Chill for 45 minutes or until thickened, stirring frequently; do not allow to set. Beat egg whites until soft peaks form. Beat in ¼ cup sugar gradually until stiff and glossy. Fold into pumpkin mixture. Beat whipping cream until soft peaks form; whisk in confectioners' sugar and vanilla. Layer half the pumpkin mixture, half the whipped cream and remaining pumpkin in pie shell. Pipe remaining whipped cream around edge. Top with nuts. Chill for 2 hours. Yield: 6 servings.

Sandi Dalton, Preceptor Delta
Ashland, Ohio

RUM-RAISIN CHESS PIE

½ cup raisins	3 eggs
1 cup water	¼ cup milk
1½ cups sugar	½ cup melted margarine
1 tablespoon cornmeal	1½ teaspoon rum extract
1 tablespoons all-purpose	½ cup coconut
flour	1 unbaked 9-inch pie shell

Preheat oven to 350 degrees. Cook raisins in water in saucepan for 10 minutes. Cool. Mix sugar, cornmeal, flour, eggs and milk in bowl. Stir in raisins and next 3 ingredients. Pour into pie shell. Bake for 45 minutes. Yield: 6 servings.

Dorothy Golden, Laureate Alpha Beta
Cambridge, Ohio

RASPBERRY RIBBON PIE

1 3-ounce package	3 ounces cream cheese,
raspberry gelatin	softened
¼ cup sugar	⅓ cup confectioners'
1¼ cups boiling water	sugar
1 10-ounce package	¼ teaspoon salt
frozen red raspberries	1 cup whipping cream,
1 tablespoon lemon juice	whipped
1 teaspoon vanilla extract	1 baked 9-inch pie shell

Dissolve gelatin and sugar in boiling water in bowl. Add raspberries and lemon juice. Stir until raspberries thaw. Chill until partially set. Beat next 4 ingredients in bowl until smooth. Fold in ¼ of the whipped cream. Fold in remaining whipped cream. Layer half the cream cheese mixture, all the raspberry mixture and remaining cream cheese mixture in pie shell. Chill for several hours. Yield: 6 servings.

Cathy Helleny, Xi Rho
Energy, Illinois

RHUBARB PIE

1 cup all-purpose flour	¾ cup sugar
¼ teaspoon salt	1 tablespoon all-purpose
1 egg yolk	flour
1 tablespoon sugar	3 egg whites
½ cup margarine	⅓ cup sugar
2 cups chopped rhubarb	¼ teaspoon cinnamon
2 egg yolks, beaten	

Preheat oven to 350 degrees. Mix first 5 ingredients in bowl. Pat into 9-inch pie plate. Bake for 10 minutes or until light brown. Combine rhubarb and next 3 ingredients in bowl. Pour into crust. Bake for 30 minutes. Beat egg whites until stiff peaks form. Add sugar and cinnamon, beating until very stiff peaks form. Spread over filling; seal to edge. Bake for 30 minutes. Yield: 6 servings.

Marjorie La Fever, Preceptor Alpha Psi
Menlo Park, California

SIN PIE

1 cup walnuts	8 ounces semisweet
1 cup all-purpose flour	chocolate, melted
½ cup packed light brown	¼ cup Frangelico liqueur
sugar	2 eggs
6 tablespoons melted	1 cup whipped cream
butter	¼ cup sliced toasted
10 tablespoons butter,	almonds
softened	
1⅔ cups confectioners'	
sugar	

Preheat oven to 350 degrees. Process walnuts, flour and brown sugar in food processor. Blend in melted butter. Press over bottom and side of 10-inch pie plate. Bake for 10 minutes. Cream softened butter, confectioners' sugar, chocolate and liqueur in bowl. Beat in eggs 1 at a time. Pour into pie shell. Chill. Garnish with whipped cream and almonds. Yield: 10 servings.

Carol Drake, Preceptor Xi
Winnemucca, Nevada

STRAWBERRY CREAM PIE

1 3-ounce package vanilla instant pudding mix	2 teaspoons grated orange or lemon rind
1 cup sour cream	3½ cups whipped topping
¼ cup milk	1 graham cracker pie shell
	1 pint strawberries

Combine pie filling mix, sour cream, milk, rind and whipped topping in bowl. Beat with whisk until well blended. Spoon half the filling into pie shell. Arrange strawberries over filling. Spoon remaining filling over top. Chill for 3 hours before serving. Yield: 8 servings.

Patricia Theiss, Zeta Nu
Princeton, Missouri

SPECIAL STRAWBERRY PIE

8 ounces cream cheese, softened	2 10-ounce packages frozen strawberries, thawed, drained
½ cup sugar	
1 cup sour cream	1 8-inch crumb pie shell

Beat cream cheese and sugar in medium bowl until light and fluffy. Fold in sour cream and strawberries gently. Pour into pie shell. Freeze for 8 hours to overnight. Remove pie from freezer 1 hour before serving.
Yield: 6 servings.

Darlene M. Fleek, Xi Beta Pi
Eureka, California

FRESH STRAWBERRY PIE

3 tablespoons cornstarch	3 tablespoons strawberry gelatin
1 cup sugar	
1 cup cold water	1 quart fresh whole strawberries
2 tablespoons light corn syrup	
	1 baked 9-inch pie shell

Mix cornstarch and sugar in saucepan. Add water and corn syrup. Cook for 5 minutes or until clear and thick, stirring constantly. Remove from heat. Add gelatin. Cool slightly. Arrange strawberries in pie shell. Pour cooked mixture over top. Cool. Serve with whipped cream.
Yield: 6 to 8 servings.

Ida Marie Smreker, Preceptor Gamma Zeta
St. Louis, Missouri

STRAWBERRY AND BANANA PIE

1 3-ounce package strawberry-banana gelatin	1¼ cups water
	1 quart strawberries
⅔ cup sugar	2 large bananas, sliced
2 tablespoons cornstarch	1 baked 9-inch pie shell
	Whipped topping

Combine first 4 ingredients in saucepan. Bring to a boil, stirring constantly. Cook for 4 minutes or until mixture is clear and thick. Combine strawberries and bananas in bowl. Pour gelatin mixture over fruit; mix well. Spoon into pie shell. Chill in refrigerator. Top with whipped topping at serving time. Yield: 6 to 8 servings.

Joanne Tauber, Preceptor Delta Sigma
Tampa, Florida

SWEET POTATO PIE

2 cups mashed boiled sweet potatoes	1 teaspoon cinnamon
	½ teaspoon ginger
2 eggs, well beaten	¼ teaspoon cloves
¾ cup sugar	1⅔ cups evaporated milk
½ teaspoon salt	1 unbaked 9-inch pie shell

Preheat oven to 425 degrees. Combine first 8 ingredients in mixer bowl. Beat until well blended. Pour into pie shell. Bake for 15 minutes. Reduce temperature to 350 degrees. Bake for 45 minutes or until knife inserted in center comes out clean. Yield: 8 servings.

Linda Boyle, Beta Theta
Columbia, Maryland

SUNNY SILVER PIE

4 egg yolks	⅓ cup cold water
Juice and grated rind of 1 lemon	4 egg whites
	½ cup sugar
⅛ teaspoon salt	1 baked 10-inch pie shell
½ cup sugar	1 cup whipping cream, whipped
1½ teaspoons unflavored gelatin	

Combine egg yolks, lemon juice, rind, salt and ½ cup sugar in saucepan. Cook until thickened, stirring constantly. Soften gelatin in cold water. Add to cooked mixture, stirring until dissolved. Cool. Beat egg whites in bowl until soft peaks form. Add remaining ½ cup sugar. Beat until stiff peaks form. Fold gently into lemon mixture. Pour into pie shell. Chill for 2 to 3 hours. Top with whipped cream. Yield: 8 to 10 servings.

Maxine Burns, Laureate Lambda
Beloit, Wisconsin

ZUCCHINI CRUMB PIE

3 cups sliced zucchini	¼ cup sugar
1 unbaked 9-inch pie shell	1 cup all-purpose flour
2 teaspoons lemon juice	¾ cup sugar
1 teaspoon cinnamon	½ cup margarine

Preheat oven to 425 degrees. Place zucchini in pie shell. Sprinkle lemon juice, cinnamon and ¼ cup sugar over zucchini. Combine flour, ¾ cup sugar and margarine in bowl; mix until crumbly. Sprinkle over pie. Bake for 12 minutes. Reduce temperature to 350 degrees. Bake for 30 minutes longer. Serve warm. Yield: 6 to 8 servings.

Nora Fann, Xi Kappa Theta
Du Quoin, Illinois

---

*Delicious pies for a crowd are extra easy for **Pat Reece, Sigma, Northpart, Alabama**. She mixes ½ gallon softened vanilla ice cream and 12 ounces lemonade concentrate, spoons it into 3 graham cracker pie shells and freezes them. She garnishes them with whipped cream and lemon slices.*

STRAWBERRY TARTS

1½ quarts strawberries	1 tablespoon lemon juice
1 cup sugar	6 to 8 baked tart shells
3 tablespoons cornstarch	Whipped cream
½ cup water	

Purée enough strawberries to measure 1 cup. Cook puréed strawberries, sugar, cornstarch and water in saucepan over medium heat until thickened, stirring constantly. Blend in lemon juice. Cool. Add remaining whole or sliced strawberries; toss lightly just to coat. Arrange in tart shells. Chill until serving time. Top with whipped cream. Yield: 6 to 8 servings.

Shirley Lab, Xi Omicron
Harlingen, Texas

ZIPPY FRUIT TART

1 cup all-purpose flour	1 16-ounce container
1 tablespoon sugar	whipped topping
1 tablespoon butter	1 21-ounce can
8 ounces cream cheese,	blueberry, cherry or
softened	peach pie filling
1 cup confectioners' sugar	

Preheat oven to 350 degrees. Mix flour, sugar and butter in bowl. Press into pizza pan. Bake for 20 minutes or until brown. Cool. Beat cream cheese and confectioners' sugar in bowl until fluffy. Stir in whipped topping. Spread on baked layer. Spoon pie filling over cream cheese layer. Chill until serving time. Yield: 8 servings.

George Ann Jackson, Chi Lambda
Crystal River, Florida

ALMOND PIE SHELL

1 cup all-purpose flour	3 tablespoons
¼ cup chopped toasted	confectioners' sugar
almonds	¼ teaspoon vanilla extract
6 tablespoons butter	

Preheat oven to 400 degrees. Beat all ingredients in mixer bowl at low speed for 2 minutes or until well mixed. Press over bottom and up side of 9-inch pie plate. Bake for 8 minutes or until brown. Cool. Yield: 1 pie shell.

Marna Morgan, Preceptor Gamma Beta
Osceola, Iowa

GOOD PIE CRUST

3 tablespoons light brown	1 teaspoon baking powder
sugar	2½ cups shortening
5 cups all-purpose flour	1 egg, beaten
1½ teaspoons salt	2 tablespoons vinegar

Combine brown sugar with sifted dry ingredients in bowl; mix well. Cut in shortening until mixture resembles coarse cornmeal. Combine egg, vinegar and enough water to measure ¾ cup liquid. Pour over sifted dry ingredients. Toss lightly with fork until flour is uniformly moistened. Shape into ball; wrap in waxed paper. Chill for 30 minutes. Roll on floured surface. Yield: 2 pie shells.

Ruth Bailey, Preceptor Alpha Xi
Rushville, Missouri

NEVER-FAIL PIE PASTRY

1½ cups butter-flavored	6 tablespoons water
shortening	1 egg, beaten
3 cups all-purpose flour	1 teaspoon vinegar
1 teaspoon salt	

Preheat oven to 450 degrees. Cut shortening into mixture of flour and salt in bowl until crumbly. Stir in mixture of water, egg and vinegar. Roll on floured surface. Fit into 12-inch pie plate. Fill with favorite fruit filling. Cut remaining pastry into long lattice strips. Twist strips and coil over pie to cover. Bake for 10 minutes. Reduce temperature to 350 degrees. Bake for 30 minutes longer. Yield: One 2-crust pie pastry.

Billie Overton, Preceptor Gamma
Dumas, Texas

PIE PASTRY

1½ cups shortening	1 egg
3 cups sifted all-purpose	2 teaspoons vinegar
flour	5 tablespoons ice water
½ teaspoon salt	

Cut shortening into mixture of flour and salt with pastry blender until crumbly. Beat egg, vinegar and water in bowl. Add to flour mixture. Mix with fork until mixture forms ball. Roll to ⅛-inch thickness on lightly floured pastry cloth with covered roller. Yield: 3 pie shells.

Mary Gaylor, Xi Beta Omicron
Yarba Linda, California

RICH PIE PASTRY

14 tablespoons shortening	1½ teaspoons vinegar
2 cups all-purpose flour	¼ cup ice water
2 teaspoons sugar	1 egg
2 teaspoons salt	

Cut shortening into mixture of flour, sugar and salt in bowl until crumbly. Combine vinegar, ice water and egg in bowl; mix well. Add to dry ingredients; mix well. Roll on floured surface; fit into 9-inch pie plate. Fill as desired. Yield: 1 pie shell.

Peg Baldwin, Preceptor Gamma Tau
Kenton, Ohio

VERY FLAKY PASTRY

2 cups sifted all-purpose	½ cup vegetable oil
flour	5 tablespoons ice water
½ teaspoon salt	

Preheat oven to 475 degrees. Sift flour and salt together into bowl. Beat oil and water together in bowl until creamy. Add to flour; toss with fork to mix well. Shape into 2 balls. Roll out between 2 pieces of waxed paper. Peel off top paper. Invert pastry into pie plate. Prick surface; flute edges. Bake for 12 minutes. Yield: 2 pie shells. Note: Pastry must be baked immediately.

Della D. Reynolds, Tau Theta
Archie, Missouri

Certificate of Merit Winners

APPETIZERS & BEVERAGES
First Place
Thompson, Kim, page 57
Second Place
Hood, Deborah J., page 58
Third Place
Rochford, LouAnn, page 54
Honorable Mention
Arnold, Mary Elizabeth, page 37
Ballmer, Jessie R., page 56
Barnes, Velma J., page 51
Beirth, Anne, page 52
Brackett, Marie, page 35
Clapp, Yvonne, page 52
Combs, Wanda, page 60
Cox, Carol, page 48
Cumpton, Elaine, page 34
Davis, Peggy, page 59
Doud, Judy, page 50
Dyer, Dayna, page 54
Erickson, Laurie, page 52
Erikson, Connie Anne, page 45
Fahl, Rosanna, page 53
Fawley, Virginia, page 42
Fulcher, Sue, page 34
Gish, Wanda, page 40
Gray-Tingler, Carey, page 50
Hanson, Elaine, page 33
Harper, Linda, page 55
Hebbert, Betty Jo, page 39
Hebensperger, Terry, page 48
Heyland, Linda, page 34
Highmiller, Judie, page 31
Hinsch, Ruth, page 56
Holloman, Judi, page 58
Hood, Deborah J, page 58
Hunter, Nancy, page 30
Jerret, Janet, page 29
Johnson, Chris, page 42
Kelly, Loretta, page 32
Lab, Shirley, page 58
Lassiter, Carla, page 58
Loach, Vickie, page 30
Lockwood, Joyce, page 46
Luse, Donna, page 40
McCarrick, Kay, page 37
McMurry, Debbie, page 55
Merrihew, Linda, page 34
Miller, Cheryl, page 42

Oakes, Sally, page 28
Pearson, Eva Marie, page 32
Pessano, Jean, page 38
Potts, K. D., page 32
Reddell, Jody, page 60
Robbins, Tammy, page 34
Rochford, LouAnn, page 54
Schnitman, Donna, page 43
Short, Anita K., page 53
Swingley, Nancy N., page 58
Tanksley, Nancy, page 33
Thompson, Kim, page 57
Van Ryswyk, Pam, page 29
Vinson, Jo Beth, page 34
Warren, Peggy, page 47
Zambo, Rosemary, page 60

BREADS
First Place
Smith, Zeilla, page 164
Second Place
Robinson, Helen, page 176
Third Place
Lovell, Sara, page 172
Honorable Mention
Anderson, Ada, page 170
Bell, Mary Louise, page 164
Berger, Norma J., page 168
Brown, Tami, page 173
Burgess, Ruth M., page 165
Colflesh, Ellen Christine, page 168
Curtis, Nancy, page 167
Dalrymple, Gyl, page 164
Daniels, Elisabeth Ann, page 172
Davis, Judi, page 167
Donaldson, Martha, page 172
Edmonds, Janet, page 166
Grimsley, Lisa M., page 166
Keef, Linda, page 172
Kutcher, Judy, page 171
Lewnfield, Eleanore B., page 171
Marsh, Jennifer, page 180
Mihlmester, Linda, page 168
Parker, Dortha L., page 165
Rogers, Linda, page 169
Rosenstengel, Virginia, page 177
Spears, Jill, page 175
Venrick, Janice, page 173
Williamson, JoAnn, page 177

CAKES
First Place
DySard, Sally, page 208
Second Place
Borras, Marilyn, page 218
Third Place
Bishop, Lea Ann, page 203
Honorable Mention
Adkins, Esther, page 207
Allen, Pam, page 207
Ault, Betty J., page 207
Baker, Cheryl, page 218
Berguist, Marilys, page 217
Cook, Melody L., page 208
Cowan, Tamara D., page 205
Dewey, Patricia, page 216
Ditmore, Gail Ann, page 219
Dudley, Wanda E., page 206
Duncan, Sandra, page 202
Faut, June, page 211
Fisette, Rosemary L., page 217
Gillett, Pat, page 213
Hayes, Marcia, page 218
Krenitsky, Katherine, page 214
Kusmaul, Cathy, page 205
LaRocco, Lucie D., page 215
Lewis, Lawana, page 212
Lozano, Blanca, page 215
McGarraugh, Carol, page 215
McLeod, Juanita, page 213
Minor, Clella Rogers, page 209
Muninger, Mary, page 210
Neal, Dorris, page 206
Nepita, Janice F., page 210
Oliver, Wanda, page 202
Osborn, Barbara, page 201
Painter, Connie, page 209
Pessano, Jean, page 216
Rodler, LaVerna J., page 210
Sadler, Billie Jo, page 219
Swanson, Kathy, page 212
Trimble, Jan, page 215
Weingeroff, Linda, page 219

COOKIES
First Place
Phillips, Georgia, page 227
Second Place
Hill, Lora, page 230

Xi Iota Epsilon, *Roaring 20's Five-Star Dinner*, page 14
Xi Lambda Xi, *Black and White 40th Birthday*, page 14
Zeta Kappa, *Oriental Cook-Out*, page 10

PIES
First Place
Aimo, Elizabeth, page 231
Second Place
McConaughey, Bev, page 236
Third Place
Edmison, Teresa, page 234
Honorable Mention
Baron, Linda, page 237
Dalton, Sandi, page 238
Golden, Dorothy, page 238
Gray, Bonnie, page 231
Hannon, Shirley, page 233
Harmon, Karen, page 236
Helleny, Cathy, page 238
Johnson, Norma M., page 232
Jones, Barbara J., page 233
Reagan, Pat, page 236
Snape, Linda D., page 234
St. Clair, Doris, page 237
Veltri, Marcia, page 238
Willard, Shirley A., page 237
Wilson, Nancy, page 235

POULTRY & SEAFOOD
First Place
Wakefield, Bonnie, page 119
Second Place
Kaufman, Kathy, page 132
Waugh, Jeanie, page 132
Third Place
Kollman, Brittany M., page 140
Honorable Mention
Allen, Pam, page 134
Bertler, Rita, page 119
Buck, Nancy, page 126
Christensen, Cindy, page 123
Condon, Joni L., page 130
Conrad, Betty, page 130
Dewey, Patricia, page 128
Dyck, Mary Leigh, page 131
Fort, Roxane I., page 121
Fromdahl, Diana, page 137
Gardner, Joanne, page 117
Glassco, Bea, page 132
Gonzalez, Casey, page 124
Gruss, Mary A., page 137
Hanam, Judith A., page 132
Henry, Isabelle, page 118
Herrick, Sherri, page 123

Hobson, Esther, page 138
Ingram-Butts, Shirley, page 122
Johnson, Phyllis, page 130
Kubik, Debbie, page 120
Lammert, Georgia, page 118
Lemon, Linda Faye, page 129
Marples, Janine, page 142
McCoy, Merline, page 130
McDaniel, Suzi, page 134
McGuire, Maxine, page 121
McReynolds, Kathy, page 121
Mikeworth, Estelline, page 131
Miller, Colleen B., page 115
Morgan, Cammy, page 127
Morse, Donna, page 116
Myers, Frances A., page 128
Pippin, Vikki, page 133
Roberts, Vera, page 136
Runo, Diane, page 136
Sowards, Geraldine E., page 140
Thomas, Betty L., page 141
Thompson, Jennifer S., page 132
Vogler, Jackie, page 140
Winchell, Ellen, page 131
Yates, Debbie, page 119

SALADS
First Place
Orlob, Ruth, page 64
Second Place
Runo, Diane, page 68
Third Place
Faltz Lembright, Muriel, page 73
Honorable Mention
Ables, Helen, page 62
Akelewicz, Margie, page 67
Allen, Linda S., page 77
Azar, Jeanette, page 80
Bahl, Linda C., page 62
Baker, Jean, page 82
Berning, Kathy, page 69
Blakely, Janet, page 79
Briggman, Phyllis, page 71
Carroll, Bonnie J., page 63
Crockett, Janice, page 65
Crowell, Holly, page 78
Dottore, Maribeth V., page 73
Drake, Carol, page 81
Emry, Linda, page 78
Fatale, Molly, page 75
Flood, Marcia, page 68
Franklin, Paige, page 65
Glasgow, Eva, page 76
Hadlock, Betty, page 79
Hood, Eloise, page 68
Kaufman, Kathy, page 79
Keck, Sherie L., page 70

Kellerman, Marlene, page 83
Kirby, Helen A., page 62
LeSueur, Pat, page 86
Martin, Donna, page 83
Mendiola, Gloria F., page 84
Miller, Maria, page 70
Monty, Josephine, page 78
Morgan, Betty, page 81
Morrow, Christine L., page 69
Myers, Susie, page 73
Needels, Jeannette, page 67
Norris, Dixie, page 75
Partsch, Jeannine, page 71
Pelling, Rosella, page 69
Phillips, June, page 63
Reid, Olivia C., page 72
Restvedt, Barbara, page 70
Rice, Dorothy, page 74
Rieder, Susan, page 72
Riggs, Gigi, page 71
Roberts, Vera, page 72
Roper, Jo, page 85
Sandusky, Dolores, page 85
Schlenz, Elfreda, page 65
Sheen, Beverly L., page 64
Sides, Linda, page 67
Vineyard, Jeri, page 68
Waugh, Jeanie, page 79
Wheeler, June, page 80
Zenthoefer, Maye, page 75

VEGETABLES & SIDE DISHES
First Place
Steele, Joyce, page 157
Second Place
Mullis, Emily, page 150
Third Place
Smith, Billie J., page 148
Honorable Mention
Anthony, Mary Ann, page 162
Azar, Jeanette, page 160
Bender, Connie, page 159
Cloninger, LaNita, page 156
Cox, Carole, page 157
Ferrara, Sarah E., page 154
Gillingham, Lillian M., page 155
Harms, Marjorie, page 146
Hess, Kathleen, page 153
Hilbig, Jamie, page 149
Hinkle, Peg, page 153
Humphreys, Maureen, page 162
Jackson, Linda, page 161
Jarvinen, Laura, page 158
Jasionowski, Gail, page 151
Konishi, Bessie, page 154
Loudat, Cecile, page 148
Lubeski, Beverly, page 145

Menu Recipe Index

Almond Pilaf, 160
Anise Sugar Cookies, 228
Apple Pancakes, 172
Aspen Salad, 75
Avocado with Tomato Freeze, 76
Barbecued Shrimp, 139
Basil Fettucini, 159
Beer Nut Clusters, 54
Biscochitos, 228
Biscuit Tortoni, 191
Blueberry Muffins, 171
Caesar Salad, 77
Carrots in Champagne, 47
Ceviche, 133
Chocolate Raspberry
    Cheesecake, 184
Cold Broiled Chicken, 115
Colorado Crunch, 174
Corn Bread Sticks, 167
Cornish Pasty, 94
CousCous, 160
Cucumber Salad with Yogurt, 79
Curried Onions, 150
Curried Turkey, 131
Fettucini with Scampi, 139
Fireside Fondue, 39
Fresh Fruit Napoleons, 190
Fried Fish, 134
Frosty Fruit, 190
Frozen Strawberry Salad, 67
Frozen Waldorf Salad, 68

Green Beans Italienne, 145
Green Chili Hor d'Oeuvros, 57
Green Chili Quiche, 158
Grilled Beef Tenderloin, 89
Grilled Tomatoes, 151
Ham and Rice Quiche, 111
Hors d'Oeuvre Pie, 54
Keftethakia, 100
Kona Krunch Pie, 235
Lemon Squares, 226
Linguine with Asparagus, 159
Maids of Honor, 229
Mandarin Orange Toss, 80
Macadamia Bar Cookies, 226
Mexican Strata, 57
Mock Caesar Salad, 77
Nasi Goreng, 141
Natillas, 196
Nippy Potato Salad, 81
Orangy Rum Sherbet, 193
Oriental Grilled Pork Chops, 107
Overnight Bloody Marys, 60
Peachy Keen Witches Brew, 60
Pecan and Rice Dressing, 161
Petite Dinner Salad, 75
Piñata Salad, 80
Pork Au Vin, 108
Polla de Kiev con Salsa, 119
Red Pepper Pasta, 160
Roast Leg of Lamb, 114
Rocky Mountain High, 192

Royal Chicken Crêpes, 128
Salmon Champagne Sauce, 136
Salsa Sauce, 46
Sauerbraten Over Noodles, 94
Sausage, Rolls, 55
Scallops in Seafood Sauce, 139
Smoked Beef Brisket
    with Buns, 88
Spinach Salad Flambé, 83
Spinach-Stuffed Mushrooms, 150
Spinach Salad with Poppy Seed
    Dressing, 84
Stegt Rodspaette, 135
Strawberries Chantilly, 199
Stuffed Easter Ham, 110
Stuffed Snow Peas, 56
Sweet Potato Pie, 239
Sweetly Spiced Oranges, 196
Tabbouli, 84
Tandoori Cornish Hens, 132
Teddy Bear Cakes, 219
Tomato and Avocado Salad, 76
Tomato and Mozzarella Salad, 85
Tomato and Squash Quiche, 158
Tortillas de Harina, 174
Waikiki Crêpes, 200
White Wine Sangria, 60
Baked Yams and Chestnuts, 154
Yeast Biscuits, 74

Index

Beta Sigma Phi Cookbooks

available from Favorite Recipes Press are chock-full of home-tested recipes from Beta Sigma Phi members that earn you the best compliment of all . . . "More Please!"

Every cookbook includes:
- 128 to 250 pages
- 300 to 1500 delicious family-pleasing recipes
- color photos
- black-and-white photos
- lay-flat binding
- wipe-clean color covers
- easy-to-read format
- comprehensive index

To place your order, call our **toll free** number

1-800-251-1520

In Tennessee call collect
1-615-391-2899
or clip and mail the convenient form below.

☐ **YES.** Please send me the cookbooks I've checked below. I understand that if I'm not completely delighted I may return any book within 30 days for a full refund.

BETA SIGMA PHI COOKBOOKS	Item #	Qty.	Retail Price	Total
The Beta Sigma Phi Party Cookbook	79774		$ 9.95	
The Cook Light Cookbook	72567		$12.95	
The Cook Quick Cookbook	65889		$12.95	
All-Occasion Casseroles Cookbook With Menus	28029		4.50	
The Dining Room	13595		5.95	
Gourmet Cookbook	13617		5.95	
Save & Win	13676		5.95	
Bicentennial Heritage Recipes	13560		6.95	
Shipping and Handling	36579	1	$ 1.95	$ 1.95
TOTAL AMOUNT				

☐ Payment enclosed.

☐ Please Charge My ☐ MasterCard ☐ Visa

Account Number _____

Signature _____

Name _____

Address _____

City _____ State ___ Zip _____

No COD orders please.
Call our **toll free** number for return information.
Prices subject to change.
Books offered subject to availability.
Please allow 30 days for delivery.

Mail completed order form to:

Favorite Recipes Press
P. O. Box 305141
Nashville, TN 37230